OUR BELOVED KIN

THE HENRY ROE CLOUD SERIES ON AMERICAN INDIANS AND MODERNITY

Series Editors: Ned Blackhawk, Professor of History
and American Studies, Yale University, and
Kate W. Shanley, Native American Studies, University of Montana

Series Mission Statement
Named in honor of the pioneering Winnebago educational reformer and first known American Indian graduate of Yale College, Henry Roe Cloud (Class of 1910), this series showcases emergent and leading scholarship in the field of American Indian Studies. The series draws upon multiple disciplinary perspectives and organizes them around the place of Native Americans within the development of American and European modernity, emphasizing the shared, relational ties between indigenous and Euro-American societies. It seeks to broaden current historic, literary, and cultural approaches to American Studies by foregrounding the fraught but generative sites of inquiry provided by the study of indigenous communities.

OUR
BELOVED KIN

A New History of King Philip's War

Lisa Brooks

Yale

UNIVERSITY
PRESS

New Haven & London

The publication of this book was supported (in part) by Amherst College.
Published with assistance from the foundation established in memory of
Philip Hamilton McMillan of the Class of 1894, Yale College.

Yale University Press books may be purchased in quantity for educational,
business, or promotional use. For information, please e-mail sales.press@yale.edu
(U.S. office) or sales@yaleup.co.uk (U.K. office).

Set in Electra type by Newgen North America.
Printed in the United States of America.

Library of Congress Control Number: 2017947666
ISBN 978-0-300-19673-3 (hardcover : alk. paper)
ISBN 978-0-300-24432-8 (pbk.)

A catalogue record for this book is available from the British Library.

10 9 8 7 6

For Rick, who has always understood

The first step in liquidating a people . . . is to erase its memory. Destroy its books, its culture, its history. Then have somebody write new books, manufacture a new culture, invent a new history. Before long the nation will begin to forget what it is and what it was. The world around it will forget even faster.

—Milan Kundera, *The Book of Laughter and Forgetting* (1978)

pili kisos, "the new moon"
pildowi ôjmowôgan, "a new history"

—Joseph Laurent, *New Familiar Abenaki and English Dialogues* (1884)

CONTENTS

MAPS

A NOTE ON THE MAPS

The maps included in each chapter and on the website are designed as interactive guides. Readers are encouraged to refer to them as they read. Full-scale color versions and additional maps can be viewed at http://ourbelovedkin.com. These maps do not represent all Native territories and place names or all colonial towns, but highlight places mentioned in the book. Please note that these maps are not designed to delineate fixed territories, but to locate the reader in and convey the author's conceptualizations of Native space. Concentric circles convey a sense of homelands spreading outwards from a center, rather than indicating a single point on a map.

The maps were created using ArcGIS 10.3, courtesy of Amherst College. Lisa Brooks and Andy Anderson, lead GIS Specialist, led a team that included Aida Orozco, Micayla Tatum, Cassandra Hradil, Lauren Tuiskula, Heru Craig, Maggie King, Allyson LaForge, and Griffin Harris. Special thanks to the Andrew W. Mellon Foundation and the Gregory S. Call Academic Interns Program for supporting a research tutorial and funding for research assistants, and to the Whiting Foundation for supporting the development and piloting of the website.

ACKNOWLEDGMENTS

This book did not start out as a project on King Philip's War but emerged gradually from the intertwining of several different inquiries. Many conversations and collaborations along the way contributed to my understanding. All mistakes and misunderstandings herein are my own.

Ktsi wliwni, great thanks, to the writers, educators, and historians who read the manuscript, in whole or in part, and offered incisive critique and encouragement, including Cheryl Savageau, Cassandra Brooks, Gordon Russell, Susan Power, J. Kēhaulani Kauanui, Melissa Tantaquidgeon Zobel, Elizabeth James Perry, Jonathan Perry, Judy Dow, Cheryll Toney Holley, Pam Ellis, Linda Coombs, Darius Coombs, Jill Lepore, Barry O'Connell, Colin Calloway, Neal Salisbury, Kevin Sweeney, and Tad Baker.

Wliwni to the many additional people who, through ongoing conversation, contributed vital insights to this project. In the Nipmuc country and in Cambridge/Boston, thanks to Bruce Curliss, Keely Curliss, Mary Anne Hendricks, Kristen Wyman, Larry Mann, Patrik Johansson, Shelly Lowe, Dennis Norman, Malinda Maynor-Lowery, Werner Sollors, Steve Biel, Jeanne Follansbee, Andy Romig, Jim Engell, Leah Price, Mark Schiefsky, and Sally Livingston. Special thanks to the students who contributed to translation and research, including Wampanoag scholar Tiffany Smalley, Rebecca Cohen, and Vanessa Dube, and to everyone who organized and participated in "From the Gospel to Sovereignty: Commemorating 350 Years of the Harvard Indian College" in April 2005.

In the Wampanoag and Narragansett country, *kutaputash* to Tobias Vanderhoop, Judith Sanford-Harris, Bettina Washington, Jessie Little Doe Baird, Patricia Perry, Leah Hopkins, Dawn and Cassius Spears, Berta Welch, Ramona Peters, Jim Peters, Tall Oak Weeden, and Donna Mitchell. At Mohegan and in Connecticut, *taputni* to Lynn Malerba, Stephanie Fielding, Rachel Sayet, Trudie Lamb Richmond, and Ruth Garby Torres. In Haudenosaunee territory, *Nia:wen* to Kahntineta Horn, Kahente Horn-Miller, and Alyssa Mt. Pleasant. Thanks also to Mary Beth Norton at Cornell for supporting this project early on.

In Wabanaki, *wliwni* to Roger Paul, Carol Dana, Gabe Paul, James Francis, Donald Soctomah, Natalie Dana, Kyle Lolar, Natalie Michelle, John Banks, Chip Loring, Mark Ranco, Maria Girouard, Marge Bruchac, Louise Lampman-Larivee, Alex Larivee, Lester Lampman, and everyone at Missisquoi. Rick Pouliot and Lillie Rose Brooks were my constant companions on this journey, and I am grateful to them for sustaining me. Thanks also to my mother, Christine Brooks, for offering vital support while I wrote. A special thanks to Michael Johnson, Sabine Klein and all my colleagues and students at the University of Maine at Farmington, for collaboration, conversation, and research support.

In the Connecticut River Valley, thanks to Barbara Moseley, Ed Lonergan, and to all my generous, engaged colleagues in the American Studies and English departments, and in the Five College Native American and Indigenous Studies community. Special thanks to our mapping and website research team, including Dr. Andy Anderson, Aida Orozco, Micayla Tatum, Cassandra Hradil, Lauren Tuiskula, Tim Gaura, Heru Craig, Maggie King, Allyson LaForge, Griffin Harris, and Lehua Matsumoto.

Thanks to colleagues at University of Texas at Austin, including Jim Cox and Polly Strong, for good questions, and to those who hosted and participated in discussions at UConn, Rutgers, Yale, Concordia, UCLA, University of Illinois, UC Berkeley, Plimoth Plantation, Historic Deerfield, Primary Source, UMass NEH Summer Institute, and NAISA.

Yale University Press carried this manuscript through to fruition, and I am grateful to Kate Shanley, Laura Davulis, Chris Rogers, Adina Berk, Eva Skewes, and all those working behind the scenes through publication, as well as to David Pritchard, an unparalleled copy editor. I also want to thank Writers House, especially Michele Rubin, for seeing the vision, and Geri Thoma, for key advice.

Finally, I am grateful to those institutions who provided the time, space, and support for research and writing, including Amherst College, Harvard University, University of Maine at Farmington, New England Regional Fellowship Consortium and Colonial Society of Massachusetts, Ford Foundation, Whiting Foundation, New England Historic and Genealogical Society, Rhode Island Historical Society, Massachusetts Historical Society, Massachusetts Archives,

American Antiquarian Society, Fall River Historical Society, and Maine Historical Society, with special thanks to Nicholas Noyes and Bill Barry.

Parts of the introduction and chapter 7 were previously published as "Turning the Looking Glass on King Philip's War: Locating American Literature in Native Space," in *American Literary History* 25, no. 4: 718–50. Parts of the prologue and chapter 6 were previously published in "The Reciprocity Principle and ITEK: Understanding the Significance of Indigenous Protest on the Presumpscot," with Cassandra M. Brooks, in the *International Journal of Critical Indigenous Studies* 3, no. 2 (2010).

INTRODUCTION

THE ABSENCE OF PRESENCE

As the first leaves of sassafras and strawberry emerged in the Wampanoag country during the spring of 1623, a leader stepped forth to confront Plymouth colonist Edward Winslow and the Wampanoag diplomat Hobbomock as they entered the Pocasset town of Mattapoisett, on the banks of the Kteticut (or Taunton) River. All were preoccupied with the illness that had overcome a beloved man, Ousamequin, or Massasoit (his title)—a "great sachem" of the Wampanoags and leader of the adjacent region of Pokanoket. Hundreds gathered at Ousamequin's council house, and both Hobbomock and Winslow were en route to pay their respects, a "commendable" Indigenous custom in this land, as Winslow noted in *Good News From New England*. This Pocasset leader, however, had remained at Mattapoisett, perhaps to help begin cultivating the fields, process the spring fish, or look after children and elders who required care. A gunshot had sounded beyond the river just prior to Winslow's arrival, putting the leader on edge, prepared to defend those kin who also remained. From the well-worn path ahead, the leader may have heard heavy English boots, or Hobbomock's voice, lamenting and singing Ousamequin's praises. Winslow later reported that a rumor had circulated that Ousamequin had already passed away. Indeed, their diversion to Mattapoisett was in part necessitated by his concern that the sachem of this town, a man who held a much more suspicious view of the English settlers who had so recently planted on the Wampanoag coast, "would succeed" Ousamequin[1] (see maps 1 and 4).

Upon entering Mattapoisett Winslow approached the great *Sachimo Camoco*, the council house where leaders deliberated, where the sachem and his family lived and hosted guests. However, he quickly discovered that "Conbitant, the

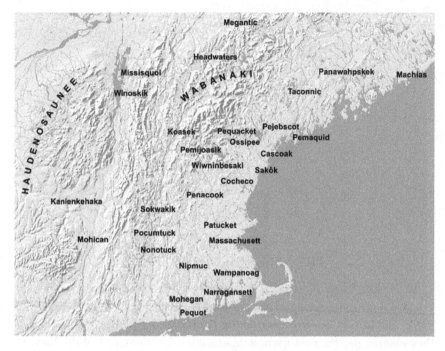

1. Native homelands of the Northeast, highlighting places mentioned in the book

Sachem, was not at home, but at" Pokanoket, tending to Ousamequin and his kin. Instead, Winslow remarked, he was greeted and given "friendly entertainment" by "the Squa-sachim," translating to an audience in England, "for so they called the Sachims wife." This was his mistranslation. *Saunkskwa,* or "sachem-squa," was not simply the word for spouse but rather the word for female leader, suggesting that this woman who "entertained" him was perhaps more than Conbitant's wife, particularly given that by local custom she would have come from a leadership family.[2]

The saunkskwa must have carried a legitimate suspicion of this English newcomer who, by his own account, had raised a gun at her and her family during the previous year's spring gathering at Nemasket, a neighboring Wampanoag town, acting rashly on false rumors that Conbitant had killed Plymouth's interpreter, Tisquantum. Indeed, that spring, on the return journey home from Pokanoket, Conbitant would raise this encounter when Winslow assured him of Plymouth's good intentions, asking, "If your love is so great and it grows such good fruits, why is it that when you come to our places or we go to yours, you stand as if ready to fight, with the mouths of your guns pointed at us?" Yet, despite the gun Winslow carried, the saunkskwa responded to his arrival with diplomacy. She hosted Winslow and his small party, offering hospitality, food, and rest, as well as assistance and information, when she allowed Winslow to "hire" one of her runners to seek news from Pokanoket of Ousamequin's status. Perhaps this impulse arose in part from her awareness of the danger of rumors in Winslow's hands. But it also arose from her responsibility as a leader, a choice she made about how to deal with this stranger in her space. Her response was emblematic of the ways in which Native leaders often acted as diplomatic hosts to unexpected European guests.[3]

Indeed, two years before, the Wabanaki leader Samoset, of Pemaquid (far up the coast), had greeted the startled newcomers at Patuxet (or Plymouth) in their language, saying, "Welcome Englishmen!" This reflected not only Indigenous diplomacy, but experience with over one hundred years of trade, cultural and linguistic exchange, as well as violence, disease, and captivity with "Englishmen" and other western Europeans on the coast. Indeed, Samoset was one of many Wabanaki and Wampanoag men who had been captured by European "explorers," learning a new language by necessity, and in his case, returning to serve as an intercultural diplomat. This exchange was not new to the Wampanoags or Wabanakis, who also had been traveling by canoe to exchange with each other for millennia. What *was* new about this "encounter" was that these Englishmen had come to stay, marking a discernible move from extractive colonialism (including the harvesting of trees and fish and the capture of Indigenous bodies) to settler colonialism. These newcomers also carried a vision that "Englishmen" would replace the Indigenous people, including women planters, as the rightful inhabitants of this land.[4]

Winslow's is the only account of this important woman in the Puritan narratives. She was a leader, the wife of Conbitant, and a relation to many. She experienced the arrival of the newcomers and their incorporation into Native networks of exchange and diplomacy. She hosted Winslow, and other leaders, at her large home. Like other women, she cultivated and sustained the fields that fed the families. She felt the dire impacts of the diseases that ravaged her relations. Living through the epidemics and the first wave of colonization, she experienced unimaginable grief and loss. Yet she birthed and raised at least two daughters, Weetamoo (or Namumpum) and Wootonakanuske, who survived several epidemics, as well as threats of violence, to mature into leaders among their communities. Yet in Winslow's account, this significant mother and leader was not even named.

Although well remembered within Native New England communities, like her mother, Weetamoo has often not been named in the histories and literatures of early America, despite her prominent leadership role. Weetamoo emerged as the saunkskwa of Pocasset after Conbitant's death, recognized by Ousamequin as his relation and "true heir" to the Pocasset sachemship. In fact, the title of this book is taken from Ousamequin's description of Weetamoo as "our beloved cousin" and "kinswoman." An influential Wampanoag diplomat, Weetamoo presented a political and cultural challenge to the Puritan men who confronted her authority. Her strategic adaptation to the colonial "deed game" enabled her to protect more land than nearly any surrounding leader (a history explored in chapter one). She married Wamsutta, Ousamequin's eldest son, in a dual marriage alliance with her sister Wootonakanuske and Wamsutta's brother Pometacomet, more commonly known as Metacom, or "Philip." She played a key role and forged alliances during the infamous colonial conflict known as "King Philip's War." One Puritan chronicler portrayed her "as potent a Prince as any round about her" with "as much corn, land, and men, at her command" as Metacom, insisting she was "much more forward in the Design and had greater success than King Philip himself." Yet in many histories of the war, she is relegated to a trivial role in comparison to Metacom or colonial leaders such as Plymouth governor Josiah Winslow, Edward's son. Even recent scholarly accounts mention her briefly, a footnote to history.[5]

Weetamoo's striking presence in primary documents and her conspicuous absence from many secondary sources led me down a long winding road of historical recovery. Tellingly, this process began with a simple question regarding the role of women leaders in King Philip's War. However, the deeper I dug the more I found myself pursuing a decolonizing process of expanding the strategies through which we might do the work of history, which in the Abenaki language is called *ôjmowôgan*, a cyclical activity of recalling and relaying in which we are collectively engaged. Thus, if you hold this book in your hands or are viewing it on a screen, I am asking you to follow these strands and storylines with me. I am saying, "Welcome," although I will warn you that, for some readers, this landscape may seem unfamiliar and unsettling. Others, of course, may find it strikingly familiar. I acknowledge that it may be difficult to follow me at times. Yet, if you come in the manner of a guest to the "place-world" I've created, and immerse yourself as I have in the documents and maps of our history, I hope your participation may be rewarded with the gift of seeing a world we all inhabit with greater insight and clarity.[6]

This book also focuses on the recovery of the Nipmuc scholar James Printer, another compelling figure absent from most histories, who was accused of "revolt" during King Philip's War. Wawaus, or James, was from a leading family in the Nipmuc mission community or "praying town" of Hassanamesit. After attending English preparatory schools in the Massachusetts Colony, James became an apprentice to Cambridge printer Samuel Greene, and helped usher in American publishing history. He worked the first printing press in New England, which was housed in the Harvard Indian College (another project of historical recovery covered in depth in chapter two). Here, the man henceforth known as James Printer set the type on the first bible printed in North America. Printer adapted to a changing and challenging environment, using his linguistic skills to survive the ravages of war, serving as a scribe and negotiator for Native leaders, and leveraging his invaluable talent to negotiate his way back to the Press. He went on to serve as a leader at Hassanamesit, enabling the protection of Nipmuc lands and the survival of his kin and community. Laboring at the Harvard Press after the war, he set the type for one of the first publications by a woman in the English colonies, a text that would become a classic of American literature. In the process, he encountered himself in the print. He was not only the printer of *The Sovereignty and Goodness of God . . . A Narrative of the Captivity and Restoration of Mrs. Mary Rowlandson,* but a character within it, credited with helping to negotiate the "redemption" of the Puritan mistress Mary Rowlandson, by her (and his) own hand.[7]

Both the Nipmuc printer and the Puritan mistress survived King Philip's War, but the conflict upended their lives. Both experienced forms of "captivity" and "restoration." As Jill Lepore observes, however, "The lasting legacy of Mary Rowlandson's dramatic, eloquent, and fantastically popular narrative of captivity and redemption is the nearly complete veil it has unwittingly placed over the experience of bondage endured by Algonquian Indians during King Philip's War." Captivity has most often been seen as a condition faced by settlers, particularly women and children. Until recently, as Pauline Strong relays, scholars often "neglected or distorted" the "Native American context of captivity." Margaret Newell notes that "we still know more about the relatively few Euro-American captives among the Indians than we do about the thousands of Native Americans" who were enslaved. This "absence," as both Newell and Strong suggest, is particularly grievous when we consider that "in numerical terms, the captivity of English colonists among Indians pales in comparison to the abduction, imprisonment, and enslavement of Indians by the English, and indeed, to the captivity of Indians by Indians during the colonial period."[8]

For example, in August 1675, James Printer was captured by colonial forces and falsely accused of participating in a raid—on Rowlandson's town of Lancaster, Massachusetts. Although he ultimately averted conviction, establishing that he was in church, James was imprisoned for a month in a Boston jail and "barely escaped lynching" by an English mob (a story relayed in full in chapter five). Five months later, James's brother traveled eighty miles on snowshoes to deliver a warning to ministers at Cambridge that another raid on Lancaster was imminent. However, Massachusetts military leaders did not respond quickly enough, and in February 1676 Mary Rowlandson was captured by Narragansett men during a winter raid. As detailed in chapter seven, Mary was carried to the Nipmuc stronghold of Menimesit, where she encountered James and his extended family, held in "captivity," according to missionary Daniel Gookin, by their own relations. In an intriguing twist of fate, at Menimesit, Rowlandson was given to Weetamoo, whom she followed deep into the interior of Nipmuc and Wabanaki countries, as the saunkskwa sought protective sanctuaries for families evading colonial troops. Years later, in 1682, as James set the type on Rowlandson's narrative, he helped preserve the most detailed portrait of Weetamoo and her movements in the colonial record.[9]

As historian Neal Salisbury has insisted, "Our understanding of the cross-cultural dimensions of captivity will remain incomplete until the stories of the . . . James Printers and Weetamoos throughout American history are fully fleshed out and placed alongside . . . more familiar narratives" like Rowlandson's. This book seeks to answer his charge. All too often, histories of war focus on male soldiers and warriors, the victories and losses of captains, generals, and chiefs. In drawing James and Weetamoo's stories together, a different picture of war, captivity, and resistance arises, one that reveals the determination of a mother, who was a valiant leader, and the compromises of an erudite scholar, who became a diplomat and scribe. These stories reverse the narrative of absence and reveal the persistence of Indigenous adaptation and survival.[10]

As Anishinaabe historian Jean O'Brien and others have observed, American readers have often been drawn to the "national narrative of the 'vanishing Indian,'" including the death of Native leaders like Philip, rather than the more complex stories of Native adaptation, as with James Printer. The persistent narrative of "extinction," to which O'Brien refers, "has falsely educated New Englanders" and Americans "for generations," engendering a mythological history in which the English, and their American descendants, "replace" Indians in the land. Likewise, in writing about "King Philip's War" colonial ministers and magistrates sought to contain Indigenous resistance within narratives that would justify their replacement. Following colonial structures, many authors and historians have also contained such wars within an orderly "chain-of-events" or thesis argument. A decolonial process might reverse that trend by resisting containment and opening possibilities for Native presence. As exemplified by the expansive and connective approach of chapter six, where multiple narratives intertwine, this book seeks to focus narrowly at times on the alternative stories revealed by tracking Weetamoo, James Printer, and their network of relations, while at other times expanding far beyond that scope to vast Indigenous geographies, including the Wabanaki northern front, where many Native people sought refuge from colonization and war.[11]

The book is organized episodically, to offer scenarios, like the encounter between Winslow and Weetamoo's mother, and insights for contemplation and critical reflection. Section breaks and subheads signal a pause in the narrative, offering an opportunity for deliberation.

LANGUAGE: NAMING WAR

One of the most crucial lenses to viewing history anew is Indigenous language, a vastly underutilized archive of place names and concepts. A new generation of Hawaiian scholars, some trained in the Ka Papahana Kaiapuni immersion schools, is bringing forth a revolutionary understanding of the historical relationship between Hawai'i and the United States, based on a vast archive of Hawaiian newspapers and documents which past historians have largely ignored, in part because they lacked literacy in the language. Our understanding of Wampanoag and New England history will be transformed as a new generation of Wôpanâak speakers, led by Jessie Little Doe Baird, turns the lens of language on the body of place names and understudied Wôpanâak language texts. Language keepers are among the most important scholars we have with us today. Their insights into a single word can reveal layers of history which we cannot understand from documents alone. As a student of Abenaki language and a scholar of history, I have benefitted tremendously from conversations with language keepers in northern New England such as Roger Paul, Carol Dana, the late Cecile Wawanolet, her son Elie Joubert, and her student, Jesse Bruchac, as well as language keepers and tribal scholars in southern New England like Jessie Little Doe Baird, Bettina Washington, Linda Coombs, Elizabeth James Perry, Jonathan Perry, Cheryll Holley, Pam Ellis, Stephanie Fielding, and Melissa Tantaquidgeon Zobel. My understanding of Indigenous language is only that of a student, not of a fluent speaker, but being able to understand the nuances of language has at times shed remarkable light on the historical landscape.[12]

The "war" in which Weetamoo and James Printer became embroiled would not have been known to them, in any language, as "King Philip's War." As Jenny Pulsipher notes, that appellation arose only in the eighteenth century, perhaps with the publication of Benjamin Church's *Entertaining History of King Philip's War*. Thomas Church published his father's boisterous memoir in 1716, forty years after Benjamin Church led a company to capture and kill Metacom. If Custer had survived the Battle of Little Bighorn, he may have relayed a similar account of that war. Church's narrative formally marked the "end" of the conflict with his own successful containment of Metacom. The hyperbolic narrative implied that it was Church's leadership and tracking skills that enabled his company to locate and ensnare the elusive Wampanoag sachem, even though Church acknowledged that a Pocasset Wampanoag man, Alderman, struck the fatal blow. Naming the conflict "King Philip's War" created an impression of finality. The Indigenous "rebellion" had been squashed with the death of Philip, the subjugation complete, titles cleared. This act of naming contained the "war" from an ongoing, multifaceted Indigenous resistance, led by an uncontainable network of Indigenous leaders and families, to a rebellion, an event that could be contained within one year, by a single persuasive insurgent, who had taken his exit and vanished.[13]

As Lepore notes in her landmark work on the narratives of "King Philip's War," "Names of wars are always biased; they always privilege one perspective over another." In New England, when the first narratives of the war emerged, the conflict was known more broadly as "the Warr with the Indians in New-England," as Massachusetts minister Increase Mather entitled it, or "the Indian War," as Rhode Island leader John Easton and Massachusetts merchant Nathaniel Saltonstall described it. Later, this struggle would be acknowledged as part of a longer engagement, "the first Indian war," the beginning of resistance against increasing English expansion that continued in the northern Wabanaki country for the next hundred years. Indeed, the Mohegan leader Owaneco, who led an influential company of Mohegan scouts *for* the English in this "first" war and those that followed, referred to this conflict as "the warres with the Generall Nations of Indians," suggesting a series of wars waged by the English with a regional alliance of Native nations. This Mohegan naming may be the most accurate.[14]

Moreover, most of the Native people who were impacted by this war would have named the conflict in their own languages. To them (and for many Native people today) this was not New England, but *ndakinna* (to use the Abenaki word), "our land," the place "to which we belong." This is a word that denotes kinship, similar to *nigawes*, "our mother." Long before it was reinscribed as "New England," this place was named Wôpanâak or Wabanaki, "the land where the sun is born every day." The tribal names Wabanaki and Wampanoag reflect an originary embeddedness in this land, as well as the first peoples' responsibility to welcome the sun's emergence and return. Wabanaki and Wampanoag people are born of, and continually born into, this easternmost place. While neighboring Native nations used these terms to describe the nations the English termed "Indians" of "New England," they called themselves simply "the people," the human beings (*alnôbak* in Abenaki). When introducing themselves, the people would have acknowledged the families and places to which they "belonged," like James Printer's town of Hassanamesit, in the Nipmuc or "freshwater" interior, or Weetamoo's homeland of Pocasset, on the coast.[15]

Likewise, Native people in the Northeast had multiple names for war. In Western Abenaki, with which I am most familiar, *aôdowôgan* is an activity in which people are engaged, a state of being which is temporary. In this language there is a distinction between being caught up or immersed in a conflict, *matañbégw*, or *aôdin* ("we are fighting, we are in a war"), and "to wage war against something or someone," *nedaiwdwôdamen*, or *nañsekañsw*. There are also multiple words that refer to counselor-warriors, such as *pniesesok*, in Wôpanâak, and *kinôbak*, in Abenaki, both of which translate more precisely to those who have the courage to pursue difficult courses, similar to words that describe steep terrain. Edward Winslow acknowledged that "the pnieses are men of great courage and wisdom," among the "Sachims Council," who would "endure most hardness, and yet are more discreet, courteous and humane in their carriage than any amongst them."[16] One of the most intriguing questions raised by the study of language is to consider which "name of war" a man like James Printer, a woman like Weetamoo, a pniese like Hobbomock, or Metacom himself would have used to describe the conflict in which they found themselves entangled, and which Metacom was accused by the English of waging. Native languages also have precise and complex terms for peace, and this book, especially in its final chapters, highlights the processes and places of peacemaking that the existing narratives of war obscure.

REENVISIONING "NARRATIVE FIELDS"

Both Jill Lepore and Amy Den Ouden, among others, have highlighted the important role of narration in establishing accounts of war and legal justification for settler colonialism in New England. Den Ouden provides an incisive, if somewhat ironic, comment by Peter Hulme:

"The particular difficulty associated with the establishment of the European colonies concerned what might be called the planting of a narrative, the hacking away of enough surrounding 'weeds' to let flourish a narrative field in which the colonists could settle themselves."[17]

Among the goals of this book is to provide, reveal, and restore alternative "narrative fields," which have sometimes arisen quite unexpectedly from the archive of colonial documents, like "weeds" breaking through soil into that well-established "field." Perhaps this "unsettling" process, in which I have engaged, could be better described as allowing multifaceted "plants" to emerge into the "narrative field," transforming that field into a (narrative) swamp which requires different kinds of navigation, or reading practices.

READING IN THE ARCHIVE

When I embarked on this project, I thought it would focus on recovering the stories of James Printer and Weetamoo, revealing different perspectives on the war . . . and it does. I thought this book would be about reading narratives of the war like Mary Rowlandson's text anew . . . and it is. I believed that extending our historical vision to include the vast land of the northern front was crucial to understanding the war and its aftermath, and that proved true. What I did not know at the outset was how much new material would be revealed by focusing so closely on the lives of James, Weetamoo, their families, and those who traveled north. So much had already been written about the war, so many archives mined by historians. I did not realize how many more documents would arise in the process of research that previous historians had not located or acknowledged. I could not have anticipated how such documents would challenge and unsettle the narratives of the war.

So many of the histories that have been written about "King Philip's War" over the last two centuries rely on the veracity of the narratives written by seventeenth-century colonial military and religious leaders, such as Increase Mather, William Hubbard, and Benjamin Church. Yet I found many instances where these foundational narratives are either not supported or entirely contradicted by primary records from the precise time and place about which they were written. For example, the oft-cited, contradictory narratives of the death of Weetamoo's husband, the Wampanoag sachem Wamsutta, are undermined by the records of the Plymouth Court (see chapter one). The accounts, written postwar, emphasize a suspected collusion between Wamsutta and the Narragansetts, which led the Plymouth colonial government to capture Wamsutta. Mather and Hubbard place Wamsutta's capture and death (by either illness or poisoning) within a larger narrative of longstanding Indigenous rebellion and conspiracy. In particular, Mather offered his account as proof of the "notoriously known" "jealousies" of the "Narragansetts and Wompanoags." However, the court documents reveal that rather than conspiracy with the neighboring

Narragansetts, Plymouth's real concern was Wamsutta's purported land deals with settlers in the competing colony of Rhode Island.[18]

Land stands at the center of those narratives. Mather's "history" of the war opens with a clear claim to the land he called New England, portraying Indigenous people as interlopers in a divinely gifted space. The Boston minister asserted "that the Heathen people amongst whom we live, and whose Land the Lord God of our Fathers hath given to us for a rightfull possession, have at sundry times been plotting mischievous devices against that part of the English Israel which is seated in these goings down of the Sun, no man that is an Inhabitant of any considerable standing, can be ignorant."[19]

Mather's geographic orientation is revealing. While Wampanoag and Wabanaki people recognized this region as the land of the dawn, Mather regarded New England as a place "seated" in the "going down of the sun." For Native people, this was the easternmost land, a place of origins. For English settlers, this was their final resting place, the end of their journey to a remote place to the west of their home. Yet it was also a birth place for them, a "new" England, a new "Israel" that would provide a fertile ground in which to plant their fields and raise their sons. The problem, as we will see herein, is that another people were already planting here, and they had their own new generations to cultivate, their longstanding responsibilities to this land holding greater weight than the promise of a distant "Lord God." While ancient planting fields and bonds of reciprocity rooted the Wampanoag, Narragansett, Nipmuc, and Wabanaki families deeply in these places, men like Mather also claimed a "rightful possession" to these lands, which they imagined had been granted them by a higher authority. At this intersection of competing claims, "rights" and responsibilities often conflicted. The puzzle that is both perplexing and disturbing to unpack, if our orientation is east, is the way in which men like Mather sought to portray the practice and defense of those longstanding Indigenous responsibilities to land and kin as a "mischievous" plot against "the English Israel" which had planted itself "amongst" them.

The records also reveal a much more complex role for Weetamoo. In Mather's postwar narrative of Wamsutta's capture, she is reduced to a scorned wife who erroneously believes her husband had been poisoned by settlers. In general, colonial narrators downplayed her role, and the conflicts between the colonies, while building a narrative of Indian treachery. But in the documents, she appears as a diplomat and leader who strategically manipulated and circumvented Plymouth's interests in her lands in order to protect them.

Two overlooked manuscript letters concerning Weetamoo, explored in chapter three, shed new light on the origins of King Philip's War. John Easton, the

Quaker governor of Rhode Island, composed a letter to Plymouth governor Josiah Winslow, one month before the outbreak of war, detailing Weetamoo's concerns regarding Plymouth Colony's encroachment on her lands, and urging Winslow to restrain this imposition on "the Queen's Right." Rather than addressing her pressing concerns, Winslow himself wrote to Weetamoo on the eve of war, hoping to persuade the influential leader to remain neutral. The letter makes clear Winslow's intent to contain Metacom, a neighboring sachem and Weetamoo's brother-in-law. Both letters illuminate the context of the causes of war in striking ways, as well as the reluctance of later historians to acknowledge the importance of Weetamoo's leadership or the strategies Plymouth pursued in its invasion of Metacom's stronghold. Thus, homing in on two extraordinary but neglected actors—Weetamoo and James Printer—led me not only to recover crucial documents, but to uncover a radically different "narrative field."

READING SCENARIOS

In my research, I also focused on reading the primary sources closely for what was happening on the ground—interpreting actions against statements, reading depictions of geography, paying close attention to behavior, movements, and exchanges. Influenced by Diana Taylor's *The Archive and the Repertoire*, and approaches from Native literary studies, I considered the "scenarios" contained within primary documents, reading people's actions in places of cultural and ecological significance, through a culturally specific lens. In writing, I also sought to imaginatively reconstruct these "place-worlds." This style may be especially evident beginning with chapter four, on the opening of the war, where storytelling evokes the interruptive, chaotic nature of war, even as critical close reading sheds light on events and causes.[20]

This process was enabled by language study—dwelling on a place name or title, or utilizing multiple language resources to recover a more accurate conceptualization of a practice like "tribute" or a category like "captive." But it also entailed reading texts, such as deeds, within a network of related documents. For example, one mistake that historians sometimes make is to assume that a court grant can be read as the beginning of colonial settlement, or as a marker of legitimacy. In contrast, I would often find that a "grant" issued by the Plymouth or Massachusetts Court did not lead to immediate settlement but rather to protests by Native people who inhabited those places. Sometimes the resistance to "improvement" was overt, such as dismantling built structures or assaulting livestock. In other cases it was a matter of discerning the evidence of continued inhabitation and signs of protecting lands against encroachment. Often, statements made in court years later demonstrated that although English people claimed title, Indigenous people continued to inhabit, cultivate, and know land as their own, retaining their ancestral rights and responsibilities.

READING THE LAND AS ARCHIVE

Likewise, a large part of the research for this project has entailed walking, paddling, and driving through the places where these events took place. The land itself is an archive that demands interpretation. My own education often involved my father, along with Abenaki community leaders like Lenny Lampman, Louise Lampman Larivee, Lester Lampman, and Larry Lapan, and my tracking mentor Gordon Russell, taking me out on the land and showing me the stories it has to tell. Those excursions entailed learning to recognize the rocks that revealed the remains of homes and council houses, understanding how apple trees planted by grandmothers were still feeding deer, which in turn were still feeding families through the winter, and learning to read the flow of the river in rapids and trout pools, or, as I learned from Wampanoag tribal historians, seeing the cliffs where councils were held at Metacom's stronghold of Montaup. These ancient and ongoing places all have stories attached to them — features that evoke memories, embed oral traditions, and map subsistence and survival, and that can reveal acute insight into a historical document.

My teachers in Abenaki country consistently emphasized the importance of oral history, learned on the land and at the kitchen table. When I began this project, I imagined the same might be true in southern New England, but I learned that I had as much to learn from Wampanoag readings of the documents as I did from hearing oral histories. When I visited Massachusetts and Rhode Island, out came books, illuminating readings of the printed word, laced with ironic humor about all of the misguided interpretations that have been published over the years. We have a tendency to think of Native people, of the past and even of the present, as "oral cultures," but this characterization fails to account for adaptation. The Wampanoags and their neighbors swiftly and adeptly adopted reading and the culture of the book in the seventeenth century, making them a highly literate people. Moreover, these communities have been engaged with the historical record for multiple generations, producing analysis, synthesis, and knowledge, which is informed by their oral traditions. Consultation and exchange regarding the interpretation of documents, places, actions, and motivations is an ongoing process in which I am engaged, a process that

will never be complete. Thus, as you reach the end of this book, you will encounter more openings than closures, inviting the process of research, recovery,
and exchange to continue.

My own obsession with land and place, swamps and rivers, led to many hours
immersed in maps, as I strove to comprehend routes of movement, tracked
particular places, and attempted to reconstruct subsistence and recreate the
historical space in my mind. The maps would inevitably lead me back to those
swamps and rivers, where my legs would become snagged in brambles, my
feet wet and muddy. In southern New England, one of the greatest challenges
was figuring out how to access and understand places that had been radically
transformed by colonialism and industrial development. I encountered a stark
difference in southern New England than what I had previously experienced
in northern New England. Whereas so much of our forested land in Wabanaki
has either been sustained or recovered, in Wampanoag country the development is overwhelming, in some places erasing any traces of the Indigenous
landscape that preceded it. I will never forget the experience of traveling to
Mattapoisett (in Somerset, Massachusetts), where Weetamoo grew up, to find a
massive power plant overshadowing the entire peninsula.

Readers will be able to travel in digital space to many of these places, via
the book's website, at http://ourbelovedkin.com, which features a wide array
of maps, images, and related documents as well as "connections" that offer
additional context. These online maps, created for the book, are often key to
understanding Indigenous networks, places, and movements in each chapter.
The website provides multiple options for navigation. From the website's table
of contents, you can select "Navigate Alongside the Book." You can also follow
the embedded link to each chapter's digital "path," provided in the first endnote
of each chapter in this book. Or you can select individual embedded links,
which appear in additional endnotes throughout the text. Through this website,
the interested reader will be able to journey beyond the page, linking to key
documents, places, and contexts that further illuminate the stories contained in
the book, allowing participation to extend into digital space, and perhaps, out
onto the land.

ACKNOWLEDGING THE STORIES OF OUR ANCESTORS

In my travels, I realized that it was my own unique family that has compelled
me to tell this story anew. The most obvious is my father's influence, teaching

me to read the land and waterways, to understand the depth of history that lies within the land, to laugh at our human fallibility in the face of so much power. Still, the more I wrote, the more I realized that an equally strong influence came from the stories I heard from my cherished *Babcia*, my mother's mother. At the beginning of World War II, my grandmother found her family suddenly displaced by a war in which she had no commanding role and no power of resistance. She lived on a farm in rural Poland with her parents, three young children, and my grandfather, who once pulled a plow by the strength of his broad shoulders when the oxen gave out. They were displaced from their home by opposing armies, coming from both Russia and Germany, and she soon found herself separated from her husband, her parents, and her siblings, as she and her children were transported on cattle cars, often in bitter cold, between Nazi labor camps. *Babcia* was a phenomenal storyteller, and her harrowing tales have stayed with me. Her ability to strategize in the midst of chaos was astounding, and led to the survival of seven children, three of whom were born during the war, including my mother. I know that but for the strength and intelligence of this woman, who never had a formal education, I would not be here.

Yet among the most important realizations I drew from her stories was that for most people in the world, war simply arrives at their door, an unwelcome invader. It is not the carefully orchestrated series of causes, effects, strategies, and events that historians often construct in the aftermath. For most people, war is a relentless storm that arrives without warning, a swirl of chaos that upends their lives in untold ways. For most mothers and many fathers, the goal of war is merely striving to ensure that their children will survive. Inevitably, this understanding shapes my reading of the documents as much as my training as a scholar. Rather than striving for objectivity, I've taken a cue from my grandmother and father.[21] I aim to strive for integrity in my research and interpretation, and pursue a relentless determination to document the strategies of survival. I acknowledge, and even cultivate, a sense of embeddedness (rather than distance) through my writing. In doing so, I draw on and respect the language of this land, which privileges participation. This includes using writing as a tool, and this book as an *awikhigan*, to draw you, the reader, into this Native space, to use the techniques of storytelling to draw you into "place-worlds," with the goal of deeper understanding.

Opening the door to Weetamoo's story meant understanding her as a mother, a sister, and a leader responsible for protecting all of her "beloved kin." Likewise, James Printer's story revealed his family's remarkable efforts to find sanctuary for their relations when it seemed that no place in their homeland was safe. This project also changed when I became a mother, transformed by my newfound understanding of the lengths to which a parent will go to protect a single life. It brought not only deeper understanding of the actions of Weetamoo and James Printer, but also, quite unexpectedly, of Mary Rowlandson, and most assuredly, of those ancestors who found refuge in the north country and survived.

Prologue: Caskoak, the Place of Peace

THE "QUEEN" OF CASKOAK: CASCO BAY, 1623

It was spring, the salmon streaming upriver, when English explorer and colonial agent Christopher Levett arrived at Caskoak, the "place of herons," in
Wabanaki, the land of the dawn (map 2). Wabanaki leaders greeted him, hosted
his visit, and diplomatically opened the way through the extensive coastal region. The leaders of Cascoak invited Levett to remain, and, he recounted, the
"Queen" of "Quack" formally welcomed him, his men, and the fishermen who
came to her homeland: "The woman or reputed queen, asked me if those men
were my friends. I told her they were; then she drank to them, and told them
they were welcome to her country, and so should all my friends be at any time;
she drank also to her husband, and bid him welcome to her country too; for you
must understand that her father was the sagamore of this place, and left it to her
at his death, having no more children."[1]

In welcoming Levett into "her country," the Queen initiated a diplomatic
relationship. She spoke on behalf of a community, a "gathering" of extended
families bound to each other through longstanding inhabitation, intermarriage,
and interdependent relationships. The people who "belonged" to this place
included those whose ties reached back through oral tradition and kinship to
time immemorial, as well as others, like her husband Cogawesco, who had
been incorporated through marriage or adoption. Belonging entailed not only
residency, but kinship to a particular place and people, of which the *sôgamo*
(sagamore or sachem) or *sôgeskwa* (saunkskwa) was the symbolic leader. The
Queen's leadership may have seemed anomalous to Levett, explained by the
apparent lack of male heirs, but *sôgeskwak*, or female leaders, were not uncommon, particularly in communities reliant upon horticulture, where oral

17

2. Caskoak and surrounding territories

traditions emphasized the power of women. Evidence of women's labor and management, in cultivating fields and allowing some to lie fallow, was all around Levett, who witnessed "a great quantity of cleared ground" from his position on the coastal waterways.[2]

Located near the northeasternmost limits of horticulture, the people of Caskoak occupied a critical position in a distributive trade network, mediating between planting communities and northerly kin who relied on hunting, fishing, and gathering (see map 1). *Sôgamak* and *sôgeskwak* were responsible for ensuring distribution of resources within their homelands, and between territories, through a well-established ceremonial and economic system of exchange. A breakdown in the redistributive system could yield conflict, particularly in times of scarcity. Therefore, effective leaders facilitated the renewal of relationships and amelioration of disputes through diplomatic councils and annual ceremonies at places like Caskoak, where people of all ages participated in symbolic and material exchange, celebrating intercommunity marriages, relaying deep-time stories, sharing artistic and practical knowledge, and negotiating rights and responsibilities among contiguous communities, thus enabling social and ecological sustainability.[3]

Diplomatic negotiation was crucial at this juncture, as Wabanaki communities increasingly encountered European vessels and fledgling fishing and trading settlements on their coast, imposing a different system of exchange. At the same time, foreign diseases devastated Native communities. These transformations ushered in a time of great grief and change, where conflict could abound. Exchange was vital to diplomacy. Wabanaki men were already traveling between Ktsitekw (the St. Lawrence River) and the coast, participating in an extensive inland and maritime trade network, which included both Indigenous people and French, English, and Basque visitors. They adapted their language to accommodate the trade and even commanded European shallops. Some of their relations had been taken captive by English and French men, carried away in ships, far from their homes and their kin. Thus, Wabanaki leaders understood that there were dangers inherent to their interactions with European visitors and vessels; the Queen's diplomacy was designed to bring both neighboring leaders and newcomers into right relations.[4]

Levett participated in such a diplomatic council at the Indigenous meeting place of Casco Bay with Wabanaki leaders from the region, who expressed a desire to bring him and his family into their kinship network. He humorously expressed that he "was not a little proud . . . to be adopted cousin to so many great kings at one instant, but did willingly accept of it." In this world, one could not inhabit a place without belonging to a particular family, and as Levett witnessed at Caskoak, this "belonging" could be cultivated. The Queen explained that her husband belonged through marriage, and Levett himself was offered a place within her family and territory. However, these relationships also entailed commitment. Whether Levett realized it or not, his "acceptance" came with responsibilities."[5]

The problem, of course, was that English guests all too often misinterpreted such hospitality—when the Queen said they were "welcome" to her country, she did not mean they were "welcome" to possess it. Nor did she mean that the English and French fishermen were welcome to harvest all the fish from the sea, an abundance they misunderstood as endless. Having lived in this place for so long, dependent upon it for their survival, the people of Caskoak understood through experience the complex of belief, practice, story, and ceremony that enabled them to sustain balance among finite resources. This included the crucial role of leaders like the Queen in ensuring fair distribution at Caskoak, a place name that conveyed a meeting of multiple tributaries and nations, a site of diplomacy and exchange. When the Queen welcomed Levett and his "friends" into this space, she invited them to enter into its network of people, diplomatic practices, and reciprocal relations. It was up to him, and those that followed, to reveal whether they would "abide with" them and "share" in the first mother's power and strength, or fall among the "brutes," who would "steal" her "body" and refuse to "share in it" as she had intended.[6]

A REBALANCING: CASKOAK, 1631

Christopher Levett acknowledged that the Native nations had a "natural right of inheritance" and received praise from local leaders for "acting in a right fashion," but others posed a direct challenge to the system of reciprocal relations. For example, Walter Bagnall, the first European to *settle* in Casco Bay, displayed little regard for either Indigenous rights or the protocols of exchange. In 1628, he set up a trading post on "Richmond" island, and became infamous for hoarding goods and repeatedly cheating Wabanaki people in trade. Bagnall neglected to acquire title from either his own government or local Indigenous leaders, but became wealthy through deception and "extortion." In the Wabanaki world, such behavior represented the worst of infractions against the community. In 1631, Skitterygusset, whom Levett had acknowledged as a local sagamore, killed Bagnall and burned down his trading post, enacting a violent redistribution and asserting jurisdiction in this diplomatic space.[7]

"A BUSHEL OF CORN," OWASCOAG, 1659

Skitterygusset belonged to a wide network of related leaders along the coast, who participated in negotiations that led to deeds, often signed by multiple representatives. He was the first to appear on a deed for land at Caskoak, in which "fisherman" Francis Small acquired the right to settle land from "the marshes and uplands of Capissic" to the fishing falls at Amancongan, on the south side of the Presumpscot River (between the contemporary Fore River and Cumberland Mills). Small pledged an annual "pay" of "one trading coat," a symbolic recognition of Skitterygusset's leadership, and "one gallon of liquor." The exchange of wampum and tobacco, as Small later testified, in this and subsequent agreements, sealed a pledge to share space, creating a negotiated relationship as much as an economic transaction. He later sold the rights to part of this tract, including a mill privilege at Capissic, to John Phillips, who transferred it to his son-in-law George Munjoy, both of whom had come to Casco from Boston. In 1666, Skitterygusset's sister, the saunkskwa Warrabitta, signed a deed with another leader, Nannateonett, allowing Munjoy to extend his claim to the "other side" of the Presumpscot, from "the lower-most planting ground" of Amancongan to the great falls at Sacarappa (Westbrook), an area far from the English settlements clustered on the coast. Four years later, War-rabitta, known also as Jane or Jhone, apparently consented to a local colonial land grant at Casco Bay to Anthony Brackett for "twenty shillings," with her brother Sagettawon, who had married into a leadership family to the south, on the Saco and Kennebunk Rivers. Warrabitta and Skitterygusset also appear on deeds with leaders to the north, including Moxus, Sheepscot John, and the influential Androscoggin leader the English called "Robin Hood"; documents such as these often recognized the intersecting relationships and jurisdictions of "neighboring sachems" in the coastal region.[8]

At Owascoag, just south of Caskoak, where Warrabitta and her mother lived and planted, they had allowed a group of settlers, represented by Andrew and Arthur Alger, to live among them. This produced the earliest record in which Warrabitta appeared. The documented agreement between Warrabit-ta's family and the Alger brothers is typical of deeds in this region, although more revealing than many of those recorded in Plymouth, where Indigenous rights were often subsumed. In the document, dated September 1659, "Jane alias Uphanum" declared that she, "her mother namely Naguasqua the wife of Wickwarrawaske Sagamore, & her brother" Skitterygusset (who may have died by this time), had "coequally," eight years previous (in 1651), "sold unto Andrew Alger, & to his brother Arther Alger a Tract of Land" on the Owas-

coag River (Scarborough). The deed reveals patterns of contiguous and overlapping inhabitation and resource use that had to be negotiated in order to
maintain peaceful relations. The deed recognized the name of the river "in
Indian" while naming several places that denoted recent settlement, such as
"the great hill of Abram Jocelyns" (probably Orchard Hill). It also recognized
the right of Warrabitta and her mother to continue to plant in this territory "so
long as" they "both live." Most important, the agreement required the Algers to
give "one bushel of corne for acknowledgment every year so long as they both
shall Live."[9]

This annual bushel of corn, recurrently pledged on deeds and treaties, was
similar to the contribution a Native family would be obliged to make to their
community. Rather than simply acquiring an outright purchase, the Algers
engaged in an agreement by which they, too, could belong to this place,
through their annual "acknowledgement" to the local family leaders, enacting
a formalized relationship to the land and its longstanding community. "Uphanum," translated to "our sister" or "our woman," acted as speaker for the extended leadership family, acknowledging that the agreement had been in place
since 1651. Warrabitta reaffirmed the agreement again in 1672, three years before her death and the commencement of the war.[10]

While Warrabitta was party to multiple deeds over these decades between
1651 and 1675, the 1659 Owascoag deed bears close examination, revealing a
great deal about the larger context of diplomatic negotiations and conceptualizations of relationships among people and places. Owascoag was "the place of
good grass," and the name may have translated more precisely to "Olaskikak," or
"sweetgrass gathering place." This was the grass—known to some Algonquian
nations as the "hair of Mother Earth," a sacred plant used in ceremonies, art,
basketry, and medicine—that is uniquely adapted to annual summer harvesting. Sweetgrass flourishes in brackish marshes, which were and are often tied
to particular family territories. Owascoag was likely the place where Warrabitta
and her family handpicked the blades of grass, distributing carefully woven
braids and baskets among the networks to which they belonged.[11]

This was also a place where they planted "our mother" corn, a practice
clearly continuing here even as settlers like the Algers began their own plant-
ings. Oral traditions relay that the Corn Mother, known in story and song as
Nigawes, "our mother," instructed that her own body be planted in order to feed
her starving children, the Wabanaki people. And it was unlikely that Warrabitta
and her mother planted alone; like other Native women, they must have shared
the fields with their female relations. Naming here was important as well. The
name given to Warrabitta and Skitterygusset's mother was Naguasqua, which

may have been an Anglicized spelling of *nigawes* (with the gendered ending
"skwa"), recognizing "our mother's" right to continue to harvest and plant in
this place. Thus the deed recognized Owascoag as the place of "our mother," on
multiple levels, where "our mother" lived, planted and was planted, harvested
and was harvested, to enable the peacemaking protocols for which Cascoak was
well known.[12]

Like their predecessor, the Queen, these leaders of Cascoak were entrusted
with diplomacy. Thus, part of their role was to create responsible relationships
with the newcomers. With this agreement, they gave the Algers and their extended family permission to live at Owascoag, but negotiated some of the terms
of sharing space and required "acknowledgment" of their continuing relationship to and leadership in this place. As Alice Nash has observed, such "deeds
should be read more like proto-treaties" or councils in which rights, land use, and
jurisdiction were negotiated, rather "than as simple property transactions."[13]

This agreement was made at harvest time, when both the Algers and Warrabitta and her mother were gathering in the corn. Like any family in the territory, the Algers were expected to make a contribution that could be distributed
to the whole. As Nash points out, the annual "acknowledgment" was not an act
of charity, as Warrabitta clearly could plant her own field, but a symbolic act
that embedded settlers in an Indigenous redistributive system. In giving them
corn, the Algers were at least symbolically acknowledging not only the women
leaders, but "our mother" from whom they also were drawing nourishment.
The old stories warned that the newcomers would crave the Corn Mother's
body, would try to steal it. Part of Warrabitta's responsibility was to encourage
them instead to follow her original instructions, to "divide among you the flesh
and bone of the first mother," corn and tobacco, "and let all shares be alike" in
order to "carry out" the "love of your first mother."[14]

Part I

The Education of Weetamoo and James Printer

Exchange, Diplomacy, Dispossession

Namumpum, "Our Beloved Kinswoman," Saunkskwa of Pocasset: Bonds, Acts, Deeds

"Squa Sachim, Our Beloved Cousin, Kinswoman," Nonaquaket, July 1651

A unique "Indian deed" is the earliest surviving *awikhigan*, or written instrument, to which Weetamoo of Pocasset set her mark. In the document, dated July 26, 1651, the "great sachem," Ousamequin, his son Wamsutta, and his son-by-marriage Tuspaquin recognized Weetamoo, then known as "Namumpum," as both the neighboring "Squa Sachim" and their "kinswoman." They declared, as "neighbor sachems" who "bordered upon" the "confines and inheritance of our beloved cousin," that only Namumpum held the symbolic and legal authority to permit settlement at Pocasset. While acknowledging her right to allow an individual settler, Richard Morris, to inhabit a "tract" of land in her territory of "Nunequoquit or Pogasek Neck," the document also mapped crucial Indigenous relationships.[1]

The "deed" concerned a small "neck" of coastal wetland in Pocasset, on the east side of Kteticut (Taunton River), the great waterway of the Wampanoag country. At the center of Pocasset was the river Quequechand, a series of fishing falls, which flowed from Watuppa, a long spring-fed pond. Namumpum maintained a town, with her kin, by the deep pool at the falls, but they relied on a vast ecological range, including cedar swamps to the south and forested uplands to the north. They maintained several planting fields, including one at Nonaquaket, beside crystalline coastal waters. Trails and canoe routes enabled travel from Quequechand southward past Nonaquaket Pond to the neighboring saunkskwa Awashonks's territory of Sakonnet and coastal Acoaxet; and northwards via the Kteticut to Ousamequin and Wamsutta's territory of Pokanoket, Tuspaquin's town of Nemasket, and Cohannet, where the Pocasset path joined the Kteticut trail.[2]

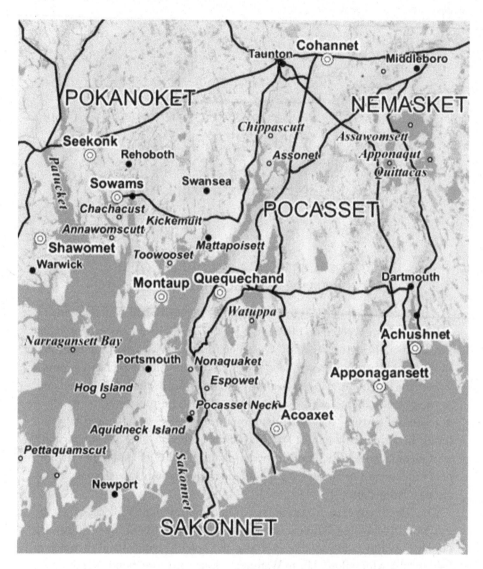

3. Pocasset and Pokanoket, highlighting places in chapter 1

In the heat of July, Pocasset families would have been living on the coast and ponds, fishing, gathering shellfish, harvesting plants from the salt and cedar marshes, and returning periodically to check the growth of their planting fields. To the west of Nonaquaket's planting grounds, on the "neck," their English neighbor, Richard Morris, with their permission, left his cattle to graze on the copious salt marsh grasses, the cows confined by water on both sides of the peninsula. Yet summer was not all subsistence, but a season of diplomacy. While this deed confirmed Morris's right, it also recorded a council among sachems, Indigenous diplomatic rhetoric intertwining with English legal discourse. The deed signals the ways in which leaders like Ousamequin and Namumpum had begun to adapt the tool of writing to play a role similar to wampum, the powerful shell bead which bound people together, and bound words to deeds.[3]

Adhering to traditional protocols, the sachems opened their statement by invoking bonds of kinship, the framework on which governance rested, declaring they were "of the blood and kindred" of Namumpum. Algonquian languages express kinship through pronouns like "my," "our," and "his." Yet these terms do not denote possession, but rather evoke responsibilities and shared histories that bind people to each other and the land. Every pronouncement of kinship invokes a bond. While *nigawes*, "my mother," evokes the birth cord that connects the infant to its mother, *ndakinna*, "our land," evokes the cord that ties the people to our nourishing mother-land. Moreover, these terms embed inclusivity and exclusivity. To Ousamequin and his "neighboring sachems," Namumpum was "*my* kinswoman," "*our* cousin," as well as his "brother's daughter,"[4] deceptively simple words which, like wampum, bound their expression of reciprocal kinship to their deeds. Yet his words also drew bounds around "our land," making clear that those outside the bonds of kinship, in this case, the Plymouth settlers, could claim neither Weetamoo nor her land as their own.[5]

The bonds of kinship also required sachems to respect the bonds and "bounds" between their territories, "our land," on which families relied for sustenance. In the deed, Ousamequin, the leader recognized as "Massasoit," the "great sachem" of the Wampanoag, and Plymouth's most valued ally, spoke with reverence for his "kinswoman," insisting he commanded neither obedience nor authority in the territory of her "inheritance." Further, Ousamequin stated, "I Never did nor intended to put under plimoth any of my kinswomans land but my own inheritance and there fore I do disalow of any pretended claime to this land." Marking a clear boundary between Plymouth's "pretended" assertions and Namumpum's jurisdiction, Ousamequin expressed Namumpum's *exclusive* relationship to Pocasset, a symbolic representation of the "collective right" of Pocasset families, which he was obliged to respect as her kinsman and "neighbor."[6]

Indeed, one crucial function of summer councils and *this* written instrument was to cement and clarify relationships between neighboring peoples and their territories, including settlers. In the discourse of English land tenure, the deed allowed Rhode Islander Richard Morris the right to claim this "neck" at Nonaquaket as "property," a "tract" cut off from Pocasset, which he could pass down to his descendants or sell to another individual. Yet, in the context of Indigenous councils, the writing registered Namumpum's protection of the usage rights of a single settler whom she had allowed in her territory *against* the claims of Plymouth men. The fledgling colony of Plymouth "pretended" to claim preemptive rights to the entire Wampanaog country, through their alliance with Ousamequin; the legitimacy and bounds of their "patent" rested in part on their treaty with him. Plymouth interpreted Ousamequin's role as "chief Sachem" and his "inheritance" of "a great tract of land" as rule of and rights to all Wampanoag territory. Yet this deed represents a clear example of Ousamequin denying that he had the power of a "king." Although he may "have put my land under plimoth government," he formalized in writing that he "never did nor intended to put under plimoth any of my kinswoman's land."[7]

The use of the word "under" is telling. While Ousamequin and Namumpum acted within an Indigenous rhizomatic system of kinship, the English settlers at Plymouth sought to incorporate them into "interlocking hierarchies" of governance. In the first treaty between Ousamequin and the settlers, shortly after their arrival at Patuxet in 1620, Edward Winslow and his fellow émigrés declared that "King James would esteem of him as his friend and ally," implying equality between the "great sachem" and the king. In subsequent renewals, the Plymouth men tried to place Ousamequin and his sons "under" the English king, who imagined all these territories as his own, setting out the boundaries on paper, lines of latitude and longitude that crossed lands "from sea to sea," upon which he would never step foot. Likewise, although most of the Plymouth men had never been to Pocasset, they claimed it "under" their imagined jurisdiction, by right of their patent from the king and their treaty with Ousamequin. That spring of 1651, they had already imagined dividing "Puncateesett [Pocasset] Neck," including the cove of Espowet, among themselves, "over and against Rhode Island." But, in an ironic turn, Ousamequin's role as *Massasoit*, a great ambassador, compelled him to use his diplomatic ability to make his allies comprehend Wampanoag territorial relationships and Namumpum's authority. Namumpum maintained here and throughout her lifetime that her Pocasset mother-land was her just "inheritance." She had the right and responsibility to maintain its integrity, and she, in consultation with her families, would decide whom she would allow to enter her network of kin. With this deed, Massasoit recognized Namumpum's exclusive right to grant usage rights to an individual settler in a particular place in her territory. Although Rhode Islanders like Morris and the Plymouth men regarded "Pocasset Neck" as potential pasture, to Namumpum, the ancient cove of Espowet and marsh of Nonaquaket sustained a vast network above and below the ground, which she was bound to preserve.[8]

This chapter will explore a number of deeds in which Weetamoo (Namumpum) appears as a major diplomatic figure, setting a crucial, complex stage for her alliance-building during King Philip's War. The *saunkskwa* materializes only on the eve of the war in most histories, which too often rely on postwar narratives that displace both her diplomacy and the war waged against Indigenous women. Thus, this chapter necessarily fills a substantial gap in the record; these documents demonstrate Weetamoo's leadership prior to the war, as well as the challenge she posed to Puritan men and their colonial desires. Moreover, these documents, read in the context of Native networks of kinship and geography, reveal that Wampanoag leaders did not merely acquiesce to or resist progressive land loss and dispossession, but devised "strategic adaptations" to colonization, including the deeds and "improvements" that settlers imposed upon the land.[9] Each section will present a document and lead the reader through interpretations, illuminated through geography and Indigenous cultural frameworks. Juxtaposing Weetamoo's struggles and strategic adaptations with some of the women and men in her extensive network, this chapter asks us to read rhizomatically from the time and place of particular deeds to contiguous locations and scenarios, which provide crucial context for interpretation. While Weetamoo's appearances in the historical record may first appear sparse, this chapter builds a frame through which we will be better able to understand her motivations and adaptations prior to King Philip's War.

"YOU HAVE RATHER BINE A HUSBAND THAN A WIFE"

If Ousamequin and Namumpum stood on Nonaquaket Neck as they exchanged words, they would have seen a small village across the narrows, which the English settlers called Pocasset—a name likely borrowed from the neighboring Wampanoag territory. The origin story of this fledgling English settlement, where Morris lived, elucidates the challenge Namumpum posed to colonial men, as a woman whose authority was recognized by the most influential Native men they knew. The story also reveals early competition for jurisdiction among English colonists. Indeed, Plymouth leaders desired to claim the land at Pocasset Neck "against" the people of Pocasset, not only because of the land's resources, but to enforce their power versus wayward settlers who had rebelled against their neighboring colony in Massachusetts Bay and set up their own colony which came to be known as Rhode Island.[10]

Pocasset, later renamed Portsmouth, had been established on "Aquidneck Island" in 1638 when Narragansett leaders, including Canonicus and his nephew Miantonomo, granted occupancy rights to a group of exiles, in a series of councils brokered by Roger Williams (see map 3). Their words bound with strings of wampum, the sachems gave the English families permission to exclusively inhabit the island, where they could plant, graze livestock, build houses and a church. Likewise, Ousamequin gave them permission to cut grass from neighboring necks and coves, and they agreed to give annual "rent" in the form of a coat, acknowledgement of his sachemship, and their usage rights in Wampanaog territory.[11]

These first settlers of the island had been expelled from Massachusetts Bay in 1637 as a result of the Antinomian Controversy, a conflict associated with the notorious Anne Hutchinson, who deigned to take on the role of teacher, gathering a small congregation of women in her Boston home who posed questions about John Cotton's weekly sermon. At the root of the "blasphemy" was her belief, shared with the minister John Wheelwright (her sister's husband), that pre-destined salvation, or "justification," could be discerned only through "inner assurance" of "God's grace," not through reading the signs and "evidence" of salvation, known as "sanctification," in outward behavior. This notion posed a threat to the authority of the ministers; if an individual could, through inner reflection and prayer, discern the presence of grace, she did not require confirmation by any outside body, including her minister. Hutchinson was by no means the first to propound this belief, but she was regarded as its most vexing proponent and, as a woman, the most vulnerable one. Using gendered language, Edward Johnson called her "the grand Mistris of all the rest" and her nemesis, Governor John Winthrop, suggested she was the mother of the Antinomian Controversy, "the breeder and nourisher of all these distempers." Still, it was Hutchinson's appropriation of a masculine leadership role that caused the greatest offense. During her church trial, the minister Hugh Peter chastised, "'You have stept out of your place, you have rather bine a Husband than a Wife and a preacher than a Hearer; and a Magistrate than a Subject." As Mary Beth Norton has observed, Hutchinson was punished by the ministers for "her refusal to occupy a woman's proper place."[12]

After two protracted trials, first in the General Court and then in Boston's First Church, the Bay Colony's leaders banished Hutchinson, along with Wheelwright and other defenders. Roger Williams, likewise exiled for controversies over religious doctrine, brokered a council with the Narragansetts to make space for the exiles in the fledgling colony of Rhode Island.[13] Thus, the first English village settled adjacent to Weetamoo's town and named for her territory originated with a woman who stepped out of her "place" to assume a leadership role.

Hutchinson and Weetamoo challenged the beliefs and structure of Puritan society by asserting a space of authority for women. In Weetamoo's country, banishment was reserved for the worst offenses—unthinkable acts of violence and family betrayal that threatened the whole. However, Hutchinson's world rested on a firm hierarchy of male authority, in which families, farms, towns, and colonies needed to be "husbanded" into order by men designed by God to govern those below them. The rebellion of a woman, or the failure of men to control and "yoke" their subordinates, threatened to push the entire social order toward chaos.[14]

PLANTING POCASSET

That July of 1651, as she returned from the council, Namumpum (Weetamoo) might have joined her kinswomen to check on their planting fields nearby Nonaquaket and Quequechand. By midsummer, the corn stalks likely reached toward the sun, tassling, drawing bees to light among them. Beneath the stalks, squash vines would extend across the mounds, wide green leaves expanding to provide shade, blossoms beckoning to bees. From among the leaves, bean tendrils would spiral around the stalks, climbing toward sunflowers and sunchokes, delicate white flowers promising fruit. Working alongside the plants, the women would have coaxed soil up the mounds with noninvasive shells and hoes, ensuring the shallow corn roots were protected, not only by squash leaves but their own hands. The Plymouth and Portsmouth settlers might have seen a terrible chaos of tangled vines. But this "ecological cornucopia" had its own order, a network of relationships that fostered long-term sustainability.[15]

Across the Sakonnet river, Namumpum might have noticed a stark difference in the planting fields at Portsmouth. No large mounds rose from the earth. No women cultivated communal fields. Even Anne Hutchinson, allowed comparable freedom at Aquidneck, would have been confined in her work to the domestic household and kitchen garden, tending orderly rows of lettuce, turnips, and herbs. One of the first acts of the English men at Pocasset was to divide the land into household lots, each owned and governed by a husband. They divided lots into parcels, designated for a house, pasturage for cattle, outbuildings to house livestock and fodder in winter, and a fenced planting field. If as a child Namumpum had observed the Hutchinson household, across the narrows of the river, she might have seen William standing on the neck of the cove in his field, accompanied by two massive horned creatures, yoked to a plow. In the soil, he would have commanded the oxen to make parallel furrows in long, deep uniform lines. When this arduous task was completed, William would have taken his oxen to the other side of the rectangular field and compelled them to repeat the parallel rows to cross the previous ones. If William planted in the manner typical of Plymouth colonists, he would sow the English grains of wheat, barley, and rye in the rows, and plant corn in small hills at the intersections, or alternatively, he might have planted English and "Indian" crops in separate fields. Just as the English king placed an imagined grid over the continent, and settlers placed imagined grids over Native territories to make towns, thus a man "husbanded" the land into an imagined order, creating a grid to contain native corn and English grain within his properly bounded fields.[16]

The English men in Portsmouth and Plymouth, the saunkskwa may have already known, gazed longingly across the narrows at her "meadows" and fields. They desired her planting grounds, cultivated and fallow, her marshlands, salt and fresh, with the passion of the righteous, believing that the land's destiny was to be converted with the plow, yoked like oxen, husbanded to its "proper" purpose, and transformed to field and pasture.

"NAMUMPUM, SQUA-SACHEM OF POCASSET"

While Portsmouth men solidified their identity as "planters" by husbanding the land into orderly fields, Pocasset women derived strength from cultivating the intertwined mounds. Weetamoo's leadership arose from her role as a cultivator of diplomacy. The 1651 Nonaquaket deed recognized Namumpum's title as "squa sachem," a phrase English men erroneously translated as "queen" or "sachem's wife." English women's status was defined primarily by the men to whom they were bound, by birth to their father's rank, and by marriage, to their husband's. Thus it was challenging, despite the recent reign of Queen Elizabeth I, for English settlers to conceive of a Native woman governing in her own right, particularly given that, in their hierarchies of race, class, and gender, an "Indian" woman would rank far below themselves.[17]

Nevertheless, in Algonquian communities and languages, the title "saunkskwa" was commonly applied to women leaders like Warrabitta and Weetamoo, as equals to their male relations. They were the "rock women" on whom entire communities relied. These titles contain the most important role that *sôgemak* and *sôgeskwak* played. They were not ruling "kings" and "queens," but rather ambassadors, "hard-bodied" diplomats who traveled to other nations, carried their community's deliberative decisions, communicated effectively and persuasively with other leaders, and traveled swiftly to return the wider deliberations home.[18] Rather than singular authorities, they formed part of a leadership network, which also included counselors and elders. Their collective responsibilities are embedded in the rhetoric of the Nonaquaket deed. The Pocasset families entrusted Namumpum to represent their intertwined interests and their collective sovereignty in their territory. She had inherited this role from her father, Conbitant, as well as her mother, but had risen to this capacity through her community's trust. In council, she received acknowledgment from "neighboring sachems," including Ousamequin's commitment to uphold the saunkskwa's right at Pocasset against the claims of Plymouth. Likewise, she ensured that the right they had allowed to their Portsmouth neighbor would be respected. She ensured the bonds with their Wampanoag kin and the more delicate strands that connected them to their new neighbors would be cultivated and upheld.

"THIS WOMAN TATAPANUM," PATUXET, 1659

Sometime after Ousamequin made his declaration regarding Weetamoo's authority in 1651, Weetamoo married Wamsutta, his eldest son, in a dual marriage alliance joining her sister Wootonakanuske with Metacom, further cementing the bonds between these Wampanoag leadership families, ensuring peace, security, and exchange between them. It appears, however, that soon after this marriage, the Plymouth men sought to use this bond to access Weetamoo's lands.

According to the Plymouth Book of Deeds, on Christmas Eve, 1657, Plymouth leaders James Cudworth, Josiah Winslow, Constant Southworth (William Bradford's stepson), and the tavern keeper John Barnes cornered Wamsutta regarding a debt to Barnes that had come due that very day. They compelled him to sign a "bond" for "a parcel of land, which they say is granted by the court of Plymouth unto themselves with some others." Yet, according to their testimony, Wamsutta insisted he was "not willing at present to sell all they doe desire." Much of the court's "grant" was on Pocasset land, which Wamsutta had neither the right nor the authority to concede. The Book of Deeds recorded that over a year later, in April 1659, "Tatapanum" (Namumpum/Weetamoo) released her husband from the bond, by her signed consent to convey those lands to a group of twenty-six "freemen," including those who compelled the bond. The large "tract" included "all the upland and meadow . . . on the easterly side of the Taunton River," from Quequechand to the "narrowing of Assonet neck," as well as the "meadow on the westerly side of Taunton river" to the "head of the Weyposet river" (see map 3). The document reported that Wamsutta and Weetamoo had relinquished for themselves and their "heirs" "any right and title . . . unto any part and parcel thereof." Then, in June 1659, the Book of Deeds recorded, Wamsutta and "this Woman Tatapanum" "appeared before" Josiah Winslow and William Bradford Jr., "acknowledging" that the previous agreement was their "free act and deed."[19]

These documents demonstrate a stark contrast with the Nonaquaket deed, which recognized Namumpum as saunkskwa and conveyed to a single settler the right to use a small "tract" of land. The "Freeman's" deed encompassed much of northern Pocasset and authorized a large group of settlers to divide the land into lots which could be sold for profit and developed into farms, mills, and pasture. The deed registered a different set of relationships as well. While acknowledging Wampanoag authority to convey land, the instrument invested the Plymouth men and the English king with jurisdiction *over* them, asserting that "Ossamequin, Wamsutta [and] Tatapanum" were "natives inhabiting and living within the government of New Plymouth in New England in America." With such deeds, the Plymouth men further constructed their vision of New England as colonial space, in which "Natives" were "inhabitants," rather than sovereigns. Although only Wamsutta and Namumpum's marks were affixed to the deed, the document also implied that these leaders consented to this construct and to their status in the colonial hierarchy. Moreover, while no titles or kinship ties appeared, Namumpum's gender was marked, in English terms.[20]

Some historians looking back upon the few words that the Plymouth men recorded might regard these documents simply as land transactions, but the records reflect merely the surface of the waters below, often concealing oral and symbolic exchanges and the acts that followed. Even the record itself reveals a compelling anomaly: all of these statements, from December 1657 to June 1659, were recorded in the same place in the Plymouth Book of Deeds, at the same time. Written on two sides of the same page, they immediately precede the division of the lands in question, in 1666. Their veracity relies on the testimony of Plymouth men *to the consenting acts of Wamsutta and "this Woman Tatapanum."* Although the historical record is sparse and sometimes confounding, composed largely of the brief phrases recorded as acts of the court, we can use a network of documents to read the scenarios that took place at both Pocasset and Plymouth and, drawing on Indigenous language, geography, and other cultural frameworks, we can begin to interpret what might have taken place on the ground.[21]

THE ROAD TO PATUXET

Ironically, the men who claimed jurisdiction over the whole Wampanoag country had only recent and limited familiarity with its geography; Winslow and Southworth were foreigners who claimed the rights of "first born sons." In contrast, when Weetamoo went to Plymouth, she traveled through territory she knew intimately. For her, this was not "New England" but Wôpanâak, ancestral ground (see map 4).

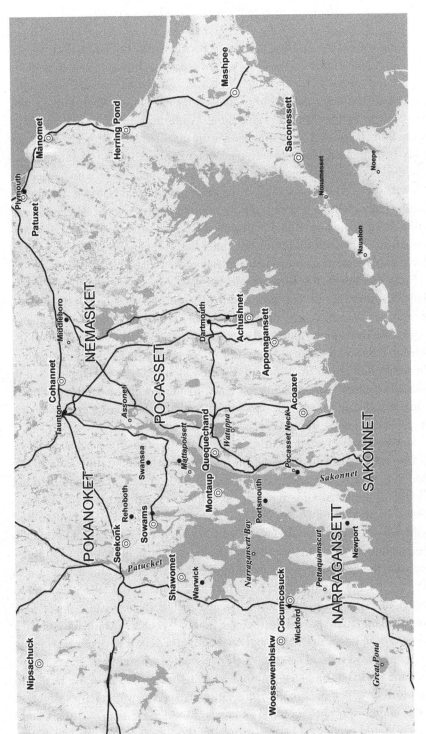

4. From Pocasset to Patuxet, wide view of places in chapter 1

As she walked the familiar path from Pocasset with her counselors, Weeta-moo would have followed the Kteticut north, passing through the ancient plant-ing grounds at Assonet, grown high with grasses and edible plants. New plants intermingled among native ones—dandelion, red clover, Englishman's foot, first brought to these lands in cattle dung. Wamsutta could have joined her en route from Pokanoket at the junction with the Kteticut trail near Cohannet, a key fishing place. Some twenty years before, the settlement of Taunton had emerged here when a high-ranking "spinster," Elizabeth Poole, who had left the Massachusetts Bay Colony, made an agreement with local Native leaders to live nearby Cohannet, on a stream off the main trail. Here, when Weetamoo was still a child, Poole had tended her cattle, relying for support on her brother and a small group of settlers who followed after her. Weetamoo may have passed by Poole's old house or seen her cows grazing as she walked by the stream.[22]

From Cohannet, the Kteticut trail led east, a road long traveled by diplo-mats. A canopy of nut trees provided shade from the sun's rays. At Nemasket, Weetamoo, Wamsutta, and their company could stop to refresh and exchange news with Tuspaquin, Amie, and their kin. From there, the Nemasket trail led them to the coast and the old town of Patuxet, where the English settlement of Plymouth had arisen from ground depleted by disease. As she approached it, Weetamoo must have encountered cows, roaming without constraint during warm months, and men from the outlying settlements, drawing cattle or carry-ing meat and cheese to market.[23]

As Weetamoo entered the English village, she must have been struck by its structure: square houses built on long, narrow lots lining the sides of the road, fences separating gardens from fields. In the center, upon the hill, stood a building similar in form and purpose to their council house. While its walls were composed of rough-hewn boards, the rectangular structure, built to host gatherings of leaders, would have been a relatively familiar sight. Outside the meetinghouse, Weetamoo would have seen another sight familiar to summer councils: the gathering of people to trade. At Plymouth, "court day" was also "market day." Weetamoo's ancestors had long come to the falls at Patuxet to engage in exchange, but the scene had changed dramatically in just a genera-tion. Walking uphill toward the meeting house, Weetamoo would have heard a cacophony of voices in English and Algonquian, as people bartered, interacting by gestures and signs. The salty smell of fish smoked and fresh, game, salted beef and pork, intermingled with the odor of cheese turning in the heat, and the pungent stench of manure. Here in the market, she would have seen oxen, cattle, and horses yoked for travel and trade, a strange sight; no one in her com-munity would deign to yoke a deer and offer her for trade. Yet this "stock" was the most prized "commodity" Plymouth settlers possessed. According to the Plymouth Court records, this was the main reason that Wampanoag leaders attended the court in June 1659, to protest against livestock that was inundating their fields.[24]

FROM PLYMOUTH TO POCASSET: THE FREEMAN'S DEED AND THE OLD COMERS GRANT

Just as Plymouth was situated in familiar Indigenous geographies, so, too, were the lands described in the 1659 deed. The acts that led to the deed's creation were rooted in conflicting systems of land tenure, law, and language as well as different perceptions of the land. Traveling the Kteticut trail on a diplomatic visit to Pokanoket in 1621, Edward Winslow noted: "As we passed along, we observed that there were few places by the river but had been inhabited, by reason whereof much ground was clear, save of weeds which grew higher than our heads. There is much good timber, both oak, walnut tree, fir, beech, and exceeding great chestnut trees. The country, in respect of the lying of it, is both champaign and hilly, like many places in England. In some places it is very rocky both above ground and in it. And though the country be wild and overgrown with woods, yet the trees stand not thick, but a man may well ride a horse amongst them."[25]

To the generation that followed, including Josiah Winslow and his peers, the meadows and forests presented uncultivated land ripe for husbandry. The grasses might be cut for hay, the forests converted to lumber to build homes and feed hearth fires. Lush meadows might be claimed to plant furrows of wheat, without the labor of felling trees, while marshes could be converted to pasture. Such acts would fulfill their god's grand design, that men should husband the land, as a wife, to become fruitful. Successful improvement might even be evidence of salvation, while profits from harvested commodities, whether lumber, livestock, or rye, could be read as a "visible sign of God's favor."[26]

Absent from Winslow's description was recognition that the land was already successfully managed. Native women and men had over time developed complex systems of horticulture and forestry that fostered diversity and long-term sustenance. In his travels, Winslow saw "few places" along the great river that did not show the signs of planting fields, understanding these meadows had once been "clear." Yet his description displaced the labor of women who cultivated the soil. While some fields had been emptied by epidemics (then left alone in respect for the dead), others lay fallow as part of a cyclical horticultural system. For example, at this time, while Weetamoo and her relations cultivated substantial fields near Quequechand falls, the ancient planting grounds on the west side of the Kteticut, which had appeared "overgrown" to Winslow, were resting. In a few years, these old grounds would be burned, fire harnessed as a tool of renewal. In the spring, the women would turn ash into the soil, mixing with decayed leaves and grasses in a nutrient balance. Then women would rebuild their mounds, starting the planting cycle anew. This Indigenous resource management system did not arise from altruistic impulse, but was an adaptation vital to survival for people who had remained in the same place for thousands of years.[27]

The English newcomers likewise possessed long-term practices and environmental knowledge, with beliefs derived from both Christian religion and pagan folklore, which were adapted to an entirely different place. The English plants that grew among Kteticut grasses were uniquely adapted to cattle husbandry, regenerating as cows stomped and chomped. Cattle had adapted to wander among meadows, grazing on grass, saplings, and small plants, eating as much as they could consume. Indigenous plants, on the other hand, were accustomed to browsing deer, which covered wide ranges and fed on a variety of plants. For domesticated grazers like cattle and oxen, Wampanoag grasslands presented a feast, but to the plants that had adapted to this cultural environment, livestock posed a significant threat. Indigenous plants were, however, well adapted to fire; some even relied on it for regeneration. The abundant open forest Winslow witnessed was a cultivated environment, annual controlled burns encouraging the growth of nut trees and edible plants, inviting game and facilitating hunting and gathering. Yet, as Native people discovered, new growth also drew English livestock, while open forests caught the eye of settlers like the Winslows.[28]

It was likely during one of these trips, following in their fathers' footsteps, that Josiah Winslow and Constant Southworth first conceived of acquiring the "meadows" along Kteticut, between Assonet and Quequechand. Unbeknownst to Weetamoo or Wamsutta, the Plymouth Court had issued a grant to these "first borns" and their fellow "freemen" in 1656, for "all the uplands and meadows . . . on the east side of Taunton river, from Assonate Neck to Quaquerchand, alias the Plain, commonly called by the name of the Falls." Yet, it is important to recognize that the "Court" was not an independent body. Southworth and Cudworth were members of that court, while Winslow had served the previous year, immediately following his father's death. The Plymouth men granted Pocasset land to themselves. Still, under English law, the colonial grant would prove fruitless unless they acquired consent from the rightful sachem.[29]

Ousamequin had recognized Weetamoo's "inheritance" of jurisdiction in Pocasset, but the "first born sons" of Plymouth also claimed inheritance of large tracts of Wampanoag lands granted them by their fathers, the "Old Comers." The "Plymouth patent," granted by the Council of New England, endowed the men with a sense of ownership from the Atlantic Ocean "to the utmost bounds" of Ousamequin's territory at Pokanoket, or "Sowamsettt," and as early as 1639 the first Plymouth settlers endowed themselves and their sons with first choice to those lands. They selected three loosely defined tracts in the Wampanoag country "for future use and distribution," including the "garden" of "Sowamsett" (reserving the "cheefe habitacion of the Indians" on "Causumpsit Neck" or Montaup), on Cape Cod (near Yarmouth and Namskaket), and on the coast between Acoaxet and Acushnet (later Dartmouth). However, the "Old Comers" and "first born" had to secure their shares by "purchase [of] the said land of the natives."[30]

The "Old Comers," including Winslow, first made an agreement with Ousamequin, through the exchange of wampum, to build a small settlement at Sowams (Rehoboth). In 1652, concerned with competition from other colonies, they sought full legal possession of the three large tracts they claimed. They pursued deeds at "Sowams and parts adjacent," and between Acoaxet and Acushnet, with acknowledgment in wampum and goods given to both Ousamequin and Wamsutta. Simultaneously, they sought deeds with leaders on the Cape. Yet, as Laurie Weinstein has explained, early colonial "land sales," often "symbolized two contradictory agreements" wherein Native leaders understood they were "granting co-occupancy rights to use the land" within a particular territory, rather than the permanent alienation of a bounded "tract." Still, as settlers encroached on Native subsistence places and imposed jurisdiction, Native leaders progressively grasped "the full meaning" and potential power of written deeds.[31]

The "Old Comers" had initially included Pocasset Neck in their plans, presuming it was contained within the "bounds" of "Pokanoket." Ousamequin and Wamsutta had maintained, however, that these lands were under Weetamoo's jurisdiction. Rather than respecting the 1651 deed at Nonaquaket, the Plymouth men sought to circumvent the saunkskwa's authority. In December 1652, they secured an "Indian deed" for "Punkateesett," signed by an obscure man named "Ekatabacke." Through this instrument, the Plymouth men created a competing claim to Pocasset Neck *against* Weetamoo *and* Rhode Island Colony. During the June 1659 court, when Weetamoo supposedly confirmed the Freeman's deed, Plymouth also called Richard Morris to appear, offering to authorize his "Indian deed" if he would acknowledge their jurisdiction and "submitt himselfe unto this government," instead of Rhode Island Colony. Although Morris did not immediately consent, the Plymouth men granted themselves authority to seek suitable replacement land nearby. Yet Weetamoo did not put any mark, that June or ever after, to any deed for Pocasset Neck, and settlement did not commence.[32]

Indeed, one of the most important questions we can ask, as we try to understand these documents, is: What happened on the ground, in these places, *after* the deeds were signed? What do subsequent acts tell us about the agreements behind the deeds? Earlier agreements, like those at Sowams, resulted in immediate settlement, but fostered conflicts in overlapping spaces. At the June 1659 and 1660 court sessions, Wamsutta and other Wampanoag leaders implored the Plymouth leaders to contain the encroachment of livestock on their fields, including the peninsulas of "Kekamewett" (Kickemuit), "Annawamscutt," and "Causumsett Neck" (Montaup), all adjacent to or overlapping English settlements in "Sowams and parts adjacent" (see map 3). Such records also reveal that Wampanoag people continued to plant and live in Sowams, even as settlers built the towns of Rehoboth and Swansea. A major motivation for Wampanoag leaders' participation in this council was their responsibility to compel the magistrates to control the livestock and planters over whom they claimed jurisdiction. And, indeed, this negotiation between leaders is the only reason recorded in 1659 for Wamsutta's presence in the court, with no reference to either him or Weetamoo consenting to further expansion of Plymouth's settlements. In the court records of 1659, she is not even mentioned.[33]

COUVERTURE AND CAPTIVITY

Colonists preferred to do business with Wamsutta, as a male and son of their ally. As historian John Strong has noted, although English men "were somewhat uncomfortable in dealing with women" in land "transactions," they were compelled "by the realities of Indian customs to negotiate with Algonquian women."[34] Although Ousamequin had made clear that Plymouth could not claim jurisdiction over Weetamoo's lands through their agreement with him, marriage may have offered a new inroad, adding another layer to the 1659 deed. As Norton has observed, "power in colonial America lay in the hands of men, who expected to govern women," as members of their household, alongside children, servants, and livestock. Under *English* law, Wamsutta would have gained authority over Weetamoo and her lands when they married. According to the doctrine of *couverture*, all of a woman's property rights transferred to her husband upon marriage, including those inherited from her father. This practice was so ubiquitous in the colonies that it would have seemed a natural part of how the world worked. It would have appeared as an anomaly that Conbitant's daughter, upon marriage to Ousamequin's son, would retain her "inheritance" to Pocasset land.[35]

However, in Native space, the authority to negotiate over usage and resource rights remained with the sachems and saunkskwas as symbolic representatives of the community, regardless of marriage or gender. The union of Wamsutta and Weetamoo did not negate the responsibilities they had in their respective territories, but rather bound them together. Although the colonists sought to empower Ousamequin, then Wamsutta as a single male leader with whom they could negotiate, the strength of the Wampanoags rested more in the union of families than consolidation of power in any single leader.[36] Still, even if they could not apply couverture, the Plymouth men could manipulate this Indigenous *kinship bond* to enforce the *legal bond* of debt they had imposed upon Wamsutta.

This was fast becoming common strategy. During the court sessions of 1659, the neighboring Massachusetts Colony held the Wachusett leader Nanamocomuck, son of the great Penacook sachem Passaconaway, in a Boston jail. Coveting Penacook lands to the north, the trader John Tinker had drawn a number of Nashaway men under Nanamocomuck's jurisdiction into debt and held him responsible for their bond. In the spring of 1657, when Nanamocomuck traveled to the Massachusetts Court to negotiate on behalf of his kin, the Boston men imprisoned him for failure to pay the debt. Nanamocomuck was confined in captivity for over two years, until his father and brother sold their people's cherished planting and fishing grounds on the Molôdemak River island of Wicasauke in November 1659.[37] Weetamoo and Wamsutta were likely well aware of Nanamocomuck's presence just north of Plymouth. The capture revealed a powerful leader's inability to free his son from the pretended jurisdiction of the English. Further, this case made clear how far English men would go to acquire land they desired, including imprisoning the son of an influential ally. If Weetamoo did give her consent, this was, to paraphrase Scott Lyons, consent in the context of acute coercion, particularly since the men who held the bond were also magistrates on the court.[38]

ACTS ON THE GROUND

According to the Plymouth Book of Deeds, Winslow, Southworth, and Cudworth went "upon the land" between Quequechand and Assonet, took "view of it," then "divided it into twenty-six parcels" in 1660, with the list of grantees recorded in 1666 and 1667, including themselves. On paper, it would seem that Weetamoo permanently alienated land between Quequechand and Assonet, agreeing to relinquish her "right and title" and that of her "heirs." Yet, although the land was "divided" into imagined "parcels," as with Pocasset Neck, none of the grantees moved onto their "lots," failing to "improve" the land, the most significant marker of ownership in colonial law. Wampanoag people, on the other hand, continued in their longstanding relationships to this place.[39]

Local historians have suggested that the "Freeman's purchase" was "speculative."[40] That is, the Plymouth men invested in fertile land on the Kteticut and Assonet rivers, along a major travel route, "for future use and distribution." In the deed, they attempted to set the northern bounds of "Pocasset" at the Quequechand River, the "cleft rock" and deep pool around which the houses of Weetamoo's families were gathered. Perhaps they assumed they could eventually persuade the Pocassets to live on a smaller, reserved tract below the falls.[41] However, their claim was not performed, through either "improvement" or force. Is it possible that Weetamoo never appeared in Plymouth in April or June 1659, and that she did not sign the deed? Or was she compelled to a compromise through the force of her husband's debt? The only proof of her consent was the testimony of the very men who would profit most. Few English homes were built even in the northernmost part of her territory, and local histories suggest that Assonet was "jealously guarded" by its Indigenous inhabitants. Not until after King Philip's War did grantees, their "heirs," or their "assigns" move onto the land. Weetamoo and the Pocassets maintained the jurisdiction recognized by their "neighbor sachems," despite the grants and deeds created by Plymouth men.[42]

ATHERTON DEEDS: "A DEPRAVED APPETITE AFTER THE GREAT VANITIES," NARRAGANSETT COUNTRY, JUNE 1659

That summer of 1659, another saunkskwa, the Narragansett leader Quaiapin, faced a parallel predicament. Quaiapin had lost her husband, the sachem Mixanno, but maintained leadership at her fortified town of Woossowenbiskw (in present day Exeter, Rhode Island) alongside her sons, Scuttup and Quequegunent. Her brother Ninigret was the longstanding sachem of nearby Niantic.[43] In June, just after Weetamoo allegedly attended Plymouth's court, a group of colonial leaders and speculators "seduced" Cojonoquant, cousin to Mixanno, into signing a deed for some "six thousand acres of the best Narragansett land," a gift "in consideration" of his English "friends'" "great love and affection." These "friends" included Governor John Winthrop Jr. of Connecticut, the local trader Richard Smith and his son, trader John Tinker of Nashaway, and Major Humphrey Atherton. The deed included a "tract of land . . . called Wyapumseatt, Mascacowage, Cocumcosuck," which included Quaiapin's lands.[44]

These settlers formed the Atherton Company to forge a competing claim, on behalf of the United Colonies—Massachusetts, Connecticut, and Plymouth—

to the lands that Rhode Island held by right of its treaty with the Narragansetts. The Atherton Company's claim centered on Pettaquamscut, an ancient Narragansett planting ground, but eventually encompassed nearly all of Narragansett territory. The members of this company pursued their claim by coercing a "mortgage" through force and deceit from the leading Narragansett sachems, including Quaiapin's sons, her brother, and the elder Quissucquansh, as well as Cojonoquant. Using a raid on Mohegan as a pretext, Winthrop and the United Colonies sent armed forces to Narragansett (in September 1660) to demand payment for damages to English property and "sundry other crimes," which Atherton subsequently offered to cover with a "mortgage" as collateral. On payment of an astounding amount of wampum—six hundred fathoms—in six months time, Atherton promised, "this writing" would "be void and of none effect." However, the company refused to accept payment when the Narragansett leaders delivered the wampum, preferring instead to convert the mortgage to a deed. They had begun dividing the shares before the mortgage even came due.[45]

The company included Edward Hutchinson (Anne's son, returned to Massachusetts) and the Smiths, who lived at Cocumcosuck (Wickford), but other Rhode Island settlers saw the "mortgage" as a ruse and feared its potential impact on their colony. The mortgage circumvented a recent Rhode Island law, which required the court's approval for all purchases of Indian land. At his "first going up" to Narragansett, Atherton had offered Roger Williams a cut, asking him to "interpret for them to ye Sachems," but the Rhode Island leader had "refused," later condemning "this Business" as "an unneighborly and unchristian Intrusion" which was "Contrary to your Laws as well as ours." Writing to Winthrop's rival John Mason, Williams eloquently expressed his concern that the scheme arose from "a depraved appetite after the great vanities, dreams and shadows of this vanishing life, great portions of land, land in this wilderness, as if men were in as great necessity and danger for want of great portions of land, as poor, hungry, thirsty seamen have, after a sick and stormy, a long and starving passage."[46]

AN "ABUSE" AGAINST "A SQUA SACHEM, CALLED NAMUMPUM," WAMPANOAG TERRITORY, JANUARY–AUGUST, 1662

In midwinter of 1661–62, Peter Tallman, a Portsmouth, Rhode Island emigrant, produced a deed for "a parcel of land" that encompassed nearly all of Awashonks's territory of Sakonnet and part of Weetamoo's territory of Pocasset.[47] Neither saunkskwa appeared on the deed. Rather, it proclaimed that Wamsutta, "the greatest and chiefest prince or sachim here about" "freely" gave the land to his "beloved friend." Ousamequin had recently passed away, leaving the people in deep grief. Tallman sought to extend Wamsutta's new role to claim a great "parcel" for himself.

In the deed, Tallman claimed Wamsutta's consent to grant not only the land, but also the usage rights and resources, including "medows" and "hearbidge" for grazing and "timber" for houses, fences, and fuel, as well as the "coves" and "islands," to lease or sell for pasture. These words transformed the land into an English style patchwork of property for agriculture and resource extraction, eliminating the possibility of Native subsistence. The deed explicitly included the "under-woods" which the Wampanoag men fired, as well as the fishing places, routes, and water resources of the "creeks," "fresh rivers" and "springs." The deed excepted Morris's "purchase" at Nonaquaket and Plymouth's claim to Pocasset Neck, but made no allowances for the Wampanoag people living at Pocasset and Sakonnet.[48]

The deed reveals no hint of the circumstances under which Wamsutta might have been compelled to "give" such a vast tract of land to a single settler. No compensation or exchange is noted. Tallman may have orchestrated a deed of "gift," like the Atherton men, to circumvent Rhode Island law.[49] Likewise, since he had first purchased land at Portsmouth from Morris, Tallman must have known his deed defied Plymouth's claim to jurisdiction as well. Yet Tallman did recognize jurisdiction for Wamsutta, including the right to alienate land, as "the greatest sachem" in the Wampanoag country. Mimicking the rhetoric of kinship, the deed implied the sachem's "gift" was motivated by generosity toward his "beloved friend, a merchant who traveled frequently to Barbados, carrying cattle and bringing back tobacco, sugar, and rum. However, later records reveal that this document was more "bond" than deed. And nearly twenty years later, the witnesses Richard Bulgar and Thomas Durfee testified "that the Indian Sachim called Wamsetta . . . was in a very Sober Condition and not any way Over-come in or by drink" when he signed the deed, the subtext suggesting speculation that the "gift" was induced by rum. Weetamoo's next appearance in the Plymouth Court, in June 1662, arose from her multifaceted strategy to ensure she would not be "put off her ground by" Tallman.[50]

Six days after Tallman's deed, a "terrible" and "prodigious" earthquake struck the Wampanoag country. As darkness set, the land trembled beneath the cover of snow and a deep howl arose from below. As the rumbling intensified, the earth "shook the houses" of the English and "caused the Inhabitants to run out into the Streets." Over the course of a month, "three violent shocks" shook the land, knock-

ing people to the ground and tearing chimneys from English roofs. Weetamoo and her relations may have interpreted the earth's trembling as a warning that erupted from the lower world, calling for restoration of a world off-balance, which the people felt in their bellies, even as they witnessed its impacts. The rumbles continued through spring, and "the earth did not cease to quake until the following July."[51]

As the "great earthquake" shook Aquidneck Island, Ann Tallman must have held her five children close. In contrast with Weetamoo, Ann's fate had rarely been in her own hands, and her story provides a salient counterpoint to that of the saunkskwa's. (Reader, bear with me, as I appear to diverge.) Raised in Barbados among plantations and trade ports, the English girl had lost her father, leaving her mother a widow and her brother to manage the family's affairs. As an adolescent, Ann caught the eye of Peter Tallman, a German merchant who dealt in the trade to New England. He married her, and in June 1648 the two set sail on *The Golden Dolphin*, along with Ann's mother and brother, an indentured servant, "at least ten tons of cargo, including rum, cotton and tobacco," and "three slaves," all designed to bring wealth to Peter Tallman's new household in Newport, Rhode Island.[52]

In one of the earliest records regarding slavery in the colony, in 1650, one of these enslaved men, an African called "Mingoe," escaped from Tallman's household, breaking his bonds, asserting his will and moving freely, if furtively, within the Wampanoag and Narragansett country, where he may have found refuge. Apparently, the attempt at recapture was so unsuccessful that Tallman sold the right to hold Mingoe as a slave to John Elton, who had married Ann's mother, on the condition that Elton would seek out the "fugitive" and return him to his proper place within the colonial hierarchy. As Tallman recorded, "The Negro is named Mingoe & but a yong man & hath the marke of I:P: on his left shoulder: & did unlawfully depart from my house in Newport about six months since."[53]

The Rhode Island ports must have presented a strange sight to Weetamoo. Not only did she witness the "yoked" and branded animals shipped and sold at market, but other human beings. Settlers transported bound men and women as commodities from the West Indies to be sold at market in the ports of Narragansett Bay, transforming the coastal landscape to harness wealth. The enslaved then became members of settler households, both property and living beings who could be harnessed to husband the land. While slaves remained rare in Rhode Island at this time, Africans had already begun to adapt in this new environment, sometimes resisting the physical and legal confines imposed upon them. Over the decades, some Africans and African Americans would join local Native communities, marrying in and sometimes replacing relations lost to war and at sea, entwining with kinship networks. As more enslaved Africans were "imported" *from* the West Indies, Rhode Island enacted a law that authorized the enslavement, sale, and shipment of "Indians" who damaged or confiscated English cattle and goods *to* those southern ports, part of a growing legal code which criminalized and commodified Native people.[54]

An active merchant in the coastal trade, Tallman left Newport and built a house at Portsmouth on land bought from Morris. In addition to his remaining slaves, he held a young English man in indentured servitude, Thomas Durfee, who then served as witness on his deed. One year later, in 1663, Tallman brought Durfee up on charges of "breach of his bond" and "insolent carriage" toward his wife. By that winter, it was clear that Ann was carrying Durfee's child, a truth she did not conceal from her husband. Like Mingoe, Ann and Thomas broke their bonds. Did Ann find inspiration in women like Weetamoo? And in women like Ann, did Weetamoo see the ways in which men like Tallman bound their wives, as well as the land?[55]

Colonization, as a project, is tied to gendered concepts of land and power. When the English explorer Bartholomew Gosnold first viewed the Wampanoag country at Acushnet in 1602, he recorded that he and his men stood in awe, "like men ravished, at the beautie and delicacie of this sweet soil." Portraying the coastal land as a bountiful woman, pregnant with possibility, he believed the "fat and lustie" quality of the earth, which made even the "most fertile[e] part of al[l] England" seem "barren," was simply a contribution of "God and Nature," not realizing the hand that the Wampanoag women had in its regeneration. The women had located their fields in the fertile floodplains of Kteticut in part because of the river's cycles of revitalization, to which their agriculture was uniquely adapted, with the annual spring runoff renewing and replacing the soils. Settlers' conversion of the land, including the deforestation of the open, parklike woods that Gosnold and Winslow admired, disrupted this cycle severely.[56]

Just as Ann Tallman might have seen possibilities for independence in the women at Pocasset, Weetamoo would have witnessed the possibilities for the loss of independence in the changing environment. As settlers felled the great forests to the north and west of Pocasset, Weetamoo and her kin may have noticed the snow melting more rapidly under the spring sun and the spring runs traveling with greater ferocity, which in turn compromised the fertility of the soil. As English farms spread, the streams dried in summer while insects, worms, and disease increased, affecting plants in the fields and marshes, even as English monocrop planting and plowing drained nutrients from the soil, increasing settler demands for land.[57] These environmental impacts were not limited to the places where the English settled, but the closer those settlements were, the greater their impact on Native women's subsistence.

Yet it was not only "changes in the land" that threatened the capacity of Indigenous women to care for their communities, but more subtle changes in governance. If either Tallman or the Plymouth men planted at Pocasset, they would assert greater political influence over this territory as well, with real consequences for women. To the north, in some of the "praying towns," women's roles were becoming constrained, as men became "rulers" and took hold of the plow and missionaries imposed Puritan laws on sexual relations. In the Wampanoag country, a woman could "put away" her husband if he acted against the welfare of her family. Under Indigenous law, if she divorced, Weetamoo would retain her position as saunkskwa and the governance of Pocasset. Like any Wampanoag woman, she would keep her house and her children. Under colonial law, the husband owned all the property and divorce had to be authorized by the court, with the burden of proof on the party who claimed just cause. Ann Tallman, for example, could not leave Peter unless she proved a violation of the marriage contract, such as permanent desertion, adultery, or impotence. Rather than accusing him, she openly acknowledged the evidence that she had violated the contract herself. Yet, in doing so, she risked losing the means to sustain herself and her children. Wampanoag women planters held greater economic power, providing more than half of the food to their communities—as long as they continued to hold the land.[58]

These gendered systems of power also influenced diplomacy. When Peter Tallman's 1662 deed came to light, the saunkswkas Weetamoo and Awashonks joined together in protest, compelling the Plymouth men to rein in this neighboring settler. According to the Plymouth records, on June 3, 1662, "a squa sachem, called Namumpum" appeared in court to protest the illegitimate deed, an "abuse" of justice against her. In its record, the court did not acknowledge that she was married to Wamsutta, the purported seller. Instead, Namumpum (Weetamoo) was flanked by Tatacomuncah, counselor and brother to Awashonks, who also "complained against Wamsitta for selling away a necke of land called Sakonnet, which hee saith belongeth to him." They referred to the Tallman deed, but the court phrased the "complaint" in a way that suggested fault lay with the Pokanoket sachem. For Plymouth, the greatest issue was

Wamsutta's purported authorization to convey land to a Rhode Island settler, in territory to which they claimed preemptive right. The king's continued recognition of their colony rested on their insistence that "Wampanoags dealt in land affairs exclusively" with them. Perhaps Weetamoo and Awashonks understood it was in Plymouth's interests to nullify the deed, seeking their intervention to prevent Tallman from carrying out his intent on their grounds. Still, their complaint also enabled Plymouth to strengthen its own claims.[59]

According to their record, "the Court agreed to doe what they could in convenient time for her relief," bolstering their claim of a "protectorate" over Wampanoag lands. Tallman was prevented from executing the deed, and the saunkskwas' rights were recognized, but the Plymouth Court also took this opportunity to forcefully assert jurisdiction. In March, they had authorized Seekonk settler and militia commander Thomas Willet to travel to Sowams in arms, to discuss the controversial deed. Willet was instructed "that incase the squa sachem should bee put of her ground by Talmud [Tallman], to see that shee bee not wronged in that behalf." "Likewise," he was "to speak with Wamsitta about his estranging land and not selling it to our collonie."[60]

"THEIR KING'S BROTHER CAME MISERABLY TO DY BY BEING FORCED TO COURT, AS THEY JUDGE POYSONED."

In the midst of this maneuvering during June of 1662, tragedy struck the Wampanoag country, driving Weetamoo, Metacom, and their relations into mourning. Most accounts of King Philip's War foreground Wamsutta's suspicious death, a story recounted repeatedly, with little questioning of the Puritan narratives that give muddled explanations for his capture. All three existing accounts are postwar narratives, rife with conflicting evidence and inaccuracies, and all defend the actions of Plymouth and its wartime governor, Josiah Winslow.

The accounts by Increase Mather, William Hubbard, and John Cotton all agree that Wamsutta's death occurred mysteriously after Winslow "surprised" him at his "hunting house" on Munponset Pond, north of Nemasket, only twelve miles from Winslow's estate. Willet went to speak with Wamsutta at Sowams, they recount, to request his presence at the next court. When Wamsutta failed to appear, increasing suspicions, Winslow led a group of armed Plymouth men to approach Wamsutta and his kin in the midst of a morning meal, their hunting guns resting outside the arbor. After confiscating the guns, Winslow delivered his orders from the court—via the Massachusett interpreter, Roland Sassamon, conveniently nearby—then led the sachem towards Plymouth.[61]

Yet these accounts diverge on numerous points. Did Wamsutta greet Winslow with welcome or suspicion? Did he calmly explain the misunderstanding between them, then travel willingly with Winslow to Plymouth, as Cotton suggested? Or did "the proud sachem" fall "into a raging passion" and refuse to go, as Mather recounted? In Mather's version, Winslow proclaimed that "his order was to bring him to Plimouth, and that, by the help of God, he would do it, or else he would die on the place," pointing "a pistol at the sachem's breast."[62] Oddly, all sources agree that when Wamsutta complied, he declared he would not travel alone, but accompanied by his counselors: "he would go as a sachem . . . and not as a culprit or a prisoner." When offered a horse, Mather relayed, the sachem chivalrously declined, saying if his wife and kinswomen were going to walk, so would he. The tale has the feel of an apocryphal story, the last noble speech of an admirable "chief" who knows his fate lies before him.[63]

The accounts also agree that the court authorized the expedition because Wamsutta was suspected of rousing the Narragansetts toward a "rebellion" against the English, and had failed to attend court as he had "promised" Willet. Instead, "at that very time," Mather insisted, he "went over to the Narragansetts." Yet, despite the dramatic accounts, no evidence appears in the court records of any order to bring Wamsutta to court on these grounds. No records suggest concern that Wamsutta was embroiled in such a "rebellion," nor are there instructions for Winslow or anyone to question the sachem's relationship to the Narragansetts. Winslow was not even on the court during the spring session. Furthermore, no documents suggest that Wamsutta was expected at court. The only mention of Wamsutta in the spring and summer court records concerns his "estranging land" from Weetamoo and "not selling it to" Plymouth. The available evidence suggests, as Francis Jennings long ago discerned, that the real "rebellion" concerned Wamsutta's dealings with *Rhode Island*, and the Tallman deed was but one example.[64]

The narratives recounting Wamsutta's treatment at Plymouth are even more ambiguous than those of his capture. According to Cotton, the available magistrates gathered quickly to meet with Wamsutta and sort the matter out congenially. In contrast, Mather and Hubbard reported that Winslow held Wamsutta at his house, awaiting Governor Thomas Prence's arrival. In either case, while at Plymouth, Wamsutta became "violently sick." Winslow purportedly called on the "physician" Matthew Fuller, who administered "a working physic," which failed to cure him and may have worsened his condition. Wamsutta then persuaded Winslow and the magistrates to allow him to go home, promising to return. En route (according to Cotton) or at Sowams (according to Mather), the sachem died. Before these narratives were published, Metacom reported to Rhode Island leader John Easton that his brother "came miserably to dy by being forced to Court, as they judge poysoned." If, as Metacom suspected, Fuller administered a "physic" that killed Wamsutta, he had motive. He and his cousin Samuel, as "first borns," had been granted lots in a planned settlement in Sakonnet, within the tract claimed by Tallman. Winslow and his family, of course, had substantive claims at Pocasset as well.[65]

In the Puritan ministers' narratives, Wamsutta's role in a fictional "rebellion" was dramatized, while Weetamoo's role as a leader was erased. They portrayed only Wamsutta's chivalry toward his wife, demoted by Mather to "his squa," a phrase which, by the end of the war, had begun to take on derogatory connotations. The narratives elided the saunkskwa's influence in court, along with the possibility that Winslow may have pursued Wamsutta's capture extra-legally, a warning by Plymouth's first-born sons that Wampanoag leaders should not "rebel" by making land deals with other colonies.[66]

Moreover, these narratives displaced the cause of Wamsutta's death onto the sachem himself. Mather blamed Wamsutta's fiery "distemper," which kept him "vexing and fretting in his spirit." Hubbard insisted that, in line with contemporary beliefs about the relationship between "humors," emotions, and illness, "the very surprizal of him, so raised his choler and indignation, that it put him into a fever." This narrative proved a crucial pretext to the war: evidence of recurring "Indian conspiracy," an example of the "insolency" of the Wampanoag men, and a displacement of colonial violence to Indigenous offense, with death an inevitable result of the fiery nature of Indian men. Or perhaps, as Cotton suggested, the death of Indians was merely the regrettable cause of sickness, the clash of savagery with civilization. Yet the brief records of Weetamoo's interactions with Plymouth regarding the Tallman deed reveal a much more complex political landscape, with contests over colonial jurisdiction and increasing threats to Native lands prompting actions that might simultaneously protect and threaten a woman leader's network of relations. Nothing, the documents show, was inevitable, or as orderly as the later narratives would have us believe; rather, at times, these documents reveal the multifaceted impacts of human actions and choices within competing systems of land tenure, jurisdiction, and belief.[67]

"PHILLIP, ALIAS METACUM, SACHEM OF POCANOKETT"

As the summer of 1662 reached its peak, the corn came into green, drawing families to Sowams. Weetamoo surely attended the festival at her sister's town, carrying gifts to Montaup. As John Cotton reported, after Wamsutta's untimely death, "There was great solemnity in the Congratulating of Philip's coming to the crowne, by the flocking of multitudes of Indians from all parts, Sachems & others, with great feasting & rejoicing at Mount Hope [Montaup]." Yet, rather than attend the feast, "this caused the Gov'r to call a meeting" with Metacom, requiring "his appearance att the Court held att Plymouth" to renew the "former covenants" made "betwixt our predecessors and his ancestors" and to "make answer" to the "rumors" moving "too and frow of [the] danger of the rising of the Indians against the English, and some suspicion of theire ploting against us to cut us off." Although he must have been wary, Metacom traveled the path through Mattapoisett and Nemasket to arrive at Plymouth on the requested date of August 6.[68]

Ironically, although no court records indicate that Wamsutta was called to court on rumors of an Indian conspiracy, Plymouth did call Metacom to court for that suspicion, following Wamsutta's death. Such "feastings and rejoicings" happened every summer and were no cause for "suspicion," although as foreigners to this land, settlers may have interpreted these gatherings through a distorted lens. Metacom's travel to Plymouth made sense in an Indigenous context, a response to Prence's request, but also part of the annual summer councils to renew relations and resolve conflicts with neighboring nations.

At Plymouth, according to their record, "Phillip, allis Metacum, sachem of Pocanokett" expressed his "desire" for "the continuance of that amitie and friendship that hath formerly bine between" Plymouth and his "father and brother." Perhaps, in the wake of their harsh treatment of his brother, he proposed a renewal of more diplomatic relations. The "Court" agreed they were willing "to continew with him and his the abovesaid friendship." They recorded little of the pledges they made, beyond their generous "promise" to give Metacom "friendly assistance by advise" and to "require our English att all times to cary friendly towards them." From Metacom and his counselors, however, they required a profession that he and his people would "for ever remaine subject to the Kinge of England." Importantly, while Metacom made his acknowledgement to the *king*, as his father had, he did not "subject" his people to the colony of Plymouth. Thus, Metacom maintained an equal if not greater standing in relation to colonial leaders even within the English hierarchy. Along with other pledges, the court recorded Metacom's "promise" that "hee and his will" not "give, sell, or any way dispose of any lands to him or them appertaineing to any strangers or to any without our privity, consent, or appointment." This, of course, was the crucial guarantee in the wake of Wamsutta's death. While Metacom might not have been fully subject to Plymouth's jurisdiction, they secured his pledge that he would sell land only to them.[69]

Yet Metacom may have secured a more comprehensive agreement in the oral exchange of this council. Sometime later (the exact date is unclear), he had a letter composed, in which he expressed his regret that he could not attend the next meeting with the court, explaining that his interpreter was injured and his sister Amie was "very sick." Yet Metacom's scribe reiterated the "promises" exchanged at their last council: "This last sumer he maid promis with you that he would not sell no land in 7 years time, nor that he would have no English trouble him before that time, he has not forgot that you promis him." Metacom entreated that if any "English or Engians [Indians] speak about aney land, he pray you to give them no answer at all." Thus, Metacom may have understood his "promise" not to "dispose" of land to "strangers" as part of a reciprocal agreement, by which the Plymouth men agreed they would not "trouble" him about selling land for "seven years time" and he would likewise pledge not to sell land to any settler during that time.[70]

Metacom used the tool of writing to make his intentions and understanding of their "covenant" clear. He recalled the pledges the magistrates made to him, and his writing would make permanent the words they neglected to include in their records. Furthermore, the letter shows Metacom's effort to prevent any manipulation of "Indians" to sell land without authorization. He not only bound the Plymouth men and himself in agreement, but sought to rein in both settlers and Natives from engaging in acts or deeds that would result in dispossession. The conversations that took place at Sowams with leaders who came "from all parts" surely influenced the pledges the new sachem secured during that first harvest time council with his father's old allies at Plymouth.

"TURBULENT SPIRITED FANATICS" AND "FILTHY CUTTHROATS," PETTAQUAMSCUT, FALL 1662

In September 1662, Edward Hutchinson wrote an urgent letter to John Winthrop Jr. concerning a "report" that the Narragansett sachems had sent "two agents to the King . . . to complain against the English, and in special against ourselves, for taking away their lands," asking the king to rein in "his subjects here." The same year, the Atherton men also sent to England a complaint that "some turbulent spirited fanatics" had "disturbed" their improvements, "cutting down their houses in the night." These "fanatics" were not Narragansetts, but "inhabitants of Rhode Island," settlers who sought to improve the same "lands."[71]

The 1660s brought a population explosion among the English settlements, with the number of people in Plymouth Colony alone tripling between 1640 and

1660. The rise in "first borns," the sons of immigrants coming of age, produced rising demands for land and competition among colonists for jurisdiction, as well as "an increasing number of land-related complaints registered by both Indians and colonists." These included Native protests against incursions by livestock, one of New England's most valuable and productive commodities.[72]

As colonists in towns like Boston and Plymouth depleted pastureland, demand for fresh and salted meat from the outlying settlements grew. Simultaneously, demand for cattle and beef in the West Indies, where colonial planters did not want to squander fertile plantation land for raising livestock, fostered a lucrative export market on the New England coast. When a horse export tax was imposed in England, the colonists "rushed to produce a homegrown supply." Tallman and Hutchinson were among the competitive merchants who, with "vessels laden with barrels of salted pork and beef, as well as with live animals," made "regular runs from New England ports to Barbados, Jamaica, and other island destinations." This trade likewise motivated further expansion. Tallman's neighbor Samuel Wildbore and Massachusetts merchant John Hull competed directly with Hutchinson and the Atherton Company, when, with a group of Rhode Island settlers—those "turbulent, spirited fanatics"—they sought to purchase and develop "twelve miles square of prime meadow land" at Pettaquamscut "to raise cattle to sell in the Caribbean." By 1660, as Virginia DeJohn Anderson notes, thousands of "neate beasts and hoggs" were slaughtered annually for shipment to the islands, and "much to the Narragansetts' dismay, their territory was fast becoming both a giant pasture and a thoroughfare for horses" and other "cattle" "driven to the bay for shipment overseas."[73]

Livestock ranged freely outside the colonial settlements, particularly during the seasons when Native women's fields were growing. As Anderson observes, "From the moment they arrived in the New World, English animals intruded upon nearly every activity that contributed to Indians' subsistence." Cows and pigs could "devastate" a field "in a matter of hours," with "cornstalks and other plants stripped bare or trampled to the ground." Pigs uprooted seedlings and trampled mounds, even digging up baskets of corn stored below the ground, leading Native people to "roll the bodies of trees" over their storage pits. Native women, Roger Williams wrote, called hogs "filthy cutthroats" for the damage they did to the clam banks. Pigs devoured nuts and berries as they roamed the woods and marshes, often clearing the area before Native women and children could harvest, and likely defending their "territory" when the competitors arrived. Sometimes, before an Englishman set foot in Native territory, "roaming livestock" would "herald" the planting "of a new English plantation" nearby.[74]

These animals represented the only beings that Native people *wanted* English men to confine. Instead, they moved without constraint . . . anywhere outside the fenced English fields. Although settlers went to great lengths to constrain people who rebelled against them, they failed to restrain the animals that actively destroyed Indigenous subsistence places. While there is a reasonable explanation—that the fencing needed to confine livestock, as commonly practiced in England, would have been too laborious for settlers who had to clear the land for plow agriculture—there was also strong motivation to *allow* the animals to move freely onto Indigenous lands. They were, as Anderson has convincingly argued, "the means by which colonists established exclusive control over more and more territory. As agents of empire, livestock occupied land in advance of English settlers, forcing native people who stood in their way either to fend the animals off as best they could or else to move on." Unwittingly, as they sought new sources of food, cattle laid claim to Native lands, "improving" them by their presence, clearing high grasses in fertile meadows, preventing saplings from growing into trees, and initiating the clearing of bushes and low lying plants from the forests, all the while encouraging Native removal with their intrusions onto key subsistence grounds.[75]

As Native leaders increasingly protested the encroachment of livestock, Englishmen proposed they build fences around their fields and restrain their relations' behavior. Laws passed in multiple colonies required settlers to help their Native neighbors construct fences. Yet cattle, horses, and pigs, adapted to their newfound freedom, made their way around fences in search of succulent greens. Even as colonial magistrates made efforts to ensure that Native people could be compensated for damage, they enacted legislation that prohibited Native people from capturing, killing, or "damaging" encroaching livestock. Their recommendation was to capture the offending animal and either imprison it within a fence or lead it to the nearest settlement to "demand satisfaction," if the owner could be located. Many colonists did not want to engage in direct conflict with their neighbors, but they were highly motivated to find ways to expand their claim to neighboring lands. They were not averse to cattle, pigs, and horses, as members of their households, doing that work for them, on the front lines of colonization.[76]

Both the Pettaquamscut "proprietors," led by Wildbore, and the Atherton Company sought to use cattle to demonstrate their improvement of the ancient planting ground of Pettaquamscut, envisioning it as the perfect pasturage and shipping port. Circumventing colonial law requiring Native consent, they produced competing deeds in which the same group of Narragansett leaders purportedly granted the land to them, and petitions that portrayed their competitors as deceitful rogues. In 1662, for example, the Atherton men sent to England a series of deeds to support their claim, along with a petition by Ninigret, Quissucquansh, and Quaiapin's sons, Quequegunent and Scuttop, complaining that Wildbore and his associates had "forceably" "possess[ed] themselves" of Pettaquamscut by "both building and bringing catell," thereby "pretending title" to the land. The Narragansetts had purportedly warned them off, but the Rhode Island settlers did not "take theire cattle from all the lande, but, on the contrary resist[ed], and one of their number" shot "a gun at us."[77]

The petition appeared to advocate for Native rights, but it was used to support the Atherton Company's competing claim. One of the first decisions the Atherton shareholders made was to create a common for pasturage at Pettaquamscut. In August 1661, when the Atherton men made plans "to take possession of the Lands by building" houses and fences, they asserted their ownership in opposition to that of the Rhode Island settlers, who responded by "pulling down" those houses "in the night." Hutchinson and the Atherton men wrote to the king, insisting this was an assault against the "many places built and planted upon the said Lands" intended to "enlarge your Majesties Empire."[78]

Even as the Atherton men sent this trail of documents to England, their larger political counterpart, the United Colonies, joined the effort to rein in Rhode Island. Plymouth Governor Prence, writing for the colonies, proclaimed that such "Intrusions" were "very Insolent and Injurious to all the Colonies." Acting as a mediator, Prence proposed to Rhode Island a United Colonies hearing "where they will bee equally heard and answered," but also threatened to use the Narragansetts against them. Quoting the Narragansetts' request for a "tryall" for "Wildbore and his company," which "it seemes they have refused," the United Colonies warned that the Narragansetts believed they would be well within their rights to "drive away their Cattle and force them to desist." The Rhode Island governors should use their "best Indeavor to keep your people from Injuring the heathen or others which they may draw upon your selves and us uncomfortable consequences." Thus, the United Colonies used the threat of "heathen" violence to compel Rhode Island settlers to submit to their jurisdiction and receive protection through their intervention. Together, these documents supported not only the Atherton Company's claim against Wildbore, but the United Colonies' assertion of more legitimate jurisdiction over Narragansett against Rhode Island, an entire colony of "spirited fanatics." However, Rhode Island was not interested in mediation by their competitors, and instead sent their own "agents" to England, armed with paper, including the Narragansett leaders' confirmation of their original agreements, as well as a separate petition by the sachems themselves. Hutchinson was especially concerned that the sachems' message was accompanied by "a great parcel of peague," the wampum giving greater weight and legitimacy to the writing.[79]

"ENTERTAINING NARRAGANSETTS," PATUXET, OCTOBER 1663

While the United Colonies was attempting to bolster its position in the Narragansett country, Plymouth was also attempting to assert and demonstrate its jurisdiction through Wampanoag country, by acting as an arbitrator. Weetamoo's next appearance in court, in October 1663, was prompted by the Plymouth men's perception of "controversies" that had arisen "between Phillip[,] the sachem of Sowams[,] and Quiquequanchett and Namumpam, his wife, and som Narragansett Indians that are with them." The court reported that Weetamoo and her new husband were "entertaining . . . Narragansetts against" Metacom's "liking."[80]

In all likelihood, Weetamoo had simply been hosting Narragansett relations; her new husband was likely the Narragansett saunkskwa Quaiapin's son, Quequegunent, who, like Weetamoo, had been learning from the colonial "deed games." The Plymouth men had long been apprehensive about encroachment from Rhode Island. In this case, Plymouth claimed that Metacom himself expressed concern that the visiting Narragansetts made claims of "proprietie and royaltie to such places as they have bine soe entertained." The court determined that the territory in question "hath bine originally in the said Phillipes predecessers, and is acknowledged by the other to have bine from Phillipes father conveyed to him." By upholding a patrilineal inheritance, Plymouth bolstered its interests, particularly against Rhode Island's claim to Pocasset. Further, the court argued, if Narragansett visitors were living "under him," in Metacom's jurisdiction, they "should always observe such orders and costomes as they had found amongst them, the nonobservance of which hath bine a great cause of theire present troubles." At the same time, the magistrates could not afford to alienate either Weetamoo or the Narragansett sachems. They urged Metacom to return the "canoes" he had taken from the visitors, and suggested that if he was amenable they all might work out a deal to enable the Narragansetts to remain in Wampanoag country on "their promise of better carriage."[81]

By its actions, the Plymouth Court appropriated the role of a sachem, mediating a conflict between neighboring leaders, while asserting colonial jurisdiction over Wampanoag people. Yet, even as they portrayed the court as the ultimate arbitrator, Plymouth magistrates found themselves enforcing Indigenous "customs" longstanding in this land. The Plymouth magistrates did not express

concern about Weetamoo's "entertaining" and forging alliance with Narragansetts, or call her to answer for a "conspiracy" to "cut off" the English. Rather,
they seemed preoccupied with interposing their court as a just authority among
the peoples over whom they claimed jurisdiction and shoring up their claims to
a colonial "protectorate" in the Wampanoag country.[82]

The records do not reveal whether any of the parties consented to the court's
decision, but they do demonstrate that Weetamoo forged alliances on the
ground that fortified her authority and territorial integrity, even as colonial
competition challenged the bonds of kinship. Appearing in court during two
annual sessions, flanked by neighboring leaders, she demonstrated the respect
she commanded in the region. Quaiapin may have become a key mentor and
advisor during these challenging times; throughout her "sachemship," the "old
Queen" steadfastly resisted pressure to sell land. Even as colonial men pursued
the division of territories, Weetamoo pursued a strategy of intertwining, joining
with other leaders and their families to protect the many beings who depended
upon them. Together, they steered a course of strategic adaptation to the colonial system that had begun to entangle itself in their roots.

A ROYAL COMMISSION AT PETTAQUAMSCUT, JULY 1664–AUGUST 1665

In July 1664, a ship arrived on the coast carrying a Royal Commission, empowered by the newly restored English king. They traveled with a fleet authorized to capture "New Netherland" from the Dutch, a colonial conquest
that would send ripple effects through Native networks. New England had to
respond quickly to the dramatic change in governance following Charles II's
restoration. Each colony scrambled to make its case for validation and expansion amidst competing claims and complaints of Puritan oppression. Reassert-
ing the power of royal arbitration, one of the commission's many objectives was
to "investigate the Narragansett country."[83]

In March 1665, the Royal Commissioners traveled from Plymouth to Rhode
Island to meet with all the parties entangled in the contest for Narragansett
lands. The Narragansett sachems had sent to England their "long petition complaining of violence and injustice from the Massachusetts, amongst others," saying "that they had caused them to be fined, and then took their whole country in
mortgage." Calling for the king's intervention, they insisted that "there could be
no redress" in the colonies. That spring, Quissucquansh and Ninigret traveled
to meet the commissioners with heavy hearts. Quaiapin's sons Quequegunent
and Scuttup had recently died, at least one of a persistent "sickness." Shortly

before the commission's arrival, Hutchinson had made a last effort to validate the Atherton deed by bringing the ailing Scuttup and his sister Quenemique to Boston to sign a confirmatory deed in loyal "friendship." Quissucquansh and Ninigret carried the burden of contradicting, with persuasive oral testimony, the authenticity of the many writings the Atherton Company presented to support its claims to the "whole" Narragansett homeland.[84]

The Royal Commissioners met at the "narrow river" of Pettaquamscut, on the contested land, where they engaged in formal exchange and mutual acknowledgment with the sachems. Quissucquansh and Ninigret presented them with wampum "crowns" and clubs, to be delivered to the king in recognition of his leadership, as well as a "feather mantle" and "porcupine bag" for the queen. In return, the commissioners presented the sachems with "scarlet silver-laced coats," accompanied by swords and belts, on behalf of King Charles, recognizing their status as leaders. The Narragansett speaker, Quissucquansh, gave formal testimony, illuminating the situation on the ground. First of all, he asserted, the deed with Cojonoquant was a fraud. His younger brother was "simple," Quissucquansh explained, and "had not power to sell land." The Atherton men had taken advantage, Quissucquansh insisted: "he was seduced Being made drunk, & kept so for some days, & carried to Boston, where this sale was made," consisting of "about 6000 acres of the best" land in the Narragansett country, "for about 25 pounds" or "300 fathom of [wampum]peag." Not only Connecticut men, but also "Major [Josiah] Wenslo of New Plymouth colony," "joined together with these of Massachusetts" in the scheme.[85]

Furthermore, while conned by Atherton and his "mortgage," Quissucquansh reported that the Narragansett leaders had attempted to make payment, once they understood the trap in which they were ensnared. As Commissioner George Cartwright later observed, "For the Indians never knew what selling of land, or mortgaging meant, till the English taught them, yet it was proved before the Com[mission]: that the Indians sent to know where they would have the mony payd, before the time in the mortgage was expired; and answer was returnd, they could not receive it now, because Mr. Winthrop was in England, yet after that seized upon the country as forfeited." John Winthrop Jr. had indeed been abroad, arguing for a royal charter that would give Connecticut jurisdiction over those very lands. In England, Winthrop "had cozened the crown into recognizing the Atherton title." The king had even authorized the United Colonies to protect Atherton and his collaborators against Rhode Island's competing claims. Yet, standing among the salt marshes of Pettaquamscut, hearing testimony from all parties, the commissioners declared both the fraudulent deed of "gift" and the "pretended" mortgage "void." They ordered that the Atherton

Company and its hired associates "shall quit and goe of[f] ye said pretended purchased lands, and shall not keep any cattle of any sort upon ye said land."[86]

Despite this victory in their favor, the Narragansetts were asked to make major concessions as the commission declared jurisdictional authority for their king. The commissioners insisted they pay the wampum "owed" to the Atherton Company, as well as the "three hundred fathom of wampum" that, it was discovered, was paid to Cojonoquant for his "gift." Moreover, while the Narragansetts received a hearing regarding the "many injuries which they say they have received from several of his Majesties English subjects, against whom they desire justice," the price was the symbolic renewal of their "submission" to the king, through a ceremony whereby they laid "downe their armes as at his Majesties feet" and formally accepted his "protection." Finally, although their lands would be "protected," the commission declared that the Narragansett country would "be henceforward called ye Kings Province," with administrative responsibilities going to the Narragansetts' allies, the newly chartered colony of Rhode Island, who would serve as "justices of the peace" for the king.[87]

One of the commission's most provocative decrees, inspired in part by the sachems' testimony, was a validation of Indigenous title, ruling that lands must be acquired by consent and not conquest. Massachusetts had attempted to justify its claims to Native lands by arguing that they were not owned because they were not improved. As John Cotton put it, "In a vacant soyle, he that taketh possession of it, and bestoweth culture and husbandry upon it, his Right it is." John Winthrop Sr. had cited Psalms 115:16 to support this argument: "The heaven, even the heavens are the Lords: but the earth hath he given to the children of men." The argument embedded was that "Indians" were not truly "men" because they were not civilized. The commission dismissed this argument, saying, "'Children of men' comprehends Indians as well as English; and no doubt the country is theirs till they give it or sell it, though it not be improved." The new policy was solidified in the royal charter of Rhode Island, a colony that rested almost entirely on its agreements with the Narragansetts, in the "midst" of whom they "did transplant themselves." The commission applied this ruling to past deeds as well as future transactions, declaring some grants "null and void," and chastised the United Colonies for seizing "more power than was ever given, or entended them."[88]

In the wake of the commission's decisions, Plymouth scrambled to sanctify its boundaries and "confirm" its deeds, particularly since it held no such royal authorization. Rhode Island's new charter extended its bounds "three miles"

inland to the east of Narragansett Bay, including the Pocasset and Sakonnet coasts and the Montaup peninsula. Further, during its council at Pettaquamscut, the commissioners had discerned Josiah Winslow's involvement in fraudulent land schemes, including a share in the Atherton Company. Winslow and Prence had accompanied the commissioners on their journey from Plymouth to Narragansett and attended the proceedings. Despite the collegial relationship, the revocation of the Atherton deeds, along with Rhode Island's royal charter, must have sent shockwaves through Plymouth, which now turned its attention to strengthening its claim to the Wampanoag country.[89]

Both during and after the commission's visit, the Plymouth men called Metacom to court to sign a series of deeds confirming the validity of former grants. Sachems regularly discussed territorial relationships at annual councils, but Plymouth used the pretext of these negotiations to solidify their claims against other colonies and answer the demand for more land. In 1664, Thomas Willet arranged a confirmation of the oral agreement that had created Taunton and an expansion of the Rehoboth deed. On paper, Metacom acknowledged that an eight-square-mile "plantation . . . named Taunton" had been "bought of Osamequin" in 1638 by "sundery persons" including William Poole, "whoe there sett downe" on the "meadows" of "the Great River." Metacom's sign thereby legitimated a colonial town for which a deed either did not exist or had disappeared. However, the retroactive document also *expanded* the extent of those "meadows upon the great river downward" to include "all the meddow of Acconett [Assonet] and broad Cove."[90]

These "confirmatory" deeds expanded the original grants into Weetamoo's territory, perhaps circumventing Metacom's pledge to sell no additional land. In October 1664 and June 1665, according to the Plymouth Book of Deeds, Josiah Winslow and Thomas Southworth acquired Metacom's consent for a confirmation and survey of the Dartmouth settlement. The original deed for Acoaxet and Acushnet required that settlement go only "soe high that the English may not bee annoyed by the hunting of the Indians in any sort of theire Cattle." However, the newly incorporated town of Dartmouth was expanded by the survey and revised deed, with the northern bounds extending to Watuppa Pond and the eastern bounds extending, with additional local "purchases," nearly to Cape Cod.[91] In March 1664, the Plymouth men, anxious about "encroachment" from Rhode Island, likewise moved forward on a "survey" of the "lots" at Pocasset Neck. Concerned about local colonial and Indigenous opposition to their settlement, the court authorized Thomas Southworth (and two others) to "treat with Phillip" to "procure of him an evidence" to validate their "interest" in the land and acquire "full confirmation" of the dubious "Ekatabacke" deed.

This "evidence" was produced at the same June 1665 court, authorizing settlement from the Espowet marsh to Dartmouth "bounds."[92]

These deeds beg the question, why would Metacom sign documents that further alienated land and infringed on the jurisdiction of a neighboring sachem, who was also sister to his wife? One possible answer lies in the problem of interpretation and translation. Since Metacom did not read English alphabetic script, someone, most likely a Native speaker, had to convey to Metacom the words on the deed and translate his speech to the Plymouth men. From the moment these colonial councils regarding lands had been initiated, the role of interpreters had been critical. Few Wampanoag and Narragansett people spoke English fluently and even fewer could read the words recorded on English acts and deeds. Likewise, few English men could speak Wôpanâak or Narragansett, and even fewer could be trusted to communicate clearly and truthfully. Even Roger Williams was reported to have "softened" the words of English magistrates in interpreting them to Narragansett sachems. While colonial magistrates held significant influence in composing deeds, Native interpreters also wielded considerable power. Only a small group, during this time, held both literacy in English and fluency in Indigenous languages. One was the Massachusett scholar, John Sassamon.[93]

Although Sassamon eventually became a relative to Metacom, when he began his interpretive work he was a man without strong family ties.[94] An orphan of the epidemics, Sassamon was raised among the English in Massachusetts Colony. "Instructed . . . in the principles of religion" by John Eliot, who had "known him from a child," Sassamon was the first Native "scholar" to attend Harvard College, although he did not graduate. Highly educated in the colonial world, Sassamon was embroiled in many of the questionable deeds to which Native leaders put their marks, including every deed signed by Metacom in 1664–65. He even walked the lands with Winslow and Southworth to "survey" the bounds of Dartmouth, "in behalf" of Metacom, which expanded the deed's northern boundary into Pocasset. Later, as Metacom himself revealed to John Easton, Sassamon devised a will in which Metacom gave away "a great Part of the Land" to a single inheritor, John Sassamon. Eventually ostracized for his deceitful behavior and betrayal, Sassamon, Metacom conveyed, was "a bad man" without conscience for his kin. Metacom's understanding of the confirmation deeds likely differed substantively from the versions printed by the court; Sassamon played a key role in the legal documentation of Metacom's consent.[95]

Colonial chroniclers often referred to Sassamon as Metacom's "scribe"; however, as Lepore has written, "while Sassamon used his literacy skills as a tool in acquiring status and prestige in the Indian community, it is difficult to know if Sassamon's work for Metacom at this time represents a genuine change of heart or whether he was essentially acting as a spy for the English." The commissioners of the United Colonies paid Sassamon for his service as an interpreter and teacher, recorded as "incouragmt" for teaching "Phillip and his men to read." Of course, the commissioners had more lucrative ventures than Indian education in play. Sassamon's linguistic dexterity in council may have been the talent for which he was most highly valued.[96]

Sassamon's dubious influence extended further still, providing yet another layer of context to deeds which involved Weetamoo and the Narragansett sachems. He was listed as a "witness" to the Freeman's purchase, which the Plymouth men recorded in 1666 as they scrambled for confirmations, attesting to both Wamsutta's bond and Weetamoo's consent. He was likewise listed as interpreter for Peter Tallman's deed and as "Witness" to the August 1662 treaty between Plymouth and Metacom. The earliest deeds in which Sassamon participated were the "Petequoimscutt" land "sales" to Wildbore and associates, yet he also acted as interpreter and witness to the Atherton Company's "confirmation" deed signed by Scuttup and Quequegunent for the same lands. Both John and Roland Sassamon's names, along with Thomas Southworth's, appeared on a June 1664 deed in which Metacom purportedly "sold" his wife's childhood home of Mattapoisett, with Wootonakanuske's consent (her mark), along with seasonal pasturage rights at the planting peninsula of Toowooset. Finally, as noted, Sassamon witnessed the confirmation of Pocasset Neck, the expansion of Taunton into Assonet, and the expansion of Dartmouth into Watuppa, all places that would be fiercely defended in the war to come. The track record of deceptive documents in which Sassamon was embroiled makes nearly any deed in which he appeared as witness or interpreter highly questionable. Moreover, it demonstrates that these deeds themselves are *unstable* historical documents. Sassamon's presence on the Freeman's deed may provide some explanation for the gap between Weetamoo's alleged words of alienation and submission and her acts in protecting those very lands she supposedly sold. We will never know what words were actually exchanged, but we can consider how the saunkskwa took action on the ground to ensure that the lands at Pocasset and Assonet would not be captured by English deeds.[97]

As the Royal Commission delivered their judgment at Pettaquamscut in the spring of 1665, and the Plymouth men authorized Southworth to "treat with Phillip" regarding Pocasset Neck, the fish runs began to come in. At Pocasset,

Weetamoo must have gathered with the families to welcome the return of their nourishing relatives to Quequechand and Assonet Neck, even as she grieved the death of another husband. Quaiapin, also deep in grief, may have traveled the short distance from her town to Pettaquamscut to watch the herring come in through the bay with her brother Ninigret. Her ancestors had witnessed this wondrous spectacle, countless streams of fish making their way from the sea to the rivers of their birth, at this place, for thousands of years. Perhaps the commissioners were feasted with fish, newly caught, as they marveled at the sight. Across the Bay, in Portsmouth, Ann Tallman nursed her newborn son, awaiting trial.[98]

As Weetamoo and Quaiapin knew, a Native man could easily be imprisoned, or even shipped to Barbados along with cattle, for "stealing" livestock or an unpaid debt, but they were not the only ones who faced confinement. A majority of people, not to mention animals and plants, in colonial America were under threat of being contained. Still, at the same time, this land offered opportunities for breaking free of the confinements to which many were subjected.

In May 1665, the newly established Rhode Island General Assembly called Ann Tallman to Newport to answer "whether she owned herself to be an adulteresse," as her husband alleged. Standing before Governor Benedict Arnold, Deputy Governor William Brenton, Roger Williams, Samuel Wildbore, and John Easton, among others, Ann admitted that she had informed her husband in writing "given under her hand" that the son she had recently borne "was none of his begetting, and that it was begotten by another man." Indeed Thomas Durfee's first son, Robert, had been born three months prior to her trial. Thomas had already left Tallman's house, and had been sentenced and fined for "breach of bond" and "insolent carriage." As members of the merchant's household, Thomas and Ann's rebellion posed a major challenge to Tallman's authority. However, he was positioned well, as a deputy to the General Assembly, which tried his wife and former servant. One of the greatest "freedoms" of the colonial system, for "freemen," was their ability to grant themselves authority to assert control over those who rebelled against them.[99]

The mother was found guilty of adultery and sentenced to be publically "whipt at Portsmouth, receiving fifteen stripes; and after a weeke respite, to be whipt at Newport, receiving fifteen stripes, and to pay a fine of ten pound." Thomas was also sentenced to receive "fifteen stripes." In an effort to restore order, the court asked Ann if she would be willing to rejoin her husband's household. She responded "that she would rather cast herselfe on the mercy of God if he take away her life, than to returne." Without regard for her newborn, the court ordered that Ann be confined to jail until her whipping, a sentence she resisted by leaving Rhode Island. In August 1665, Portsmouth settler John Archer was summoned to Plymouth Court "to answare for abusive speeches and for entertaining the wife of one Tallman," most likely at his outlying house in Pocasset. Seeking to escape her sentence, Ann Tallman apparently headed across the Sakonnet River, taking the Indian ferry to Weetamoo's territory of Pocasset. Once she crossed over, Archer's would have been the first, if not the only, English house she would see.[100]

In the summer of 1667, when Ann returned to Rhode Island and visibly renewed her relationship with Durfee, the Portsmouth constable brought her to court, under a warrant for her arrest. That spring, as she addressed the assembly, Ann may have been carrying Durfee's second son. With few options left, Ann petitioned for "mercy." The magistrates generously offered to reduce her sentence to "one whipping" and a fine. Still, they would not condone her relationship to Durfee, which had transgressed the bounds of marriage.[101]

Although they spent the rest of their lives together, raising five children, colonial authorities never did allow Ann and Thomas to forge a legal bond. The assembly had granted Peter a divorce when Ann was sentenced, but, as the "guilty party," Ann was not permitted under colonial law to remarry, as Peter did shortly thereafter. Ironically, her neighbors repeatedly persecuted her for the crime of fornication but would not allow her to lawfully wed the father of her children. Like the fictional Hester Prynne, Ann Tallman was marked as an "adulteress" for the remainder of her adult life, although Durfee was finally admitted as a "freeman" to Portsmouth in 1673, sometime around the birth of his fourth son by Ann.[102]

Ann Tallman's English neighbors regarded her extramarital relationship as a grave offense, but she may have experienced a different view across the river. Over the course of her lifetime, Weetamoo married at least four men. She would leave her third husband on the eve of war, and freely marry another within months. The kinship ties made in Indigenous marriages were highly respected bonds, but they did not confine men and women to an exclusive relationship for a lifetime. In fact, it was not uncommon for a man to make a second marriage while his first wife was focused on the first years of her child's life. Moreover, Weetamoo's multiple marriages over the course of a lifetime would not have been seen as out of the ordinary. Women like Ann Tallman may have found in these neighboring communities an alternative model for viewing marriage and heterosexual relationships. Although her bond with Thomas Durfee was not recognized by any court, perhaps Ann took heart that in this "new world," a woman might have more influence over the partner with whom *she* chose to live out her life.

"BOTH CORN AND PEAGUE TO SECURE
HER LAND," PATUXET, JUNE 1668

In October 1667, only five months after Ann Tallman had been hauled to court, she may have heard disturbing news about the man who had once offered her safe harbor. As the Plymouth Court reported, "John Arther" was "disposed" of the house he had built "att Pocasseeset near Rhode Iland ferry" by "several Indians," most likely belonging to Weetamoo. In the rhetoric of the time, Weetamoo sought to "put" Archer into his "proper place," to "govern" in her territory, to "direct" and "manage" affairs in her jurisdiction. In this act, and in words presented to the court, Weetamoo sought to "deal definitively" with Archer's claims at Pocasset.[103]

The following year, Dartmouth settler John Cooke submitted to the Plymouth Court the testimony of two witnesses, which explained the context under which Archer acquired his deed and the reason for his "disposing":

> The testimony of Richard Sisson, aged sixty or therabouts: John Archer, being att my house, did speake as followeth, and said, the deed of gift made by Namumpum [Weetamoo] to John Sanford and himselfe was a cheatt, and the intent therof was to deceive Namumpam, squa sachem, of her land; and they were to have both corn and peague to secure her land from Wamsutta or Peter Tallman, and was to resigne up the deed att her demand . . .
>
> And I, Mary Sisson, doe testify, that I heard the same words att the same time; and further, when my husband was gon out of the house, I heard them both say they were troubled in conscience that they had concealled it soe longe, and did refuse to take pte [part] of the grattification.[104]

This document represents a rare reversal. Rather than recording the deed, the court recorded the oral accounts of witnesses who testified to the verbal and symbolic exchange between parties and the story behind the paper deed (which has not survived). If the deed alone had survived, historians might relate simply that Namumpum sold to Portsmouth settlers John Sanford and John Archer a parcel of land at Pocasset. The deed would not reveal the circumstances of its creation, or its relationship to the Tallman deed; rather, it would be evidence of a legitimate transfer of land.

Instead, this documentation of oral testimony reveals a glimpse of Weetamoo's strategic adaptation to the deed game, as she attempted to protect her lands and jurisdiction by turning the power of this colonial instrument back on itself. Even as Tallman orchestrated a play for her land, she used the power of the written word to protect it. She made an oral agreement, sealed with wampum, with Portsmouth leader John Sanford Jr. and Archer to put their names to a false "deed of gift," with the stipulation that they would "resigne up the deed att her demande." In exchange, she gave them corn, symbolic of her role as a female leader. They would hold the false deed and the wampum that symbolized the true meaning of their pledge. Simultaneously, she enabled Plymouth to assert its presumed power against the controversial German merchant. However, if Tallman asserted his claim before authorities in Rhode Island, she could demonstrate that she had already allowed that right to the upstanding John Sanford and his neighbor. Through this strategy, rather than being outwitted by the deed game, she strove to turn it to her advantage.

Yet, clearly, Sanford and Archer thought they had successfully swindled the "squa sachem" out "of her land." After all, they had the deed. Although gained collusively, they now possessed the authority to develop, divide, and sell the land, with the potential of great profit. However, for Weetamoo, the real power was not in the paper, but in the words and wampum exchanged between them. And it is clear, from the guilt Mary Sisson witnessed in the men, that they understood this pledge as well.

Bringing English witnesses to the stand, Weetamoo used the power of the spoken word to counteract the authority of the written deed. Richard Sisson was Archer's neighbor and had served as Portsmouth's constable. Although Sanford came from a powerful family, the "heathenish" Archer may have presented a more vulnerable target. Again, Plymouth could shore up its claims against Rhode Island by intervening on Weetamoo's behalf. Through this strategic reversal, Weetamoo compelled the colonial court to enforce both Wampanoag custom and a shared sense of justice, reversing the power of the deed by invoking the authority of wampum and oral exchange. Yet, at the same time, the document demonstrates the increasing threat that land sales and expanding settlement posed to the women who cultivated the corn that Weetamoo offered.[105]

STRATEGIC ADAPTATIONS, PLANTING REVITALIZATION, WAMPANOAG AND NARRAGANSETT COUNTRY, JUNE 1669–JUNE 1673

That June, as the Sissons testified at Plymouth, Metacom pursued his own "strategic adaptations" at Pokanoket. A year following, John Sanford, serving as the Portsmouth town clerk, was instructed by his fellow freemen to write a letter to "Phillip, Sachim of Mount Hope" who "hath putt Severall Swine on hog-Island therin intrudeing on the Rights of this Towne," demanding that he "remove such Swine or other Catle" or they would be "constrain[ed] . . .

to defend their Legall Rights against him." Facing a debilitating decrease in the deer herds, Wampanoag leaders, including Metacom and Awashonks, had turned to free-ranging pigs as an alternative source of game. Chesawanocke, an island to the east of Montaup and Portsmouth, provided an ideal location for Wampanoag men to keep and hunt hogs. They had learned to isolate their hogs by surrounding waters, in colonial fashion, from their planting grounds. However, while the original use of "Hog Island" corresponded to its English name, several Portsmouth settlers had received permission to plant there, including John Archer and William Sisson. Thus, Sanford's order represented an ironic reversal: a complaint that Wampanoag livestock encroached on English fields. Rather than pursuing the husbandry of "docile" cattle, as missionaries and magistrates had hoped, Wampanoag people instead adapted swine, the most "slovenly" form of European livestock, to their hunting and trading practices. Perhaps the worst offense to the English, as well as the shrewdest adaptation, was that Native people carried their surplus meat to the Boston market for trade. By 1669, as Anderson has noted, Plymouth settlers were losing profits to Native pork traders.[106]

Meanwhile, to the south and east, families gathered, renewing ties to each other and to the land that sustained them. In late July 1669, as the corn ripened, Quaiapin's brother hosted a festival that drew families from all around to "the greatest dance . . . that ever was in the Narragansett" country. Several of Ninigret's men returned to build the arbor, harvesting cedar from the marshes, traveling from Pocasset, where they now lived. While the Plymouth men had repeatedly sought to expand their bounds at Taunton, "desir[ing] the Neck of Assonet for pasturing young beasts," Narragansett and Wampanoag protectors were planted at Assonet, which became known as "One of ye most considerable Seats of the Indians in this Part of ye World."[107]

Shortly after the festival ended, the General Council of Rhode Island called Ninigret to Newport, riled by rumors that the dance fomented a great conspiracy. Among the reports they received was a letter from Plymouth, saying when their messengers confronted Ninigret, asking why Metacom's "ancient men" had been with him "together" for "nine or ten days," Ninigret dismissed it incredulously, with a laugh. The court asked him to answer for reports from Connecticut and New York that he "was contriving to cut of all the English and that hee, the said Ninicraft, had reported hee would draw as many Indians as hee could into the combination." Ninigret dismissed the accusation and even identified the source, a "Long Island Indian" who was now "forsaken by all his kindred, and is in a very sad condition, laying his hand over his face" for "the lyes he hath made."[108] After giving long speeches as to the falsity of the report and his fidelity to the English king, when the council "demanded what was the reason of this great dance," in exasperation Ninigret reiterated the significance of the annual corn festivals: "it is knowne to you it is noe unusuall thing for us soe to doe; but that it is often used from the time after the weeding of our corne till such time as wee doe eat of it; and farther said it was a kind of invocation used among them, that they might have a plentiful harvest."[109]

Five months later, Ninigret received another request to attend the Rhode Island General Assembly,[110] this time to answer for his nephew, Quinnapin. The young "lusty" Narragansett sachem and "war captain," had replaced his father Cojonoquant after his death. The rising leader resisted the bounds that the English attempted to place upon him. On December 26, 1669, he had "brocke the prison," "escaped" the Newport jail, and, with his conspirator John Carr, had "got over to Narragansett, where they both gave out threatening to doe mischief to the English, &c., thereabouts residing." The magistrates had been unable to apprehend the men, who they said, during the last few months, had been "preparing to fight, and drawing the Indians into their conspiracye soe to keep themselves from justice." Or, perhaps from their perspective, they sought a form of "justice" which would not involve their own containment. The assembly invoked the agreement Ninigret and Quissucquansh made during the Royal Commission's visit for mutual "defence" to demand they "apprehend the said John Carr and Quinnapint," and "deliver them" to "his Majestyes officers in this Collony." If the sachems refused, and Quinnapin and Carr carried out the rumored "conspiracy," the "Collony" and "his Majestye" would hold them accountable as "accessaryes with the malefactors."[111]

Regardless of the threat, Ninigret and Quissucquansh did not turn in their nephew, and Quinnapin continued to operate outside the bounds of colonial jurisdiction. The following year, the court observed that the young leader had taken under his protection a Narragansett man who stood accused of "ravishing" a settler's daughter. The stakes were high and apparently Quinnapin did not want to draw consequences upon his kin. Instead, it appears he went north, joining other protectors who had gathered at Pocasset, the root of a crucial alliance with Weetamoo.[112]

Several years later, in June 1673, "Wetamo, Squa Sachem," put her mark to one final deed, marking the bounds of "Assonet Neck" against English settlement. She put the land in the name of "Piowant," likely one of the men bound to protect it, understanding that in the colonial system, planting lands that belonged to an individual man would be respected more than those that belonged to a collective of women. This land, the deed recorded, has been "for many years . . . the Posession," that is, *property*, "of Piowant; without disturbance."

Piowant's "improvement" counteracted the deeds that would extend Taunton, making a stronger claim to ownership.[113]

The Piowant deed, according to Fall River historian Arthur Phillips, was "designed to establish the boundary lines of colonial lands" and it clearly laid out "the line between the English men and him." The deed conserved the entire Assonet peninsula, including the planting grounds and "remarkable" fishing places, setting a northern boundary at the headwaters of Mastucksett brook, which fed into Assonet Bay, and a western boundary at Kteticut. Taunton men could occupy land from the Three Mile River to Chippascutt (Smith's cove), but Assonet and its resources were off limits. The "writing" recorded Piowant's "cleare Testimony," which was confirmed by the saunskwa, and "was by Captaine Bradford ordered to be Recorded" at Plymouth. This was the son of Governor William Bradford, one of the first generation of colonial leaders to be born in Wampanoag country, and half-brother to the Southworths. Unlike the "Freeman's Purchase," this deed was marked not only by Weetamoo but several men, likely her counselors. They included "Benjamine, the husband to Wetamo," a common man who could claim no rights to her land, and the Narragansett leader Quinnapin.[114]

This instrument reversed the deed game. Whereas settlers used deeds to alienate Native people from their lands, Weetamoo and her counselors adapted it to protect the fields. Where Plymouth men used geographic description to mark the bounds of land to be surveyed and sold, they marked the land that would be retained. Where lines had been drawn to divide their lands, here, fences were built with words to prevent encroachment upon them. Oral testimony was recorded in writing, used like wampum, to formally bind the Plymouth men to the words they dutifully entered into their records. For now, the ancient planting grounds at Assonet, with the marshes and grounds surrounding Quequechand, would be protected — by word, bond, act, and deed.

2

THE HARVARD INDIAN COLLEGE
SCHOLARS AND THE ALGONQUIAN
ORIGINS OF AMERICAN LITERATURE

FIRST FRUITS: ORIGINS OF HARVARD AND THE
INDIAN COLLEGE, CAMBRIDGE, 1636–1659

In early fall 1662 two young Wampanoag men arrived at Harvard Yard for commencement, the opening ceremonies that honored the graduation of the past year's class. Having traveled the shore by ship from their island homeland of Noepe (Martha's Vineyard), the young men faced a challenge that none of their relatives had assumed before: completing their first year of university education at Harvard College. Joel Iacoomes, the son of the Wampanoag convert leader Hiacoomes of Nunnepog (Edgartown), and Caleb Cheeshateaumuck, the son of the sachem Cheeschumuck of Nobnocket ("Holmes Hole," Vineyard Haven), had prepared intensively for this endeavor. They had attended lessons on the island as boys, then emerged as top scholars at the grammar school in Roxbury and at the Latin school in Cambridge, before passing the intensive entrance exam for the college. At Harvard, they joined "an unusually clever group of candidates," and together the Wampanoag and English students performed their scholarly exercises in Harvard Hall, mastering not only English but Greek, Hebrew, and Latin. Joel and Caleb lived and studied in the college's first brick building, the Harvard Indian College. In a chamber on the first floor of this same building their fellow scholar Wawaus, or James, labored at the first printing press in the colonies, alongside his mentor, the printer Samuel Green, to complete the printing of one of the earliest texts to be published in an Algonquian language—the first bible in North America.[1]

This chapter recovers the history of the Harvard Indian College and highlights the multiple cultural, literary, and oral traditions that intersected in this space. The Indian College provides a vital foundation for understanding the complex role of "praying Indians," or members of Indigenous mission communities, as scholars, scribes, scouts and political intermediaries before, during, and after King Philip's War. Finally, the chapter shows that Indigenous scholars like Joel Iacoomes, Caleb Cheeshateaumuck, and Wawaus—also known as James Printer—were not merely students who received, or were subjected to, a colonial education, but significant contributors to the emergence of a multilingual American literary tradition, beginning with the Indigenous language publications of the Harvard Press, which was housed in the Indian College.

The Massachusetts Colony's coastal settlement of Cambridge was not at this time the thriving city and intellectual center it is today, but rather a "well-ordered" English outpost in Native space. English settlers, led by Thomas Dudley, had forged the settlement in the salt marshes and "great tidal estuary" of the Massachusett coast, on the north side of the Mishaum River, which John Smith had christened the "Charles" for his king. The settlement was built on the bank opposite Boston, a "port" "facing London," with the extraction and shipment of resources, particularly cod and wood products, and the importation of English goods in mind. The first planned town in the English colonies, "Newtowne" aspired to be the capital of Massachusetts Bay. In 1636, at the heart of the town, Harvard College was established, four buildings surrounded by cow pasture, located on a street aptly named "Cow Yard Lane." The settlement was then renamed "Cambridge," for the university town in England. Harvard's first president, Henry Dunster, envisioned that Harvard would become "the Indian Oxford as well as the New English Cambridge."[2]

Shortly after the establishment of the college, settlers sought out formal recognition of their growing settlement from the local Massachusett saunkskwa, acquiring "title" to plant in her homeland even as they pledged acknowledgment of her leadership with the annual gift of a coat. This influential leader, recorded by settlers only as the "Squa sachem" or "Massachusett Queen," made an agreement in 1639 to allow the settlement of Cambridge, but also insisted that her own town at Missitekw (Mystic river and its ponds), to the northwest, and her community's subsistence rights on the headwaters pond, would be respected.[3]

This agreement was especially critical because the towns of the Native Massachusetts had been devastated by epidemics. The saunkskwa had suffered massive loss of her kin, including her brother and two of her sons, fellow sachems who had formed relationships of exchange with the newcomers. In their absence, the coast lay exposed. Her husband, the great sachem Nanapashemet, had been

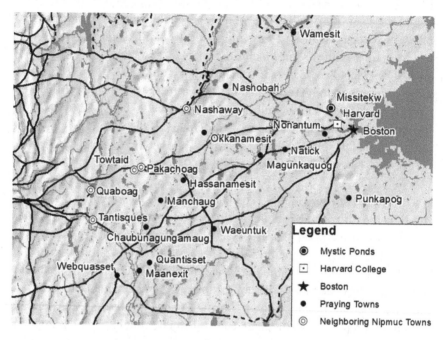

5. Hassanamesit and the mission communities, with Missitekw, Cambridge, Boston

killed in a raid by Wabanaki traders from the far north, a potential threat that remained. The agreements she made with settlers in places like Cambridge, Charlestowne, and Concord served as a protective bulwark in these vulnerable, chaotic times. Although the colonists sought clear title, she may have believed that this agreement to share space represented the newcomers' pledge to "come to their aid in the spirit of family."[4]

Some Massachusetts Bay settlers, such as John Winthrop, had, by their own reports, come to the aid of the saunkskwa's kin and nursed them through the sickness. Yet they regarded that emptying of the Native population as an opportunity, a gift from their God. Prior to the epidemics, the Massachusett sachems had held their jurisdictional ground, even as they offered hospitality to the newcomers. "Without the epidemic, according to the Charlestown records," historian Neal Salisbury notes, "the hundreds of English settlers who poured in annually 'would with much more difficulty have found room and at far greater charge have obtained and purchased land.'" However, the massive depopulation apparently put the burgeoning "quarrel with them about the bounds of Land" to rest. As Winthrop wrote to a colleague in England, "God hath hereby cleared our title to this place."[5]

These recurring epidemics nearly annihilated the majority of the Massachusett villages that had only recently flourished on the coast, but leaders like the Massachusett Saunkskwa repeatedly responded by shoring up ties, through marriage and diplomacy, with neighboring nations, including the Patucket-Penacooks to the north, the Nipmucs to the west, and the Wampanoags to the south. Collectively they engaged in a process of recovery, strengthening kinship networks through marriage and seeking ways to draw their new neighbors into their social and economic system even as they worked to repair the tears in their social tapestry. While some sought solutions in ancient ways, others strove to acquire alternate routes to survival in a changing environment, as their ancestors had done for generations.[6]

On the island of Noepe, in Wampanoag country, a number of families were drawn by the power of a new force in their territory. Struck by "a strange disease" in 1643 and again two years later by "a universal" and "mortal" "distemper," "which shook survivors to their core," they observed that a common man named Hiacoomes and his family seemed impervious to the dreadful disease, which had sent so many running in frenzy. Following the first wave of sickness and the apparent blessing of his own family's preservation, Hiacoomes began openly preaching about the powerful protection of the spirit Jehovah. Traveling among survivors, he carried a talisman: a primer, which held, he said, the words of the spirit that had protected him. He promised that they, too, could access this "wellspring" of Manitou, the power of transformation.[7]

Hiacoomes proved a powerful example. He had forged a new path for himself when he welcomed the English settlers, offering hospitality in his town of Nunnepog, when others were more cautious. Although not a sachem or spiritual leader, he initiated an intensive exchange with Thomas Mayhew and with his son, Thomas Jr., who aspired to be a missionary and teacher to the Natives. While Hiacoomes taught him the Wôpanâak language, Thomas Jr. taught the young Wampanoag man the principles of Christianity and the potentially powerful skill of reading. Native people had, from the beginnings of exchange, regarded books as instruments that held Manitou, but this was an ambivalent power, which could be turned to creation or destruction. Some sought to acquire this new skill, which once adopted, proliferated among networks of kin, but others, including some of the traditional spiritual leaders, advocated caution, wary of the words and deeds of the missionaries whom they observed.[8]

The Mayhews willingly encouraged a syncretic adoption of their religion, describing God as Manitou, the spirit that flows through all beings, and comparing him to Kiehtan, the powerful life-giving spirit of the upper world, the giver of corn at the center of Wampanoag ceremonial life. Yet they imposed a

simplifying framework on a complex Indigenous system of dualities, conflat-
ing Cheepi, a powerful and sometimes dangerous spiritual figure of the lower
world, with Satan, and the world of separated souls with "hell." Similarly, the
missionaries portrayed themselves in diametric opposition to Indigenous spiritual leaders; whatever cautions traditional leaders urged the missionaries interpreted as words motivated by "diabolical" forces and "dreams." To support their
argument, the missionaries were not above pointing to the deaths around them
and the spiritual leaders' inability to heal their kin.[9]

It was in the midst of these destructive epidemics and confrontations that a
son, Joel, was born to Hiacoomes, and in a nearby town another boy, Caleb, was
born to the sachem Cheeschumuck, a man equally fortunate to see many of his
children survive. Even as Hiacoomes became an influential "Teacher" through
conversion, Cheeschumuck maintained his traditional leadership while weaving the "emergent" religion into the fabric of his community. Both men sent
their children to the newly established day school on the island, where they
flourished. It was likely Thomas Mayhew Jr. who encouraged Hiacoomes and
Cheeschumuck to send their sons north to familiar Massachusett territory to further hone their skills. With the diffusion of reading and writing, the Wampanoag
communities of Noepe acquired "access" to a "sacred language," which many
believed would reveal a route out of the chaos in which they found themselves
embroiled. Although Mayhew brought the mission to the island, "the most
active disseminators" of the emergent syncretic religion "were Wampanoags
themselves, beginning with Hiacoomes" and expanding through sachems like
Cheeschumuck and students like Joel and Caleb, some of whom went on to
become teachers and ministers in their homeland. Retaining its original name,
Noepe continued to be a place of confluence, where "currents" of traditions
from multiple places merged. Neither "blank slates" nor "traditionalists," Joel
and Caleb were born into and raised within a community that had already
begun to "transform Christianity into a bulwark for Wampanoag communities
and an expression of their own culture." [10]

Similarly, in the inland Nipmuc country, the new religion made its way to
Wawaus's family at Hassanamesit (Grafton) through a relation from a neighboring town. The "word" arrived in their own language, carried by Wabun, or
the "wind." Like Hiacoomes, Wabun was not a sachem, but rose into a leadership position as he advocated for the healing and protective power of that great
spirit Jehovah. And like Hiacoomes, Wawaus's father Naoas was blessed with
the survival of his wife and sons during the epidemics. This apparent protection
must have deeply influenced his decision to send two of his sons to attend the
preparatory schools alongside Joel and Caleb in Roxbury. As Jean O'Brien has

discerned, "Epidemics produced penetrating doubts in survivors," and men like Naoas "considered English lifeways and religion as alternative to Indian ways that failed to control European diseases." Where faith in traditional healers was shaken, Wabun's proclamation that Christ was "a physician of souls" proved compelling. In the words of John Speen, a leader at Natick, upriver on the Charles, "I heard that Christ healed all manner of diseases, therefore I believed that Christ is the son of God, able to heal and pardon all." Yet some were also swayed by the fear of punishment which missionaries claimed Jehovah had brought upon them. As Speen painfully recalled, "I remembered that many of my children are dead; This is God's punishment on me because of my sins." At least half of the Nipmuc and Massachusett men who participated in public "confessions," O'Brien has demonstrated, "singled out the death of friends and family as a factor in persuading them to pray." [11]

This dual-edged message of punishment and protection was most fiercely advocated by Wabun's mentor, the missionary John Eliot, who assumed a role in the interior similar to the one Mayhew played on the island, although he did not live among the Nipmucs. The Roxbury minister first appeared at a Massachusett town upriver from Cambridge, later known as Nonantum, "place of rejoicing," then simply as "Newton." Here, Eliot was received graciously by Wabun, who served as his interpreter. As O'Brien notes, Eliot "preached the harsh message of English Calvinism in the Native tongue to the best of his ability," but he relied on Native ambassadors like Wabun to communicate his message through Indigenous frameworks and methods of persuasion. For example, while explaining the pervasive presence of God, Eliot perhaps unwittingly joined with his Indigenous interpreters in comparing Jehovah to the spirit of the upper world. He explained that God was akin to "the light of the sun," which shines in so many places at once, "here at Massachusets," at "Quinipeiock," and "in old England" simultaneously. Eliot's metaphor would have been easily understood by his audience, who, like many people of the east, already associated Kiehtan with the power of the sun and understood that different peoples had various names in their own languages for the same being. They also understood the concept of a force, Manitou, which pervades all beings and places. And, as Mayhew later assured Waban, they learned that this great Manitou, or spirit, "doth understand all Languages in the World." [12]

It is not clear from Eliot's account if this comparison originated with him or if it was an insightful sleight-of-hand performed by his Indigenous teachers. Either way, the message was compelling enough that some men responded to Eliot's invitation to send their sons to be schooled, at home and in colonial towns, where they might learn to read "the book of God." Wabun was among the first who "offered his eldest son to be educated and trained up in the knowledge of God." By the following year, the young man was dressed in English-style clothes and lived with an English family in Dedham, a settlement south of Cambridge. An early Nipmuc convert, Wampus, whose name signified the coming of "light," sent his young son John to live with Elder Isaac Heath nearby Eliot's home in Roxbury, where the first grammar school to educate young Indian scholars emerged. Naoas divided his sons, sending Wawaus and Job Kattenanit to the new grammar school, while keeping his eldest Annaweekin and Joseph Tukuppawillin at home, under the tutelage of Monotunkquanit, the local Nipmuc schoolteacher.[13]

Although Eliot had his own missionary motivations for urging Native men to send their sons to English schools, it had long been a tradition in eastern Indigenous networks for neighboring nations to engage in an "exchange of sons" to build and "seal" the alliances among them. These young men were educated in another community's ways to become effective and "knowledgeable interpreters and mediators," enabling communication and conflict resolution in regional space. Maintaining kinship and social relationships with their families and communities, they brought knowledge and information about neighboring people back home. Sustaining loyalties to both communities, they became careful and reliable mediators in intertribal councils. In sending their sons to neighboring territory at *Missitekw* to live among the English and be educated, men like Hiacoomes, Cheeschumuck, Naoas, and Wampus were preparing their young men to take up this role.[14]

This project was especially crucial given how "foreign" the ways of the English were to the Nipmuc and Wampanoag people, and how vulnerable they were in the wake of devastating epidemics. Roger Williams wrote of the neighboring Narragansetts, "'Awaunaguss, suck': This they call us, as much as to say, 'These strangers.'" This was the best way, in Algonquian languages, to describe "foreigners," meaning not only those who were "not from here," but also those who are "not kin." And the best way to make these strangers "known" was to forge relations with them, to draw them into the regional network as allies and friends. Although Eliot and his fellow Englishmen envisioned that these young men would grow up to educate their people in the Christian religion, the Nipmuc and Wampanoag people also hoped that these boys would help to teach them about the ways of the English, enabling them to prevent and ameliorate the conflicts that might arise between them.[15]

Other children, however, were drawn into English households and colonial education as a result of the epidemics. Following the death of the Massachusett Saunkskwa's sons and many of their kin, Massachusetts colonists "removed a number of Indian orphans from their villages," who then became servants in colonial homes. According to one of the first publications of Harvard's press, *New England's First Fruits*, Wonohaquahan, or "Sagamore John, the Prince of Massaquesets . . . being struck with death" proclaimed that although "the God of the English" might "destroy me . . . yet my Child shall live with the English, and learn to know their God." Likewise, Wampus in "his last breath" reportedly entrusted Eliot and Heath with the care "of our Children" who "dwelled" among them, "that they may be taught to know God, so as that they may teach their Countrymen." The dying men may have been earnest, but these published deathbed proclamations provided legal grounds for settlers to capture and retain custody of Native children.[16]

One of these orphaned children, John Sassamon, briefly attended Harvard alongside John Eliot Jr. and Increase Mather before the Indian College was formally established. He did not graduate, but by 1656 Eliot's ledger noted payment for his services as an "interpreter and schoolmaster," along with the Nipmuc teacher Monequason. As shown in chapter one, as early as 1657 the "cunning" Sassamon began appearing as an interpreter on dubious deeds. It may be important to note that he was raised to be a useful servant to his English masters. Witnessing the example of this displaced Massachusett man, Native leaders learned to be cautious about colonial education. Students might acquire beneficial knowledge and skills, but such "learning" held potentially destructive power.[17]

Englishmen like Eliot, though, had other motivations for "the education of Indian youth." Eliot commenced his missionary project when the situation in England was dire for Puritan dissenters like himself. They envisioned planting a "new" England in this place that would not only provide religious refuge, but would expand the Christian kingdom into a "new" world, fulfilling a convoluted biblical prophecy that the conversion of the Lost Tribes of Israel would bring about the return of Christ. When the English Civil War (1642–1651) temporarily overthrew the monarchy and brought forth Puritan rule (the Commonwealth of England, 1649–1660), refuge was no longer a necessity, and new fervor was brought to the mission of Indian conversion as a justification for continued support of the colony.[18]

In one of the first works of literature published by the Harvard Press, proponents of the colony's missionary activities celebrated their initial success—at Harvard College and the colony at large—while seeking funding to support their efforts. *New England's First Fruits* (1643) began by describing the "hellish darknesse" in which the "poore Indians" lived, referring both to the physical environment and to the natives' imagined spiritual state, "adoring the Divell himselfe for their GOD." The authors asked readers to take pity on these "miserable Soules" and described the stories of transformation signified by these "first fruits" of the mission project, including the Indian student-converts and the fledgling English plantations, their success a "sure pledge" that a "greater harvest" would emerge "in His owne time." The tract promised and promoted the conversion of a wild land and a wild people into a domesticated space and a tamed populace, which would gratefully serve the work of the Lord. In *First Fruits*' reading of the landscape, "God" the planter offered a grand design and a "pledge" of promised success, while the faithful were urged to act as patient cultivators of his divine garden.[19]

Tropes of captivity and redemption were prevalent in this promotional pamphlet; *First Fruits* portrayed Indians as "a people held captive by Satan" who must be redeemed by English saviors in the service of their heavenly planter. Thomas Mayhew similarly described them as "miserable Captives," who were "slaves to the devil from their birth," a state of entrapment from which the English must set them free. Yet, as Kristina Bross explains, Christian Indians' own accounts of their conversion reveal that they "did not see themselves as captives," of Satan or anyone else, and they did not regard their "preconversion state" as a form of captivity. Their mediated words do reveal, however, a tendency to "mark their colonized state as a captivity," including descriptions of being "hemmed in" by colonists.[20]

Like Weetamoo, the Massachusett Saunkskwa and her kin found their lands inundated by "invading livestock." Cambridge settlers compensated her with corn and built a half-mile-long fence at "the town line," but this contributed to the sense that the community was "hemmed" in upriver, impeding seasonal travel to the shore. Missionaries sought to "hem in" Native culture as well, by instituting "practices and values" such as "male plow agriculture, private property holding, monogamous lifelong marriage," regimented work schedules, and restrictive clothing that "covered nearly all of the body." By Eliot's "third meeting" with the people at Nonantum, he sought to impose restraints on women's bodies, including a "law" that they cover their breasts and wear their hair "tied up," under penalty of fines. Men were likewise discouraged from wearing "long locks," while "unmarried" men and women faced fines if they dared "lie" with one another. Native ways were increasingly constrained by English domestication — including the cultural conversion of those "first fruits" of the missionary project.[21]

Indeed, for all the talk of "redemption," a primary goal of conversion was the containment of Native peoples and homelands. Writing to Eliot in 1651, the Connecticut Commissioners expressed concern that alleged converts might adopt the appearance of conversion "for loaves and outward advantage, remaining enemies to the yoak and government." Missionary supporters viewed Christianization and education as a potentially effective means to contain a perceived threat, portraying converts as captives or "conquered enemies" who should be tamed and restrained, like domesticated animals, by the "yoke" of the colonial "government."[22]

Fear of Indigenous uprising also motivated settlers to contain their own communities. For example, in the wake of the Pequot War (1636–1637), amid rumors of an Indian "plot," when "settlers' foothold . . . was still tenuous," Harvard Hall was surrounded by an "expensive" stockade, designed to keep potential enemies, and perhaps "the boundless forests," at bay. Through missionary education, colonial leaders sought to reverse that vulnerable condition, bringing the Native people and territories that surrounded them under the "yoke" of colonial governance. The missionaries were thus involved in a complicated verbal dance, a play on words in which conversion would free the Natives from their enslavement to Satan even as it would capture them within the divinely ordained garden of colonial subjection.[23]

Apart from these grand schemes, there were also pragmatic economic motivations that wedded the missionary project, colonization, and Harvard College. When *First Fruits* was published, the young college and colony were in financial crisis. With both Puritan funds and sons flowing back to England, Harvard faced an uncertain fate. Enrollment was low; no students graduated in 1644, for example. Its buildings, not well constructed for the coastal Massachusett environment, were already breaking down. The only local revenue, other than tuition and donations, were profits from the Charles River ferry donated by the General Court of the colony, consisting largely of wampum, mainly of the "badd and unfinished peague." Tuition itself could be paid in wampum, the trade shell adopted by the English as currency, but most of the students paid in turnips, wheat, barley or other domestic goods. Harvard's leaders faced the possibility that the fledgling college might collapse. The greatest prospect for survival lay in the vision advocated by Eliot and set forth in *First Fruits*—funding for the intertwined projects of "conversion" and "preparation" of "the Indians" and "the progresse of Learning in the Colledge at Cambridge." The tract beseeched its readers in London "to pitty those poore Heathen that are bleeding to death[,] to eternall death." Potential donors could "reach forth an hand of soule-mercy" by "affording some means" to send "fit instruments . . . to preach to these pore wretches," and thereby do "as the tender Samaritan did to the wounded man." "The Colledge" in "Massacusetts Bay" was uniquely situated to train such "instruments" for this worthy mission. In addition to educating the sons of colonial leaders in the manner of Cambridge and Oxford, Harvard would cultivate Native teachers and ministers to be "raised up amongst themselves."[24]

With the goal of Indian conversion moving to the forefront as Puritans gained power in England, support for the missionary effort and the college gained momentum. In 1649, the newly established Rump Parliament passed An Act for the Propagating of the Gospel, which pledged sustained financial support to the effort by "some of the godly English of this Nation," to convert "the Heathen Natives of that Country." The Act itself constructed nativity and foreignness, portraying the colonists as wholly of English nationality, pursuing a worthy project in a foreign land, to which England laid claim. While lumping all the "Natives" together as a poor people in dire need of Christianity, the Act portrayed their "country" as largely uninhabited, with additional funding required because the colonists had "in a great measure exhausted their Estates" in building "many hopeful Towns and Colonies in a desolate Wilderness." The Act included funding for the establishment in that "wilderness" of "Universities, Schools, and Nurseries of Literature settled for further instructing and civilizing them." One year after its passage, in 1650, the Harvard Charter was adopted, signed by the colonial Governor Thomas Dudley, declaring its mission to be "the education of the English and Indian youth of this country in knowledge and godliness," creating a bicultural foundation for the college. The charter "still serves as the constitution and frame of government" for the University today.[25]

By the commencement of 1655, in accordance with the request of the newly formed Society for the Propagation of the Gospel, "a brick Indian college through whose windows could be seen the only printing shop in the English colonies" had risen in the Yard. The two-story building was designed to house twenty Indian scholars, who would study alongside English students, and engage in language exchange, "preserving their owne language" that "they may attaine the knowledge of other tounges and disperse the Indian tounge in the Collidge." The "strong and substantial" edifice had been constructed in adaptation to the Massachusett environment, built to withstand the native climate, and to educate its sons.[26]

One year later, Caleb Cheeshateaumuck, Joel Iacoomes, Wawaus, and his brother Job Kattenanit entered Daniel Weld's preparatory school, in Eliot's town of Roxbury, with the promise that they might be among the first students to enter the Indian College. Among their classmates were a young woman named Joane, her public education a rarity in New England, and four boys. These boys may have included John, the son of Wampus (who would later attend the college), Samuel Numphow, son of the Patucket sachem Numphow (among Eliot's first converts), and William Mammanuah, son of the Wampanoag saunkskwa Awashonks, both of whom attended the preparatory schools.[27] It is critical to understand that, unlike the Indian boarding schools established by the United States in the nineteenth century, Native students in seventeenth-century Massachusetts were not trained as a servant class, educated separately from Anglo students and forced to abandon their languages. Rather, the Harvard Indian College was designed to educate the sons of leaders, who were to be trained alongside the sons of English clergymen and magistrates.[28]

At the Roxbury grammar school (which continues today as Roxbury Latin), Caleb, Joel, James, and their peers learned to read and write in Latin, and to cipher (arithmetic), while also learning to adopt, and adapt, English social customs and the "practice of logic." Modeled on Elizabethan grammar schools, Roxbury was a traditional one-room school, with Indian and English students sitting on benches, each pupil reciting Latin phrases from their books, as schoolmaster Daniel Weld called upon them. They read and memorized passages from books such as Comenius's *Janua*, a Latin phrase book, and Cicero's *Ethics*, formally quizzing each other to retain their knowledge of Latin grammar. The students' early Indigenous education in the art of *memorate* and aural/oral recall likely served them well. Native students learned to read in English and Algonquian, most likely from Thomas Shepard's *Catechism* and Eliot's *Primer* (both published in 1654, the latter by Harvard Press), which provided basic exercises and recitations of the principles of Christianity. Thus, while learning Latin and English, the scholars were encouraged to maintain their own language. This would make them more effective teachers to their people, but also had the effect of maintaining Indigenous systems of communication. The commissioners of the United Colonies observed, in 1660, that Native students had "so much exersice of their own language" that there was "no fear or danger of their forgetting of it."[29]

At the same time, Native students were introduced to English methods of "education" that differed vastly from those at home. Students who diverged from their studies, or the routine, were subjected to corporal punishment, which may have been rare in practice, but when enforced, was carried out against its victim by the schoolmaster, with the assistance of the other students, who would hold their classmate down while the schoolmaster hit him with the "birch" switch. This was one of many English "customs" which would have seemed strange, and probably horrifying, to the Nipmuc and Wampanoag youth who attended the grammar schools. Before the arrival of missionaries, the physical punishment of children was not practiced in Native space. At Aquinnah, David

Silverman notes, Wampanoag people "rejected missionary arguments to 'break the will' of their young people." Well into the eighteenth century, Englishmen like Cotton Mather bemoaned that Native children were "the most humored, cockered, indulged things in the world." At school, however, there were no adult advocates to intercede on the students' behalf, and shame became a potent force for imposing self-restraint.[30]

The discipline imposed upon the students also included a regimented, rigid schedule, with little room for play, which was dictated by an unfamiliar temporal system whereby the day was divided into particular segments regulated by a clock, which in the Western Abenaki language became known as *papeezokwazik*, "that thing which makes much noise and does nothing useful." Shepard's *Catechism* gave the students a divine reason to follow the schedule. As the primer stated, the existence of God could be proven by the existence of this temporal system. In answer to the "Question, 'How may it be proved that there is a God?,'" students would have learned to repeat by rote, "From time, for we see that months come before years, and weeks before months, and dayes before weeks, and houres before dayes . . . and a minute of time before an hour, and therefore there must necessarily be some minute of time before the world began, & therefore a God who gave it this beginning." It was a tricky but potentially persuasive form of circular reasoning: the existence of this particular conception of linear, divided time was a fact of the world, evidenced by our own progress from birth to adulthood to death, and since it could presumably be observed by all mankind, it clearly demonstrated the orderly vision of God and the world he created, as well as the juxtaposition of his eternal existence. Therefore, time was a creation of the divinity, and the divinity could be witnessed in time.[31]

Yet, in their own language, students like Caleb, Joel, and James also would have read and recited a different version of the same question as asked in the bilingual "Some Helps for the Indians": "*Oohgôkje korâmen neh átta Mandouh?*" or "How know you that there is Manitou?" Among the answers, they would reply "that there is Manitou common to all men, nor is it changed by the changes of times; therefore it must arise from some light which is common to all men." This Indigenous depiction reflected and reinforced the presence of an indefinable force inhabiting a cyclical, spatialized conception of deep time, permeating all spaces and temporalities. The awesome "light" would manifest in such forces as "Thunder, Earthquakes, fights in the Aire, blazing Stars, &c.," all representations of the Sky World associated with Kiehtan, "which shewes that" men "know there is a power above the creatures, though they see him not, who will punish sin, and can do it when he will. And this is God Jehovah."

Thus, even at school, Native students could continue to practice the syncretic religion of their home, where "God Jehovah" and Manitou were manifestations of the same power, bolstered by their reading of bilingual texts open to multiple interpretations. At the same time, such passages utilized familiar references to perform a shifty doubleness in which the fluid spirit of Manitou and the upper world creator spirit of Kiehtan became interchangeable with a fearsome, all-powerful God who would "punish sin."[32]

As evidenced by these passages, the rigid disciplinary system went hand-in-hand with the goal of training young minds in the "practice of logic," the "art of thinking" that the English believed would "tame" the "wildness" and "natural depravity" of children. Some students, English and Indian, would focus on the art of self-discipline and the classic "Three R's"; others, who demonstrated the greatest aptitude for "absorbing Latin," were identified by Weld as potential scholars—those who would most "benefit from a classical education." These young men, exhibiting exceptional learning and discipline, were encouraged to master the classical languages and literatures, with the goal of qualifying for Harvard College. "From the beginning," Richard Hale Jr. observes, "the founders of Roxbury Latin intended" that a major and "perpetual" goal of the school would be "the teaching of 'Good Literature,'" meaning "Latin literature, for in 1650 this was the universal language." Thus the Native students were not merely being trained to be missionary teachers, but literary scholars. At these schools, the teaching of Christian religion and classical literature were intertwined, with the dual goal of "giving instruction in the classics and producing Christian citizens."[33]

Caleb Cheeshateaumuck and Joel Iacoomes excelled at their studies, advancing to Elijah Corlett's Latin School, next to the college in Cambridge, where they were joined in their lessons by the son of their missionary, Matthew Mayhew, and the son of the former Governor, Joseph Dudley. Observing their progress, Harvard president Charles Chauncey remarked that when "Caleb and Joel were called forth" to "be examined" by himself at "the publick Commencement," they "gave good contentment . . . to them that were present," translating "part of a Chapter in Isaiah into Latine, and sheweing the construction of it so that they gave great hope for the future of their perfecting." At Corlett's, Joel and Caleb mastered Latin, Greek, and English and by rigorous examination, they were admitted to Harvard College in 1661. Here they studied beside the sons of colonial leaders, developing their knowledge of classical literatures, while learning to read the scriptures in the original Hebrew. Ironically, hopeful missionary Matthew Mayhew was not allowed to advance to the college, in part because he was not able to master the Wôpanâak tongue. The young woman,

Joane, who had studied with Joel and Caleb, was not advanced beyond the grammar school; women were not allowed to attend college, or participate in the colonial government. Wampanoag women did, however, become teachers, in their homes and day schools on the island of Noepe.[34]

James and Job were steered in a different direction. Having acquired literacy in English, Latin, and their own language, Naoas's sons were "put to apprentice" at the end of their tutelage at the grammar school. Job was to be trained as a carpenter, although he returned to mission education shortly thereafter, joining his brother Joseph Tukuppawillin back in the Nipmuc country, where both served as teachers. As Caleb and Joel furthered their studies at the Latin School, James joined the printer Samuel Green at the Indian College, where the colony's only press was now housed. Recruited by Eliot as a printer's apprentice, he would help to produce the first run of bilingual literature in the colonies, with readers in England and in his home country. Hereafter, the young Wawaus would be known as "James the Printer," or simply "James Printer."[35]

THE HARVARD PRINTING PRESS AND THE ORIGINS OF AMERICAN LITERATURE, CAMBRIDGE, 1659–1663

The funding that flowed from across the Atlantic to the mission project was essential to the first flowerings of American literature. As George Parker Winship has noted, it was the moneys intended "to Christianize the natives of New England" that kept "the Cambridge Press active for more than thirty . . . years."[36] When we focus on the productions of the Harvard Press, it becomes evident that American literature from its origins was a bilingual, bicultural endeavor, utilizing the linguistic skills of Wampanoag, Massachusett, and Nipmuc natives and English immigrants to produce a literature that could be read by multiple audiences.

John Eliot is often credited with producing the famous "Indian Library," which, in the words of Bernd Peyer, "initiated American publishing history." However, as Peyer and numerous scholars have acknowledged, this publishing endeavor would have been impossible without young men like James Printer and his peers.[37] Eliot's benefactors knew his language skills were not strong enough to achieve such an ambitious publishing project, and Eliot himself expressed his need for Native translators, writing to Edward Winslow in 1649:

I do very much desire to translate some parts of the Scripture into their language, and to print some Primer in their language wherein to initiate and teach them to read, which some of the men do much also desire; and printing such a thing will be troublesome and chargeable, and I having yet but little skill in their language . . . I must have some Indians, and it may be other help continually about me to try and examine Translations.[38]

Eliot's first translator, a captive named Cockenoe, had recently returned to his Montauk community on Long Island. However, when Wampus sent his son to Roxbury, a young Massachusett man, Job Nesuton, joined them in traveling to the coast and became Eliot's primary translator. Eliot acknowledged his role in translating *The Indian Grammar Begun* (published by the Harvard Press in 1666), calling Job a "pregnant witted young man." When Caleb, Joel, James, and Job Kattenanit entered the preparatory schools, Job Nesuton was already working with Eliot toward the ambitious goal of translating the Christian Bible.[39]

Still, one man was hardly enough. Eliot expressed great doubt about his ability to translate and publish the bible in his lifetime. In 1658, he wrote to the colonial government and to the Society in England that he required a "Journey man Printer" "at the presse in Harvard Colledge" to assist the English printer Samuel Green, "to expedite the work . . . in impressing the Bible in the Indian language." Shortly thereafter, James was "put to apprentice" as a "printer's devil," and he and Green were joined by the "London printer" Marmaduke Johnson. There were only a handful of young men in the colony who were both fluent in the language in which the "Indian library" was published and familiar with the Roman alphabet in which it was printed. James's dual fluency made him invaluable to the printing process.[40]

Eliot had noted that the "printing" of "the Scripture" would be especially "troublesome" with "little skill in their language." A printer had to be able to read each page of the handwritten manuscript and then set the tiny type letter by letter in order to produce the printed sheets. Without literacy and fluency in the language being printed, a printer like Green or Johnson would have to read letter by single letter in order to select and set each type. James, on the other hand, could read and recognize a phrase and set the letters with comparative speed. Without James Printer, who learned the very rare art of typesetting and was literate in the Indigenous language, the process would have been maddeningly slow and "grossly inefficient."[41]

It is probable that Joel and Caleb—who lived in the building where the bible was printed, and would have regularly conversed with James, Job Nesuton, and Eliot—were also involved in its translation and production, as they studied at Corlett's school and the college. It cannot be mere coincidence that this development of literature, marked by "Eliot's" translation and publication of the

"Indian Library," was accomplished during the years that Caleb, Joel, and James were living on the campus. Eliot first proposed the idea of translating the bible in his 1649 letter to Winslow. By 1655, with the assistance of Job Nesuton, only one full book, Genesis, and one part of the gospel of Matthew were printed. However, after 1659, when Caleb, Joel, and James arrived in Harvard Yard, the project gained momentum. By 1661 the press had published a first print run of 1,500 copies of the New Testament in the Wôpanâak language. By 1663, the entire bible was ready for publication.[42]

Working two presses, twelve to thirteen hours a day, on the lower floor of the Indian College, printing one sheet at a time after setting out each piece of type by hand, Green, Printer, and Johnson were able to produce a full version of the Bible entitled *Mamusse Wunneetupanatamwe Up-Biblum God*, which was distributed in wide-ranging networks of trade. Published in "huge print runs," the bible circulated among Native converts (and potential converts) in the Nipmuc, Patucket, and Wampanoag towns to the west and south, and also among curious benefactors and collectors in England. From there, the books continued to travel within both Native and European networks. The press quickly printed enough copies that there could be one bible "for every Christian Indian family in New England." Within a decade, the press published ten Indigenous language texts, some of which were published in a bilingual, interlinear format to assist both Native speakers and English readers. Likewise, English students being prepared for missionary work, such as Matthew Mayhew, could use the primer to hasten their acquisition of Wôpanâak. "Formally educated Wampanoags" like Joel and Caleb "generously shared their knowledge," Silverman relates, "so the entire community could benefit from the Indian Library." On the island and inland, Native teachers like Hiacoomes and Job Kattenanit utilized the primer and the bible to instruct youth in their communities.[43]

Over the fifty years of its existence, Lepore observes, "the labor behind the Indian Library was phenomenal, and the output of the Cambridge Press unparalleled." At least one hundred books and pamphlets were printed during this time, along with countless broadsides, the laws of the colony, which every English family was required to purchase, and the commencement programs or Latin "theses" of the college. Its publications included not only the first bible to be printed in America, but also literary texts, such as Michael Wigglesworth's *Day of Doom*, which became staples of the early American canon. This New England "bestseller" was circulating widely in Cambridge when Joel and Caleb arrived at commencement. They might have huddled with other scholars, reading the vivid but dogmatic poem with both excitement and trepidation. Like many students, they may have memorized "all 224 stanzas," reciting the lines dramatically for each other.[44]

On "the day of doom," predicted in the Book of Revelations (a chapter Native people, ironically, were *not* encouraged to read), God's "Power Imperial" would reach all corners of the earth, driving into the open all people who might hide from his wrath "in Caves and Delves and woody Mountains." This vision inspired hope that Native converts could be among the saved even as it inspired fear that their relations faced imminent danger, providing an urgent motivation for young men like Caleb and Joel to become teachers to their kin. After all, this literature taught them that it was not their race that made them "infidels" but their imprisonment in ignorance of God's law. Yet it also marked a clear divide between believers and "the sons of men" who "refused" or "condemn[ed]" the "Threatnings of God's Word." Even as such texts promoted the possibility of kinship with the English, through an imagined mutual descent from Adam, they also fostered fissures in Native networks. Like Sassamon, the "scholars" were encouraged to value the bonds to their fellow sons of Adam more deeply than their bonds to their "heathen" kin. "Before the Throne of Christ," Wigglesworth's poem warned, the scholars would want to be "found" standing among their English brethren. Yet it also promised, if successful in their education, they might become the "Peace-maker[s]" who could save the "num'rous bands" from "anguish" on the "day of doom."[45]

This consideration of the circulation of texts in multiple languages—Algonquian, Indo-European, Semitic—in both ancient and modern forms, raises key questions about our understandings of the origins of American literature. What would it mean to read Wigglesworth's poem alongside Eliot's bible, as Caleb and Joel must have done? Why aren't we reading excerpts from Wôpanâak books alongside Bradford's *Plimoth Plantation* and Anne Bradstreet's poetry today? What would the American canon look like if these texts were restored? What would it mean to ask twenty-first-century students to wrestle with the few extant writings of the Harvard Indian College, the multilingual and multinational texts revealing the intersections among the numerous languages read, written, and spoken in "early America"? What might those texts reveal about the diverse cultural frameworks that formed a confluence at Cambridge?

Speaking to efforts toward the inclusion of Native American literary texts within the American canon, Creek literary scholar Craig Womack has asserted that "tribal literatures are not some branch waiting to be grafted onto the main trunk. Tribal literatures are the *tree*, the oldest literatures in the Americas, the most American of American literatures. We *are* the canon."[46] Taking into account the collaboration which produced the voluminous "Indian Library," this statement becomes relevant, not only for the longstanding oral traditions and understudied glyphic writing systems of the Americas, but also for the first printed publications in Algonquian, Latin, and English. Yet *how* we read these texts matters as much as whether we read them. Following is merely one example of how we might look anew at a very old text, written by the Indian College's most famous graduate.

THE POWER OF THE POET'S SONG:
READING CALEB'S ADDRESS

The scholars who attended the grammar and Latin schools also became composers of literature, including poetry, essays, addresses, and petitions. Although the students were apparently prolific, only three texts from the Indian College, as far as scholars are aware, have survived: an elegy, written in 1678 by a student known only as Eleazar; an eighteenth-century poem by Benjamin Larnell; and a missive composed in 1663 by Caleb Cheeshateaumuck. Caleb addressed his eloquent epistle to the "Honoratissimi Benefactores," or "honored benefactors," who had supported the Indian College mission.[47] He opened by recounting the Greek myth of Orpheus:

Referunt historici de Orpheo musico et insigni Poeta quod ab Appolline Lyram acceperit eaque tantum valuerit, ut illius Cantu sylvas saxumque moverit et Arbores ingentes post se traxerit, ferasque ferocissimas mitiores rediderit imo, quod accepta Lyrâ ad inferos descenderit et Plutonem et Proserpinam suo carmine demulserit, et Eurydicen uxorem ab inferis ad superos evexerit: Hoc symbolum esse statuunt Philosophi Antiquissimi, ut ostendant quod tanta et vis et virtus doctrinae et politioris literaturae ad mutandum Barborum Ingenium: qui sunt tanquam arbores, saxa, et bruta animantia: et eorum quasi matephorisin efficiendam, eosque tanquam Tigres Cicurandos et post se trahendos.

Following is an English translation:

Historians tell about Orpheus the musician and remarkable poet, that he received a lyre from Apollo, and that he was so excellent upon it that the forests and the rocks were moved by his song. The song's power was so great that he made the great trees follow behind him, and made the wild animals tame. Indeed the lyre was so powerful that, having received it, he descended into the underworld, softened even Pluto and Proserpina with his song, and led Eurydice, his wife, out of the underworld into the upper world. The most ancient philosophers make this a symbol in order that they might show how strong the power and virtue of education and of refined literature are in the transformation of the barbarians' nature. They are like the trees, the rocks, and the unthinking animals, and a metamorphosis, as it were, of them must be brought about. They have to be tamed like tigers and must be drawn to follow behind.[48]

The first observation that might strike a reader of the opening paragraph is Caleb Cheeshateaumuck's proficiency in Latin and knowledge of classical literature. With his exegesis Caleb proved that, like many learned people in New England, he could read and interpret classical poetry, including Ovid's *Metamorphoses* and Virgil's *Georgics*, the primary Latin sources for the Orpheus myth. Further, as Wolfgang Hochbruck and Beatrix Dudensing-Reichel have explained, Caleb demonstrated his comprehension of the appropriate placement of this "pagan" literature within a Christian context, citing the "ancient" Christian "philosophers" such as Clement of Alexandria, who read the *type* of Christ in the figure of Orpheus. Further, Caleb seemed to emphasize to his Puritan benefactors that he was familiar with the proper *Calvinist* interpretation of that myth, exemplified by Arthur Golding's English translation of Ovid's *Metamorphoses*. Likely read by Caleb, as by other religious readers in New England, Golding's *Metamorphosis* was the version on which Shakespeare and Spencer drew. Caleb's interpretation may have been informed by the popular literature of his peers, such as George Sandys's much admired *Metamorphosis Englished* (1626), the first "American" translation of Ovid, completed while the author was treasurer of the fledgling colony of Virginia, making it perhaps "the earliest piece of English verse written in America." Whether read in the original Latin or in English translation, Ovid's *Metamorphoses* was among the best-known works of the "heathen poets" in colonial New England. With his erudite analysis of both classical literature and Calvinist theology, Caleb did not merely perform as a student, but asserted his place among an elite group of New England scholars.[49]

Despite these rich influences, some scholars have accepted a simplistic interpretation of Caleb's address, considered one of the earliest texts composed by a Native American author in a European language. For example, while Hochbruck and Dudensing-Reichel have provided a nuanced translation and useful contextualization, they offer only a fleeting analysis of the text, observing that the "analogies the author draws are obvious." That is, they write, the teachers and benefactors "are likened to Orpheus; their efforts and missionary work to the lyre; and lastly, the wildness of the stones, forests, and animals to the savageness of nature's human inhabitants, among which were the Indian students themselves."[50] However, other lenses might invite less "obvious" readings of the address and offer more complex possibilities for Caleb's interpretation of the classical Greek myth and the Latin literature.

✦ ✦ ✦

In this letter to his "honored benefactors," Caleb not only demonstrates his knowledge and skill, but advances a thesis or "disputation" on the transformative power of literature. Caleb interprets not just the text but the landscape in which he finds himself: he is one of those "barbarians," both a "foreigner" to the culture that surrounds him and an "uncultivated" youth who has been transformed by the word, by "education," and by "literature" into a learned man. Moreover, in the story of Orpheus, literature also transforms the "uncivilized" land. Although Caleb's reading refers most directly to the transformation of the Native people, in his emphasis on and depiction of Orpheus's transformation of "the forests and the rocks" by his song, he argues several provocative, and perhaps contradictory, propositions simultaneously. First, that literature, or the missionary project, has the potential to cause a transformation of the wilderness, the forested land that surrounded Cambridge and the college. And second, that the "trees," rocks, and "wild animals" of the forest are agents in this transformation. In his portrayal, following Virgil and Ovid, they are animate, alive. The forests and rocks, are "moved" by the poet's song. The song makes "the trees" willingly "follow" Orpheus.[51]

And yet, in the classical myth and in Caleb's address, those powerful animate beings are tamed. Caleb's diction implies that this domestication is to their benefit. The trees, the rocks, the beasts are not destroyed, but instead enraptured; following Virgil, they are "softened" by Orpheus's song, made calm and peaceful in its power. It is the beauty of the poetry and ironically, the depth and integrity of Orpheus's grief that engenders this tranquility, producing a desire to "follow" its source. In a homeland torn asunder by chaos and disease, such music must have been tempting indeed. As Gary Gibbs and Florinda Ruiz note, Ovid's version "departed" from Virgil's in its message that the deepest grief could ultimately lead to "personal transformation." Furthermore, Christian interpretation insisted that the route to virtuous metamorphosis was accessible only through the redemptive "song" of Christ. As Clement of Alexandria proclaimed, "Truly, the [New Song] alone . . . tamed men, ever the wildest of beasts." Indeed, the interpretations of some "ancient" Christian "philosophers" likened Orpheus's taming of the beasts to "Christ's triumph over death." Joel Iacoomes's father had undergone this very transformation, creating a model for young men like Caleb and Joel, who also faced great loss. Joel had seen his father remain silent, stalwart, and "patient" in the face of the loss of his sibling at an early age, his "softness" attributed to his conversion. Ovid's poem, which Caleb may have seen as a lens on his own life, promised that such grief could have a purpose, that it could lead his kin to a "metamorphosis" that would result in salvation.[52]

If we are to read into Caleb's expressed view of his education as well as his impressive performance as a literary scholar, then we can imagine that he was a lover of literature, a classic reader who saw in the stories that he read inspiration and guidance in reading his own complex life. At the same time, given what we know of the missionary education project, we can see that the promise carried an ironic, if not sinister, subtext. After all, Orpheus's power was not only associated with music and literature, but in early Christian Europe, with the power of priests and missionaries, those who spread the song of Christ. Men like Hiacoomes, his son Joel, and Caleb were led by the powerful persuasion of their missionary teachers to play the role of Orpheus—like the pied piper who leads the children to follow him, in this case, to participate in the colonization of their homeland. After all, the forest could only be tamed through its felling; those "great trees" were even then being led to their destruction, shipped from Boston harbor to be transformed into ships and staves or devoured locally by wasteful, inefficient open hearths. Caleb may have seen those trees floated downriver, "following" English men to the sea. Were Caleb and the other students "moved" to follow an English path to their own destruction? Were they participants in the domestication of their homelands, serving colonialist ends?[53]

The turn in the language of the address, from past to present and toward force and compulsion, would certainly seem to support this suggestion. Yet before turning to the contemporary transformation of the "barbarians," Caleb mentions the crux of Orpheus's story, his attempt to rescue his beloved Eurydice from death. Having described the lyre's effect on the trees, rocks, and animals, Caleb pauses, recalling that, "indeed," the lyre was so powerful that Orpheus was able to descend to the "underworld" and "soften" the gods "Pluto and Proserpina," allowing the poet to lead "Eurydice, his wife, out of the underworld into the upper." The possible interpretations of the underworld here are a fascinating lens through which we might discern deeper readings of Caleb's allegory. To begin, there is, of course, Caleb's clear reference to the "world which lies beneath the earth," in the translated words of Ovid, "hither we all make our way" upon death. In the moving story of Orpheus and Eurydice, one repeatedly told in many nations' literature and song, Orpheus is able (at least temporarily) to rescue his beautiful wife from captivity and premature death by softening the powerful and dangerous "lord of the shades," bringing even "the bloodless spirits" to tears. His is an especially impressive feat, as he achieves her redemption not through physical prowess or battle, but through the power of his song, made potent by his passion for his wife and his profound anguish at her loss.[54]

To add another layer of meaning, in the Christian typology through which Caleb read the Orpheus myth, the underworld was transformed into the Christian space of hell. The Calvinist Golding, for example, characterizes Pluto as the "king of Ghosts" who "like a lordly tyrant reignes" in "Shady Hell." In Puritan imagination, this "tyrant" held unconverted Native people captive, "With dismal chains, and strongest reins, like Prisoners of Hell," to quote Wigglesworth. In this reading, Orpheus, "the poet" and typological symbol of Christ, "lull[s]" the "Gods of Hell" and frees his wife from captivity. Caleb's address emphasized the power of Christian literature and education to cultivate a missionary teacher (which he aspired to become) who might likewise save his kin from "captivity" by Satan. Later in the address, he reveals that one of his "hope[s]" is that he and the other scholars might "become instruments to spread and propagate the gospel among our kin and neighbors," carrying out the promise of *First Fruits*. The scholars would "become" Apollo's lucid, harmonious lyre, through which Christ, in the "ancient philosopher's" reading, would sing. Harvard, in this sense, may have represented that dangerous place through which Caleb must travel in order to become that man of words, that "instrument" of Christ. Or, alternatively, since he had spent so much of his childhood in Roxbury and Cambridge, perhaps he had absorbed enough of settler worldviews to see Native space as that dangerous realm of chaos and temptation to which he must eventually return to transform (convert) and "save" his relations, enabling their journey to a heavenly "home" above.[55]

Yet, given that Caleb spent the earliest years of his childhood on Noepe and absorbed the oral literature of that place, the story can also be read through an Indigenous literary framework. The lower world and upper worlds of the classical literature and biblical allegories also had Indigenous analogies which missionaries like Mayhew did not fail to exploit. Most Native people in the eastern woodlands share a common cosmology of three connected, overlapping worlds—the upper world of sky, the lower world of waters, and this world in between—that of human beings. Powerful beings are said to inhabit the lower world of waters, among them the many forms of great horned snakes portrayed in Indigenous stories and iconographic art. Although Caleb does not mention it in his address, the opening of the Orpheus story reveals that the beloved Eurydice's premature death was caused by a serpent's bite. As Miller's translation of

Virgil puts it, "She, doomed girl, running headlong along the stream . . . did not see the fierce snake, that kept to the riverbank, in the deep grass under her feet." Christian theologians and English translators did not fail to see the obvious: as with Eve in the Garden of Eden, Satan took the form of "a viper" "lurking in the grasse." Caleb would also have seen the obvious parallel to the great horned snakes of the lower world who figured in the oral traditions and their associated emergence places in the home where he was raised, applying Christian typology to his own tradition of "pagan literature" just as the "ancient philosophers" had done. At the same time, Wampanoag oral traditions also offered him a framework for reading the classical myths.[56]

In Wampanoag country, the lower world was associated with ambivalent, potentially dangerous beings, some of whom might take the form of a snake. Like the stories that the poet Orpheus sings, tales of transformation abounded in the oral traditions on which Caleb was raised. Such beings could travel between worlds and, like Orpheus's song, could bring about "metamorphosis." Indigenous stories across the continent feature certain powerful *human* beings who were, or are, able to travel between worlds—women who married those underwater creatures, seducing them or being seduced by them, and men who gained power through escaping their capture or defeating them. Those humans who encountered these lower-world beings risked death or capture, but those, akin to Orpheus, who survived were often transformed by the experience, becoming people of great power and influence. Spiritual leaders or *pawwauak* could call upon such forces to help them heal their kin, while war leaders might beg assistance to defend their homelands. It may also be worth noting that Roger Williams described Moshup, the most prominent figure in Wampanoag oral tradition, as a man of "miracles" who could walk "upon the waters," likening him to "the Sone of God," while missionaries, in their desire to eradicate Indigenous cultural traditions, likened Moshup to "the devil." In the Wôpanâak bible, the word for hell is Cheepiok, literally, the place of Cheepi, the place of separated souls, those shadowy spirits who wandered in the afterlife, separated from their kin. The similarity to the lower world that Virgil described could not have been lost on Caleb, a place filled with "insubstantial shadows, and the phantoms of those without light," who "came from the lowest depths of Erebus, startled by his song."[57]

Likewise, there was an Indigenous counterpart to Jove, "the king of the gods," and Jehovah, the sovereign of the heavens. Like Jove, Kiehtan, bringer of corn, was associated with the upper world of the sky, symbolized by thunderbolts and thunderbirds, the small ones who still today signal the coming of stormy weather. Caleb must have recognized this similarity, with

Orpheus's description of the "power of Jove," the "victorious bolts hurled on the Phlegrian plains," the spirit who "did not deign to take the form of any bird save only that which could bear his thunderbolts." In Golding's English translation, that bird took the form of an eagle, a symbol associated with ascension to heaven in Christian allegory and a being affiliated with Kiehtan in Algonquian belief. If Caleb did indeed read Golding, he would have been able to join with the English translator and the ancient philosophers in making the connection between Jove and Jehovah. Ovid's Orpheus made the plea, "From Jove, O Muse, my mother—for all things yield to the sway of Jove— inspire my song!" In comparison, Golding's Orpheus proclaimed, "O Muse my Mother frame my song of Jove. For everything is subject untoo royall Jove. Of Jove the heavenly King I oft have shewed the glorious Power." Although Ovid's "king of the gods," like a sachem, held the power of persuasion, Golding's "heavenly King" resembled the Calvinist God, commanding subjection from all beings, including the Native people whom the English desired to rule, as his preordained representatives in New England. Thus, in the hands of the theologians, translators, and teachers, it was not only the trees and beasts who would be transformed by Orpheus's song, but the "pagan gods" like Jove and Kiehtan. Or . . . would Jehovah himself undergo a metamorphosis on this continent, in the hands and songs of Wampanoag people, and become a being more like Kiehtan?[58]

The encounter "between worlds," whether the lower world and this world, or the English and Algonquian, held the potential for danger, death, destruction, and capture; the potential for transformation; the potential for a transformative experience or "metamorphosis" that could allow a man or his entire community to gain great positive power. The key was in the strength and the will of the man or woman who wrangled with the horned snake. The strongest and cleverest survived. The most arrogant were often killed. Those who survived could return to this world and use their newfound power to transform the troubled state of their people—to return water to a community suffering from drought or to provide food to children who are starving. However, sometimes those who encountered the snake actually chose to stay in the underworld, embracing a new life, seduced by the power of its own songs. In this case, the effect on this world of such a union could still be tremendous, but its impact—positive or negative—was much more ambivalent. Whether Caleb's education would work to free the people or enslave them was in part dependent on the strength and skill, the actions and motivations of the scholar himself. That he was learning a powerful song was a given. How he would be able to wield it, how he would choose to use it, and what impacts it would have on his relations was an ambivalent question that, like the story of Orpheus, even now remains open to interpretation.

Our reading of this story within the framework of Caleb's landscape becomes even more complicated as we encounter his forceful turn to the allegorical interpretation of "the ancient philosophers," a dogmatic reading of the myth which was likely favored by his missionary teachers. Shifting the tone abruptly from the lyrical to the didactic, he contends that the story of Orpheus serves as a "symbol" for the "power and virtue of education and of refined literature . . . in the transformation of the barbarians' nature." The song no longer has Ovid's magical, "moving" quality which might lull us into a state of calm, but, like Golding's Jove, is propelled by coercive strength. Orpheus's song is a metaphor for "education," a virtuous power that can transform the "nature" of "barbarian" people, who are likened to "tigers" that "have to be tamed." Thus, Caleb's own education becomes a brute but necessary force, through which he is compelled to change. Likewise the poet's "song" becomes a power or instrument that he "must" use, and which must be used upon him, to enact this necessary metamorphosis in his "nature," as well as upon his people and in his homeland.[59]

Yet there is an intriguing parallelism at play in Caleb's use of the Latin which appears to be quite strategic. The phrases *post se traxerit* and *post se trahendos* are essentially the same, creating a parallel structure in poetic phrasing as well as meaning. Just as Orpheus with his song made the trees and wild animals follow behind him, the "cultivated" teachers or "instruments" who would affect a "metamorphosis" must make the "wild" people follow behind them. The key difference is in Caleb's use of the "puzzling phrase" *quasi matephorisin efficiendam*. Although Ovid used the nominative form of the Latin word, *metamorphoses*, to describe a world where transformation is occurring all the time, for good or ill, with or without deliberate human or divine will, Caleb uses an accusative Greek form, *matephorisin* (albeit imprecisely spelled), which insists that metamorphosis must be effected by the "instruments" of God's will. Christ's "new song" might hold the power to "move," but the realization of that metamorphosis required a "powerful" lyre: the benefactors would play an important role in the transformation which "must be brought about." As Caleb declared in the paragraph that immediately followed, "God delegated you to be our patrons."[60]

Even as literature itself became an "instrument" of dangerous and ambivalent metamorphosis, Caleb's literary text was itself operating as a tool. The power of his words served to achieve a particular pragmatic goal, the continuance of his education. Among Native peoples in the northeast, writing emerged as an instrument of persuasion, with the effectiveness of the text often rooted in the beauty of the speaker's words, his song. Caleb's address thus served as a tool to advance the educational project in which he was engaged, or of which he had himself been made an instrument, depending on our reading of that project. The writing of the epistle may have been urged by his own teachers, to "move" the "benefactors" of the college to continue in their financial and political support of this transformative project. In it, Caleb appeals to the benefactors' sense of the "refined" nature of literature and its "power" to "soften" the "barbarians." He appeals to the possibility that Native children could become "tamed" through the power of education. At the same time, he appeals to the colonial sense of force, arguing that these same people can and "must be" subdued through this process. These petitions may in fact have been directed at different kinds of benefactors, those who regarded themselves as motivated by benevolence, as well as those who were motivated by fear and a desire for submission and containment of the Native populace. Yet, Caleb also asserts that the "benefactors" are themselves "instruments," like Orpheus's lyre, invoking a divine plan for continued support of Native education. The patrons, like Orpheus, are merely vessels for Jove or Jehovah, and if *they* had read Golding, they would know that they must be "subject" to his "Glorious power."[61]

Furthermore, Caleb demonstrates the success of the project and the evidence for his thesis in his *performance* of the address. In this sense, his use of the classical texts to "read" his own landscape and to translate it appropriately to the "benefactors" becomes even more significant. The address is a performance of knowledge and aptitude, but also a performance of his comprehension of the *correct* reading of both the text and the landscape, which, if carried out successfully, will sway the benefactors as to the efficacy of the education project. He will "soften" them with the recital of his own song, compelling them to continue funding the college.

Through his interpretive display, Caleb persuades his audience of his argument that literature and education are indeed effective tools in the "transformation" of "barbarians," the vision of *First Fruits* manifested in his writing. He reveals how "refined" he has become through his education, presenting his ability to write eloquently of literature and religion, his capacity for reading classical literature, his knowledge of the appropriate critical interpretations, and his ability to formulate interpretations and theses. Finally, he makes clear that he understands the divinity, righteousness, and benevolence of the education project. In the paragraphs that follow his exegesis, he praises the "divine mercy" and the "loving" actions of these benefactors, who "have poured forth immense—the greatest—of resources," referring both to their literal financial gifts and to the more symbolic gift of civilization and Christianity to "us pagans," making the connection evident between the Classical Greeks and Romans and the Wampanoags. This "metamorphosis" has taken place as a result of their "blessings" and patronage: "We used to be naked in soul and body, alien from all humanity, led around by all sorts of errors." But, now the Indian scholars have been transformed into knowledgeable and refined Christian men, a thesis that Caleb supports not through a description of their transformed state, but through a performance of its evidence in his address. He stands as the ultimate proof of his argument.[62]

LOOKING BACK, MOVING FORWARD

A final look at Caleb's use of the Orpheus story reveals one more lens through which we can read his interpretation. We can consider what is absent from his address to his patrons. As Hochbruck and Dudensing-Reichel have observed, Caleb's account of the myth, following early Christian typology, "specifically omits the loss of Eurydice and the final failure of Orpheus's rescue attempt." By focusing on the power of Orpheus's song to transform the wild beings of the forest and to lull the gods of the underworld, this reading elides the tragic ending to Orpheus's lower world journey, in which the bard is unable to resist temptation and loses his beloved forever. In Ovid's recounting, "And now they were nearing the margin of the upper earth, when he, afraid that she might fail him, eager for sight of her, turned back his longing eyes; and instantly she slipped into the depths." The condition that Pluto and Proserpina had set for the poet was that he "should not turn his eyes backward until he had gone forth . . . or else the gift would be in vain." Yet just as they reached the precipice of the lower world, Orpheus looks back, and Eurydice is lost permanently to him and to this world.[63]

Caleb was surely familiar with the tragic heart of the story. However, a recounting of Orpheus's failure might have signaled ambivalence to the benefactors who wanted clear evidence that the "transformation" of this "first fruit" promised the conversion of the wilderness to a garden. The ancient philosophers interpreted this passage allegorically; as the "twelfth century Platonist William of Conches" explained, "This fable applies to all of you who seek to raise your minds to sovereign day. For whoever is conquered and turns his eyes to the pit of hell, looking into the inferno, loses all the excellence he has gained." If Caleb were to look back, responding to "desire, the passional part of man's soul," he would, the "ancient philosophers" warned, "lose" all the progress he had made toward "excellence." Those "affections" which might draw him closer to his kin, moving him to look back longingly at the faces of those he loved, might be the very act that would cause him to lose them to the underworld below.[64]

The loss of Eurydice raises many questions, which may have been circling in Caleb's mind. Would his relations, despite the power of the Christian "song," look back? Would some, like the women who married the horned snake, choose to remain in the "desert" of Native space? Would his kin be divided, like the people in Wigglesworth's *Day of Doom*, into flocks of "sheep" and "goats," permanently separated souls?[65] Would those trees, rocks, and animals, whose animate agency Caleb recognized, resist those who would have them subdued? Or, was it his own doubt that he would refuse to acknowledge to his benefactors? Was he not fully swayed by Christ's lyre? Would Caleb look back and be tempted to rejoin his kin in the world of his birth? Was his own "metamorphosis" incomplete?

One of the most striking aspects of reading the classical literature alongside Caleb's address is the flashes of symmetry and congruence between two "pagan" traditions that emerged in entirely different and distant places. The literary and theological traditions of two continents formed a confluence at such sites of intersection, just as classical and Christian traditions intertwined in the ancient European world. In this way, Indigenous traditions about the horned serpent of the lower world of water (a place of "separated souls") with a penchant for seduction weave with traditions about a snake that bites a maiden's foot, carrying her to the lower world of Hades (a place of shadows), and with traditions about a fallen angel named Satan, who takes the form of a snake to tempt maidens, and who inhabits a fiery underworld called hell, where the unrepentant and unconverted go after death. For Caleb, who had witnessed the loss of many, narrowly escaping death during the epidemics, the lower world must have seemed to be always looming beneath him, ready to take him and more of his kin at any moment. It was a subject worthy of great contemplation, to be sure, and the correct assessment of its existence would have the most significant of consequences imaginable.

Still, Caleb had good reasons to look back. Although his teachers promised heaven, life in the preparatory schools and at Harvard was anything but. And although there is a persistent tendency to assume that life in the "Indian wigwam" was less hospitable than life in a colonial English home, historical and archaeological research has revealed that the opposite was true. Consider food as an example. At home, Caleb and Joel would have enjoyed a steady diet of corn in its many forms, with a variety of fresh and smoked fish, shellfish, game meats, along with vegetables and fruits determined by the season, including beans, squash, pumpkin, sunchoke, groundnuts (small native potatoes), plums, berries, and numerous other edible plants. The meal, a social activity shared among the families, would have been accompanied by spring water or tea made from local leaves like raspberry or wintergreen. They would have eaten outside, perhaps under an arbor, with the smell of the cook fires still wafting through the air. The timing of their meals would have been regulated by the rising and falling of the sun. However, Joel and Caleb would have had to spend a part of their day helping their relatives procure the food that would sustain them, joining their relations in hunting, fishing, planting, gathering, and trade. Although most of the time food would have been available in abundance, there was always the possibility that they would hit a period of scarcity, particularly in winter, depending on weather, last year's harvest, and the health of community members. Still, families could regularly offer a feast, made all the more significant by their gratefulness at having acquired it.

Meals at Harvard must have paled in comparison, although the food was pretty much guaranteed. Here, at the tolling of the mealtime bell, Caleb, Joel, and (likely) James gathered with the other students at the "buttery" where they received a steady diet of beer and bread, with a midday "dinner" of small portions of beef, lamb, or pork, sometimes accompanied by turnips or peas, and a similar "supper," a meat pie or hasty pudding. Social hierarchy was established at mealtime. More affluent students ate from silver, their diet supplemented with fresh fruit, mulled cider, and "other luxuries." Like other common students, Joel and Caleb would have eaten from wooden "trenchers, using their own knives and spoons," and drunk from pewter cups. When they first enrolled at Harvard they might have acted like servants, as younger students had to carry the "bevers" to upperclassmen's rooms. Later, they would take their "bevers" back to their quarters, or, if the weather was good, they could eat outside in the Yard. For more formal "supper" and "dinner," they would eat together in the hall, with prayers of thanksgiving opening and closing the meals. Served in the same manner in the same amounts at the same time every day, meals were formal and consistent, regulated by the clock and the budget. For variation, they might sneak out to the local tavern, where they could buy a dinner of oysters, a brief reminder of home.[66]

On the island, Caleb and Joel would have been constantly surrounded by their kin, who also led their education. The instruction of the day would have been determined by the season—as small children, they would have assisted their mothers in planting the fields and gathering plants in the spring and summer. Increasingly, formal religious instruction in the day school was incorporated into their seasonal education. As they became young men, they would have joined their uncles, brothers, and fathers, learning to paddle the ocean and rivers, mastering the art of carving, hunting and fishing while acquiring knowledge of the territory and its multiple habitats, and learning to work co-operatively and think collaboratively as part of a group. Through the coldest months, they would have learned how to be human not only from observing their relatives, but through their elders' stories, recounted so the teachings embedded in ancient literature would lodge firmly in their minds. Increasingly, these stories wove elements from the bible into Indigenous traditions. While participating in family subsistence activities, they would also learn important lessons about how to behave properly toward other beings, including humans, plants, and animals, related through story and example, including the rousing lectures delivered on Sundays by Joel's father and Caleb's sister's husband in the Wôpanâak tongue.[67]

At Harvard, the students were confined to the small space of the Yard. Learning was delivered according to a strict daily schedule, divided into clear segments, regulated by the clock and bell. The routine balanced worship and scholarship, with prayers opening the day, and lectures scheduled at 8:00, 9:00, and 10:00, the students breaking for "dinner" at 11:00. Caleb and Joel joined the other students in performing "disputations" at hourly intervals in the afternoon, where they learned the art of arguing a thesis, and participated in "evening prayers" at 5:00 p.m., including "more translation and logical analysis," followed by "supper" by candlelight at 7:30 and study in their chambers. At home, Caleb would have retreated from outdoors at night to sleep in a *wetu* (round house) or longhouse, depending on the season, lying on raised mats close to the ground, surrounded by family (for better or worse) and the warmth of fire. At Harvard, he slept alone, with Joel and perhaps James as his only company in the drafty upper chambers of the Indian College. The next morning, with the exception of Sundays, they would begin the entire process again.[68]

Research to date suggests that only five Native students actually attended the Harvard Indian College. Two, Eleazar and Benjamin Larnell, who came after Caleb and Joel, both died as a result of disease (and perhaps malnutrition) prior to graduation. Joel Iacoomes was so successful in his studies, according to a local tradition at Harvard, that he was allegedly slated to graduate with "top honors" in the class of 1665. His cohort included Benjamin, the youngest son of John Eliot; Edward Mitchelson, the son of the Marshal-General of the colony; and Joseph Dudley, who would go on to become the governor of the Massachusetts Colony, following in the footsteps of his father, Thomas, who signed the Harvard Charter. Of Joel, the missionary Daniel Gookin wrote, "He was a good scholar and a pious man, as I judge. I knew him well; for he lived and was taught in the same town where I dwell. I observed him for several years, after he was grown to years of discretion, to be not only a diligent student, but an attentive hearer of God's word, diligently writing the sermons, and frequenting lectures; grave and sober in his conversation." Unfortunately, in one of the greatest tragedies of the college's history, by Gookin's account, Joel "took a voyage to Martha's Vineyard to visit his father and kindred, a little before the commencement [in 1665]; but upon his return back in a vessel, with other passengers and mariners, suffered shipwreck upon the island of Nantucket." Caleb thus became the first Native American graduate of Harvard, and the only graduate of the Indian College. Remaining in Boston, he, too, died of consumption shortly after his graduation in 1665. But his story must not end there.[69]

In her hauntingly beautiful short story, "First Fruits," Dakota novelist and Harvard alumnus Susan Power imagines that Caleb, in his death, "returned to Martha's Vineyard." As she paints the scene, through the eyes of a contemporary Harvard freshman and young Dakota woman, "His relatives are all there, and his mother steps forward to help him remove the double-breasted woolen jacket buttoned to his throat." She has made him a full-length coat woven of turkey feathers, which he puts upon his shoulders, in grateful relief. Caleb's father offers a bow of "witch hazel," his little sister "a basket of bright red pearplums, their flesh taut with ripe juice." Exploring Noepe, reacquainting himself with the flowing "sea lavender," the painted turtles, the starfish and spotted salmon of his "favored" cove, "reclaim[ing] the island" as his home, Caleb sits down with a "sheaf of pulpy yellow paper and a lead pencil he sharpens with a knife" to "mark down letters, words, writing feverishly." But rather than working to preserve them in print, he folds the sheets into paper birds, and then launches them into the sea." Power's young narrator observes, "I immediately grasp what he's doing: letting go of the languages . . . Algonqui[a]n is the only language he remembers."[70]

Although we can imagine multiple scenarios, perhaps none so potent and peaceful as Power's portrayal, we also have accounts available from the time that show the continuing impact of Joel and Caleb's education, their kin carrying on their intellectual and spiritual work. When Harvard alumnus and missionary John Cotton Jr. arrived at Noepe only one year after Caleb's graduation, he found a learned community brimming with challenging, precise theological questions. Neither innocent pagans nor ignorant savages, they were interested in debating the details of doctrines and biblical exegesis. The texts of the Indian library circulated widely in Wampanoag networks, and the spoken sacred word traveled even more rapidly. When they returned to Noepe for visits, Joel and Caleb were welcomed by kin who boasted a "sophisticated knowledge of Christian principles" and were critically engaged with the bible. When they went home, the scholars carried Latin, Greek, and English words with them. They probably carried copies of the Wôpanâak bible, providing their own readings and interpretations to their families. Perhaps Caleb related the ancient story of Orpheus in Wôpanâak. Caleb and Joel's expanding knowledge of both religious and classical literature could only contribute to this ongoing conversation, posing new questions and providing possible answers to those raised by their relatives. And their legacy was carried on by their kin, long after their deaths.[71]

During Cotton's fairly brief time as a missionary on Noepe, "dozens of Wampanoags" peppered him with "questions about more than 200 passages of scripture." At Chappaquiddick, Joel's father, Hiacoomes, asked "what are the false Christs, and when will they be?" Joel's brother John asked, "What is it to seek God early?" A man named Matthew questioned a passage in Revelations, a book the missionaries did not encourage them to read: "How doth," he asked, "Christ come as a thief?" Perhaps he was concerned about the connection between the missionaries and their neighbors who had already begun to swindle land. Cotton, as Silverman notes, did not include his own answers to the questions. At Takemmy, the Wampanoag teacher and "minister" Wunnanauhkomun, who married Caleb's sister, asked several thought-provoking philosophical questions: "Can a good man at any time desire to sin? How can the soul know things done before the world began? Can a man quench the motions of the spirit of God?" Back at Chappaquiddick, the influential Christian sachem of Nunnepog, Towanquatick, perhaps demonstrating knowledge of Orpheus's story gained from Caleb, asked "whether a man may not walk in God's way, till he come near to heaven, and then go back again quite to hell?"[72]

The questions Joel and Caleb's relations posed to Cotton suggest that they were especially concerned with the spiritual fate of their beloved kin. They asked "whether our fathers that died before they heard of God or knew him are saved or not." They wanted to know where the souls of babies who passed prematurely traveled. They queried whether "God hath promised that the children of all godly men shall go to heaven?" Joseph of Chappaquiddick asked "whether faith" would "heal the sick," while Joshua, the son of the teacher Monmatchegin, wanted more explanation for the meaning and virtue of Luke 14:12, which stated, "When thou makest a dinner or a supper, call not they friends, nor thy brethren, neither they kinsmen, nor thy rich neighbors; lest they also bid thee again, and recompense be made thee." Most poignantly, Joel Iacoomes's mother wanted to know "Whether those that are buried in the sea shall rise again at the last day, as well as those that are buried on land?" The recent death of her son at sea must have weighed heavily on her mind. The texts Joel had read at Harvard, whether the bible or Wigglesworth's *Day of Doom*, promised that the faithful would rise again, joining Christ and their kin in the heavens, but the underworld of water had claimed him. Would he be forever held in the grasp of Cheepi, Pluto, or Satan? Had he been captured, confined to the world below? Or would Christ's song lead his soul from the waters and carry him to the precipice? Would his grieving mother, through the powerful song of her prayers, be able to carry him to complete the journey to the world above?[73]

Although the records of mission education are rife with tragedy, it is important to acknowledge that not all encounters with Harvard or education ended in death. Joel's brother John, schooled on the island, became a preacher at home and a teacher to Wampanoags on the mainland, while his brother Samuel became a magistrate. Samuel, like Joel, was a scholar who "could read well, both in Indian and in English," but he lived a more colorful life. "Notwithstanding all these Advantages" of education, noted Experience Mayhew, "he was in his youthful Days a carnal Man." He indulged in drink, "folly," and "lust," balancing the Apollonian logic of his education with the Dionysian impulses of independent youth. Samuel was even hauled into colonial court for "fornication" with a local English girl, a very rare charge for a Native man, for which he paid a fine of five pounds. In his adulthood, he was a valued religious and political leader, always distributing food and goods to the community and serving as a "principle Provider" for community feasts.[74]

Caleb's brother Ponit Cheeshateaumuck also became a leader, assuming the sachemship of "Holmes Hole" from his father. His sisters likewise played key leadership roles in the community. Nattootumau, or Hannah Nahnosoo, was a healer and keeper of plant knowledge, who specialized in aiding women who had trouble conceiving. She married John Nahnosoo, a prominent Christian leader and preacher at Sanchakantacket and had many children and grandchildren. Ammapoo, or Abigail, was "taught to read while young" and became "a diligent instructor of her Grandchildren, as well as of her own." She also married "an Indian minister," Wunnanauhkomun, mentioned above, who "used frequently to catechize the Children of the Town." It seems the two sisters lived in the same place, perhaps even in the same house, after their husbands died during the same year. Like her brother Caleb, Abigail was known for her eloquent disputations on religion, describing death as a "Ferryman, by which we have our passage out of this life" and "this world" "into the next." When her own death came near, Abigail's daughter said that "she saw two bright shining Persons, standing in the white Raiment at her Mother's Bed-side, who, on her

Sight of them, with the Light attending them, immediately disappeared." Joining Christian and Wampanoag traditions, the daughter took comfort in her mother's words, that "her Guardians were already come for her." This daughter may have been the one that gave birth to a son named Caleb.[75]

The stories of the youth who inhabited the Indian College take us well beyond its confines. Several of Caleb and Joel's peers survived to become complex men who negotiated within colonial political systems and Indigenous networks. After Caleb graduated, John Wampus was admitted to Harvard, residing in the Indian College for only one year. As the story, which is commonly told at Harvard even today, goes, Wampus "left to become a mariner," seemingly disappearing into the unknown abyss of a life at sea. Yet, in truth, John Wampus, like many other Native men, went to sea for a short time to earn money. Only a year later, he had purchased a home on Beacon Hill in Boston, with his earnings and a mortgage, and was living there with his wife, the daughter of a Mohegan sachem. His neighbors included the son of the future governor of the colony. While John Wampus chose to live in Boston, James Printer pursued another course. He remained for a time at the Indian College after the deaths of Joel and Caleb, where he continued to work the press and to publish bilingual literature. But shortly thereafter, he returned to Nipmuc country. The same year that Caleb died, Annaweekin, James's eldest brother, and his wife brought a son into the world. Now, James's responsibilities at Hassanamesit surpassed those at the college. James Printer left Cambridge and went home, joining his brother Job. There, they would see how their newfound skills might serve the community of Hassanamesit as it underwent its own significant "metamorphosis" in the wake of great change.[76]

Interlude: Nashaway

NIPMUC COUNTRY, 1643–1674

While trading pelts in the recently established Watertown settlement, in Massachusett territory, the sachem Showanon invited trader Thomas King to establish a trading post in his territory of Nashaway, drawing the English trade closer to Nipmuc country. Their formal agreement was among the first regarding shared space in the "freshwater" inland. It allowed for a trading post, at the junction of indigenous trails and "the Bay Path," and limited settlement, at the "fording place . . . where the Nashaway Trail crossed the Nashua River," but preserved Nipmuc subsistence rights and jurisdiction in the wider region, while strengthening Nashaway's reputation as a crossroads of exchange. Nashaway sat at the junction of multiple trails, which connected it to Penacook, the Connecticut River valley, and other Nipmuc towns. At the confluence of rivers, the "between" land was especially well-suited to horticulture and fishing. Settlers who migrated from the coast to the inland intervale lived "in close geographical proximity to the Nashaway," including Showanon, who lived at the "largest settlement" at Weshawkim, on the high ground between two ponds. The English town did not "replace" the Native one, but was rather contiguous to it, similar to the configuration that emerged when a settlement was established at nearby Quaboag in the 1660s. This arrangement enabled economic and social exchange between the two communities, while allowing separate spaces for planting, fishing, and inhabitation. The community at Weshawkim also remained tied to the Nashaway town at the foot of the mountain Wachusett.[1]

Still, the intial motivation for the colonization of Nashaway was neither the trade that Showanon cultivated, nor the fertile fields, but rather resource extraction to support a struggling colonial economy. John Winthrop Jr. and his

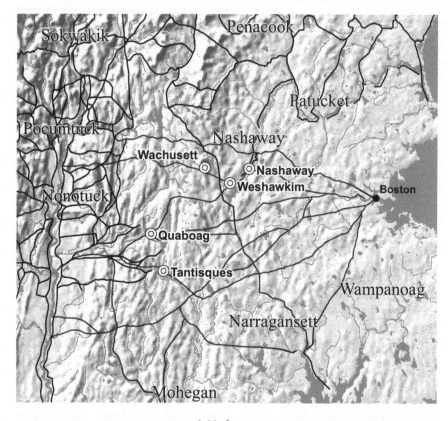

6. Nashaway

entrepreneurial partners sought inland sources for mining and were encouraged by a report that "black-lead" had been found at Tantisques, in Quaboag territory. Winthrop secured Stephen Day, the Harvard Press's first printer, to lead the effort to locate mines and obtain "purchase of the interest" from local sachems, with King's assistance. Day also involved himself in the trade, claiming he hosted "both English and Indians at my house from day to day for some years together." Although the mining effort failed, the promise of silver and iron motivated the inland migration of Massachusetts settlers and their capital, both of which found fertile ground at Nashaway's crossroads.[2]

Shortly thereafter, in the wake of intertribal and colonial violence on the coast and inland, Showanon joined several Indigenous leaders, including the Massachusett Saunkskwa and Ousamequin (representing allies at Quaboag), to join a covenant with the burgeoning Massachusetts Colony. Colonial leaders recorded this 1644 council as an act of "submission" and acceptance of their "protection," as well as a pledge to adhere to colonial laws. However, the formal exchange of wampum and long red coats, symbols of acknowledgment, suggests a bond of alliance among equals. The covenant was enacted the same year the "Nashaway Company" was established to forge a settlement in Showanon's territory. For the Massachusetts colonists, this agreement solidified on paper their right to colonize both the inland and the Massachusett coast. For Native leaders, the agreement solidified in wampum a significant relationship of mutual exchange and protection with their new neighbors in Massachusett, the settlers pledging "to protect them" from both "outside attacks and encroachments on their lands." This alliance paralleled the Mohegan sachem Uncas's league with Connecticut and provided a buffer for inland towns from Mohegan raids.[3]

Ten years later, when the revered Showanon died, Massachusetts magistrates attempted to influence the choice of successor, using the 1644 covenant to assert that the "great people" of Nashaway had "submitted" to the "jurisdiction" of Massachusetts. The magistrates' interest in Nashaway had increased since they had recently approved the small settlement as a township, renamed Lancaster. John Eliot, who had early interest in the Nashaway "plantation," served as the colony's intermediary. As the Nipmuc people deliberated, choosing among "two or three" potential leaders within the sachem's extended family, Eliot advocated for Matthew, a "very hopeful" convert, and against Shoshanim, or "Samuel," whom the magistrates portrayed as "a very debased, drunken fellow" who was "no friend to the English." Claiming jurisdiction, they encouraged Eliot to speak like a sachem, arguing by way of "perswasion and counsell, not by compulsion" that Matthew would provide "good service to the country." Whether it was Eliot's "persuasion" or other factors, Matthew became the next sachem. The same year, originary proprietor John Prescott established a grist mill in Lancaster, damming the river, and recent Harvard graduate Joseph Rowlandson arrived, becoming minister of the developing town. He married Mary White, daughter of one of the town's newest and most significant landowners, John White, who had migrated from Salem the previous year. As Matthew assumed the sachemship and Mary assumed her role as Mistress Rowlandson, vast changes came to Nashaway.[4]

Prescott had taken over the "trucking house" in 1647, but by 1656, John Tinker assumed the trade. Although Eliot prohibited drunkenness, traders like Tinker made alcohol a useful tool in the declining fur trade. Before arriving in Nashaway, he faced fines for selling liquor to Indians, but the profits likely far outweighed the fines and, at Lancaster, no magistrates would witness his trading practice. Moreover, Tinker kept all the records for the new town. As local historian Henry Nourse observed, "prominent men of the Nashway tribe became so deeply indebted to him as to mortgage the prospective gains of two hunting seasons for payment." Stephen Day was likewise "admonished for defrauding the Nashways." As Salisbury has observed, "some Lancaster traders pressured their Nashaway creditors to satisfy their debts with land in lieu of furs." After Tinker left Nashaway in 1659 to operate "a liquor business," Simon Willard, who had established a trade monopoly on the Merrimack River, purchased Tinker's post and right to trade. Only three Lancaster settlers held the title of "Mister"—John Tinker, Samuel Willard, and Joseph Rowlandson, all of whom occupied prime land. "Goodman" Prescott also continued to play a leadership role in the town, and during Matthew's sachemship, both Prescott and Willard extended their landholdings, pushing northward toward Penacook and Wachusett, and westward toward Weshawkim. Through debt, Day acquired "150 acres of upland" via a deed from Matthew, while Prescott acquired one hundred acres of land near Weshawkim from James Quananopohit, who would later serve with the colonial forces. By the time Shoshanin became sachem, following Matthew's death in 1674, Lancaster was upon Weshawkim.[5]

During Matthew's sachemship, Nashaway also suffered from losses in Mohawk raids. In 1663, the Massachusetts Court instructed Willard to provide Nashaway men with weapons to defend themselves, under the 1644 agreement. Kanienkehaka warriors were elusive, tactical raiders, ambushing Nipmuc and Connecticut River men as they traveled in small hunting parties. These strategies inhibited subsistence, and many Native men turned to working as day laborers for colonists, including Prescott and Edward Hutchinson, who held a farm near Hassanamesit. Colonial households, like the Rowlandsons', hired Native people as servants, transforming their status in English hierarchies. Meanwhile the Nipmucs pressured the English to honor the covenant in which they promised protection. When five "well armed" Mohawks came into Cambridge in September 1665, Gookin recounted that "the Indians, our neighbors" encouraged their English allies to "put them to death. For, said they," using an English metaphor, "these Maquas are unto us, as wolves are to your sheep. They secretly seize upon us and our children, wherever they meet us, and destroy us." But colonists did not want to risk any Mohawk attack on their own towns. After holding the Kanienkehaka men in prison, they set them free with some coats and a letter to their sachem "to forbid them" from assaulting "any of the Indians under our protection," which "they might distinguish" by their English clothes and the cut of their hair. Nashaway men like Shoshanim, Monoco, and James Quananopohit were largely left to defend their places and people themselves.[6]

Still, Gookin and Eliot assured Native converts that they were under a higher form of "protection" under their covenant with "God," noting that none of the

English towns or established praying towns, like Natick and Hassanamesit, were attacked by Mohawks. When the Nipmucs and Massachusetts gathered a great "army" to strike the town of Kahnawake on the Mohawk River, the missionaries advocated against it, even as their allies followed English advice, to bring the battle to the Mohawks and fight them face-to-face in a large company, "openly and in a plain field." The strategy proved disabling. The "army" made it to the Kanienkehaka town and engaged them on the ground, but war parties followed the Massachusett and Nipmuc men back east, ambushing them along the way. Nashaway was particularly devastated. As Gookin observed in 1674, "These have been a great people in former times; but of late years, have been consumed by the Maquas' wars and other ways; and are not above fifteen or sixteen families." Although describing the devastation of Mohawk warfare, Gookin acknowledged neither the lack of English intervention nor the impact of trade. Combined with leaders' imprisonment, traders' deceit, and cattle and settlers' increasing encroachment on the "meadows" near Weshawkim, the failure of Massachusetts to protect the people of Nashaway, under the covenant of 1644, laid ground for the mistrust that the sachem Shoshanim and the war leader Monoco increasingly held toward their wayward neighbors and allies.[7]

Part II

No Single Origin Story

Multiple Views on the Emergence of War

3

THE QUEEN'S RIGHT AND THE
QUAKER'S RELATION

THE QUEEN'S RIGHT, POCASSET, SPRING, 1675

In the spring of 1675, as the women planted at Pocasset, "Weetomuw the queen of Pocasset" and "her husband" Petonowowet (or "Benjamine") met with John Easton, the deputy governor of Rhode Island, to discuss an urgent point of concern. Easton, a Quaker leader from Newport, listened attentively. Weetamoo "showed" him "a letter," signed by Constant Southworth and others "dated aprell 30: [16]75, by which thay have great feare of oppretion from the English." It was May 24, 1675, one month, to the day, before the outbreak of the conflict that the English would come to call King Philip's War.[1]

In meeting with Easton, Weetamoo sought to maintain the still considerable expanse of territory at Pocasset, including her town at the falls of Quequechand, where no Englishman had yet dared to plant. The town was seated near the ferrying place from Portsmouth, a likely site for the meeting. From the highland, Weetamoo had a clear view across the bay, enabling her to observe travelers in the river and to keep a close watch on her sister and kin who lived at Metacom's protected hill town of Montaup (map 7).[2]

After exchanging greetings with the Rhode Island governor, Weetamoo and Petonowowet said that they were hesitant to trust Easton, expressing concern that he would "join" with the other English to "do them wrong." Easton reassured them, using the language of kinship and political alliance, that he considered himself "as much ingadged" with the neighboring Pocassets "as if they were my Country men, and I of their nation." He gave his pledge that he would do his best to see "that they should not be wronged."[3]

Weetamoo had good reason to fear "oppression." Two months previous, Constant Southworth, Josiah Winslow, and James Cudworth had captured two of

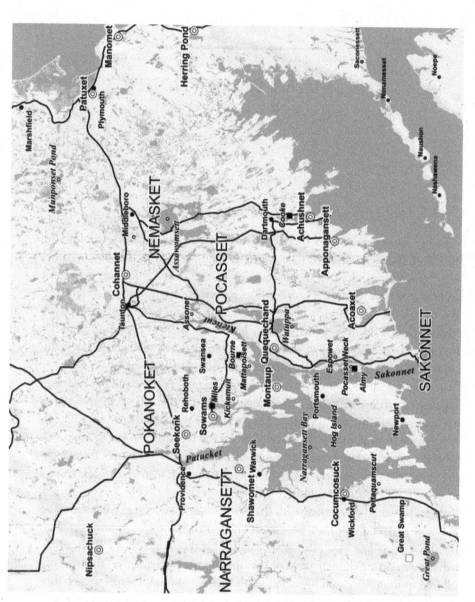

7. Pocasset and Pokanoket, highlighting places in chapters 3 and 4

her relations, a respected counselor named Tobias and his son, charging them with murder. The Plymouth men took Tobias and Wampapaquan during the spring fish runs, as the families gathered at Nemasket and the herring streamed into Assawomset Pond. Weetamoo may have recalled that spring when Edward Winslow had come to Nemasket for her father, charging him with a similar crime. Conbitant had eluded capture, but Tobias and his son were imprisoned in the Plymouth jail, his "bond" the land itself. Only fifteen years had passed since the elder Tuspaquin, the sachem of Nemasket, had stood alongside Ousamequin and Weetamoo at Nonaquaket, confirming her right at Pocasset, but the political landscape had transformed. Tobias's "trial" was set to begin at the Plymouth Court in six days. Rumors spread that the Plymouth men were coming for Philip next.[4]

As these conflicts erupted to the north, at the south, a related crisis spiraled out of control. A month before Weetamoo met with Easton, Awashonks's son, the Cambridge-educated Mammanuah, had signed a deed granting all of the land at Sakonnet to Constant Southworth, Josiah Winslow, Nathaniel Thomas, and a large group of "purchasers." Despite vigorous protests the previous summer by his mother and their kin, Mammanuah and his brother Osamehew had agreed to sell all of the land from Pocasset Neck south to the sea, including Sakonnet Neck, where Awashonks maintained her house and town. Having gathered a number of Wampanoag men around him, amassing power, Mammanuah had been recognized by the Plymouth Court as the "chief sachem" and "proprietor" to Sakonnet. This act authorized the patrilineal authority of Mammanuah alongside those "first born" sons who sought to improve the rights their fathers had long ago granted to them. In March, just as the planting season was about to begin, the court had declared "Saconnet" a "towneshipp," ready to be converted to a "plantation."[5]

As Pocasset women planted below Quequechand that spring, several English men were "improving" their "rights," plowing furrows at Sakonnet and on Pocasset Neck. Benjamin Church was among them, planting his fields for the first time, as his wife, Alice, tended their firstborn son in a house newly built from the timber of Sakonnet woods. As Church later related, "I was the first Englishman that built upon that neck, which was fully of Indians. My head and hands were full about settling a new plantation where nothing was brought to; no preparation of dwelling-house, or out-houses, or fencing made. Horses and cattle were to be provided, ground to be cleared and broken up; and the utmost caution to be used, to keep myself free from offending my Indian neighbours all round about me."[6]

When Church's son Thomas published his *Entertaining History* forty years later, it appeared Church's settlement at Sakonnet occurred by happenstance. "In the year 1674," he recounted, he "fell into acquaintance with Captain John Almy" who "invited him to ride with him, and view" the "pleasant" country of "Pocasset and Sakonnet," persuading him on the journey, to "purchase . . . some of the Court grant rights." Struck by the "very rich . . . soil," he was inspired to "make a purchase" and shortly thereafter "settled a farm."[7]

However, the documents of the time suggest a different history. In 1667, Church, a "carpenter," married Constant Southworth's daughter Alice and shortly thereafter, he assumed the role that Southworth and Winslow had long played. In the spring of 1670 he witnessed a deed authorized by Philip and Tuspaquin, transferring "a tract of land" at "Nemassakett Pond" to Southworth and the Plymouth men. In the fall of 1671, he participated in the survey and division of those lands. By the summer of 1673, he was orchestrating the sale of Nemasket land and leading the survey of the "Punckateesset" lands. In return, Church found that his marriage alliance and service to the colony entitled him to tracts of land at Pocasset Neck and Sakonnet as well as Nemasket. By 1674, Church had emerged as a major player in Plymouth Colony's deed games. However, the young man's greatest asset was his willingness to plant. Southworth had not possessed the courage to improve the lands at Pocasset he had acquired so forcefully on paper. His son-in-law was among the first persuaded to execute his "claim." Church acquired a "right" at Sakonnet by July 1673, and, with Southworth and Winslow clearing conflicts over the deeds in their court, he began to build in the summer of 1674.[8]

The circumstances of the land deals at Nemasket and Sakonnet are critical to interpreting Easton's letter, a rare document which has not been previously taken into account by historians. This context is even more vital to achieving a clear understanding of the origins of the war, providing a perspective more elucidating than that offered by Church's dubious memoir, on which so many narratives of the war have relied.[9]

SOUTH: BOUND TO THE LAND, SAKONNET, SUMMER 1671–SUMMER 1674

In the summer of 1671, the leaders of Plymouth Colony formed a Council of War. They aimed to press a key adversary into submission and to secure the fertile lands they had promised to their first-born sons. On July 8, the council declared they would gather one hundred men "at or near" Assonet to march upon a saunkskwa who had "put upon" them much "trouble" by "too long standing out against the many tenders of peace we have made to her and her people."

Josiah Winslow led the charge, with Constant Southworth as commissary and Matthew Fuller as lieutenant. All three held interest in the lands that motivated the military expedition. Companies from Plymouth, Taunton, Rehoboth, Bridgewater, and Swansea would meet at John Tisdall's farm in Taunton, just north of Pocasset, and they would "procure" forty "of our trustiest Indians" to accompany them. They gave the saunkskwa a month to come in to Plymouth and "submit." Amid rumors of Indian uprising, they feared the reaction of the powerful woman and her counselors. Nevertheless, as Thomas Hinckley and Nathan Bacon wrote to Governor Prence, the day before this order was recorded, "It is better for us to find them at their homes than for them to find us at ours."[10]

Under this imminent threat of violence, Awashonks traveled to Plymouth Court on July 24 and signed "tenders of peace." The magistrates expressed some measure of satisfaction "with her voluntary coming in now at last." The "articles of agreement" recorded that she had "submitted her lands" and her people "to the authority" of the colonial "government," although subsequent correspondence suggests both her "integrity and real intentions of peace" and a mutual recognition of her continued "government" in her own territory. The covenant mandated the surrender of her guns, and those of her men. A subsequent list of those "obedient to" Awashonks who agreed to the articles included John Sassamon. With this signing, the Plymouth men had the consent they needed to implement the survey and division of Sakonnet. Wherever Sassamon appeared, land deals were achieved.[11]

The articles also required the symbolic surrender of all Sakonnet arms, but the governor expressed disappointment that the list of men that would "submit to his majesty's authority here" did not include "your two sons, that may probably succeed you in your government, and your brother also." Although he acknowledged Awashonks's "government," Prence assumed her male heirs would "succeed" her. He asked, "Do they think themselves so great as to disregard and affront his majesty's interest and authority here, and the amity of the English? Certainly if they do," Prence warned, he "wishe[d] they would yet show themselves wise, before it be too late." The veiled threat played on the bonds of kinship. The prospect of military violence would influence Awashonks to act as a sister and mother to compel the "submission" of her brother and sons to English "authority." However, as they soon discerned, those bonds had already weakened. By 1673, Plymouth pursued an alternate strategy to improve the lands at Sakonnet and Pocasset, bolstering the power of one of those sons to gain full access to her lands.[12]

In spring 1674, Awashonks, encircled by her relations, confronted her eldest son for selling land on which she and other Wampanoag families were then living. According to Mammanuah's complaint to the Plymouth Court, his mother, whom he called the "pretended Squa Sachem" of Sakonnet, and "Wewayeweitt, her husband," assembled "together with divers other Indians," surrounding and "forcibly detaining" him "upon a parcel of land," which he meant to convey to settlers, including Church, who sought to establish a "township" at "Saconnet." "Then and there," Mammanuah protested, "with the help" of these "assembled Indians," Awashonks "did forcibly molest and hinder" him "from giving possession of a parcel of land to such of the English, to whom he had sold the same, by violent binding the said Mammanuah in the same place, insulting over and threatening him, whiles he lay bound before them."[13]

It was March, so the dispute must have emerged at the prospect of planting. The summer before, the Plymouth Court had recognized Mammanuah's "title to those lands" against his people's "former claim," confirming his patrilineal right to the sachemship. Mammanuah asserted that his mother and his uncle's lineage was of a "more remote stock," and the court concluded that Awashonks and Tatacomuncah should be allowed "proportions of land" to "be settled on," leaving the remainder under the control of Mammanuah and themselves. Yet, when they tried to implement settlement on the ground, Mammanuah's relations encircled him, insisting that he "relinquish his title to his said land," a right the people undoubtedly held over a son and a sachem, regardless of his status. In "binding" him to the land which he had "sold," Mammanuah's relations humbled him, reminding him of his place, his responsibilities to his mother and his kin. This symbolic, ceremonial act was not a "violent" reaction, but a formal disavowal of any authority he might hold through them. His elders removed his "title" and required him to acknowledge his failure to fulfill his obligations as the son of two leaders.[14]

Allowed to leave with his life, Mammanuah sought restitution at Plymouth. The court reasserted its power, giving Mammanuah a forum to file a lawsuit against his mother, in a "jurisdiction" which she had previously acknowledged. By July 1674, when the case was heard, Prence had died, and Josiah Winslow had succeeded him as governor. Taking the reins of his new authority, Winslow joined with Cudworth, Southworth, and their fellow magistrates to confirm Mammanuah as the "chief proprietor of the lands of Saconett, and places adjacent." They found for the plaintiff, recognizing Mammanuah's right to sell land to them. It was that summer that Benjamin Church began to build "upon the neck."[15]

Church's narrative thus masks the strategic claiming of Sakonnet lands in which he was engaged. What Southworth, Winslow, and the other purchasers needed was a young man bold enough to implement their claims at Sakonnet and Pocasset Neck, which they had pursued for more than a decade, and a young Native man who could authorize those claims. Church became involved in orchestrating and implementing claims to Native lands only after his marriage to Southworth's daughter. Serving as an agent to the magistrates, he assumed the work they now entrusted to the next generation. Thus, rather than settlement and war appearing by happenstance in Church's path, both were intricately intertwined with the intent to claim Wampanoag lands.

Even as Church felled trees at Sakonnet, the developing alliance between Mammanuah and the first-born sons threatened to infringe on the "Queen's right" at Pocasset. During that same summer of 1674, the Plymouth men sought to expand into "adjacent parts" to the north. They invited Mammanuah, "Sachem of Saconnet side," to "a meeting of the Purchasers of the Township of Dartmouth," over which Winslow presided. Here, Mammanuah acknowledged "his Resignation of his Right title and Interest in the land" claimed by the Dartmouth proprietors. This "resignation" specified the northern bounds of the grant, extended to Watuppa by Sassamon's survey, which was then recorded in the Plymouth Book of Deeds, with the "division and survey of lands." Alongside these documents, the Plymouth men recorded Philip's confirmation of Sassamon's survey and his receipt of ten pounds from Dartmouth settler John Cooke for "release" of any hereditary "claims," both given with other confirmations in June 1665, according to the witnesses, including Josiah Winslow, Thomas Southworth, and John Sassamon. Above Philip's consent, in the Book of Deeds, the mark of "Namumpum" was affixed to a "surrender of all that Right and title of such lands as Woosamequin and Wamsutta sould to the purchasers as appears by deeds given under theire hands." Weetamoo's consent to these vague deeds, apparently including Dartmouth, was purportedly given in June and October 1659, at the same time as the Freeman's purchase. All of these documents together cleared title for the expansion of the new settlement of Dartmouth into Pocasset. Acts on the ground gave new weight to the documents. At Pocasset Neck, at the head of the Acoaxet River, and at the "broad cove" across the river from Assonet Neck, English men had begun to plant.[16]

NORTH: "BINDING OVER THE LAND," NEMASKET, SPRING 1674–SPRING 1675

To the north of Pocasset, Church and the Plymouth men orchestrated grants for a new settlement called Middlebury at Nemasket, where Tuspaquin and Amie maintained their town on Assawomset Pond.[17] In narrations of the war's origins, Nemasket has been overshadowed by Montaup, but the ancient fishing place played a critical role.

Nearly all histories based upon the Puritan narratives follow a similar trajectory when recounting the war's origins. They begin with the death of John Sassamon and the trial of his accused "murderers," highlighting the event as a primary cause of the war. They consider the question of whether Sassamon was murdered, whether Philip ordered his death, and recount in vivid detail the trial and "execution" of Philip's counselors for the crime. Increase Mather offered an especially colorful account, oft repeated, of Sassamon's corpse bleeding when Tobias, Philip's counselor, was brought before it, a sure sign of the man's guilt.[18] Yet those narratives elide a central context: the "great pond" where Sassamon died, whether he drowned or was killed, was then at the center of a heated land claim, through which the Plymouth men attempted to purchase vast tracts at Nemasket. Both Sassamon and Tobias, as well as Southworth and Church, were directly involved.

On March 3, 1674, less than a year before Sassamon's death, the Plymouth Court authorized Constant Southworth and John Thompson to "make purchase of such lands in the township of Middlebury as the Indians doe or may tender to sell," utilizing "such debts as the Indians owe to any as the occasion may require" to compel them to "tender" the land. The Plymouth men sought to extend a grant of land that Church and Thompson had acquired from Tuspaquin the previous summer. However, only two days before this court session, Sassamon arranged deeds through which two large tracts of land, nearly one hundred acres, were granted by Tuspaquin to *himself*, his daughter Assaweta (Betty), and her husband, Felix. The land was at Assawomset Neck, on the pond where Sassamon died the following winter.[19]

Historians have generally assumed that Tuspaquin freely gave these lands to Sassamon despite the fact that Tuspaquin's "principle residence" was at Assawomset Neck. Given Sassamon's record and the timing of the transaction, it is equally possible, if not more likely, that Sassamon orchestrated these deeds because he knew the Plymouth magistrates were about to force a sale. He may have sought to ensure that he and his daughter were protected in lands they inhabited at Assawomset. Or, he may have attempted to claim for himself and his heir first rights to one of the choicest tracts of land in the Wampanoag country, with key access to the fishing grounds and cranberry bogs, before the settlers began to divide it up.[20]

There is also evidence that Sassamon may have been training his daughter to serve in a similar role. A deed from the previous fall (November 1673) shows Assaweta joining William Tuspaquin and Tobias in granting a large tract of land at

Nemasket to Plymouth settlers, with acknowledgement by "old Tispquin" and Southworth. One month later, William and Tuspaquin ostensibly deeded land directly to Assaweta, with Tobias as a witness. Why would Assaweta, neither saunkskwa nor counselor, represent the people of Nemasket in a land transaction? What might it mean that Tobias and Assaweta appear on two deeds, a year before Tobias and his son were accused of Sassamon's murder? These questions seem especially relevant when we consider that the land concerned was just below Assawomset Pond. If Sassamon was killed, perhaps it was because of his role in dispossession, including the division of Assawomset. Yet, as Easton heard from some "intelegabell and impartiall" Native people, although a leader would have been within his rights to "execute" someone who had done such damage, they had never heard of obscuring such a fatality as an accident. Rather, they believed that Sassamon most likely "fell in and was so drowned," breaking the precarious ice at the edge of the pond while duck hunting, the "ice" injuring "his throat." Either way, his death became a pretext for Plymouth Colony's arrest of a counselor who was tied not only to Philip but also to Tuspaquin and Amie, one of the "the chief men of Assowamset." Tobias's name does not appear on any later deeds, suggesting he did not consent to further land sales. His primary "crime" may have been developing a keen awareness of the deed game at Nemasket.[21]

The court records reveal a greater cause for the capture of Tobias than the claim that he killed Sassamon at Philip's bequest. The magistrates made a unique exception for their prisoner, allowing bail, which under the colony's laws, was not permitted for those accused of murder. Why would they allow such a dangerous man to post bail, contrary to their own law? Apparently, they desired the "bond" more than they required his imprisonment. On March 1, 1675, one year after announcing its intent to purchase more land from the Indians of Nemasket, the court arranged a debt to compel the sale. To ensure the "personal appearance of an Indian, called Tobias, before the Court, to make further answer" regarding the "sudden and violent death of an Indian called John Sassamon," the court required the "said Tobias" along with "Tuspaquin, the black sachem, of Nemasket, and William his son" to "bind over all their lands, to the value of one hundred ponds, unto the Court." Only days before Tobias and his son were tried for murder, this "bond" was followed by a "deed" in which "Wetuspaquin . . . and William Tuspaquin" did "bind and firmly make over to Constant Southworth, John Thompson and the rest of the proprietors of Middleberry . . . all that Tract or Tracts of land which we now have in possession and Goes Commonly by the Name of Assowamsett Necke or Neckes and places adjacent."[22]

As their records show, the Plymouth Court resolved all claims to Assawomset with one fell swoop. Holding his son hostage, they compelled Tobias and the Tuspaquin sachems to sign a document which gave the Plymouth men the rights to "*all*" of their lands at Nemasket, including their primary residence at the neck. In the past, when the men of Plymouth and Boston had held the sons of leaders, a deed nearly always resulted in their release. As Lepore notes, the evidence against them was "slim to vanishing," but political pressure was high. Having capitulated to Plymouth's desires, the Nemasket leaders had reason to believe that their kin would go free.[23]

It cannot be a mere coincidence that the deed resulting from the bond encompassed the very pond on which Sassamon was killed. With the deed signed and Sassamon dead (his own deed set aside), the land surrounding the pond, now formally acknowledged as part of the town of "Middlebury," was clear for improvement. The only impediment that remained was the women and men who might oppose settlement on the ground.

POCASSET: SETTING THE BOUNDS OF THE QUEEN'S RIGHT

Meeting with John Easton in May 1675, Weetamoo responded to the overwhelming evidence before her, and sent a strong message to Winslow and the Plymouth men, through Easton, that she would "stand upon" her demand that the "bounds" of Pocasset land be set—by her—and "confirmed" in their court "records." As Easton conveyed Weetamoo's intentions, "for what they would now have" as "their bounds north and south is to maintain a river at each end by which they have great dependence for fish," emphasizing their reliance on this crucial resource and the centrality of riverways in the Pocasset homeland. Yet Weetamoo also offered a compromise: she was willing "to accommodate" those people from Plymouth "whom" she and her counselors "shall admit" with "four mile square of land," within areas previously deeded, "at the head of dartmouth bounds" and/or "the lots on the other side of the falls river."[24]

At the time, only one settler lived anywhere near the "head": Rhode Islander John Sisson, who had testified on Weetamoo's behalf in the case against John Archer. At Watuppa, where Pocasset families fished, the marks Sassamon had etched into oak trees had likely faded, but Sisson had recently built a house at the headwaters of the Acoaxet River, just four miles southeast of Watuppa, one of a handful in the newly established township. The Plymouth men may have objected to Sisson's settlement in a territory they claimed. Weetamoo offered the opportunity to securely settle some Plymouth men "at the head" and allow limited settlement in the "lots" at Pocasset Neck (or within the Freeman's Purchase), while she would reestablish the bounds of Dartmouth below Watuppa. The recent experience of her relations at Nemasket demonstrated that Plymouth sought to forcefully expand, and the agreements with Mammanuah gave her cause to believe her ponds might be next on their list.[25]

Although Weetamoo faced colonial expansion on all her bounds, with her kin she had maintained a greater hold on Pocasset than other Wampanoag leaders had been able to sustain in their territories. A few settlers may have built houses in the northern part of the "Freeman's purchase," but the falls of Quequechand, the ponds and cedar swamps of Watuppa, and the forests extending to Assonet Neck, remained free of English settlements, and the interior paths saw few English travelers. Southworth, Winslow, and Cudworth still worked their plans for Assonet, laid long ago at Barnes's tavern, but they preferred to stake their claims by extending established settlements on the west side of the river, at Taunton and Swansea, rather than directly contending with protectors at Assonet. At Pocasset, Weetamoo held her ground.

Still, the "new plantation" at Sakonnet must have alarmed her, particularly since the bounds between the two territories had been somewhat fluid. As Weetamoo's statement to Easton made clear, those boundaries now required firm defense. The houses and fields being raised at Sakonnet bolstered Plymouth's old claims to Pocasset Neck, and opened the path that connected the two territories to further depredations by settlers and their cattle. Her proposal sought to prevent both encroachment and greater conflict.[26]

The promise of settlement had also drawn more travelers to the trail that paralleled the Kteticut and moved through the length of Pocasset. Yet settlers had to walk or guide their horses through fully inhabited villages and hunting grounds to travel between Sakonnet and Plymouth. The daunting cedar marshes and the prospect of armed Wampanaog warriors hunting in the oak and pine forests kept most English men near the coast, taking a route through Dartmouth. Indeed, a key motivation for the new plantation at Nemasket was the promise of safe haven and a secure midway point on "the Dartmouth path," an alternative route from Sakonnet and Dartmouth, which led to Plymouth.[27]

Rather than having the bounds repeatedly "set" by the Plymouth men's desires, Weetamoo sought to solidify the boundaries of Pocasset in writing, based on subsistence needs, traditional waterways, and the agreements *she* had made with individual settlers and Plymouth leaders. Rather than acquiescing to a small "reserved" tract of Pocasset land within a larger "grant" of land to Plymouth, Weetamoo once more sought to reverse the deed game, allowing for limited, bounded "lots" on the edges of a clearly defined Pocasset territory, which would continue to provide sustenance and protection to the families under her house.

Following his meeting with Weetamoo, Easton wrote to Winslow, presenting her request and entreating the Plymouth governor to seek a just resolution by having "the difference decided" in court. In his letter, Easton reinforced Weetamoo's request, saying, "it appeareth to me" that "they desire only of you what is their reasonable due." The "Queen's right," he told Winslow, had been "confirmed" by dozens of settlers whom she might call to testify in a higher court, and it encompassed "a far greater tract of land beside" which she now proposed. Weetamoo was still in a position of considerable power, not only among Native people, but among the neighboring English with whom she had formed lasting relationships of exchange. Easton also stressed that the saunkskwa offered a compromise, which, if not taken, could result in the loss of the unimproved "rights" that Plymouth held.[28]

With suspicions of English "oppression" circulating widely, Easton emphasized that, during the meeting, he was "largely engaged" to "manifest to them that I am not false," and he "endeavored they may have right according to English Law." He urged Winslow to be an "instrument" for "peaceable settlement" and to demonstrate fair treatment to the Pocasset people. Playing the diplomat, he deferred to Winslow's authority, saying he would "hope it will not be in any opposition to your desires or to your rule in your Colony" to "proceed to try the Case at your Court," where, Easton said, he would willingly serve as Weetamoo's attorney. In a provocative turn of phrase, Easton expressed his "great desire that they [the Pocassets] may not be" led "to do wrong" to the English out of their "fear" of having "wrong" done to them. A hearing of "her case" was an urgent matter, he insisted, as this "fear" might erupt into violence if her legitimate concerns were not addressed, potentially causing suffering to both of their colonies. Just as he had conveyed his sense of loyalty to Weetamoo, Easton likewise emphasized that he was Winslow's "true friend" and desired only a peaceful resolution to the conflict between these neighboring groups. Through fair arbitration, he insisted, "both may be so satisfied."[29]

The Plymouth Court never heard Weetamoo's case and Easton's request was not entered into the court records. Instead, one week later, at the General Court's June session, Tobias, his son, Wampapaquan, and the counselor Mattashunannamo were judged guilty for the "murder" of John Sassamon and sentenced to death, "to be hanged by the head until their bodies are dead," and, according to the court record, it "accordingly was executed, the 8th of June, 1675, on the said Tobias and Mattashunannamo." Wampapaquan "on some consideration," that is, an eleventh-hour "confession" of guilt, was given a temporary "reprieve." As Easton later related, "The three Indians [that] were hunge, to the last denied the Fact; but one broke the Halter as it is reported, then desired to be saved, and so" he "confessed they three had done the Fact." Regardless, "afterwards" Tobias's son was "shot to death within the said month."[30]

The brief trial and sentencing of the three Wampanaog men was only one among many cases on the June court docket. The *only* business concerning Weetamoo's lands at Pocasset pertained to her old nemesis John Archer. Rather than answering her request to set her bounds, the Plymouth magistrates took further action to shore up their jurisdiction, calling Archer to court with Matthew Boomer and John Lawton, all living at or near Pocasset, to answer for "their residing in the government without order, and not attending the public worship of God, living lonely and in a heathenish way from good society." Witnessing the sentencing of the Wampanoag men may have given Archer cause to take the charge seriously.[31]

Following the death of the three Wampanoag counselors, the fear from oppression of which Weetamoo had spoken increased dramatically. Historians have made much of the "first shots" fired in the war, but surely we should also count the shooting of Tobias's son among them. Certainly the assassination of three Wampanoag counselors could be interpreted as an act of war. Moreover, with Wampapaquan's confession, Plymouth had secured cause to capture Philip. Rumors abounded that Plymouth was amassing an army to move on Montaup, with the goal of apprehending the Pokanoket sachem. Meanwhile, Plymouth magistrate and Rehoboth resident John Brown reported that men came in from Narragansett, Coweset, and Pocasset to protect him, stirring further rumors of an Indian uprising. (Winslow later characterized these relations as "strange Indians.") Brown added that the Wampanoags were moving families from Montaup to Narragansett in fear of an assault by Plymouth. As Easton related, "the English were afraid and Philip was afraid, and both increased in Arms."[32]

Shortly thereafter, Philip sent a message by Samuel Gorton, conveying "his great desire of concluding of peace with neighboring English," in response to a letter from Winslow requiring him and his counselors to lay down their arms and come to court, which they were not willing to do. Winslow may have been following the protocols of just war, offering a formal tender of peace before pursuing war. Gorton explained that they were "not at present, free to promise to appear at court" because of "harsh threats to the sachem" and "suggestions of great danger that" would "befall them" should "they there appear." Thus, as Roger Williams observed, "Phillip (fearing apprehension) stood upon his Guard," and the towns of "Taunton, Swansie, Rehoboth and Providence stood upon ours." Yet, on June 13, Williams wrote to John Winthrop Jr., "Praised be God the storm is over. Phillip is strongly suspected but the honr'd Court at Plymouth (as we hear) not having evidence sufficient, let matters sleep and the Country be in quiet."[33]

Unfortunately, Williams's sense of relief was premature. Even as he wrote, Winslow sat at his desk in Marshfield, composing missives, hoping to isolate Philip and draw allies to Plymouth's assistance. Soon letters would arrive at Providence and Boston, and on June 15 Winslow directed a letter to "Weeta-moo, and Ben her husband, Sachems of Pocasset." While neglecting to address her request to set her bounds, Winslow entreated Weetamoo to consider his position with respect to her sister's husband. Addressing the Pocassets as "Friends and Neighbors," he proclaimed, "I am informed that Phillip the Sachem of Mount Hope, contrary to his many promises and engagements," and "upon no provocation . . . in the least from us," is causing "new troubles to himself and us." Winslow's depiction represented a developing official narrative of the war, in which Plymouth would be forced to defend itself against "groundless" actions by Philip and his men. Winslow then raised his concern that Philip had "endeavored to engage you and your people with him, by intimations of notorious falsehoods as if we were secretly designing mischief to him, and you, such unmanly treacherous practices as we abhor to think of."[34]

This statement was the only indication that Winslow had received Weetamoo's message that her people feared English "oppression." However, he attributed the cause to rumors of "mischief" spread by Philip, denying any violations on Plymouth's part. Winslow may have received information regarding Philip's "endeavors" from Church, who, he later wrote, had met with "Weetamoo and some of her chief men" on "the 7th of June." In his memoir, Church recounted the rumors and his conversations with Weetamoo and Awashonks, emphasizing his position as a neighboring settler rather than an agent of Plymouth. He recounted that, while he was "diligently settling his new farm," he "had it daily suggested to him that the Indians were plotting a bloody design," led by "Philip, the great Mount Hope Sachem," who was "sending his messengers to all the neighbouring Sachems, to engage them into a confederacy with him in the war." Further, Church claimed, during a visit to Sakonnet, Awashonks asked him whether the English "were gathering a great army to invade Philip's country" as "Philip had told her." Petonowowet, Church said, also revealed that "Philip expected to be sent for to Plymouth; to be examined about Sassamon's death, who was murdered at Assawomset Ponds, knowing himself guilty of contriving that murder," attributing words to Petonowowet retrospectively which corresponded perfectly to the official narrative of war.[35]

There are numerous correspondences *and* significant discrepancies between Winslow's letters and Church's "history." For example, Church claimed he met with Weetamoo and Petonowowet only days before the outbreak of war, attributing to "Peter Nunnuit, the husband of the Queen of Pocasset" the direct knowledge that "Philip had held a dance of several weeks continuance, and had entertained the young men from all parts of the country." Conclusively, "Peter told him that there would certainly be war," and that Philip had promised his men, that "on the next Lords Day [June 20], when the English were gone to meeting, they should rifle their houses, and from that time forward kill their cattle." However, as noted, Winslow reported that Church had met with Weetamoo on June 7, and then he sent his own letter on June 15, which Church may have delivered during a second meeting. The timing is crucial. Church's narrative portrays a war gathering, led by Philip, spiraling out of control, but the documents suggest a longer period of strategic planning on Plymouth's part. It seems especially significant that Church, as an agent of Plymouth, sought out Weetamoo the day before Tobias was executed, and four days before John Brown reported growing numbers of armed men at Montaup, who "stand upon their guard on reason say they is because they hear you intend to send for phillip."[36]

The tone and purpose of Winslow's letter also differs markedly from Church's memoir. Winslow sought to exploit Weetamoo's diplomatic position to sway her to Plymouth's side, but Church portrayed Weetamoo as an indecisive woman wavering between two men: Philip, who was of her race and nation, and Winslow, who was her "friend." Nathaniel Saltonstall's contemporary narrative portrayed Weetamoo "as potent a Prince as any round about her," and claimed that Philip's "first errand" was to ensure her support, yet Church retrospectively diminished Weetamoo's influence and represented her caution as feminized fear, recalling he found "few of her people with her. She said they were all gone, against her will to the dances" at Montaup, "and she much feared there would be a war." To the contrary, in his letter, Winslow reported that Church had met with Weetamoo "and her chief men." Further, he communicated to her his understanding that Philip had "prevayled very little unto you," except for engaging "some *few* of your giddy inconsiderate young men" (my emphasis). "If it be fact," Winslow continued, "you shall find us always ready to acknowledge and incourage your faithfulness, and protect you also so farr as in us lieth from his pride and tyranny."[37]

As an experienced leader, Weetamoo was acutely aware that armed conflict with the English could bring about the destruction of her entire community. Yet Church depicted her as a helpless, impotent queen, to whom he offered chivalrous protection, ironically, from his own forces. The "protection" Winslow offered, to a powerful leader, contained a veiled threat. If Philip "prevailed" with her, she would face the same fate as he. However, he promised, "if you continue faithfull, you shall assuredly reape that fruit of it to your Comfort, when he by his pride and treachery have wrought his owne ruin." Thus, Winslow insinuated, Weetamoo and her husband might, with Winslow, "reap the fruit" of Montaup's planting fields, if they severed ties with Philip and demonstrated "faithfulness" to Plymouth. "As a testimony of your continued friendship," Winslow continued, "I desire you will give us what intelligence you may have, or shall gather up."[38]

Winslow's offer proved more persuasive with Petononowet (Peter Nunnuit/ Benjamin) than with Weetamoo. Church may have first sought out Weetamoo's husband because he was more mutable than his wife. However, Petonowowet was not a leader, as the Plymouth Court recognized in its records, listing his "title" as "husband to Wetamo," the "Squa Sachem." When Winslow, for the first time, referred to Petononowet as a "sachem of Pocasset," he may have been dangling the "fruits" of assumed leadership, should he "remain faithful," just as he did with Mammanuah. Although Church and Winslow's attempts to sway Weetamoo proved futile, "Peter Nunnuit" was later rewarded with land and guardianship at Dartmouth for his "faithfulness" in the war. Still, even Church revealed that "Peter Nunnuit" did not divulge any information in Weetamoo's presence, providing intelligence *before* leading Church to meet Weetamoo "up the hill." Petonowowet proved a more helpful informant than his wife, but his betrayal probably cost him his marriage, as Weetamoo "put" him "away" shortly after.[39]

While Church sped off to Plymouth, to give "an account of his observations and discoveries," and Plymouth "hastened their preparation for defense," Weetamoo must have sent runners to Montaup. Although Winslow had sought to persuade Weetamoo to remain "faithful" to Plymouth, he overlooked the bond she shared with her sister. Weetamoo likely shared the contents of the letter with Wootonakanuske, giving her sister and Philip the "intelligence" they needed to comprehend that war was imminent. Surely, they could discern the not so subtle invitation to join Plymouth in a defensive war against Philip's "pride and tyranny." Winslow tried to persuade Weetamoo that Philip was a prideful young man who had overstepped his bounds and would bring about "his own ruin." Neither she, if she gave intelligence and isolated herself from Philip, nor the Plymouth men would shoulder the blame if he came to a bad end.[40]

Rumors may have been flying, but this letter was one more piece of hard evidence in Weetamoo's hands that Plymouth was about to strike. Her response, as always, was to gather her families together and strategize the best means to protect them from the approaching storm, which, despite Williams's beliefs, was just beginning to gather force.

THE QUAKER'S RELATION, MONTAUP, JUNE 1675

"NOW THEY HAD NO HOPES LEFT TO KEEP ANY LAND"

In June 1675, just weeks after he met with Weetamoo, John Easton likewise sought council with Philip. Endeavoring to "prevent" war and propose mediation, "We sent a Man to Philip," Easton wrote, to offer that "if he would come to the ferry we would come over to speak with him." Philip insisted the meeting take place on his grounds. Easton, with three "magistrates" and another man, took the ferry from Portsmouth to the south end of Montaup, and Philip met them at the ferrying place, with "about 40 of his men." According to Easton, they "sat very friendly together" under the midsummer sun.[41]

Easton assured Philip their "business was to endeavor that they might not receive or do wrong." Philip and his Counsellors replied "that was well" since "they had done no wrong." Rather, "the English wronged them." Easton acknowledged that both sides blamed the other, but stressed their "desire was the quarrel might rightly be decided, in the best way, and not as dogs decided their quarrels." The Wampanoags "owned that fighting was the worst way" and asked Easton "how right might take place." When Easton proposed "arbitration," they told him that it was by supposed "arbitration they had had much wrong, many miles square of land so taken from them."[42]

Referring to decades of experience in colonial courts, Philip told Easton there was no fair arbitration, as "all English agreed against them," and the end result was loss of land. "Once," they explained, "they were persuaded to give in their arms, that thereby jealousy might be removed," but "the English having their arms would not deliver them as they had promised, until they consented to pay a 100" pound fine, "and now they had not so much land or money." Referring to their reliance on those "arms" and the land for subsistence, the counselors said that "they were as good be killed as leave all their livelihood."[43]

In this statement, Metacom alluded to councils with Plymouth and Massachusetts during the spring and fall of 1671, when Plymouth was also pressuring Awashonks to "submit." Amid spring conflicts over marauding cattle, armed settlers searching for missing cows, and rumored gatherings of warriors at Montaup, Philip and his counselors met on midway ground at Taunton in April to council with the Plymouth men, pursuing "arbitration." Rather than hearing

their complaints, the magistrates "persuaded" Philip and the counselors to lay
down their guns, as proof of fidelity and peaceful intent. "Having" confiscated
"their arms," they then refused to return them as "promised," the court later ruling them "justly forfeit," by claiming that Philip admitted he had been preparing for war. The Plymouth men demanded "submission" to their jurisdiction
and a permanent surrender of all arms, a ludicrous request given Wampanoag
families' dependence on hunting.[44]

Plymouth's plan for Wampanaog containment was fueled by flying rumors.
Knowing the danger that fears of "conspiracy" could cause, Philip "exclaimed
much against [John] Sausiman" for fueling these fires by reporting collusion
between Wampanoags and Narragansetts. Meanwhile, Winslow told Governor
Prence the Wampanoags schemed to capture them both to demand ransom and
dictate the terms of peace, a very unlikely scenario. When Thomas Mayhew
questioned his Wampanoag neighbors at Noepe, they said "there was no manner
of plot known to any of the heads of this island." Yet another rumor circulated
that Daniel Gookin spoke words "to animate Philip and his Indians against"
Plymouth, which the missionary fiercely denied. Acknowledging the many
"false" reports among both "Indians" and "English," Prence assured Gookin
that he did not give such rumors credit. Further, he agreed that "fighting with
Indians about horses and hogs" was a matter "too low to shed blood."[45]

In truth, men like Winslow sought not "arbitration" of these conflicts over
"horses and hogs," but the imposition of power and control, including the confiscation of guns that Wampanoag men and women could use to defend their
planting grounds and their rights. When, as could be expected, Wampanoag
people at Montaup, Sakonnet, Nemasket, Showamet, and Assawomset did not
deliver their arms as requested, and Philip "entertained" Wampanoag relations
from Sakonnet, Winslow and his men pursued a campaign to "reduce them to
reason," to secure submissions and "fetch in arms" from Wampanoag towns.
Thus, their pursuit of Awashonks in the summer of 1671 was part of a much
larger scheme to assert jurisdiction over Wampanoag people and lands, and to
protect themselves by attempting to isolate Philip and his followers from this
larger network, a plan that proved difficult to carry out.[46]

When, in August, Plymouth sent an emissary empowered by their Council of
War to take Philip to Plymouth "to endeavor his reducement by force," the sachem dismissed him via a messenger, saying he awaited travel to Boston, where
the Massachusetts magistrates, via Natick messengers, had offered to arbitrate
the dispute. Demonstrating his knowledge of English law, Philip further insisted he was not subject to Plymouth. Rather, he said, Governor Prence "was

but a subject of King Charles of England," and as a sachem, he "would treat of peace only with the King, my brother"—his equal. "When" the king "comes" to the Wampanoag country, Philip said, he "would be ready."[47]

Philip traveled to Boston in early September, to make "complaint" against Plymouth to the Massachusetts magistrates, who then acknowledged that Plymouth's political relationship to the Wampanoags was more like a "neighborly and friendly correspondency," not absolute title or jurisdiction. They asserted civil as well as biblical authority, conveying to Plymouth that war against the Wampanoags could not be justified under the United Colonies' Articles of Confederation. They "tendered theire healp," offering to mediate, even as they asserted authority. Plymouth ultimately accepted, inviting the "commissioners of the Massachusetts and Connecticut" to "come to Plymouth to aford us theire help."[48]

Unbeknownst to Philip, Massachusetts offered to help "reduce" Philip "to order" and to secure the Wampanoags under the reigns of the United Colonies, once Plymouth's dependence on Massachusetts was reinforced. When Philip reluctantly traveled to Taunton at the end of September, he faced the drama of a "trial," rather than the diplomatic space of a council, betrayed by both Massachusetts and the Natick diplomats, including Sassamon. Rather than mediating, the combined leaders of the United Colonies, including Prence, Winthrop, and John Leverett, chastised Philip for his "insolent" carriage and his violation of the April "covenant," including "his entertaining of divers Saconett Indians, professed enemies to this colony." Demanding he "humble himself unto the magistrates" and "amend his ways," the governors ordered the sachem and his counselors to surrender their remaining arms, pay a 100-pound fine for failing to fulfill this obligation, and pledge an annual tribute of five wolf heads to Plymouth. If they did not have the funds, the court would take the fine in land. Philip had agreed to meet, hoping for the fair "arbitration" promised by Massachusetts and the Natick messengers. However, he discovered at Taunton that the English of Massachusetts ultimately "agreed" with Plymouth "against them." As he told Easton, he would accept no more of such "arbitration."[49]

Although many historians, quoting the Plymouth Court Order, have represented this meeting as a "treaty" by which Philip acknowledged himself and his people to be "subjects to his majestie the Kinge of England, &c, and the government of New Plymouth," Easton's relation demonstrates that Philip and his counselors expressed great exasperation with these increasingly invasive attempts to assert colonial authority.[50] In 1671, Metacom may have hoped for negotiations over a breakdown of reciprocal relations between allies, but the

English clearly had other motivations for supporting each other and solidifying the alliance among the colonies.

Many of the prominent leaders of the United Colonies, including those present at the Taunton council, were embroiled in land grants and speculation, as Douglas Leach and Francis Jennings long ago discerned, and they had nurtured rumors of Indian conspiracy and "defiance" for years. The "covenant" produced in Taunton ensured that Plymouth would have the support of the colonies of Connecticut and Massachusetts if and when the Wampanoags "broke" the articles, as long as Plymouth also acknowledged the authority of the United Colonies. Philip's actual consent may not have been as important as his signature on paper. Indeed, the "war scare of 1671" produced a rash of Wampanoag signatures. Those "binding" documents, like deeds, provided legal proof that Wampanoag people and land were under the jurisdiction of Plymouth Colony, the United Colonies, and the British crown, and would serve as justification for imprisonment and military action if Wampanoag "subjects" made a move to "rebel" against the crown's agents in New England. As Jennings wrote of the covenant, "On paper, Plymouth's triumph was complete."[51]

If not for Easton's relation, this "covenant" might stand on its own as "history." We would be left to believe that Philip consented to sign away Wampanoag rights to land and self-government, and willingly "subjected" his people to the Plymouth colonists, something he could not do without their consent. However, the Wampanoags who met with Easton in June 1675 revealed a different perspective. They expressed frustration with English failure to adhere to an *Indigenous* code of values, a persistent determination to maintain self-governance, and an urgent concern over the widening loss of land so necessary to their survival. Standing at the carrying place between nations, the Wampanoag counselors reminded the Rhode Island men that "they had been the first in doing good to the English, and the English the first in doing wrong." They "said when the English first came their king's father was as a great man and the English as a little child, he constrained other Indians from wronging the English and gave them corn and showed them how to plant and was free to do them any good."[52]

Following Indigenous diplomatic protocol, Philip and his counselors opened the council by recalling the historical relationship between the Wampanoags and the English, reminding settlers that it was they who first extended a hand to Plymouth, and to Rhode Island. Recalling Massasoit's generosity and protection, Philip and his counselors asserted that the sons dishonored the agreement between their fathers, failing to return this hospitality. In the next generation, they recalled, "their king's brother," Wamsutta, "when he was king Came miserably to die being forced to Court as they judged poisoned." Just as many colonial statements censured the Wampanoags' failure to act as proper subjects to the colonial government, the Wampanoag leaders' statement critiqued the newcomers' failure to participate in the Indigenous system of reciprocal relations. If, as Easton warned, they should avoid war at all costs because the English "were too strong for them," "then," they retorted, "the English should do to them as they did when they were too strong for the English."[53]

As Wamsutta and Philip's experience had demonstrated, the court was a place where their lives and lands might be taken by force. Pointing to Tobias's recent trial, they complained that "another grievance was if 20 of their honest Indians testified that an Englishman had done them wrong, it was as nothing, and if but one of their worst Indians testified against any Indian or their King when it pleased the English that was sufficient." A key example was William Tahaton, who had betrayed Philip to Massachusetts and Plymouth in 1671, then testified with "hearsay" against Tobias and his son. Easton knew the case had been a sham. In his *Relation*, he revealed that Patuckson, the Christian Indian who had "accused" Tobias and the two others of "murder," had owed "a coat" to one of the men. Patuckson falsely "informed" on them "in order not to pay" for the coat, "knowing" this deceit "would please the English so to think him a better Christian." Indeed, he "showed" the coat to the Plymouth magistrates, claiming "they [Tobias, etc.] gave" it to him to "conceal" their secret. Although the magistrates took this "Christian" testimony as truth, Easton recalled, they did not hear testimony from any of "the honest men" who could have provided the background. In the *Relation*, Easton revealed his grasp of the irony that Englishmen would call the swindler "a better Christian" for providing the story they desired to pursue a conviction. The Wampanoag counselors said "that they had great Fear to have any of their Indians should be called or forced to be Christian Indians. They said that such were in everything more mischievous, only Dissemblers, and then the English made them not subject to their Kings, and by their lying to wrong their Kings." Easton admitted, "We knew it to be true."[54]

The Wampanoag delegates expressed particular concern with the manipulation of their sachems. Referring to the betrayal of Wamsutta, among others, they testified, "when their kings sold land, the English would say it was more than" the leaders "agreed to and a writing must be proved against all them, and sum of their kings had done wrong to sell so much." Some, they said, "being given to drunkenness, the English made them drunk and then cheated them in bargains." How could Winslow's "Court" be trusted to "arbitrate"? Yet Philip and his counselors had learned from their predecessors' experience. They emphasized that the people retained the ultimate power *as a group* over the land *and* the sachems. "Now," they insisted, "their Kings wear forewarned not for to part with Land for nothing." Still, they had reason to fear the most recent colonial strategy. Perhaps referring directly to Awashonks and Mammanuah, they said, "now [whom] the English had owned for king or queen they would disinherit, and make another king that would give or sell them their land." With this new scheme, "now they had no hopes left to keep any land."[55]

These encroachments led to other violations: "The English cattle and horses still increased." Even "when they removed 30 Miles from where English had any thing to do, they could not keep their corn from being spoiled." Philip's stronghold was located on a peninsula at a strategic distance from English towns, but newly built colonial farms now extended from "Swansea" onto the neck. They acknowledged English admonitions about fencing, but "they never being used to fencing" in their own land, "thought" that "when the English bought Land of them they would have kept their cattle upon their own Land." The Wampanoags recognized that the roaming livestock served the ends of colonization, and although settlers demanded that Native people respect the town boundaries they set, the Wampanoags sardonically observed, they did not seem to require the same of their animals. "Another grievance" was that "the English were so eager to sell the Indians liquors, that most of the Indians spent all in drinks" and then "hurt the English cattle, and their King could not prevent it."[56]

As Easton documented these two key "grievances," he drew attention to several interrelated factors which contributed to the outbreak of violence. The tension reached its boiling point during planting season, as marauding cattle destroyed seedlings. "New English towns . . . hedged ancestral Wampanoag lands on all sides," as Anderson has noted, rendering Wampanoag and Narragansett people even more "vulnerable to encroachments by colonists and livestock." The conflict Mammanuah had reported at Sakonnet might have served as a warning. Already, conflicts had arisen *within* communities when family loyalties and tensions combined with the pressures of dispossession and the fuel of alcohol. As Philip and his counselors implied, it would not take much for a young man, brimming with a desire for justice and incited by a draught of rum, to strike out at those signs of settlement that had crept so close to home.[57]

In contrast with other portrayals of Philip (e.g., Winslow, Church, Mather, etc.), Easton showed a leader and his counselors expressing sincere apprehension that the escalating acts and impacts of colonization were leading to violence, a chaotic combination spiraling around them, which they could not control. Easton may have had the clearest vision, among his contemporaries, of the precipice upon which they all stood. Summarizing Wampanoag grievances, he wrote, "We knew before, these were their grand Complaints, but . . . we endeavored to persuade that all complaints might be righted without war." Easton offered Philip another alternative. He said that "they might choose a Indian King and the English might choose the Governor of New York," who were not "Parties in the Difference," suggesting a forum of equals, where both sides might be heard by neutral parties and both Indigenous and English principles would be considered. In Tobias's trial, the Plymouth Court had appointed themselves the ultimate arbiters of a case that concerned not only "murder," but a conflict over legal jurisdiction and land. They appointed a "jury," which included English freemen and select "friend" Indians as "nonvoting" advisors, giving the appearance of just "arbitration." However, Easton proposed the Wampanoags might themselves choose a sachem, who would mediate alongside a governor from outside New England, unconcerned with their land. Philip and his counselors responded, saying, "They had not heard of that way, for the Governor of York and an Indian King to have the hearing of it, and said we honestly spoke." Easton and his ambassadors "were persuaded if that way had been tendered they would have accepted."[58]

Winslow and Church claimed that Philip directed all his energy toward gathering men for war, yet, in June, he was meeting with Easton, still responsive to diplomacy with a *trusted* ambassador. Easton portrayed Philip as a leader, who, while backed into a corner, was nevertheless willing to consider a solution that might restore justice, without resorting to war, which he agreed was "the worst way." Easton's letter and *Relation* reveal that both Weetamoo and Philip had similar positions in their roles as sachems. They sought a restoration of balance in their homelands, and felt strongly their responsibility to ensure that their families would have the lands they required for sustaining life. Both demonstrated keen awareness that war would bring untold consequences. Further, both leaders gave the Plymouth men, through Easton, the opportunity to address their "difference" in a fair forum. Contrary to the narratives that highlighted the murder of Sassamon as the origin point for the war, the issue stressed repeatedly by Wampanoag leaders was the English threat to the survival of their homelands.[59]

Easton "honestly" believed he had found a potential route to mediation. He left Montaup prepared to carry his proposal to Plymouth, but upon returning home, "suddenly had [a] Letter from Plimoth Governor" that "they intended in arms to conform [subdue] Philip, but no Information what that was that they required or what terms" they sought. "In a week's time, after we had been with the Indians," Easton lamented, "the War thus begun."[60]

"AN IDLE LAD'S WORDS"

Circulating after Saltonstall's first two publications, but before Mather's, the *Relation* presented an elucidating perspective on the first outbreak of violence, which contrasts with other narratives of the beginning of King Philip's War. According to Saltonstall, in spring 1675, "Several Indians were seen in small Parties about Rehoboth and Swanzey, which not a little afrighted the Inhabitants. Who demanding the Reason of them, wherefore it was so? Answer was made, That they were only on their own Defence for they understood that the English intended to Cut them off."[61]

Although Wampanoags had inhabited these territories of Sowams and Mattapoisett for millennia, Saltonstall portrayed them as threatening strangers skulking on the edges of well-established English towns. He neglected to mention that these recent settlements were encroaching onto Montaup, which he noted was "judged to be the best land in New England." Saltonstall also acknowledged a key Wampanoag motivation, highlighted by Easton's *Relation*: they "understood that" the colonists intended "to cut them off."[62]

Two years later, William Hubbard described a necessary war of defense against invading Indians, eliminating Indigenous motivations and using passive language to describe an English act of violence: "At last their Insolencies grew to such an Height, that they began not only to use threatening Words to the English, but also to kill their Cattle and rifle their Houses; whereat an Englishman was so provoked, that he let fly a Gun at an Indian, but did only wound, not kill him; whereupon the Indians immediately began to kill all the English they could."[63] The English, embodied in this one settler, did not instigate violence; they allowed the inevitable to occur—being "provoked," he/they "let fly" a bullet. Indians were the active agents of warfare: they "began to kill all the English they could."

Forty years later, Church excluded this "first shot" by a colonist, instead recounting that "the enemy, who began their hostilities with plundering and destroying cattle, did not long content themselves with that game; they thirsted for English blood, and they soon broached it, killing two men in the way near Miles garrison." Church portrayed bloodthirsty hunters seeking English men on the roadway, but Samuel Drake, in editing Church's account, felt the need to clarify: "It appears that an Indian was wounded while in the act of killing cattle; or as tradition informs us, the Indian who was wounded, after killing some animals in a man's field, went to his house and demanded liquor, and being refused attempted to take it by violence, threatening at the same time to be revenged for such usage, this caused the English man to fire on him."[64]

Easton's *Relation* provided the most complex explanation of this incident:

Plimouth Soldiers were cum to have their Head Quarters within 10 Miles of Philip; then most of the English thereabout left there Houses . . . we had Leter from Plimouth Governor to desier our Help with sum Boats if thay had such Ocation, and for us to looke to our selfs; and from the Generall at the Quarters we had Leter of the Day they intended to cum upon the Indians, and desier for sum of our Boats to attend . . . in this time sum indians fell a pilfering sum houses that the English had left, and an old man and a lad going to one of those houses did see 3 indians run out therof. the old man bid the young man shoote so he did and a indian fell doune but got away againe. it is reported that then sum indians Came to the gareson asked why thay shot the indian. thay asked whether he ws dead. the indians saied yea. a English lad saied it was no mater. the men indevered to inforem them it was but an idell lads words but the indians in hast went away and did not harken to them. the next day the lad that shot the indian and his father and fief [five] English more wear killed so the war begun with philop.[65]

Easton's account revealed the "pilfered" houses were abandoned, and settlers left not merely because of fear of Wampanoag action but because the Plymouth forces were amassing in their midst, not only in defense but to apprehend Philip. It acknowledged that Winslow sent letters, stating his intent to marshal forces and "come upon the Indians," before the first shot "flew." Easton also revealed that the young man of Swansea, John Salisbury, fired that "shot" while the Wampanoag man was running from an abandoned house, a detail Hubbard omitted. Easton allowed for variance in the colonists' positions. When a young "lad" announced that the death of an Indian was "no matter," another man was moved to ameliorate the damage of the remark. Yet another man, William Salisbury, urged his son to "shoot." Hubbard described a mass of Indians in growing insurgence, but Easton recognized differences between individuals, whether English or Indian, and the complexity of conflict. He represented the war as emerging in a swirl of anger, misunderstanding, and burgeoning chaos, which he struggled to comprehend.

4

HERE COMES THE STORM

How do we write about the myriad, complex ways in which war enters into a community and into Indigenous homelands? This chapter explores multiple possible answers to that question by approaching the "beginning" of "King Philip's War" from multiple places and viewpoints—ranging from mothers and leaders like Weetamoo and her sister Wootonakanuske to scouts embedded in colonial companies like James Quananopohit and his brother Thomas—bringing multifaceted Indigenous characters and perspectives to the fore, while also considering the tactics and experiences of colonial leaders and soldiers. The chapter makes no attempt to encompass or balance *all* viewpoints, but rather seeks to evoke the experience of the storm of war as it spirals through the land, using Indigenous frameworks for interpretation. The chapter begins with an italicized section, which places us within that spiral as it entered Pocasset. These italicized segments, which appear throughout the book, signal my use of the techniques of historical fiction to bring readers into plausible scenarios, to animate the historical landscape through Indigenous frameworks and to give a sense of humanity to historical characters whose stories have been silenced, repressed or misunderstood. This is one of my approaches to addressing the "absence of presence" discussed in the Introduction. These italicized sections often bring to life elements from the primary sources, informed by knowledge drawn from Indigenous places and languages, discussions with tribal historians, and understandings of the deep-seated and diverse causes and effects of war.

MONTAUP

POCASSET, FOLLOWING SOLSTICE

She was picking berries in the cedar swamp with her daughter; the tart, succulent fruits burst on their tongues. The little one delighted in her work, small fingers grasping berries of the most vibrant red as she navigated vining branches and thorns. The song of cicadas filled the canopy of trees. The rains had cleared, leaving the air crisp and temperate. Later, they would bring the berries back home to share. A familiar sound interrupted, coming from up the path. Weetamoo called to her daughter and they ran toward the sound of her sister's voice.[1]

Wootonakanuske had paddled across the river, taking a familiar route to Weetamoo's town, with many other families, seeking counsel and shelter. It was true that they had been holding dances, but they had always hosted gatherings in the summer. At Plymouth, the people did not dance. They brought their fears with them. Now, the people of this land had every reason to fear they would be taken, dispossessed, even killed. Many who came to Montaup had been displaced from their family's planting grounds, fishing places, and deer yards by English houses, cattle, and deeds. Many had lost family, acts of war that had been answered not with violence but with gritty tolerance and determined diplomacy. Others had been hunted for "infractions"—men who had defended their mothers' fields against cattle, women from the praying towns, like Ahaton's wife, who had been whipped for "adultery" or banished for wearing "heathen" symbols, children whose parents had been imprisoned for debt.[2]

During the solstice, they had met at Montaup, surrounded by cedars that formed the four poles, as their ancestors always had. They danced, grateful the plants had given fruit. They gathered together in families before the great cliffs, the light of the moon reflecting off the gray stone, the undulations of the ocean rumbling behind them. The dome of the sky flickered with stars, a reminder of the world to which they would return. They heard stories from the elders who had remarkably endured. Their mothers, aunties, and grandmothers urged them to consider the road that lay before their children and grandchildren. Men who had seen the Pequot towns razed urged forbearance, while others recalled driving back the Mohawks. They heard stories of loss and regeneration. They saw every being in motion, together and in opposition, yet always striving toward balance. All around them, springs and rivulets lit by the moon sought the path of least resistance through the ground, finding their way home to the ocean, its waves governed by the moon. They understood the motion that always finds its way to stillness. They knew they were only expressions of these impulses. At the same time, they understood that every child there that night, held in her grandmother's *arms or perched in the crook of an old oak, was, without doubt, the most precious being in the world.*

Now, at Pocasset, Wootonakanuske confirmed that the Plymouth men were gathering, planning a last thrust toward Montaup. Word was they had sent messages to Massachusetts, Rhode Island, and Connecticut requesting support, invoking their loyalty to the king. Even Easton had said that by their own law, the English men must stand with Plymouth if they pursued war. Weetamoo could not have found this news surprising; she had received such a letter herself. The forces had arrived on solstice, posted at houses in Mattapoisett and Sowams. Old Cudworth was there, leading the young men in their marches, with Southworth to goad him on. Winslow was a coward. He stayed at home in Marshfield, sending orders with his pen.[3]

Any day now, the Plymouth men would march forward and try to take Metacom from them. Past experience had proven that some would not hesitate to threaten a woman's children to force her husband to comply. Wootonakanuske's son, and all the children, would be safer at Pocasset. Together, as they skillfully secured green branches with twine, building shelters in the refuge of the cedar swamp, the sisters and their kin deliberated how to navigate the coming storm.[4]

Countless stories told of the cedar swamp's power, a place of nourishment and a world of ambivalence. It sheltered many animals in the thickets, which in turn became settings where skilled hunters could find game. It hosted medicine plants that could heal, or cause illness. Springs bubbled up from pockets in the earth, offering cool water even on the hottest days. Yet a wayward traveler might find his body merging with the muck. To the sisters, the swamp was the most familiar place on earth, a place that had taught them to survive. When they gathered here, they stood under the greatest arbor in the land, the pungent aroma of cedar surrounding them, evergreen branches rising high, enveloping them like their mother's arms.

COUNCIL AT GREAT POND, NARRAGANSETT, JUNE 21–27

Quinnapin, Quaiapin, and the other sachems had refused to go to Smith's house to meet with the men from Massachusetts. They knew that Plymouth men marched at Sowams, seeking Metacom. They had reason to believe that Anne Hutchinson's son, who had long conspired with Smith to take their lands at Pettaquamscut, and his men might join them.

The sachems had little motivation to trust Edward Hutchinson's proclaimed intention for peace. Only a few years before, he had placed a piece of paper before them, claiming that Quinnapin and "the Queen" had granted Pettaquamscut to the Atherton Company. It was a paper the two sachems had signed in a tense council after Narragansett men had tried to prevent settlers from planting at Pettaquamscut. The war could have started then, as Narragansett men were "burning hay, killing sundry horses," and "assaulting" English men "in the high way as they rode about their occasions." Just as young Wampanoag men protested at Sowams, Narragansetts had often attacked horses and cattle, and "used many threatening speeches" to try to "force" English men "from their labors in mowing grass" and sowing grains on Narragansett marshes and fields. Their diplomacy had prevented war. Now, even Roger Williams, their old friend, spoke of "quenching the Phillipian fire." If the English joined in alliance, the Narragansett leaders had reason to suspect the "fire" would soon reach their lands.[5]

The sachems insisted they meet closer to their towns, near a great pond eight miles west of Pettaquamscut and fifteen miles south of Smith's house in Wickford. Here, Quinnapin, Quaiapin, Canonchet, Ninigret, and Quissucquansh (now known as Canonicus) listened to emissaries from Rhode Island and Massachusetts, including Governor John Leverett's message, asking that they restrain themselves and their young men from joining with Metacom in "rising against the English." They responded that they held "no agreement with Philip" that would bind them to him. "They had not sent one man" to Montaup, "nor would" they. As for "those of their people who had made marriages" with Wampanoags, some of whom lived at Montaup, they "should return or perish there."[6]

However, in responding, the Narragansett leaders reversed Leverett's proposal. They inquired "why Plymouth pursued Philip?" and asked "why the Massachusetts and Rhode Island" men "rose, and joined with Plymouth against Philip, and left not Philip and Plymouth to fight it out?" If the commissioners asked them to refrain from joining Metacom, did the sachems not have an equal right to ask their allies to refrain from joining Plymouth? Such alliance would likely bring war to their door. Why invite violence in their mutual territories? Why not make demands on their neighboring colony, or leave Metacom and Plymouth to resolve the conflict between them?[7]

The sachems could not have been satisfied with the answer of the commissioners, who replied that since "all the Colonies were subject to one King" it was their duty "for one English man to stand to the death by each other, in all parts of the world." Because of their fidelity to the King, they claimed, the English men of Massachusetts, Connecticut, and Rhode Island were bound to join with Plymouth. The commissioners asserted that Metacom had "broke all laws, and was in arms of rebellion against that Colony, his ancient friends and protectors," and it was "believed that he was the author" of the "murdering of John Sossiman."[8]

The Narragansett sachems responded by invoking their own alliance with the English king and the loyalty the Rhode Island and Massachusetts men owed to them. If, they said, the colonies had now abandoned their "law of leaving Indians to Indian justice," and instead joined together to prosecute Indians for crimes against other Indians, then they wished to raise again their own claim against Tatuphosuit (Owaneco), the son of Uncas, who had killed "a sachim, one of their cousins," a much greater offense than the death of lowly Sassamon. They asked that Tatuphosuit "may suffer impartially as now the English have dealt with the three Indians which killed John Sossimon." They had heard that Tatuphosuit had been taken by the Connecticut men, but released, and now he held a "great dance in triumph." The case paralleled that of Plymouth and Metacom, and the dances at Mohegan, like those at Montaup, could threaten the men of Rhode Island and Massachusetts. The Narragansett leaders had heard news, they warned, that Uncas "had sent twenty men to Philip" and they advised Hutchinson and his men to turn their attention to Mohegan. Either Massachusetts and Rhode Island should back their Narragansett allies, as they were willing to back Plymouth, or they should enable the Narragansetts "to right themselves" and seek their own justice against the Mohegans. They should likewise refrain from interfering with Plymouth and Metacom, allowing "justice" to fall where it would.[9]

Roger Williams, as interpreter, agreed to "write to the Governor and Council of Massachusetts" with the Narragansett sachems' reply and request, which Hutchinson and his men agreed to deliver. The commissioners had traveled to Narragansett to intimidate and persuade the sachems to isolate themselves from Metacom and pledge fidelity to the neighboring colonies, but instead they had received some cool-headed advice to isolate themselves from Plymouth and prove their fidelity and fairness to the neighboring Narragansetts. This was not the subject that the commissioners had expected to discuss, but in return for bringing this request forward, they received the Narragansett sachems' assurance that they would not send men to Metacom and "if Philip or his men fled to them," they said "yet they would not receive them, but deliver them to the English." The "yet" here may have been crucial. They would await answer from the Massachusetts governor and would watch their neighbors in Rhode Island carefully. Their agreement, therefore, was conditional.[10]

As disturbing news came in from Montaup, Quinnapin may have sent runners to Pocasset, with the message that Massachusetts and Rhode Island rose to "join with Plymouth against Philip." He may have been among the one hundred disciplined warriors who "marched to Warwick" the day after the commissioners' departure, conveying a warning of the consequences should Rhode

Island men allow "the fire" to be directed at Narragansett. Although they refrained from violence, the warriors' imposing presence "frightened Warwick" and "all the inhabitants there," as did news that the sachems may have been less than forthcoming at Great Pond. In less than a week, Williams wrote to John Winthrop Jr. that he had reason to "suspect" that the words of "the Indian sachems to us were but words of policy, falsehood and treachery." Now, Williams reported, "the English testify, that for divers weeks (if not months) canoes passed to and again (day and night between Metacom and the Narragansetts) and the Narragansett Indians have committed many robberies on the English houses."[11]

Williams had multiple reasons for apprehension. Those canoes might carry protectors allied with Metacom, but also messengers, who conveyed information on English movements and communications, including those from Rhode Island. In closing his letter, Williams lamented, "Sir, many wish that Plymouth had left the Indians alone, at least not to put to death the three Indians upon one Indian's testimony, a thing which Philip fears" for himself. Echoing the words of the Narragansett sachems, Williams implored Winthrop, then negotiating with Uncas for support, that many also wished that Winthrop and his people "could leave the Mohegan and Narragansetts to themselves as to Tatuphosoit, if there could be any just way by your General Court found out for the preventing of their conjunction with Metacom, which so much concerneth the peace of New England." As Williams now believed, those canoes also carried families from Montaup to Narragansett. If the Narragansetts gave shelter to Wampanoags, Williams had good reason to believe his neighbors would bring the war to Rhode Island.[12]

Traveling along those same canoe routes, word soon reached Narragansett that some Wampanoag men had killed five English settlers at Mattapoisett and had "brought their heads to Philip." Canonicus, meeting with his old friend, said that "his heart affected and sorrowed" for the families' loss. Still, he explained to Williams, sachems "could not rule the youth and the common people" nor "persuade others, chief among them," such as Quinnapin and Quaiapin. He held sway only over his brother's son, Canonchet, who would rise as a key diplomat and strategist in the coming months. Canonicus urged Williams to advise his neighbors "to stand upon their guard" and "to fortify one or more houses strongly, which if they could not do, then to fly" from their settlements to a safer place. Messengers had come to Narragansett, both men knew, laying English heads at the sachems' feet. Canonicus told Williams he had "advised a refusal" of the messengers. However, Williams later heard, Quaiapin rejected that advice, offering the young men food and shelter from the storm.[13]

THE EVICTION OF JOHN ARCHER, POCASSET, JUNE 25

Mamuxuat and his brother Waweapunet watched John Archer's house from a distance. They lay hidden with their two kinsmen as if behind a hunting blind, "about ten rod distance," where Archer and his son could not see them. They had him in their sight. The one beside him whispered, "Should we shoot . . . or not?" Before Mamuxuat could answer, a shot rang out, flying by his ear, and hit John Archer. Archer faltered, and Waweapunet rushed passed him, hatchet in hand, with a deafening cry. He ran at Archer, but the wounded man, fury pounding through him, fought back, wrestling Waweapunet's hatchet from his hand. Fear for his brother rising, Mamuxuat shot out like a frightened rabbit and fell upon Archer, his hatchet thrusting through the man's head.[14]

He was reluctant, but his brother insisted, threatening and persuading, then handing him his shirt to use as a satchel, to carry it up the path to the town, to carry it to her.[15]

When the four men arrived, bearing their offering, she was already surrounded by her relations who had come from Montaup, all the families who now drew close to her, anxious to protect their children, to go on about the business of their daily lives. Whether or not she accepted it mattered.[16]

She had gone to the Plymouth Court . . . they had done nothing. They lacked the power to regulate their own "subjects," never mind those who lived in her territory, beyond their reach. Those orders they had sent to Archer had gone unheeded. Furthermore, the letter from Southworth confirmed they still pursued access to her territories, without her acquiescence. Now, more had come under her house, seeking not only protection but also assistance. They had presented her with a choice. She may not have wanted war; she knew the danger it could bring to her home, the consequences to mothers and their children. But she also knew they had tried every possible strategy to seek balance through "arbitration." As in the old stories, the force of hunger had become too great. Something had to be done to put the world back in balance. Like the earthquake, the pulsing wave of war came from the lower world of waters. It came coursing through the bodies of those who struck at English cattle. It flowed through the young man who brought her the head of her enemy. It moved on bullets that danced through the air, appearing to strike from within trees. It lodged in the hearts of men. It was here; it was moving, spiraling tendrils from the earth. There was no escaping its movement. War had arrived at Pocasset.

ECLIPSE, JUNE 26

War emerged like the earthquake had fifteen years before, shaking the land with its force of reversal. The moon became a disc of wampum, revolving from white to black. The world as they knew it had turned. In some places, leadership would also turn in time of conflict—from the leaders of peace to the leaders of war. The protectors, those men (and women) of courage who could navigate this rough terrain, were that force of rebalancing in motion. The English, so new to this place and its ways, did not know how to read the signs, but nonetheless, they felt the dread creep into their bodies. A change had come, perhaps invoked by their leaders, but they were marching and there was no way they could turn back now.

POKANOKET, JUNE 26–30

When the Massachusetts forces under Captains Thomas Prentiss and Daniel Henchman went out from Cambridge and Boston on the afternoon of June 26, only three Native men marched with them: James Quananopohit (or Rumney-marsh), his brother Thomas, and Zachary "Abrams" (Abraham). All three were converts. James and Thomas may have been among those orphans raised as servants in English households, being originally from Winisimet, or Rumney Marsh, and probable kin to the Massachusett Saunkskwa. Zachary Abraham was likely from Natick, a place James and Thomas knew well.[17]

The three men must have been considered trustworthy and knowledgeable in order to accompany the troops on this expedition. James's linguistic skills may have been useful, but his experience in tracking and warfare were invaluable. The Massachusetts troops' primary purpose was to assist in the defense of the Swansea settlements, the containment of Montaup, and the capture of Metacom. They had no idea how necessary these scouts would become. Most of the colonists had little military experience. Some had fought in recent wars with the Dutch for New York, although that seaborne conflict provided little experience on the ground. One of the Massachusetts companies, led by Captain Samuel Mosely, included privateers and released prisoners, who had experience on the seas, and with hand-to-hand combat. Although local militia had spent years practicing their marches and drills, loading and firing their arms, they were underprepared for woodland warfare.[18]

James Quananopohit, on the other hand, had recently defended Natick, Nashaway, and other inland towns against incursions from the Mohawks. The formidable Kanienkehaka warriors had inspired fear in the praying towns, but James had accepted training and leadership from Nipmuc relations to stand up to the threat. Training and observing in the field, James had learned to apply the skills he acquired in hunting to warfare—to move stealthily through the woods in small parties; to evade detection, using both camouflage and mental training to blend into any environment; to use the element of surprise. The goal, in raiding the Mohawks, had never been to take or raze the Kanienkehaka towns but to strike fear in those who would lay claim to Nipmuc places and people, and to restore the balance. Such tactics, they believed, would ensure that their families could live in peace. Of course, Kanienkehaka men still listened to their clan mothers, who by their Great Law had the power to authorize or halt war. English settlers were a different case altogether. Just as the majority of English men could not anticipate the experience of woodland warfare, the majority of Native people could not anticipate what a relentless "total war" would look like in their country, with men who did not take counsel from their wives and mothers, particularly in matters of governance and war.[19]

That afternoon, James and Thomas Quananopohit rode out on horseback, leaving Cambridge as the sun began its descent. Night soon overtook them, but the Massachusetts troop had no plans to stop for sleep. The moon lit their way as they traveled the long road toward Rehoboth. Yet, as they rode, the brothers must have noticed the shifting illumination, the thin edge of darkness that crept across the moon. As the lunar eclipse progressed, Prentiss called a halt to the troops, pausing alongside the Neponset River. Most of the men did not know how to read the sign, or how long this total darkness would last. Surrounded by forest, they must have craved the light of fire. Some steeled themselves against apprehension; others prayed to God. Still others "read a melancholy Omen of the divine Displeasure" in the shading of the moon. Everyone, throughout the Native towns and English settlements, experienced the darkness that night. Like a skillful warrior, it came unexpectedly, and instilled fear.[20]

Enshrouded in darkness for well "above an hour," the men must have contemplated the news they had recently received from their chief commander, Thomas Savage. As the first small troop from Massachusetts had traveled this path, approaching Swansea, they had encountered the remains of a raid, the corpses of "five Englishmen." Now, this troop knew they might see similar sights, as they marched to the outlying Plymouth settlements. Some, certain of their valor and superior training, boasted "that one Englishman was sufficient to chase ten Indians," and "many reckoned it was no other but *Veni, vidi, vici.*" They imagined they would "come" to Montaup, they would see, they would conquer, a resolution swift and complete. Others, more reluctant, feared they were drawn into a conflict that arose from "Plymouth's stern and unyielding policy," which should be left to Plymouth and "its" Indians. Still others, feeling apprehensive, wished they could be home with their families, worrying over their fields of wheat.[21]

When the Massachusetts troops safely reached Swansea on June 28, James Quananopohit would have heard that those settlers had been killed "at the head of Mattapoisett neck," in the heart of Conbitant's old town. Two more had died of their wounds. Among them was William Salisbury and his son, who had "let fly" the first shot and killed a Wampanoag man. The next day, the fallen man's kin returned, and as the Salisburys and their neighbors gathered corn near an abandoned house, they struck swiftly. This was a raid on specific targets, who had violated land and kin, not on random "Englishmen."[22]

On arrival at Sowams, the Massachusetts company found Constant Southworth and his Plymouth troop holed up in the minister's house. On the night of the raid at Mattapoisett, their sentry, posted outside the makeshift garrison on the Sowams River, had been "shot in the face and slain by an Indian that crept near unto him," and two more lay injured nearby. When Southworth's men looked outside, they saw no sign of those who had fired. They had not left "Miles garrison" since. From Marshfield, Winslow had sent cutting words of disappointment in his troops' "neglect of action." The reinforcements from Massachusetts should turn their "discouragement" to "encouragement." Having reconnoitered in Rehoboth, the Massachusetts company was poised for battle. Church later related, "Some of Captain Prentice's troop," of which the Quananopohit brothers were members, "desired they might have liberty to go out and seek the Enemy in their own quarters." Thus, that afternoon, a party of twelve men marched from the garrison toward the bridge, heading for the small narrows that led to Montaup. They had as their "pilot" William Hammond, a Rehoboth and Swansea settler, who they hoped could lead them through the peninsula to Metacom's town.[23]

Yet no sooner had they crossed the bridge, than they found themselves barraged by shot, which came "upon them" from "out of the bushes." Prepared to confront the Wampanoags in open combat, they "could see no enemy to shoot at, but yet felt their bullets out of the thick bushes where" warriors "lay in ambushments," camouflaged "from the waist upwards with green boughs." The ambush was over before it began. Hammond was dead, and two commanders lay wounded. A few remaining "troopers" set off after "those Indians that ran away," but others fled back toward the garrison. Church later claimed he had to persuade the runners to return to collect Hammond's corpse, a wounded officer among the only volunteers.[24]

James and Thomas may have been among the twelve troopers. More likely, they witnessed the spectacle from Miles garrison, alongside the rest of the troops. The speed of the strike may have astounded those from Plymouth and Cambridge, but the ambush was a familiar sight to James. Wampanoag warriors, seeing the obvious buildup of troops around Miles's house, had kept watch by the woods near the bridge, guarding the entrance to Montaup and placing a snare at the narrow "neck." In a plan James must have found perplexing, the troopers imagined they would march to Montaup and impress Metacom with their force, or engage him in face-to-face combat, for which they had been trained. James may have been bold enough to tell them that this expectation was misguided.

James may have received a colonial education, but he also had Indigenous training. He had learned to evade, capture, and protect alongside the Nashaway leader, Monoco. From him, and from the Mohawks, James had learned how to move in fast and strike quickly, leaving his enemy stunned and surprised. He had learned that warfare was about affecting another man's mind, creating a space where fear swirled around him, eventually overtaking his capacity for rational thought. When a Nipmuc or Kanienkehaka war party ambushed, they employed a carefully planned strategy, allowing for multiple scenarios and outcomes, designed to foster a perception of chaos. From the perspective of the strategists, the process had a clear order, with varying stratagems employed by particular men, who made use of their environment. But from the perspective of the targets of the operation, strikes seemed to emerge from nowhere, spiral around them, and evaporate quickly, leaving fright and confusion in their wake. When a man recovered his senses, he would see before him the corpse of a friend, a kinsman, or rival. He would experience relief at his survival, mixed with grief and apprehension that the warriors could return, any moment, to take him.[25]

That afternoon, a barrage of rain prevented further action.[26] With one dead, two wounded, and all discouraged by the failure of their first expedition into enemy territory, James watched one of the troopers from Watertown, "a stout man" named William Sherman, fall into the mental trap that had been set for him. "Seeing the English slain, hearing many profane oaths" from Mosely's privateers, and experiencing how the "unseasonable" cold "weather" and rain had come upon them, as if "nothing could be done against the Enemy," he dashed about, "distracted," shouting that "God was against the English." Although Sherman was sent home, shamed as "a lamentable spectacle," his words surely left doubts lurking in the minds of other men. Plymouth's ministers, on the day of humiliation, had warned that their sin had brought this scourge upon them. Wampanoag men had carried out their first ambush that very day. Those snares set by protectors would produce a deadly brew of impotence and doubt mixed with anger, which, while impelling a man to take revenge, would also invite him to act rashly.[27]

Thus, when Mosely led the troops out the next morning, determined to take the peninsula, they were in some respects fulfilling another strategy, acting out a scenario the Wampanoags likely anticipated. That morning, the men around the garrison heard voices in the distance, and a handful of Wampanoag men appeared outside the minister's house, teasing the soldiers. James Quanano-pohit might have recognized the classic strategy designed to draw them out, often into a waiting ambush. In response, Henchman's "horsemen," including the Quananopohit brothers, and "the whole body of Privateers under Captain Mosely . . . ran violently down upon them over the . . . bridge," toward the bushes, anxious and irate, revved to shoot before being shot.[28]

According to Church, "having passed the bridge," they marched ahead "down into the neck" in formation. Ordered to "extend both wings," they spread out to the left and right, which must have taken them off trail into brush and woods. This military strategy was designed for the open fields of England, not the Wampanoag country. Since the "center" was "not well headed," and they were immersed in gloomy gray light and plummeting rain, they lost sight of each other. Hearing movements in the brush, perhaps thunder overhead, someone let loose his gun, sparking reaction among the tense troops. James Quanano-pohit must have strained to discern the action around him as "some of them mistook their Friends for Enemies, and made a fire upon" those in "the right wing." When Thomas Savage, the commander of the Massachusetts forces, finally arrived at Miles garrison that night, they had to explain why his young son had a bullet "lodged in his thigh." The young man was not only the son of their commander, but nephew to Edward Hutchinson, who had also arrived at Rehoboth. Perhaps they made up the story on the spot. Two years later, William Hubbard claimed the troops had engaged in a battle wherein "Ensign Savage, that young martial Spark," was injured "while he boldly held up his colours in the front of his company." According to his embellished narrative, they killed "five or six of the enemy" before they "ran away into a swamp" and the rain forced the troops to retreat.[29]

The next morning, the combined Plymouth and Massachusetts troops, led by Savage and Cudworth, were once more determined to march on Montaup, to engage and capture Metacom. Savage may have been emboldened by his newly vested authority to employ his men in "fighting, killing, subduing and de-stroying the enemy." While Wampanoag and Narragansett warriors were mov-ing freely, the settlers were shut up in three garrison houses, and makeshift bar-ricades and tents, barraged by rain. By the time they set out, it was "near noon" and the sky remained dark and ominous. They crossed the bridge, this time avoiding ambush, and once more set out in files, with men upon horseback at the "wings." The Quananopohit brothers flanked the troops with their horses, searching for signs on the woods' edge, scanning for tracks on the ground. But the recent downpours had washed any trace away. The men advanced warily, but after marching for over a mile, they had discerned no sound or sign of threat or prey.[30]

Approaching the recently constructed colonial enclave below the narrow opening of the peninsula, they found abandoned fields and "some houses newly burned," the only signs of activity. While fear stirred, they heard only wind and rain. As they marched onward, horses straining against the wet flowing ground, they found leaves from a bible "newly torn" and "scattered," the words of God blown about on the wind, fallen on the earth, saturated and muddied. Perhaps some wondered if the stout Sherman's proclamation had been right. They continued, marching along the main trail, until they were halted at the narrows of Kickemuit by a sight that stunned them all. Posted aside the trail were eight massive wood poles; atop each was an English man's head. Those men from Swansea and Rehoboth recognized the disfigured faces; they belonged to their neighbors who had been killed at Mattapoisett. Inspiring shock and fear, these staves served as a warning to those who would go further. It was work Wampanoag men had ample time to accomplish while the soldiers were holed up in their garrisons. The poles resembled crude fences, mocking the advice of English magistrates to fence their fields. They were also a recognizable adaptation of the English practice of mounting criminals' heads on pikes, which Wampanoags had witnessed and now applied, marking the crimes of those they killed at Mattapoisett. Perhaps the Quananopohit brothers, at this juncture, warned the troops to turn back. Perhaps some fought the urge to run in retreat. An ambush, like the one at Mattapoisett, could be just around the trail, this spectacle designed to stun them into a vulnerable stupor. Their heads could be next.[31]

Yet as the troops marched forward "two miles further," they found neither an ambush, nor a company of warriors prepared to defend their sachem. When they arrived at the hill town of Montaup, wet, exhausted, blood pumping in anticipation and fear, they found only abandoned *wetus*, some dogs, and Metacom's herd of pigs, an empty village surrounded by "many fields of stately corn." In his letter to Winslow, all Cudworth could report was that they "burned" some "empty wigwams" and "took" some "corn." Mosely's privateers let loose their dogs, but all they brought back was a few "young pigs." They had believed that, with their post at the northern entrance of the peninsula, and Rhode Island boats patrolling the surrounding waters, they had Metacom "penned up," trapped like a hog on a neck. Instead, they found themselves trapped in unfamiliar territory, no enemy left to fight. They had thought this expedition would be contained to one battle, but instead they confronted chaos, fearing ambush but facing silence, ominous clouds still roiling above. Soon, word traveled that Metacom "had left his place" and the Plymouth men "know not where he is."[32]

MONTAUP, JUNE 30–JULY 1

The commanders, now without clear course, decided to march to the southern reach of the peninsula. Trekking "two miles further," the troops "came to the seaside," perhaps the point where Metacom had met with Easton. Drenched and drained, they lay down in a "plain," their great expedition having dissipated before them. When patrolling boats from Rhode Island arrived, the Plymouth men accepted their offer of "refreshment" at Portsmouth. Savage stubbornly refused the invitation. Thus, the Quananopohit brothers, with the Massachusetts troops, spent a cold, wet night on an open field beside Narragansett Bay, the nearest English house miles to the north. Unlike the Wampanoag women, the English men did not build shelter from the trees; nor did they risk traveling back to the town to sleep in the recently abandoned *wetus*. Metacom's warriors might come upon them, their eyes drooping and bellies empty, their clothes heavy with rain.[33]

The men kept watch all night, sleeping fitfully. In the morning, Savage led the retreat back through Montaup and Kickemuit, to seek shelter at Rehoboth. To save face, he claimed his troops had "taken" Montaup and announced his plan to build a fort at Metacom's town. But as Church later admitted, "to speak the truth, it must be said, that as they gained not that field by their sword, nor their bow; so 'twas rather their fear than their courage, that oblig'd them to set up the marks of their conquest."[34]

James and Thomas must have proved helpful on the expedition, despite its failures, and on the return journey. Encountering a Wampanoag party near Swansea, Thomas "kild one of Philip's cheefe men" and "brought in his head to the Governor of Boston." Shortly thereafter, Daniel Gookin was asked to raise a company of over fifty men from the praying towns "to be sent to" Major Savage and "the army at Mount Hope" in order "to deal the better with the enemy in their own ways and methods, according to the Indian manner of fighting." As Gookin related, their troops "could not . . . find an enemy to fight with, yet were galled by the enemy." Despite their belief in the superiority of English ways, they needed Native men to guide them in the tactics and strategies that would be effective in this unfamiliar environment. The praying towns, which formed a defensive circle around Boston, sent "one third" of "their able men" to assist their allies. James Printer's brother, Job Kattenanit, was among them.[35]

Constant Southworth had had enough. Enough of the stink of men, crowded into a stuffy house, enough of the aimless trekking about; enough of the driving rain, enough of the blood-pumping fear of an Indian behind every tree. He was a magistrate and a money counter, not a soldier. He should be at his desk, like Winslow, writing letters. He would ride to Rehoboth, take some sustenance, and return to Plymouth. He would not die in this wilderness. He handed over the title of "Commissary" to his son-in-law, who seemed eager to seek out "the enemy" in the swamps. Before he left, the young man was assigned with Matthew Fuller to lead a small company over the water to Sakonnet and Pocasset, while others roamed the woods about Swansea and Rehoboth. They might as well have been chasing a deer which had successfully dodged their bullet. But he would not worry himself with the matter. Church had proven useful in negotiating deeds, but if he should falter on the field, there were other young men he could choose for his daughter. If Church should succeed, he would take credit for the young man's promotion, having acted the part of the admirable father in selecting him for the post. From his desk, he would write a letter praising his protégé's feats.[36]

POCASSET

POCASSET, JULY 7–8

More than a week had passed since Metacom and his men had paddled to Pocasset, their movement shielded by the storm. Their strikes and fearful displays had effected a diversion. While Savage built his fort and militia roamed the woods at Montaup, Sowams, and Mattapoisett, "the Wampanoags were undisturbed for several days" at Pocasset, allowing leaders to make plans in peace, as their scouting parties watched English movements. On the morning of July 7, the Pocasset scouts likely witnessed Church and Fuller prowling between Sakonnet and Acoaxet with a group of wayward men, all armed, trudging under the "light and heat of the sun." Some wore leather boots that creaked as they walked. Fuller and Church were among those who claimed land at Sakonnet, so they knew the area better than most. But a place that Church knew as "fully of Indians" now seemed emptied of them.[37]

However, two days later, Cudworth reported to Winslow that "40 men under Capt Fuller and Benajmin Church have been on Pocasset side and had a hot dispute." Although the parties had diverged, both were ambushed. As they approached Pocasset, some "Indians fell on" Church's men, and they "skirmished" for "two hours" until the soldiers "spent all their ammunition." Church would later convey a romanticized story of the "pease field fight," on Pocasset Neck, describing countless Indians emerging from a hillside, cascading downward as they "closed a circle" around the soldiers in John Almy's field, a hill in motion, in Church's portrayal, "covered over" with warriors, "their bright guns glittering in the sun."[38]

On Church's return to the "fort" at Montaup, Cudworth demanded the number of enemies killed, but in the chaos, Church could not say. Winslow's suggestion that they imitate Hutchinson's commission at Narragansett and pursue a "purpose to the same intent with Wittamoo" was lost in the wake. Yet, in the ambush, the Wampanoags had achieved their purpose, which was not the death of English men, Church and Fuller reporting only seven wounded. The families lay safe in the swamps to the east of Almy's field, the protectors having driven Church and Fuller back across the Sakonnet River.[39]

While one group handled Church at Pocasset, other decoy parties headed north to Nemasket and east to Apponagansett. On the same day, Totoson drew his men home to raid the dispersed settlement of Dartmouth on the east side of the cedar swamps, blocking access to Pocasset via the Dartmouth path. Entering quickly, they caught the settlers off guard, firing the houses, some of which were already abandoned, with arrows aflame. "Nearly all the dwellings . . . were reduced to ashes." At the same time, Tuspaquin led a fighting force north, where they set fire to Middleboro, as John Thompson, who had all those Nemasket deeds in hand, watched powerless, his neighbors too few and frightened to "take the raiders on" and defend their improvements. As he reported, "towards night" Wampanoag men ran "to the top of Tuspaquin's Hill with" a "shout" of "great triumph and rejoicing." Local settlers attempted to shoot at the men with a "long gun," but they quickly escaped, leaving the town burning in their wake.[40]

Meanwhile, Wampanoag protectors continued to strike the settlements in Sowams and Cohannet, burning houses at Swansea and Taunton. All of these raids fostered fear in the settlers who had laid claim to Wampanoag lands, provoking many to abandon their homes. More important, the colonial forces were divided, dispersing to multiple locations, diverted from Pocasset. As they moved through the settlements, warriors struck livestock and burned hay and corn "in great quantities," simultaneously clearing the signs of "improvement," eliminating an old enemy to the planting fields, and destroying a key "supply of food." Even as Dartmouth and Middleboro smoldered, none of the English forces knew that Metacom and the families from Montaup were at Pocasset. As Easton wrote, the Plymouth forces were "hunting Philip from all sea shores, yet they could not tell what was become of him." Meanwhile, the majority of

Massachusetts troops had traveled to Narragansett, to prevent the "Phillipian fire" from spreading west.[41]

PETTAQUAMSCUT, JULY 7–15

Job Nesuton had traveled to Narragansett with the Massachusetts forces to serve as an interpreter. He had gone out with the other volunteers from the praying towns and, upon arrival, was drafted into diplomatic service. He was a long way from Cambridge, where he had been safe among his books and translations. As a scholar, he now kept strange company, surrounded by Mosely's ragtag band of ruffians, some of whom had just been released from the Boston jail. Savage and Hutchinson, accompanied by "five score" (100) of Mosely's privateers, intended a display of military bravado to discourage the Narragansetts from "joining with Philip." As Hubbard later observed, the commission "resolved" to "make a peace with a sword in their hands." They had to make a strong impression on the nation considered the "potentest of all our neighboring heathen." Job's long life had not prepared him for war. He must have been grateful they had the sense to send him to the council, where he might make himself useful.[42]

After several days of waiting at Pettaquamscut, Savage and Hutchinson realized the Narragansett sachems were not coming. The seasoned leaders were not fooled. Hutchinson had asked them to meet him on the same land that he had repeatedly attempted to swindle from them, and the irony could not have been lost on them. He had planned to employ his usual tactics, including intimidation by Mosely and his men, to compel them to sign a document acknowledging their submission. Massachusetts's commission wanted the Narragansetts to pledge neutrality and to send scouts to assist the English forces in hunting Metacom. They had sent messages "again and again," but the sachems did not appear. The commission represented an alliance with Connecticut and Plymouth, but Rhode Island was excluded from the council. Some Rhode Islanders were concerned that Massachusetts, coming into their territory "without our consent or informing us," as Easton observed, would provoke violence rather than peace. Warriors, from where they could not be sure, had lately burned "many farm houses about Providence," wounding three Englishmen, and the Providence men had "killed five or six" Indians. Williams had consented to "accompany" Hutchinson from "Swansea to Nahiggonck," but he seemed unsurprised that the sachems and commissioners could not "agree upon a meeting." He feared that if they did, there would be "blows and bloodshed and the fire [would be] kindled."[43]

Hutchinson staged a council anyway, compelling four "unimportant and obscure" men "to sign a one sided treaty" as "Attornies" for the sachems Canonicus, Ninigret, Canonchet, Pomham, and "the old Queen" Quaiapin, although these men "had no such power of attorney." Job Nesuton signed as a witness, his fellow scholar Joseph Dudley, a classmate of Joel and Caleb's and the former governor's son, standing nearby. Job was accustomed to the work of translation, finding precisely the right word in his language to communicate a Hebrew concept or Latin phrase. Here, at Pettaquamscut, the precision mattered less than the force. The words had to carry a message that would strike hard and travel far.[44]

Job was one of the few Native men present who could read the "treaty," which required the sachems to "deliver" to the English "all and every of Philip's subjects, whatsoever" who "shall come or be found" in "their lands," and to raise parties to enter Metacom's "lands or any other lands of the English to kill and destroy the said Enemy." This "promise" gave Josiah Winslow, reading the document in Marshfield, false hope that the Narragansetts would send warriors to capture Metacom, a goal his men had proved unable to accomplish. The "treaty" also required the sachems to "search out and deliver all stolen goods" taken by any Narragansetts "from the English," and a pledge to "forever" cease to pilfer or kill settlers' cattle. Finally, Hutchinson slipped in a formal renewal of his claims to Narragansett land, including Pettaquamscut, and in generosity, included confirmation of all grants to "the English" in Narragansett country. It lay upon the "attorneys" to convey these messages to the sachems. Although Hutchinson did not acknowledge it, the only authority these Narragansett men might have had was the ability to carry the Massachusetts men's words back to their communities.[45]

One message was designed to travel throughout Narragansett country. The commissioners pledged that any Narragansett person who brought Metacom to them would receive "forty trucking cloth coats," and also offered rewards for Metacom's head and the capture of his "subjects." If the Massachusetts commissioners could not compel the Narragansetts as a whole to pledge cooperation, they would offer bounties to individuals, who might join the English or pursue an independent campaign. If even a handful of Narragansett warriors could be coerced to send out parties to the surrounding swamps in search of Metacom and his men, the colonial officers might have the most difficult part of their work done for them.[46]

The document may have carried little weight with the Narragansett sachems, who had not themselves agreed to its articles. But that would not stop colonial leaders from using it as a tool for enforcement, as families from Wampanoag country made their way to Narragansett, or as Narragansett men went out on their own, seeking bounty against old enemies. The "treaty" served as a message from the United Colonies about their expectations, their willingness to compensate "fidelity," and their resolve to punish aggression. And it created a layer of comfort for those, like Winslow, who saw a war spinning beyond their control, making them believe that the war's spread had been contained, and that they could anticipate assistance from the largest neighboring populace of Native people. As Winslow imagined, "the Narragansetts" would soon "enter in their business against Phillip" and surely they, or the Massachusett Indians who "are our friends" would "very probably . . . force him to an engagement, or impound him on a narrow neck of land or on sum of ye Islands, from whence he cannot easily make his escape."[47]

SAKONNET, JULY 14

As families built shelters at Pocasset, and word of the commissioners' arrival spread through Narragansett, Awashonks and her son Peter made plans to paddle across the river with their family. As Peter later testified, "When the English army went out, we were afraid, and desired to go over to Rhode Island." They tried to traverse the Sakonnet River by canoe, "but the young men there kept such a strict watch that we could not get over in safety." Easton also reported that Awashonks "practiced much" that "the Quarell be decided without War, but some of our English also, in fury against all Indians, would not consent she should be reserved to our Island, although I preferred to be at all the charge to secure her and those she desired to come with her." Finally, he "prevailed" that "we might send for her," but "then our men had ceased some canoes on her side, supposing they were Philip's." Their passage prevented, Peter Awashonks testified, "Then we were forced to hide ourselves in swamps, and the English army came and burnt our houses." He acknowledged that "an English house there" was also burned, but reported that this house had already been abandoned.[48]

For Awashonks and Peter, the first events of war were not the looting and burning of houses at Swansea, but the arrival of the English army at Sakonnet. They experienced the destruction of their canoes, the blocking of paths to possible safety, the drawing off of their men to both sides of the burgeoning conflict. They witnessed the abandonment of English houses near Pocasset and the burning of at least one house by a Wampanoag relation. Having finally decided to retreat into the swamps for protection, they faced pursuit by William Bradford Jr., Church, and their troops. As Bradford reported, the Sakonnet families "outran" them, but as they escaped, the soldiers "burned" their "habitations," then "dispa[t]c[h]ed" the "two old men" who remained. Following these acts of violence, Awashonks and Peter made their way across the bay, "wee understanding," Peter later testified, the Narragansetts "were friends to the English, wee went to them."[49]

Wampanaog people, like human beings across the world, reacted in multiple divergent ways as war arrived in their homeland. Narratives written about war tend to create false binaries, as if every person faces a clear-cut decision between two sides. Such narratives obscure the multifaceted responses and strategies of individuals and families who have often sought simply to protect themselves and their kin in the present moment. A Sakonnet man named George later reported, "At the first breaking forth of the war, divers of them sat still and minded their work at home, but some of their Indians did then go to Philip, and fight with him against the English." Thus, some Sakonnet people sought safe haven with Awashonks and Peter in Rhode Island and Narragansett. Others went about the daily work of subsistence and caring for their families, hoping the storm would pass. Many hid in the swamps just to avoid English militia. Yet some did join Succanowassucke, "the first man" at Saconnett "that stirred up" their relations "to joyne with Philip to fight against the English." Still others, with Mammanuah, gave "service" to the army, along with Alderman, a Pocasset man who sought refuge with his family on Rhode Island, perhaps secured by the intelligence he gave to Church, when he confirmed that Metacom was "on Pocaset side."[50]

POCASSET, JULY 16

Deep within the swamps of Pocasset, far off the main path, nearly one hundred *wetus* had been built on some "four acres of ground" among the cedars, "standing thick together," with all the resources the families needed. Fish ran through the streams that fed in and out of the swamps, tender plants grew along the banks, and deer, rabbit, beaver, and muskrat abounded. They still had corn meal from last year's harvest, which sustained protectors as they moved through Wampanoag territory in small, elusive parties. While some men, women, and children gathered food, others scouted and guarded the edges of the forested swamp, the access trails and crossroads. They would hear the soldiers long before they arrived. They had remained undisturbed for days with ample time to plan and prepare, the swamp their fortification.[51]

Thus, on July 16, their scouts must have seen Church, Cudworth, and Bradford when they docked a sloop at Quequechand, returning to Pocasset with an army. Among the troops were at least two of their own relations, including

Thomas Hunter of Nemasket (and perhaps Alderman or Mammanuah as "pilot"). As more than one hundred men marched through Pocasset, they espied "two Indians," and after shooting one dead, they compelled the second to reveal information to better guide them, with Hunter as a forceful interpreter. As Cudworth later reported, "Before we killed him, he declared by pointing, whereabout the squaw sachem was, and whereabout Philip was." And "so," moving toward the swamp, they "marched to find out the squaw sachem," seeking Weetamoo first.[52]

There were few possible trails from the west, through which Hunter or the "pilot" could lead the Army. With awareness of the troops' movements, the protectors had ample time to position themselves strategically, behind trees, within bushes, nestled between boulders. Their chests and arms blended into green and they smelled of the marsh that surrounded them, their minds stilled to make them part of the place. They could wait as long as was needed. It was what they trained, since childhood, to do.[53]

As Bradford, Church, and their men made their way into the marsh, their prey finally within reach, "the thick cedar swamp" came alive around them. The call of a hawk, somewhere nearby. From the bushes and trees, movement, then a sudden, reverberating hail of small pistol balls and swan shot bursting from every direction, including the ground. As some men stumbled backward in instinctive retreat, shot exploded on the path through which they had entered. On the trail, they had unwittingly passed protectors who never made a sound. Having moved into the swamp, the army was caught in its grasp. They pushed on, their pilot leading, with nowhere to go but forward. Those who moved to the sides found their limbs caught in brambles and thorns, their feet sucked into spongy mud. Their leather armor offered little protection, and worse, it slowed them down. They shot madly at the bushes in volleys, as they had been trained, but they had no clue if their shots struck anything at all. They struggled to reload as they moved. Although the day was clear, they could discern few human shapes in the dark, shady swamp. It seemed the trees themselves had become their enemies.[54]

While the protectors held off one hundred English men, Weetamoo led the mothers and their children out of the encampment, deeper into the swamp, the women striving to quiet their children as they moved. They stepped over familiar rocks and hummocks, crossing streams, navigating the thickest part of the swamp. They mashed their lips, holding back cries, when the greenbrier or raspberry brambles pricked their skin. They carried babies on their backs, children on their hips, and baskets of food and supplies. They concealed themselves in rock crevices and caves, hollowed out logs and trees, deep thickets where deer and rabbits eluded even the most skillful hunters.[55]

When the troops finally pushed through to the encampment, Weetamoo "and [the] children [had] fled." They found a village of empty *wetus*, several of which they "fired." Even that proved a useless task as they had been "newly made of green barks." Instead of taking captives, the soldiers took "diverse pots and kettles" that the women had left behind, proof they had found the targeted place, if not the person. Now, their choice was to enter the maze of the swamp, where countless ambushes waited, or retreat in reverse. They chose the latter, planning a return to Weetamoo's "headquarters" with more men and ammunition. Yet, as they moved out of the swamp and back toward their sloop, the protectors pursued them. Although Bradford later claimed the troops had "beat them out of their place," it was just as likely the Wampanoag protectors "beat" the troops back to the sloop, which ferried them back to the "fort" at Montaup.[56]

Even as the Wampanoag force continued to fire upon the soldiers, their goal, it seems, was not to take lives, but to repel the colonial troops and send a message to their leaders. According to officers' reports, despite all the fire, the troops lost only two men, with four others wounded, one "lost by accidental providence by one of our own people." Patrick Malone has emphasized the marksmanship of Native hunters; however, historian Kevin Sweeney argues that during an ambush, Native men utilized their "knowledge of the terrain and skills developed hunting with traditional weapons and firearms to close the distance to their targets and compensate for the inaccuracy of the period's firearms." In this instance, they most likely "unleash[ed] a volley" of shot "at close range," but with the intention to "wound and disorient, rather than kill." As Malone and others have recognized, in traditional Native warfare, "relatively few participants were killed." Elders and clan mothers instilled respect for life in all its forms, while warriors and hunters were trained to practice restraint. At the same time, communities had been pushed to the breaking point. Wampanoag people's demonstration of strategic agile force, their adaptability and use of the environment, made clear their formidable capacity to circumvent colonial plans for their containment. They reasserted their primacy in this place, their responsibility for all its many inhabitants, and their determination to remain.[57]

MARSHFIELD, PLYMOUTH COLONY, JULY 18

A week had passed since Josiah Winslow had heard news from any of his men. He sent orders, but had not a clue what had happened in the field. He had heard word of a skirmish at Pocasset from Leverett, but Cudworth had not managed to send a report. Winslow had believed they would easily corner and capture Metacom. He had envisioned his troops descending on Montaup, filling the town with volleys, and taking the insolent man down. But now all he had was a useless fort, which he directed his officers to abandon, and men ranging the woods, searching for an elusive enemy. He gave Cudworth instructions to release the majority of the men, who should return to their homes. The fields needed planting, and with unexpected fires breaking out at Taunton, Dartmouth, and Middleboro, the men's homes required defending. He knew the people at Dartmouth had "suffered very much"; word had arrived that the "whole plantation" except the garrison houses had been "burnt and six or eight of the people killed besides several wounded." On the same day, his fellow magistrate John Freeman wrote from Taunton, where the troops had gathered, saying, "the town of Taunton seemeth to be greatly destroyed." He reported that "Mosley and Hinksman [Henchman] with there companies are with ours," waiting at Taunton, and they planned to "meet with them at the fall river on Monday morning," the following day. Writing to Leverett on Sunday, Winslow observed, "It is supposed that phillip and the strongest party of his men are about Pocasset or Sacconet near Dartmouth." His plans to capture Metacom foiled, Winslow was much disturbed by news that "The Pocasset squaw seems to have been deeply ingaged with and for him, and William Tuspaquin," which meant the three hundred men reportedly under her command were likely engaged, as well. Those vines of kinship had proven stronger than Winslow could have imagined. He wrote to Cudworth that the captain should retain one hundred of his "best men," to join with the Massachusetts forces and "our Indian allies" in "small parties," which should "range downwards through the country from Swansea and Pocasset towards our Eastern bounds" in search of signs "of the enemy." Winslow's letter would not reach Cudworth until after Weetamoo and Metacom had escaped his forces once more.[58]

POCASSET, JULY 19

Weetamoo's "camp" had dispersed, and the families trekked north in small parties. A huge army was on the move, taking the wide trail from Cohannet and heading south through Assonet. By now the scouts must have seen the English patrols about Assonet Neck, which discovered nothing, and the small boat patrolling the great river for signs of their passage. Among the army, Weetamoo's scouts would have reported, there were "50 Indians from the Massachusett," and Felix, Sassamon's son-in-law from Nemasket, was among them.[59]

Weetamoo would have sent word to the families to stay off the main road, to stick to the minor trails in the cedar swamps and hunting grounds. She would have warned them to watch for those Massachusett scouts, who could discern their movements more easily than the marching troops. She would meet them up north, at places they knew well. Warriors remained to redirect and draw in the English soldiers. Weetamoo would not leave until that morning, after she was certain all the families were on the move. An elder volunteered to stay behind. He was an old man, he must have persuaded her, who would not make it anyway. If he stayed, he could divert them, a kinsman's last honor.[60]

James Quananopohit and Job Nesuton marched with the combined forces as they made the long trek toward Pocasset. The commanders aimed to return to Weetamoo's "headquarters," a place Cudworth and Bradford had described as a "hideous dismal swamp." Joined "together" with the Massachusetts troops returned from Narragansett, the Plymouth men were determined to "discover Philip." They had been in the field for nearly a month and had yet to catch a glimpse of their target.[61]

Dusk descended as they approached the trail that led toward the swamp. They had traveled the whole day, eighteen miles from Taunton, and Job Nesuton could feel the ache in his old bones. He was not prepared for a fight. Job stole a look back at the river as it merged with the sky, turning the color of fading flames and swollen, too-ripe berries, making him recall his childhood home in Massachusett, the family he long ago lost. Following the other Massachusett men, he trudged forward as the sky darkened under the canopy of cedar. The officers, with their sons, traveled with relative ease along the path; they made the scouts and privateers go before them, spreading out in flanks into the woods. It was a foolish way to navigate the swamp. Their boots betrayed their every step, leather and cloth heavy on their sweaty bodies, the smell of fear and soil giving them away long before they were seen. Even a small child would catch their scent. Grunts and an occasional high-pitched scream, as legs and arms got snared, announced their presence. They glanced around at every birdcall, every rustle in the brush, surrounded by animals and plants they knew vaguely, people of whom they were terrified, and nameless other demons that, in their minds, waited behind every bush. That was how the shots came, not from the hands of men in their sight, but from behind the shadowy trees.[62]

Later, they conveyed in their letters and stories that Wampanoag warriors "encased themselves in green boughs," but while they were in the swamp, they believed the great trees and bushes had come to life with the gradual setting of the sun. Thorny tendrils of greenbrier grabbed at their ankles, disabling their knees, pulling them to the ground. Grapevines looped around their necks, halting their movement. As they lumbered on, their eyes "muffled with leaves," their heads became "pinioned" in the "thick boughs of the trees." They tripped over roots that "shackled" their feet. Branches seemed to move toward them. Raspberry brambles grabbed at their arms, piercing through fiber and breaking skin. Ensnared in a net of shadowy green, they could not discern shapes even a few feet before them. And, just as the animated swamp had them in her grasp, a shot sailed through the air from behind a tree and hit one of the privateers in the chest. He howled, staggering forward, ready for a fight, but no one appeared. A second shot flew from the trees in the opposite direction, hitting another, as the first fell to the ground. The men started shooting at the bushes, and another fell, by the hand of one of his own, then a young warrior fell to the ground. The younger soldiers ducked, screaming as the thorns scraped their faces. But they found themselves hugging the ground, terrified the plants were demons that would pull them into the bowels of the earth, even as they avoided shot sailing from the trees. They waited, listening to the deafening sound of crickets as they resumed their evening song.[63]

A man, whom Job recognized, materialized from the surrounding darkness to drag in the struggling young warrior who lay on the ground. He had been a scholar at Cambridge; he had gone home, used his skills to serve his own people, and had become a "Councellor." Job watched as James Quananopohit, hidden behind a large oak, steadied his flintlock against the trunk of the tree, and aimed directly for the counselor's heart.[64]

Job leaned against a tree to quiet his rumbling heart. He feared the thunderous noise made him an obvious target; he could smell fear pouring in rivulets from his tired old hide. This was not the role for which he had been trained. The long days he had spent doing translations in a dark English room had numbed his senses. He was not made for mucking through a swamp with a bunch of fools. All the labor, the pages he had deciphered so carefully had seemed so important at Cambridge. But here in the swamp, he could make no sense of it all. Some of his own relations said that Jehovah was not with the English, who had imagined that God would rush to their side and overpower the heathen. But the thunder and rain from the sky had only covered the Wampanaoags' tracks, allowing their escape, as the Massachusetts men lay a sleepless night on an open plain, unable to build their own shelter. Job could feel many forces around them as they lay quiet in the swamp, but none so powerful as fear. A shot rang out, from just behind, sailing past to hit one of Mosely's men, pressed to a tree. Job stole a glance behind but saw only shadows and hints of rapid movement. The forest opened in a cacophony of shot, most of it coming from English men's guns. Their flanks had been disrupted; in the shadowy forest they could not discern each other's positions, and they fired at an "enemy" they could not see. A stinging pain seared his side, clenching, as darkness enveloped him, his body crumpling against the tree. His last thoughts were of forgiveness. He was not sure for whom, or to whom, he was petitioning, but his prayerful words went out on the last wind of his breath.[65]

The protectors "retired deeper into the swamp," drawing the English forces in. When the troops finally made it through the barrage of fire, to their desired destination of Weetamoo's camp, they encountered a familiar sight: abandoned *wetus* and no sign of Metacom. They found only "one old man" in a *wetu*, "who told us that Philipe & the squa sachem" had both been "there with their men." He said that "Wittoma" had been here "that day," and "that Philip had been there the day before" but that "all women and children" had fled. Most likely, the elder told them what they thought they wanted to know, giving them hope that "Philip's place of residence was about half a mile off," directing them deeper into the darkening woods. They may have imagined they had pushed through a wall of warriors to make it to Weetamoo and Metacom's camps. But, as they moved forward, chaos descended. The "swamp was so boggy and full of bushes," their anxiety so intense, that if they saw "a bush stir," they would "presently" shoot, and every man was in danger of being hit by fire from his own men. As Mather later related, "It could not there be discerned who were English, and who the Indians." Not long in, Cudworth called a retreat, as "it was judged to proceed further therein would be but to throw away men's lives." The old man had led them on a wild goose chase. As the army "withdrew," carrying their "dead and wounded men" through the darkness, as Church later observed, "Philip and his gang had the very fortune to escape as Weetamoo and hers had."[66]

As Metacom and Weetamoo pursued a strategy of tactical withdrawal, heading north through Pocasset hunting territory and the network of cedar swamps, the English commanders made a decision. Rather than going back into the swamp, where they imagined Metacom and his warriors lay in wait, Cudworth thought it "best . . . to maintain" their "garrison at Mount Hope" with a small party of men, and to build "a garrison at Pocasset." Here, they argued, they might be able to "keep the enemy from their corn," and "starve them out of the Swamp." This logic would soon prove faulty, demonstrating their lack of knowledge of the swamp's bountiful resources, the many routes out, and the subsistence and navigational knowledge of the people they pursued. They understood, however, that their current strategy had failed. Cudworth wrote to Winslow, "We shall never be able to obtain our end in this way, for they fly before us, from one swamp to another," and "pick off our men." Rather than returning to Pocasset, he advised they "have a flying army, to be in motion" to defend the settlements, "to keep the Indians from destroying our cattle, and fetching in supply of food." While imagining a strategy of starving the Indians out, the army was so sorely in need of provisions that unless they pursued a different course, there was "no possibility for men to hold out." The flying army would protect the men as they tended the fields, the harvest vital to sustain the military campaign.[67]

Already discouraged, Cudworth soon received the devastating news that Wampanoag forces had once more raided Dartmouth, and many of the soldiers, including Church's, were diverted to Apponagansett. Likewise, the Massachusetts officers had sent three companies back to Boston, and one north to Mendon, raided by the Nipmucs on July 14. The Dartmouth strike once more divided English forces, preventing pursuit through Pocasset. Cudworth's "flying army" moved to defend the southeastern settlement while Weetamoo, Metacom, and Tuspaquin led the Wampanoag families from immediate danger, heading north to Assonet. Eluding scouting parties and the boat patrol, they crossed the great river, landing on the north side of Weetamoo's childhood town. Still undetected, "a considerable party" stopped for a rest on their old planting and fishing grounds, built some "forty" cooking fires "hard by the side of the river," then traveled on in dispersed groups, "beating 14 or 15 trails into the woods" at Mattapoisett.[68]

Henchman had men building a garrison at Pocasset, while Cudworth had left Nathaniel Thomas in command of the fort at "Mount Hope," a largely fruitless charge. Thomas, a Sakonnet claimant, anxious for an opportunity to pursue, soon brought news to Henchman, which he had gathered at Rehoboth: Metacom and Weetamoo, with their warriors and families, had escaped across the Taunton River. Meanwhile, about July 26, Uncas's son Owaneco arrived in Boston with "40 or more" Mohegans, prepared to assist the Massachusetts troops alongside their Connecticut allies. Three "praying Indians" from Natick would also serve as "guides." Together they traveled from Boston to Rehoboth, prepared to track Metacom and Weetamoo through Sowams.[69]

SOWAMS AND NIPSACHUCK, JULY 30–AUGUST 1

The Wampanoags and their allies passed through familiar territory north of Rehoboth without detection, and, crossing over the Patucket River, drew on their kinship ties to set up two temporary camps at Quaiapin's town of Nipsachuck. Although the "considerable party," composed mainly of "many women and children" had maintained great strength and persistence, eluding English troops for days, they were weary and "afrighted," in deep need of respite and rest.[70]

Stationed at Rehoboth and moving about in small scouting parties, the Mohegan and Natick scouts picked up a track crossing Seekonk plain, and followed "a very obvious path" to the Patucket River, and beyond "the wading place," to the west bank, where the troops captured "an Indian" who had been with Metacom and Weetamoo. He confirmed their movements, and disclosed that though they had not lost a man in the Pocasset swamp (on July 19) or in their escape, they were "disheartened" and running out of powder. Rehoboth minister Noah Newman, sending his report to Thomas, hoped to "apprehend them before they swamp themselves and while their weariness is still upon them." But by the time Thomas arrived, reconnoitering with over a hundred English men from Providence, Connecticut, Massachusetts, and Plymouth, as well as the fifty men from Mohegan, Weetamoo and Metacom had already led the families to refuge, and "swamped" themselves deep within the woods.[71]

The Mohegans and Natick men tracked the Wampanoags to Nipsachuck and Thomas, moving the troops close under cover of night, made plans "to surprise the enemy" at "the dawning of the day" near a planting field. They marched before sunrise, "while it was" still "dark," and stopped "to consult" regarding the formation they should take "to surprise the enemy without danger to one another," when they saw "5 Indians from Weetamoo's camp," who, they "supposed," had come "to fetch beans from the . . . field." However, it is also possible that the troops were also being tracked by Weetamoo's scouts, the five in the field decoys designed to draw them toward Metacom's men who were placed on a hill nearby. According to Thomas's report, the English shot two, but "the others fled, whereby Wittamas and Philip's Camp were alarmed. Wittama's camp then being within about an 100 rod of us, whom we had undoubtedly surprised, while they were most of them asleep and secure, had it not been for the said alarm; who immediately fled and despersed, who we pursued, slew some of them, but while we were in pursuit of them, Philip's fighting men showed themselves upon a hill unto us, who were retreated from their camp near half a mile to fight us. Philip's camp was pitched about 3 quarters of a mile beyond Witamas."[72]

The English troops killed a significant number of Wampanoags at Nipsachuck, including Woonashum, one of Metacom's counselors, and at least four of his "captains." This loss may have represented a significant achievement to the English, but their primary goal continued to elude them. Even with Mohegan assistance, the troops failed to capture the sachems or even to block Wampanoag travel. Soon, Weetamoo, Wootonakanuske, Metacom, and the

Tuspaquins once more led the families north, traveling further along the networks of kinship to cultivate the ties of alliance. Weetamoo traveled with Metacom on their way northwest, avoiding the open water and Rhode Island settlements which would have given away her plans and exposed her to attack, then turned abruptly south, heading for Narragansett country with her company. Metacom proceeded northwest toward Nipmuc territory, where protectors had already begun striking English settlements. Soon the Nipmuc sachems would send a message, offering to "conduct him up to Squabaug [Quaboag]" where they would shelter his families and "protect him."[73]

Word spread quickly through kinship networks after the attacks on Montaup, Pocasset, and Nipsachuck. Although historians have named this conflict "King Philip's War," it is better described as a multitribal Indigenous resistance movement during colonial expansion, a complex series of alliances forged by multiple leaders, including Metacom and Weetamoo, to reclaim land and rebalance relations in a shared Algonquian homeland. As Saltonstall reported, "after King Philip had secured his Interest in Squaw Sachem . . . he privately sent Messengers to most of the Indian Sagamores and Sachems about him, telling them that the English had a design to cut off all the Indians round about them, and that if they did not Joyn together, they should lose their Lives and Lands."[74]

5

THE PRINTER'S REVOLT: A NARRATIVE OF THE CAPTIVITY OF JAMES THE PRINTER

One month after Weetamoo and Metacom fled from Nipsachuck, James Printer was drawn toward Cambridge. Commencement had just concluded, the Yard was filled with scholars, the air thick with the robust smell of harvest. As James passed through the town, he must have seen the familiar red brick of the Indian College, although it was not his destination. James was yoked by the neck to fourteen other men, accused of murdering settlers at Lancaster, neighbors of Mary Rowlandson. Towing the roped converts was Samuel Mosely, who, while failing to capture Metacom, had easily apprehended these "friend" Indians. Despite their pleas, Mosely led James and his relations neither to the college nor to Eliot's house in Roxbury; instead he hauled them directly to the jail.[1]

CULTIVATING A COVENANT, HASSANAMESIT, JUNE 1675, AND BOSTON, MAY 1668

That spring, James and his brother Job had been living in the Nipmuc country, traveling back and forth from their town of Hassanamesit to neighboring villages, where they served as teachers to their kin. They also moved freely between their towns and the settlements in Boston and Cambridge, following familiar roads and rivers. While James had been in residence at the preparatory school and the press, Hassanamesit had emerged as an active mission community, or "praying town," the second established inland, with his family as leaders in its conversion. As Daniel Gookin observed during a tour of the Nipmuc country in 1674, Hassanamesit had "not above 12 families . . . but is capable to receive some hundreds," predicting its emergence as a central gathering place for Christian

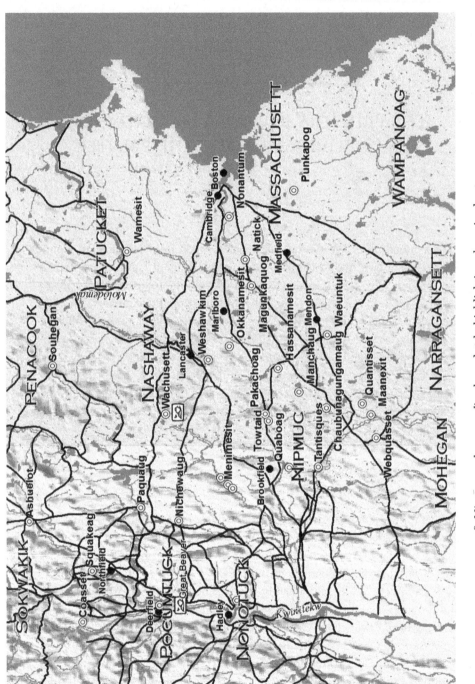

8. Nipm̄uc and surrounding homelands, highlighting places in chapter 5

Indians. Hassanamesit was a particularly fertile "village," with some "eight thousand acres" of "rich land," and "plenty of meadow, being well tempered & watered." Its fields yielded "plenty of corn," and, adapting English agriculture, the people planted "grain" and harvested "fruit" from orchards. Gookin observed that Hassanamesit was also "an apt place for keeping cattle & swine; in which respect this people are the best stored of any Indian town of their size."[2]

James's "father, mother, brothers, and their wives," Gookin noted, were "the principal studs of the town"—the foundation and framework of its leadership. Naoas served as "deacon," and James's elder brother, Annaweekin, as a primary leader or "ruler," alongside their kinsman, Tom Wuttasacomponom. James and his brothers had married converts and were busy cultivating the next generation. Annaweekin's son, Joseph, already ten years old, would have attended school at the house of his uncle, Joseph Tukuppawillin, the town's teacher. While living primarily at Hassanamesit, James taught and "preach[ed]" at the newly established school in Waeuntuk, ten miles downriver. Job, described by Gookin as "a person well accepted for piety and ability among them," served as a teacher at Okkanamesit, a town northwest of Hassanamesit, and as both teacher and "preacher" at Magunkaquog, the "place of great trees," located "midway between" Hassanamesit and Natick.[3]

Acting as a leader and interpreter, Job was one of ten "native Indian sagamores" from the "peoples of Nipmuc" who signed an agreement with Massachusetts Colony in the spring of 1668. According to the document, "the inhabitants of Quanutusset [Quantisset], Mônuhchogok [Magunkaquog], Chaubunakongkomuk [Chaubunagungamaug], Asukodnôcog, kesepusqus, wabuhqushish [Webquasset] and the adjacent parts of Nipmuk" pledged to "give up ourselves to God" and to English laws. Furthermore, "We finding by experience how good it is to live under laws & good government," and recognizing "how much we need the protection of the English[;] We doe freely out of our own motion and voluntary choyce do submit our selves to the government of the Massachusets." This covenant may have been crafted during a spring gathering, but it was executed in Boston, "before God & this Court." Tom Wuttasacomponom was the primary signer, but below his mark was Job Kattenanit's signature, demonstrating the scholar's literacy as well as his role as a mediator in this court.[4]

Although historians have commonly interpreted this document as the "submission" of the Nipmucs as a nation, the signers represented the "freshwater" people whose towns were "within the bounds of the [royal] patents of Massachusetts" and "adjoining the English seats of Mendon and Marlborough," not all of the Nipmuc communities.[5] The agreement named towns that lay on the frequently traveled path from Massachusetts to Connecticut.[6] There remained several places beyond the settlements, not contained by this covenant, including the central gathering place of Pakachoag and the substantial inland regions of Nashaway and Quaboag. The agreement solidified a relationship previously accepted by those Nipmuc families who formed mission communities under Christian rule. They could give their consent to colonial governance, but could not give consent for others. This distinction is crucial if we are to understand the coming of the war into the Nipmuc country, including the expansion of Massachusetts's jurisdiction *through* the mission communities, and the precarious political position of Native converts on the eve of war.

Nipmuc communities maintained multiple political affiliations, kinship ties, and alliances that bound particular families to communities on the coast and to inland rivers like Kwinitekw. Likewise, each town cultivated and maintained distinct relationships to neighboring sachems, which were challenged by the imposition of colonial rule. Both coastal sachems and Massachusetts missionaries and magistrates offered "protection" to vulnerable inland towns, a "need" highlighted by the 1668 covenant.

As Dennis Connole has observed, this agreement arose during a legal case through which the Nipmucs of Quantisset sought intervention from missionaries and magistrates against Quaiapin, after she sent warriors to reassert jurisdiction over them in "love" and kinship, seeking to renew a longstanding commitment and demand the acknowledgement which "belonged" to her within a framework of reciprocal relations. Likewise, the Mohegan sachem Uncas continued to assert jurisdiction and safeguard those towns, like Webquasset, with which *he* had agreements of affiliation, in opposition to Massachusetts missionaries. The 1668 "covenant" did not necessarily supersede local alliances, but created conflict and competition in overlapping spaces. Moreover, although English magistrates sought "subjection," instated at the moment of signing, as perpetual, this notion was foreign to Indigenous logics. In Algonquian languages, alliance is an activity, a state of being that can adapt and change. Relationships of belonging, protection, and acknowledgement required renewal, sometimes enforcement, but always negotiation.[7]

At this particular time, the greatest "need" for "protection" arose from the west. The covenant was made while the Nipmuc country and Kwinitekw Valley were besieged by Mohawk warriors, who may have been enforcing the protection and jurisdiction of their own Great Law. In response, Nipmuc people cultivated an alliance with their new, militarily powerful neighbor, who filled a gap in regional relations: the colony of Massachusetts Bay had begun to occupy, geographically and diplomatically, the place of the Indigenous people of Massachusett, who had been ravaged by epidemics and contained or dispersed by colonial rule. To the mission communities in particular, the Massachusetts men offered a spiritual, geographic, and military buffer against outside threats (whether Mohawk and Mohegan raids, Satan's temptations, or disease) in exchange for political allegiance, religious obedience, and ultimately, access to land.[8]

Indeed, as Uncas had discerned, the Massachusetts court that mediated this agreement and related legal cases included a number of land speculators, who held great political sway in the colony. In 1668 this group included the trader John Pynchon, involved in countless land transactions in the Connecticut River Valley; Simon Bradstreet, an Atherton proprietor; and Boston magistrate Edward Tyng and trader Simon Willard, whose monopoly was solidified by the marriage of their children in 1673, extending from Nashaway and Penacook to Casco Bay. Indeed the rapid acquisition of vast tracts of land by the Willards and Tyngs, including a two-hundred-square-mile plantation on Molôdemak, was "probably an immediate cause of King Philip's War." Military officers in the war, including Caleb's classmate Joseph Dudley, who married Tyng's daughter, and Daniel Henchman, benefitted directly from these acquisitions. Although they demanded no "tribute," these Massachusetts men had strong motivations for "extending" their jurisdictional power inland, increasing access to valuable land. For them, the mission communities also created a buffer between the settlements they sought to improve and the unknown territories to the north and west, protected by Wabanaki and Mohawk warriors.[9]

"n'ahteuk": bounding the land

Thus, even as Nipmuc converts sought English protection, they faced English encroachment. Indeed, some Native people were motivated in part to establish mission communities to ensure that their neighbors would recognize their rights and bounds. "For many," Kristina Bross writes, "the decision to pray [in an English manner] was reached when they realized that the only way to avoid giving up their lands was to convert to Christianity." As John Speen, a leader of the first "praying town" of Natick, declared in his conversion narrative, "I saw the English took much ground, and I thought if I prayed, the English would not take away my ground." Although Eliot is often credited with Natick's "founding," as both Pam Ellis and Jean O'Brien have observed, this leader, who carried the title Qualalanset, and his family were fundamental to its creation. When Eliot sought to move his mission from Nonantum to the falls, he needed consent and cooperation from local leaders. Thus, in making a covenant with Eliot and Massachusetts, Natick's boundaries were recorded in English law, while the Speens retained their leadership role, becoming "rulers" of the re-structured town.[10]

The name of the town sheds light on this adaptation to colonial property law. As O'Brien notes, "N'ahteuk" means "my land," a deceptively simple phrase, which is more complex when viewed through the lens of Algonquian languages. This translation, also meaning "my field," corresponds to the related Abenaki term *ndaki*, which denotes bounded (individual) property—but also to *ndakinna*, "our [exclusive] land," the greater, collectively held homeland. It is significant that the inhabitants of "N'ahteuk" used the exclusive term, and not the inclusive term, *kdakinna*, which would suggest that this place was "our [inclusive] land," shared with many others, perhaps even including the English settlers. When the people of the falls renamed their town, they emphasized delineated bounds that would be registered in an English legal system. "N'ahteuk" translated colonial law into Indigenous language, requiring respect from both groups for the exclusive Nipmuc rights to this "field" where families planted, while retaining in language their relationship of belonging and responsibility to, as well as reliance upon, their land.[11]

However, the transformation to N'ahteuk also signaled a change in relationships. In the mission communities, families were exhorted by ministers and required by colonial law to adopt colonial social and political practices, enforced by "teachers" and "rulers" like James Printer and his kin, including the division of planting grounds into smaller, fenced fields, and the reversal of gender roles. Ministers encouraged men to plow and plant, and attempted to "banish" women "from the fields" and restrict them to "domestic" duties such as spinning. When Joseph Tukuppawillin later grieved the loss of "my corn" and "cattle, my plough" and "cart," he referred to the instruments *he* used in plowing *his* field. These attempts to transform land and gender roles also affected saunkskwas like Quaiapin and Weetamoo. When Quaiapin sought to "reclaim" Quantisset's acknowledgement, her men took swine and corn that were likely tended by male converts, who were encouraged not to acknowledge female planters. While Eliot praised the male "rulers" as sober leaders, he characterized Quaiapin as a "wicked woman," who, "having buried her husband and son, is now in some power," undermining the legitimacy of her authority. He asserted that Quaiapin "picked a quarrel with the Nipmuc Indians," like a temperamental sister in need of restraint, and "robbed" their property. During that same year, one of Eliot's converts had escaped the confines of a praying town, leaving her ruler husband and eluding a "whipping" for adultery, to seek refuge at Montaup. Thus it was not only saunkskwas who resisted missionary rule, but their male relations, including Metacom, Ninigret, and Uncas, all of whom maintained affiliations with people of the mission communities.[12]

As O'Brien has succinctly summarized the English goals for towns like Natick, Quantisset, and Hassanamesit, "The ideology of conversion John Eliot developed involved fixing Indian candidates for conversion in geographically bounded places called 'Praying Towns' where English ideas about land use and ownership would prevail, gender roles would be transformed, and English institutions would instruct Indians about their place in the social order."[13] Thus, as Qualalanset and his kin sought to bound their lands to protect Native space, missionaries and magistrates sought to contain Native peoples within colonial space—polities within circumscribed towns, women within domestic homes, and "subjects" within a colonial legal system. Once contained, by covenant and deed, the missionaries and magistrates imagined subjection as permanent; yet Native people proved much more adaptive, retaining their language and their land in common, while moving within the colonial system and often outside it, resisting its bounds and negotiating multiple relationships of alliance.

"THEY WOULD NOT FIGHT AGAINST THEMSELVES," HASSANAMESIT, JUNE 1675

In the words of antiquarian Samuel Drake, "it was owing to the *amor patriae* of James-printer that he left his master and joined in Philip's war." Perhaps a love of "our land" did motivate James to join his relations in their resistance against colonization. However, the increasing containment of his and his family's freedom of movement within that beloved country likely provided the greatest impetus. This chapter develops the context of the beginning of war in the Nipmuc country, focusing not only on the Native resistance, rooted in responsibility toward and deep knowledge of places like Pakachoag, Quaboag, and Menimesit, but also on the colonial drive toward containment, charged by fear of unknown spaces and increased racialization of "Indians," which ultimately drove men like James into a conflict over which they had little control. Contrary to claims that he "ran off" from his apprenticeship at the press, James was already living in the Nipmuc country when violence erupted in the summer of 1675. Like many converts, James and his kin at first attempted to avoid any embroilment in the burgeoning war.[14]

On June 24, as Plymouth forces gathered at garrisons and Wampanoag men approached Swansea, James Printer was likely home at Hassanamesit, perhaps assisting his brother Joseph with his teaching, fishing on the river, or tending his field, when a messenger from Massachusetts rode into town. Ephraim Curtis, a man many Nipmucs regarded as a trusted interpreter and trader, had traveled from Sudbury, accompanied by two men from Natick. James and his family had already heard of mounting tension between the Wampanoags and Plymouth settlers to the south. When Curtis raised rumors that Metacom was stirring a coalition against the English, "Captain" Tom Wuttasacomponom assured him the men of Hassanamesit would "not assist Phillip." They "did not know," he said, "of any of their men that are gone" to Philip and moreover, they had little reason to join him. As Christians, they "accounted themselves as the English, and they would not fight against themselves."[15]

Wuttasacomponom offered a critical, complex description of the Hassanamesit peoples' relationship to the neighboring English. During a moment brimming with tension, he diplomatically conveyed that his relations considered themselves to be in the same political position as the settlers in the Bay, with no stronger bonds or loyalty to Metacom than that of Massachusetts. Indeed, he communicated, their close political and religious ties with Massachusetts made their English neighbors like kin, and they "would not fight against" themselves, their own. It is essential to understand that English constructions of race—particularly the distinction between groups of people based on skin color and other physical attributes (as well as geographic origins)—were only beginning to enter Native space. Nipmuc converts had little reason to "account" themselves loyal to Metacom on the basis of shared "race" or "ethnicity," or for that matter, out of a sense of *amor patriae*, or nationalistic patriotism.[16] Their responsibility was to honor the relationships of alliance made with neighboring nations, and in this case, their stronger loyalty was to the English of *Massachusett*, regardless of their "national" or "ethnic" origins. Men like James and Job had grown up alongside Massachusetts settlers and had maintained a "friendship" with them. Moreover, in forming their mission communities and accepting English "protection," they had not only pledged to honor the religious "sovereignty of God," but to acknowledge the political authority of Massachusetts Colony. Even as Nipmuc families maintained self-government within their town, Hassanamesit was tied to both the Massachusetts Colony, as a political and religious structure, and the Massachusett homeland that the settlers occupied. To diverge from that relationship would be to surrender the protection afforded the mission communities, as well as the commitments Hassanamesit leaders had made to live in peace with their English neighbors and each other. Leaders like Wuttasacomponom sincerely hoped that war would not come to their town. At this meeting, the people of Hassanamesit were not asked to pledge their assistance to the English should violence break out, but only to inform their neighbors if they heard word "of any hereafter" going to Metacom, which they promised to do. As Curtis left Hassanamesit with his Natick guides, the crisis averted, Wuttasacomponom and his kin must have expressed a deep breath of relief.[17]

Curtis continued to the other Nipmuc mission communities and to Quaboag, where he secured similar pledges, while the people of Hassanamesit returned to their daily work. They could not have known that even as they met with Curtis, violence had exploded to the south. The next time Curtis visited the Nipmuc country, in mid-July, everything had changed. While Hutchinson negotiated at Narragansett and Church scouted at Sakonnet, Nipmucs from Pakachoag, led by Matoonas, had reclaimed their territory at Quinsigamon, where Curtis's house had been ransacked. Even as Nipmuc protectors struck, their convert relations responded to Gookin's call for scouts; Hassanamesit men, including Job, were even then among the Massachusetts troops. The families from Hassanamesit took shelter at Okkanamesit, where Native converts had built a fort near the church at neighboring Marlborough, in a relationship of mutual protection. News and goods traveled rapidly through Native networks—when Curtis arrived at Okkanamesit, his friends openly showed him belongings Matoonas's men had taken from his house, reporting that the Pakachoag leader joined "in company with" Wampanoags. Even as they spoke, warriors ranged between the Nipmuc and Narragansett countries, from "Chabonkongamog and Quanteseck [Quantisset]" to "Mendum [Mendon] and Warwick," creating a sphere of surveillance for colonial companies. The Okkanamesit men cautioned Curtis that "it was very dangerous for [him] to go into the woods"; they advised against continuing his mission to discern the "motions of the Nipmug or Western Indians." If he traveled deeper inland, the guides warned, and came upon "the Nipmug Indians which were gathered together . . . they would be ready to shoot" him.[18]

Curtis's three Natick guides took this warning seriously, telling Curtis "they were not willing to go with" him further, without reinforcements. They would soon lose the protection of a Mohegan company, which had gone to Boston to "give assurance" of Uncas's "friendship and to offer his service against Philip." Responding to his "friends'" advice, Curtis recruited two settlers and another guide from Marlborough, and proceeded down the Connecticut Path towards Hassanamesit. At Webquasset, the Mohegan messengers gave thanks and headed "homewards," while Curtis's party headed northwest on the Nipmuc Path, moving deeper inland.[19]

ENTERING MENIMESIT, JULY–AUGUST 1675

The Massachusetts Council had become increasingly concerned about the "motions of the Nipmug Indians," particularly because these "Western Indians" eluded colonial surveillance. Their movements and intentions seemed increasingly inscrutable, and rumors of "gatherings" in the nearly inaccessible inland forests represented a frightening prospect for the English. Colonial leaders sought surveillance and containment of a "field" that was unsettlingly foreign to them, their pursuit circumscribed by their lack of knowledge. Still, scouting missions like Curtis's posed a real threat to Nipmuc people. Mission communities, in locations known and accessible, were particularly vulnerable to violence, as many settlers, abiding by a racial logic, believed "all Indians" would prove "false and perfidious."[20]

Yet Nipmuc people sought secure, private spaces not just to strategize assaults on the English, but to deliberate among themselves. Shortly after the outbreak of war, Nipmuc leaders began to form three towns in an area known as Menimesit, a protected "island place," northwest of Quaboag, far from the newest settlement. As Curtis described it, they had "newly begun to settle themselves up on Island containing about four acres of ground, being compassed round with a broad mirey swamp on the one side, and a muddy river with meadow on both sides of it on the other side, and but only one place that a horse could possibly pass, and there with a great deal of difficulty."[21]

Nipmuc people utilized their geographic knowledge in a time-honored strategy of protection: they relocated to an area within their homeland, which they knew well, but was unknown to their potential assailants. The land offered refuge *and* sustenance—plentiful fish, edible plants, berries near peak ripeness, and access to fields at Quaboag. For Curtis, the thick vegetation and heady wildflowers must have presented a nearly impenetrable fortress, daunting in its indecipherability.[22]

Thus Curtis himself relied upon the environmental knowledge of his scouts. A "volunteer Indian" from Okkanamesit, recently returned from the gathering at Menimesit, told Curtis "he would find them out" for him. As they rode horseback on the Nipmuc Path, the scouts found "an Indian path newly made" and pursued it for "many miles," encountering recently inhabited but emptied camps along the way. Near Tantisques, they tracked down two men, who "being surprised with fear could scarcely speak to us, but only told us that the Indians were but a little way from us." The Okkanamesit scout rode ahead to deliver Curtis's news that "the Governor of Massachusetts his messenger was coming with peaceable words," however, he quickly returned saying that "when he came to them they would not believe him."[23]

As the scouting party approached the river, their horses' hooves sinking into dense wet ground, the Natick and Okkanamesit men must have felt deep trepidation, perhaps even regret. Before they could cross the river, "at least forty Indians" appeared before them, "some with their guns in their hands ready cocked and primed." Among these men were their own relations, but that did not mean they were safe. Curtis, too, noticed men among them he considered "acquaintance[s]," yet, he said "they would not know me," despite his use of proper diplomatic protocol, asking politely after "their welfare." Although "many of them could speak good English," they did not return his words. At this point, any English expedition would have been met with suspicion. News of troop movements to the south must have already arrived, and recently, the people at Menimesit had received word "that the English had killed a man of theirs about Merrymak river," in Penacook territory, and "had an intent to destroy them all."[24]

Standing on the riverbank, the men from Natick and Okkanamesit did not say a word. They watched the tense encounter, listening, as Curtis proclaimed his message from "my Master the great Sachem of the Massachusetts English," and reminded the Nipmucs of their longstanding mutual friendship. He tried to assure them that "I came not to fight with them or to hurt them, but as a messenger from the Governor to put them in mind of their engagement to the English." However, the men on the opposite bank could hardly regard Curtis's intrusion as diplomatic. For all they knew, militia would soon follow. The unexpected visit required delicate diplomacy. If they did not show force, Curtis might report that they made an easy target. If they demonstrated too fierce a reaction, and Curtis was indeed a peaceful messenger, they would have war at their front door before they were prepared. Finally, his arrival meant that their position at Menimesit was exposed. "There was a great uproar amongst them," Curtis wrote, "some of them would have had me and my company presently killed, but many others, as I understood afterwards," from his guides, "were against it."[25]

The scouts must have cringed when Curtis proclaimed to the Nipmucs that he "required their sachems to come over the river." Not surprisingly, "they refused, saying that I must come over to them." It may seem strange that the Nipmucs would allow this English envoy into their sanctuary, yet if they were going to meet, they would receive him on their ground, on their terms. Although Curtis attempted to claim jurisdiction and retain a safer position, the Nipmuc protectors reversed his request, escorting him and his company into the encampment, flanked by armed men. The guides felt "themselves in very great danger where we were," a condition they believed would deepen should they "come over the river." An ambush could be imminent. Yet Curtis insisted they continue, and "with much difficulty we got over the river and meadow to the Island," where some two hundred people "stood to face us at our coming out of the mire."[26]

Approaching the central town, Curtis and the guides faced a gauntlet. Still mounted, "we rushed between them, and called for their sachem; they presently faced about and went to surround us, we rushed between them once or twice, and bid them stand in a body, and I would face them; but still the uproar continued with such noise that the air rang." Completely oblivious of the traditional performance of strength, Curtis had the gall to ask them "to lay down their arms." Instead, "they commanded" the small company "to put up [their] arms first and come off [their] horses," which Curtis initially "refused to do." One man even teased that he would "neither believe" Curtis nor his "master," unless the governor would "send them two or three bushels of powder," a comment that surely received a round of laughter from the gathering. Amid the tension, the Natick guides attempted diplomacy, striving to "still the tumult" and "persuade" their relations of the legitimacy of their mission. Finally, the "tumult" subsided, and they were brought before five sachems, who agreed to meet with them, whence Curtis and his company "dismounted" and put down their "arms."[27]

Mattawamp of Quaboag served as speaker for the group, which included his relation Konkewasco, Shoshanim, Willymachen, and Keehood and Noncatonso of Webquasset, with at least "twelve" members of their council. "I had a great deal of speech with them by an interpreter," Curtis reported, "being brought to their Court and sent out again three or four times." On return to Boston, Curtis neglected to report the full conversation, but said, "I left them well appeased when I came away." Still, a sense of unease must have permeated Menimesit, knowing their location was exposed.[28]

There may have been another reason for the tension at Menimesit. At least one leader was absent when Curtis arrived. Even as Nipmuc leaders held council with Curtis, Matoonas of Pakachoag, whose son had been executed by the English several years before, led a force to raid the settlement of Mendon, neighboring Weauntuk and just twelve miles southeast of Hassanamesit, drawing the war to James Printer's front door.[29]

Matoonas was motivated in part because his people believed the English had launched a war against Natives who refused conversion and containment. When Curtis was dispatched on a second visit to Menimesit, several days later, the sachems, including Keehood, Willymachen, Monoco, and Shoshanim, conveyed they were wary because "Black James, the constable of Chabonagonkamug, had told them that the English would kill them all without an exception, because they were not Praying Indians." Although Curtis assured them of the council's good intentions, and the sachems likewise treated him with respect, even "promis[ing]" to travel to "speak" with "the Great Sachem" of Massachusetts, both departed with grounds for suspicion. Twelve miles outside of Menimesit, one of Curtis's scouts revealed that while Curtis was "treating" with the sachems, he learned that an emissary had arrived from the Wampanoag country, carrying English goods, along with firsthand accounts of the English assaults on Montaup and Pocasset.[30]

By July 27, word had arrived in Boston that the Narragansetts had sent "100 armed men" to "the Nipmuck country," prompting the council to send Hutchinson and Curtis back toward Menimesit, backed by militia, to evaluate the situation and demand the sachems "deliver" their "enemies," any among them who joined with Metacom or Matoonas, lest they be considered "aiders and abettors" in war. Unlike their previous diplomatic instructions, the council now ordered Curtis, Hutchinson, and Captain Thomas Wheeler, that if any at Menimesit might "stand in opposition to you," then "you are ordered to engage with them . . . and endeavor to reduce them by force of Arms."[31]

WHEELER'S FLIGHT, OR MATTAWAMP'S "SURPRISE," QUABOAG AND MENIMESIT, AUGUST 2, 1675

His family secured at Okkanamesit, Job Kattenanit remained with the Massachusetts troops and Mohegan scouts, tracking Metacom. Exhausted from the "long march" through Seekonk and "sharp fight" at Nipsachuck, the men were allowed a night's rest "in the woods." The company consisted of sixty-eight Massachusetts men and at least as many Mohegans and Nipmucs, with the recent addition of seventeen men from the mission communities. Job may have preferred a small elusive group, but the Englishmen favored a large body, with Native men scouting ahead. With the sunrise, on August 2, they began their "march into the Nipmuc country," following Metacom's track north "toward Quaboag."[32]

That morning, as Job moved toward the Nipmuc country, his kinsmen and fellow teachers Sampson and Joseph Petavit stood upon a plain at Quaboag, with Hutchinson, Wheeler, Curtis, and "about twenty men," awaiting the Nipmuc sachems' arrival. Unaware of activities to the south, the captains imagined they'd offer stern counsel, or if the sachems resisted, a battle on the open field. Instead they stood sweating in the midmorning sun, mosquitoes nipping at their necks, alert to every sound.[33]

AT THE PLAIN . . .

Sampson waited with Joseph, their fellow scout George "Memecho," several settlers from the nearby settlement of Brookfield, and the Massachusetts men. They had received word that Matoonas might be sheltered at Menimesit, with Brookfield a vulnerable target. Hutchinson was concerned not only with his property at

Pettaquamscut, but his "farm" near Hassanamesit, where the Petavits may have been among the local leaders he hired to work. The night before, Sampson and Joseph had witnessed a tense meeting, as a force of some one hundred fifty armed men agreed to take the message regarding "a Treaty of Peace" to their sachems, who would meet them at the field in the morning. Yet now, the sun rose high, and they stood alone, several miles north of the settlement on the hill, surrounded by woods that few among them knew. The commanders grew restless. Sampson and Joseph urged them to return home, "earnestly" appealing to Hutchinson and Wheeler "not to adventure to go to them at the swamp," while the local militia leaders urged them on. Hutchinson had read Curtis's report and was confident they had a way in. The captains turned toward the brothers, not for their advice, but for their knowledge of the territory, their ability to guide them on a course that the Petavits knew to be a path of fools.[34]

AT MENIMESIT . . .

Monoco and Mattawamp sat with the other leaders who had come from the inland places. Since Metacom's brother had arrived from the Wampanoag country, carrying the stories of Montaup and Pocasset, they understood that if the English came seeking a "treaty," the protectors should move fast. Metacom was on his way north, carrying families with him. They needed a distraction. They needed to ensure this sanctuary would be protected. Monoco, his whole life, had watched the English slowly encroach on the space that they had once shared at Nashaway. He saw John Prentiss's furrows come increasingly close to the women's fields at Weshawkim, he saw Tinker and Willard trading rum for deeds, taking captive their strongest leaders, encroaching not only on their lands but their governance. He saw Shoshanim begin to turn back the tide and the English attempt to dam its flow. He and Sam had grown up fishing these rivers along the Nashaway trail; they knew how to make a good weir, how to forge a trap amid the marshes and hills. They councilled, making plans, as they awaited the return of their scouts from the fallow field.[35]

FROM THE NORTH . . .

Andrew traveled homeward with his son, returning from a hunting and fishing trip in the lake country. Although life within the mission communities could be restrictive, Andrew and his kin moved freely within a wide network of relations and knew this country well. Traveling to deeper inland lakes in summer, the father and son were heading back to the Nipmuc country as harvest drew near. As Andrew and Aaron moved southward, they may have had no knowledge that violence had come to their homeland. When they arrived at Menimesit, the large gathering may have surprised them. Once informed, they wisely decided not to move on, as it could be dangerous to travel alone with colonial forces out looking for Indian men. They hunkered down with their relatives to await the storm.[36]

ON THE PATH LEADING NORTH . . .

Sampson Petavit marched for miles with the troop, most on horseback, alert to every movement in the surrounding woods. The men tired as the road climbed into the uplands. They had long since passed the gristmill, the last sign of the settlement, and had little sense of their destination as Sampson and Joseph led them to the river where men had long built weirs.

ON THE ROAD LEADING SOUTH . . .

Monoco and the protectors laid their trap, and waited among the trees and brush, their knowledge of the marshes and hill country around them their best asset. They heard the clop-clop-clop of hooves long before the heavily clad, sweaty men came around the bend, plodding, their horses weary. Monoco caught Mattawamp's eye, making a subtle sign, from behind a massive oak. Others hid among the branches of the tall pines, behind the moss-covered boulders, aside old stumps, among makeshift blinds in the brush, their legs hidden by tall ferns and sassafras on the hillside. An equal number perched on the other side of the trail, in the marsh, behind old beaver dams and lodges, under cover of bush, their skin protected by a sheen of bear and hog grease. Breezes cooled them beneath the forest canopy as they awaited the approach of the troop.[37]

FOLLOWING THE BROOK THAT LED TO MENIMESIT . . .

Sampson Petavit assured them the encampment was just ahead, as they descended into the bowl made by the brook and its many marshes. Sampson pointed out a familiar landmark to Curtis, who rode alongside him, and might have recognized the place. To the others, it was just a mass of relentless trees and brush. They swatted at flies and mosquitoes, tried to wipe from their skin the sweaty dust that rose in a cloud from the horses' hooves. Just ahead the trail began to close into "a narrow defile." To their left, the marsh expanded: watery hillocks, dense brush, and deep mud warming in the sun. To their right, a steep rocky hillside, thick with trees. Although the road was dappled in shadows, they could see a long *straightaway ahead, which gave them comfort even as they slowed their pace to allow the horses to form a single line.*[38]

As Sampson and Joseph coaxed their horses, who sniffed the air, urging them ahead, they may have heard a bird call, a flicker of sound from the trees. Perhaps Sampson turned his head toward the call before a rain of bullets suddenly came down upon them, as if the sky had opened in "a shower of hail." The horses bolted, acrid smoke filling the air. While some of the men cowered down, others turned back the way they had come, facing sudden fire from the rear, protectors emerging from the hillside and arising from the marshes that Sampson and Joseph had just foolishly passed, blocking any rear retreat. Finding little "room to fight," and barraged on all sides, some attempted to move toward the swamp, their horses' hooves sinking in the "miry" mud. It appeared as if hundreds of warriors had them surrounded, with no route of escape. Shots flew from the marshes and the hillside. Sampson watched, perhaps under cover, as the three men from Brookfield went down. Horses fell below their riders, and soldiers tumbled to the ground. Among the men firing from the swamps and the hillside, he may have recognized the sachem from Webquasset, whose council house he had attended on the Sabbath, Puckquahow, a leader of the ambush, and "the constable," "Black James." No one could have predicted their actions better than he, who had lived alongside these men.[39]

FROM BEHIND THE OAK . . .

Monoco watched as the English men filed past him, unaware. They moved slowly, steadily into position, like fish swimming upstream. Time slowed to a deep summer trickle, as protectors hidden on the hill above him simultaneously opened fire, on a single signal from Mattawamp, a plan conceived at Menimesit. He watched as horses reared, faltered, and fell. He watched Englishmen cower, covering their heads as bullets rained down. He watched them turn back toward him, toward the direction from which they had come. His face painted for intimidation, he emerged onto the road, his gun raised, his voice joining with those of his men.

AT THE DEFILE, UNDER FIRE . . .

There was no time to regret the foolhardiness of Hutchinson and Wheeler's decision. Sampson had to act fast. He gathered his brother and signaled Curtis to follow him. He knew another route out, but it would not be easily gained. He forced his way up the hillside, away from the source of heaviest fire, navigating rocks, stumps, and branches. *Joseph, Curtis, and Wheeler were not far behind. At first Wheeler seemed content to escape but then (according to his own account) he bravely wheeled about and began to shoot, inviting another volley of fire from the hillside and swamp, and his horse was "shot out from under him and himself was shot through the body." Wheeler's son nobly put his wounded father upon his horse, walking uphill aside him, nursing a wounded arm. (Although Sampson would perhaps tell a different story of Wheeler's wounding and flight from Menimesit.)*[40]

FROM COVER BELOW . . .

Monoco watched as the English soldiers fled. A few, caught in the trap or heading uphill, attempted fire, aiming into the woods and marsh. He watched a man he knew fall, and then saw one of his relatives deftly aim, firing through the shooter's thumb and shoulder, preventing him from firing again. Monoco watched as the magistrate that many of them knew, reacted, his plan for a treaty by force overtaken by this unanticipated ambush. Monoco saw young Aaron, cowering behind the brush, as Hoorawannonit took aim. He saw Edward Hutchinson cry out, falling from his horse to embrace the soil he so badly craved, his face covered in sweat, blood, and dust, his eyes searching for meaning, for help, for some explanation of his fate.[41]

FROM THE ROAD BELOW . . .

Those English men still ensnared caught wind of the movement above, and followed Sampson and Joseph as they struggled uphill through the trees. They carried their wounded, including Hutchinson, on the backs of surviving horses, leaving the dead, including the three Brookfield leaders, behind. If they could escape the gauntlet of gunfire, Sampson knew, they could find the old "by-trail" that would lead them back to Quaboag.[42]

While Sampson and Joseph escaped, credited with the "skill and bravery" that enabled their company's survival, their kinsman George "Memecho" (Camecho), left with the Nipmuc leaders, later explaining he was captured by Mattawamp and carried to Menimesit.[43] Monoco, Mattawamp, and the protectors did not follow the troop. There was only one possible destination for the fleeing party; whether they reached it would rest largely on how well they followed their guides. There, in the Quaboag uplands, Nipmuc leaders had set another trap in this country they knew so well. Sending a small group back to Menimesit, they moved south toward the settlement on the hill.

EN ROUTE TO QUABOAG, WEBQUASSET, AUGUST 2–3

Having covered some fifteen miles, tracking Metacom and Weetamoo from Nipsachuck, Job Kattenanit's company diverged toward "Webquasset," where they might seek sustenance. Moreover, Henchman believed the company could "cut" Metacom "off" by getting ahead of him on the trail. When they arrived, they noted the town flourished with "great quantities of [es]peciall[y] good corn & beans" and "stately wigwams," but "not one Indian" was "to be seen." Job and the scouts "judged they were all gone to Squabaug," where there was an "Indian fort & Plantation" with "great swamps and places of security for them." The next day, the company was joined by a second troop from Plymouth and Rhode Island, including Lieutenant Thomas, "carrying provisions and ammunition" from Providence. In following Metacom's trail past Henchman's divergence, Thomas's troop had noticed "an Indian track newly made," which "wheeled about from west to south toward Narragansett." Backtracking from Webquasset, the Mohegan and Nipmuc scouts confirmed the track had "divided," with "one part going on to Squaboag & the other turned toward Narragansett." Metacom and Weetamoo had eluded them once more.[44]

At Webquasset, Owaneco and the Mohegans, "overloaded with . . . plunder" from Nipsachuck, once more opted to go downriver and return home rather than lead English troops deeper into Nipmuc country. The company would not move on without them. Lieutenant Brown went south with the Mohegans, promising to gather "more supplies of men & provisions" before undertaking a "march" to "Squabaug," which the scouts reported was still another "20 miles" northwest. The remaining company waited at Webquasset, doing little, for five days (until August 7), but Brown did not return. Like Hutchinson, Henchman and Thomas imagined they would march to Quaboag and boldly entreat the leaders there to "deliver" Philip, should he come to Quaboag, or they would "locke them up as enemies." They had no idea that while they "tarried" at abandoned Webquasset, Brookfield was under siege, its people desperate for relief. Nipmuc leaders from Webquasset, Nashaway, and Quaboag, with their relations, had confined the Brookfield settlers and Wheeler's troop in a single garrison house, while Metacom continued to make his way north.[45]

BLOCKADE AT QUABOAG, AUGUST 2–5, 1675

As protectors arrived on the hill, they struck the signs of settlement, claiming what was useful from hastily abandoned houses and barns, then setting fire to the structures. In the heat of that August afternoon, the simple wood and thatch-roofed buildings blazed, fueled by hay and flax. The protectors began at outlying houses, then moved toward the center, where nearly all the settlers and soldiers were confined within the two-story tavern house of John Ayres, who had died in the ambush. Gathering on a hillside above the tavern, Mattawamp, Monoco, and their men forged a blockade. They shot from behind a massive boulder, which provided near perfect protection. From the hill they possessed a perfect angle to aim downward at the house, while gunfire from within would fall short. To the settlers, it seemed that hundreds of Indians had converged upon Brookfield. Yet the protectors, skilled in clever maneuvers, could give the appearance of greater numbers, and with freedom of movement, could easily exchange positions with replacements from Menimesit over the course of the "siege."[46]

This is one of many ways that an understanding of Indigenous strategies and logics can illuminate and revise colonial narratives of events like the Brookfield "siege." Hubbard portrayed the warriors as "wolves" relentlessly "yelling and gaping for their prey," and Wheeler reported that they "would have swallowed us up alive," seeking "our destruction by fire," but for the intervention of "the Lord." Yet Mattawamp and Monoco's "design" was not, as in colonial warfare, to fight as long as they could stand and kill as many "enemies" as possible. Their goal was not to destroy the inhabitants—indeed, few were killed—but rather to strike fear into them; to clear the structures and signs of colonization, and to prevent future incursions by the militia and their Native guides. Rather than simply striking "Brookfield," they created a sphere of defense at Quaboag. From the hill, Nipmuc men sent flying arrows tipped with fire, made from dipping cotton and linen in sulfur, the signs of "civility" turned back on themselves. From Ayres's barn, they carried bales of hay, cattle fodder, and placed them at the sides of the tavern house, setting them on fire. They shot a "ball of wildfire" at the "garret of the house," to land in "a great heap of flax," which rapidly combusted. With Hutchinson and Wheeler nearly immobile inside, they "killed or drove away almost all the horses" of their "company," preventing recruitment of reinforcements.[47]

Although after the raid Wheeler proclaimed God's intervention, during the ordeal the settlers could not be so certain. Nearly one hundred people remained in the garrison house for three days, having gathered little provision or clothing before they fled their homes in fear of attack. Two women were in labor, their two sets of twins, according to local lore, born during the siege, in sweltering heat. Although the wealthy Ayres's house was spacious compared to most of the houses at Brookfield, the windows provided little air. Shots penetrated the windows and wood walls, fear preventing sleep. According to Wheeler, when one man stuck his head out to get air and survey the hill, he was shot and wounded. Sampson and Joseph, along with some settlers and the few soldiers who had not been wounded in the ambush, could occasionally shoot out the windows at the warriors, but nearly all of the men remained in the garrison. They used up nearly all their water putting out fires, and, according to Wheeler, when one of the young men ventured out to try to draw water from the nearby well, warriors shot at him. Another, William Pritchard's son, attempted to fetch more supplies, probably from his house across the road, and within minutes he was killed and decapitated, his head posted outside his father's house. When a few men emerged from the house to put out the fire, praying and reassuring each other that "god is with us, and fights for us, and will deliver us out of the hands of the heathen," the warriors teased and taunted them, shooting guns and arrows, saying "now see how your God delivers you, or will deliver ours." The Petavits, contained within the house, must have wondered, truly, which side "God" was on. For the protectors, the brothers' presence was vital. Assuming they survived, they would take this story back to the mission communities. They would know that despite the boasts of their leaders, the English were not so powerful after all.[48]

To prove their point, the protectors took over the meeting house, where the settlers had recently held Sabbath on the very day that the troops invaded Nipsachuck. They sang an exaggerated version of an English psalm, mocking settler decorum, while inviting the settlers trapped within the house to "come and pray." Here, they reversed in war the invitation the missionaries had given to them, under the pretense of a gift. They demonstrated their knowledge of the new religion, but showed they saw through the pretense of its prayers. Although settlers could only see the act as blasphemy, Sampson and Joseph must have understood their relations' sense of irony.[49]

During the blockade, the Nipmuc men destroyed all signs of English improvement, even as they mocked them. As the afternoon skies darkened with storm clouds, they constructed a makeshift cart, the kind settlers used to travel over rocky trails or plow fields, and turned it into a chariot of fire, which they drove toward the house. As the rain began to fall, it put out the fire, signaling a natural end to the drama. Nipmuc scouts, placed in strategic positions in a perimeter around the settlement, made their way to the hill to inform their relations that the elderly trader Samuel Willard, a man Monoco knew all too well, was heading for the settlement, leading men from Nashaway. Willard had left his post, after several traveling settlers reported seeing the devastated houses on the outskirts of Brookfield. After three attempts Curtis had also managed to escape, crawling on hands and knees through the grass and brush, then running for Marlborough. Still, it would take several days for troops to respond. Outside Ayres's tavern, the warriors parleyed briefly with Willard, killing the horse of Willard's son and wounding two of his men, before he retreated into the house, bringing the number of people contained within to a staggering 162. That night, Nipmuc men killed more of Willard's horses, preventing the militia from following them as they returned to Menimesit. Then they made their final strikes against the greatest signs of English improvement, burning the great Ayres barn, its thatched roof quickly catching flame, the meeting house adjacent to the tavern, and the remaining cattle. (It may be telling of the settlers' great state of fear that no one emerged to defend the meeting house from destruction). Their goals accomplished, they left at dawn on August 5 to return home. Escaping with their lives, the settlers abandoned the smoking settlement, now made uninhabitable—it would remain so long after the war. Once more, in a twisted turn of their roles, the warriors had cleared the fields by fire.[50]

Perhaps the most important goal achieved through the blockade at Quaboag, missed by colonial narrators and even subsequent historians, was to create a crucial diversion; the warriors left the settlement only after the Wampanoags had passed through Quaboag undetected. For, on that same day, August 5, George Camecho later reported, "Philip and his company" arrived at Menimesit, "about 48 men," as well as "women and children many more," led through Quaboag by two Nipmuc men, including "Caleb of Tatumasket." At this safeguarded sanctuary, the beleaguered Wampanoag families were welcomed and fed, and Metacom was reunited with his brother. He could report that Weetamoo "and her company" had also escaped Nipsachuck, although their companies had diverged to avoid capture. That evening was likely their first night of rest in relative safety since the families had left Montaup.[51]

At Menimesit, the Wampanoag sachem had to prove to the Nipmucs that this was not "Philip's war," but a crucial struggle involving all the inhabitants of a shared homeland. Where Ousamequin had offered protection to the people at Quaboag, Metacom sought and received reciprocity. He had lost many since he left Montaup for Pocasset. As George Camecho observed, the warriors who remained with him were "weak and weary." To continue, they needed help. To demonstrate his humility and desire for equal leadership, he broke up his esteemed "coat" of wampum and distributed the shell beads "plentifully" among the Nipmuc sachems. Camecho witnessed as Metacom gave "a peck of unstrung wampum" each to Monoco, Mattawamp, and "Quanansit" of Pakachoag, acknowledging their leadership, their homelands, and their recent victories, while sealing an alliance among them. Then, sending messengers along old trails, the united sachems sent wampum "to the Eastward," to Penacook, to the "Southward," to Narragansett (where some of Metacom's relatives were now sheltered), westward to the Connecticut River, "and all round about."[52]

Metacom followed old examples. Numerous traditional stories from the region emphasize the distribution of power. To the west, the Great Beaver loomed over the Connecticut River, reminding Natives and colonists alike of the danger of hoarding and the compelling force, personified by Hobbomock, that would release the flow to all the valley's inhabitants. To the east the Corn Mother reminded her children to divide her body among their kin. More recently, the Narragansett leader Miantonomo had sought to forge alliance against English colonization through a renewal of these values; in a speech to the Montauks in 1642, he recalled:

> Our fathers had plenty of deer and skins, our plains were full of deer, as also our woods, and of turkies, and our coves full of fish and fowl. But these English having gotten our land, they with scythes cut down the grass, and with axes fell the trees; their cows and horses eat the grass, and their hogs spoil our clam banks, and we shall all be starved.[53]

Invoking a renewal of distribution and reciprocity to counteract destruction, "whereas Miantonomo formerly received presents during his visits, he now gave them to his listeners." Miantonomo called for a recognition of shared resources and, for perhaps the first time, shared identity based on kinship and collective experience, telling his relations: "Are we all Indians as the English are, and say brother to one another; so must we be one as they are, otherwise we shall be all be gone shortly." A generation later, Metacom and Weetamoo joined in alliance with Monoco and Mattawamp, and took up Miantonomo's call.[54]

THE CAPTIVITY OF JAMES PRINTER

OKKANAMESIT AND CAMBRIDGE, AUGUST AND SEPTEMBER, 1675

The ambush and blockade at Quaboag touched James Printer and his kin in ways they could not have anticipated. Some effects were immediate, but they were exacerbated by increasing settler anxiety as colonial commanders proved unable to navigate the interior, locate targets, and contain the uprising. This pervading sense of anxiety and failure intensified racial assumptions and apprehension, provoking settlers to associate neighboring Native allies with those beyond their reach. Settlers moved to contain "Indians" within one racial category, morphing kinship ties into a conspiracy based on a racial divide that was clear only to them. This categorization was different from Miantonomo's call for alliance and recognition of collective identity based on a shared *experience* of colonization and its impacts on the land. Settlers rather imagined an inherent racial *nature* would cause converts to revolt and revert to their "savage" ways. Yet their Native neighbors continued to engage multiple ways of reckoning alliance and loyalties, some of which came into stark competition during the war. James and his family chose to abide by the covenant they had made with each other and with the people of Massachusetts, serving as scouts, confining themselves to one town, and actively protecting both their families and those of neighboring settlers. However, they could only have felt great apprehension as they watched their neighbors consolidate "the enemy" along racial lines, seeking their containment. At the forefront of this movement was Samuel Mosely, who returned to the Nipmuc country in August, in search of Indians.[55]

On August 7, about twelve miles east of Webquasset, Job Kattenanit encountered Mosely, with his pack of dogs and mounted ruffians. The captain carried provisions from Providence, having planned to join the expedition to Quaboag, which Henchman had just abandoned. The company knew nothing of the ambush and siege, or of Metacom's arrival at Menimesit. Mosely confirmed that Metacom had circumvented Henchman's company, and by way of intelligence from a captured elder, that he had "gone to Squabaug," while Weetamoo headed toward Narragansett. Rather than following either lead, Henchman and Mosely "retreat[ed]" to Mendon to await orders from Boston. There they "heard the unwelcome news of Captain Hutchinson and Captain Wheeler," their own plans to boorishly confront the sachems of Quaboag and capture Metacom long gone.[56]

With orders from Governor Leverett, Mosely soon joined Willard and several other officers at the charred remains of Brookfield, to guard and evacuate wounded soldiers and homeless settlers, while Henchman returned to his futile post at Pocasset. For the next two weeks, colonial troops trekked through the inland, from Quaboag to Nashaway, west to Kwinitekw, and east to Tyng's new settlement on the Molôdemak, searching for an elusive enemy. Massachusetts forces found "no sign of any Indians around those woods and swamps" near the site of the Quaboag ambush; Mosely found only "a parcel of wigwams beyond the swamp," which they burned. Whether they found Menimesit at all is doubtful, but even if they located the first town, the Nipmucs and Wampanoags had likely moved into the upper towns, eluding surveillance again.[57]

Mosely and Willard speculated that the center of the resistance might have shifted far northward. Acting on intelligence of an Indian gathering "above Chelmsford," Mosely left his headquarters at Lancaster and traveled up the

"Penacook River" and the Molôdemak into "Pennicooke" country, where he expected to find "ye great Randevous of ye Enemy." Major Richard Waldron of Dover was to join him there, where, despite the leader Wanalancet's pledge of neutrality, the combined colonial forces planned "to pursue kill & destroy them . . . unless" they would "willingly deliver up their armes & themselves or sufficient hostages to secure their peaceable behaviour." Wanalancet had received "messages" from the alliance, but had led his people inland, to avoid the war entirely. Thus, when his scouts detected colonial troops, his people simply moved deeper "into the woods and swamps." As Gookin later observed, Wanalancet had every advantage, with "opportunity enough in ambushment, to have slain any of the English soldiers, without any great hazard to themselves." Even though "several of the young Indians inclined to it," Gookin wrote, "the Sachem Wannalanset, by his authority and wisdom, restrained his men, and suffered not an Indian to appear or shoot a gun," although "they were very near to" and badly "provoked by the English, who" burnt some houses and destroyed some dried fish. Their plans foiled, Mosely returned to Lancaster, frustrated by fruitless wanderings and failure to flush out or surprise any "enemies."[58]

When Mosely arrived at Lancaster, he learned that Hutchinson had died of his wounds, a disturbing reminder of the ambush. The news must have also reached James Printer at Okkanamesit, as Hutchinson was buried at Marlborough. With Brookfield in ruins, Marlborough lay exposed. The men at Okkanamesit knew they were as vulnerable as their neighbors, having received reports from the Quananopohit and Petavit brothers. James may have even heard firsthand accounts from Job. In response, James Printer, along with several other Nipmuc men, began scouting the woods near their "fort." They formed the troop to protect their families and their neighbors, fulfilling their covenant. During one of these scoutings, James and his fellows found Andrew and Aaron in the woods near Marlborough, making their way back to Okkanamesit. Demonstrating fidelity to their neighbors, James and his company "conducted them to the English."[59]

With the death of Hutchinson at his headquarters on August 19, and his fellow settlers calling for blood, Mosely was anxious to capture men he could hold responsible for the siege. Failing to find leaders or warriors in those interior woods, he went after easier prey. When James's company turned in Aaron and Andrew, according to Saltonsall, Mosely "took the old man and bound him to a tree" and "sent away the son by a file of men out of sight." Andrew pleaded with Mosely that "he was a Praying Indian" who had "only" been "hunting for deer thereabouts." Through his usual tactics, Mosely forced a "confession" from Andrew that his son "was one of those men that wounded Capt. Hutchinson." Then, having "pumped him as much as they could, they fired a gun with no bullet in it over his head, untied him, and sent him another way with a file out sight." Then, they fetched Aaron, "bound" him "in like manner" and told him "they had shot his father, and would shoot him also, if we would not confess." Aaron also pleaded that he was a "praying Indian" and "his father" had forced him to "go with him to the Nipmoog Indians," to the ambush, where "they shot three or four times a piece." Then Mosely's men tied the father and son together, and "at length they confessed they were both among the Nipmoogs, and that the Son did wound Captain Hutchinson." After confessing, "they were both shot to death." Shortly thereafter, the news of Andrew and Aaron's death reached Okkanamesit, where not only James Printer, but Andrew's brother David resided.[60]

On August 21, James Printer went out hunting with a group of men north of Okkanamesit. Together, they successfully tracked and shot three deer and divided the meat among them, returning that evening. The next morning, Sabbath, they attended church at "their fort," remaining "in worship" all day. On that Sunday, while Mosley and Willard scouted for "enemy Indians" in other places, Monoco returned to Nashaway and raided their headquarters. A quick strike, the kind he mastered during the Mohawk wars, it inspired fear and showed how little power or control Willard and Mosely had in these inland woods.[61]

Shortly thereafter, Mosely returned to Okkanmesit, and captured "Great David," Andrew's brother, formerly a sachem of Quaboag. Under the pretense that David was "suspected for shooting" a servant at Marlborough, Mosely "apprehended" David and, like his brother, bound him "to a tree to be shot to death." He accused David of assaulting the servant and participating in the raid on Lancaster, guilty by reason of association with his brother. David, according to Gookin, "being fastened to a tree, and guns bent at him, feared death, and being offered a reprieve if he would confess truth, he promised something and so was unbound." He then "accused eleven of the Indians then at the fort to be murderers of the English at Lancaster." Still, David insisted, he had not been "there," but only "heard some speak so," perhaps referring to local settlers, who, Mosely reported, suspected the men from Hassanamesit of "singing and dancing," keeping ammunition "hid in their baskets," and acting suspiciously, as they returned from hunting. Although Mosely sought to build cause for capture, this suggests alarm over the lack of containment of the behavior and movement of convert Indians and the way that suspicion could rapidly transform to accusation.[62]

AT THE FOOT OF THE GREAT BEAVER, NONOTUCK
AND POCUMTUCK, AUGUST 1675

With Quaboag in ruins and scouting near Menimesit proving fruitless, some colonial officers suspected that the "enemy" encampment may have moved closer to the Connecticut River Valley. Although their expeditions between Menimesit and Kwinitekw found no sign, by August 23, eastern Massachusetts Captains Thomas Lathrop and Richard Beers had established a "headquarters" at Hadley, with a force of a hundred and eighty men. Holding a "war council," the officers determined that the "neighbor Indians" must "surrender their arms to them." The nominally "christianized Indians" living at Nonotuck, "on a bluff above Hadley," were suspected for their close kin ties to Quaboag, and Uncas's son Attanwood and his Mohegan warriors, who had arrived on August 9 to bolster Hadley's defense, warned that they might not be trustworthy scouts. Acting from their "great feares" and uncertainties, colonial officers prepared to march upon Nonotuck to surprise and disarm its inhabitants. On August 25, the people of Nonotuck left their "fort" under cover of night and took shelter upriver with their relations at Pocumtuck. The next day, Lathrop and Beers, with one hundred men, pursued them all the way to the foot of the Great Beaver. Here, they made a grave mistake. After the Nonotuck people refused to surrender their arms, the officers spilled the blood of the Pocumtucks's relatives on their home ground, symbolically invoking the narrative of the Great Beaver and provoking a wide network of relations in the Kwinitekw Valley and beyond. The Nonotucks' sensible choice, to preserve their autonomy and seek shelter among kin, was held up as proof that even neighboring "praying Indians" would "prove perfidious."[63]

On August 30, James Printer was at Okkanamesit when Mosely arrived "with a guard of soldiers." Mosely's men forced him at gunpoint from the fort and bound him like a captive. His father and brothers had to stand by and watch as James's arms were shackled behind his back and a rope tied round his neck, which Mosely then used to bind him to the men with whom he had recently hunted and scouted. The eleven men, all affiliated with mission communities, must have feared they would face the same fate as Andrew and Aaron, whom they had handed over to the colonists. Mosely had a reputation for brutality that would only have been reinforced by reports from James Quananopohit and Job Kattenanit, who had fought with him in the Wampanoag country. Mosely had little regard for Christian fairness or rules, and he was known for spontaneous cruelty, including feeding captives to his dogs. James and his relations were powerless to defend themselves, since the day before, an officer had come from Marlborough to demand "delivery of their arms and ammunition," which they had used only for subsistence and protection. Ironically, "their common stock of powder and ball" had been "given to them by order of the commissioners of the United Colonies" and carried from Boston by the "principle Indians" for "their defence against the common enemy." Now it was distributed to English soldiers as "plunder" as the men were left defenseless against Mosely's rage.[64]

From Okkanamesit, Mosely and his men rode on horseback, leading James and his ten companions by rope along the Bay Path, a forced march of thirty miles to Cambridge. Only days before, some Webquasset relations, under Uncas's protection and encouragement, had turned over a group of more than a hundred "of Phillip's men, women and children," who were marched to Boston in like manner and shipped as slaves to the West Indies. James must have wondered whether this would be their fate, as well. He must have marveled at how quickly the accusations could be turned against them, their English clothes and prayers no defense. He may have hoped that, although their pleadings of the proof of their innocence fell uselessly on Mosely's ears, the missionaries and magistrates in Cambridge would give them fair hearing. How suddenly the storms had turned upon them. They had faithfully abided by their covenant. They had removed their homes, in the middle of the planting season, to reside closer to the English, and provided their own brothers to help catch Metacom. They had scouted about Marlborough, exposing themselves to enemy attack. They had faithfully attended the Sabbath, worn English clothes, followed the laws of the gospel. They had turned from some of their own relations. They had surrendered their guns. And now, for no reason they could discern, they were fastened like cattle, their eloquent words of prayer and protest dissipating in the dusty air. As Drake observed, these "eleven" were suspected but four more were dragged to prison "for no other reason but their being accidentally, at that time, at Marlborough, or for the *crime* of being Indians" (emphasis in original). The fifteen included Abram Speen, John Choo, Tantamous or "Old Jethro" and his two sons, "James the printer," James Acompanet, Daniel Munups, John Cquasquaconet, John Asquenet, George Nonsequesewit, Thomas Manuxonqua, and "Joseph Watapacoson, alis Joseph Spoonaut," likely the son or nephew of Tom Wuttasacomponom. Great David was imprisoned with those he accused.[65]

On the same day that James and his kin were imprisoned, the Massachusetts Council challenged the covenant and changed the rules of diplomacy and war, with an order "declaring that all Christian Indians be forthwith confined" to five of "their plantations": Natick, Punkapog, Nashobah, Wamesit, and Hassanamesit. Criminalizing independent movement, the order required them to set their houses in a more "compact" manner, "in one place," and prohibited travel more than a mile from that "center," lest they be "taken" as an "enemie," unless "in the company of some English, or in their service." Henceforth, any praying Indian found outside the bounds of these towns could be "taken" or killed, without trial; their "blood," the council declared, would "be upon their own heads." Indeed male settlers were empowered, if they found "any Indian travelling in any of our towns or woods," to "command them under their guard and examination, or kill and destroy them as best they can." By this order, Gookin wrote, the mission communities were subjected to poverty, "hindered from their hunting" and the tending of "their cattle [and] swine," and "getting their corn," or even traveling to do day labor. They were permitted to gather their corn, "with one Englishman in company," since the council had no plans to supply food, but as Anderson has observed, this order was devastating to those outside these five "plantations" who had not yet gathered in their harvest, leaving it open to livestock and settlers. Gookin recalled they were "daily exposed to be slain or imprisoned," despite the fidelity their men had displayed as scouts. Men like James Quananopohit and Job Kattenanit found themselves nearly powerless to advocate for their relations. When Job returned from the war front, he faced his inability to retrieve his brother from the Massachusetts prison or, perhaps, even to feed his children and extended family.[66]

Both the capture of James Printer and the confinement order represented a colonial effort to contain the only Indians over which settlers could still successfully assert jurisdiction and force. It gave some semblance of control over those who had rebelled against colonial rule. Mobilizing a racial logic, male settlers were empowered to take any Indian they deemed a threat, justified in their fears and assumptions, even as the real "enemy" lay far beyond their reach. Most of the inland territory that housed both neutral Penacooks and a growing resistance movement lay in wooded waters and uplands beyond colonial knowledge or surveillance. Between Lancaster and the Kwinitekw hills was a deeply wooded corridor, more than fifty miles long, extending twenty miles to the south and nearly infinitely to the north, "an unknown land to the English." It now created a blockade from Nashaway to Pocumtuck. As Monoco had proven, protectors could move from within that corridor to strike key settlements, undetected by patrols. Gookin insisted that had the mission communities been left alone, they would have acted "as a wall of defense to the western frontiers of Massachusetts Colony; where most of our danger lay." The restrictions on the movements of

"faithful Indians," including hunting expeditions like those of James and Andrew, ultimately put the erstwhile allies and their towns at great risk.[67]

James Printer and his relations remained in the stifling prison for three weeks
before they were allowed to stand trial for the crime of "being instigated by
the devil" to "murder" several settlers with "severall Indians at Lancaster," or
of being "confederate with several Indians as an abettor or concealer of the
murder." The magistrates on the court included Governor Leverett, Edward
Tyng, Simon Bradstreet[68] (an Atherton man), William Hathorne, and Daniel
Gookin, who was their sole advocate, bearing witness to their "great sufferings"
in confinement. The surrounding settlers "clamor[ed] against those praying
Indians accused," as if the men had committed "very great" crimes. Their vision clouded, "as things appear in mist or fog," Gookin reported, "Some men
were so violent that they would have had these Indians put to death by martial
law, and not tried by a jury, though they were subjects under the English protection, and not in hostility with us." Recalling the covenant, Gookin insisted
that James Printer and his relations were allies who had served with them and
whom they owed protection, not enemies to be punished and slain. "Elliot's
Indians" were "several times" over "tried for their lives and condemned to die,"
and, according to Saltonstall, Gookin and Eliot "pleaded so very hard for the
Indians, the whole council knew not what to do about them." Gookin "daily
trouble[ed]" his fellow magistrates "with his impertinences and multitudinous
speeches," knowing the imprisoned men were innocent. Still, Captain James
Oliver, whom Printer knew from his time at Cambridge, suggested that perhaps
Gookin should "be confined among his Indians, than to sit on the Bench,"
questioning the Irishman's racial loyalty. One night, just past dark, while James
sat in prison, a mob of forty men advanced on Oliver's house to ask him to
"joyn together" with them "and go break open the prison," so they might "hang"
an Indian. Oliver balked, reporting the escalating level of fury to Governor
Leverett. Thus, as Lepore has noted, James Printer and his relations "narrowly
averted" a lynching.[69]

Meanwhile, Owaneco had arrived in Boston with "about twenty-eight" Mohegan men to meet with the commissioners of the United Colonies, including
Leverett, "then sitting in Boston." Before committing to aid the colonies further,
the Mohegans presented three requests. First, they required that their lands at
Mohegan, and at Webquasset, would be protected, their "ancient inheritance"
confirmed; second, they complained that "a party of Narragansetts" had taken
"about one hundred prisoners of Philip's people" from them by force. Lastly,
the Mohegans interceded "on behalf of the eleven Marlborough Indians that

were now on trial," insisting that they were "not guilty" of the crime for which they were charged. Here, the network of relations took force. Several of the Nipmuc men's relations had either fought alongside the Mohegans, like Job, or come under their protection, like many from Webquasset. Job may have even solicited the help of the Mohegans directly. Perhaps Sampson Petavit, drawing on his connections to Mohegan through Webquasset, lobbied on their behalf. Job did not possess the power to force the release of his brother, but Owaneco and Uncas did. Not only were many of the colonists intimidated by Uncas, but they needed the Mohegans to carry out their mission against Metacom and his allies, particularly as the war spiraled beyond their control.[70]

BLOCKADE AT THE GREAT BEAVER

In the first days of September, while James Printer lay in the Cambridge prison, allied protectors raided the northern settlements of Deerfield (Pocumtuck) and Squakeag (later Northfield), recently built upon fertile Native towns on Kwinitekw, at the southern door of Wabanaki. At Deerfield, they burned nearly all the houses, "killed many horses, and carried away horse-loads of beef and pork up the hill" to their towns. At Squakeag, they also burned houses and killed cattle, although seventeen cows reportedly escaped and were "fetched into Hadley." On September 3, Captain Beers led a company of thirty-six men toward Squakeag to reinforce a recently established "garrison," unaware that eight male settlers had been killed there the day before. He was ambushed near a swamp just south of the settlement the next morning, losing twenty men, and then fell himself as his company retreated toward a nearby hill. Through these actions, the protectors created a blockade, discouraging soldiers from moving past the Great Beaver and sending settlers south toward Hadley. Changing the course of the war, the Nipmucs and their Kwinitekw relations reclaimed their towns and reset colonial bounds, while sheltering families far from English reach.[71]

On September 18, on the west side of the Great Beaver, protectors once more ambushed a large company (eighty men), led by Lathrop, who were evacuating settlers from Deerfield, their carts full of corn. When Mosely and his men arrived to "rescue" Lathrop he, too, was cornered by the Great Beaver. Warriors obliterated the companies and upset the carts, reclaiming corn from Pocumtuck. Michael Oberg notes that Mosely, "overrun . . . must have feared that he would face, at last, some of the violence he had meted out upon his Indian opponents." Although Mosely was credited with saving the "beleaguered troops," Oberg acknowledges another source. "At the last possible second," he writes, "'threescore of Unkas his Indians' along with a force of one hundred Englishmen under Major Robert Treat [of Connecticut], arrived 'in the nick to time' to rescue Mosely." Mosely's arrival apparently did little to intimidate the local warriors, but the Mohegans presented a more formidable opponent. The allied Native forces moved north that night, while the Mohegans "returned home" several days later, after the trial of James Printer, begun on the same day as the ambush, was complete.[72]

Thus, in late September, with pressure from Mohegan allies, James Printer and his relations were finally released to stand trial. One of the Nipmuc men, James Akompanet, "a very understanding fellow," was allowed to "peruse the evidence against them" and speak on their behalf. Mosely and the Marlborough settlers claimed the men had been "tracked from Lancaster to Marlbrough" about the time of the raid, that one wore "a bloody shirt," and that another had possession of "a pair of bandoleers belonging to one of the persons slain." Evidence was presented of murder, not an act of war. Still, "the Indians proved by many witnesses," that they had only been out hunting, that "the shirt became bloody by venison newly killed," which one of the men "carried upon his back." James Quananopohit had given one among them the bandoleers, a trophy from the fight with Philip. Furthermore, witnesses confirmed that on the day of the raid, James Printer and the others "were all at Marlborough the whole Sabbath day, at the worship of God in their fort." Meanwhile, "before the conclusion of the trial," colonial forces captured "two prisoners," who revealed, "at two distinct times," that the raid at Lancaster had been committed by Monoco and warriors allied with Metacom, not by these men standing trial. Moreover, as James Akompanet explained, their accuser, David, had given their names "to save his own life" and "to revenge himself." David admitted that the ten men standing trial with him were among those who "had seized upon his brother Andrew and his son, and delivered them to the English." Of that betrayal they might be guilty, but it only proved their fidelity to the English. The crime for which they stood, and for which they were nearly lynched, was without grounds. With Gookin's incessant advocacy and the Mohegans' intercession, the court found James Printer and nearly all the men not guilty, and released them into the hands of Wabun, the ruler at Natick, from where they might return to confinement in one of the five "plantations" where their families remained. There was no apology for their extended imprisonment. Yet the clamoring settlers would also have their Indian execution. Joseph Watapacoson, "tried by another jury," was found "guilty of conspiracy" and of "murder" by the "testimony" of Groton settler Samuel Scripture, and sent into slavery. Likewise David, originally charged with killing an Irish servant, and now of falsely accusing his relations, was sold by the colony, to be carried "to any place out of this Continent." Finally, "Little John" was "proved" to be a "messenger and murderer" and was therefore "executed," "led by a rope about his neck to the gallows," and "hoisted . . . up like a dog, three or four times, he being yet half alive, and half dead." "Thus," wrote Nathaniel Saltonstall, "with the Dog-like death (good enough) of one poor Heathen, was the peoples rage laid in some measure" and contained.[73]

Part III

COLONIAL CONTAINMENT
AND NETWORKS OF KINSHIP

Expanding the Map of Captivity,
Resistance, and Alliance

6

THE ROADS LEADING NORTH:
SEPTEMBER 1675–JANUARY 1676

"SHE IS KIND TO SUCQUAUCH"

On August 5, as Metacom reached Menimesit, Richard Smith, the trader from Wickford, Rhode Island, reported to Governor John Winthrop Jr. of Connecticut that "Weetamors the Pacusset Sachim squo" had arrived in Narragansett territory. Among the English, only Smith and "two others" had any "intelligence of it." Three hundred Narragansetts had just "come home," bringing "seven heads" to Smith, and carrying with them "at lest 100 men—woman and Children of Wettamors." Smith was aware that "she & her men hath bin in aicion Agaynst the Einglish," but, he reported, "She is kind to Sucquauch: & he deseyers all fauor for her thatt Can be."[1]

From the outbreak of violence Smith had maintained communication with the Narragansett sachem Quissucquansh, now known as Canonicus, who, he believed, "inclines to peace rather than war." When Weetamoo arrived at Narragansett, under the protection of Narragansett warriors, she must have sought out the elder diplomat, who appealed for leniency on her behalf, the good will and graciousness owed a leader of her standing. Although his men carried heads as proof of their fidelity to previous agreements, they did not bring the Pocasset families to Smith's post.[2]

Expressing gratefulness for Narragansett "endeavours . . . against the enemy," colonial leaders, including Winthrop and the Connecticut Council, also demanded clarification of the status of "the squa sachem & that company with her," inquiring "whether they came in voluntarily or were taken prisoner." This question would persist, as Weetamoo and "her company" remained at Narragansett through the fall. Was she a "captive," a "prisoner" owed to the English? Or a neighboring leader who could expect sanctuary? Was she a woman in need

9. Northern Front Territories, highlighting places in chapter 6

of protection? Or a persuasive diplomat striving toward alliance in war? When the Narragansett sachems had met with the commissioners at Great Pond in June, they agreed "that if Philip or his men fled to them, yet they would not receive them, but deliver them up unto the English." Had Weetamoo so transcended gender boundaries in her "actions" that she was considered "one of Philip's men?" Did the covenant require that the Narragansetts deliver up the women and children who had come from Pocasset, regardless of Indigenous relationships and protocols?[3]

Narragansett leaders emphasized the complexity of this situation. It was true that both Wampanoags and "inland Indians" had "come hither" to Narragansett, seeking "shelter" from "English soldiers," but the Narragansetts had longstanding responsibilities to protect those to whom they were tied by alliance and kinship. Quaiapin in particular may have felt bound more to the Pocassets than the English, while Canonicus strove for "mediation." Canonicus continued to provide proof of their fidelity, delivering "in all 14 heads . . . some of which" they claimed were from "Phillips Chief men." Nonetheless, in September, Smith expressed concern that "several of Phillips Company" remained among them, brought in with "Wittamore and her Company," for whom "the Narragansetts still request favor." Awashonks and her kin had also taken shelter at Narragansett and the leaders sought "favor" for her as well. Yet, as Connecticut's deputy governor William Leete conveyed to Winthrop, "Sucquansh & the rest of those Sachems who have many captives . . . plead some difference betwixt such as are *taken* by them, & those that so have surrendered themselves to mercy, *especially sundry of them being of their blood relations & affinity*." When Smith noted that Weetamoo "was kind to Sucquauch," he was not simply communicating that Weetamoo treated the sachem kindly. Rather, he informed the governor that the saunkskwa was *kin*, whom Canonicus was obliged to shelter.[4]

This obligation arose as a primary concern during an oft-overlooked but crucial council that took place in Wickford in September 1675. Meeting in Boston, the commissioners of the United Colonies sent an emissary to Wickford to "persuade" the Narragansetts to "amicable compliance," a "treatie" which, they assured the sachems, would lead to "a good road for the future." The commissioners sought a steadfast commitment to "deliver" the Wampanoags among them, a request to which the sachems replied with reserve. Canonicus, Quaiapin, Ninigret, Canonchet, and Quinnapin met the emissary at Wickford, but as interpreter Thomas Stanton noted, "We found a great strangeness in the spaerites of the satchems heare such . . . as I never observed . . . before," which he attributed to the arrival of "the Wampanoags which have come in to

Canonicus Quanapan Nanontanow & the old queene & some others," bearing "gifts." Stanton acknowledged that nearly all the sachems, excepting Ninigret, had "received" the symbolic gifts offered by Weetamoo and her relations, signaling their commitment to give them sanctuary.[5]

Perceiving the power of kinship as well as the fragility of "peace," both Smith and Leete urged moderation. Rather than pursue a "vigorous & hasty attempt to inforce" in "hostile wise" the delivery of captives, resulting in a country "more enflamed, with more enemyes in armes," several subtler strategies were proposed. Leete recommended a quid pro quo: the Narragansetts might "retaine & redeeme" their "captives" (with "actuall murderers excepted") in return for more vigorous participation in the "quarrel" against the "Philistines now in hostility." Stanton suggested that if the Narragansetts could be persuaded to turn over some of the Wampanoags as hostages, this might prevent Metacom's men and the "uplanders" from further "bloody acts." Finally, Ninigret, diverging from the others, reaffirmed his "resolution" toward the "deliverie" of the captive Wampanoags "to the English according to contract," and offered to send his elder Counselor Cornman to Winthrop, with a proposed solution.[6]

Stanton noted that Ninigret "carried it well in our presence" and "avowed" to "keep his agreement made with the English as much as in him lieth." Further, he was willing to "make protest against" the "other satchums" if they "will not do the like." He would join with the English to "cause them to keep their covenant" to which they "are bound . . . as well as him selfe." He was motivated by his covenant with the king and the colonies, but also his enmity for Metacom. As Stanton told the commissioners, he "saith he will not hazard his people nor the pease of his peopall, for a company of bloody parsons that have not onlie killed the English but killed his peopall like wise." Relationships of kinship also bound Ninigret to his English neighbors through the most recent "agreement." Stanton told Winthrop that Ninigret would not have attended the July council, nor "subscribed to those articles above named," if "your son captain waeght [Wait] . . . had not been there." Stanton assured the governor that "Ninigrat doth much confide in your hous[e], as both a man of peas and wisdom." Although the Wickford council revealed a widening "split between the Niantics and the rest of the Narragansetts," all of the sachems present were motivated by their obligation and loyalty to their covenants and their kin.[7]

Both Ninigret and the four Narragansett sachems sent representatives to Boston following the Wickford meeting. Cornman delivered Ningret's "private" proposal, which if he approved, Winthrop might make public to the other commissioners of the United Colonies. Ninigret suggested he would turn over the Wampanoag captives he held, and the English should then return them to him, demonstrating their fair treatment. This performance, he suggested, might bring more Wampanoags to seek their mercy. Moreover, he proposed a diplomatic journey to Sokwakik and to the Mahican and Mohawk countries to persuade the neighboring sachems to reject any proposal for alliance they might receive from Metacom and his confederates. This, he urged along with Stanton, would have the greatest potential to "put out this fire that Philip has kindled."[8]

These contexts of kinship and diplomacy prove especially crucial to our understanding of the events that led to the notorious Great Swamp massacre, in which hundreds of Narragansett and Wampanoag people died and a central Narragansett town was destroyed by English troops. An understanding of the vital kinship relationships among Weetamoo, her Wampanoag families, and the Narragansett leadership, as well as the ties between those leaders and their English neighbors, is essential to interpreting the movements, strategies, and decisions of Indigenous actors, as well as the United Colonies' advance toward war in the Narragansett country. At the same time, these ties reflect only a microcosm of the vast networks of kinship and diplomacy suggested by Ninigret's proposal. This chapter will develop these crucial contexts in the fall of 1675, moving out into northern networks and deeper into the Narragansett country, juxtaposing and interweaving multiple historical strands to show how all of these spaces and stories, like the networks of kinship, are intertwined.

THE NORTHERN FRONT

A VIEW FROM THE KENNEBEC RIVER: "YOU CAME HERE WHEN WE WERE QUIET & TOOK AWAY OUR GUNS"

In early September, while James Printer sweltered in prison and Weetamoo harvested at Narragansett, a force led by Plymouth Captain Gorham and Massachusetts Lieutenant Upham, "destroy[ed] much of the corn and burn[ed] the wigwams" at Printer's home of Hassanamesit.[9] With the families confined at Okkanamesit, several men jailed and the rest disarmed, there was little possibility for protest. Meanwhile, the war spread north. As violence erupted in the Wampanoag country that summer, Plymouth and Massachusetts had sought to extend their nascent policy of containment up the coast, demanding that Wabanaki people from Newichwannock (Salmon Falls) to the Kennebec surrender their guns, knives, and powder. Colonial leaders did not comprehend the dire strategic mistake they made; rather than containing the fire to the south, this preemptive policy instead sparked embers in the north (maps 1 and 13).

Trader Thomas Gardner, writing from the "northernmost" English "outpost" at Pemaquid, regarded this offensive assault on Wabanaki sovereignty and subsistence as a major cause of war on the northern front. In September he told Leverett, "I Conceive the Reason of our Troubles hear may be occa[s]ioned not only by som[e] southern Indianes which may Com[e] this way But by our owne Acctings." Other Kennebec River traders, empowered by Plymouth and Massachusetts, made a "clumsy attempt to disarm" Wabanaki people, who initially had no desire "to become involved in the conflicts that were breaking out" to the south. Fair trade and diplomatic exchange engendered trust; these actions engendered suspicion, giving credence to arguments made by visiting ambassadors and local counselors.[10]

Shortly thereafter, in reaction to these threats, some of the Wabanaki families withdrew from their "fort" on the Kennebec and left their "corn" fields "to our great loss," to shelter their families further upriver, beyond the traders' reach. Two years later, the leader Madoasquarbet conveyed the consequences of disarmament in a letter to "the Governor of Boston": "Because there was war at narragans[et] you c[a]m[e] here when we were quiet & took away our g[u]ns & mad[e] pris[o]ners of our chief sagamore & that winter for want of our g[u]ns there was severall starved." Settlers were motivated by a fear for "a general rising of the Indians against the English all over the country," but the most deleterious impact of this policy was on Wabanaki winter subsistence. In his letter, Gardner implored Leverett, "these Indians live most by Hunting as your Honnor well Knoweth how we cant take away their armes whose livelihood dependeth of it."[11]

As Gardner recognized, the Massachusetts men also failed to understand complex coastal relationships and regional differences. He urged Leverett to practice restraint: "I do not find anything I can discerne that the Indians east of us," that is, on the north side of the Kennebec, "are in the least our Ennimies." They "only fly for fear from Any boats or English thay se[e] & good Reason for thay well Know it may Cost them their Lives if the wild fishermen meet with them. Sir I doubt whether we should Kill these Kennibeke Indians if we meet with them that have not Killed any of us." Gardner understood that many seamen and settlers in the fragile coastal settlements wanted to "sease on all Indians they find," taking vigilante action against Indians in their midst. With violence rising, he sought to explain and quell the real causes of conflict. "These Indianes in these parts," Gardner insisted, "did never Apeare dissatisfied until their Armes wear Taken Away." When Gardner wrote his letter, already smoke had begun to rise from the northernmost settlements on the Presumpscot and Saco Rivers, but he observed, "who those persones are that have killed our friends in Casco or Rob[be]d the houses on the south side of Kennibek doth not yet Ap[p]ear."[12]

In October, as leaves turned to scarlet and goldenrod, the Patucket teacher Samuel Numphow left his home of Wamesit and headed north up the deep river Molôdemak. Like fellow scholar James Printer, he had experienced increasing constraints on his movements, and like Job Kattenanit, his unique skills proved useful to his colonial neighbors. Increasingly anxious about the spread of war on the northern front, Leverett and Henchman, Numphow's Chelmsford neighbor, "commanded" Numphow to travel north to ascertain the location and status of the Penacooks and to "carry a letter" to Wanalancet. Although the vast Wabanaki country to the north was an uncharted expanse for these colonial leaders, to Samuel Numphow it was familiar ground. Samuel was from a leadership family, the son of Numphow, a praying town "ruler" who was "of the blood of their chief sachems." A teacher to his kin, he was a rising leader of his generation, a mediator and articulate writer. His familiarity with this country is unmistakable in the report he wrote for Leverett on his return to Wamesit on October 12.[13]

As Numphow conveyed, he and his company traveled upriver, moving through Souhegan, the northernmost reach of Eliot's missionary work, and up the Molô-demak to the central town of Penacook, where Mosely had burned empty wig-wams in a rage. Unlike Mosely, Numphow knew he had to travel "a little further" to find "some of the Pannacook Indians." On arriving, after exchanging news, Numphow asked "where Wanna[lan]cit was." The Penacooks said that he had gone north to "Pemechowasick." So they continued up the Molôdemak, navigating around the falls (at present-day Franklin, New Hampshire), as the river changed to the swift Pemigewasset, and then eastward to "Wennippesa-cick," which "was our way to go to" Pemijoasik, an Abenaki town tucked into a fertile intervale in the midst of the western White Mountains. Only a handful of Englishmen had traveled as far inland. Few English people had heard of Pemi-joasik and even fewer, perhaps none, had traveled there (map 10).[14]

Yet Numphow wrote of his journey to the mountain towns with ease and familiarity, this lake region well known to him and his kin, although they were a hundred miles from Wamesit. Pemijoasik and Wiwninbesaki were part of the same waterway, the same network of trails and relations—a place Wanalancet could also call home. Among the northernmost planting places, Pemijoasik was deeply protected by mountains on either side. Wiwninbesaki, the great

10. Samuel Numphow's journey

lake where Numphow and his party stopped to inquire about the sachem, was a major gathering place, particularly in summer, when fishing in the coves was especially good. At the crossroads of northern trails, Wiwninbesaki was also a gathering place for news.[15]

From the "Indians" at Wiwninbesaki Numphow learned that although Wanalancet had been there, "he went away three weeks agone from Pemechowasick" and "went toward the French." Numphow (or his northern relations) may have been purposefully vague in describing Wanalancet's northerly direction. Wanalancet had carried families to one of the most protected refuges in Wabanaki, the headwaters of Kwintekw, a dense forest of marshes, ponds, and lakes, protected from English incursions by an insurmountable palisade of mountains and impenetrable fir and spruce. Here, as Gookin rightly observed, they could find plentiful "good hunting for moose, deer [and] bear," two hundred miles from colonial settlements. This was not an uncommon strategy for Wabanaki people, accustomed to seeking inland shelter from winter storms. Many people from the coastal rivers remained protected in their mountain towns during the war, even as Wabanaki protectors sought to reclaim their planting and fishing places.[16]

News traveled swiftly up these rivers and trails to Wiwninbesaki, where Numphow first heard of the raids on the coast. The people at Wiwninbesaki told Numphow that "today," "two Indians came from Pascattoway," seventy miles to the south, reporting on the exploits of a "company" of "ten Indians." "They told us," he wrote, "they killed two English men and take one alive." They referred to a September raid on the New Hampshire settlement of Oyster River in Piscataqua, where warriors "killed two men in a canoe" and took an "Irishman" captive. They also had news of "some more Indians" who "went out afore these last" from Ossipee. At Caskoak, these warriors "killed some English and brought two children and one maid alive." From Ossipee, "fifty more" were "going out," but when he asked his hosts where, they replied, "we cannot tell."[17]

In Numphow's account, the view of the first raids, which ignited the northern front of war, was from Wiwninbesaki and Ossipee, not "Falmouth" (Portland) or Boston. A Wabanaki town at the confluence of the Saco and Ossipee Rivers, Ossipee extended upriver to Ossipee Lake, northeast of Wiwninbesaki. Trails connected it to upper Saco towns, including the Pequacket intervale, and the coast, including Caskoak. Just as Numphow could navigate between Wamesit and Wiwninbesaki, Wabanaki protectors could move covertly between coastal settlements and the upper towns. With no settlements or forts upriver, Ossipee was essentially beyond reach.[18]

In nearly all other accounts of the first Casco Bay raid, on the house of settler John Wakely, the details are personalized, reconstructed from the account of Falmouth militia commander George Ingersoll, who discovered Wakely's corpse amidst the remains of his charred house, and reported it to Andrew Alger. The raid is portrayed as a horrifying assault on a domestic space: a planter brutally murdered, his pregnant wife scalped, two children killed, and three others taken, his aging parents seemingly crawling over the threshold as the house erupted in flames. Historian of Portland William Willis reflected, "Why this family was selected for a sacrifice we have no means of determining," but Maine historian William D. Williamson held up the raid as evidence that "the Indians" were "guilty of shedding the first blood," a common portrayal, strikingly similar to narratives of the Wampanoags' first strike at Swansea.[19]

William Hubbard portrayed the first raids as misplaced acts of revenge by the Wabanaki leader the English called "Squando." The "strange enthusiastical sagamore" appears only with the dawning of war, the "chief actor" and "the beginner" of violence, according to Mather and Hubbard. While oft repeated, Hubbard's is the only account that suggests the Saco River leader pursued war because "some English seaman" accidentally drowned his son, while testing a myth that Indian babies could float. Squando, "filled with malice and revenge," Hubbard maintained, took vengeance on settler families. Through this story, Hubbard displaced any cause arising from colonial encroachment, suggesting the war was instigated by the "rude and indiscreet act" of a fisherman and the "natural" proclivity of savages for "bloody and deceitful actions." Thus, Kenneth Morrison astutely observed, "The English excused themselves for causing the war." "By obscuring the actual causes of the ensuing three-year conflict," he wrote, "Hubbard's published justification misled English readers. He made the Abenaki seem hot-blooded when they actually were defending themselves . . . by implying that the Indians were lawless, he glossed over repeated English provocations."[20]

Hubbard also revealed, unwittingly, that the first shot came from an English gun, when a group of twenty-five settlers traveling by boat to gather "Indian corn" from the Casco Bay settlements came across several "Indians" seemingly pilfering goods from a settler's house. His account is scattered, but he admitted that one Indian was killed and another wounded "in pursuit." Hubbard depicted the accused pilferers as nameless "Indians," lacking the family connections and personalized names that color his (and all others') portrayal of the Wakelys. Surely, this Native man's death was just as horrifying to *his* neighbors and kin. This is not to say that Hubbard's account should have been more "sympathetic" toward the Indians, but rather to point out that Hubbard's narrative of the first shot against a Wabanaki man is just as abstract as Numphow's account of the first shot against a settler. Such abstraction occurs on both sides, shifting our perspective as readers of history. In our first reading of Numphow's account, our eyes, too, might quickly move over the "English" who were killed, seeming simply one act of many in war.[21]

On the other hand, viewing the raid from Ossipee enables a broader, more concrete perspective on the beginning of the war. Ossipee's riverside trails led southeast to Amancongan, the planting grounds and fishing falls of Warrabitta and Skitterygusset, *and* the site of the Wakely raid (see maps 2 and 10). The Wakely family had first settled on Back Cove, southwest of the Presumpscot River's mouth, along with most other Falmouth settlers. John was among the second generation of "planters" who sought the fertile land upriver. Until the 1670s, no settler houses existed on the north side of the Presumpscot, above "Skitterygusset Creek." John Wakely was one of three men who built houses north of the creek between 1672 and 1675, just before the outbreak of war. His house was only three-quarters of a mile below the Presumpscot falls, where John Phillips had built the first sawmill, both structures encroaching on the village where Skitterygusset had lived with his extended family. The raid enacted the reclamation of Amancongan.[22]

As Numphow's report suggests, this incident did not take place in isolation but was part of a network of coastal raids. At the beginning of September, Wabanaki protectors plundered Thomas Purchase's trading post and house on the Pejebscot (lower Androscoggin) River. On September 15, "3 guns" appeared "out of the bushes" and two men fell "in the marsh," shot down as they attempted to gather grass, or salt "hay," from Owascoag. Several days later, Wabanaki warriors burned down seven houses at Scarborough, including two second-generation Alger homes, and killed Andrew and Arthur Alger. According to the original deed, the Algers would "suffer" Warrabitta and her mother "to plant" in the field until the death of Warrabitta, which, according to local histories, occurred in 1675. Her descendants may have been attempting to reclaim these fields, particularly if both their usury rights and acknowledgment were disregarded, terminated by the deed.[23]

Just south of Owascoag, Squando and his relations turned to the Saco falls, striking at the mills. As trader and military commander Richard Waldron reported from Cocheco (Dover), on September 18, "36 Indians came over ye [Saco] river in english canooes & which come Ashore cut holes in ym and turned ym Adrift." Then "they went to Major Phillips Saw mill" and set it "on fire" and "did like to his corn mill." With Phillips and some fifty settlers holed up in a garrison, the protectors set to burning houses and barns. According to Phillips, they lay in wait in the "thick bushes" outside his house, and when he peered out to investigate a "stirring" among the "ferns," a shot came flying "immediately" to hit him in the shoulder. Then the "shot came thick" from the woods, answered by return shot from the garrison. The protectors, "decked with ferns and boughs" moved stealthily toward the house, and even designed a contraption with "old truck wheels . . . boards and slabs," filled with "combustible matter," a mix of birch bark, "pitchwood," and powder, which they drove toward the house, an act reminiscent of Quaboag. Before they left the next morning, they set fire to an outhouse stuffed with hogs, a message ripe with satirical symbolism. Within days, Phillips abandoned his post and "removed down to Winter Harbour," where Waldron recorded his story. "Within a fortnight" his house was burned. Even as he wrote, Waldron must have feared for his own house and mills at Cocheco.[24]

It is no coincidence that among the first raids were strikes on mills near traditional planting grounds and fishing falls, including Saco and Oyster River. The mills were fed by the massive white pine trees that were daily cut and harvested from the forests, logs carried downriver by the natural waterpower. Settlers built over fifty sawmills on the Wabanaki coast, which "produced up to a thousand feet a day of white pine boards." The mills powered the local settlements, but the exports of lumber, fur, and fish produced by the Waldrons, Phillips, and other traders also "fueled the Massachusetts economy, providing the colony's major source of income." While supporting colonial growth, this intensive logging disrupted Wabanaki subsistence, radically transforming the habitat where men hunted, destabilizing the riverbanks where women planted, and impeding the fish that migrated annually for spawning, some already compromised by intensive commercial fishing on the coast. Additionally, Phillip's gristmill harnessed the river's power to grind corn from the lower Saco fields, now cultivated by English planters and plows.[25]

The physical and symbolic act of burning mills would be repeated along the coast throughout the war, a demolition of these instruments of destruction, which were so vital to colonial production. Without mills, wood could not be processed to build houses, shipped on boats, or used to build masts. Wabanaki women ground corn with mortar and pestle, but settlers were reliant on the water-powered mills to process their corn into meal. That fall, at Newichwannock and Cocheco, warriors directed overhead shots and insults at millers, burned corn storage barns, and gathered corn from settler fields. At Newichwannock they took "one hundred barrels of corn" from Captain John Wincoll's barn and then torched it, taking their acknowledgment by force, while he, under Waldron, was likely out scouting for them. A "founding" settler, Wincoll had established the first mill at a vital fishing falls. Protectors targeted the sawmills that obstructed the waterways and fisheries, and reclaimed corn from the gristmills, preventing settlers from renewing the pursuits that sustained their "plantations."[26]

Protectors also strove for rebalancing at the falls by targeting traders, including Phillips and Waldron. During the raid on Purchase's post on the Pejebscot, warriors evened the scales on his stores, taking "what they like[d] without even asking the price of it," when previously, one Androscoggin man recounted, Purchase had once charged him "one hundred pound for water drawn out from Mr. P his well." Purchase was one of many traders with a reputation for swindling Wabanaki hunters, which further undermined the social responsibilities and political relationships integral to trade. Although Wabanaki leaders had initially been willing to share coastal resources with smaller populations of fishermen, traders, and settlers, they quickly learned that this "welcome" had opened the door on a wave of settlement that had upset a balance they had maintained for millennia.[27]

Indeed, viewing these raids from Ossipee and Winnipesaukee, it is clear that assaults on coastal settlements might also have been motivated by a desire to *prevent* settlers from coming upriver, to deforest Ossipee, displace their towns, and plant on the banks where families were even then gathering their harvest. If settlers made it to Ossipee, what would prevent them from moving further upriver, to Ossipee Lake, and then west to Wiwninbesaki and the well-hidden Pemijoasik? Perhaps learning from the experience of the planting people to the south, Wabanaki people still saw the real possibility of halting further destruction.

Indeed all of the raids Numphow mentioned in his report corresponded to this motivation of protection and prevention. In late September and October, Wabanaki warriors moved south "towards Piscataqua" and "the several branches of that river," including Oyster River and Newichwannock. The Newichwannock (Salmon Falls) River and trail (along the current New Hampshire–Maine boundary) led north from the coast all the way up to the Ossipee and Wiwninbesaki region. Further settlement pushing upwards from the logging and trading operations of Waldron, Wincoll, and their neighbors at Cocheco, Caskoak, and Newichwannock would threaten both places. Andrew, one of the men who led a raid on Newichwannock, came originally with his relation Symon from the mouth of the Molôdemak; they surely brought harrowing stories of settlement to Ossipee. Nearly a decade before, Nanamocomuck, Wanalancet's brother, had arrived at Pejebscot with stories of his capture by Boston men, and their successful attempt to dispossess his family of their planting grounds. His daughter and his son, Kancamagus, remained among the Wabanaki people. Andrew and Symon's families, at the mouth, may have been related to others on the Molôdemak, including Wanalancet, Nanamocomuck, and Numphow. Unlike Numphow, however, Andrew chose early on to join with protectors on the northern front.[28]

Although Numphow's relations at Wiwninbesaki would not reveal the location, as they predicted, a party of over a hundred men went out from Ossipee
on October 16 to strike for the second time the English settlement at Newichwannock, with Andrew and Hopehood, the son of "Robinhood," leading. As an
early snow fell, they fired houses and barns, killed the founding settler family
of Richard Tozier, "about a half mile above the mills," and ambushed the men
who emerged from the garrison. They burned the house of Wincoll, preventing
his return to the mills. Shortly thereafter, they also burnt a mill belonging to
Edward Hutchinson, whose land dealings extended not only into the Nipmuc
and Narragansett country, but also Wabanaki territory.[29]

Hopehood had kinship ties that bound him to multiple places, from Pejebscot
to Newichwannock. These raids represented not only a strike against the logging operations and mills of the Piscataqua region, but a network of Wabanaki
planting towns that stretched from the mouth of Molôdemak to the Kennebec.
The headwaters of all of these rivers—Molôdemak, Piscataqua/Newichwan-
nock, Presumpscot, Saco, Androscoggin—were in the lakes region and White
Mountains. Andrew and Hopehood represented a regional alliance of "closely
related" agricultural peoples determined to "pursue strategic objectives," to protect their planting towns, fishing places, and hunting territories from further
encroachment. As Emerson Baker and John Reid have astutely observed, with
the advent of this war, "The safeguarding of boundaries—stemming originally
from expectations based on environmental considerations and resource harvesting—increasingly influenced Wabanaki demands on New England." War
was far from "the preferred method" of Wabanaki leaders, but it became an
increasingly important strategy for resource management and community security. If earlier deeds represented an attempt to share space and accommodate
settlers in the desire for exchange, then these acts of war represented a reversal
of that policy towards an enforcement of borders, to support the defense and
reclamation of Wabanaki space. This strategy would become even more crucial
as Wabanaki people began to accommodate survivors from the south, forging a
blockade from Sokwakik to Ossipee.[30]

"ALL THEIR WAR IS COMMOTION"

THE CAPTIVITY OF NUMPHOW'S RELATIONS

At the Kwinitekw headwaters, Wanalancet and his families likely spent the
fall fishing the lakes and ponds, then hunting in the marshes and mountains,
secure through the deep winter in longhouses, listening to old stories, protected
by a cover of snow. No English man from the coast would find them here,

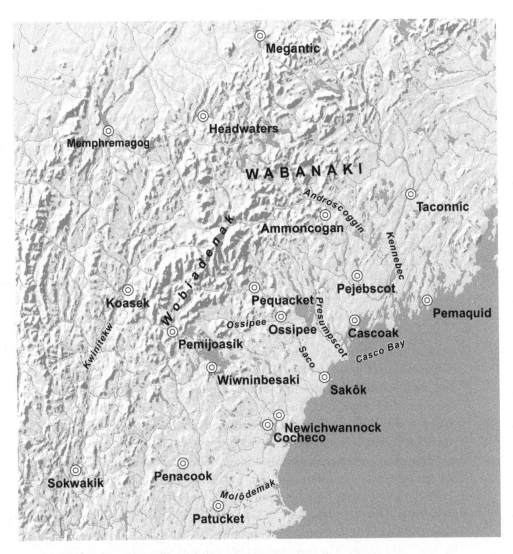

11. Wanalancet's journey

where they could "wholly avoid the storm." Come spring, they could travel north to visit relatives at Megantic, the lake at the bottom of a lone mountain, east to the upper villages on the Saco, Androscoggin, and Kennebec Rivers, or west to Memphremagog, all places yet unknown to the English.[31]

In contrast, when Samuel Numphow returned to Wamesit, he found his town in chaos. While he was at Wiwninbesaki, some hay had been set on fire at neighboring Chelmsford, a minor infraction compared to the raids on the coast.

Within days of his return, the Massachusetts Court sent Edward Oakes with forty armed men to apprehend the "Wamesit Indians" who were "vehement[ly] suspected to be actors and consenters to the burning of a haystack." They captured one hundred forty-five "men, women, and children," including "sundry infants."[32]

Amos Richardson, whose haystack was burned, protested their prosecution, telling Gookin his neighbors were innocent. Numphow himself had reported that on the way "home," he and his company had stopped "at Penakook," where they "met with" some "Groton Indians" who "were afraid to come into" Wamesit because, they admitted, some men from their town had burnt the haystack at Richardson's house. With these "Groton Indians" beyond reach and Chelmsford still exposed, the court rounded up Numphow's kin, regardless of his service. Indeed, the magistrates may have used his report as a pretext to seek those "Groton Indians" among them.[33]

The women, children, and elders were ultimately allowed to return to Wamesit to live under guard, but thirty-five men were marched to Cambridge prison. The court did not record their names. "Examined singly and apart," then in groups, "they all vehemently denied" that any of them burned the haystack, or knew who had done it. At first, Gookin recalled, "a vote passed in the House of Deputies, as I heard, finding all the Wamesit Indians guilty of burning the hay, but it was not consented unto by the magistrates." Instead, they culled out those who had come to Wamesit "since the war," deemed more "suspicious" than the rest. William Hawkins, a Christian Narragansett who had formerly worked at Salem, but, following colonial policy, had taken shelter at Wamesit, was "sent away" to slavery in the West Indies. The court generously offered his wife the opportunity to accompany him, but being "examined," she said she was "not willing to go with him, being an old woman." Two others, Monnipaugh, an elder, and his son Mannasett, who had traveled to the colonies on a *diplomatic* embassy from Penacook, were deemed "strangers" and also sentenced to be "sold" into slavery. The two men had been visiting their relations at Wamesit when the Cambridge force arrived. The court realized their "mistake" in November, acknowledging that Monnipaugh and Mannasett had come "in from Wannalancet upon a safe conduct from the council." It is unclear how the magistrates became so confused as to not only imprison them, but sentence them to slavery, when they had granted the men "safe conduct" as diplomats.[34]

As for the remaining men, at least twenty were released and "sent back to their wives and children at Wamesit," marching "under guard" toward a town now "secured" by armed settlers. As they passed through Woburn, where the local militia were "exercising," a "soldier named Knight" shot and killed "a stout young man, very closely allied to the principal praying Indians of Natick and Wamesit, whose grandfather and uncle were pious men, his father long since slain in the war with the Magues." The men returned to Wamesit with the weighty responsibility of informing this man's kin, as well as the relations of those still imprisoned, that their sons, nephews, and husbands were not coming home. News would soon reach Wiwninbesaki that those who remained at Wamesit under Massachusetts's protection, as colonial leaders had urged Wanalancet to do, had not fared well. This "ancient and capital seat of the Indians" had become a pen.[35]

Wamesit was representative of a larger movement. In the same session, the magistrates implemented an extreme policy of containment aimed at Native converts, on whom they had drawn for military support since the beginning of war. They "ordered that all the Natick Indians be forthwith sent for, & disposed of to Deer Island," an isolated isle in Boston harbor, a "place appointed for their present abode." They also forbid the presence of Indians in Boston, unless under "guard," including those "owned" or "entertained" as servants, while prohibiting employment or hosting of "strangers" who were not British subjects. During the same session, Daniel Denison, magistrate and commander of the eastern forces, sought containment of the northern front. Having received intelligence from Numphow and the northern settlements, the court "approved" a proposal to "raise a force" to "resist the ennemys headquarters at Ausebee." In their response, they remarked, "Without doubt, if their squawes & papooses, &c, be at Assabee, & God be pleased to deliver them into our hands, it would be much for our interest." At the same time, the United Colonies held a "conference" in Boston with Canonchet and Cornman, demanding the surrender of Wampanoags held "under" their "c[u]stody."[36]

These multiple "orders" were reactive strategies to contain a "fire" that had rapidly spread beyond the colonies' control. Although rumors abounded, colonial leaders lacked knowledge of Metacom's location, and the sources of many of the raids. Nearly all Natives had left the visible Connecticut Valley towns, yet warriors continued to hit settlements on the river with regularity—whether from Menimesit or upriver colonial leaders did not know. According to conflicting rumors circulating throughout the colonies, Metacom may have been with those companies, striking in the Valley, or among the Narragansetts, urging them toward war. Or perhaps he had gone west to the Mohawks, or east to Ossipee, where the Boston magistrates received reports that the "Eastern Indians" had their headquarters and were receiving warriors from the south. Since they could not find Metacom or any northern "headquarters," colonists pursued containment closer to home, targeting Indians in the praying towns, aiming threats at the neutral Narragansetts, and even turning toward settlers in their midst who might be offending their god.

Writing to Leverett just prior to the October court, Roger Williams expressed concern for these misplaced projections. Had they become so distracted by war that they had forgotten to listen to "what the Eternal Speaketh" toward "peace"? He cautioned against "the growing tendency" to speak out against the "false worship" of Quakers and other dissenters. Many colonists believed the war was a manifestation of God's disapproval, Indians merely tools to punish sinful children into obedience and ministers, the instruments to reinforce divine order. Williams recognized the psychology behind these acts—rising anxiety and loss of control drove colonial leaders to assert order where they still maintained power.[37]

Of course, Williams understood the true source of the desire for control. "All their war is commotion," he wrote, "They have Commootind our Howses, our Cattell, our Heads, etc. and that not by their Artillerie but our Weapons." The war seemed an active rising tumult, an insurrection against the structures settlers built, their own guns appearing to rise from the surrounding trees to turn against them. Williams described New England as one "Whole Ship" caught in a turbulent storm at sea. Alone, the ship could not request assistance from the home country, and military support was never offered from the king. Yet, as Williams discerned, the source of the storm lay in the Indigenous style of warfare, indiscernible and unpredictable to its targets. Pettaquamscut proprietor John Hull observed, "They are like wild Deare in the Wilderness," who "will Never stand to maintaine any fight but come upon some of our out plantations & burne some of the remote houses & kill one or two & take there scalps & get away that our souldiers can rarely find any of them." Urian Oakes, president of Harvard and son of Edward, described "a despised & despicable Enemy, that is not acquainted with books of military Discipline, that observe no regular Order, that understand not the Souldier's Postures, and Motions, and Firings, and Forms of Battle, that fight in a base, cowardly, contemptible way."[38]

This apparent lack of "Order" was the problem, as colonists saw it, but the conundrum lay in the apparent effectiveness of "disorder" as a military strategy. As Lepore has observed, "Nearly all of the damage to the English during King Philip's War—the burning of houses, the spilling of blood, the English becoming Indianized—was understood as attacks on bounded systems. While disorder threatened to rule New England, military strategists sought means to draw a line to keep Indians—and chaos—out." But Native warriors understood war as actively invoking chaos. Their strategic actions and inscriptions, upon houses, mills, and fields, upon bodies and livestock, planted fear that would take root and spiral within those who remained. They created spectacles, like the heads at Kickemuit or the bodies splayed below the Presumpscot falls, which inspired waves of anxious foreboding. It was not simply the elimination of houses and structures that moved settlers to flee, but the relentless worry that they would be next. Ambushes cultivated a sense that a warrior could be "lurking" around every tree, on the edge of every field, outside every garrison door or window. The "commotion" inspired a persistent state of anxiety, flowing within the subconscious of its targets, who could never know what lay ahead. The colonies themselves became unbounded.[39]

Rumors were a key force in this swirl of chaos. Colonists spread reports orally, and in writing, of all kinds of violent acts (true, false, and exaggerated) as well as predictions of impending bloodshed. In his letter, Williams reported, "Since the doleful news from Springfield, here it is said that Philip with a strong Body of many hundredth Cutthroats steeres for Providence and Secunk." A rumor traveled that "Philip's great Design" was "to draw C[apt]. Mosely" and the Massachusetts forces "into such places as are full of long grasse, flags, Sedge, etc. and then inviron them round with Fires, Smoke and Bullets." Providence settler Mary Pray wrote to Captain Oliver in Boston that "These fals[e] trecher[o]us imps the Naraganset Indians" told men at "Warwick that Captain Mosley an[d] 3 hundred men with him are al[l] cut ofe," and she feared that "our poer nation are neerely ensnaered."[40]

Such rumors sent some people packing, abandoning houses and cattle. As Rhode Island settler Samuel Gorton reported, "Many people in these partes are like soules distracted, running hither and thither for shelter." Richard Smith likewise related that "the inhabitanc here are many goone and most removing for feare of dainger." From the Kennebec, Thomas Gardner reported, "The Inhabitants of these parts ar[e] fled & Left their houses Corne Cattell & all to the Ennimy." Most of the Kennebec settlers went to isolated Monhegan Island, with little protection or provisions, finding themselves contained, like settlers in many of the towns who were "shut up in our garrisons, and dare not goe abroad." From Piscataqua to Saco, Waldron observed, many "forsake their plantations," leaving "their Corn & Cattle to the enemy." Concerned for the provision of the settlers who remained, he suggested they "contract the people into as Small a Compasse as may be" within town "fortifications," so that they could best be protected. In pursuing a policy to foster security Waldron fulfilled a major goal of Indigenous resistance, drawing the colonies to a narrower compass.[41]

The Massachusetts Court supported Waldron's plan, but also prohibited settlers from abandoning their settlements. Although some towns, like Salem, had already taken in fleeing settlers from the north, Massachusetts sought to halt the flow, ordering settlers to maintain and defend their improvements. Men who left without "license" from the court, would "forfeite theire interest in that place."

Settlers, including women, who remained thus became casualties of the war on colonial structures and the United Colonies' determination to maintain them.[42]

At the same time, this Indigenous strategy enabled the restoration of a network of relationships, particularly among people who planted. The growing resistance necessitated the creation and renewal of bonds to foster a wide network of protection. Alliance in war depended on the *dispersal* of people and resources to multiple places—warriors striking in diverse regions, laying ambush in multiple strategic locations, and working together within particular homelands. What settlers discerned, even in their fear, was the decentralized character of the Indigenous military effort. Even the push to characterize Metacom as the commander of these forces represented an attempt to impose English order on a complex Indigenous system.

CANONCHET'S LOOKING-GLASS AND MARY PRAY'S CALL TO "BATTEL"

While Weetamoo remained hidden at Narragansett, the community sent a diplomat to continue negotiations on their behalf. In his letter to Leverett, Williams recalled a conversation he had with "the young Prince," Canonchet, "in his return lately from You." Canonchet and his counselors were traveling over the Seekonk River on their way home from their early October meeting with the commissioners in Boston. Williams ferried them in his "great canoe" from "Secunk to Pawtuxet side," noting "no Indian comes to Providence." He advised Canonchet "that Phillip was his Cawkakinnamuk, that is Looking Glasse, he was deafe to all Advice and now was overset: Cooshkouwawi."[43]

In Williams's metaphor, it was not the English "ship" that had overturned, but rather Philip's canoe, its captain "over his head, about to be drowned," with no hope of getting "ashoare." This, he warned, would be Canonchet's fate as well, should he fail to take the proper course. Williams implied that this vision of Philip's "overset" canoe represented Canonchet's mirror image and possible future. Williams spoke while paddling across the river, as if Canonchet could glance at the rippling water and imagine his own canoe capsizing, and comprehend Williams's vision of English allegiance carrying him safely through the rapids. Williams expressed certainty about Philip's and Canonchet's fate, and confidence in the combined colonial army's ability to carry out a decisive war come winter. "I told him I would not aske him newes" regarding his conference with the governor or the "captives" at Narragansett "for I knew matters were private. Only I told him that if he were false to his Engagements we would pursue them with a Winters War, when they should not as Muskeetoes and Rattlesnakes in Warme Weather bit[e] us."[44]

As Williams noted, Canonchet did not give a full response, but acknowledged his words: "He answered me in a Consenting Considering Way[:] Phillip Cooshkowwawi." Yet, it was probably neither Metacom nor Williams with whom "the young prince" was most concerned. That October, news came in regularly to Narragansett of captured kin. Only days before, Canonicus had gone once more to Smith's post, emphasizing he was "not inclined to make war"; he pleaded for the release of a Narragansett named "Bolt," who had been wrongly "sesed" when he was mistaken for a "wompanooge," and for other Narragansetts held "aboard" a "vessel," whom he prayed "may not be sent away" as they were "all innocent men." Canonicus likely referred to a group of captives taken at Prudence Island, in Narragansett Bay. As settler John Paine reported, a Narragansett family under his protection—"Jack, an Indian," his wife and baby, and their companion, Caleb—had been "surprised by night in their wigwam," even as Paine slept in the house next door, by Fuller and Gorham, under Cudworth's command. Jack and his family were not only "innocent" but had provided their neighbors with crucial assistance at the outbreak of war, and had promised "upon their lives" to remain with Paine and offer any "intelligence" that came their way, in return for his promised protection. Yet, Fuller and Gorham could not be persuaded to release them, and even now, Jack's family was upon a boat to Plymouth, along with two other Indian servants. All "innocent," they were taken captive simply for being Indians, who lived in proximity to Pocasset, where Plymouth still operated a pointless "fort," the Pocasset people just beyond reach at Narragansett.[45]

With family members being captured and some "sent away" into slavery, it would be hard for Canonicus to dissuade those inclined to war. The policy of containment sent shockwaves of grief into kinship networks. When he returned to Boston to meet with the commissioners on October 18th, Canonchet would have seen the jail full with Christian Indians from Wamesit and Okkanamesit, including his kinsman, Will Hawkins, sentenced into slavery, along with numerous others, including "Great David." Most disturbing, Canonchet may also have seen the families of these "Indian captives," who were taken to Boston and "examined" by the court regarding their willingness to join the men. David's wife, Sara, "with one child at her back," said she would be willing to go with him "if to King Charles his country." Apparently, the magistrates were not transparent in their intents. Sara believed they might be carried under protection to England, not sold into slavery. With her were David's mother, "very old," and his sister, "with a little child," who also said she was "willing to go with her husband," an Abenaki man named John Humphry, imprisoned with David. Among the "9 women with 6 children" examined was "Mary," whose husband Sampson had taken shelter in Narragansett, "at hilling time last." She was among several women who made clear their husbands were not even among those imprisoned. Yet the court ordered all of the women and children to be either sent into slavery, if so willing, or to the Boston harbor islands; none would be allowed to return home.[46]

Such evidence in the world around them could only have further convinced Narragansett leaders that they needed to shield Weetamoo and the Wampanoags who had come to them. As Canonicus had stressed in September, many among them were kin, "whome to surrender for slaughter or forraigne captivity, doth run hard against the graine of nature" as well as Indigenous custom. It is not difficult to understand why Canonchet may have signed a sweeping document in Boston that proclaimed he would "deliver" all the people among them "whether belonging unto Philip, the Pocassett Squa [Weetamoo] or the Saconnett Indians [Awashonks], Quabaug, Hadley, or any other Sachems," even if we assume that he understood the words on paper before him. He had to have understood that refusal to sign would likely result in his own imprisonment, as well as calling an army onto his people, unprepared. He made his mark, and returned home. By the end of October, as Smith reported, rumors circulated "amongst Indyns and English" that "an armey" was "coming up." As historians Michael Tougias and Eric Schultz have observed, the signing ensured that "Canonchet would have had almost two full months to prepare his defensive strategy." He would not return to Boston again. He would not release the Wampanoags to colonial custody. Instead, he continued to forge structures to protect the many families now sheltered by his house.[47]

Two days after the signing, Providence settler Mary Pray wrote a furious letter to Captain Oliver in Boston, relaying many rumors and the growing state of fear among her neighbors in Rhode Island. One rumor suggested that Canonicus had given Canonchet "20 bushel of corn which he divided to fourscore Indians and sent them out," suggesting an immediate threat, while another warned that "the Indians doe not desire to fight this winter" but would strike in the spring, "when the leaves are green." Referring directly to the Wampanoag "captives," she challenged Oliver: "Are our friend[s] of Boston satesfied that Naragansets are not true by detaining those murderus wreches?" She urged Oliver not to hesitate, to strike the Narragansetts in winter, writing, "It is deemed by al here that now is the time to try what the Lord God of power an mercy wil do for us against them." Appealing to divine justification and manly duty, Pray urged the Boston men to heed the call of "the God of Battel." If they waited, she insisted, Philip's prophecy would soon be fulfilled—they would turn to devour each other, lacking the "corn and hay" even to sustain their livestock in this war. To her great relief, before she had posted the letter, hushed "private" news had arrived from Williams that the Massachusetts "gouernor doth intend to send up an army to Naraganset."[48]

A NARRATIVE OF THE CAPTIVITY OF JAMES THE PRINTER, II: THE SOVEREIGNTY AND GOODNESS OF OUR NIPMUC RELATIONS

At the beginning of November, Job Kattenanit and James Speen came into Mendon with disturbing news. The scouts had just barely escaped an "enemy" raid on Hassanamesit. Their corn taken and their families "carried away captive," the two men, being "a little distance from the rest," were able to make "a shift to get away," along with some women and children. Job expressed great concern for the safety and welfare of his kin. Among those "captivated" were James Printer, Joseph Tukuppawillin, their "aged father," and Job's children, his wife having recently died.[49]

The frost already hardening the soil, the mission communities had been in the midst of "gathering, threshing and putting up in Indian barns," their "considerable crop of Indian corn that grew in that place and parts adjacent."[50] Many who had previously taken shelter at Okkanamesit had joined Printer's family in their return to Hassanamesit, to gather the late harvest. Although Gorham and Upham had destroyed much, together they retained enough corn to carry them through the coming winter, and hoped they might remain in their homes.

Still, "they were in a great strait," knowing if they returned to the settlements, "they sho[u]ld be sent to Deere Iland, as others were." Just days before, the Natick Indians had been carried away in horse-drawn carts in the middle of the night, then taken by canoe down the Charles River, past the Indian College, and loaded on ships to cross the fierce windy harbor. The faithful "friend Indians" of Natick had become captives, isolated on an island off the coast, long deforested and barren of shelter and resources. They faced harsh ocean winds and nor'easters that covered the island with snow, which, combined with meager shelter, led inevitably to death by freezing. The deer for which the island had been named (by the English) were long gone, and the people could eat mainly what shellfish they could gather from the freezing sand and sea. The islands had been planting places for their ancestors, not winter homes. James Printer and his relations were especially afraid of this possible future, knowing that "there corne being at such a distance about 40 miles from Boston," there was no way "it could . . . bee carried to susteyne their lives." If they were forced to Deer Island, "they should bee in danger to famish."[51]

News had also arrived of the capture of the men from Wamesit and the slave ships that left the coast, with praying Indians in their cargo holds. Some at

Hassanamesit "feared they should bee sent away to Barbados, or other places." Some among them, like Job, had gone to great lengths to assist the colonial troops. Yet that service would not shield them. After all, the men from Boston claimed they were taking the people of Natick for their own protection. All of the men previously taken at Okkanamesit and "imprisoned in Boston," were among them at Hassanamesit. They knew how close they had come to losing their freedom and their lives.[52]

On that brisk November day, as the women and men hung corn in the rafters, some three hundred of their Nipmuc relations came down from the north. Perhaps they had expected armed English troops, coming to round them up. Instead, they recognized the armed men as those whom they had fought beside in the Mohawk wars, with whom they had hunted and fished. They carried compelling words, asking the families at Hassanamesit to "go with them quietly" to Menimesit. If "you go to the English again," they warned, they would "force you all to some Island as the Natick Indians are, where you will be in danger to be starved with cold and hunger, and most probably in the end be all sent out of the country for slaves."[53]

The Nipmuc warriors came to gather their relatives under their protection, but also to gather the harvest they needed to sustain Menimesit through the winter. As James Quananopohit later reported, "to stay at Haasanamesho these Indians our enemies would not permit them, but said they must have the corne, but promised them if they should goe with them they should not die but bee preserved." "These praying Indians," he said, "were carried away by the enemy somewhat willingly, others of them unwillingly, as they [later] told him," "captivated" by the warriors' words. For some, perhaps those who had been imprisoned or lost kin, the arguments were persuasive. Tom Wuttasacomponom, the influential "ruler" of Hassanamesit, "yielded" to the warriors' "arguments, and by his example drew most of the rest." For others, the choice was more difficult. As James Quananopohit explained, "Most of them thought it best to go with them though they feared death every way." Some in Job's family, as Gookin later recalled, went "with heavy hearts and weeping eyes." His father, Naoas, and his brother, Joseph Tukuppawillin, "lamented much." Even as the Nipmuc force carried them north, Joseph "would faine have come back to the English after they were gone as far as Manchange but the enemy mockt him, for crying & drew him . . . the rest that were unwilling along with them."[54]

Was James Printer a "captive" or a "revolter," in joining Tom to travel north? Should he, as Gookin insisted, "rather have suffered death, than have gone among the wicked enemies of the people of God"? Perhaps, having been jailed, James did not share his brother and father's despair. Or perhaps, pragmatically, he understood their chance for survival was greater at Menimesit. Did James go willingly or was he taken by force? Was he a passive victim, or did he join the resistance? Job and James Quananopohit were remarkably silent on the matter. However, in characterizing *all* of the people at Hassanamesit as "captives" taken by "enemies" against their will, Job provided his kin protection with his words, the best possible shelter being their fidelity to the English, whether faltering or sustained. Job and James emphasized that the men were "unarmed," portraying peaceful Christian planters, crying with their wives and children, not fifty potential warriors leaving for the Nipmuc stronghold. Yet, even as the Massachusetts men pursued plans to contain the praying Indians, Nipmuc leaders were reclaiming the fields and families under their jurisdiction. James Printer and his family may have been "carried away captive," as Gookin described, but perhaps they were likewise "redeemed" by their relations from a narrowing compass of confinement.[55]

WEETAMOO: CAPTIVE OR PRINCE?

Amid the flying rumors in the colonies were reports that Narragansetts were among the warriors that "captivated" the Indians at Hassanamesit and that praying Indians had fled to Narragansett. The commissioners, led by Massachusetts, moved to "reach a decision for action." During the last "conference" with Canonchet and Cornman, they had set a date of October 28 for the Narragansett leaders to "deliver" Weetamoo and her relations. On October 27, Smith sent an important letter, communicating the Narragansett sachems' request for patience. Many of the Wampanaogs were still "out hunting," they relayed, and would be suspicious were the sachems to call them in; furthermore, they did not have the capacity to command their return.[56]

In early November, as the commissioners met in Boston, Gookin replied to Smith, on behalf of Massachusetts, dismissing the request as a ploy: "We evidently perceive the Narragansetts still make pleas & excuses for their not performance of their covenant to deliver up our enemies, that are among them, we cannot but thinke if they had been real, but they could easily have performed. Therefore wee Judge they do but juggle with us." Instead, they believed "that the womponoages & Narragansetts" were "abroad, (though they pretend at hunting)" in the woods west of Providence and Boston, "in conjunction with some of Phillips company." Revealing a surprising connection to James Printer's capture, Gookin said they "judge[d]" those pretended hunters were "of those that last weeke seased & carried away about 140 of the praying Indians" at "Hassannamesit; together with some of their corne." Failing to discern regional distinctions among "Indians," colonial leaders transformed evidence of Nipmuc warriors at Hassanamesit into supposition that allied Wampanoag and Narragansett "hunters" lurked "in parties upon our southwest borders" just "waiting for an opertunity to doe som other mischief." Thus the capture (or redemption) at Hassanamesit became one more pretext for a preemptive invasion of Narragansett.[57]

Meanwhile, Narragansett leaders were increasingly troubled by reports of captivity. From Boston, Canonchet had brought news of Christian Indians imprisoned in the colonial jail, and just recently, Smith's letter revealed, Quaboag messengers had ridden into Narragansett on horses, carrying news that their "fr[i]ends all the Prayinge indyans were seased first & then killed by Boston men, only they escaped," referring to rumors regarding the Natick Indians, and perhaps those captured at Wamesit. If this news reached Narragansett from Quaboag, it must have also motivated the warriors who "carried away" the families from Hassanamesit. The same news fueled the Boston men to action, infuriating Gookin. He told Smith that this "intelligence" was "false," insisting that "we had seased . . . their friends at Natick & other places" and put them "upon an Island" only for "their & our security" with "no purpose of doing them wrong." Despite this assurance, his admonition that those who delivered the news should be "punished" for their "flight and false report" could only have added to the Narragansetts' concerns about containment, which they had every reason to fear would soon be directed toward them. The Quaboag messengers also carried news from Boston, warning that the United Colonies "intended a war with the Narragansets sudenly."[58]

The intelligence from Quaboag was not off the mark. In his letter, Gookin asked Smith "to signify to the sachems of Narragansett that wee expect a speedy & punctual performance of their article touching the delivery of the enemy & that wee cannot accept of their pleas & alegations, which wee conceive are only deceits & delusions." If they did "not perform *very* speedily," Gookin wrote, "they must expect to heare from us an other manner besides words" (emphasis in original). Gookin may have been a strong advocate for "his" converts, but he joined with his fellow magistrates in constraining the unconverted. Privately, he responded to Smith, "The commissioners of the United Colonies & our Generall Court are come to a resolve; not to suffer themselves to bee baffled & abused by those Narrogansetts." It would not be "much longer" before they would "(by God's Assistance) reduce them to reason."[59]

As Gookin predicted, on November 12, the United Colonies declared they would raise an army of "one thousand" soldiers, in addition to those already serving, "to march into the Narragansett Country." They held the sachems culpable for "harbouring" the "actors" of war, "relieving and succoring theire women and children and wounded men; and detaining them in theire custody." There was "suspicion and probability" that Narragansetts had "killed and taken away many Cattle from the English theire Naighbors" and expressed shouts of "triumph" at the raid on Hadley, some joining with "the Phillipians and the other uplanders" in the Connecticut Valley, "destroying many of the English, their houses and goods." However, it was the "detaining" of Weetamoo and her kin, combined with their "feare" that those "captives" lurked "in parties" near inland towns, that gave the commissioners solid cause to declare war.[60]

Yet, like the Nipmucs who reclaimed their relations at Hassanamesit, the Narragansetts not only "detained," but *"retained"* their Wampanoag kin under their protection. Settler narratives portrayed both groups through a framework of captivity: the Hassanamesit families as captives taken by the enemy, the Wampanoags as captives held too long by wayward friends, turned suspicious "actors." The English asserted jurisdiction over both groups. The Christian Nipmucs "belonged" to Massachusetts by covenants they had signed before the war, although the Boston men had failed in their promises to protect them. The Wampanoags held in "custody," they claimed, belonged to the United Colonies by right of war, and were owed to them through the "covenants" of peace that the Narragansetts had signed in July and October. In truth, these invocations of covenants and claims were part of the frenetic policy of containment, an attempt to assert jurisdiction and control, through forceful persuasion, intimidation, or outright violence, over *all* Indians. Indeed, although the United Colonies' initial order was to raise a military force to compel the Narragansetts to the "actuall performance of theire Covenants . . . by delivering up those of our enimies that are in theire custody," ultimately, the commissioners sought their total containment, and to break up the alliances they feared were emerging throughout the land. By the time they delivered formal instructions to Winslow, the commander-in-chief of the expedition, the order had been transformed: "You shall . . . endeavour to secure any of our English plantations . . . to discover, pursue, encounter, and by the help of God, to vanquish and subdue the cruel, barbarous and treacherous enemy, whether Philip Sachem and his Wampanooucks, or the Narrigansets his undoubted allies, or any other their friends and abettors."[61]

Shortly after the commissioners made their formal declaration, Nathaniel Saltonstall completed a "letter to a friend in London," one of the first narratives of the war to be published in England. *The Present State of New England with Respect to the Indian War* portrayed Weetamoo as a major actor and stressed the urgency of the looming campaign against the Narragansetts. As Saltonstall described her, Weetamoo was "as Potent a Prince as any round about her, and hath as much Corn, Land, and Men, at her Command" as any sachem. Even as James Printer's father and brother were feminized as praying Indians help-less against the "enemy" in this portrait, Weetamoo was gendered masculine, a "potent" military leader and inheritor of great wealth. The lands that she had labored to protect became a symbol of her power, and she had so fully inhab-ited a male role that she was able to "command" men in war. Weetamoo was so influential, Salstonstall claimed, that Philip's "first Errand" was to ask her to "joyn with him in this Conspiracy." Weetamoo "was much more forward in the Design," he maintained, and "had greater success than King Philip himself."[62]

Saltonstall's timing was crucial. His letter was not simply a representation of the "present state" of the war, but an argument in support of the Narragansett campaign. The first clearly preemptive strike, against such a large nation of England's Indigenous allies, had to be justified. The major argument, from Saltonstall's point of view, was the "delivery" of Weetamoo and the Wampanoag warriors under her "command." Although rumors circulated that Metacom was at Narragansett, there is no real evidence that he was there at any time during that fall. All of the Wampanoags had come in with Weetamoo, or on their own, drawing on kinship and alliance.

In his letter, Saltonstall also suggested that Weetamoo had used her feminine wiles to draw in the Narragansett sachems. "Having ran very far in her Engage-ments with King Philip, and fearing lest she should be taken," he wrote, "she committed her Person to the Possession of . . . Ninicroft, judging herself safe by Virtue of his Protection, where she hath continued ever since July last." Saltonstall sometimes confused Narragansett leaders; here he erroneously re-ported that Weetamoo went to Ninigret rather than Canonicus. However, what is most interesting is the gendered manner in which he described her move-ments. Having gone "too far," with a feminine fear of being "taken," she sought out male "protection." The elder sachem, whether Ninigret or Canonicus, took "possession" of her "person," offering a chivalrous shield. Saltonstall suggests this "friend" of the English was duped by Weetamoo's feminine plea, evoking the guileful femme, a keen strategist who manipulates men to her advantage.[63]

According to Saltonstall a company of Connecticut men were sent "to the Narragansetts, to require them to deliver the Queen, and withal to Ratifie that long Peace they had maintained with the English." He recounted the July peace and the September council with Ninigret's counselor, as well as the "agreement" of the Narragansetts to "deliver" the Wampanaogs. At every turn he emphasized the singular role of Weetamoo as a subject of negotiation. The Massachusetts Council required that Ninigret "come to Boston, to treat concerning the deliv-ery [of the] Squaw Sachem." In renewing the "Peace" and making their final "Agreement," the Narragansetts "were to deliver the Squa Sachem within so many Days at Boston." Writing even as the commissioners met, Saltonstall provided strong motivation for offensive action. "The Narragansetts," he wrote, "we fear more and more every Day, will be perfidious to us, the Time being past that they should have delivered Squaw Sachem at Boston."[64]

Reporting on the commissioners' declaration, he continued, "Our Fears the more increased, as well in that we understand several of them appear up and down in Arms; however here is a Levie now coming out for a thousand Englishmen to wait on them, which we hope may reduce them to good Order, as well as recover Squaw Sachem out of their Hands; which if she be taken by the English, her Lands will more than pay all the Charge we have been at in this unhappy War."[65]

In this powerful passage, Saltonstall revealed the most important motivations for the Narragansett campaign: the containment of the growing resistance — reducing the Narragansetts and those appearing "up and down in Arms" "to good order" — and the claiming of Wampanoag lands. Narragansett lands were at stake, as well. The Massachusetts Council promised soldiers who successfully "played the man, took the Fort, & Drove the Enemy out of the Narragansett Country . . . a gratuity in land besides their wages." Among the United Colonies commissioners and key military officers were Atherton men and those with financial interest in Pocasset and Sakonnet, including Josiah Winslow, Richard Smith Sr. and Jr., John Winthrop Jr., Wait Winthrop, Thomas Stanton Sr. and Jr., Daniel Dennison, Matthew Fuller, Benjamin Church, and William Bradford. The bitter catastrophe that would come to be known as the Great Swamp "Fight" was not merely motivated by the need to suppress an Indian insurrection, but was driven by Englishmen's desperate desire for Native land and the containment of Native leaders.[66]

However, leaders like Canonchet and Weetamoo were engaged in strategies and deliberations far more complex and innovative than the commissioners imagined. Even as Canonchet met with the commissioners, Weetamoo actively forged bonds while the Narragansetts built a defense. In Saltonstall's next letter, he reported that one of the Narragansett sachems had "since [been] Marryed to the Squaw Sachem; which Marriage doth signifie a near Alliance."[67]

A NARRATIVE OF THE CAPTIVITY OF JOB KATTENANIT

Even as the commissioners met in Boston, the Massachusetts Court sent a company from Cambridge toward Hassanamesit, responding to Job Kattenanit and James Speen's report. After gathering "intelligence" at Hassanamesit, the Cambridge company under Syll would meet with Henchman's troops at

Mendon "to jointly seek out the enemy" who "hath killed and surprised some of our neighbor Indians that were gathering corn there." James and Thomas Quananopohit, along with three other scouts, would serve as guides. James Speen and Job's report was among the best intelligence they had of the location of actual "enemy" warriors.[68]

Gookin advised Syll to "use your best skill & force to surprise, sease, kill and destroy the enemy and to receive and release any of our friends either English or Indians that are taken or injured by him." Although Gookin continued to equate "Praying Indians" among the "enemy" with English captives, suspicion was high among settlers and soldiers. Some believed converts might be hiding behind the "camouflage" of English clothes and prayers, just as warriors cloaked themselves in ferns. Recent reports from Rhode Island warned, "The Indians boast and say those indians that are caled praying Indians never shut [shoot] at the other Indians, but up into the tops of the trees or into the ground," and many feared those shots would be turned on them. Still, Gookin urged Syll to trust in their scouts, send them ahead, but to avoid "thickets" and aim to strike at night.[69]

As James Quananopohit arrived at Mendon with Syll's troop, his brother, and his friend Eleazar Pegin, he encountered a scene of desolation. All of its settlers were "contracted" into "two houses," lacking the "necessities" to sustain them. Henchman's troops, only five days out from Boston, were in no better shape, having consumed nearly all their provisions. James would have heard from Henchman's men that they had already scouted Hassanamesit, finding no Indians present. Nipmucs had gathered a robust harvest of corn, nuts, and apples, but left before the colonial troops arrived, leaving an apple smoking on the fire, and a tobacco pouch behind. Although Henchman portrayed this as evidence of hurried escape, James may have recognized a clear intent—the tobacco attached to purposeful words, a single piece of fruit designed to show that warriors remained nearby. The effectiveness of this tactic was evident in Henchman's subsequent actions—he began to make preparations for Boston, writing from Mendon that his men had not brought enough food and the promised support had not arrived. The council replied with further orders: Syll's arrival was imminent, biscuits were coming, and he should return to the "other side" of the Nipmuc river to "bring away the corn & secure it from the enemy." The council also sent news of another raid—the elusive warriors had attacked a mill in Marlboro, nearly killing the miller's son and taking his apprentice captive.[70]

Although Henchman's company had failed to find a single Indian, captive or "enemy," once Syll arrived, his company, guided by James Quananopohit and Eleazar Pegin, soon "discovered seven of the enemy and one of them leading an Englishman," the miller's apprentice. They fired upon the man and "pursued them so close" that the captor "was forced to leave his prisoner" as he escaped. James Quananopohit led the startled young man back to Syll, with a "recovered" musket, taken from Marlborough the night before.[71]

Gookin imagined that the warriors "lurking about" the Nipmuc country were allied forces that included Narragansetts and Wampanoags, seeking to violently surprise bordering settlements. Yet this group consisted mainly of Nipmucs with a pragmatic motivation, the harvesting of food. They still had an ample harvest at Pakachoag, where no settlers remained. When Henchman's company marched there, they found "above one hundred bushels of Indian corn newly gathered, and a great quantity of corn standing." Yet they could "discover" no "enemy," although, "in all probability" the Nipmucs "saw them in all their motions," as they trudged among the fields.[72]

Only when Thomas Quananopohit doubled back, ordered to retrieve correspondence Henchman had left in the "wigwam," did he espy the men who had been watching their movements. Riding up Pakachoag's hill, Thomas came upon the round house at the top to find six men, four sitting by the fire inside and two emerging from the door, who immediately saw him. Thinking quickly, Thomas pretended an army was "coming up the hill" behind him, calling them to "encompass the enemy." One of the Nipmuc "presented his gun," but "the gun missing fire," due to damage from the rain, they quickly "ran away." Thomas had lost the use of his hand at Pocasset, and at Pakachoag he would have been nearly unable to defend himself, having "only a pistol," a young unarmed medic, and a soldier who had lost his flint. His stratagem saved their lives. Yet many soldiers in the company still "murmured greatly against . . . their guides," and Syll reluctantly sent three "home," to quell fears and potential violence among his troops. They retained only the Quananopohits, who moved on with Syll toward Marlborough, while Henchman continued to scout between Mendon and Hassanamesit.[73]

As these Nipmuc men later told James at Menimesit, after *his* company left, they returned to Hassanamesit "to get the corn," when a family dog alerted them to an intrusion. Despite the barking, Henchman and his "two files" of twenty-two men descended, clumsily attempting to "surround them." As the Nipmucs reported, "The English came upon them in the wigwam at Hassunnamesuke & there they killed two Englishmen." Henchman's report to the magistrates described a scene of utter chaos and their good fortune in escaping, admitting the death of two officers. Gookin, who later received reports from the Quananopohit brothers, observed, "having no Indian guide with him," Henchman "sustained a great loss." After this incident, the Nipmucs regrouped, continuing to harvest: they "carried away all the corne at Pakuahooge & in the Nipmuck country unto their quarters" at Menimesit, enough to sustain the many families gathered there.[74]

Only three days after Henchman's botched expedition, Gookin sent another scout on an important mission. Following an "order from the council to gain intelligence of the enemy," he engaged Job Kattenanit, who might have the best chance of tracking the captives from Hassanamesit, as well as their captors, and observing the imagined alliance in the western woods. Job most desired to find his three "children," taken "captive" at Hassanamesit, and "endeavor to get them out of the enemies' hand," believing they would be better protected among the English. "Alleging that his affections were so great to his children, (their mother being dead,) and he in a widowed estate," Gookin wrote, Job "was willing to venture his life among the enemy, in order to the recovery of his children." Gookin composed a pass to authorize Job's mission in the Nipmuc country, relaying that he was "a trusty Indian" under the protection of "the Governor and myself."[75]

When Job came near to his family's town of Hassanamesit, he "met with some of Capt. Henchman's troops," still scouting. As Gookin noted, Job "could easily have concealed himself." But unlike the warriors they feared, Job "not fearing to speak with the English, from whom he was sent with a pass, stood in open view." Yet neither the writing nor his articulate speech could persuade them of his purpose. The soldiers only debated whether to kill or capture him. They stripped him of his clothes and his gun, "seized him" like a prisoner and "carried him to Capt. Henchman." If it had been only days earlier, James Quananopohit could have told Henchman that Job had provided the very intelligence that prompted Henchman's mission. Thomas could have reminded him that Job was among his troops as they pursued Philip to Nipsachuck. But Henchman could not see Job, the "preacher," scout, and "faithful" ally. Having lost two of his best men, amidst a burgeoning loss of control, he, like Mosely, captured the only Indian over whom he had power, ironically subverting the best chance at gathering intelligence on the "enemy" he sought.[76]

After interrogating him, Henchman brought him to Boston, where Job, like his brother James, was confined to prison, joining "many" other "Indians" in the small "noisome" place. Like James, Job was subjected to the "clamors" of settlers who called for his death, "though," Gookin wryly observed, "they knew not wherefore." Gookin himself was once more accused of conspiracy, with the baseless charge that Job was "sent forth to give intelligence to the enemy." Job Kattenanit spent three weeks in the crowded prison. Upon his release, he was sent to Deer Island. Meanwhile, Henchman and Syll's troops, minus their scouts, were "diverted" from the Nipmuc country to join the forces heading toward Narragansett.[77]

"THEY COULD NOT COME HOME AGAIN"

While Job was imprisoned in Boston, a letter arrived from the leader Numphow, Samuel's father, and his counselor, John Lyne. Writing to Henchman, their neighbor, they explained they had left their "home" at Wamesit, and gone "towards the French, we go where Wanalancet is." The tone of the letter is regretful, but their reasons boiled down to one point: Massachusetts had failed to provide shelter from the storm. The "help" they received "from the Council . . . did not do us good," and did not prevent "wrong by the English." Referring to the haystack burning, the Wamesit leaders said, "When there was any harm done in Chelmsford, they laid it to us and said we did it." But, they insisted, "we know ourselves that we never did harm to the English, but we go away peaceabley and quietly." They understood the looming threat of containment and sought to avoid forced removal: "As for the Island, we say there is no safety for us, because many English be not good," and "they" may "come to kill us, as in the other case."[78]

Here, Numphow and John Lyne referred to past incidents and the most recent violence at Wamesit. Even as Henchman was bringing in Job, a group of fourteen vigilantes from his town had gone down to the "wigwams" of the Wamesit people, who were under Richardson's guard, with the intent to "kill them all." According to Gookin, the men "called to the poor Indians to come out of doors." Like Job, "both men, women, and children" readily showed their faces. Then, "two of the English being loaded with pistol-shot, being not far off, fired upon them and wounded five women and children," in view of their relations. The men also shot and killed a young man from influential leadership families in front of his mother, Sarah, who was also wounded. This violence led the people of Wamesit, including Sarah, to head north. Yet, "as soon as the Council were informed that the Indians were fled, they sent out order to Lieutenant Henchman to send after them, and endeavor to persuade them to return." Henchman sent a Native servant, who returned with their letter, likely composed by Samuel or their "teacher" Simon Betomkin. They insisted, they could "not come home again."[79]

Even as the Massachusetts men demanded that the Narragansetts fulfill their "covenant," they failed to fulfill the covenant they had made with the Nipmuc and Patucket praying towns. Sarah and Numphow were inheritors of the original agreements between the Massachusett Saunkskwa, Passaconaway, and Massachusetts, and yet, as Numphow and John Lyne showed, the magistrates had failed even to protect their Native allies from settlers under their jurisdiction.[80] Leaders like Job and Numphow realized, with great regret, that they could not even expect protection of the most vulnerable among their kin, and both the policy of containment and vigilante violence hindered their own efforts to protect their families. Still, Numphow's letter reveals they had options beyond suffering containment and exposure at Wamesit or "the Island." In heading north, they followed the path of "Wanalancet," seeking shelter among kin who *could* protect them, while insisting in writing that they pursued a "peaceable" course.

While captives like the "maid," Elizabeth Wakely, were forced to move through unfamiliar northern spaces, James Printer and his relations became captives confined within familiar homelands. Despite longstanding relationships, settlers increasingly treated Native converts as unfamiliar, less-than-human suspects. Ironically, even as colonial narratives, laws, and oral accusations constructed them as foreigners, men like Samuel Numphow, James Printer, and Job Kattenanit were confined in part because of English fears of their familiarity with both the interior of their Native homelands and the social spaces of the English.[81]

PLANTING ALLIANCE

Neal Salisbury provides a salient description of the agricultural practices of Native women from Wabanaki to Wampanoag country, which is also an apt metaphor for the ways in which they cultivated alliance:

> By the seventeenth century Indian women from the Saco River southward had developed a variety of crops, including several types of maize, beans, and squash, as well as pumpkins, cucumbers, Jerusalem artichokes, and tobacco. A single field was planted with all these crops, and the most prominent feature was the regularly spaced mounds or "hills" in which several corn and bean seeds were planted. One effect of these hills was to strengthen the plants against winds . . . by allowing the roots to intertwine.[82]

Even as the bounds around mission communities constricted, Weetamoo expanded her bonds at Narragansett to fulfill the covenant of protection with her Pocasset kin. Like many women before her, she used the twine of marriage, which "linked" families together in "a complex network" of relationships that ensured reciprocal exchange and mutual support. Many colonial narrators claimed Weetamoo fled to Narragansett seeking "protection." Yet Pocasset families found here a temporary refuge from their war-torn home, a harvest to replace their destroyed fields, and a coalition against "a common threat"—all of which was expected from families bound by marriage. Weetamoo's alliance-making shows that she understood the importance of forging a stronger bond with the Narragansetts, whom Mather called "the greatest body of Indians in New England." Metacom had pursued alliance in the Nipmuc country, where protectors already struck English towns, yet Weetamoo assumed a greater challenge. Weetamoo had married once to unite the Wampanoags; now, she conceived a transnational confederation.[83]

When she arrived at Narragansett, Weetamoo may have called on her ties to Quaiapin, just as she relied on Canonicus's diplomacy. Yet she solidified alliance by marrying Quinnapin. Described as "a midling thick-set man of a very stout fierce countenance," Quinnapin was "the second man in Command in the Narraganset Country, next to" his cousin, Canonchet. When Rhode Island authorities had tried to imprison him, Quinnapin had received shelter in Weetamoo's house. Recognizing the reversal of their roles, Quinnapin must have offered Weetamoo shelter in return, creating a relational structure that ensured her people's survival. Marriage bound her to his uncles and cousins, obliging them to provide sustenance and loyalty. Although the English would not accept kinship trumping political allegiance, in Weetamoo's world, there was no stronger bond. The English tried to contain the Narragansetts as "subjects" and force them to fulfill a tenuous pledge. Yet, in "failing" to "deliver" the Wampanoags, the Narragansetts fulfilled a much stronger covenant, according to their value system and adaptable political structure, which sometimes required the "regrouping" and linking of relatively "fluid" and "contingent" extended families in order to unify against a common threat.[84]

As Weetamoo and Quinnapin engineered an alliance, a Narragansett named Stonewall John engineered a massive defensive fort to shelter it. John adapted the masonry skills he acquired while working for Richard Smith to create a refuge on the secluded wetland known as Great Swamp. Constructed of stone and earth, the fort also provided storage for their ample supply of corn. Understanding that "conferences" and "treaties" were "only" a "policie to intrap the Sachims, as they had done Phillip many times," Canonchet "yielded" to deceptive diplomacy in Boston to forestall military action, providing enough time to put up the harvest and complete the structure that would protect the families when and if the English came down.[85]

"THE PERFIDIOUS & UNJUST
DEALING OF SOM ENGLISH"

That same November, William Waldron, Richard's nephew, piloted the ship *Endeavor* up the coast, seeking to capture Wabanaki people under pretense of trade. Hearing that "they had shackles on board," Thomas Gardner sent an urgent letter to the *Endeavor's* crew, docked at Monhegan Island, "warning them not to take any Indians east side of Kenibek River because we had made peace with them." Waldron continued to sail up the coast and "did carry 9 Indians away from Michias," a Wolastokuk (Passamaquoddy/Maliseet) village two hundred miles east of Casco Bay, "and more from Cape Sables," a remote peninsula across from Machias, in Wolastokuk, far beyond the northern front of the war (see map 9).[86]

Seeking prosecution, Gardner described a "perfidious & unjust dealing": Waldron and his crew had "Stollen Eight or Nine persones from the Indianes" by deception, including, according to other reports, a sachem and his wife, who had no involvement in the violence to the south. This was, he later wrote, a chief "Cause of the Indianes Riseing" in the north. "Being Incensed for their loss," Wabanaki people asked Gardner to pursue action against the offenders, but Waldron's ship had sailed directly from the Wabanaki coast "to Azores to sell them into slavery."[87]

GREAT SWAMP

On December 10, two detachments went out from Massachusetts to attempt to simultaneously contain the southern and northern fronts of the war. A northern detachment under Daniel Denison sought to "subdue the Indians in their winter quarters" at Ossipee and Pequacket. The southern detachment, part of a force of more than one thousand (1,300) soldiers from three colonies, pursued the same goal at Narragansett. Both companies had little idea of where their targets were or how they would find them. The expedition to Ossipee never got off the ground. As Williamson wrote, "The snow had fallen to the depth of four feet upon a level; and they, being unfurnished with snowshoes, could not travel a day's journey into the woods without great hazard of their lives; therefore the enterprize was abandoned." Hubbard, writing two years later, still (erroneously) believed it was a journey of "about an hundred miles up into the country northward." Lacking crucial Indigenous technology, navigational skill, and geographic knowledge, the colonial troops were nearly powerless to implement their plan for containment of the northern front. On the other hand, Indigenous knowledge — of travel technology, geography, and colonial (in)capacities — enabled Wabanaki warriors and their families to travel in these same environments and to plan ahead, moving into their interior towns long before the winter came down, knowing the snow would serve as a deep, extensive fortress against colonial invasion.[88]

The conditions were similar at Narragansett. Experiencing an exceptionally bitter winter, by mid-December, Saltonstall reported, "the weather now being extreme cold . . . both frost and snow" had accumulated to a depth of "two Foot," and "in many Places three Foot deep." Marching from Boston and Plymouth to Seekonk, companies arrived by foot and sloop at Smith's fort in Wickford, which became a base for the United Colonies army. The colonial forces were initially "at a Stand, not knowing which Way to go in Pursuit of the Indians," so Mosely pursued a hunt for captives who might provide the "information" they required.[89]

COCUMCOSUCK (WICKFORD), SHAWOMET (WARWICK), AND SURROUNDING AREAS, NARRAGANSETT COUNTRY, SATURDAY–SUNDAY (SABBATH), DECEMBER 11–12

Some of them went missing. Some family, having gone out that day, did not return. But others, who made it home, might have glimpsed the familiar face of Mosely, heard the crunch of boots breaking through the crust, the heavy breath of dogs. The Wampanoags among them might have recognized Benjamin Church. Seeing their tracks, they must have understood.

In the night, scouts may have seen men from Warwick, as they guided a Cambridge troop, trudging through the snow towards Shawomet. Already emptied, the soldiers found no one in the snowy woods of "Pomham's country," closest to the settlement of Warwick.[90]

COCUMCOSUCK (WICKFORD), MONDAY, DECEMBER 13

Disappointed and frustrated, Cambridge Captain Oliver arrived at Smith's garrison the next morning, joined by companies from Plymouth and Massachusetts. Mosely and Church, having scouted beyond Wickford the day before, presented their newly arrived commander, Josiah Winslow, with thirty-six prisoners, including "Indian Peter," the only one who, under threat of hanging, gave up "information" regarding the "number and resolutions" of the Narragansetts, including the location of their "towns" (see maps 4 and 7).[91]

WOOSSOWENBISKW, TUESDAY, DECEMBER 14

From beneath the ground, she could hear the plod of horse hooves coming toward them, the trudge of heavy boots upon the snowpack. She could hear the low rumbling of voices as they approached, now moving at a crawl, their paths diverging. Perhaps at a distance, the sound of men uncovering woven mats, rustling through corn the women had laid below the now frozen ground in winter stores, as her own heartbeat echoed in her ears. In stillness, some of her men may have regretted their position, wanting to move stealthily to the surface, feeling the lost opportunity of ambush. But Quaiapin had built this sanctuary in the womb of the earth, hidden by stonework and glacial boulders, now camouflaged by snow, for this very purpose. An entire company could move through her "fort" and never realize they were there.[92] They could steal the corn, if they found it, they could even destroy by fire the hundreds of homes nearby, but they would not find the people, hidden in this full size underground "chamber" and the other great stonework to the west. Elsewhere, on that day, families grieved more missing kin, one man and one woman killed in the morning by Cambridge men, while seven more were killed that afternoon; twelve people taken captive, carried back to Smith's post.[93]

PETTAQUAMSCUT, WEDNESDAY, DECEMBER 15

With kin being captured and two empty towns burned, Quinnapin led the first major Narragansett strike, a forceful "retaliation" and symbolic reclamation of Pettaquamscut. Before them lay the site of deed wars among the Rhode Island proprietors and Atherton men; raids on houses and cattle; the meeting with the Royal Commission; and the most recent "treaty by sword," led by the now deceased Hutchinson. Only three months before, the settler Jeriah Bull was still "promot[ing] settlement in Narragansett Country," in the midst of great tension, "witnessing a deed to land six miles west from Pettaquamscutt Rock at the edge of Great Swamp." The warriors targeted Bull's "large stone house" and "stone wall yard," along with the "dozen" soldiers sent by Connecticut to protect it. Burning the garrison to the ground, the protectors enacted a perfect reversal of the attack on Quaiapin's town, then left, leading cattle to the refuge at Great Swamp.[94]

The raid was a violent reassertion of sovereignty over this highly contested place, as well as a symbolic message designed to instill fear and a sense of Narragansett power. Bull's fortified house was the very location where the Massachusetts and Plymouth forces were to rendezvous with those from Connecticut. As Ebenezer Peirce would later observe, "This was a daring feat on the part of the Indians, with so large an army not far distant and large reinforcements to that army daily and hourly expected." Neither settlers nor soldiers detected their movements. When Prentice's troop rode to the rendezvous the next day, they fully expected to see Connecticut troops, flanked by Mohegan scouts, and wood smoke signaling a warm fire. Instead, from the road, they espied the charred remains of the building and bodies lying upon the hill. The remote town was emptied of the living and no troops had yet arrived.[95]

COCUMCOSUCK (WICKFORD)

Meanwhile, at Smith's post, the Narragansett mason John had "stonewalled" the troops as the Narragansett protectors moved east, proposing a council to make "peace." At Cocumcosuck, John may have been able to observe captive family members, to determine who among them was still alive, and report back the conditions of the garrison's fortifications. He may have gathered information on the numbers and intents of the troops, their provisions, their lack of snowshoes.[96]

Once the "rogue" John left, as Oliver reported, some of the Salem men, scouting nearby (and perhaps looting corn), were ambushed by warriors, who shot three men from behind a hill "within a mile" of the garrison. Two more were killed "at a house three miles off." When Mosely, Oliver, and Captain Gardner "went off" to warn and "fetch in" a Massachusetts company, they found themselves facing a barrage of shot from behind stone walls nearby the Queen's Fort, the multilevel structure they could not discern and would never locate during the war. These walls formed a defensive network, the bulwarks of which were Quaiapin's hidden chamber and the impenetrable fort at "their great swamp" at Canonicus's "quarters," where "Indian Peter" reported over four thousand people were sheltered, "joined all in a Body."[97]

On this same day, chaplain Joseph Dudley delivered Peter's intelligence to the magistrates in Boston. Writing from Smith's garrison, he noted, "By ye help of Indian Peter . . . we have burned two of their Towns," including "ye Old Queens quarters consisting of about 150 Many of them large wigwams." Over the last several days they had "seized & slayne 50 person in all our prisoners being about 40," among whom were "10 or 12 Wampanoags." Unaware that only nine miles away, Pettaquamscut was burning, Dudley stated simply that "this day we Intend the removal or spoyle of ye Corn" they had already found. Peter had revealed that "the whole body" of Narragansetts, Wampanoags, and their allies had "removed into their Great Swamp." Once the Connecticut troops arrived, Dudley wrote, they "hoped to Coop them up," a simple goal of containment, not unlike rounding up cattle. Already gathered together, in one single location, the Indians would be drawn under control by the impressive military force. Dudley expressed confidence that the combined troops would capture the corn for their own sustenance, and then capture the Indians "in one body." The troops would remove them from the country, and claim the planting fields, finally, for their own.[98]

COCUMCOSUCK (WICKFORD), PETTAQUAMSCUT, GREAT SWAMP, FRIDAY–SUNDAY, DECEMBER 17–19

The next day, the news arrived that Pettaquamscut had been burned. On the following day Connecticut troops arrived at the ruins with a hundred fifty Mohegans and Pequots, led by Owaneco and Catapazet. As Oliver briefed from Smith's fort, "That day we sold Capt. Davenport," leader of the Cambridge company, "47 Indians, young and old for 80 [pounds] money," the captives moved to Aquidneck Island "for safekeeping" en route to the Caribbean. Whatever profit Davenport made, he would not be able to spend. Two days later, he was shot dead at Great Swamp, his claims to profit from the sale of captives or land in the Narragansett country gone.[99]

On December 18 the full contingent of Plymouth and Massachusetts troops marched and rode to Pettaquamscut to meet their allies from Connecticut. They spent a bitter night in "an open field," amidst a rising snowstorm, with no buildings to shelter them, no hearth to warm them. With sleep a hazardous option, the combined forces, with the Mohegans and Pequots, began the march from Pettaquamscut before break of day, according to Dudley and Oliver, on the "Sabbath" of December 19. Mosely "led the van."[100]

The Great Swamp fort was well protected by its geographic isolation and environment. Surrounded by marsh and thick with brush, the fort had only one opening that allowed access. Without prior knowledge, navigation would be impossible. However, below freezing temperatures turned the icy swamp to solid ground and packed snow allowed for foot travel, while "Indian Peter" guided the troops. Thus, as Dudley reported from the field, "a tedious march in the snow, without intermission, brought us about two of the clock afternoon, to the entrance of the swamp, by the help of Indian Peter."[101]

Saltonstall, narrating the story for his English readers, described the scene witnessed by Dudley and the troops: "In the Midst [of the Swamp] thereof was a Piece of firm Land, of about three or four Acres of Ground, whereon the Indians had built a Kind of Fort, being Palisado'd round, and within that a Clay Wall, as also felled down Abundance of Trees to lay quite round the said Fort, but they had not quite finished the said Work."[102]

Dudley reported, "Within the cedar swamp we found some hundreds of wigwams, forted in with a breastwork and flankered, and many small blockhouses up and down, round about; they entertained us with a fierce fight, and many thousand shot, for about an hour, when our men valiantly scaled the fort, beat them thence, and from the blockhouses."[103]

Although they intended to intimidate the Narragansetts and Wampanoags into quick surrender, the troops were taken aback by the sight of the immense fort and "blockhouses," startled by the blasts of gunfire that emerged from the edifice. According to historian George Bodge, the Great Swamp "wigwams" were "rendered bullet-proof by large quantities of grain in tubs and bags, placed along the sides. In these many of their old people and their women and children had gathered for safety," while protectors shot from "behind and within these defenses." The Narragansetts used corn to fortify their homes and to protect their families from being wounded in the fighting. As in planting, they found strength in intertwining adaptation, combining European building techniques with Indigenous guerilla warfare strategies to create a multifaceted bastion against English troops.[104]

According to Dudley, the Narragansett and Wampanoags "beat us out of the fort" within hours, but eventually, having lost several officers, with many more soldiers slain and wounded, Winslow pursued an annihilative strategy. Dudley reported:

> We reinforced and very hardily entered the fort again, and fired the wigwams, with many living and dead persons in them, great piles of meat and heaps of corn . . . were consumed; the number of their dead, we generally suppose the enemy lost at least two hundred men . . . a captive woman, well known to Mr. Smith, informing that there wer three thousand five hundred men engaging us and about a mile distant a thousand in reserve.[105]

Historian George Bodge has suggested that the Narragansett strategy was successful in beating back the English until the colonists decided to utilize the tactic that had so devastated the Pequots fifty-five years earlier. They set fire to the Narragansett homes, burning the people within and sending bullets into those who ran from the chaos of the flames that were rapidly devouring the town. Captain Oliver reported that "by the best intelligence, we killed 300 fighting men; prisoners we took, say 350, above 300 women and children. We burnt above 500 houses, left but 9, burnt all their corn, that was in baskets, great store." These figures mentioned only male casualties. Considering that fire rarely discriminates on the basis of age or sex, surely just as many women and children were killed. According to Bodge, "Indian prisoners afterward reported seven hundred killed."[106]

It is these accounts, told from the perspective of the troops, and debates over the actual numbers of the dead that dominate the published histories of Great Swamp. Historian Christine DeLucia reminds us that there are other stories, other accounts to be remembered, not only of the massacre itself, but of the ways in which it has been recounted. Describing the picture of survival after the war, and accounting for Narragansett perspectives, she writes, "The immediate aftermath was chaotic, with prisoners being sold into slavery, widows and children begging for subsistence, wounded and dead unaccounted for. Record-keeping suffered as community fragmentation made it difficult for anyone to accurately tabulate total human losses. One Narragansett, captured and sent for execution, was asked by Massachusetts officials in August 1676 to 'say how many Indians were killed at the Fort-Fight' at Great Swamp. 'He replyed . . . that as to old men, women and Children, they had lost no body could tell how many.'"[107]

The fires at Great Swamp had erupted in desperation and chaos. Although they killed hundreds of people, including children, a crime from which they could never be redeemed, the United Colonies failed to "coop up" either the Narragansetts or the Wampanaog "captives." The obsession with tabulating the numbers of dead seems one way colonial leaders tried to regain control, attempting to contain the Narragansetts and their allies by measurements, and claim victory, while continuing to estimate the numbers yet uncontained. As this statement by a Narragansett captive suggests, the loss, of those sold and those killed, was in truth unknowable and unfathomable. Yet key leaders, including Weetamoo, had escaped, and were reconfiguring, gathering families together. We do not have the saunkskwa's report or her relation, but it is possible to imagine fragments and impressions of her experience and the experience of the women who survived:

What She Witnessed

In the membranes of her nostrils, on her tongue
The overwhelming smoke of parched corn
Blue flames climbing
Bark mats burning
From inside
Her nostrils filling, resisting
Saturated with seared flesh

Corn husk dolls, corn husk mats
Devoured by relentless orange tongues
Her ears filling with their cries
With the exhalation of their feverish breath
Limbs responding with rapidity

The sinews of her arms giving way
Still pulling, grasping those she could carry
Then the weight of her own child against her back,
Legs moving
The cold wind biting the exposed skin of her cheek
A relief

Despite the unfathomable loss, many of the Narragansetts and Wampanoags survived, taking shelter in Quaiapin's hidden fort and other remote locations in the Narragansett Country. It was one of the coldest winters they had seen and the troops continued to march through their land, seeking captives and corn. As Saltonstall proudly related, after burning Great Swamp, "Our Forces foraged the Country, and brought in great Quantities of Indian Corn to the Army," a tactic designed not merely to feed the undernourished troops, but as part of the military campaign. Oliver reported, "We fetch in their corn daily and that undoes them."[108]

As survivors gathered together, deliberating the best strategy for survival in the midst of deep snow, the sachems sent runners north, carrying reports of Great Swamp to the Nipmuc country and beyond. In January, the troops found an English man, Joshua Teft, living among the remaining Narragansetts. When interrogated, he reported that the main body of survivors was already gone, "three days on the march" toward "Quaboag amongst a great many Rocks by a Swampeside." Two weeks later, Edward Palmer reported to the Connecticut Council, "Yesterday Daniel the Pequitt Sachem brought in two Naragansett Indyan men which ware in the fight against ye English, one of them being shot through the hand. They say the Indyans are scattered; the two sachems Suikquens [Quinnapin], Nononanto [Canonchet], & ye Queene beeing neere ye Nipmug Country." Joined together, Weetamoo and the Narragansett sachems led survivors north, where they would be received in alliance at Menimesit.[109]

Interlude: "My Children Are Here and I Will Stay"

Job Kattenanit was at Deer Island, doing his best to survive the frigid cold and starving conditions, when Daniel Gookin arrived on the rocky shore. He must have hoped the boat carried food and blankets. But as the missionary later observed, "After the great fight at Narraganset, it was greatly desired to learn the position and movements of the Indians to the westward, towards the Connecticut River," and he was enlisted to recruit from Deer Island two men "to go as spies amongst the enemies." The news that Gookin carried of Great Swamp could only have increased Job's concern. With the United Colonies turning attention back to Menimesit, Job was anxious to retrieve his children. When Gookin asked him to go to the Nipmuc country, Job agreed, so that he could "know their state" and "the condition of the praying Indians of Hassameske and Magunkoog that were hee thought in the power of the enimy." If the colonial troops marched on the Nipmuc country as they had on Narragansett, he would do well if he could convince them his Christian kin were still "faithful," held against their will. He also desired to attempt mediation between the Nipmuc leaders and the English, hoping that his relations might return to Hassanamesit, and those held on Deer Island would be "restored to their places." With news of the fires at Great Swamp, the Deer Island captives knew the same could happen to them. Many settlers were clamoring to be let loose upon them; it was only the continual defense by Gookin and Eliot that kept them back. Still, Job and James Quananopohit, who would travel with him, were motivated by their "love for the English," according to Gookin, and their desire to prove their "fidelity."[1]

The journey would be dangerous. At any point, Job could be assaulted by those same settlers, clamoring for Indian blood. He could be rounded up by

Mosely, like his brother. He could be taken by the "enemy," revealed a spy for the English. He could die alone of exposure on the long road. He did not even hold certain knowledge of the survival or location of his children.

Job and James left Cambridge on December 30, traveling through Natick, where they stayed with Job's friend James Speen, left behind to care for elders who could not make the journey to Deer Island. Then, they trudged through snow to Job's empty town of Hassanamesit, "where they lodged" a night. Crossing the Nipmuc River, they traveled to Manchaug, then Maanexit, where, for the first time, they "met with seven Indians of the enemy," some of whom were armed. Convincing them that they had escaped the "bleak place" of Deer Island, Job and James were led the "next day to Quabaage old fort," where they conversed with others, and finally, "conducted" to Menimesit, where they found the people sheltered in several "small towns," well fed and well housed, with plenty of firewood, a striking contrast with the island. While there, they feasted on venison, filling their bellies and regaining their strength.[2]

To Job's great relief, his children were safe, under the care of "Pumham," and his father and brothers, with all "the Christian Indians belonging to Hassannmiske & Magunhooge" were secure. They exchanged stories, Job relating how despite all his "services" to the English, he had been captured by Henchman, imprisoned, and sent to Deer Island. As advised by Gookin, Job described the "great sufferings" of the people at Deer Island, where they had "little wood for fuell," "very little provision," and only "poore wigwams such as they could make . . . with a few mats." His brother Joseph Tukuppawillin likewise spoke of their anguish in having been taken by the "enemy." They continued in the practice of their faith, reading the bible every day.[3]

In reporting back to Gookin, Job and James Quananopohit took pains to confirm the faithfulness of Job's family in captivity. They also mentioned that James Printer was there, along with "Captain Tom" and the Petavit brothers, and they framed their report to distinguish these "Christian Indians" and captives from the "300 fighting men" of Quaboag, Pakachoag, Weshawkim, Nashaway, and other Nipmuc communities who were also housed at Menimesit, along with their familes, consisting of "double" the number of "women and children." On his return to Cambridge in early February, Job did not reveal that his elder brother Annaweekin had just become embroiled in a raid on settler Thomas Eames's house near Magunkaquog, where Job had taught. He did "inform" Gookin that "six of Eames his children," were safe "with the Indians."[4]

At Menimesit, James Quananopohit also tried to convincingly present his story. He admitted that he and his brother had been among the English. Yet, despite his many feats and sacrifices, he was forced into the meanest conditions at Deer Island, prompting him to escape and "see how things were with the Indians in the woods," where perhaps he might "fight with & for them." Among the sachems, Matoonas was the most suspicious of James and Job, distrusting their intentions. As they reported, Metacom was far to the west, on the Hoosic River, but Joseph Tukuppawillin "secretly informed" them that Metacom knew of James's deeds and had asked anyone who "met with" him or his brother to either "bring them to him or put them to death." Indeed, Matoonas and his sons tested James's claims by requesting to "borrow" his hatchet and knife, and asking him to travel with them to meet Metacom.[5]

Yet it was James's kinship relations and alliance that saved him. The Nashaway war leader Monoco sheltered James in his house at "the second town," saying he had fought with James in "the war with the Mauhaks," and knew him as a "valiant man." No one, he proclaimed, would "wrong" or "kill" James, "but they shall first kill me." Yet Monoco also reminded the scout of his "special love" for him, the bonds of brotherhood between them, inviting him to recall his commitments. When Monoco offered James protection, he expected reciprocal fidelity in return.

While James stayed with Monoco, the war leader and his relations pointed out that their supplies were sufficient and "that all this war their loss of men was inconsiderable." Further, Menimesit remained a central hub for messengers and news that moved through Native networks of communication, despite the cold and deep snow. Traveling by snowshoe, runners had gone out from Menimesit toward the north and west, renewing old networks of trade and exchange.[6]

As Monoco observed, while the Nipmucs were sheltered at Menimesit, their allies and relations from Kwinitekw were sheltered at Sokwakik, above the old village, far beyond the northernmost English settlement, now deserted. Many of Metacom's people were there with them, and Metacom had traveled the old riverside trails west over the mountains, to cultivate alliance with the Mohawks and Mohicans, and Wabanaki people from the north. Monoco and his relations told James that they "had sent" formal requests "to the Wompeagues and Mawquas to aid them in the spring, that the Wampeages promised them help, but the Maquas said they were not willing to fight with the English" but would "fight the Mohegins & Pequots that were brethren to the English." Neal Salisbury suggests that by "Wompeagues," they may have meant the Wappingers of the lower Hudson River. However, it is more likely that they were referring to Wabanaki people in the north, who, already embroiled in the war, were meeting in council at Hoosic that winter, and would, indeed, begin raiding again as the weather warmed. If so, news of Great Swamp may have also been traveling through those northern networks, reaching Wabanaki.[7]

This intelligence, which James carried to Boston, must have disturbed colonial leaders. Although they had tried to justify Great Swamp by spreading rumors that Metacom was among the Narragansetts, James's report that Metacom was to the west, had recently been confirmed by the governor of New York. Moreover, this news signaled that the network of alliances was spreading to the west, as well as to the north. Monoco also revealed to James that they had supplies at the ready. They were hunting deer in their homeland with ease, and he showed James "a kettle full of powder" and "two horns full beside." Through their networks, the Nipmucs sent beaver and wampum to the Mohawks, who gave them "Dutch" powder in return. Come spring, they expected "armes & ammunition" from the northern "hunting Indians" and the French, through relations who had gone north for winter. They might even expect a French company, drawn to the fertile Connecticut River, from which the Sokokis had traveled to fledgling Catholic missions on the St. Lawrence in the wake of war.[8]

The Massachusetts colonists could take heart, however, in the news that the "Pennakooge Indians," as James relayed, were still "quartered about the head of the Kenecticut river & had not at all ingaged in any fight with the English & would not." Indeed, James offered news that the young Penacook warriors had nearly ambushed Mosely and his men, "when he was at Pennakooge last summer" and could have "destroyed" them, but Wanalancet and "their sagamores" "restrained the young men," and "would not suffer them to shoot a gun." This report confirmed colonists' fears that an ambush lay around every bend, but also assured them that Penacooks would not be among the northern forces that might descend upon them in the spring. At the same time, it also demonstrated the vast extent of Menimesit's networks, reaching even in the cold heart of winter into places far to the north, well beyond Boston's reach.[9]

As Monoco and his relations informed James, messengers had also come from the south. "The Narragansetts," James disclosed, "told these Indians that the English had had fight with them, & killed about forty fighting men & one Sachem, & about 300 old men women & children were kild & burnt in the wigwams, most of which were destroyed." The English reports emphasized a large number of warriors killed, but James's report of the official Narragansett message indicated a massacre of families, with comparatively few warriors and only one leader killed in the "fight." Most disturbingly, James's report revealed that many of the English suspicions, which had justified the invasion, were false. The Nipmuc leaders had initially doubted the Narragansett messengers who came from Great Swamp, even though they carried proof of English scalps. Prior to the violence at Great Swamp, the Narragansetts, James understood, had *not* been in alliance with Metacom or the Nipmucs; nor had Narragansetts been with them in their raids the previous summer. Rather, the Nipmuc sachems "looked on" the Narragansetts as "friends to the English all along til now," the massacre instigating their change in course toward war. Now, Narragansett leaders had sent messengers to "solicit" the Nipmucs "to send them some help." Even as James reported this news to Gookin, several "companies" were traveling north; the first had arrived at Quantisset, consisting of "above 200" people, including "several wounded." A company of Nipmuc men had asked Job Kattenanit to accompany them on the journey south, to bring in the first group of Great Swamp survivors.[10]

"Upon the same day," James reported, "Mawtaamp the sagamore said hee would goe with another company up to Phillip, to informe him & those Indians of the breach between the English & Narragansitts." He requested that James "should goe along with him to Philipp to acquaint him of the state of affayres among the English & praying Indians." James's identity was increasingly ambiguous and contested. Monoco protected him as a fellow warrior; his services were requested as a messenger, yet if he followed Mattawamp to Metacom, he might become a prisoner, subject to punishment for betraying his kin. Above all, he was a fierce survivor who judged his time was short. After hunting with Job the next morning, and suspecting "their motions" were watched, James advised, at night, "let us escape away if we can."[11]

However, Job was not yet willing to leave, saying, "I cannot carry my children with me, and I have not yet considered a way to bring them off." His family was his priority and he still trusted in his faith. "My children are here and I will stay longer," Job insisted, "If God please hee can preserve my life; if not I am willing to die." He would go with the Nipmuc company to Quintesset, and if he survived, he would return to see what he could do to "get away my children." Having heard about the number of children who died at Great Swamp, Job, above all, sought their protection from harm. Perhaps he feared the arrival of the Narragansetts would make Menimesit a greater target. Perhaps he feared, should the warriors discern his real purpose, they would retaliate against his family. Although Job had to have known that bringing them with him would also put his children in danger of starvation and exposure at Deer Island, he wanted to be the one responsible for their protection, and he still believed that his "faithful" service might persuade the Boston men to allow them to go home. All the while, as he collected intelligence, he made plans with his brother Joseph and his father, Naoas, for their family's escape.[12]

James left Job, with his apologies, saying "I am sorry for you Job, lest when I am gon they will kill you for my sake," but, he said, "you may tel]l] them I runne away from you & was afrayd to goe to Philip." Job should tell them that

James intended to prove his worth as a warrior on "some exploit" before facing the Wampanoag sachem. James left Job at the pond, and returned to Cambridge through deep snow, bringing much news with him.[13]

As James and Job's testimony attested, while at Menimesit they moved freely and were well fed. The hunting was good that winter, the deep snow slowing down the deer, and the cold hardening the surface, making travel on snowshoes fairly easy. The Nipmucs still had stores of corn, successfully gathered from their towns, as well as the pork and beef they had taken from Quaboag. Still, with the arrival of hundreds of Narragansett survivors, whose corn had been pilfered and burned, they would have many more to feed. As James reported to Gookin, Monoco admitted to him that "ere long, when their beefe & porke & deare is spent & gone," they would "be in want of corn," but they had plans to "com down upon the English townes" about the Nipmuc country, and then they would have "hope to have corn enough." They planned to raid the towns of Lancaster, Marlborough, and Groton, and "they intend[ed] first to cut off Lancaster bridge," so that "no relief" could "come to them from Boston." It was crucial intelligence, and yet, "it was not then credited" by the magistrates or military leaders.[14]

Job remained at Menimesit for more than two weeks, making plans for his family's escape, when news arrived that Monoco was about to make his raid. Since he could not yet take his children, Job left them in his family's care, and took to the snow. His commitment to his English friends still remarkably strong, Job traveled eighty miles on snowshoes through the bitter February night, a journey that had originally taken James and him six days, to carry the alarm to Gookin that Lancaster would be hit the next day. They had heard the news from James, but had not acted on his intelligence, suspecting the Christian Indian of false reporting. It was a great mistake. English families, like Mary Rowlandson's, were left unprotected, and had to fare for themselves. Her minister husband in Boston (ironically, pleading for military support), and few militia stationed at her garrison house, the mistress Mary found herself and her children surrounded, with few options and little protection, as they were barraged by shot, flying "like hail," and flames.[15]

Even as Monoco and his force moved toward Lancaster, Gookin "rose out of his bed" to alert the council, who gave credence to Job's report, and sent a post to Marlborough, ten miles from Lancaster. Arriving the next day, the troops found the bridge burned, their access across the Nashaway River obstructed. After finally making their way across the icy river, they found the "minister's house" in "flames" and some fourteen settlers dead. An even larger group of captives, "the minister's wife and children among them," were already gone.

Job's warning and Gookin's fast action were credited for preventing further violence, as the arrival of the troops appeared to drive the warriors away. Still, as
Neal Salisbury observes, the settlement in the heart of the Nashaway country
"was fatally damaged," and by "the end of March," with provision "dangerously
low" and the fear of further attacks frighteningly high, the formerly "prosperous
town" of Lancaster had been "evacuated."[16]

James's relation of Monoco's plans provides crucial context for the raid on
Mary Rowlandson's town. The primary purpose was to increase the supplies of
corn at Menimesit, redirecting the flow of colonial goods toward Native families
and reclaiming the fruits of Nashaway's fields. The raid was likewise directly
related both to the colonial army's confiscations of Indian corn and to the massacre at Great Swamp. Lancaster's corn (and livestock), grown on the Nashaway
intervale, would help to feed and heal the survivors. Indeed the Rowlandson
house and pasture were situated on prime fertile ground.[17] Moreover, this was
the first raid in which the Nipmucs took captive substantial numbers of English
women and children, which they may have hoped would prevent soldiers from
setting fire to their towns, should they gain access to Menimesit. During their
stay in January, James and Job reported only the presence of one male captive at
Menimesit and two more with Metacom. This scene changed radically within
the next month. It was unlikely, Indigenous leaders must have supposed, that
English officers would burn down a town that contained English mistresses and
their children, even if a town full of Native families did not give them pause.
Therefore, it was no simple coincidence that Mary Rowlandson was taken by
a Narragansett protector. She became the leverage that might protect his kin,
who had survived the fire at Great Swamp, her body a crucial addition and
adaptation to the defensive environment at Menimesit.

7

The Captive's Lament: Reinterpreting Rowlandson's Narrative

CAPTIVE GEOGRAPHIES, NIPMUC COUNTRY, FEBRUARY 1676

Following the raid on Lancaster, according to her own account, Mary Rowlandson and her captors camped the first chill night on a snow-covered hill only a mile from her town. Monoco and his men spent the evening singing and feasting, watching smoke rise from the ruins below. Rowlandson asked to sleep in an abandoned English house on the hill, "to which they answered," she wrote, "what do you love English men still?" This may have been the original trading post, built by Thomas King at the Nashaway crossroads. As the company began to move west along these old Nipmuc trails the next day, they traveled, in Rowlandson's words, "into a vast and desolate wilderness, I knew not whither."[1]

In her narrative, Rowlandson described her regret as she was pressed to "turn my back upon *the* Town" and follow her captors into "*the* wilderness," constructing two spaces, diametrically opposed (my emphasis). "The Town" represented cleared colonial space, resembling the old towns of England. Although she acknowledged the existence of Native "towns" in her narrative, because the Nipmuc country remained a forested environment, held by Native people, she equated these homelands with an "uncultivated," "ungoverned," and "alien" expanse, using the familiar trope of "wilderness" to depict a place uninhabited, or inhabited only by the "barbarians" she feared, a "boundless and unknown" landscape awaiting transformation. For Rowlandson, the "wilderness" also represented a place of inner "solitude" and danger, where she could potentially "lose" her "way." As the "Pilgrim" traveler "walk'd through the Wilderness of this world," *Pilgrim's Progress* warned, the danger of chaos and uncertainty threatened to undermine faith in the order of God's design.[2]

12. Mary Rowlandson's removes

Yet, rather than being enmeshed in solitude, Rowlandson entered "an intricately webbed landscape," known intimately to the Nipmucs with whom she traveled. This "vast" space was a "wilderness" because "whither" she went she "knew" it "not." For Rowlandson, born in South Petherton, England, and raised in Wenham (outside Salem), her travel as an adult largely confined to Lancaster and "the Bay," this was foreign territory. Indeed, the very place where she entered the "vast and desolate wilderness" was a mere ten miles from her home. Ironically, Rowlandson's captivity was not marked by confinement, but rather forced movement through unfamiliar space. Her description of the "severall Removes we had up and down the Wilderness" reflects a discomforting disorientation. Rather than moving west or north on defined riverways or trails, the company, in her estimation, moved vaguely "up and down" in their travels. Her lack of geographic knowledge made the forested landscape a prison. Her captivity laid bare her estrangement in the land that she called home. Her narrative itself fosters an uneasy dialectic, as the foreign is made familiar, and the Indigenous is constructed as foreign.[3]

The war party moved along a well-known route, some on snowshoes, some on horseback, traveling through snow-packed trails and biting cold. Monoco led with confidence and certainty, moving swiftly to avoid any English militia that might follow. Rowlandson struggled on foot, in trepidation and "sorrow," until one of the men who had raided her town dismounted and allowed her to ride on horseback, her injured child in her lap. On one side of the trail, snow-covered and tree-lined ridges rose, protecting them from wind and the sight of colonial scouts. On the other side lay a network of frozen wetlands, thick pines reaching toward gray skies.

The further into the interior Rowlandson traveled, the more frightening and unfamiliar the land became. Swamps appeared dark and foreboding. Hills loomed before her—no vista provided a landmark for her location. The deeper she went, the more vulnerable she felt. Moving further from home, she had "no Christian friend near." Her older children had been taken, "I knew not where." Her husband, she noted, was "gone . . . separated from me, he being in the Bay." He could not protect her, and if he came toward them, she said, her captors "told me they would kill him." She could not even pray for rescue, without endangering him. She was especially concerned for the welfare of the six-year-old child she carried, "looking that every hour would be the last of its life." Although her captors offered food, she refused it, wondering whether she and her "babe" would make it through the night, sleeping fitfully "upon the cold snowy ground."

The further Monoco traveled along the trail, the more confident he became. He led his company from danger, toward a known destination, a place he had probably fished every spring and summer of his life. The swamps and forested ledges promised protection. The deeper he went, the more secure he felt. He knew he was moving toward his family, secluded and safe at Menimesit. Every step deeper into the interior made it less likely an English man would follow.

Indeed, any scout who tracked them would be heard or seen, defense easily accomplished. An unfamiliar traveler who attempted escape would be trapped by steep rises on the south and swamps to the north, sheer sheets of ice giving way to mucky waters; snow-covered hillocks, stones, fallen trees, and beaver dams would ensnare those on the run. For captives, the trail was effectively a prison. For militia, it presented a risky and treacherous venture into unknown space. For Rowlandson's captors, it was an ideal route to inland sanctuary.

A "TOWN CALLED MENIMESIT"

On the third day (Rowlandson's third "remove") of their travel, the raiding company arrived at their destination: in Rowlandson's words, "This day in the afternoon, about an hour by Sun, we came to the place where they intended, *viz.* an Indian town called Wenimesset, northward of Quabaug." The trail opened to a wide plain, full with the sounds of chattering families, the smoke of cook fires, and the barely discernible sensation of safety. Monoco had led them to one of the three encampments at Menimesit.[4]

To Rowlandson's surprise, Menimesit hardly fit her image of an unpopulated wilderness; she expressed astonishment at the large number of people who were gathered there: "Oh the number of Pagans (now merciless enemies) that there came about me, that I may say as *David*, Psalm 27.13, *I had fainted, unless I had believed.*" While straining to portray a nameless, faceless mass of foreign others, she revealed that this judgment was unmoored by her experience of this place and its populace. Although only twenty-five miles from Lancaster and ten miles from Brookfield, colonial scouting missions had been unable to locate the sanctuary. For Rowlandson and her fellow captives, this place was far from home, in their perceptions and their lack of geographic and social knowledge, if not in actual mileage. For Monoco and the protectors, it was a homecoming, and they were likely received with shouts of victory and gratitude for their safe return. After the celebration, the gift-giving began.[5]

Rowlandson was rapidly assimilated into an Indigenous social network, not only as an actor but also as an object of exchange. Soon after her arrival at Menimesit she was presented by her captor, the "Narhaganset Indian, who took me when first I came out of the Garrison," to "Quanopin, who was a Saggamore," and his wife, "King Philips wives Sister." Although Rowlandson later acknowledged that she "lived and served" with Weetamoo during most of her time in captivity, in her first mention of the saunkskwa, Rowlandson acknowledged neither her title nor her name. Recognizing Quinnapin and Metacom as "sagamore" and "king," she labored to downplay Weetamoo's status, using multiple possessives to identify her only through her relationships to powerful men. For Rowlandson "wife" was a static aspect of Weetamoo's identity; she did not recognize or reveal that the saunkskwa's marriage to Quinnapin was a strategic alliance forged in the crisis of war to protect the families she led.[6]

Here, at Menimesit, this multifaceted alliance was cemented and extended through such exchange. Captives like Rowlandson became symbolic objects in Indigenous networks, which incorporated English "value." Weetamoo recognized the "mistress" as a high status captive, who would harness leveraging power in future negotiations, because Rowlandson was highly valued within her own society as the daughter of Lancaster's largest landowner and the wife of the town minister. When the "Narragansett Indian" gifted her to Quinnapin and Weetamoo, it was a significant honor, a symbolic recognition of the power of their joint leadership in these precarious times. In these networks, Rowlandon's *social* status as a "mistress" increased her *economic* value as "*awak8n*," a captive, someone who is used, who is made useful.[7]

JAMES PRINTER'S AWIKHIGAN

Soon after Rowlandson arrived at Menimesit, another Nipmuc raiding party formed to strike the settlement of Medfield, just south of Natick. "There was . . . about six miles from us, a small Plantation of Indians, where" her son, Joseph Jr., "had been during his Captivity." She learned from him that, "at this time, there were some Forces of the Indians gathered of our company, and some also from them (among whom was my Sons master) to go to assault and burn Medfield." Among these "Indians" was James Printer.[8]

During February and March, raiding parties emerged from Menimesit to reappear in their wider homelands, with Nipmucs leading raids on "English plantations" in their territory. Striking quickly, they then returned to Menimesit, beyond reach of colonial troops. This strategy proved so effective that colonists feared God's abandonment; as Daniel Gookin recalled, "Weekly, yea almost daily, messengers with sad tidings were brought into the Council, insomuch that the lord seemed to threaten great calamity to ensue upon the English nation." When men like Monoco returned to their homelands and took captives, they reasserted jurisdiction over the people who inhabited their places, while challenging the claims the "English nation" made over them.[9]

The Nipmuc leaders had also successfully reasserted jurisdiction over the inhabitants of the mission communities. Some men from Hassanamesit joined Monoco in the raid on Medfield, perhaps including Tom Wuttasacomponom, James, and his brother, Annaweekin. On the morning of the raid, James Printer may have lain concealed with his kinsmen on the outskirts of the town, the forest forming a blind. Before first light, warriors entered the town without detection, securing strategic locations. As the sun rose, James likely saw an English man emerge from the house that lay along the old Nipmuc path, which he had walked many times on his way to Cambridge. James may have felt the hair on the back of his neck rise as the man went out to the barn, unaware, to feed his cattle, watching his kinsman rise from the stacks of hay, cradling birch bracket, to light the dry grass mown from fallow fields. The fire spread rapidly to houses and barns, destroying the signs of English ownership, scattering startled soldiers and disoriented families in multiple directions, toward the waiting warriors.[10]

As the warriors left the town, heading west down the old path, carrying captives, trophies, and goods, they set fire to the bridge that crossed the Charles River, symbolically breaking the chain that had bound them to the Massachusetts colonists. James would have walked that bridge as he traveled between Cambridge and Hassanamesit, but that route was now "cut off" by war. James is credited with writing this *awikhigan*, posted "at the foot of the bridge which they fyred":

> Thou English man hath provoked us to anger & wrath & we care not though we have war with thee this 21 years for there are many of us 300 of which hath fought with thee at this time, we have nothing but our lives to loose but thou hast many fair houses cattell & much good things.[11]

The proclamation expressed anger, asserted blame, and pledged continuance. It provoked fear, even as it accused settlers of provocation. For those English men who read it, in the midst of Medfield's ruin, it was both a threat and a sign of "insolence." Yet, the *awikhigan* also functioned as a marker of jurisdiction. Hunters in the northern territories posted birchbark message maps on trees to mark family territory and inform each other of their movements and intentions. Here, Nipmuc men used the English tool of writing to reclaim their territory and express a "communal" message to a neighboring community and former ally on behalf of "300" fighting men. The bridge had been burned, the relationship broken, and the blame lay with the settlers. The authors took English men to task for their obsession with property, insisting that although they may have been pushed to the interior of their territories, the loss of their own homes and "cattell" would mean "nothing." They had their "lives," they had "300 men," and they had the resilience and determination to "war with you" for "21 years," an entire generation.[12]

If we imagine that this message came from Monoco, with James Printer acting as scribe, the note represents the adaptation of writing as a weapon of war. For the English, this prospect was frightful enough. As Kristina Bross has observed, "Perhaps the most shocking and frightening aspect of the war for its contemporary historians was the adaptation of English technologies and belief systems by Indian foes for their own purposes." Among settlers, there was a great fear of "revolters" like James who could read and write, and such "signs of transculturation," Bross observes, "were equated with the camouflaging bushes and trees." Thus even the thought that someone like James might be among the "enemy ranks" was a disturbing consideration. Was he compelled to act as scribe, composing this note on behalf of the group? Did he "print" Monoco's message, just as he set the type for the bible? Or did he participate willingly, using his unique literary skills to wage war?[13]

When we consider that this may represent James' own voice, the note takes on greater significance. In this brief "publication," the scholar may have provided a reading of the conflict in which he was embroiled. "Thou, English man" assumes a more specific and personal context. There was an entire troop of Cambridge cavalry at Medfield that day. Acting on Job's intelligence, Cambridge magistrate Edward Oakes had led "a company of twenty horsemen" to Medfield just days before to fortify the town. Yet Oakes and his men failed to detect the warriors who embedded themselves within the town before dawn. James would have recognized Oakes and other Cambridge men as they emerged, startled, from the garrisons, flintlocks firing. Indeed, Oakes's son Urian was then acting president of Harvard. In using the archaic scriptural term "thou," James may have been addressing Oakes, or any of the owners of "fair houses" with "much good things" that he had encountered daily in Cambridge. By this time, all the pretension of the Cambridge ministers and Harvard scholars must have seemed a ruse.[14]

James Printer lived for years among the English, counting many as familiar, but too many acts of confinement and captivity in such a short time may have made them strangers in his eyes. Nothing in his education could have prepared him to be falsely accused of murder, imprisoned, and nearly lynched, while magistrates like Oakes kept silent. Nothing could have prepared him to live in fear of being taken or killed by either side, to be confined in a fort in Marlborough, a prison in Cambridge, or on Deer Island, where his brother Job lay now. Nothing could have prepared him for the stories he had heard from the survivors of Great Swamp. For James, it must have been disturbing to learn that his former classmate, Joseph Dudley, a governor's son and minister, had joined the forces there. (James had just lost his own "aged mother," and the grief was a fresh wound.) For him, it may have been equally disturbing to see English homes burning before him in Medfield, men and women running from the flames.[15]

But in this note, he did not blame his own. "Thou, English man," he accused the colonial leaders and militia, formally addressing a group that included fellow scholars, teachers, and former neighbors. In the language of his training, he called them to account for the violence that had transformed the Nipmuc country and satirized the intense desire for "fair houses" and "good things" that had ushered in that metamorphosis. Families, including his own, had been torn asunder, and from his vantage point, this was not a conflict between demons and angels, nor between God's chosen and the fallen. It was rather a matter of base greed and human volition.

The symbolic house that settlers had built rested upon a "foundational belief" in their "rightful possession," to quote Increase Mather, and their identity as God's chosen people in this "new" land. What leaders like Monoco understood, and converts like James had begun to comprehend, was that this belief also functioned as a mask for baser desires. This kind of psychological warfare required "cultural literacy" regarding the complexity of colonial "English belief about value," an understanding that although greed and materialism were devalued by Puritan theology, property like houses and cattle were highly valued in the English economic and social structure. Mary Rowlandson's value as a captive, after all, was tied to the value of her father and husband's estates. As Philip Round has suggested, James demonstrated in this note his awareness that some settlers had themselves begun to admit that they had "become more enamored with 'their fair houses and cattle' than with their souls," a theme that arises repeatedly in Rowlandson's narrative. Yet James did not join Mather in proclaiming that Indians were tools in God's hands to punish the settlers for their materialism. Instead he called the "English men" to account. If the war was not the "apocalyptic battle of good against evil" that Mather imagined, then the ultimate cause was the *sin* of greed and desire for material wealth. The *awikhigan*, then, may have been the revelation of a Christian Nipmuc scholar, or a tool to plant the seeds of self-doubt amid the burning meadows, a psychological ambush of the settlers who remained.[16]

Finally, this *awikhigan* reflects the state of mind that James would have had to adopt to participate in such a raid. His performance of this "strategy of separation" revealed a developing belief in a clear line between the "English man" and "us," an act of writing that enforced boundaries of land and identity. Thus, it reveals the transformation that may have taken place within James himself. He left this text as a message, to inform his former friends of his position, and a territorial marker, nearby the ruins of an English construction that had previously joined these two communities in exchange.[17]

As Rowlandson described the return of the men from Medfield, "all the company . . . came through the town," celebrating their victory. She could hear the warriors "roaring and hooping" from a mile away, performing a call and response with their relations who had remained at Menimesit. By their calls, they "signified how many they had destroyed . . . Those that were with us at home," she observed, "gathered together as soon as they heard the hooping and every time that the other went over their number, these at home gave a shout, that the very Earth rung again." Collectively, they moved toward "the Sagamores Wigwam," Rowlandson wrote, "and then, Oh, the hideous insulting and triumphing that there was over some Englishmens scalps that they had taken (as is their manner) and brought with them."[18]

Just as James Printer portrayed the English as foreigners in Nipmuc land, so did Rowlandson use strategies of separation to portray the Nipmucs, Wampanoags, and Narragansetts as foreigners in an English, Christian world. Their triumphant calls were, like Printer's note, "hideous" insults against the people they had "destroyed," a cacophony that shook the Christian "Earth." Portraying a mass of sounds and a faceless "company," she emphasized the display of scalps as a symbol of savagery. Yet even in this stark portrayal there are slips in her construction. She called Menimesit "home," suggesting she had become, reluctantly, a part of this place. She also revealed her developing familiarity with Indigenous geography, even as she used terms that emphasized foreignness. She recognized the place of the central Council House, which, she said, its leaders likened to their "Court," because she had participated in councils.[19]

This was the House to which James returned, and from which Weetamoo must have emerged to greet the returning protectors. Here, the people gathered to deliberate, strategize, and heal from the devastations of war. Here, men like James were invited to speak and translate, even as leaders like Weetamoo and

Quinnapin were encouraged to take their seats beside the Nipmuc leaders, as they renewed and reconstructed the bonds among them. Although temporarily displaced from their homelands, leaders could regroup as they strove to represent the voices and needs of their communities. The convergence of people on the Council House symbolized this unity and sense of shared space. The Council House became the symbolic microcosm of the larger territory shared and defended by all. When warriors returned from battle, they brought their victories "home," and gave their relations hope that they would soon reclaim their lands.

INTO THE COUNTRY OF CORN, NICHEWAUG, PAQUAUG, SOKWAKIK, MARCH 1676

CROSSINGS

Rowlandson had been at Menimesit for about two weeks when "the Indians began to talk of removing from this place, some one way, and some another." Scouts, traveling familiar trails to colonial headquarters, had discerned that troops were mobilizing to launch a raid on Menimesit. James Quananopohit and Job Kattenanit had betrayed its location, and the Massachusetts Council had released them, along with four other men, from Deer Island to serve as guides. Observing the troops at Marlborough, the scouts may have seen their own relations among the colonial force. When colonial military leaders arrived at Quaboag, the thousands of people that had assembled three towns at Menimesit had already left. When Savage, Mosely, and their six hundred men finally pushed through the hills north of Quaboag, they found empty meadows and the wet coals of abandoned fires.[20]

Leaving Menimesit, Weetamoo headed north on an old through-trail, accompanied by many families, their captives with them, once more moving through rugged, yet familiar country, deeper into the interior. In Rowlandson's estimation, they traveled through snowy woods to "a desolate place in the Wilderness, where there were no Wigwams or Inhabitants before." Yet this place, known as Nichewaug or "between land," entrenched in deeply protected marshes, icy waters, and thick pine forest, was at the crossroads of trails. Among their company were likely those who had hunted and fished here. Nichewaug was not their destination, but a camp where they could safely regroup and rest, dry off by a fire, and perhaps hunt, en route north. Here they camped for "about four dayes," leaving "this place," Rowlandson "thought," only when they believed "the English Army" was "near."[21]

"They went," Rowlandson observed, "as if they had gone for their lives, for some considerable way, and then they made a stop, and chose some of their stoutest men, and sent them back to hold the English army in play whilst the rest escaped." Her evasive use of "they" here is telling, since Weetamoo was likely among the leaders who devised this strategy. Just as they had done at Pocasset, decoys distracted the militia from tracking the families as "they marched on furiously" towards the north.[22]

"In this travel," the captive relayed, "because of my wound, I was somewhat favored in my load; I carried only my knitting work and two quarts of parched meal. Being very faint I asked my mistress to give me one spoonful of the meal, but she would not give me a taste." While Rowlandson characterized this rejection as hardhearted, Weetamoo was required to distribute corn equally among "hundreds," over the long haul. Long journeys required strategic rationing; even in peaceful times, traveling companies consumed only limited amounts. In camp, the "two quarts" of ground corn would be transformed into bread, porridge, and stews. In winter and in war, Weetamoo had to conserve the short supply.[23]

Furthermore, Weetamoo was clearly toughening the Puritan "mistress," teaching her to carry her weight like any other woman. Rowlandson observed that "the greatest number at this time with us were" women and "many" carried babies "at their backs." They traveled "with their old, and with their young: some carried their old decrepit mothers, some carried one and some another. Four of them carried a great Indian upon a Bier; but going through a thick Wood with him, they were hindered, and could make no haste; whereupon they took him upon their backs, and carried him, one at a time, till they came to Baquaug River." At the crossing they built rafts from deadwood and cushioned them with evergreen "brush," then traversed the wide Paquaug River. Crossing during rapid spring melt, some carried wounded kin and elders. Rowlandson reported, in dismay and disgust, that "on that very day came the English army after them to this river, and saw the smoke of their wigwams, and yet this river put a stop to them." In her narration, she seemed at a loss to explain how Native women were able to accomplish what English men could not.[24]

"A SEVERE AND PROUD DAME SHE WAS"

The Wampanoag saunkskwa and the English mistress "read" each other's behavior through culturally specific frameworks. Although mystified by Native women's strength and power, Rowlandson appeared most troubled by Weetamoo's failure to adhere to the bounds of English frames of race and gender.

Rather than acknowledge Weetamoo's respected authority, Rowlandson depicted it as imagined royalty: "A severe and proud dame she was, bestowing every day in dressing herself neat as much time as any of the gentry of the land: powdering her hair, and painting her face, going with necklaces, with jewels in her ears, and bracelets upon her hands. When she had dressed herself, her work was to make girdles of wampum and beads."[25]

Throughout her narrative, Rowlandson never acknowledged that Weetamoo was a leader equal to a sachem, although this was common knowledge in the colonies. Rather, she labored to represent Weetamoo's authority as a pretension. Rowlandson hinted at Weetamoo's role by comparing her to "gentry" and calling her a "dame," but her derisive tone diminished the Wampanoag woman's power, even as it elevated the status of the English as the proper "gentry" in this "land." She represented Weetamoo's acts as a faulty imitation of bourgeois English womanhood that an Indian woman could never attain. Salisbury has observed that the Native people with whom Rowlandson was most personally familiar prior to captivity were servants in her household. In captivity, she experienced a troubling role reversal, in which a Native woman became the household "mistress" and she became a servant. With her comments, Rowlandson used words to restore the balance of power. Perhaps to appease male authorities like Mather, the Puritan mistress implied that Weetamoo was too "proud" for an Indian and a woman, requiring a stronger male hand to put her in her place, something that Mather himself would seek to impose through his narration of the consequences of Weetamoo's resistance.[26]

To further diminish Weetamoo's authority, Rowlandson portrayed the crafting of wampum belts as "work," suggesting that she was more like a servant than a leader. In truth, given the ceremonial role of wampum in alliance building, this "work" signaled the highest status in Algonquian society. In this context of war, in which the survival of thousands depended on the alliances among multiple nations, the making of wampum belts was of utmost importance, "work" involving great deliberation, skill, and knowledge of community histories and relationships. Weetamoo was entwining the bonds between nations, weaving a multifaceted tapestry of northeastern political networks. Yet Rowlandson downplayed wampum's significance, portraying the belts Weetamoo wore as an accessory she adorned to enhance her beauty, rather than symbols of leadership.

By focusing on her physical appearance, Rowlandson feminized Weetamoo, fixing her in a familiar European type: the vain woman obsessed with physical beauty. Rowlandson further characterized her gravitas as "severe," portraying her uncompromising behavior as an essential personality trait, rather than a result of loss or the necessary command she shouldered during a harsh colonial war. Even as Rowlandson familiarized Weetamoo's femininity, she performed a "strategy of separation." In contrast to her humanizing portrayals of male leaders such as Metacom and Quinnapin, Rowlandson's depictions of Weetamoo emphasized the saunkskwa's otherness and "arrogance," revealing her own resistance to accepting Weetamoo's role, her fear of being associated with the dangerous power that Weetmoo represented, as well as a clash over the place and role of women within conflicting political and cultural systems. After all, if Rowlandson accepted Weetamoo's position at Menimesit, she might question her own in New England.[27]

Just as Rowlandson criticized Weetamoo's failure to behave as a proper goodwife, Weetamoo likewise reprimanded Rowlandson for failing to act like an *Algonquian* woman, particularly for displaying weak or selfish behavior. Women in Weetamoo's community were expected to be strong and self-sufficient, carrying their weight. In contrast, when Rowlandson was made to travel with her "load at [her] back," she found it tremendously challenging. "One hill" in Sokoki uplands made her faint; it "was so steep that I was fain to creep upon my knees, and to hold by the twigs and bushes to keep myself from falling backward." Rowlandson, "reel[ing]" as she "went," became another burden that Weetamoo and the women had to carry.[28]

In Lancaster, Rowlandson had been largely confined to the domestic space of her house and town. She rarely walked far and was not required to carry large loads; she never would have traveled beyond her town without her father or husband. Although Rowlandson portrayed these challenges as part of the terrible conditions of captivity, this kind of travel would have been part of the seasonal cycles for Algonquian women (although usually not under the duress of war). Colonial chroniclers like Roger Williams attributed the comparative ease they had in childbirth to some essentialized savage state; in truth, their lifestyle defied English attitudes about the inherent weakness of women and demonstrated the physical and mental strength and endurance that women could develop from engaging in challenging physical activity. In some ways, Puritan women like Rowlandson were held captive by the cultural beliefs and practices that kept them from performing the movement that would strengthen their bodies and minds.

"A VAST AND HOWLING WILDERNESS": SOKOKI GREAT SWAMP

Having successfully crossed the wide river, Weetamoo, Rowlandson, and the families constructed shelters and encamped for several days in the Native town of Paquaug, on the north bank. Under normal circumstances, they might have encountered other families here, offering food stored from the harvest. It was one of several places that John Pynchon would send scouts, looking for corn-fields, the next summer. Those families, though, had also moved north, and after resting, Weetamoo and the women continued to trek northwards. As the "English Army" approached the river at early morning, Rowlandson observed, the women "set their Wigwam on fire, and went away."[29]

Knowing the river had halted their pursuers, Weetamoo and the families took to the major east-west Indigenous highway (now renamed, for tourism, "the Mohawk Trail"). Rowlandson characterized her journey as wandering like "one astonished" through a maze, but Weetamoo moved through a territory mapped with trails and subsistence sites. Trekking westward on this exceptionally "cold morning," they soon came to "a great Brook with ice on it," which they had to cross. While "some waded through it, up to the knees & higher . . . oth-ers," including Weetamoo, "went till they came to a Beaver dam." Following her "mistress," Rowlandson considered herself fortunate that she "did not wet [her] foot." Although Rowlandson attributed her safe passage across this natu-ral bridge to "the good providence of God," it was Indigenous knowledge of this trail and its crossings that protected her from discomfort and the danger of hypothermia. Rowlandson's unfamiliarity with and fear of "swamps," often sus-tained by such beaver dams, dominated her depiction of the landscape. As they diverged northwards onto a narrow trail, rising into the hills, she found herself surrounded by ridges and wetlands, the cold fog heavy in early March, the great pines looming overhead. "I went along that day mourning and lamenting," she wrote, "leaving farther my own Country, and traveling into the vast and howling Wilderness."[30]

Yet Weetamoo and her company traveled a well-worn trail, once followed, in fact, by Gookin, Henchman, Prentice, and Beers, seven years before, as they sought new lands on which to settle in the interior. They moved alongside a brook that would soon teem with fish and spring runoff, through marshes that would ring with the song of spring peepers. They traveled through territory that must have sustained Sokoki families, hunting deer and moose in the uplands, through many winters. When they arrived at the Sokoki "great Swamp," beside "the trail from Nichewaug to Squakeag," Weetamoo and the women stopped to camp, in a bowl sheltered among frozen waters and rising peaks, which would keep English men at bay. Yet, Rowlandson remarked, "The Swamp by which we lay, was, as it were, a deep Dungeon, and an exceeding high and steep hill before it." To her, the expanse of wetlands and surrounding high ground only solidified her feeling of imprisonment.[31]

The women took to building their camp, which Rowlandson described as the cacophony of "a thousand Hatchets going at once." Gazing upon the encampment from the trail at the "brow of the hill," she first thought they "had come to a great Indian Town" because, although the group consisted only of "our own company," the "Indians were as thick as the trees." Looking "before" her, "there was nothing but Indians, and behind [her], nothing but Indians, and so on either hand," she found herself "in the midst, and no Christian soul near." Ironically, her account displaced the other "Christian souls" around her, including fellow captives as well as the Christian Indians who traveled with Weetamoo's company. Indeed, Rowlandson did not name a single Native person during this travel from Menimesit to Sokwakik. Instead, the multifaceted community appeared a nameless, faceless mass of "Indian" others, swinging "hatchets" in the foreboding, dank "dungeon," resembling devilish creatures in some underworld hollow.[32]

Yet, as Weetamoo knew from her experience with English troops at Pocasset swamp, such places could function as a snare for colonial troops on their trail. Weetamoo and her company had successfully made the Paquaug River a barrier to the militia, and then diverged to a rugged, lesser-known trail, utilizing the swamps as camouflage, hiding even their large company. Their longstanding knowledge of the environment enabled their survival. Still, at any moment, the Christian Indian "souls" among the English troops might utilize their own environmental knowledge, leading the troops to discern their track northward in the mud and snow. Yet, here, in this protected swamp, scouts could keep watch, and potentially ambush any English parties before they got to the families, as they had at Menimesit and Pocasset. Still, if they remained too long, the swamp could prove a trap for the families, who could not quickly traverse those steep hills or frozen wetlands to seek safety. If they were to secure sanctuary, they could not rest for long before continuing their journey north, not toward an unmapped wilderness, but toward Kwinitekw, a country of corn.

TO BE MADE USEFUL: ADAPTATION AND EXCHANGE

After "a restless and hungry night" in the great Sokoki swamp, they climbed the "high and steep hill," and continued northwest. To Rowlandson's surprise, rather than moving deeper into "wilderness," signs of English settlement appeared along the descending trail: "As I went along, I saw a place where English cattle had been: that was comfort to me, such as it was." Soon after, she recognized a distinct change in the road ahead: "we came to an English Path, which so took with me, that I thought I could have freely lain down and died." The trail opened to a wide intervale, on which stood the burnt remains of English houses. Arriving at "Squakeag," Native families took to reclaiming the harvest the settlers had left behind, "quickly spread[ing] themselves over the deserted English fields."[33]

While Rowlandson recognized the signs of settler space, Weetamoo and the women recognized the fields as abundant bowls that Native planters like themselves had long cultivated, before English men availed themselves of the fertile valley. The region of Sokwakik was the southern gateway to the Abenaki country, located on the transnational trade route of Kwinitekw, but the settlement of "Squakeag" was the northern outpost of the Massachusetts colony, renamed "Northfield" as the "northernmost" English "field" on the "Connecticut River." Sokwakik was both an ancient gathering place and a boundary between the English and Wabanaki, which remained under Native control.[34]

For Rowlandson, who divided the world between English "towns" and the Indian "wilderness," the encounter with furrowed fields, cattle-mown meadows and rutted dirt paths brought a wave of familiarity. Yet Massachusetts settlers had abandoned this space. That spring, the river would rise to flood the soil, saplings and seedlings would spring from the fields of shorn wheat, and deer would return to meadows abandoned by cattle. Already, Sokwakik was being renewed.

As Rowlandson observed, the women began "gleaning what they could find" in this changing, but familiar, environment. "Some," Rowlandson observed, "pickt up ears of Wheat that were crickled down, some found ears of Indian Corn, some found Ground-nuts, and others sheaves of Wheat that were frozen together in the shock, and went to threshing of them out." Likewise, men dressed the livestock settlers left behind. Rowlandson "asked" one man "to give me a piece" of the horse-liver he carried in a basket. Heretofore, she had expressed hesitancy and disgust at the food her captors offered. Now, the man teased her, "What . . . can you eat Horse-liver?" and, probably chuckling, gave her a piece to roast upon the fires that others had built. "That night," she observed, "we had a mess of wheat for our Supper." Just as the Native women adapted wheat to their early spring diet of dried corn, *winozal* (wild onions), and *apenak* ("ground-nuts" or small potatoes), Rowlandson learned to adapt to her new place in Native space. As these "removes" carried her farther from "home," she began to adopt the skills and strategies of an Algonquian woman, who could seek out food and sustain herself, even as she recognized her dependence on others.[35]

"On the morrow morning," Rowlandson recalled, the group traveled by canoe from the lower Sokwakik town "over the River, i.e. Connecticot, to meet

with King Philip," who was returning from his diplomatic expedition to Mohican country. Yet this reunion was cut short by "their espying some English
Scouts, who were therabout." The groups split to avoid detection, with Weetamoo's party paddling "four or five miles up the River father Northward." They
stopped for a midday meal on the riverbank, where Rowlandson encountered
her son, returned with Metacom's company. Then they "traveled on till night,"
their "crew" camping on the east bank. In the morning, they paddled across
the river, where "about three thousand other Indians from throughout New
England" awaited. From the canoe, Rowlandson expressed her amazement at
"the numerous crew of Pagans that were on the Bank on the other side. When
I came ashore, they gathered all about me, I sitting alone in the midst." They
had arrived in a Sokoki town above "Northfield," nearly unknown to colonists,
sheltered by the pine forests of "Coasset" (Vernon, Vermont).[36]

This multitribal gathering included Sokoki hosts and their Kwinitekw relations, as well as displaced people from the Wampanoag, Narragansett, and
Nipmuc countries. At Coasset, Weetamoo exchanged news with her sister Wootonakanuske, Metacom, and countless relations. Far from Lancaster, Rowlandson offered a rare humanizing portrait of Native families gathered in a remote,
northern sanctuary, where, as Rowlandson observed, they "asked one another
questions, and laughed, and rejoiced over their gains and victories," exchanging
stories, embracing their mutual survival.[37]

Witnessing the reunion, Rowlandson broke down in tears. A man reassured
her that "none will hurt you" and "then came one of them" to give her some
cornmeal "to comfort" her, while another gave her "half a pint of Pease." Metacom welcomed her to sit and smoke with him, treating her like kin, a member
of *his wife's sister's* house. Indeed, Wootonakanuske and Metacom may have
lived in the same dwelling. While they sojourned at Coasset, Rowlandson's
"service" extended to Weetamoo's relations. As Rowlandson wrote,

> During my abode in this place, Philip spake to me to make a shirt for his
> boy, which I did, for which he gave me a shilling. I offered the money to my
> master [Quinnapin] but he bade me keep it; and with it I bought a piece of
> horse flesh. Afterwards he asked me to make a cap for his boy, for which he
> invited me to dinner. I went and he gave me a pancake, about as big as two
> fingers; it was made of parched wheat, beaten, and fryed in Bears grease, but
> I thought I never tasted pleasanter meat in my life. There was a squaw who
> spake to me to make a shirt for her *sannup*, for which she gave me a piece of
> bear. Another asked me to knit a pair of stockings, for which she gave me a
> quart of peas. I boiled my peas and bear together, and invited my master and

mistress to dinner; but the proud gossip, because I served them both in one
dish, would eat nothing.

As a temporary member of the community, the captive was drawn into the net-
work of exchange that flowed between extended families, and nations, even in
time of war. Metacom instructed Rowlandson in the rules of reciprocity, while
Quinnapin and (unnamed) women demonstrated redistribution and exchange.
Although she may have missed the meaning of the lesson, Weetamoo, her "mistress," schooled her in customs related to gender. The community identified
Rowlandson's talents and encouraged her to participate in trade. However, as
Michelle Burnham has pointed out, this cultural "journey" which "separate[d]"
her from home, threatened to transform her. In order to redeem herself from
censure as a woman who perhaps unwillingly stepped outside the bounds of
settler space, Rowlandson constructed a portrait of resistance to Weetamoo, and
the gender role that she performed.[38]

Although Rowlandson acknowledged that it was Weetamoo with whom "I
have lived and served all this while," when Metacom gave her "a shilling" in
exchange for her work, she attempted to hand it over to Quinnapin, "the master," she implied, to whom she "belong[ed]." In acknowledging his authority,
the Puritan mistress continued to act in accordance with English gender conventions, despite the fact that it was an *Indian* male to whom she showed sub-
servience. However, Quinnapin refused the money, showing her that she was
entitled to the goods she had earned with her labor, and that she was an equal
participant in exchange. Or perhaps, he implied her goods did not belong to
him. He then taught her a second lesson by making a trade with her himself,
demonstrating reciprocity and hospitality.[39]

The flow of exchange came to an abrupt halt, however, when Rowlandson
prepared a "dinner" for Weetamoo and Quinnapin, and her "mistress" refused
to eat from the same dish as her "master." Representing Weetamoo's actions as
inscrutable and haughty, offensive to a faithful Christian wife, she characterized Weetamoo as a "proud gossip," in colonial English idiom, a woman who
does not adhere to her position as a wife. In censuring this conduct, Rowlandson anticipated and refuted similar criticism she might receive as a woman
who dared to write, and distanced herself from association with this dangerous
woman. Even though she shared a home with Weetamoo and traveled in her
company "this long while," Rowlandson made clear her own foreignness in this
space; she had not been transformed, she had not "gone Indian," she knew her
place as a woman.[40]

Similarly, although she may have become familiar with Algonquian conventions regarding the separation of men and women in particular times and

spaces, due to the perceived power of women precisely because of their capacity to give birth, Rowlandson did not admit it here. This was not likely the first time that Rowlandson had noticed that men and women did not eat from the same dish. But it was Weetamoo's refusal that she constructed as inappropriate. Ironically, while Rowlandson denounced Weetamoo for stepping outside appropriate gender boundaries, the saunkskwa acted in accordance with those conventions within her society.[41]

A COUNTRY OF CORN: NORTHERN NETWORKS

Reading Rowlandson's narrative at the crossroads of gender and geography reveals a broader context for *Weetamoo's* "removes," as Rowlandson followed her upriver. Weetamoo led families into a country of corn, where women planters still held sway, largely unfettered by male settlers, their courts, plows, and cattle. Before and after the war, their names appeared in deeds and other documents of diplomacy. Kwinitekw was hardly a "wilderness," but a valley of horticultural hamlets, long inhabited by "mobile farmers" who cultivated some of the most fertile fields in the world, enhanced by spring freshets and deep alluvial soils, and who utilized the surrounding floodplains and upland forests for seasonal hunting, fishing, and gathering. Rowlandson experienced this adaptive mobility firsthand, as her company moved from "Squakeag" to "Coasset," then across the river to the Great Bend at the mouth of the Ashuelot River, from where she traveled a mile to visit her son at another encampment. These sites were not merely temporary camps for displaced Wampanoag and Narragansett people but "seasonal encampments within" the "well defined homelands" of their Sokoki hosts. At "Squakeag" and at Coasset, intervales lay fallow on both sides of the river, while nearby "granaries" provided storage for corn. Opportunities for fishing abounded in the region, including this confluence, and waterfalls to the south at Peskeompscut (Turner's Falls) and north at Ktsipontekw (Bellows Falls). The people of Kwinitekw had multiple places within their immediate homeland and within the larger networks of kinship where they could seek shelter and subsistence, without leaving familiar country.[42]

That winter, Metacom followed their trails of diplomacy to Hoosic, at the western edge of the mountains where Mohican and Sokoki men hunted, north of the colonial center of Albany. Hoosic, like the upper Sokoki towns, provided sanctuary that winter, beyond New England's reach, in Mohican territory. When they received reports in January that "Philip & 4 or 500 North Indians, fighting men" were "within 40 to 50 of Albany northerly, where they talke of continuing this winter," New England could not act on this "intelligence," since New York had asserted jurisdiction. Instead, Connecticut's council urged Governor Andros in Albany to take advantage of this "opportunity" to "destroy these bloody upland Indians" and Metacom by urging Albany's allies, the Mohawks, to strike "in the winter season" and "extirpate this bloody generation."[43]

The Kanienkehaka had received messages from multiple quarters, early in the war. Ninigret had proposed a diplomatic delegation, and Uncas advised "that the said Mohucks were the only Persons likely to put an End to the War." But it was not until Metacom appeared at their eastern door that Kanienkehaka warriors became involved. As they later told the New England colonies, "You had wars with the Indian Enemyes before we, for when diverse of your towns were burnt down, then our Governor General [Andros] did incourage us, & told how his friendes in N. England were Involved in a great war with Indians and that some of your Enemys were fled to hosack, Incourageing us to goe out against them." Connecticut leaders, raising the specter of raids on New York, urged a strike "before the weather permitts the Indians to disperse themselves, and fall to burning and killing upon Hudson's River also." Yet while Connecticut, Massachusetts, and Plymouth portrayed this conflict diametrically, as a war between "Indians" and English, prompted by the savage and unpredictable actions of this "bloody generation" of Natives, Andros was not reluctant to hold New England accountable for bringing "your Indyan Warr upon Philip & North Indians" to his colony. He consistently asserted that he provided crucial aid to them and acted in faithfulness to the Crown in containing *their* "Indian War."[44]

In traveling to Sokwakik and Hoosic, Weetamoo and Metacom entered a complex network of alliances, with a recent history of conflict. At the Great Bend, they camped near the hill where Mohawk warriors had dealt a hard blow, less than a decade before, to the Sokoki "fort," destroying corn stores and dispersing families. The Sokokis' Mohican allies had only recently renewed a fragile peace with their Mohawk neighbors, facilitated by the English at Albany. Seven years before, Mohicans had permitted the Massachusett and Nipmuc warriors to raid Kahnawake, a recent memory in Kaniekehaka warriors' minds. Indeed, in 1676, when Connecticut sent a message via Albany, encouraging the Mohawks to strike, they claimed "our English" had "guarded the Mohawkes from Boston to Springfield, when they were in danger of the Plimouth Indians," associating the 1669 raid by Massachusett and Nipmuc companies with Metacom's recent actions, although the Wampanoag leader had not participated. "Now," Connecticut urged, they had "a season to destroy all their old enymys together, being soe neere them and locked up with snow." Strangely, in 1669, when Massachusetts had pledged and failed to protect the Massachusett and Nipmuc allies under their jurisdiction, Connecticut claimed New England had provided protection

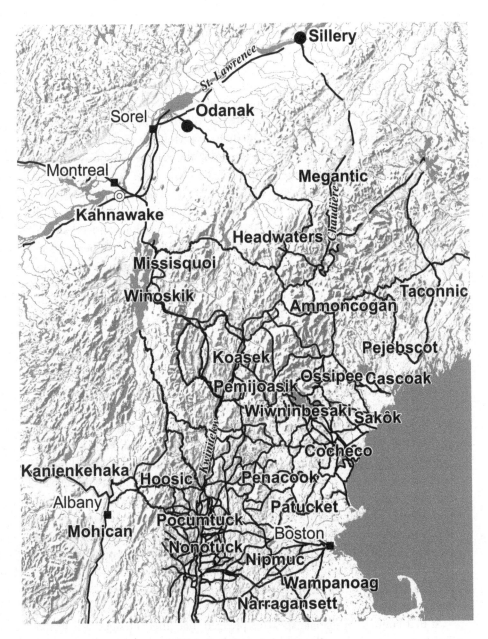

13. Hoosic and northern networks

to the Mohawks. In 1676, the New England colonies demanded fidelity of the praying towns, even as they requested assistance from the Mohawks who had only recently struck those communities under their protection.[45]

Asserting jurisdiction and upholding alliance, at the "opening of the river" in late February, the Mohawks, "being as it were one body" with Andros, "went out" with three hundred warriors to Hoosic, killed "some and Putt ye rest to ye flight." Andros supplied arms and sheltered Mohawk families in Albany. An English expedition followed, "to demand" the release of "Christian Prisoners" among "Phillip and the North Indians," who were "lately within this Government." This company was authorized to go "as farr as Caneticut river." Although no such demand for the return of prisoners was made, the English "scouts" espied by Metacom's men above Northfield, on the west bank, could have been the company from Albany. Later, Rowlandson relayed her son's report that "his Master (together with other Indians) were going to the French for Powder; but by the way the Mohawks met with them, and killed four of their Company which made the rest turn back again."[46]

This report opens the context to a wider geography, to the French settlements on the St. Lawrence and the northern Wabanaki interior. Indeed, at midwinter, Hoosic had hosted a great council, "led by a mighty Sachem" with thousands of "well armed" warriors in attendance. A "released" English captive witnessed at "the Indian Rendevouz" "some 2100 Indyans all fighting men," including the "600 Indyans" who'd been at Hoosic since he arrived, and "5 or 600 Indyans with Strawes in their Noses, which they called the French Indians." These "young men" were most likely from Winoskik and/or Missisquoi, on Betowbagw (Lake Champlain), Wabanaki communities who offered refuge to displaced relations from the south after the war and resisted English expansion long beyond. Trading with French allies on the St. Lawrence, they carried French powder downriver to their relations at Hoosic. As the report of Rowlandson's son suggests, it was through these networks that Metacom and other leaders sought material support for the continued resistance. Although New England most feared supply from Albany settlers (including the Dutch), perhaps the most reliable source of ammunition traveled through interior Indigenous networks.[47]

At that council, Wabanaki speakers pledged that "their Designe was in the Spring to goe to Hadley, Hartford &c. and Coneticut Col[ony], and having destroyed them to goe to Boston," the colonial center, "in the harvest." This plan was no secret; the warriors "themselves" drew "out into three Ranks" before the captive, making him recount "three times over" the strength of their numbers. They then turned the captive over to the Mohicans, who "released" him to carry that warning to Albany. The northern Wabanaki towns were "separated from"

Albany and Massachusetts "by 200 or 250 miles of hostile wilderness travel" and "their chances for observation were few." Dependent on neither Albany nor Boston for trade or negotiation, they were in a strikingly different position from their kin on Kwinitekw, Molôdemak, and the coast. Yet they knew those stories of dispossession and displacement, and were prepared to help reclaim their relations' homelands, harnessing the necessary force to keep the English from their southern door.[48]

To the surprise of New England leaders, Metacom and his men were not among these ranks. Although his comparatively small company had been "received . . . kindly" and hospitably "furnish'd . . . with provision" at Hoosic, the captive reported, the Wampanoag leader held "little" position or "authority amongst them." Colonial narrators labored to represent the Wampanoag sachem as the master in command, but captive reports demonstrated that the resistance was much wider and more decentralized than they imagined. Wabanaki warriors had their own motivations; yet they expressed confidence in the collective capacity to repulse the valley towns and take the war to Boston, ideas that emerged as central goals of the alliance that spring.[49]

On return to Kwinitekw, as Rowlandson observed, allied Indigenous forces carried out a stealthy raid on Northampton, across the river from Hadley, the very place the "French Indians" had said they would strike come spring. Minister John Russell reported a force of some one thousand. The men returned with horse and sheep meat to feed the families sheltered upriver. Overhearing the conversations about Hoosic and seeing live horses among them, Mary Rowlandson recognized the opportunity and her potential value: "I desired them, that they would carry me to Albany, upon one of those horses, and sell me for powder," offering herself as an object of exchange.[50]

CAPTIVE CORN

Weetamoo and Quinnapin remained on the east bank, just below the Ashuelot, for "awhile," probably about a week. As Rowlandson reported, "when we were at this place, my master's maid came home; she had been gone three weeks into the Narragansett country to fetch corn, where they had stored up some in the ground." This kinswoman of Quinnapin had left Menimesit (at the time of the dispersal) on a courageous expedition with Canonchet, who led over seventy women and men toward the Narragansett country to recover "a store of seed corn from secret granaries near Seekonk River," even as colonial scouts hunted Narragansett caches. Canonchet would give his life, engaging a party of two hundred Mohegan, Pequot, Niantic, and English warriors on the banks of the Nipmuc-Narragansett (Blackstone) river, to ensure that his kinswoman and the corn were able to make their way north. She carried twelve quarts of corn on her back and traveled, through forests teeming with colonial scouts, to gather sustenance and seeds for thousands.[51]

While this Narragansett woman was able to make her way to Sokwakik, few English men could navigate or discern this northern territory. On colonial maps, the land between Deerfield and Quebec was condensed, as settlers could not map that space between New England and New France. It remained "a maze" to English captives who traveled through it. Although Rowlandson had "liberty" to visit her son a mile away, she became "quickly lost . . . traveling over Hills and through Swamps, and could not find the way to him." Yet, as she "turned homeward," back toward the Great Bend, she "met with" Quinnapin, who showed her "the way to [her] son."

Beyond Northfield, Rowlandson lacked the language to map her journey and, even retrospectively, could speak only in vague terms about direction and geography, observing whether the company was moving up or down "the river" and when their "course bends" east, or "homeward," her only compass the sun. She understood that Lancaster and "the Bay Towns" were to the east and that the "Connecticut River" traveled north and south. However, other than the river, there were no English names for the places through which she traveled during her eighth through fourteenth removes. Moreover, although Massachusetts claimed jurisdiction far to the north (their boundary determined by the location of Winnepesaukee) and a single Northfield deed claimed land twelve miles to the north, encompassing the Great Bend, so few English men had traveled beyond Northfield that they held no common knowledge of place names. Lacking the linguistic capacity to recall the place names of the country through which she traveled, Rowlandson was unable to record the locations of her journey through *Sokwaki* space. Yet because of her descriptions, however vague, and *our* knowledge of the geography of Native space, it is possible to re-map the journey that Rowlandson, Weetamoo, and Quinnapin took as the ice broke on the rivers, and to better understand their motivations for movement.

TRACKING WEETAMOO

Kwinitekw's environs were intricately mapped according to Native scale, with ancient towns spread out along the river, protected by vast mountains and marshes. From Great Bend, tributaries and trails led north to fertile towns nestled among pines at Koasek, then to the headwaters of Kwinitekw, where Wanalancet took shelter. They led east up the Ashuelot, with multiple trails leading south to the Nipmuc country and northeast toward Penacook.

Although Rowlandson may not have perceived their motivations, Weetamoo and Quinnapin pursued purposeful travel into this protected northern country. Following the return of Quinnapin's kinswoman and major raids to the south, Rowlandson relayed that Weetamoo and Quinnapin "took their Travel," bringing "a small part of the Company" with them. They first camped less than a mile from Great Bend, below the Ashuelot River crossing, where they ate and rested. Rowlandson wasted energy by traveling back and forth to the lower town, seeking food and comfort from a woman who had been "kind" to her. The next day "in the morning" they set out, "intending a dayes journey up the River." They "wade[d] over" the Ashuelot, then headed north on the Kwinitekw trail, traveling over the hills and terraces. They trekked along the west side of a mountain opposite the Wantastegok River. To her, it seemed "tiresome and wearisome" travel, relieved only by their rest that night, at a camp near the mountain's north side.[52]

Weetamoo and Quinnapin were not leading families and captives over rugged upriver trails in order simply to seek out random camps in the wilderness. The trail between the river and the mountain made for ideal inland travel, with views of the river from the cover of forest and the defensive bulwark of the mountain flanking their eastern side. Runners could easily take the side trails leading to the ridges and peak, from which they had a full view of the country and would be able to discern any English or Mohawk war parties coming from any direction. Indeed, Abenaki warriors would continue to utilize this lookout during subsequent wars, especially after the English built a fort on the opposite bank. They likely camped by the crucial confluence of Kwinitekw and Wantastegok, where they had access to good fishing and early spring plants. Most important, just to the north was the Sokoki village at Ktsi Mskodak or Great Meadow, a fertile intervale where descendants of the women planters of Menimesit, Pocumtuck, and Sokwakik would still be living more than two generations later. If they continued northwards, they would reach Koasek, where they could plant far beyond English reach.[53]

"SHE WOULD GO NO FURTHER, BUT TURN BACK AGAIN"

The next morning, they "prepared for travel," another long day's journey. But the morning's plans had been delayed by a terrible occurrence the night before. That morning, Weetamoo had to "attend the burial" of a baby who had died en route. The baby must have been ill, perhaps with the "epidemical disease" then moving through New England; the loss to those who had come so far, must have been devastating.[54] Traveling with her child on her back, this mother must have been among those seeking sanctuary at the upriver towns. Even as warriors and leaders continued to seek alliance, the protection of these children remained at the forefront. Thus, it was not only war leaders and diplomats that were present on this journey, but the children who were the strongest argument for seeking that alliance.

That morning, as Weetamoo returned to her temporary camp from the burial, she saw that her captive had once more refused to work. It being the "Sabbath," while others were hastily packing their bags and dissembling their temporary houses, she sat reading her bible, gifted to her by a Christian Indian (taken in the raid on Medfield). Weetamoo "snatched it hastily out of [her] hand, and threw it out of doors," casting "the word" from her house. The act was ripe with meaning. Weetamoo knew the deep impact missionaries had made on the wide community, constraining and containing entire towns. When Metacom and his men had met with Easton the previous spring, one of their chief "Cumplaints" was that "thay had a great fear to have ani of ther indians should be Caled or forsed to be Christian indians," because "such wer in everi thing more mishivous, only disemblers, and then the English made them not subject to ther kings, and by ther lying to rong their kings." It was "Christian Indians" who were most well represented among the recruits hired to track their own relations. The English had made them believe that the bible held the key to their recovery, to survival of the epidemics that still claimed kin. Yet it had also been used to justify acts of extreme violence. The interpretations that colonists pulled from its pages made righteous their claims on planting fields and their destruction of towns. Moreover, Weetamoo would have seen her captive assert this same dogma as she struggled to both adapt to and resist her captors, Rowlandson believing all the while that her ethnicity and religion made her inherently superior and deserving of deliverance, if, of course, she proved obedient and faithful to her god. In throwing the bible to the ground, Weetamoo rejected that belief system and all that it justified. If her house was the microcosm, this act enacted the repulsion of colonial ideology from Native space, ejecting not the English woman but the discourse that justified her divine claim to those lands and to jurisdiction within them.[55]

In observing Rowlandson's behavior, Weetamoo surely recognized a parallel with the convert women in some of the mission communities. The gradual conversion from extended families to singular patriarchal units separated young women from their female relations, from the fields and the alliance-making practices that joined them. Weetamoo must have recognized the relationship between the bible and these forms of containment, as well as the embodiment of the gendered system in Rowlandson herself. Even in her narrative, Rowlandson struggled with the kinship system, preferring her own terms and placing Indigenous women firmly within recognizable household roles. Weetamoo and Wootonakanuske were never portrayed as sisters or aunts. Rather, Rowlandson referred to them as wives of Quinnapin and Metacom. All of their female relatives, who helped care for their children, built homes and rafts, navigated waterways, gathered and prepared food, and retrieved corn were described only as "maids." Rowlandson was so deeply enmeshed in the hierarchical household structure that she could not see beyond it to the wider network of relations, into which her captors tried to incorporate her.[56]

In casting the bible from her home, Weetamoo also insisted that Rowlandson turn her attention from the book to the world around her, and to her responsibilities as a member of this community. As Rowlandson traveled north, she increasingly focused on her interior world, her own woes. The act of sitting down and retreating to the alternate world of the bible represented inward-focused, self-centered behavior, which Weetamoo rejected. The English "mistress" would have to work, like any other woman. Moreover, the bible was an ineffective tool for navigating this space. Although Rowlandson imagined she "wept" by the "river of Babylon," she remained on the central Indigenous highway of Kwinitekw, but she could see only "Wilderness and Woods."[57]

Rowlandson's internal compass and spatial orientation was evident in her description of the route they took that morning, when they finally got on the road. She got a glimpse of purpose and hope when their course "bent" east "homeward," she thought, which "much cheared my Spirit." That hope sank when Weetamoo "on a sudden" gave "out" and said she "would go no further but turn back again, and said I must go back again with her." She called ahead for Quinnapin but he said he could not turn back with her, but had to go on. Still he would "come to us again in three days." It would be three weeks before they would see him again. "My spirit was upon this, I confess very impatient, and almost outrageous," Rowlandson lamented. "I thought I could as well have dyed as went back," across those "wearisome hills." Bemoaning their "turn back," Rowlandson failed to acknowledge the dire health of Weetamoo's child, although she had recently lost her own "babe," mentioning the child's sickness as an aside, later in the narrative. As Neal Salisbury has observed, "Weetamoo was undoubtedly turning back because her own child . . . was too sick to travel." Having witnessed the burial of another woman's baby that day, she would not "go on" but would tend to her child.[58]

Thus, to Rowlandson's dismay, they headed back west, camping for several days on that trail, not far from the river crossing where Rowlandson and others traveled to gather groundnuts. Several others remained with Weetamoo, helping to nurse her child. Her house was so full that when Rowlandson attempted to go in "to ly down" that night, "they bade me go out, and ly somewhere else, for they had company (they said) come in more than their own." Focused on her child, the needs of a lamenting captive were not at the forefront of Weetamoo's mind. But Rowlandson was given food and shelter in the homes of other families who remained with the saunkskwa.[59]

Weetamoo's child apparently took a turn for the worse, because rather than continuing on to follow Quinnapin or waiting for him at the camp, Weetamoo and her party headed back downriver, to one of the horticultural hamlets on Kwinitekw. Rowlandson described their location only as "a mighty thicket of brush" which was "five or six miles down the River." Here, Weetamoo might have sought medicine for her child, and the comfort of her sister. They stayed there "almost a fortnight," or nearly two weeks.[60]

While they were encamped on Kwinitekw's bank, a party gathered to raid downriver at Hadley. A coalition of protectors from Kwinitekw and the Narragansett, Nipmuc, and Wampanoag countries had already struck Rehoboth and Providence. Although Quinnapin was not among these parties, it is significant that the gathering occurred just days after he continued his trek north, most likely heading toward Ktsi Mskodak or Koasek. At the junction of multiple trails, Koasek was an ideal location for a rendezvous, with trails to Winoskik and Missisquoi, as well as to Pemijoasik and Wiwninbesaki. Quinnapin dependably would have sent runners ahead, and received others to usher them in. From Koasek, Wabanaki men could easily paddle downriver to join the warriors at Sokwakik. Quinnapin's influence may have been instrumental in securing support for both warriors and the families they sought to protect. Koasek would emerge as a crucial stronghold in the months to come. By June, Governor Leverett would report that "the greatest number of the enemy are gone up towards the head of Connecticut River, where they have planted much corn on the interval lands [Koasek] and seated three forts very advantageously in respect of the difficulty of coming at them." The Connecticut River functioned during this and all subsequent wars as both a sanctuary and a throughway for warriors, families, and their captives.[61]

Back on the intervals to the south, as Weetamoo attended her sick child and met with other leaders, she and her kin grew impatient with her captive. When Rowlandson inquired after her son, a man who knew his "master" teased and taunted her, saying they had "roasted him" and "he was very good meat." A woman residing in Weetamoo's house "threw a handful of ashes in [her] eyes" when Rowlandson tried to move kindling so that the heat of the fire would come her way. She showed not only self-centered, but erratic behavior, many times losing herself in reverie, then "suddenly" jumping up and running out of the house. Moreover, she often refused to work, particularly when Weetamoo or her female kin made requests. Once more "sitting" in Weetamoo's house, one of Wootonakanuske and Weetamoo's kinswomen "came in" with "the child" (likely Weetamoo's) in her arms, and "asked" Rowlandson "to give her a piece of [her] Apron" so that she could make a covering to keep the child warm. Rowlandson refused, and Weetamoo demanded she "give it" to the younger woman. Yet Rowlandson insisted she would not, her "apron" her most vital tool, in which she carried her sewing and her bible, as well as the lasting sign of her identity as an English wife. The young woman told her that if she "would not give her a piece, she would tear a piece off," and Rowlandson shot back that then "she would tear her Coat." Weetamoo, drawn from her own work, rose up to her full height, and took up "a stick big enough to have killed me," according to Rowlandson, "and struck at me with it." The captive ran from the house as Weetamoo "struck the mat of the Wigwam." Rowlandson then took off her Apron and gave it to the young woman, "and so that storm went over."[62]

One night, shortly thereafter, Weetamoo's child took a turn for the worse. Rowlandson was sent out, cared for by another family. Weetamoo's child, whom she had carried with her through Pocasset and Great Swamp, through one of the coldest and most brutal winters in memory, did not survive. The next morning, the community buried the child and mourned with the mother. Rowlandson refused to participate, but found "one benefit in it, that there was more room" for her. "On the morrow," she wrote, "they buried the papoose, and afterward, both morning and evening, there came a company to mourn and howl with her; though I confess I could not much condole with them. Many sorrowful days I had in this place, often getting alone. Like a crane, or a swallow, so did I chatter; I did mourn as a dove, mine eyes ail with looking upward. Oh, Lord, I am oppressed; undertake for me."[63]

Just as at the Council House when the warriors returned from Medfield, Rowlandson portrayed Indigenous song as "howling," base noise akin to the calls of dogs. In reality, the women who gathered around Weetamoo sang familiar songs, to express their great collective grief and to comfort the mother and leader who had suffered so much loss and done so much to ameliorate their own pain. They sat with her for several days and nights, singing songs that reminded her that her child had returned to her ancestors, traveling to a place where she would never want for sanctuary, shelter, or comfort.[64]

In order to maintain her faithfulness to her husband and her god, Mary Rowlandson could not "condole" with Weetamoo. Both women lost children to the violence of colonization. However, the same ideology that justified the violence of the colonial mission also prevented Rowlandson from seeing the space of motherhood where the two women's lives intersected, where condolence might have fostered understanding. In one sense, she simply could not accept that an Indian would feel the same emotions as a real human being like herself. More specifically, Rowlandson could not risk entering such a space of gendered grief. In Weetamoo's mourning, Rowlandson confronted an immediate conflict between her "potentially powerful" identification as a mother and her primary identification as a Puritan mistress and wife. Had she acknowledged Weetamoo's pain, Rowlandson might have recognized their mutual suffering, and been compelled to question the divinity of the colonial project, a principle on which her entire *Narrative* rested. The only pain that the captive could allow herself to feel was her own.[65]

After the death of her child, Weetamoo's decision, her course, was clear. Following several days of condolence, Weetamoo took the trail south, carrying her captive with her. She moved toward Wachusett, her sister and Metacom by her side. After crossing the river at Paquaug, they met with a messenger from Quinnapin, who had made it to Wachusett, where leaders were gathering. The messenger relayed that Tom Nepanet, a Christian Indian from Nashobah, had been led through to the stronghold, carrying a letter from Massachusetts. Governor Leverett wanted to negotiate the release of the captives. Seeking steps toward a treaty, the court had asked them to name their price, whether in wampum, goods, or exchange of prisoners. Quinnapin sent word to bring Rowlandson in. The party picked up speed and moved on.[66]

WACHUSETT, NIPMUC COUNTRY, APRIL 1676

Before James Printer lay a single blank page. When Tom Nepanet delivered Leverett's message, he had also brought this paper, and the pen and ink that lay beside him, instruments intended for the return message. Of all the converts among them, Shoshanim and the sachems chose James to write a message on their behalf. They trusted him to deliver their words. They trusted his skill. Colonial governors would call him their "scribe."

There was power in this moment before words were committed to paper. Since many of those for whom he wrote were unable to read his work, James might write anything on the page. He could reveal their location, request help, or relay a secret message to his brother, among the colonial troops. He could request redemption not only for the English captives, but also for himself and his extended family. He could compose an indictment on behalf of the sachems, which might express his own rage. He could write simply what the sachems requested, sending the words drawn from consensus in the Council House, as messengers had long carried wampum along these same trails.

James dipped his pen in the black ink and inscribed the following words, filling the page:

> For the Governor and the Council at Boston
>
> The Indians, Tom Nepennomp and Peter Tatatoquinea hath brought us letter from you about the English Captives, especially for Mrs Rolanson; the answer is I am sorrow that I have done much to wrong you and yet I say the falte is lay upon you, for when we began quarrel at first with Plimouth men I did not think that you should have so much trouble as now is: therefore I am willing to hear your desire about the Captives. Therefore we desire you to send Mr Rolanson and goodman Kettle: (for their wives) and these Indians Tom and Peter to redeem their wives, they shall come and goe very safely: Whereupon we ask Mrs Rolanson, how much your husband willing to give for you she gave an answer 20 pounds in goodes but John Kittels wife could not tell, and the rest captives may be spoken of hereafter.[67]

Mary Rowlandson knew her worth, even if the other prominent mistress among them could not name a price. Here, at Wachusett, Weetamoo guarded her claim closely, not allowing her captive to linger too long or receive too much provision at any other hearth. Neither Quinnapin's elder or younger wife could lay claim to her. As Rowlandson remarked, "I understood Wettimore thought, that if she should let me go and serve with" Quinnapin's elder wife, "she would be in danger to loose, not only my service, but the redemption pay also." Weetamoo must have been in the Council House when they called Rowlandson in to speak in their "General Court." The leaders "bade" Rowlandson "stand up" and "speak what I thought" her husband "would give" for her. Although she may not have realized she was less than twenty miles from Lancaster, the captive was closer in her journey than ever before to her home. Having contemplated her "sale" at Albany many times, she must have had some idea of how much powder could be bought for twenty pounds of goods, as did her "mistress." In her narrative, Rowlandson explained her struggle to put a price on her own head. She could not imagine what her husband might afford, given the loss of their house and belongings. She did not know whether the governor and council would contribute. To name a figure too high or low would lengthen her captivity. She had also possessed the knowledge and presence of mind to request that Tom Neponet relay a message to her husband to send "three pound of tobacco," a third of which Tom had brought with the most recent letter from

Massachusetts. Understanding its symbolic worth, she had "quickly" distributed the tobacco, opening a space for negotiation. However, to see the negotiations come to fruition and satisfy her "mistress," she had to trust James Printer to accurately deliver her request for the "redemption pay."[68]

As she noted, it was "a Praying-Indian that wrote their letter for them," referring to James. The letter revealed the important role that Nipmuc men assumed as mediators. Having traditionally occupied a middle ground between territories, cultivating alliances from the inland, they now occupied a similar role in these negotiations. Wachusett was the highest peak and a northern axis of their territory, from which they could see the alliances laid out in four directions. Kutquen, a Kwinitekw leader, was also instrumental in the negotiations, tying Wachusett to the multitribal community on the river. From Kwinitekw, the Narragansett elder Canonicus sent similar diplomatic messages to their former allies in Connecticut, answering the colony's proposal for a peace conference and captive exchange. Through writing, from the protected bulwark of Wachusett, inland leaders sought to renew their political relationship to Massachusetts, acknowledging that this war, which began with the "Plymouth men," had spun out of control, encompassing a greater scope and causing more grief than anyone had anticipated. At the same time, as Gookin noted, Massachusetts had failed to fulfill the "covenant" between "the Indians and their ancestors" that they would provide "mutual protection" to each other. Shoshanim's leadership in these negotiations harkened back to Showanon's role in the original agreement. Yet now they had their own scribes to articulate the terms of renewal.[69]

In replying to the message, Leverett and his council chastised the "Indian sachems" for not following English conventions in their letter, which was "neither subscribed by the sachems nor hath it any date, which your scribe James Printer doth well understand should be." However, Printer was responsible for following protocols required by the Native leaders, not his former teachers. The fact that he "knew" the English rules suggests a deliberate or hasty disregard for them (not a "native" ignorance). Printer did adhere to Indigenous diplomatic protocols of peacemaking, acknowledging the pain and loss of the enemy, as well as the responsibility both sides should assume for the violence that had mutually affected them. Some scholars have made much of James's use of "I" in this letter, suggesting that he used the first person singular pronoun to signify his individual point of view, or that "I" represented Shoshanim or Metacom's singular voice. However, as I read it, James referred to the council's return letter and prefaced the official response by stating, "the answer is . . . ". With this phrase, he signaled he was *transmitting* a *collective* "answer." It would have been highly inappropriate and risky for him, as the scribe or messenger, to give an individual answer to a weighty matter that concerned the whole. Moreover, in treaty literature, Native speakers commonly used the communal "I" interchangeably with the exclusive "we," when a speaker articulated the position of a nation or confederation. Here, "I" and "we" may have invoked concentric circles within the alliance, just as the sachems addressed Massachusetts separately from the United Colonies.[70]

In the message, James and the sachems distinguished between Plymouth and Massachusetts, emphasizing that "when we" (inclusive of the Native alliance but not of Massachusetts) "began quarrel . . . with Plymouth men" (excluding Massachusetts), "I (the Nipmuc leaders) did not think that you" (Massachusetts leaders and settlers) "should have so much trouble as now is." Thus the letter delineated specific, localized relationships, distinguishing between the Native alliance that formed in the wake of Plymouth's incursions on Wampanoag territory, and the breakdown of the covenant between Massachusetts and the Nipmucs, Patuckets, and, perhaps, the Narragansetts. The sachems thus proposed that because of these *particular* conditions of historical alliance and war, "I" (the mediating sachems) "am willing to hear *your* [Massachusetts Council's] desire about the Captives" and "we" (the alliance) "desire" the council to send the husbands of the two prominent captives in order to initiate the negotiations and demonstrate their good faith. Significantly, the sachems requested that Massachusetts send representatives to *their* location. They did not offer to bring the captives to Boston or to engage in a council on a midway meeting ground. The initial negotiations would take place in Nipmuc territory and the sachems only agreed to "hear" the requests. Moreover, in transmitting Rowlandson's answer regarding "the pay," they set the terms for her redemption, in consultation with *their* captive, who remained under their jurisdiction.

At this moment, the sachems negotiated from a place of confidence, believing the balance of power had been restored to more equal terms. In their previous response to the council's initial letter, transcribed by Natick convert Peter Jethro, they acknowledged the losses of the colonists, saying, "We know your heart grew sorrowful with crying for your lost many many hundred men and all your house and all your land, and woman, child and cattle." Yet they also revealed that they were aware of the position from which Massachusetts negotiated: "You know and we know . . . as all your thing[s] that you have lost" you now "on your backside stand."[71]

They were not off the mark. That spring, Gookin recalled, "The Council had used many endeavours, and raised forces and sent them forth, to beat up their headquarters at Watchusett, all those means prove ineffectual; and the enemy still kept that station, the place being near a very high mountain, and very difficult to have access to, by reason of thick woods and rocks and other fastnesses, that our English army thought it not advisable to hazard themselves in that enterprise." Once more the land served as a protective defense for the alliance, the "mountain place" proving inaccessible and unnavigable to colonial expeditions. The prospect of retrieving captives through force was unlikely. Moreover, Gookin noted, although they were daily besieged with raids, "none of our enterprises against the enemy were blessed with success, and it was groundedly feared and judged that seed-time and harvest would be greatly obstructed, and thereby occasion famine to follow the war." Colonial leaders had believed, as Rowlandson noted, that if the Indians' "corn were cut down, they would starve and dy with hunger." Yet she observed that "all the time" she "was among them," she "did not see one Man, Woman, or Child, die with hunger." The English, Gookin suggested, faced the greater prospect of famine. That spring, when Roger Williams met with a group of war leaders near Providence, he "told them planting time was a coming for them and Us," and the Kwinitekw leader Kutquen, one of the leading sachems at Wachusett, responded that "they cared not for Planting these Ten Years. They would live up on us, and De[e]r." While Gookin feared that "God seemed to put us to shame, and not to go forth with our arms," Kutquen boasted that "God was with them."[72]

As Gookin recalled, "Whilst this matter of the redemption of the captives was in agitation, the assaults of the enemy were frequent and violent, for the body of them quartered within twenty miles of the English frontiers of Lancaster, Groton, and Marlborough, and made daily incursions up on us." These were not divided endeavors; while Kutquen spoke for protectors in Providence, he also spoke with Shoshanim for the community as a whole in fostering negotiation at Wachusett. Monoco's role as war chief was in fact crucial to the Nipmuc's negotiating power. While sachems like Shoshanim and Canonicus helped to forge inroads toward peace, Monoco and Quinnapin maintained the threat of war, carrying out the spring offensive. At Groton (March 13), where Simon Willard had held many Nashaway men in debt, Monoco asserted this position of power, "entertaining" a "discourse" with his "old neighbor" Captain Parker, whom he'd known before the war. He gave his perspective on "the causes of war" and the best way to "bring about" a "friendly peace." If negotiations did not succeed, he pledged that just as he had cleared "Medfield and Lancaster," so would he clear "Groton," with "Chelmsford, Concord, Watertown, Cambridge, Charlestown, Roxbury, and Boston" to follow. In this assertion, Monoco echoed the claim the "French Indians" made at Hoosic that they would take Boston in the spring offensive. Both the Nipmucs and the Massachusetts Council were at a crucial turning point, and Monoco warned that if the English did not make good on the terms of peace, the eastern settlements would become the next target. Monoco also warned them not to be foolish enough to think that God would preserve Boston. He taunted Parker, "with several blasphemous scoffs" at their earnest "praying and worshipping God" in Groton's "meetinghouse," which Monoco "deridingly said he burnt." Similarly, when Kutquen and the protectors met with Williams, they likewise discussed the causes of war and the terms of peace. They "confessed" that the war had put them "in a strange way," but that the English "had forced them to it" and that "God . . . had forsaken" the English, who had been the first to "break the articles" of peace, "and not they." It seemed that Kutquen's statement was not his personal opinion, but a common belief held among the alliance at Wachusett, interpreting the political landscape through a syncretic lens, wherein divine will was directed toward rebalancing the scales of justice toward Indigenous continuance.[73]

This belief may have inspired some to join with Kutquen and Monoco on the spring raids. As Rowlandson observed, converts were among the company that joined Quinnapin and the warriors, that April, in raiding Sudbury, one of many towns in Nipmuc territory that encroached on the land and jurisdiction of mission communities. She did not name James Printer among those who went out, but he may have received disturbing news on return. One of the men among the English, who came in to defend the town from their successful strike, was his brother Job.

"AT HASSANAMESIT ABOUT THE FULL OF THE MOON"

As Weetamoo led families north from Menimesit at the end of February, James's brother Joseph Tukuppawillin and his family had made their escape, traveling by the light of the growing moon to their home of Hassanamesit. Moving through increasingly familiar paths under forest cover, Joseph traveled with his wife, their twelve-year-old son, their nursing baby, and several children, including Job's, as well as their father, Naoas, who was over eighty years old, and the widow who had cared for Job's children all this while, along with her grown daughter. At Menimesit in January, Job had arranged to meet Joseph and their family "at Hassanamesit about the full of the moon." The dispersal from Menimesit provided a crucial opportunity. James did not go with them.[74]

Job Kattenanit and James Quananopohit had provided crucial intelligence on Menimesit, helping the colonial troops to locate the stronghold that had long eluded them. In return for his "true and faithful account," Job had petitioned the Massachusetts Council, shortly after his February return, seeking permission to travel to Hassanamesit to meet his "friends," all "Godly Christians," and to "bring in" his "poor children." His "friends," he insisted, "do greatly mourn for their condition" and have "longed to return to the English if you please to let them live." The tone of his letter was strikingly different from the message his brother James composed at Wachusett. Job addressed the council as "your poor suplyant" and "servant" in a pleading and submissive manner, as if offering a prayer, making a "humble request," not a demand. "If you please," he asked "to send an Englishman or two with me I shall be glad, but if that cannot be done," he requested they "admit" James Speen to accompany him. He sought to pursue this journey hastily, before "the army" went "forth" to "the enemies' quarters," an expedition he was willing to join and guide, "if your Honours please," if only after his journey to bring his children to safe quarters in Boston.[75]

Job's petition arrived in the midst of a new military strategy. After the February raid on Lancaster, the court had voted to raise an "army of 600 men" for this expedition to Menimesit. However, Thomas Savage refused to "take the charge" unless he had Native men "to go with him for guides." Realizing that their efforts were nearly fruitless without adequate scouts, Massachusetts began to fully implement the strategy that had worked so well for Connecticut. John Curtis, a man "well acquainted with those Indians," traveled by boat to Deer Island "to choose six of the fittest men" for his company of guides, including Job Kattenanit and James Quananopohit, as well as Andrew Pittimee (Natick), James Speen (Natick), John Magus (another former schoolmaster), and William Nahaton (Punkapog). Their service was motivated in part by the desire to protect their families at Deer Island; in joining the expedition to Menimesit, however, the scouts also faced the prospect of violence against their kin who remained at the stronghold. Even as they demonstrated their "faithfulness" to Massachusetts, they risked betrayal of their relations. Thus, this mission "to find out the enemy at Menumesse" was starkly different than James and Job's earlier expeditions to the Wampanoag country. Job's journey to retrieve his family became all the more crucial in the context of the impending raid.[76]

Major Savage outfitted these "faithful and courageous" men with arms, and then "conducted" them to Marlborough, where Job had lived and taught, and from which he had first been recruited. In six months Job had transformed from a minister and teacher to a colonial spy and soldier. The company arrived at Okkanamesit at the very end of February, with plans to "march" with "the army" on "the first day of March." However, Gookin noted, before they could "march" toward Quaboag, a "matter of trouble and disquiet" arose.[77]

The council had granted Job's request. Yet every night during this movement from Boston to Marlborough brought the moon closer to full. In response to Job's appeals and the "order of the Council," Gookin recounted, Savage and

Dennison "gave liberty" for Job to travel, but he would "go alone" and return, with his "friends," to the army's "rendezvous" point at Quaboag. Ironically, it was the gathering of the army about Quaboag that led to the alliance's dispersal, allowing Joseph and his family a window for "escape." The army continued to gather, with no notion that their targets had moved on.[78]

As Job set out, Gookin wrote, the nefarious Captain Mosely returned to Marlborough and "made a great stir," claiming that Job "would inform the enemy of the army's motion, and so frustrate the[ir] whole design," challenging Savage and mischaracterizing Job as a traitor in their ranks. He had made similar claims about Job's brother James only five months before, and the scouts would continue to face harassment throughout the spring. The controversy swelled in the camp and town, and James Quananopohit offered to go, with two English captains, to "follow Job on horseback" and ensure his compliance and return.[79]

Meanwhile, Joseph and his family traveled on towards Hassanamesit, with little to sustain their journey. When they arrived at their town, the remains of the cornfields bare, Job was nowhere to be found. Fearful he had not been "admitted" to come to them, they moved their camp to a more protected place. Soon after, an English cavalry, en route to Quaboag, came upon them. Gookin related that the soldiers "took those poor creatures (supposing they had got a prize)," although "they were but two men (one very aged), three women, and six children," and confiscated their few goods, a couple blankets or mats ("rugs"), some bowls and utensils, and a pewter cup that Joseph used for "the sacrament of the Lord's Supper," given to him by Eliot. Gookin recounted that the soldiers took them to Marlborough, where some of the English "people of the town, especially women," so "abuse[d], threaten[ed], and taunt[ed]" them, that Joseph's wife, a nursing mother, and the widow who "had carefully kept and nourished Job's children" fled, taking the widow's older daughter and Joseph's older son with them, but leaving the baby behind. In "great fears" for their lives, the women "escaped into the woods," he wrote.

Gookin portrayed this as a case of mistaken identity, found converts initially taken for enemies, but a petition from one of the soldiers suggests the small company of "9 or so," under Captain Gibbs, had been sent to retrieve "Job's children" and relations "on his information" and with Savage's "permission," while Job continued to Quaboag with the troops. Joseph had carried his family safely to Hassanamesit, but had neither the tools nor the capacity to protect them. The soldier, Jonathan Fairbanks, took his daughter or niece, "a young girl of ten or twelve," and with Gibbs's "promise that she should be his own" Fairbanks "took her upon his horse and brought her to Quaboag." Thus Gookin's account of the harassment of families at Marlborough, may have taken place at Quaboag, and the women had even greater cause to flee, as they witnessed a soldier take this young woman as his property. These women suffered greatly; Joseph Tukuppawillin's twelve-year-old son died of starvation before they found James Printer and their relations at Wachusett. The young woman was sent to Deer Island, and when Fairbanks petitioned, it was to ask the court to formally "grant him the said girl."[80]

"Not long after," Gookin recounted, "this poor minister, Joseph Tuckapawillin, and his aged father, Naoas . . . with three or four children of the minister's, and Job's children, were all sent to Boston." There they met with Gookin and Eliot at the house of Captain Nicholas Page, who had led a company in the Wampanaog country the previous summer. Page and his wife provided needed food and shelter, as well as vital milk for the baby, even as the captain plied the father for information about "the condition and number of the enemy." Joseph lamented:

> I am greatly distressed this day on every side; the English have taken away some of my estate, my corn, cattle, my plough, cart, chain, and other goods. The enemy Indians have also taken a part of what I had; and the wicked Indians mock and scoff at me, saying "Now what is become of your praying to God?" The English also censure me, and say I am a hypocrite. In this distress I have no where to look, but up to God in heaven to help me; now my dear wife and eldest son are (through English threatening) run away, and I fear will perish in the woods for want of food; also my aged mother is lost; and all this doth greatly aggravate my grief. But yet I desire to look up to God in Christ Jesus, in whom alone is my help.

In Gookin's presence, Page then asked Tukappawillin "whether he had not assisted the enemy in the wars when he was among them" at Menimesit. He insisted, "I never did join with them against the English. Indeed, they solicited me, but I utterly denied and refused it. I thought within myself, it is better to die than to fight against the church of Christ."[81]

Joseph insisted that he had maintained the bonds of faith with the church and "God." Like Rowlandson, he used the scriptures as a map to navigate an increasingly hostile and chaotic landscape. Yet the portrait painted by missionaries had disintegrated. He could no longer expect the loyalty or protection that his fellow Christians had promised. Indeed, Tukuppawillin's lament was a plea to uphold the pledges of protection and alliance that Massachusetts men had made in God's name. The magistrates and army had failed to protect Joseph and his family, from either the Nipmuc warriors who carried them and their corn to Menimesit or the settlers who plundered his home. Rather than referring to communal fields, Joseph marked his agricultural tools and products as private property: parts of "my estate," which had been violated and stolen. The context was immediate. He had only recently traveled to Hassanamesit to find that there was no possibility for subsistence there to feed his hungry family. No store of corn, no cattle to milk or harvest for meat, no tools to plow come spring. Then, without cause, they were once more captured, this time by English troops, who did not even protect the women among them. As the "wicked Indians" at Menimesit saw, ultimately, his family's conversion had left them defenseless, exposed on "every side." Thus, as he suggested, in keeping with his faith, the only direction he could turn for deliverance was toward the sky.[82]

Despite his plea, after only "a night or two" in Boston, Joseph, Naoas, and the children were all transported to Deer Island, "sent to endure yet another form of captivity." Job's children were not secured in Boston under Gookin or Eliot's care, but left to fare as the other captives on the barren island, to dig for spring shoots and hope for harvest from the sea. The one consolation came from a generous woman, who had carried her own baby through the harsh winter, and offered precious milk to nourish Joseph's infant.[83]

Finally arriving at Wachusett, Joseph's wife must have described her ordeal to James Printer, who remained at the mountain, including the capture of his niece and the death of his nephew. The story would have struck a familiar chord. James demonstrated ambivalence and adaptability in responding to a violent world, constantly in flux. Such "ambiguity," Neal Salisbury wisely instructs us, has not been fully appreciated, and seems a common state of being for "resisting Christians" who negotiated a complex network of relations, "understanding and acting out of the many ambiguities surrounding their relations with Europeans." Here, at Wachusett, James would lay the groundwork not only for the redemption of Mary Rowlandson, but also for the redemption of his kin. With his father, mother, and two brothers gone, he was now responsible for protecting and providing for a much wider family, including his wife, her eight-year-old brother, and three women tied to him through his brothers Joseph and Job. Joseph's wife would also have carried the news that the colonial army had headed to Menimesit, with Job as a guide. If Job and James Quananopohit could locate them at Menimesit, they might also track them down at Wachusett. Her story instructed him that if they were found at Wachusett, soldiers would not attempt to distinguish between warriors and captive Christians, the women among them especially vulnerable.[84]

SUDBURY

In mid-April, as leaves began budding and spring melt coursed through mountain streams at Wachusett, returning life to the land, Rowlandson watched

Quinnapin and the protectors gather in a circle, their families with them. She watched as one of the spiritual men drew up their power with song, and a pniese invoked the words to give them strength and inner fortification, helped them to imagine and enact the battle. With every round of song and speech, they struck the land upon which they kneeled. After the last "speech" resounded, "which they all assented in a rejoicing manner," the protectors "ended their business, and forthwith went to Sudbury fight."[85]

As James Printer witnessed with Rowlandson, or participated with Quinnapin, in this gathering at Wachusett, Job Kattenanit gathered with another group of warriors in Charlestown, only three miles from the Indian College. Job mustered with a newly authorized "company of Praying Indians," forty men recruited from Deer Island. Gookin later described these men as "very desirous and willing to engage against the enemy," masking the historical memory that some regarded service as a forced obligation, following months of exposure and starvation. Many were also motivated by responsibilities for the survival of their kin. Just after the company of scouts was recruited, their families were released from the island, and carried by boat to live under English supervision in Boston. This group of families must have included Job's children and his nieces and nephews. While their families were fed, the men were supplied and "furnished" with guns by their officers, Captain Samuel Hunting and Lieutenant James Richardson, who "were well acquainted with those Indians."[86]

The company's first order was to go to the fishing falls "near Chelmsford," where they "expected the enemy would come at this season to get fish for their necessary food" and they might "scout abroad daily to seize the enemy" as they came into the falls or gathered in nearby places. However, just as they prepared to march to Patucket, numerous "messengers" came in to Boston and Cambridge reporting "that a great body of the enemy, no less as was judged than fifteen hundred" had taken the town of Sudbury, on the eastern perimeter of the Nipmuc country, within twenty miles of Boston.[87]

By all accounts, the raid was "a brilliant victory for the native alliance." The war leaders Quinnapin and Monoco had once more combined forces, and taken the easternmost colonial towns in the Nipmuc country. On April 18, warriors cleared Marlborough (on a third and final raid), destroying the signs of settler "improvement." They burned the remaining houses and barns, tore down fences, and "hacked" the "fruit trees." They destroyed a tavern and burned the house of the preacher who had blocked the path from Okkanamesit to the main road with his meetinghouse, a building which also caught fire, despite the apparent reluctance of Christian Indian warriors to assault it. Among these warriors were likely some of those same peaceful Christians from Okkanamesit who had been falsely accused by Mosely, as their neighbors stood by. From Marlborough, war parties trekked east to Sudbury, where they dealt the final blow to the military's "base of operations": killing Marlborough's current commander and his replacement in one of many ambushes. They utilized fire and smoke to drive the company from its defensive position behind a hill, and obfuscate their vision, leaving only thirteen men to escape to a nearby mill. Meanwhile, other protectors "hunted" cattle in the town to feed the people gathered at Wachusett.[88]

Job Kattenanit and his company rushed toward Sudbury, and "upon the 22nd of April, early in the morning," Gookin wrote, "our forty Indians, having stripped themselves, and painted their faces like to the enemy, they passed over the bridge to the west side of the river, without any Englishmen in their company, to make discover of the enemy." They practiced a subtle stratagem of camouflage, blending in with the environment as well as the warriors from Wachusett. But when they arrived in the smoke-filled woods, the warriors had already made their retreat. They found none of "the enemy," but rather encountered many English bodies, which they then helped to bury, earning the respect and changing the minds of many of the English soldiers and families who remained. It must have been quite a sight as they transformed before settler eyes from fierce painted warriors to "Christian" protectors, but for Job and his men, it would have been a seamless transition, all part of the commitment they had made, however ironic that they had to discard the visible markers of their conversion in order to protect their English "friends." As those settlers engaged in their own mourning rituals, Job and the scouts served as guards, "marching in two files upon the wings, to secure those that went to bury the dead." They did not encounter any of their relations on the battlefield, but, perhaps, for the "four dead Indians of the enemy" whom they found "covered up with logs and rubbish" among the English dead.[89]

At Wachusett, Rowlandson witnessed the return of her "master" Quinnapin and the protectors from Sudbury and noticed the state of grief that overwhelmed them. "They said they had killed two Captains, and almost an hundred men," she relayed, "yet they came home without that rejoicing and triumphing over their victory . . . but rather like Dogs . . . which have lost their ears." Although Rowlandson could not comprehend their glum expressions, writing in retrospect that they must have had some omen of impending defeat, they were clearly grieving the loss of their kin, both men and women, at the fight. For indeed, women, too, went out on this raid, at least one with a baby "at her back." Not all mothers sought sanctuary in remote parts. "For the enemy, to make their force seem to be very great," Gookin wrote, "there were many women among them, whom they had fitte with pieces of wood cut in the form of guns, which those carried, and were placed in the centre." Weetamoo may have been among them. This stratagem, combined with other subterfuge, worked successfully to make their numbers appear much greater than they were, leading to reports of "twelve or fourteen hundred fighting men" including "various Sagamores from all Parts with their men of Armes." Although as Rowlandson understood, they had "lost" comparatively few, "not . . . above five or six," one of these fallen protectors must have been a close relative of the spiritual man who had led the ceremony before the raid. This "Powaw" came home, she noticed, with his face painted black, a clear sign of his mourning. Her master, she noted, made it home safely, and asked her "to make a shirt" for one of his children, from "a Holland-laced" pillowcase he had carried from the raid. Even as some families grieved the loss of sons and daughters, others were now able better to clothe and feed their children from the goods and meat protectors like Quinnapin carried to the mountain.[90]

Even as he witnessed the return of Quinnapin and the protectors, his own kin must have been at the forefront of James Printer's mind. His brother Job marched with the army, and he could not know the whereabouts of Joseph, his father, or his brothers' children. His eldest brother Annaweekin died in warfare sometime that spring, perhaps at Medfield or Sudbury. And following the raid, James once more had to move his family deeper into the mountain woods. As Rowlandson observed, this was their usual practice "to remove" after a strike. Even within this sanctuary, knowing the scouts might find them, the danger to his family, on both sides, must have seemed grave. What would he do should the army arrive? Would there be any routes of escape? Would he be forced to face his brother? Would he be able to protect the children entrusted to his care? For James, the resolution of his dilemma lay in the possibility of peace.

Following the spring offensive, inland leaders were in a strong position to negotiate, having effectively cleared their homelands of settlers. As David Jaffee notes, "By late March, the Indian offensive had successfully cleared out the outer ring of frontier settlements, such as Lancaster and Groton, where the English had slowly inched their way west for over a generation." They had also cleared the northern settlements in the Connecticut River Valley. The Nipmucs, with their alliance, had pushed the English from their central homeland, and the Massachusetts men were now "on their backside" in Boston and the eastern settlements. Nipmuc leaders stood ready to renew their fields, if negotiations proceeded.[91]

The Massachusetts Council, in an ironic reversal, now sought to contain their settlements to protect the core of the colony, as the buffer of outposts collapsed and towns were "pushed back to the coast." As James Drake noted, in March the Massachusetts magistrates "put forth the idea of abandoning huge parts of the colony and retreating behind a line of fortifications, natural barriers in the form of ponds and rivers and an eight-foot palisade." They called for settlers in the outlying towns and the Connecticut Valley, to "draw into a narrow compass," a phrase that would be echoed by the sons of Kwinitekw women leaders, in satirical protest, a generation later. Colonial officers had learned they could not pursue retreating warriors into Sokwakik, "by reason of the numerousness of the enimy" and the lack of territorial knowledge. The dispersal of peoples within multiple homelands further confused them. They could not understand how they could be receiving reports that the Narragansetts were in the Connecticut Valley, even as they were raiding Rehoboth and Providence. Meanwhile, by the time peace negotiations began, commander-in-chief Savage had begun his final withdrawal back to Boston, leaving a smaller company in the Valley. He had concluded, with other officers, that they would not attempt to raid Wachusett, realizing "the futility" of trying to pursue the gathered protectors "with an army."[92]

Their solutions to the predicament rested on the men they recruited from Deer Island, to pursue the enemy and protect the towns. Lacking the numbers "to guard all towns at once while still maintaining offensive operations," Massachusetts recruited a Native company, which could navigate the land, and accepted Joseph Rowlandson and Gookin's pleas to initiate peace through the redemption of captives. Writing to Savage on April 1, the council relayed, "Wee have sent out a single Indian from ye Island to carry A letter to ye enemy aboute redemption of Captives," and noted, "hee [is] ordered to carry a flag of truce," to show he was a "messenger . . . sent in a way of treaty." This was the letter that prompted Quinnapin to send a messenger to Weetamoo, to bring in Mary Rowlandson.[93]

THE LAST REMOVE: "A GREAT DAY OF DANCING"

After moving "three or four miles," the large company with which Rowlandson traveled established a new camp at Wachusett, as the fish runs began to come in. She noted, "The Indians now began to come from all quarters" in preparation for the annual spring gathering, "their merry dancing day." For James Printer, this would have been a familiar sight, recalled from his childhood. Weetamoo and Quinnapin prepared to help host the large gathering. Rowlandson observed that, at the new camp, "they built a great Wigwam, big enough to hold an hundred Indians," an arbor for "a great day of Dancing."[94]

In the midst of these preparations, a diplomatic delegation arrived at Wachusett. Tom Neponet had returned, with Peter Ephraim, a Natick Indian who had served with the colonial troops, and Tom's neighbor John Hoar, the overseer of the Christian Indians held at Nashobah. Hoar carried the tobacco that Rowlandson had requested, along with food to offer his hosts, trading cloth for the women (perhaps for Weetamoo), and twenty pounds to "pay" for Rowlandson. While the leaders called a general council, James Printer sought out Tom Neponet. Massachusetts had sent no messages or goods for the redemption of the Indian captives, taken so long ago at Hassanamesit. James Printer negotiated with Tom on his own. That evening he witnessed the great dance, fueled by liquor Hoar had brought to ease negotiations. Weetamoo and Quinnapin hosted Hoar, allowing him to stay in their large house, as Weetamoo's mother had hosted Edward Winslow decades before. In the middle of the night, Quinnapin "went out of the Wigwam" and called for James. Rowlandson, already resting in Weetamoo's house, saw James come in and awaken Hoar. Translating, he conveyed that Quinnapin "would let" Rowlandson "go home tomorrow, if" Hoar would give him another "pint of Liquors." James may have felt foolish making the offer, which Hoar took seriously, delivering the drink and calling for Tom and Peter to confirm the pledge. Then James must have watched with a mix of humor and trepidation as Quinnapin came in once more, shouting drunken insults and praises for the Englishman, while chasing after his wives. Weetamoo left the house, leaving Quinnapin to sleep it off. The nighttime carousing was an anomaly; Rowlandson wrote that he was "the first Indian I saw drunk all the while that I was among them." In the light of day it was clear that the serious negotiations would take place only in the Council House.[95]

Two days later, the dances ended, Rowlandson recalled, "They called their General Court (as they call it) to consult and determine, whether I should go home or no." Reaching consensus, "as one man" they "did seemingly consent to it," she wrote, except for "Philip, who would not come among them," creating retrospectively an image of Metacom, stubbornly wedded to war. Accordingly, Weetamoo and Quinnapin consented to her release, a symbolic good faith offering toward the larger goal, communicated in the written message that traveled with her, calling for "an immediate truce." According to the colonial response (the original letter has not survived), the sachems "desire[d] not to be hindered by" soldiers in their "planting" as the families returned to their towns this spring. In return, they promised "not to doe damage to" the colonial "towns." For them, a resolution seemed at hand.[96]

The advocacy of mediators like James Printer, familiar with English forms and conventions, was vital to these negotiations. Like Joseph Tukuppawillin, many were anxious to return to their fields, to see the restoration of their towns. As Gookin observed, it was the "praying Indians" who "broke the ice and made way for" peace, "by their first adventuring to treat with the enemy." Although men like Tom Neponet initiated mediation for Massachusetts, men like James Printer translated, transcribed, and negotiated for the nations gathered at Wachusett. These "Praying Indians," who had formed a distinct regional community, met each other on this middle ground and had to prove fidelity to multiple relationships and to each other in order to renew the trust among them and achieve the possibility of peace. They also had to demonstrate their trustworthiness in their capacity to write, assuring Nipmuc and other leaders that they would convey messages with integrity and accuracy. Here, in contradistinction to John Sassamon, James Printer and other "scribes" had to demonstrate that they would act like kin.[97]

Mary Rowlandson's narrative concluded with her own redemption, including her sorrowful, brief return to a deserted Lancaster, en route to Boston. James Printer appeared but briefly, a glimpse of his crucial role as a negotiator and translator in the conversations that enabled her release. She did not mention his efforts to redeem his kin within Indigenous diplomatic networks. As Gookin recalled, "about two months after" her flight from Marlborough, Joseph Tukappawillin's "wife was recovered and brought in by Tom Dublet, one of our messengers to the enemy," shortly after Rowlandson. "The other widow, who went away at the time, and her daughter, were also recovered," and subsequently married Job. James remained in the Nipmuc country.[98]

The final portrayal of Weetamoo in Rowlandson's narrative conveys the unity she strove to achieve and a lasting image of her commitment to this multitribal alliance and the land that nourished it. Rowlandson wrote that Quinnapin and Weetamoo were "so busie" in their preparations for the dance that they had not time to eat the food Hoar offered. They had, after all, probably dined well after the Sudbury raid. They draped the wampum belts and strings that represented their leadership, and their multiple commitments, upon their shoulders and arms. Weetamoo wore the red coat, which the English, too, would recognize as a sign of her stately role, while Quinnapin wore the emblems of the raids he had led. Among them were their relations, including Metacom and Wootonakanuske, the saunkskwa Quaiapin, and the elder Canonicus. Weetamoo and Quinnapin were, Rowlandson observed, one of four couples who led the dance, representing the four directions from which this alliance came, and the four roads which would carry them home. She recalled, "He was dressed in his holland shirt, with great laces sewed at the tail of it; he had his silver buttons, his white stockings, his garters were hung round with shillings, and he had girdles of wampum upon his head and shoulders. She had a kersey coat, and covered with girdles of wampum from the loins upward. Her arms from her elbows to her hands were covered with bracelets; there were handfuls of necklaces about her neck, and several sorts of jewels in her ears. She had fine red stockings, and white shoes, her hair powdered and face painted red, that was always before black."[99] Weetamoo and Quinnapin, in their last appearance in the *Narrative*, danced at the center of the circle, joined with three other couples, representing multiple nations. They wore a mix of European and Indigenous adornments, representing the intertwining of tradition and innovation, and expressing a symbolic language that could be read by all of the families gathered together. The saunkskwa's face, heretofore painted black in mourning, was now painted red: the color of women, the color of war.

Part IV

The Place of Peace and the Ends of War

8

UNBINDING THE ENDS OF WAR

I will try to recount with sad grief, whom with tears the times reclaim . . .
Thus the Mother mourned Memnon, mourned Achilles,[1]
With just tears, and with heavy grief,
the mind is struck senseless, the lips are silenced . . .

But I will try to speak your praises . . .
Praises of virtue, which flies above the stars . . .

You live after death; you are happy after this fate, do you lie still?
But surely among the stars in glory you rest.
Your mind now returns to the sky; victory has been shared.
—Eleazar, Harvard Indian College, ca. 1678[2]

Most narratives of King Philip's War, whether written in 1676 or 2006, mark the late spring of 1676 as the moment when the "tide turned" toward English victory. Puritan accounts emphasized the hand of God, but even modern, secular histories often retain a sense of fatalism.[3] Although in the summer of 1675, colonial forces proved unable to navigate swamps or locate Native encampments, all accounts suggest that suddenly, in the summer of 1676, these spaces opened and "enemies" were driven, like deer, into English arms. Reports of hundreds captured, "destroyed," or sent into slavery, with hundreds more turning themselves in, then forced to "turncoat" and hunt others. Reports of destroyed corn, families captured while fishing and clamming; reports of people starved, even of children killed in fear of English capture or starvation.[4] Still, in comparison to 1675, the archive is fragmentary, making it difficult to discern what actually happened. The proliferation of contemporary narratives makes it all too easy to rely on accounts that bring the conflict to a neat end with the death of Narragansett, Nipmuc, and Wampanoag leaders, including a still resistant Metacom. Many historians rely on the mainstays of Hubbard, Mather, and Church. The story has been told so many times that authors often recount it quickly, moving swiftly to a paraphrasing of Church's sensational account of the capture of Metacom, his death at the hand of an Indian, and the "end" of the war.

In these last two chapters, I invite you to question that end. Looking at the "ends of war" from multiple places and perspectives—Nashaway, Boston/Cambridge, Nipsachuck, Pocasset, Cocheco, and the Northern Front—may enable a wider view of a complex historical space. With me, delve into the underexplored process of peacemaking initiated with the return of Mary Rowlandson. Consider the heavy recruitment of Native scouts, who brought Indigenous knowledge and tactics to colonial warfare, but also negotiated for their kin. Grapple with the United Colonies' campaign of extermination and enslavement, alongside the concrete political and environmental factors that left families exposed. Finally, this book will conclude where it opened, on the Northern Front, where the war most assuredly did not end during that brutal summer of 1676. Rather, it resolved through a rarely acknowledged treaty, the first of several at Pemaquid and Cascoak. The conflict that began in Metacom's homeland continued long beyond his death, perhaps for another hundred years. Or, as some would say, perhaps that war has never ended at all.

Most important, in these final chapters, I want to open up, not close, possibilities for further research. A common perception among scholars and publishers is that the history of "King Philip's War" has "been done," that there is little to add to the story. Yet, as much as I have sought to challenge that perception, this is not a definitive "new" history of the war. Rather it is a call to others—community-based historians and language keepers, as well as academic scholars—to engage in the *activity* of *pildowi ôjmowôgan*, recovering those stories submerged by what Jean O'Brien has termed the "replacement narratives" of settler colonialism.[5] This "conclusion" seeks to open the tributaries of our history, in the hope that informed history-makers might follow their courses, in collaboration with continuing community-based research, to discern new and ongoing interpretations that will decolonize and expand our collective understanding of this war and its legacy.

NASHAWAY: THE TREATY THAT NEVER WAS

If James's elder brother Annaweekin could have looked upon this world below, during that scorched summer of 1676, he might have seen his relations in their fishing places, some ill or recovering, others injured, all carrying the burden of grief. Some felt the lift of hope: that they might return to their planting fields unhindered by colonial troops, as their leaders had proposed.

Their grounds for hope rested upon ongoing peace negotiations among the sachems at Wachusett and Kwinitekw and the colonies of Massachusetts and Connecticut, including a preliminary treaty council held midway between Wachusett and Boston, on May 11. Connecticut's correspondence with the Narragansett sachems on Kwinitekw petered out when they proposed terms similar to those they had imposed on the Pequots. However, Massachusetts, with all of its western and interior claims threatened, was initially more accommodating in their communications with the sachems at Wachusett.[6]

On May 3 ("Election Day"), as John Hoar led Mary Rowlandson to Boston, he delivered a collective letter, "containing a desire for peace," an "overture for a cessation" of hostilities "so that they might quietly plant" in their homelands. Although in her narrative Rowlandson portrayed a division, in which Metacom dissented from the rest, this statement represented a consensus, signed by "Philip, the old queen & sundry Sachems," and the "saggamore[s] about Wachusets," including (according to the reply), Shoshanim, Pomham, and Hoorawannonit. This report appeared in a lengthy, but scarcely known, letter from Hadley minister John Russell to the Connecticut Council, conveying news from Massachusetts. Alongside related documents, Russell's letter opens wide our understanding of Rowlandson's narrative and the "end" of war. Among the most crucial revelations was that, as planting season approached, Rowlandson had been with her captors *at Pocumtuck* and, as noted, Metacom was directly engaged in the process of making peace.[7]

At Boston, Russell reported, Rowlandson revealed "that shee with the whole multitude of the Indians were at Deerfield when Northampton was burnt and lay there a Considerable space of time." Perhaps under Increase Mather's guiding hand, she omitted Pocumtuck entirely in her published narrative. When the warriors raided Hadley, she described her location vaguely as "a mighty thicket of brush." Other captives, including John Gilbert, whom Rowlandson recounted meeting in "this place," confirmed that "Deerfield alias pegunkugg" was "their" spring "headquarters." Thomas Reed, who was captured at Hadley and whose return Russell reported on May 15, relayed, "they are now planting at Deerfield" and dwelling "on both sides of the river" at "the Falls." Thus, Rowlandson's replacement narrative concealed the return of Native families to the planting fields at Pocumtuck and the resumption of fishing at "the falls" of Peskeompscut. Her portrayal of Indians wandering in a wilderness, living only by hunting and foraging, affirmed a formulaic image of a "savage" people "unsettled," bolstering colonial claims to "unimproved" lands and to "just war." The narrative displaced the presence and power of Native women like Weetamoo who lived in and cultivated longstanding, organized towns. It displaced an agricultural region and "ancient crossroads," which settlers had occupied for six years, but Indigenous people had inhabited for millennia. That spring Native leaders collectively sought to renew relations in the hope that women might "quietly plant" in their places, as they had every spring for boundless generations, without threat of violence. Ironically, it was the planting fields and deep, longstanding commitment to their permanent homelands, which Rowlandson elided, that drew so many families back to the Wampanoag, Narragansett, and Nipmuc territories, despite the risk.[8]

In the Indigenous languages of the region, the offer tendered by the sachems retained particular meanings, rooted in regional diplomacy. In Narragansett and related Algonquian languages, *aquene* or *aquyá* means to greet again, to make peace, to refrain from fighting. The first meaning is the most literal, formed from *aquay* or *kwai*, the universal northeastern greeting. When the leaders at Wachusett offered peace, they asked Massachusetts to lead the colonies in renewing greetings between neighbors and former allies. In the Western Abenaki language, closely related to those spoken at Kwinitekw, *wlakamigenokawôgan*—peacemaking—involves the renewal of "good," "calm," and "polite" relationships and interactions, neither merely the "cessation" of violence nor an act of "submission," but rather an active process *through which* respectful engagement is renewed.[9]

The sachems adapted writing to communicate their intentions, even as the English, ironically, insisted that this "great matter" could not be decided "by letters, without speaking one with another." Bringing their own customs to the process, the Massachusetts magistrates advocated for a council in Boston, alternatively "Concord or Sudbury, to meet with such cheife men as wee shall send," following their "Elders'" directive that, "if they will treate they should send their plenipotentiaries to us & not we to them." Further, Massachusetts required the return of all captives as proof "of a true heart in you to peace." In turn, they promised to "speak with you about your desires, and with true heart deal with you."[10]

Shoshanim and the sachems apparently returned a verbal message, suggesting a meeting place in Nipmuc territory, east of Wachusett. Although they did not yet address the return of captives, they released some from Wachusett to demonstrate good intent. Massachusetts appointed Peter Gardiner and Lancaster settler Jonathan Prescott as representatives, along with interpreter Tom Dublet, to meet with the sachems and deliver a written statement. In it, the magistrates conveyed their desire "to know your minde, whither you [are] willing [to] let us have our women & children you have captives." If the sachems had "any proposal to make to us" regarding peace, they were "willing to hear you." Using diplomatic rhetoric and offering compromise on location, they proposed that should the sachems "come yourselves, wee [will] send some of our sachems to treat [with] you at Concord, or some other place where best, and you have safe conduct; for wee [are] very true heart, and you tell your people so."[11]

Gardner and Prescott's instructions seemed aboveboard, suggesting that the proposed council was not merely a ruse to capture the leaders, but a legitimate step toward a "treaty." The magistrates instructed them to read aloud the written message, to communicate the court's willingness to "treat" about the "issuing," or ending "of the warre," and to "manage your whole treaty with clearness & confidence." Although their writing emphasized "true heart," the oral message would include the Elders' decree "that the English are resolved to make war theire worke until they injoy a firme peace."[12]

On May 11, the Massachusetts representatives "met" with "the sachems" "between Concord and Groton," on middle ground between extant settlements and reclaimed Nipmuc land. As before, the sachems brought a captive to symbolize their commitment, and, as he later reported, Shoshanim pledged to work to "bring" all the captives abroad "into your hands." As Canonicus had communicated to the Connecticut Council, the majority were "scattered about" in multiple locations, many up north. The treaty council record does not survive, but shortly thereafter, Shoshanim traveled toward Kwinitekw to join Canonicus, who had likewise pledged to "gather" the captives "together," in moving the peace forward. Shoshanim left his own family at Weshawkim, nearby the cleared settlement at Nashaway, believing they would be safe.[13]

PESKEOMPSCUT

Traveling west from Wachusett, Shoshanim approached Peskeompscut, where Kwinitekw coursed through granite and sandstone cliffs, then curved and pooled, an ancient fishing place. Here hundreds of people, mostly "old men and women" with children, had gathered, many coming from Pocumtuck and Sokwakik to seek sustenance in this traditional space of peace and exchange. As Shoshanim neared Peskeompscut, expecting to see his relations fishing, chatting, tending fires and racks, instead he encountered the disfigured corpses of women, children, and elders washed up on the bank of a traditional camping place; some he must have recognized as relations. Triggered by Thomas Reed's report, Captain William Turner had marched with over one hundred local men under cover of dark and thunderstorms, and, on May 19, in the shadows of pre-dawn, as families slept, the soldiers crept up on the camps, "put their guns into their Wigwams, and poured in their shot among them."[14]

"Over two hundred" died, trapped by rocks and cliffs that made escape by foot nearly impossible. Soldiers shot women, children, and elders as they ran from their houses, and as they tried to swim and paddle downriver or across to the opposite bank. Paddlers struggled against "the strong current of the River" as their canoes capsized. Many bodies were "broken in pieces" as they were dashed into the "exceeding high and steep rocks" of the falls. Only a few "did fight a little." Among them were captive children. They had been fishing and had not anticipated such a strike, particularly in the midst of negotiations for peace. Warriors later ambushed and killed Turner and several of his men on their route home, but this act could not bring back the families or return a sense of peace to this violated place.[15]

The Connecticut Council had previously urged forbearance "whilst the treaty with them is in hand," although the lack of Narragansett reply had brewed suspicion. Moreover, the Massachusetts Elders had advised that even "during the treaty" war should be "vigorously prosecuted." The Hadley men's ire was further fueled by a report that Indians had driven cattle and horses from Hatfield and penned them up at Pocumtuck, sparking fears of warriors lurking on the edges of the remaining river towns. Moreover, they strongly believed that "now" was "the time to distresse the enemy" and "drive them from their fishing," while they were "busy at their harvest worke, storing themselves wth food for a yeer to fight against us."[16]

Although Connecticut River men made the decision to strike Peskeompscut, without orders from Connecticut or Massachusetts, those governments read it as a sign of success against an "enemy" that threatened both fronts. Within a week of "Turner's fight," new initiatives took on greater force, motivated by the perception of divine approbation. Mosely had already been given free rein to range about the country unencumbered by moral restraints or explicit orders, using his "best discretions for destroying the enemy." He would soon join Captains Brattle and Bradford to scour the Wampanoag country. In Connecticut, Major John Talcott was allowed similar autonomy, as he was ordered to march upriver towards Pocumtuck, preferably with Mohegan scouts, "to use your utmost courage & endeavour valiantly to set upon them and kill and destroye them, according to the utmost power God shall give you."[17]

When Shoshanim made it home to Weshawkim, he found an equally disturbing sight. Massachusetts forces had struck his fishing place and his family, betraying his trust. News would soon arrive that a similar attack had been made on families fishing at the "falls of Pacatucke River," near Seekonk in Narragansett and Wampanoag country, only days after the massacre at Peskeompscut. And just as Massachusetts forces surprised the families at Weshawkim, Connecticut forces killed nineteen people and took thirty-two captive near Quaboag. Shoshanim no longer had an argument to make to Wampanoag warriors, still striking settlements, who distrusted colonial proposals for peace, particularly if, as according to a report by captured Native women, seventy of Metacom's relations had been killed at Peskeompscut.[18]

SHOSHANIM'S AWIKHIGAN: "WE REMEMBER IT NOW TO SIT STILL"

Shoshanim sought shelter up north, along with many others, in Penacook country. In early July, the Nipmuc sachems, including Shoshanim, Mattawamp, and Hoorawannonit sent a packet of letters by messenger to Massachusetts, with a white flag. With skillful diplomacy and sincere despair, they petitioned Governor Leverett as well as Eliot, Gookin, and Waban, praying that "our Brethren Praying to God" would "hear" their message and "keep well" the "prisoners" they had taken at Weshawkim, reminding them of their Christian duty. In his own message, transcribed by Wamesit scribe Simon Betomkin, Shoshanim recalled, "I went to Connecticot [Kwinitekw] about the Captives, that I might bring them into your hands, and when we were almost there," he found "the English had destroyed those Indians" at Peskeompscut. "When I heard it," he said, "I returned back again." But "then when I came home," he found that "we were also destroyed," referring to *his family* at Weshawkim. Shoshanim joined with the other sachems to request not only the return of his captured wife but the other "prisoners" taken at Weshawkim, including Mattawamp's wife. They also pleaded with their Christian "brethren" to "consider about the making of Peace" in which they had been engaged. Although "we," that is, their families, "have been destroyed by your soldiers," Shoshanim assured, "but still we Remember it now to sit still." The leaders did not simply express a sense of military defeat, but a sense of betrayal of their diplomacy. Even so, using symbolic language, Shoshanim and the sachems invoked calm (a state of stillness) and recalled the commitment to renew relations. They had conveyed through Tom Dublet and Peter Ephraim that they would yet "make" a "covenant of Peace" with the Christian men of Massachusetts. "Do you consider it again," they implored. Then, using sacred language, Shoshanim invoked the phrase "amen" three times, ceremonially, petitioning the peacemaker "Jesus Christ" to "let it be so," leaving open the fourth round for the response.[19]

In the narratives of war, Shoshanim's letter is represented as an expression of surrender, a meek plea for peace in the wake of colonial victories. But in the context of the treaty negotiations, the letter is much more profound. Shoshanim had gone to Kwinitekw in diplomacy, to speak with other leaders about gathering the captives. The effectiveness of his efforts is evidenced in Wanalancet's diplomatic mission to Cocheco in June, to declare the Penacooks' "good will" and "desire to maintain peace," and to "freely deliver" captives that had been among them at Penacook, fulfilling Shoshanim's promise. Wanalancet's treaty was part of this process, not a separate event. After rounds of councils, the Cocheco treaty was signed on July 3, and included the "marks" of multiple leaders, including Samuel Numphow and Atecouando. Numphow and Wanalancet must have then returned to the safety of Penacook, from where Numphow's relation Simon Betomkim helped the Nipmuc leaders compose their message on July 6, following the Cocheco treaty. Shoshanim's previous mission of "good will" was halted by the starkest evidence of colonial violence, directed at noncombatants engaged in subsistence. Even in the midst of "peacemaking," a new colonial offensive had begun to "drive them from their fishing" and catch them in their planting. These letters capture Shoshanim's alarm that his own family had been targeted, alongside his desperation to cease the violence. He conveyed that the Nipmuc leaders were "still" willing to participate in that process, rather than pursue war. Just as Shoshanim had strived to care for and return English captives, he pleaded with the Massachusetts men to reciprocate with his captured kin. He implored them to also "be still" and consider the "covenant" they had made, a collective prayer and petition for peace.[20]

Finally, in his letter, Shoshanim reported that after these places "were destroyed" both "Philip and Quanipun went away into their own Countrey againe," suggesting that Massachusetts's betrayal broke the consensus for peace, for which Shoshanim had advocated. Indeed, the betrayal undermined his integrity as a diplomat. This renewed violence had turned these leaders back toward the defense of their homelands, where troops now pursued families in their planting and fishing places. Shoshanim believed that they were "very much afraid, because of our offer to joyn with the English," leaving fewer men to fight or defend "their Countrey" against this new offensive. Yet Shoshanim still conveyed his conviction that Philip and Quinnapin "will make no warre," attempting to retain the possibility of negotiations.[21]

Indeed, although some remained on Kwinitekw, many Narragansetts and Wampanoags had returned home that spring. Josiah Winslow reported in late May that Wampanoags were "planting at Assamwamset or Dartmouth," and butchered cattle at Teticut, "as if they intended some [to] stay there." Peter

Ephraim reported in early June that "a great party" of Wampanoags had returned to Montaup where they were then "unmolested by the English." A boy
captured on the Pacatucke revealed that his relations had returned to fish and
plant at Nipsachuck, a report confirmed by allied scouts. A Native woman captured near Wachusett, where she had been visiting her cousin, reported that
near Providence, the place to which "she belonged," they "planted corn, catch
fish, sett traps to catch beaver." Before Shoshanim reported on Peskeompscut,
Quinnapin had sent a messenger to Massachusetts to convey that both he and
Quaiapin "desire peace" and "speak for peace" among the people at Wachusett;
"Canonicus," they said, "is of the same minde." Like Shoshanim and many
others, they sought a treaty that might bring about the cessation of war and the
renewal of relations, motivated by the deep desire to return to their homelands.
Speaking for many, they desired to know "whether the Narrogansets may go to
their own country, & live there." If so, the messenger would "go tell the Indians"
that they could return safely to their places.[22]

BOSTON/CAMBRIDGE: THE REDEMPTION
OF JAMES THE PRINTER

If Annaweekin could have looked upon Weshawkim, the scene of Shoshanim's deepest grief, he would have seen his brother Job among the men
who spoke to Shoshanim's wife and kin in their own language, offering "peace"
and assuring them they would come to no harm if they surrendered quietly.
Captain Henchman reported that the reply was "a volley of shot." But he also
reported that they took prisoner twenty-nine, "mostly women and children,"
and killed seven, encompassing the entire group, with no English loss. This was
only the beginning.[23]

The renewed colonial offensive arose in part because of the unexpected
"success" of the assaults on subsistence grounds like Peskeompscut and We-
shawkim, marked by the "surprisal" of large numbers of Native people and few
English casualties. At Weshawkim, the exposure and "success" was due in large
part to the skill and stealth of Native scouts. In Connecticut, the recruitment of
Mohegans and Pequots was renewed, while Plymouth sought assistance from
Wampanoags on the Cape. In Massachusetts, as Gookin observed, "after our
Indians went out, the balance turned of the English side."[24]

Massachusetts's company of forty scouts increased to eighty when guns and
ammunition, along with long-awaited food, arrived by ship from England, giving
renewed sustenance to the military campaign. While their initial commission
emphasized the protection of English towns, the scouts were soon positioned

as the vanguard of colonial troops, sent ahead to flush people into the waiting army's "net." As Gookin wrote, "At Weshakum, and at or near Mendon, at
Mount Hope, at Watchusett, and several other places, they were often made use
of as scouts before the army, and at such time when the army lay still and staid
at their quarters; in which scoutings they took several captives, and slew many
of the enemy, and brought their scalps to their commanders." Samuel Hunting,
their "commander," credited them not only with capturing hundreds, but preventing English casualties. In a year, he said, they "lost but one man of ours." A
few, like John Hunter, were motivated by the challenge to capture Metacom.
For most, their service was a condition of their release from Deer Island, and
their families, while secured near Boston with liberty to plant, remained under
close surveillance. Still, they may have been safer than their relations in the
surrounding territories, now in daily danger of military capture.[25]

On June 11, two days after the capture of Shoshanim's family, "some Indian
scouts" went out from Marlborough headquarters and found Tom Wuttasacomponom at Natick, with his son Nehemiah's wife and two children. "There was
more of them" out gathering food, including Nehemiah, who was "gone a fishing"
nearby, and James Printer. Henchman later reported that "this company" along
with "some others at other places, of which James Prenter is one, did as they say
leave the enemy by times in the spring with an intent to come in to the English,
but dare not for fear of our scouts." Furthermore, Tom and his "daughter" said
that "hearing that there was like to be a treaty with Samuel [Shoshanim]," many
had intended "to go into him," to join in the peace. Indeed, James Printer and
these relations were then living "about Natick and Magunkaquog," some having
"escaped" with Joseph Tukuppawillin, when the camps at Menimesit dispersed,
while others left Wachusett to resume subsistence closer to home.[26]

Without resistance, Tom and his family went with the scouts. Like James,
ten months before, they were taken "about ten miles" northwest to Marlborough and then to prison in Boston. At Marlborough, Tom recounted his story
to James Quananopohit. Tom had left "the Indian enemy" in the spring, when
"the army marched up to Mennimisset," which James knew had been "about
the first of March" since he was "one of the pilots." Tom's story, James added,
was confirmed by "some of the Indian prisoners that we took at Washakum
pond," who believed that Tom had "escaped to the English." Moreover, Tom
said, they had "been about" their towns of "Natick, Magunkaquog, etc. several
weeks," "hoping to meet with some English or Indians that they knew," a claim
confirmed by their location on the Connecticut Path, the main road to Boston.
He and his family had "waited for a fit opportunity to get to the English with
safety of our lives" and had even gone down the path to "Capt. Prentice's farm-

house to have spoken with him, but found no person there." These families were not in hiding, nor sheltered with those who resisted. They were living openly in their praying towns, hoping to renew relations. Yet, Tom was treated as a "prisoner att war" who had defected to the "enemy" and led others to do so. He was not a captive to be redeemed.[27]

James Quananopohit testified at length in Boston, but his account did not supersede the brief testimony of several settlers who claimed they had witnessed Tom in arms at Sudbury and Medfield. One merely said he heard Tom's voice. Eight days after his "capture" Tom was sentenced to execution (alongside John Attucks, also apprehended). Eliot's pleas for Tom's innocence fell on deaf ears. Gookin had lost his seat in the recent "election," replaced by Joseph Dudley, the chaplain at Great Swamp, leaving Tom with no advocate on the court.[28]

However, just prior to Tom's trial, James Quananopohit, Job Kattenanit, and three other "officers" submitted a petition on behalf of eighty "Indian soldiers." They appealed for "Capt. Tom, his son Nehemiah," still out, and Nehemiah's "wife and two children," and for "John Utuck, his wife and children, Maanum and her child." They "humbly" implored that "mercies be extended" to these "prisoners taken by us." They made a compelling argument for their release, giving "three reasons." First, they were "innocent," having been "against their wills, taken and kept among the enemy." If the court was not willing to "grant the lives and liberties of all," they requested "the favour to us" of releasing "the women and children." The scouts had strong grounds, for, to "encourage" their "fidelity and activity in your service," the magistrates had said they "would be ready to do anything for us, that was fit for us to ask and you to grant." Requesting reciprocity, they wrote, "We have (especially some of us) been sundry times in your service to the hazard of our lives, both as spyes, messengers, scouts, and souldiers," citing their demonstrated faithfulness to "God" and their allies. Further, "granting . . . our humble request" would "oblige" them "to remain" allies and "servants" in this "cause." They offered evidence of past service and a pledge for future service, to secure the protection of their kin.[29]

"Thirdly," the scouts petitioned for "others that are out, and love the English," that they "may be encouraged to come in." They pleaded for "the lives and libertyes of those few of our poor friends and kindred, that, in this time of temptation and affliction, have been in the enemy's quarters." They asked their allies "to shew mercy, and especially to such who have (as we conceive) done no wrong to the English." This was one of the most important aspects of their petition. Massachusetts has often been credited with offering "amnesty" to Native people who wished to "come in," yet this declaration arose in direct response to the scouts' petition. For Job, whose brother, nieces, and nephews were still "out," this plea was especially urgent. If they could not freely come in as "friends and kindred," he would face the terrible prospect of bringing them in as captives and prisoners or worse, of having them "surprised" by colonial troops.[30]

The court gave "answer" on the day of Tom's trial, asserting that they did not require "further evidence for his conviction," as Tom was judged "a lawful prisoner at war." They did, however, "grant" the "Petitioners" "the lives of the women and children," they "mentioned," forestalling enslavement and death. They also were "ready to show favour in sparing the lives and liberty of those who have been our enemys," who would "come in" and submit "themselves to the English Government and your disposal." However, those "who have been our friends" but were "found and taken among our enemies" would not be offered amnesty, regardless of their relationship to the scouts. Their kin had fourteen days to come in and request this "privilege."[31]

Although the petition did not achieve its full intent, the scouts opened a narrow path through which they might usher their kin who remained about Natick and the "Nipmuc woods." The next day, Massachusetts held a council with the company in Charlestown on the banks of the river, presenting the scouts with a medal for their service. On one side was an iconic image based on the Massachusetts seal. In the original, a stylized Indian figure proclaimed, "come over and help us," yet this medal acknowledged the "help" the English required from Indians. On the other side, engraved words honored the scouts for "giving us peace and mercy at their hands" in "the present Warr with the Heathen Natives of this Land." It was one of the few times when the colonial leaders acknowledged the scouts' sense of themselves as Christian allies. Yet it also represented the thrust of the summer campaign, which had become a "total war" to "replace" the "Natives of this land" with English settlements. There was space in "New England" for Indian converts and scouts who proved willing to submit to the colony's jurisdiction and "faithfully" serve its aims. But the summer campaign would make clear that *any* "Natives" who fell outside this narrow scope were subject to death, removal, and enslavement.[32]

Two days later, Tom Wuttasacomponom was hanged, a sign readable far beyond Boston. Eliot reported, "On the ladder he lifted up his hands and said, I never did lift up hand against the English, nor was I at Sudbury, only I was willing to go away with the enemies that surprised us." According to Eliot, he died with his hands raised in prayer toward the sky. Tom's public execution demonstrated that praying Indians judged "revolters" would be executed, with no opportunity for "repentance" in this world. Men like James had two weeks to make a plea for redemption, a window secured by their "faithful" kin.[33]

"A REVOLTER HE WAS, AND A FELLOW THAT HAD DONE MUCH
MISCHIEF, AND STAID OUT AS LONG AS HE COULD, TILL THE
LAST DAY BUT ONE OF A PROCLAMATION SET FORTH."[34]

On July 2, "the last day," James Printer "came in" to Cambridge, bringing
with him Nehemiah and a group of about twelve women and children. The
council was willing to secure them with Gookin, but also demanded that James
and Nehemiah "shew their fidelity by bringing som of the enemies heads" to
Boston. Although not part of the declaration of amnesty, evidence of "service"
in war had become a condition for peace. Perhaps leveraging his skill as an interpreter and printer, James secured amnesty for himself and the kin he carried
with him, but also persuaded the court to allow him to return to Natick and
Magunkaquog to "bring in" more people "to the benefit of the Declaration." As
he told Prentice, "they had left some Indians Behind that desired to come in
and Submit but were hindered." Securing this extension, he took a significant
risk in going back out, facing potential capture by colonial troops.[35]

The *True Account* published three months later in London was the first of
several narratives which would characterize James as a "Revolter" and elide the
context under which he came in. Mather and Hubbard's narratives, designed to
demonstrate New England's carriage of a just war to Old England and a distant
king, were built upon this characterization and elision, becoming the replacement narratives upon which nearly all subsequent narrations of the war would
rest. In his *Brief History* (1676), Mather wrote:

> Whereas, the council at Boston had lately emitted a declaration, signifying
> that such Indians as did, within fourteen days, come in to the English might
> hope for mercy, divers of them did this day return from among the Nipmucs.
> Among others, James, an Indian, who could not only read and write, but had
> learned the art of printing, notwithstanding his apostasy, did venture himself
> upon the mercy and truth of the English declaration, which he had seen and
> read, promising for the future to venture his life against the common enemy.
> He and the others now come in, affirm that very many of the Indians are dead
> since the war begun; and that more have died by the hand of God, in respect
> of diseases, fluxes and fevers, which have been amongst them, than have been
> killed by the sword.[36]

Echoing Mather, Hubbard (1677) wrote:

> Amongst sundry that came in, there was one named James, the printer, the
> superadded title distinguishing him from others of that name; who being a
> notorious apostate, that had learned so much of the English as not only to

read and write, but had attained likewise some skill in printing (and might have attained more had he not like a false villain ran away from his master before his time was out) he having seen and read the said declaration of the English, did venture himself upon the saith therof, and came to sue for his life; he affirmed with others that came along with him, that more Indians had died since this war began, of diseases (such as at other time they used not to be acquainted with) than by the sword of the English.[37]

These replacement narratives convey a clear-cut story of a revolter and the benevolent colony that granted him "mercy." We do not have James's written account of his experience. We do have documents that demonstrate the complex story of his multiple "captivities" and his attempt to redeem himself and his kin. If James had possessed the freedom to write his own narrative, there are several points at which his story would have diverged from theirs. James had not only attained "some skill" as an "apprentice" but was an invaluable printer, "the only one," Eliot later wrote, "able to compose the sheets, and correct the press with understanding." He had not run away from Samuel Greene, but had been working as a teacher at Waeuntuk and living at Hassanamesit, as he had been prepared to do by his colonial education. He did not abscond or "revolt," but was taken during the war, both at Marlborough by colonial forces, and at Hassanamesit by Nipmuc warriors. If he did join with those warriors in "mischief," his motivations were far more complex, formed *by* the war, not on its eve. In constructing James as a servant who fled his master to join a doomed rebellion, the narratives asserted colonial authority retroactively and in the future over Native peoples and spaces. Mather and Hubbard also displaced the declaration's context, masking the role of James's relations in petitioning for their kin. Instead they claimed the "declaration" arose from the colony's willingness to allow the enemy "to sue for mercy at the hands of the English," part of their argument for a just war.[38]

Both Mather and Hubbard attributed to James the claim that "more Indians" died by disease than "the English sword." Although many did fall ill, these narratives put forth an indigenized "affirmation" which replaced the reports of extreme violence that drove James to come in and made a return to Hassanamesit impossible. For example, on the same day Samuel Sewall reported that "James the Printer and other Indians came into Cambridge," he recorded in his diary that, "This week Troopers, a party, killed two men, and took an Indian Boy alive. Just between the Thanksgiving, June 29, and Sabbath day, July 2, Capt. Bradford's expedition 20 killed and taken, [and] almost 100 came in," including the "Squaw Sachem" Awashonks. "July 1, 9 Indians sold for 30 £. Capt. Hincksman [Henchman] took a little before."[39]

Just before James Printer came in, he may have witnessed or heard of the twenty-eight "killed and taken" by Henchman's company and the scouts "between Quaboag and Marlborough," whereby a "Chief councellor" was killed and "nine Indian prisoners, women and children, were brought down to Boston," corresponding with Sewall's entry. Henchman reported that "all the Indians were in a continual motion," and "lay not above a night in a place," even as he praised the success of his scouts in capturing women, children, and elders, while killing and wounding a handful of men at each encampment they found. James must have known that if he remained at Natick, he would be imprisoned again, hanged like Tom, or sent into slavery. He might be killed on site or face a similar scene of slaughter. Moreover, he would not be able to advocate for the families from prison. Even as the scouts petitioned for the possibility of amnesty, they also enabled the conditions of violence that forced so many to "come in." More than the paper declaration, these actions must have motivated James's Sabbath's day journey to Cambridge.[40]

MAGUNKAQUOG

Among those who "came in" to Cambridge in July, under the extension James secured, were William Wannukhow and his family, who also had been living at or near their home of Magunkaquog. William and his sons testified that they "readily embraced" the "tidings . . . sent by James Printer unto us . . . and came in accordingly" with their "wives and children" to Captain Prentice's house, as they "were directed to come." Three weeks later William, his wife, and their sons were apprehended at Prentice's by the constable "to answer the complaint of Thomas Eames for killing" his wife and children and "burning" his house, barn, and property.[41]

In 1669, Eames had built a substantial house above the planting grounds north of Magunkaquog's center, without a grant from Native leaders or the court. In early February 1676, the Wannukhow men traveled with a party of Christian Indians from Menimesit to Magunkaquog to retrieve corn they had put up that fall. On arrival, as Joseph Wannukhow recalled, they discovered the "corn which they expected to have found at Moguncocke" was "missing." Believing Eames "had taken our corn," Netus of Natick and "another man that were our leaders" led the charge up a familiar trail to his house. This was likely the case, as Eames later reported the loss of a great quantity of Indian corn, some "210 bushels," in comparison to ten bushels of wheat and forty bushels of rye. Thus, the men were attempting to reclaim a stolen harvest, sorely needed in late winter. The "other man," as Joseph confessed, was Annaweekin, James's brother, later "slain in the war," along with Netus.[42]

With her husband away at Boston, Goodwife Eames attempted to defend her home, according to local lore, with kitchen implements and "boiling hot soap." The Wannukhow men testified that in the scuffle, Netus and Annaweekin killed the goodwife and some of her children. They insisted that neither Joseph, his father, nor his brother John committed violence; William reported he stood "at a distance a little way off in the cornfields" the whole time. Further, they had advocated for the children; Joseph had even "carried away on his back one of Eames's sons." Even now, the girls they had "carried away" were sheltered in the north, one "at a great hill about middle way between Wachusett and Pennacook" (perhaps Mount Monadnock), "in good health and not in a starving plight," having survived not only captivity but also the massacre at Peskeompscut. Joseph had only reluctantly revealed his story, first to Prentice's son, then to magistrate Thomas Danforth, who held title to a vast tract at Magunkaquog, including the land Eames planted. Danforth assured Joseph that if he "would tell" him "plainly how all this said matter was acted," he "would speak to the Governor to spare his life." Yet after Joseph and his family "confessed," all three men were indicted by a "grand jury," tried, and convicted in a matter of days.[43]

Meanwhile, more of Printer's relations had come in, including Annaweekin's wife and sons and James's nephew by his wife. Some hundred and sixty men, women, and children arrived with the Nipmuc leader Hoorawannonit, who bargained for his life and those with him by offering Matoonas and his son, bound and captured for the court. Like the Wannukhows, Hoorawannonit and his relations were held under Prentice's "protection." The Pakachoag leader came in not only under the amnesty declaration, but also in mind of the peace process that he had helped initiate at Wachusett; his party included people "who belonged to Sagamore Sam."[44]

Although James Printer had advocated for his kin's protection, he watched in Cambridge as they were contained and dispersed: the Wannukhow men, like Tom, sentenced to death, while others were forced to scout. Joshua Assalt, accused with the Wannukhow men, avoided trial because he was out with Hunting's troop. Countless people, including the wives of Netus and Aquitakash, who had been at Magunkaquog, were sold into slavery. The children who came in were divided among colonists, bound to service until they reached full adulthood ("twenty years of age" suggested to the court), by a "Committee" consisting of Prentice, Gookin, and Edward Oakes. James's nephews became captives in colonial homes; their mother was "present" as Annaweekin's sons were taken away. Neither James nor their mothers would be able to redeem them. The committee recommended "the Court lay som penalty upon" the children "if they runne way before the time expire & on their parent or kindred

that shall entice or harbor & concele them if they should runne away." In es-
sence, under the guise of "service" and religious "education," colonial magistrates would hold children hostage to prevent the revolt of their kin. When he
later resumed his work at the press, James pursued the best possible route, of
severely limited options, that would enable him to keep watch over his younger
kin. Surrounded by other Native people who worked, many in forced servitude or slavery, in colonial homes and fields in Boston and Cambridge, James
Printer witnessed his kin converted into a labor force for settlers. Yet, even after
the war, he continued to persist within a "growing web" of Native survivors who
continued to travel and practice subsistence between their home places on the
Massachusett coast and the Nipmuc interior, a kinship network largely "invis-
ible to the colonists' gaze."[45]

William Wannukhow's younger children were also "put forth to service," his
eight-year-old son Joshua held by Gookin and his thirteen-year-old son retained
by Prentice, along with a nephew of James. William's sentence legally justified
his children's status as "captives of war." If William's wife was not sent into "foreign slavery," perhaps she was allowed to remain at Prentice's house as a servant
with her son. But her eleven-year-old son Tom was taken to Mystic, by settler
Nathaniel Wade, along with an orphaned girl of Pakachoag, taken from the protection of Hoorawannonit. Gookin noted that "above thirty" of those who came
in with him were "put out to service to the English," that is, enslaved in local
colonial households. No extant records reveal the Nipmuc leader's reaction to
this dispersal, but Hoorawannonit "escaped" from Cambridge with twenty of
his remaining relations that winter, likely heading north.[46]

Facing execution, on September 5 William Wannukhow and his sons submitted a powerful petition to the court. They cited legal documents including the
amnesty "declaration dated the 19th of June, wherein" the council "promise[d]
life and liberty unto such of your enemies as did come in and submit themselves to your mercy and order," and the July 3 decree by which the "declaration" was "enlarged to a longer time." They noted that "those orders of yours are
upon record" and they had "copies" which they were "ready to present" to the
court. The Wannukhows insisted they could not be judged among those "notorious in doing mischief." "Indeed," they said, "we were among the enemies,"
at Menimesit, "being tempted to go among them by the example of our choice
men Capt. Tom and others. But we had no arms and did not hurt the English as many others have done, that upon their submission to your mercy are
pardoned," likely referring to Hoorawannonit and those now serving as scouts.
Recounting their story of the Eames raid in full, they reiterated, "we did not act
in it." Rather, "It was done by others, who were slain in the war, and so have

answered God's justice for their demerits." Their own deaths would not add to the balance of justice. They emphasized their effort to protect the Eames children. Moreover, they insisted, "besides it was a time of war, when this mischief was done; and though it was our unhappy portion to be with those enemies yet we conceive that depredations and slaughters in war are not chargeable upon particular persons, especially such as have submitted themselves to your Honors upon promise of life, &c. as we have done."[47]

This last statement may be the petition's most remarkable aspect. The authors accurately interpreted colonial laws and declarations and adeptly articulated English wartime "doctrine." They might have received assistance from Gookin (although this was not an argument he made elsewhere), or Prentice, who testified to their coming in voluntarily. Yet it was most likely James Printer—who helped to print the colonial laws and could decipher the declarations—that composed this petition for the Wannukhows. The impassioned voice suggests someone deeply invested in their acquittal, and James had advocated for them to come in, bearing responsibility for their lives. With ties to Natick and Magunkaquog, James Quananopohit and Job Kattenanit may have had a hand in the writing as well. As a communally authored Native statement and legal interpretation, the petition presents a rare Indigenous voice, which demanded colonial authorities uphold their covenants and pledges even in war, a moment in which Native authors resisted containment by evoking colonial order. The petition argued that the crime for which the Wannukhows stood accused was not "murder" but wartime violence, which should not be prosecuted against individuals. Moreover, it cited the court's declaration which promised "lives and liberty" even "to those that have been our enemys, on their comeing in and submission of themselves to the English Government," which the Wannukhow men insisted they had done.[48]

On September 21, 1676, a "cloudy" and "rawly cold" day, William Wannukhow, Joseph Wannukhow, and John Apumatquin were hanged on Boston Common, alongside vigilante Stephen Goble, a soldier who had "murdered" three Christian Indian women, the wives and sisters of scouts, and their children while they were "gathering huckleberries in Concord." In his diary, Mather bemoaned "a sad thing that English and Indians should be executed together." At least one "impudent" woman among the spectators "laughed on the gallows, as several testified." The next day, Sewall recorded that he "spent the day . . . dissecting the middlemost of the Indian executed the day before." Eames was thereafter awarded the grant of land he desired, some two hundred acres, in reparation, along with an additional two hundred acres secured by lawsuit from the survivors at Natick, including Thomas Waban and Peter Ephraim. Moreover, Danforth's grant, originally encompassing the bounds of the Framingham plantation, was now secure, with no need to acquire Native consent from those at Magunkaquog who might challenge his title.[49]

On the day of the execution, James Printer might have noted it was nearly a year to the day that he had escaped the gallows, falsely accused of murdering colonists at Lancaster. He might have considered that had he gone with his brother to gather corn at Magunkaquog, he too would be hanging in the Common. Moreover, he may have felt the great weight of guilt for giving the message to the Wannukhow family that it was safe to come in. Neither his advocacy, nor that of Job and James Quananopohit, protected them, or the children under their care.

In October, James's nephew Joseph was called to service. Annaweekin's son was to be sent to England, as proof of the just actions and carriage of the colonies in this war. Gookin prepared Joseph and another "Indian boy" with clothing, "according to the Council's order" to travel to England with William Stoughton and Peter Bulkeley, who would address charges made against the colony regarding the validity of its land grant and its treatment of Indians before and during the war. The accusations included, ironically, evidence of forced labor, a condition to which Joseph had been sentenced. Gookin appealed to the council to "please to order some person to receive" the boys and "keep them safe," since they might try to "slipp away being possibly afraid to go for England." Gookin concluded, "I pray God they not bee put in prison for now they are cleane and free from vermin," suggesting he cleaned, kept, and clothed the boys so they could be presented as evidence in London, obscuring the real conditions they faced in the colonies. The letter reveals his fear that the boys, released from his custody, might be held in the "vermin"-infested prison, alongside their relations, while awaiting shipment to England. Even Gookin, persecuted for his defense of Christian Indians, was not above manufacturing evidence to support the replacement narratives of just war, already circulating in Boston and London.[50]

Sometime after James came in, he returned to work at the Indian College, now "converted to a printing house." He must have known Eleazar, the only Native student attending Harvard in 1678. When Increase Mather brought Mary Rowlandson's manuscript to the Harvard Press, James likely set the type, his valuable skill as a printer transformed to leverage for the protection of his kin. James must have read Rowlandson's account of her captivity, as he set the type, sentence-by-sentence, letter-by-letter. Perhaps he saw the reflection of himself, distorted through her eyes, and Mather's editorial reach. Mather and Hubbard had called him an "apostate," a renegade who had forsaken his faith and his allegiance. Yet James's story was so much more complex than the narrators of war would have us believe. James was a scholar, a teacher, a community leader, a scribe. He, too, was a captive, a prisoner, an advocate, and perhaps, a warrior. He was a tireless protector of his kin, and is remembered well among his descendants as a stone pillar on which Hassanamisco still rests.[51]

Even in his later years, James remained a "teacher" and leader among his relations. He continued to negotiate, using the power of print and pen. He helped build a coalition among the men who served as scouts, leveraging their literacy and skill in war to protect Nipmuc lands for the survivors who remained. His name appears on the deeds that preserved crucial sanctuaries as Indigenous towns. According to Nipmuc chief Cheryll Holley, James probably did not have children of his own, but his lateral descendants took his name. In the wake of Annaweekin's death, James assumed the leadership for which his elder brother had been trained. Annaweekin may have watched, his arms opening wide, as James grew to be an elder, still living at Hassanamesit among his kin, when he left this world, a new century begun.[52]

NARRAGANSETT AND WAMPANOAG

NIPSACHUCK

On the same Sabbath day that James Printer came in to Cambridge, Connecticut forces "assaulted" Nipsachuck, where they believed Narragansett families were planting. On July 1, Major Talcott reported, they "seized 4 of ye enemy," who provided information that enabled Mohegan and Pequot warriors to locate Quaiapin's encampment at the base of a hill beside the Nipsachuck swamp. Armed with this environmental knowledge, Talcott reported, "on the 2nd instant, being the Sabboth, in ye morning about sun an houre high" three hundred English soldiers descended on horseback in two flanks around the hill, rushing down upon "ye enemys place of residence," while a hundred Mohegan and Pequot warriors charged downhill between them. Talcott's force shot at the families in their homes, surprised by the swift descent. Recovering quickly, the survivors dispersed and "inswamped themselves in a great spruce swamp." Using a small land bridge to cross the wetland, water levels lowered by drought, Talcott reported "we girt the sd swamp and with English and Indian souldiers drest it." Using the language of hunting and containment, Talcott described easily surrounding and *breaking* a wild quagmire; without pause, he reported that his troops "within 3 hours slew and tooke prisoners 171, of which 45 prisoners being women and children that ye Indians saved alive, and the others slayne; in which engagement were slayne 34 men, tooke 15 armes." "Among" the "slaughter," he declared, "that ould piece of venum, Saunk squaw Magnus [Quaiapin] was slaine, and our old friend Watawikeson, Pesecus his agent, was slayne, and in his pocket Capt. Allyn's Ticket for his free passage up to his head Quarters."[53]

As Jennings discerned from the report, Talcott's forces killed thirty-four men and ninety-two women and children, while Mohegan and Pequot advocacy "saved" forty-five others from death. Others may have escaped, as archaeological research suggests that the families were able to defend themselves as they moved into the spruce swamps and took refuge on an island, which the soldiers encircled. Nipsachuck was exposed by the combination of Mohegan and Pequot logistical and navigational knowledge and a midsummer drought, which left the swamp drier, the soil more compact, the vegetation thinner, and the land thus more easily navigable than in the previous lush summer. Colonial troops, too, had adapted their tactics and relied more heavily on their Native allies, who had likewise developed knowledge of colonial stratagems. Yet the Narragansett families were also made vulnerable by their belief that a peace was still possible.[54]

Talcott took full advantage of this vulnerable condition. The next day, when Talcott "received information" that a group of Narragansett were at Warwick, hoping "to make peace with some of Road Island," his force "dressed Providence neck" and "Warwick neck," killing and taking captive over sixty people. The group pursuing diplomacy was fully exposed, awaiting the return of their leader, Potuck, a local Narragansett sachem and "emissary" sent to Massachusetts to "negotiate peace." As Jennings observed, "Connecticut's forces destroyed these Narragansetts not merely while they were waiting to make peace with Massachusetts [and Rhode Island], but in order to prevent them from doing so." In fact, Connecticut magistrates had suspected Massachusetts of claiming greater power in the region by pursuing separate peace negotiations. They were especially wary since their own negotiations had failed to produce Narragansett submission to their authority. Intercolonial conflicts increased the motivation to take the land by force. Shortly thereafter, Connecticut would lay claim to the entire Narragansett country, "deserted" and "vanquished," by right of conquest, against all other persons "both English and Indians that have or shall presented to any right or possession there." Quaiapin had presented a formidable force in negotiation and in contesting colonial claims to land, but when Talcott found her, she was planting and, like her relations at Warwick, still pursuing the possibility of peace. One of the Narragansett emissaries, Wuttawawaikessuk, was also killed at Nipsachuck, still holding the pass that allowed him safe passage to carry those messages. Talcott's expedition halted this diplomatic process. In two days, the "whole number taken captive and slayne" was "238," and as at Peskeompscut, the majority were women and children. Once more, "none of" the "English" were killed and they lost only one Native scout. But Talcott did not accept praise, which he said should be "but unto ye Lord."[55]

POKANOKET AND POCASSET

These same conditions left Weetamoo, Metacom, and their relations exposed as they returned to the Wampanoag country. On July 5, William Bradford Jr. reported from his Taunton headquarters the news of Talcott's expedition, writing that "last Friday, above Coweset, they slew and toke almost two hundred men, women and children." Bradford regretted he could not draw Talcott, or his Mohegan and Pequot allies, north, where Metacom and "all the body of Indians" hid from the army "in a hideous swamp" near Taunton. Bradford pursued a more conventional approach, but Benjamin Church used tactics that compelled those he captured to deceive their kin. Using their lives and those of their families as leverage, Church forced captives to "pretend" to be "friends" to others still free, feigning to "inform them of ye English," only to report their location so that Church could descend with his company of English and Indian soldiers. The minister Thomas Walley praised the "success [of] Benjamin Church" in bringing forth the "good fruit of the Coming in of Indians to us." He noted, "Those that come in are Conquered and help to Conquer others. I observe throughout the Land where Indians are imployed those hath bin the greatest success if not the only success which is a humbling providence of god that we have so much need of them and cannot doe our work without them."[56]

This shift happened quickly. The Wampanoag country was under siege, swamps no longer a refuge. After garnering information from an escaped captive and an enslaved Taunton man, Bradford reported taking or killing over one hundred people in less than twelve days, including Quinnapin's brother and "one of Philip's brother's daughters, one of great account among them," Weetamoo's daughter or niece. In early August, Church captured Wootonakanuske and her son, among one hundred others, a devastating loss for Metacom and Weetamoo. According to Harris, "Since then Philip and Quinnapin and nine or ten with them were seen and shot at by some Taunton men. At that time or therabouts these men captured an Indian who, to save his life, promised he would bring them to Phillip who sd yt Phillip had cutt off his haire to disguise himself & yt Qunapin was Shott Soe yt he was followed by ye bloude."[57]

In mid-August, colonial forces finally "laid hold on" Quinnapin. He and his brother Sunkeecunasuck were convicted by a Rhode Island court of "sundry crimes," including "rebellion" against the colony and king. At the court martial, Quinnapin admitted being at Great Swamp and at Lancaster, as well as to firing a garrison and driving livestock after Great Swamp. He had "nothing to say against the Indians burning and destroying" colonial structures at Pettaquamscut. For this, he was "impeatch[ed]" as a "rebel" and executed at Newport.[58]

Simultaneously, a combined Plymouth and Rhode Island company, led by Church and Peleg Sanford, pursued Metacom and cornered him "about a mile from Mount Hope." Alderman, the Pocasset man who had betrayed Weetamoo's location early in the war, is credited with the "shot" that killed the Pokanoket leader. Although Church later wrote that Alderman took Philip's hand as a trophy, signifying the savagery of his scouts, a letter from the Massachusetts Council to Josiah Winslow reveals that Church himself delivered Winslow's report of Metacom's death, along with "the paws of that monster which hath caused us so much mischief" to Boston, Metacom's hands a "welcome" gift to allies in the war. Winslow and Church's actual report did not survive.[59]

LOCKETY NECK

Weetamoo and her relations must have experienced an almost relentless pursuit, constantly on the move as colonial companies "hunted" them, "surprising" them as they gathered clams at Kickemuit and picked berries at Pocasset. There could be no greater indication that they had originally returned home to resume subsistence than the numbers of children and elders that colonial forces found among them. Returning war parties, bent on continuing the conflict, would not have carried so many children and elders with them. From the beginning, Wampanoag leaders had consistently led families to deeper shelters. Despite Mohawk attacks in the Connecticut River Valley, there were many places north of Wachusett where those children and elders could have remained sheltered (as with the captive children reported by the Wannukhows). However, once the intensive violence began, all routes north were closed off, leaving families entrapped within their own homelands.[60]

Places of sanctuary like the Pocasset cedar swamp were newly accessible to troops, while those caught in Church's snares were compelled to follow his directives. Bradford and Church made clear their pursuit would not stop all until they found and killed Metacom and his resistance was contained. Into the fall, Church pursued survivors of all ages among their kin, including those who took refuge on the island of Noepe. Even after Metacom's death, Winslow would "demand" from Rhode Island those "enemies" they had been pursuing, claiming jurisdiction and ownership over the survivors, authorizing Church to "conduct them to Plymoth" and to "sell and dispose such of them" from Rhode Island as he saw fit.[61]

It was one of those captive men, "seeking to make terms for himself," perhaps believing he could save his life or those of his kin, who revealed the hidden location of "a party of the enemy" in that "hideous swamp" to the men at Taunton in early August. The Massachusetts troops had left and Church had returned to Plymouth with his prisoners. A group of twenty Taunton men, fearing attack, according to local memory, followed the Three Mile River to its confluence with the Coweset (Wading) and Rumford Rivers and the thick swamp between them (North Taunton, now Norton). As at Nipsachuck, the forces approached the swamp from two sides, surprising the people within and attempting to drive them into the narrows of the neck, where other Taunton men remained on the south side of the confluence, to prevent them from crossing. Those people resisted, hard enough that the colonial memory of "Lockety Fight" would be embedded on maps and deeds, even though the place, "Lockety Neck," was suppressed from official narratives of the war.[62]

Mather and Hubbard simply relayed that on August 6, "An Indian that deserted his Fellows, informed the inhabitants of Taunton that a party of Indians who might be easily surprised, were not very far off, and promised to conduct any that had a mind to apprehend those Indians, in the right way towards them; whereupon about twenty Souldiers marched out of Taunton, and they took all those Indians, being in number thirty and six." Yet their narratives reveal a crucial detail, which does not arise to the surface of the local traditions: "Only the Squaw-Sachem of Pocasset, who was next unto Philip in respect of the mischief that hath been done . . . escaped alone." Mather's account continued:

> But not long after some of Taunton finding an Indian Squaw in Metapoiset newly dead, cut off her head, and it hapned to be Weetamoo, i. e. Squaw-Sachem her head. When it was set upon a pole in Taunton, the Indians who were prisoners there, knew it presently, and made a most horrid and diabolical Lamentation, crying out that it was their Queens head. Now here it is to be observed, that God himself by his own hand, brought this enemy to destruction. For in that place, where the last year, she furnished Philip with Canooes for his men, she herself could not meet with a Canoo, but venturing over the River upon a Raft, that brake under her, so that she was drowned, just before the English found her.[63]

In Mather's version, Weetamoo is delivered to colonists by "God," stripped of her life, her authority, her resistance cut off and her racialized body exposed in the place of her birth. In Hubbard's version, her woman's body is laid bare, a sure sign of conquest. In both, a divine reversal renders her unable to cross the Kteticut at the very location the authors insisted she had ferried Philip "and his men" (failing to mention her sister and the families) the summer before. In both, "some of Taunton" violate her body only after she is "drowned" (or at least "half drowned," in Hubbard's version), her death attributed to "God . . . his own hand." No mention of a battle in which she may have engaged, nor the place where her warriors were captured, only a valiant "escape," a failed struggle to cross the river, and a passive death at Mattapoisett.[64]

The deep grief expressed by those kin held imprisoned at Taunton, including those most recently captured, Mather characterized as "diabolical Lamentation," obscuring the great loss of this "beloved kinswoman," who had protected them and the land that sustained them with an enduring determination. Their "lamentations" may have been songs that honor the death of a mother, a courageous protector, and a leader. Their cries were not only for her death, but also for the violence against her sacred body, dismembered and displayed to terrify those who remained into submission. The narratives, recounted repeatedly for hundreds of years, became another form of dismemberment, questioned only by her descendants.

No primary accounts record the acts that led to Weetamoo's death, or divulge its relationship to the fight at Lockety Neck. Mather and Hubbard are the only sources, recited relentlessly to recount this leader's end. No colonial commander bragged about or even reported Weetamoo's death or a battle at Lockety Neck. No news of her conquest was conveyed in correspondence from the field. Neither Sewall nor Mather noted her death in their diaries. Rhode Islander William Harris, writing to London only six days later, reported the wounding of Quinnapin and the death of Metacom, among the capture and deaths of many others, but did not mention her name or the seizure of her warriors, only that Quinnapin and Metacom "each had a wife and child killed," by Church's force, while noting that Native men were used to having many. Church himself was silent on the matter.[65]

Yet the map showing the location of "Lockety Fight 1676" tells us something about Weetamoo's last "battle," in which "those Indians" were not "easily apprehended," as Hubbard attests, but put up a "fight." Confined to the neck, the engagement must have been intense, as local memory attests. If Weetamoo *did* "escape" from Lockety Neck, which colonial memory suggests was prevented by the strategic placement of the Taunton men, it is improbable that she ran to the south, then drowned while attempting to cross the river near Mattapoisett.

To get to the Kteticut crossing, she would have had to run six miles along the Three Mile River, the same route taken by the Taunton men, pass *through* Taunton, and travel another eleven miles downriver through Assonet to Mattapoisett. Alternatively, she could have skirted Taunton by traveling twelve miles through the woods and eight miles down the Segreganset River, which would put her close to Swansea. Even then, it would be another eight miles down the Kteticut to Mattapoisett. It is unlikely that Weetamoo would have followed either route, especially since deeper swamps lay to the north. Given the geography, it is more likely that she arrived at Taunton, not via an escape and naturalized drowning in the river, but by force. Rather than escaping and leaving others behind, Weetamoo may have been wounded at the battle, "seized" with her people or pursued and captured. In the account of her death, her nakedness might signify the violence done to her. Perhaps the silence of the record is itself telling. As Mather later wrote to John Cotton, a minister was obliged, by scripture, to maintain "faithfulness in ke[e]ping secrets & to bind ye Conscience in [that] Case. No man," he wrote, "should without necessary cause divulge ye sin & shame of his Neighbor."[66]

The divine placement of her body downriver served a kind of poetic justice for the minister-authors, who placed Metacom and Weetamoo's deaths at their perceived seats of power. Shortly thereafter, Plymouth and Taunton men claimed Montaup, Pocasset, and Assonet by right of conquest, their lands dismembered and divided, the stories of their ends also neatly closed into a narrative box.[67]

Whatever happened to Weetamoo in Taunton, surely those who went before her lay waiting to accept their beloved kinswoman with open arms. Surely, as her people grieved in prison and in sanctuaries still protected, they knew her "glory" rose "above the stars." Still now, by her relations, she is remembered. At Quequechand, the river, like the truth of Weetamoo's death, is but a trickle, buried under thick layers of pavement, concrete, highway, and degenerating mill works. Yet that stream has a sense of will and determination, breaking free from the cement that has restrained it for so long. The water, springing through cracks, actively seeks the old riverbed among the pebbles and plants below. Walking through Fall River today, Quequechand is nearly impossible to find. Yet that water has a memory of falling, an overpowering resonance. Today, you can find the river only by the sound of its name. This story, too, is just a trickle, lying beneath hundreds of years of print. Yet water has its own mind, its own course to take. Despite all efforts to dam and control it, it cannot be contained.

THIS IS NOT THE END

Pursuing the achievement of balance through war, Shoshanim, Quaiapin, Quinnapin, and Metacom sought to "renew greetings" through a process of peacemaking during the planting season of 1676. Yet this was not the peace colonial leaders desired. The war was merely one conflict among several in which England was engaged, to gain power and property, not achieve balanced relationships with the Indigenous peoples it claimed.[68] Ultimately, colonial leaders wanted to win New England and claim it fully as their own, replacing the Indigenous people in the land. Once such "success" seemed a real possibility, they no longer pursued peace negotiations that would allow for Native nations to exist independently in large territories anywhere in what is now southern New England. Any individual or group not fully contained became subject to death or enslavement. A policy first directed toward Metacom and his allies was extended to any Indian, Christian or "heathen," ally or "enemy," woman or man, adult or child, found outside colonial bounds. The military of the United Colonies were enabled in this effort, not by their sense of ethnic unity or the "hand of God," but by skilled scouts who knew the territory and a drought that no one could predict. These conditions, along with betrayal of the process of peace, left so many exposed, their locations revealed, their sanctuaries suddenly open and navigable.

Still, those who slipped past the southern settlements and scouts could make their way north. That spring, the governor of New York and the Mohicans offered sanctuary at Schaghticoke, on the Hoosic River, and Andros called the Mohawks to halt their raids.[69] At Koasek and Taconnic, the people planted. On the Pemigewasset and Saco, they fished salmon. At Wiwninbesaki, they counseled. At Ossipee they gathered. This was not the end of the war.

9

THE NORTHERN FRONT: BEYOND REPLACEMENT NARRATIVES

The literal and symbolic death of "King Philip" not only marked the "ends" of Puritan narratives, but became an iconic image for the birth of New England, exemplified in the following poem, which commemorated the 250th anniversary of the establishment of Bristol, Rhode Island, on the grounds of Montaup:

> His recreant arm the death-shot sped
> Brought to the dust that royal head,
>   The peerless Metacom.
> The last and foremost of his race!
> Where erst *he* sought a resting-place,
>   Our fathers found a home.[1]

As Jean O'Brien has demonstrated, Metacom's death has been privileged in the narrative of New England's settlement because it allows for the finality of "extinction" and "eclipse," the "replacement" of Indians with settlers. In the place where once the Wampanoag leader found a resting place is now the "lasting" home of the New England people, "found" and founded by "our fathers," the narrative granting legitimacy to colonial claims to land. Metacom's nobility and resistance are honored here only because both are contained within the past. The narrative conveys that Indigenous resistance, although noble, is futile. The story of the formative settlement of New England, leading to the American Revolution in Boston and beyond, is born of this narrative of extinction, moving forward "progressively" from this moment of early, but contained, violence. Philip's "rebellion" of 1676 is a natural and necessary precursor to the "revolution" of 1776, part of the labor pains inherent in the birth of a nation and the subjugation of the wilderness.[2]

Yet what happens to this cleanly contained narrative if we consider the history of "the Warres," of which this was merely the "first," with "the General Indian Nations," as the Mohegans called it, which continued for nearly a century? Those conflicts, which Kevin Sweeney and Evan Haefeli term the Anglo-Abenaki wars, continued until the end of the "French and Indian war," or even until the war that established the United States as a nation-state. Although narratives of the "Indian war" that mark its end with Philip's death have been persistent, the documentary record provides a different story, as scholars of Wabanaki history are well aware. As Emerson Baker and John Reid observe, "To many modern observers the defeat of King Philip and his allies is seen as a historical inevitability, part of a continent-wide conquest of Native Americans by Europeans. Those who lived through the war knew English victory was by no means assured."[3]

In truth, on the same day that Church pursued Metacom to his death at Montaup, a new series of raids erupted on the northern front. On August 11, the notorious Symon led a raid at Caskoak. Originally from the lower Molôdomak, Symon had recently escaped prison at Cocheco, with his companions Andrew and Peter, and returned to "join with the eastern Indians." Richard Waldron had attempted to capture and forcibly "employ" these men in military "service" when they "came in" with Wanalancet during the June peace councils, for "having a hand in the killing" and capture of settlers. Waldron planned to send each out in turn "against the Enemy" while "retaining & securing the other two" to ensure their compliance. Instead, they broke out of the jail.[4]

In the raid, Symon enacted strategic reversals of colonial tactics. He employed "camouflage" strategies based on his familiarity with English language and practices, creating a "counterfeited pass" and acquainting himself with settler Anthony Brackett's estate, built on land acquired from the saunkskwa Warrabitta. Symon tricked Brackett by bringing two men with him, whom he pretended to be turning in for cattle killing, using this ruse to confiscate all weapons in the house. The "rising" of Wabanaki hunters was motivated by local settlers' attempt to seize their guns. Yet here, Symon and his men claimed English arms. At Cocheco, Symon and Andrew had circumvented colonial tactics that leveraged the survival of kin for "service." At Caskoak, Symon offered Brackett a choice similar to the one Waldron had given him, asking "whether he would rather serve the Indians, or be slain by them." The "choice" was one that even then was being given to Christian Indians and other captured individuals to the south—to become servants, slaves, scouts, and informers, or to be slain. Yet Symon also offered a real choice to Brackett: to die as a warrior or submit to captivity. Brackett chose the latter.[5]

Symon's story offers a counterpoint to the countless stories of imprisonment, execution, and enslavement. Symon represents one of many Native people who found refuge and the possibility of continued resistance in the north. That same month, Thomas Gardner reported "the coming of divers Indianes from the west-wards," escaping violence and containment, which included bounties for any "sculking" Indian slain or captured "on the south side of Piscataqua River." The Jesuit Jean Enjalran reported the arrival of "a hundred fifty" Abenaki people at Sillery (at the confluence of the Chaudière and St. Lawrence) in October 1676, driven there by the "cruel war with the English of Boston and of all new England." As historian André Sevigny remarked, "At the death of Philip . . . manifold representatives of the insurgent tribes of the west came to take refuge at the home of Squando," thus strengthening Wabanaki resistance and linking the "people of the east" in common cause, a renewed strengthening of the coastal kinship networks devastated by disease and dispossession.[6]

The raid at Caskoak initiated a new wave of warfare in the north, including raids on deceitful trader Richard Hammond's post and the extensive Clarke and Lake garrison and trading post at Arrowsic, both on the Kennebec River, south of the vital Wabanaki town of Taconnic. Wabanaki protectors also pursued an innovative tactic: the capture of English "vessels." Within several days, over thirty settlers in Maine were taken captive or killed, while survivors "fled," even as colonial commanders pursued containment in the south. In the north, the war had just begun.[7]

FROM COCHECO TO KENNEBEC:
"MAJOR WALDRON DO LIE"

One year later, in July 1677, as war continued on the northern front, the Kennebec River sagamores sent a message from Taconnic via a captive, Eliza-beth Hammond, to the "governor of boston." Wabanaki people were sincerely "willing to live peaceable" but were weary of deceit. Among numerous points they raised, Madoasquarbet, a spiritual leader known to the English as "Deo-genes," urged Leverett to "understand how we have been abused," especially by Waldron:

> Governor of Boston this is to let you to understand how Major Waldin served us. We carried 4 prisoners aboard. We would fain know whither you did give such order to kill us for bringing your prisoners. Is that your fashion to come & make peace & then kill us? We are afraid you will do so again. Major Wal-din do lie. We were not minded to kill no body. Major Waldin did wrong to

give cloth & powder but he gave us drink & when were drunk killed us. If it had not been for this fault you [would have] had your prisoners long ago . . . Major Waldin has been the cause of killing all that have been killed this summer. You may see how honest we have been. We have killed none of your English prisoners. If you had any of our prisoners you would a knocked them on the head. Do you think all this is nothing?[8]

In his statement, Madoasquarbet likely alluded to three major deceits by the Waldrons: William's enslavement of seventeen or more Wabanaki people at Machias and Nova Scotia in November 1675 (see chapter 7); a purported peace council at Sagadahoc in February 1677 during which Richard captured and killed several Wabanaki leaders "under a flag of truce"; and the infamous "surprise" at Cocheco in September 1676, wherein Richard captured hundreds of Native people and sent them to Boston, where the majority were executed or enslaved. As both Gardner's reports and Wabanaki statements established, the Waldrons' deceits fueled war on the northern front and remained a lasting communal memory of colonial deception for decades. Although by no means the only treachery Wabanaki people faced, the Waldrons' actions became emblematic of colonial betrayal—by traders pretending fairness and friendship, and governors pretending peace. Moreover, Madoasquarbet's questions persist. Did Waldron act alone, or under Massachusetts's orders? Did colonial leaders consider the destructive impact such deceptions had on the peace process? Or did they regard "all this" as "nothing," their usual "fashion" of doing business? Would they *do* "nothing" to reset the balance, compelling warriors to restore it themselves? Wabanaki people would continue to pose such questions long after the war.[9]

COCHECO: SURPRISALS AND STRATAGEMS

In June 1676, Mary and Joseph Rowlandson traveled to the crossroads of Cocheco to redeem their son, who "was come in to Major Waldron's." Like the Eames girls, Rowlandson's children had traveled with Native families into northern networks, her son coming in with Wanalancet and the other leaders who met with Richard Waldron in June. Wakely's daughter, captured at Casco, had traveled as far as Narragansett, but arrived at Cocheco with Squando. Wabanaki leaders delivered these captives in response to messages that had traveled from Wachusett, symbols, as Rowlandson had been, of their intent to renew respectful relations. When Waldron later sent an invitation to meet once more at Cocheco, Wanalancet's Penacooks and those whom they sheltered came to his post in that spirit of exchange. Madoasquarbet may have recalled Waldron's pretense at peace when he referred to the "cloth & powder" the trader offered.[10]

It is difficult to discern what happened in September 1676, when Waldron hosted hundreds of Native people on "open ground" in front of his house. According to the oft-quoted colonial New Hampshire historian Jeremy Belknap, Waldron orchestrated a "sham fight," under pretense of "training" Native men for colonial service, whereby "the whole body of them (except two or three) were surrounded" then "seized and disarmed" by Massachusetts troops. "A separation was then made" according to Belknap (and Hubbard), between those belonging to "Wonolanset, with the Penacook Indians," who "were peaceably dismissed," and "the strange Indians," those "who had fled from the southward and taken refuge among them," who "were made prisoners" and "sent to Boston." Of these, Belknap wrote, "seven or eight of them, who were known to have killed" colonists, "were condemned and hanged" as "rebels" while "the rest were sold into slavery in foreign parts."[11]

In his September 6, 1676, letter to the Massachusetts Council, Waldron reported that he was able to "draw up ye Indians at Cocheco . . . under ye Notion of takeing them out into Service," in line with Belknap's eighteenth-century narration. However, Waldron's report reveals a different stratagem. Rather than a "sham fight," Waldron organized a sham feast. Once "assembled," the trader invited the people to "eat and Drink," presumably alcohol (as customary) if Madoasquarbet's statement sheds light. By hosting a meal, Waldron displayed peaceful intent, an Indigenous sign of friendship and hospitality, a ruse that ensnared his guests: "Then," Waldron wrote, the recently arrived "Army," under Captains Syll and Hathorne, "surrounded" them. "Calling ye cheife Sagamores into ye Center," Waldron relayed, "I told [them] what must bee don, only [that the] Innocent should not be damnified." Surrounded, "they surrended their Armes," which, he reported, were only "20 in Number," clearly not people expecting a fight. Most important, Waldron reported the number of people they had "taken" captive—only "80 fighting Men & 20 old men," but "250 women & children."[12] This begs the question, why had whole families traveled to Waldron's house if the purpose was to recruit men for military service? And why were so few armed? Further, if orders were to "secure" or "seize" those implicated in war, why were the majority captured women and children? Although it is possible that some of these women, like Weetamoo, might have participated in resistance, were the children judged guilty as well?

Although Belknap described "a separation" of the Penacook from the "strange Indians," Waldron's letter reveals that such a division did not take place at Cocheco. Instead, he and the officers awaited direction from Boston, regarding "the disposal" of "all." In writing to the council on the same day, local settlers Nicholas Shapleigh and Thomas Daniel, who had provided "Assistance" in "Securing" the "Indians," wrote that the "Commanders were earnest" in requesting a speedy "Removal of all of" the captives and affirmed they would "dispatch away ye Prisoners according to your Com[m]ands." Although Waldron was reluctant to include local parties to the Cocheco treaty, no "separation" seems to have occurred. Instead, soon after, Waldron and the officers received orders "to have *all* sent down to determine their Case at Boston," with the exception of "about ten men to serve in the Army," along with "their families." Waldron reported finding "among" the captives "Narraganset Indians, Groton & Nashaway Indians," but the Christian Indians of Wamesit and the peaceable Penacooks were sent along with the rest, despite the treaty they had made with Waldron two months before. The only separation made at Cocheco was between those compelled to "serve" and those shipped to Boston.[13]

NORTHERN FRONT

The "ten young men" Waldron mentioned were retained to assist the Massachusetts soldiers in navigating the "hideous" eastern country, under orders to "pursue, repel and destroy the enemy." Following the capture at Cocheco, Hathorne and Syll, along with Captain Hunting and "his Indians," awaited the court's "order" to begin their "search" in "ye Woods" of the Wabanaki country. By pressing locally knowledgeable men into service, alongside scouts from Massachusetts, the army stood the best chance of tracking their "enemy." Moreover, by holding the men's families, the magistrates and military commanders could compel their service, a strategy they had used effectively before. Yet Shapleigh and Daniel were wary that news of the capture might provoke Wabanaki people to further violence. The successful stratagem, they warned, might "prove very prejudiciall by Reason of divers of their relations that are abroad in these parts." Those relations, they feared, were like "to make Suddain Spoyle upon us." They requested that soldiers would remain among them to protect the vulnerable eastern settlements. Waldron specifically requested that "Captain Hunting may stay with his Indians," suggesting the crucial role the Christian Indian scouts continued to play.[14]

The largest colonial company, led by Hathorne and guided by local Piscataqua scouts, saw little success. For eleven days, they traveled by ship, docking at eastern settlements and scouting the surrounding territory, arriving finally at Cascoak on September 19. In all that time, Hathorne's company captured only two men: "a sagamore" from Pequacket, whom they interrogated and executed, and Aboquacemoka, a Pequacket war leader known to the locals as John Sampson, who they "killed dead in ye place" following an apparent ambush at or near Cascoak. Although the army found so few, local settlers were all too well aware of "ye nearness of ye Enemy now in our borders by whome wee daly Expect to bee Surprised," their confidence further undermined by a *loss* of protection and provision, and the apparent incompetence of the Massachusetts troops, including competition among officers. The army had compelled local colonists to leave their settlements to serve, and also had "eaten us out of bread." Meanwhile, warriors were able "to slip by them unobserved." Hathorne himself reported, "wee find itt very Difficult to Come neore them there is soe many River & soe much broken land, that they soon Escape by Canoes ye Country being full of them." Once more colonial troops faced their lack of environmental knowledge and an enemy that could neither be located nor contained.[15]

Only shortly after Hathorne's troops left the area, Casco was again under siege, with protectors led by Mogg Hegone reclaiming land at Owascoag on October 12. There, Mogg offered Henry Josselyn and the settlers safe passage if they left, and Josselyn "surrendered" the Black Point settlement, avoiding bloodshed. As Maine historian William Willis observed, the coast of Casco Bay "remained desolate during the remainder of the war." By October 19, Waldron reported a "deserted and conquered Eastern Country" to the magistrates in Boston, and warned, "ye Enemy intimates" that "hee is proceeding towards us" (settlements on the Piscataqua and Merrimack Rivers) "and on towards yourselves." Meanwhile, a colonial expedition to the perceived "headquarters" at Ossipee proved futile. When captive Francis Card escaped from Taconnic that winter, he reported that Mogg told his people "he hath found the way to burn Boston," having scoped out the city in the fall. "Four Indian women" had traveled to Taconnic, likely from Sillery or Wabanaki villages on the Chaudière, to convey that they would be able to send men and ammunition from Canada come spring. Squando preached to the Wabanaki masses, telling them that "god doth speak to him and doth tell him that god hath left" the English "na[t]ion to destroy." The people, Card said, took "all that he doth tell them" for "truth."[16]

THE CAPTURE OF MONOCO AND SHOSHANIM

Hathorne had sent no prisoners to Boston, yet within two days of his report, news arrived that "One-eyed John" or Monoco, "with about 45 of your Southern Indians, have been apprehended since the Souldiers went Eastward." Five days later, on September 26, Shoshanim, Monoco, Mattawamp, and the elder Tantamous or "Old Jethro," were executed in Boston. Although both Sewall and Mather reported the hangings in their diaries, no officer bragged about the capture. It was certainly not the result of Hathorne and Syll's fruitless expeditions "eastward." How then were these formidable leaders taken?[17]

While Hathorne and Syll organized their mission, the Massachusetts Council had ordered Gookin to recruit "two Indians" to serve as "Spyes among the enemy." This smaller group was separate from the main company of scouts under Hunting; their mission was to "travel among them all both Easterly & westerly" to "procure" captives. Although ostensibly the "spies" would pursue the redemption of English settlers, they may have simultaneously sought Native captives as well. Offered only coats for "encouragement," the spies were empowered to give "assurance" to those in the Nipmuc and Wabanaki countries who held English captives that "in case they will come in & Submitt themselves to ye mercy of" the colonial "government" they would "have their lives given them & freed from foreign slavery."[18]

Among those who helped achieve these goals was Peter Jethro, the son of Tantamous, a likely choice for a spy. Gookin and Waldron both had knowledge of the second "company" of captives shipped from Cocheco to Boston. In their correspondence, Waldron acknowledged he had given Peter Jethro incentive to "use his Endeav[o]r" to "bring in one eyed John," but denied Gookin's claim that Jethro and others of his "company" had been promised "life and liberty" in return. Jethro's position was especially precarious because he had not only served as scribe for the Nipmuc leaders at Wachusett, but had ostensibly participated in raids, including "Beer's fight" in the Connecticut River Valley. Moreover, "Old Jethro" and "his two sons," likely including Peter, were among those falsely imprisoned with James Printer at the beginning of the war for the raid that Monoco had carried out.[19]

Mather and Hubbard, in recounting Peter's "endeavor" in "bringing in" Monoco and others, displaced the roles of colonial leaders, placing blame entirely on him. According to Hubbard, "Besides those that were surprised aforesaid [at Cocheco], there were several others who had been the chief actors, that were taken up and down in those woods beyond Merrimack, and so were delivered up to justice; as John Monoco, Sagamore Sam, old Jethro with some others" noting that "young Jethro brought in 40 at one time." This supported the argument for the savagery even of convert Indians: as Mather exclaimed, "That abominable Indian Peter Jethro betrayed his own Father and other Indians of his own special Acquaintance, unto Death. Many of the Nipmuc Indians who were wont to lay Snares for others, were at last themselves taken by a Stratagem, and brought to deserved Execution." Both Hubbard and Mather effectively used passive language to attribute the unsavory capture to other Indians, without admitting the inability of the Massachusetts troops to carry out the mission themselves. Mather observed in his diary, "They were betrayed into the hands of the English by Indians," leaving English hands free of involvement in the "stratagem."[20]

Yet, in truth, it appears that the Nipmuc leaders and at least forty of their people "were induced . . . through the mediation of Peter Jethro" to "come in" to Waldron's post at "Cocheco, as they understood to make peace," in a strategy similar to the first "surprise." There, they were "seized" and "soon after carried to Boston" as prisoners, where the leaders were hanged, and others were "sold into slavery." Given Gookin's order, it is possible that Peter Jethro brought his own father to Cocheco, thinking he would be granted "life and liberty," only to find that "Old Jethro" was to be executed in Boston with the rest.[21]

As Shapleigh's letter from Cocheco suggests, local settlers were fearful of the impacts of these betrayals. More than a week before the execution, John Lake, the brother of the influential Kennebec trader Thomas Lake, who he believed had been captured that summer, advocated for the release of Shoshanim. In his petition to the Massachusetts Council, he conveyed that the news that "Sagamore Sam is to receive a sentence of death" had reached the eastern settlements, and would likely travel "to those Indians with whom my brother is, which may provoke them to proceed with him to ye same sentence of death." Recognizing this reciprocal brand of justice, Lake pleaded with the magistrates to "suspend" Shoshanim's "sentence" so that the Nashaway leader might travel among those communities, and advocate "to procure ye return of my brother," in return for which the magistrates might "be pleased to spare his life." Lake's petition demonstrates settlers' awareness of Shoshanim's influence and diplomatic skill, as well as the wide network to which he belonged. Although Shoshanim's homeland was far from the Kennebec, his relationships and reputation extended far into Wabanaki, and his death would provoke grief and retribution in both Wabanaki people and those sheltered among them.[22]

Therefore, it is no surprise that raiding resumed after Shoshanim, Monoco, Mattawamp, and Tantamous were "walk[ed] to the gallows" in Boston. Moreover, Monoco reportedly made a significant challenge to colonial authority, just before his death. According to Sewall, he revealed that Hoorawannonit, then held under Prentice's protection in Cambridge, had "fired the first shot at Quabaug and killed Capt. Hutchinson." This was not simply a revelation or confession. Rather, Monoco revealed the hypocrisy of colonial justice. While men like the Wannukhows and Tantamous, who surely deserved the "amnesty" the magistrates had promised, faced public execution, war leaders like Hoo-rawannonit had their "life and liberty." Bringing in high status prisoners, Hoo-rawannonit and Peter Jethro were granted amnesty for the betrayal of their kin, just as Waldron received accolades for his betrayal of his "friends." Monoco was reportedly willing to face death; the warrior had surely accepted this consequence early on. Yet he stood on the gallows next to a peaceable leader from nearby Natick (who had narrowly escaped deportation to Deer Island), and a fellow Nashaway leader who had strongly promoted peace. For Monoco, the injustice was evident on either side.[23]

BOSTON

The Wannukhows might have seen Shoshanim and Monoco brought in, with their neighbor Tantamous, just before their own execution. They likely witnessed the arrival of hundreds from Cocheco, just days after they had submitted their petition, as well as the subsequent execution, on September 13, when, as Sewall recorded, "there were eight Indians shot to death on the common, upon Wind-mill hill," who Mather noted were those "brought in from the eastward." Countless others were sold into slavery; during the months of August and September alone, according to Margaret Newell, Massachusetts colony "sold over 190" Native people at public auction, the profits going into the colony's "accounts for the war," while "Plymouth disposed of an additional 169." Even as the names of the Massachusetts "buyers" were noted in John Hull's account book, the names of the Cocheco captives went unrecorded. Indeed, the bulk of the September court records concerned preparations for Stoughton and Buckley's trip to London to defend Massachusetts's patent, including its just carriage in war. Nevertheless, with executions and enslavements well under way, by September 16, a "committee" was organized to "consider" what should "be done" about "peaceable Indians" and those who came in under "amnesty." Without naming any individuals, the court ruled that of "the many . . . Indian enemyes now seized & in our possession," those that "appear to have Imbrued their hands in English blood should suffer death here and not be transported to foreign partes." Thus, this ruling suggests that most of those "transported" into slavery were people not directly implicated in violence against settlers, removed from the land because of their kinship affiliations and competing claims to land. As Newell has discerned, this enslavement was justified under doctrine that "permitted enslavement" of "traitors" and "enemies," as well as their children, who were "captured in a defensive conflict," an argument put forth by the official narratives of the war.[24]

The names of Native captives from Cocheco appear in the records only as advocates like Gookin sought to keep particular converts from death and deportation. These included Samuel Numphow, who had signed the treaty at Cocheco for the Wamesits, Samuel's brother Jonathan George, and the minister and scribe Samuel Betomkin, who had composed the recent letters of Shoshanim and the Nipmuc sachems. Although the Wamesit people "came in with Wannalancet to Major Waldernes" as part of a process of "reconciliation" and "peace," as Gookin observed, they were "sent to Boston" with the rest. Once there, some settlers made "accusations against them," and regardless of the probability of mistaken identity (a kind of colonial racial profiling, which Gookin acknowledged), such "testimony was admitted, and some of them condemned to death and executed, and others sent to the Islands out of the country." Only "some few were pardoned and reconciled," including Wanalancet and "six or seven of his men," demonstrating, as Norton suggests, that even the Penacook sagamore and his relations were judged alongside the rest. Among the Wamesit captives only a few, including Betomkin, Jonathan George, "and a very few other men," along with "several women and children," survived. Numphow "hardly escaped" with his life.[25]

Another Christian Indian, "John Namesit," had been drawn out from Cocheco to scout with "the Army" while his "wife and sucking child" were "sent among others . . . to boston & there sold," contrary to "promises" that they would be allowed "life and liberty" for his service. Only by Gookin's intervention, and John's own travel to Boston in November, where his wife remained "in prison" with her baby, was Mary Namesit "released." "Life and liberty" had become a refrain in these petitions, a repeated invocation of the documents of peace and amnesty, the promises that Massachusetts had not kept. In correspondence initiated by Gookin, Waldron admitted he had "sold" Mary, but denied any culpability, saying it "was her own fault in not Acquainting me with it." Still, he was compelled to "reimburse" the buyers "what they gave me for her," so "she may be sett at liberty." This suggests that some of the Cocheco captives were sold directly by Waldron, outside the colony's public auction. Gookin was not the only advocate for the captives. James Speen secured the release of "Jacob," sold alongside Mary, promising he would "bee faithfull to the English." James Quananopohit used his influence to rescue his "kinsman" George Wenepoykin (or "No-nose") of Naumkeag, the last surviving son of the Massachusett Saunkskwa, redeeming him from slavery in Barbados. James cared for George for the rest of his life, ensuring his protection. Mary Namesit, "Jacob Indian," and George Wenepoykin offer rare stories of the redemption of Indigenous captives from "foreign slavery."[26]

REDEMPTION IN NORTHERN NETWORKS

The court permitted the surviving Wamesits and Penacooks to return to Wamesit, under the "inspection" of Jonathan Tyng, who had taken so much of their land. Some of their children were "put to service" in colonial homes. Still under a form of captivity, a year later, their northern "kindred and relations" arrived to redeem them. In September 1677, the Kwinitekw leader Ashpelon and twenty-six protectors (including a Narragansett) raided Hatfield and Deerfield, creating a distraction while another party paddled to "Naamkeke," the Wamesit fishing falls, "near Chelmsford." By persuasion or compulsion, they carried away "Wanalancet, the sachem," and "about fifty" of his people, being mostly "women and children," warning them that "the war" with the English "was not yet at an end," and they would find greater safety to the north. They loaded the summer's harvest, including "plenty of fish & many dried huckleberries," into their canoes. The timing was crucial; the people at Wamesit had grown little corn, because most of their planting grounds had been "improved" by colonists, including the Tyngs. Without it, they would not likely survive the winter. Ashpelon's company took refuge upriver at Ktsi Mskodak, where they hosted surviving "Wachusett sachems" and their families, some "four score" women and children who had been living at Nashaway. Here, before continuing northward, they "talked of" creating a sanctuary, a "fort a greate way up the river," at Koasek or the Kwinitekw headwaters, where Wanalancet had weathered the war. Penacooks were thereafter seen among their kin on Lake Champlain and the St. Lawrence, as well as at Schaghticoke. Still, within "a few years," as Haefeli and Sweeney note, "many of the Penacooks had returned" to their homeland, retaining ties to these northern networks. Over a decade later, Kancamagus, son of Nanamocomuck and survivor of the war, led a raid on Waldron's post at Cocheco. Native women, requesting hospitality from the trader, entered his house and led the reversal of a deceit that would end in Waldron's death and a "balancing" of his scales.[27]

WABANAKI: "OUR DESIRE IS TO BE QUIET"

Shoshanim's story, as John Lake's petition suggested, must have been heard throughout these northern networks, from Kwinitekw to Kennebec, and beyond. His death should not be read as emblematic of the containment of either Indigenous resistance or diplomacy. When Madoasquarbet and the Kennebec leaders sent their message to Boston from Taconnic in July 1677, they reconvened a peace process which paralleled and renewed his own. Like the leaders at Wachusett, they conveyed a communally authored statement through a female captive. Taken at their former village, she now stood among the "English friends" willing to carry their words. Elizabeth Hammond was an apt messenger, since she had also been deceived by Waldron, who, she later wrote, had "utterly destroyed" her "estate," after the previous summer's raid, "cutting of[f] her mills spoyling her Smith-shop & Carrying away her Iron work," adding to her loss.[28]

Speaking for Kennebec River people and their allies, the Wabanaki leader Moxus told Leverett, "We would find your mind," conveying that "you find us all way[s] for peace." Like Shoshanim, he used poetic oratory to express both the still state of their collective "mind," focused to follow all "ways" (paths) to peace, and their integrity in previous and present councils—advocating "always for peace." They sought to engage in peacemaking once more, offering to resume the "trade," and the return of twenty English captives, whom Hammond could attest they had treated well. Moxus also offered a distinction between themselves and warriors like Symon, who had led a spring raid on York and Wells, and Mogg, who had died in a raid on Black Point, and others of the Saco, Presumpscot, and Androscoggin Rivers who continued to raid English settlements. Yet they acknowledged this violence arose in response to colonial actions, including Waldron's deceits. Such deceit had also marked English overtures toward peace. Recalling the Waldrons' and Massachusetts men's actions, they proclaimed, "You all ways broke the peace." "This time," they insisted, they would have to "see" evidence of the colonists' commitment to cease violence and renew the trade "first," before they would release more captives. They must have known that Shoshanim had been betrayed even as he sought the full restoration of captives. The Kennebec sagamores requested that Massachusetts "send" both material and symbolic evidence of its peaceful intent and commitment, goods including tobacco and corn (as well as powder and cloth), and return the "captives you took at Pemaquid." Still, the most important message the Kennebec sachems conveyed was the firm ground from which they offered the possibility of peace. "We can fight as well as others," Moxus proclaimed. Yet, "we are willing to live peaceable—we will not fight without they fight with us first."[29]

Emphasizing this point and echoing Shoshanim, Madoasquarbet recalled, "we were quiet" when they came to take "away our guns," and "our desire is to be quiet" once more. Wabanaki people desired and cultivated the restoration of stillness and right relations. Madoasquarbet recalled the actions, by men under Massachusetts's jurisdiction, that fostered imbalance: dispossession through drink, confiscation of guns, false assertion of blame for damage to cattle by wolves, manufacture of debt for small infractions ("we must pay a 100 skins if we break a tobacco pipe"), and binding and imprisoning the people, which Madoasquarbet described as akin to death. And "now" he said, "we hear that you say you will not leave war as long as an Indian is in the country."[30]

Madoasquarbet's statement revealed Wabanaki people's ability to read the landscape through a wider geopolitical lens than Massachusetts settlers could possess. The Kennebec leaders sent their message after Waldron's botched attempt at containing the northern front in February 1677, under orders from Massachusetts (although in their reply, the magistrates did not acknowledge their role). Waldron's killing and seizure of Penobscot leaders and their kin at Sagadahoc had only fueled the fire, spreading it further east. His deceits also fueled warriors led by Squando and Symon, triggering further raids and moving the northern front closer to Cocheco and Boston. Further, before the Kennebec message arrived, Massachusetts had pursued another disastrous "expedition" with Waldron to seek out the "headquarters" of the "Eastern Indian Enemy" (with military support denied by their fellow colonies of Plymouth and Connecticut). Through Pynchon, Massachusetts had also renewed their "friendship" with the Mohawks, asking them, with three wampum belts, to pursue "our Indian Ennemy at kinnebeck &c as farr as Cannada," in response to Francis Card's report. This news traveled with Native people to the missions on the St. Lawrence, and then likely down through Wabanaki villages on the Chaudière to the Kennebec, the displacements caused by war ironically fueling communication. From knowledge of these actions arose Madaosquarbet's accusation that Massachusetts sought to fight until not an Indian remained.[31]

The spiritual leader could see clearly not only past injustice, but also Massachusetts's current pursuit of total containment, destruction and replacement. Yet Madoasquarbet, the visionary, insisted that this desire would not be fulfilled, declaring, "We are owners of the country & it is wide and full of Indians & we can drive you out." He could see the vastness of "the country" and the people who belonged to it, from the coast to the "great river" (St. Lawrence) and the "long river" (Kwinitekw), even to the new intertribal town of Schaghticoke, sheltered under the "great tree" of the Mohicans and New York colony. Massachusetts, despite its boasts, patents, and deeds, could not rightfully claim to be the "owners." In his own language, Madoasquarbet proclaimed this land "our country," *ndakinna*. His statement evoked a sense of common identity throughout the region—in his language, *alnôbak*, a word formerly meaning only "human beings," transformed to represent "Indians," those people indigenous to this "country" claimed by "New England." The word also asserted the humanness of "Indian" people in contrast to colonial objectification. Combining these two potent words, Madoasquarbet evoked a sense of confederation among the people who had emerged through war as the "Eastern Indians," the Wabana-kiak and Wôpanâak whose name now took on new meaning in the wake of war. Not only the collective people of the east, but those who belonged to and would remain in this "vast" eastern land (see map 1).[32]

PEACE AT PEMAQUID

The Kennebec leaders' message, along with letters sent by emissaries of Governor Andros, initiated a crucial yet nearly unknown treaty that effectively ended the war. The councils, held during July and August 1677, were hosted by the Kennebec leaders, in their territory of Sagadahoc, near the mouth of the river, at the long rocky point called Pemaquid; and Andros's commission-ers, Commander in Chief Anthony Brockholls, Secretary Matthias Nicolls, and Caesar Knapton, who understood the protocols of Indigenous diplomacy from many councils with the Mohawks, the greater Haudenosaunee Confederacy, the Mohicans, and allied nations. Indeed, Wabanaki people at Schaghticoke could testify to New York's relative justness in offering asylum to those Massa-chusetts regarded only as enemies. New York had used their stronger diplomatic position with the Mohawks to "call back" the warriors from raiding "Eastward beyond" New York colony's "bounds." Andros's commissioners operated under the authority of the king, who had given a patent to his brother, James, "the Duke of York and Albany," which included the Wabanaki coast from Kennebec to the St. Lawrence. Asserting this jurisdiction, New York colony had recently established a trading post and fort at Pemaquid, with a mission to negotiate a royally authorized peace between the Wabanaki leaders and English settlers, and to secure the British hold, versus the French, on this key fishing and trading region. The Kennebec leaders, who accepted New York's offer, were also apt diplomats for this peacemaking process, having long served as middlemen in the trade between the primarily hunting regions to the north and agricultural regions to the south.[33]

Massachusetts recognized the Kennebec leaders' July message as "an over-ture of a treaty of peace," and begrudgingly consented to Andros's mediation, recognizing that New York colonists, "having not been concerned in any Act of Hostility against them," would hold more "credence" with Wabanaki leaders. In their communications with Brockholls, the magistrates tried to insist, as they had in the past, on the return of all captives preliminary to peace. Yet Brockholls's communications, arising from his councils with the Kennebec leaders, demon-strated the importance of the mutual cessation of violence as the first step.[34]

The treaty council opened in July with preliminary negotiations between the New York commissioners and the Kennebec leaders, marked by a spirit of diplomacy and reciprocity. They met near the carrying place at Pemaquid, where the commissioners had established their post. The Kennebec leaders, including Moxus and Madoasquarbet, agreed to "forbear" from making war upon any of the English colonists, and to "deliver" all English captives to Pemaquid. Further, they would send diplomats to all of their people, requesting the same of their "friends & Allies." Likewise, the commissioners "promised to do the like to the English, that they may likewise forebeare all Acts of Hostility" and return Wabanaki captives to Pemaquid. This apparently included those taken at Machias, since Massachusetts at that time commissioned Captain Bernard Trott to sail to the Azores Islands and redeem them from the slave trade. The commissioners then wrote to Massachusetts, communicating diplomatically that if they were serious about making peace, they should confirm their willingness to carry out these terms, which, Brockholls relayed, "wee thinke to bee very reasonable."[35]

Massachusetts eventually consented to the terms, sending Black Point captain Joshua Scottow eastward with a cargo-hold of captives. He arrived at Pemaquid on August 5. The diplomacy of the Kennebec leaders among their relations was especially effective. On August 13, just before sunset, thirteen canoes arrived at Pemaquid, carrying multiple Wabanaki sachems and their "retinue." Their simultaneous arrival suggests a preliminary council had been held elsewhere, perhaps upriver at Taconnic. Once all the representatives had arrived, there were some sixty Wabanaki people gathered for the council, which lasted ten days. Among them was Derumkin, along with other Androscoggin River leaders, who brought in Elizabeth Hammond's son; "a Sagamore of Pegwacket"; as well as Symon and Squando.[36]

Squando's arrival was particularly significant, since he at first had rejected New York's offer of diplomacy, leaving, as the Kennebec leaders reported, for the north. Councils in Wabanaki country had long been underway. The Kennebec speaker and "chief Sachem" Moxus said, according to Brockholls, that "all the Indians from Piscataqua to Penobscot" (including Squando "and his men") had "put themselves under him," at least for the purpose of this treaty. That is, he could speak from the grounds of consensus among all of these related peoples. Squando had stepped away from that consensus, dissenting (as was his right), and had removed himself from the coast, heading inland, an effective diplomatic strategy. Massachusetts had initially imagined they could compel the Kennebec leaders to "join their forces for the suppression" of Squando, but the leaders insisted he was beyond their reach. Moreover, even when he came in, New York made clear that this was not a point of negotiation. When Squando arrived at Pemaquid, following further councils in Wabanaki, he rejoined the consensus and represented his people in the final negotiations that led to peace.[37]

Following dialogue and "debate" with the commissioners, all the Wabanaki leaders joined those of the Kennebec in "signing" and consenting to the treaty, which emphasized reciprocal terms, including mutual cessation of violence and the "mutual return of captives." It also bound "all" English settlers to the treaty, recognizing that "all ye English" were "Subjects to ye Same King." It is important to recognize that the treaty did not insist or imply that Wabanaki people were "Subjects" of the "King." The point of the treaty's first article was to bind all English to its terms and to recognize the New York commission's authority to negotiate on behalf of the Crown. Thus, Wabanaki leaders could be assured of a higher colonial authority with jurisdiction over the New England colonies, to which "all the English" settlers were obliged to adhere. Importantly, these articles were carried out on the ground. No more orders came from Massachusetts authorizing the destruction of Indians after the treaty was concluded. The treaty also created the grounds for prevention of future conflicts. If any English suffered injury by Wabanaki people, the "complaints should be made to their Sagamores, for Reparation." Likewise, should injury be done to Wabanaki people by settlers, "they were to Complain" to the New York commissioners at the new fort or to Henry Josselyn of Black Point, the local representative to the treaty.[38]

Still, as Brockholls observed, a significant conflict during the treaty negotiations threatened to cause "a new breach." Massachusetts sent a late message, in contrast to their earlier communications, requiring new "difficult terms," the return of the "vessels" or ships that Wabanaki people had taken. It was likely Penobscot people who had pursued this tactic, for messages had to be sent to Panawahpskek with this new request. Moreover, the magistrates had instructed Scottow not to release the "prisoners" until the ships had been returned. Brockholls chastised Massachusetts for this "imposition," which threatened to "spoyle all" they "had done" to create a space for negotiations. It was particularly maddening, he said, for the Wabanaki people who could see their kin held in the cargo holds, to them "a breach of promise," given the number of captives they had already released. Six Native people had spent at least a fortnight in the dark and filthy "hold," below deck, and even upon signing of the treaty, Scottow would not release them. Brockholls tried in earnest to accommodate, allowing Madoasquarbet and a Wabanaki woman to check on them, and on the day of the treaty signing, Symon and Madoasquarbet "came aboard to see ye Captives" on Scottow's ship. According to Scottow, Symon leapt to take a "little boy out of ye Hold & would have carried him away but being Hindered put him down again." Many others threatened to "rescue the Captives by force," while diplomatic leaders emphasized the promise that had been breached. Finally, Scottow consented to allow the captives up on deck so that they could see their families. Among them were two "miserable creatures," most likely the Machias leader and his wife redeemed from the Azores, who Brockholls said had "too long beene innocent sufferers."[39]

On the arrival of the Penobscot leader Madackawando and "his retinue" on August 18, the captives were finally released and "carried ashore." Brockholls acknowledged the Penobscot leader's generosity in assenting to "surrender the ketches," although not grounded in the original terms. With Madackawando's assent and signing, the treaty was complete. Brockholls declared, "Wee hope God almighty will give a blessing to the Peace now made with Indians." Madackawando could now travel to his relations at Machias, bringing home two of their kin, even as they continued to grieve the loss of those who had been lost to the slave trade. Symon could now embrace the boy, carry him from the prison of the ship's hold, and take him home.[40]

CASKOAK, THE PLACE OF PEACE

The next spring, Squando sent a message to Boston to confirm a more "firm peace." In April 1678, Boston sent local settlers Nicholas Shapleigh, Francis Champernoon, and Nathaniel Fryer to the peacemaking place of Caskoak, where they met Squando and other leaders, to finalize terms for settlers to return to the Wabanaki coast. As Baker and Reid have observed, "In the Wabanaki territory there was no native defeat, total or otherwise. Instead, the English were expelled" and the war only came to a close with the Casco Bay treaty of 1678, "which obliged English colonists to pay a tribute to the Wabanakis." "For the privilege of resettlement," Massachusetts and local leaders agreed that each family would give annually "a peck of corn," acknowledgement to the Wabanaki leaders whose territory they inhabited. A "bushel" was required of Major Philips of the Saco River, whose mills had been fired at the outset of war. This was a renewal of original pledges secured by leaders like Warrabitta, but also a formal agreement that recognized the continuance of Indigenous leadership and jurisdiction, as well as settler responsibility, in what Madoasquarbet called "our country," Wabanaki.[41]

RESISTING REPLACEMENT

The narrative of war that ends with the death of King Philip suggests that resistance to colonization is noble, yet foolish and futile. It ends with dismemberment, beloved leaders' bodies transformed into signs of colonial conquest. What remains, in these narratives, are only the remnants, contained in circumscribed towns (or reservations) under firm colonial rule and surveillance. Yet, if we consider alternative narratives, we see the ways in which resistance fostered a space for collaboration, even across previous geographical and political chasms. This is not to say that resistance was not without severe risks and losses, to individuals and families, including betrayal and great loss of life. However, it is equally dangerous to regard the history of Indigenous resistance as an exercise in futility, with successful colonial "replacement" the only inevitable outcome.[42]

Likewise, we cannot disregard the power and persistence of Indigenous diplomacy, the ways in which Native people continued to draw settlers into networks of kinship and exchange. Cascoak endured as a site of negotiations and peace councils between English settlers and Wabanaki leaders for many decades to come. If we move to consider the nearly one hundred years of war and negotiation that followed the "First Indian War," a very different view of the relationship between Indigenous people and settlers in "New England" emerges: one which must account for the French Jesuits as well as the Puritan fathers; one which must engage with the many multifaceted alliances that formed among Indigenous people in the wake of colonization; one which acknowledges, as Baker and Reid do, that "the Wabanakis effectively won the northern extension of King Philip's War and remained a serious military threat for decades afterward," as well as a serious force of diplomacy.[43]

Most important, we cannot repress or replace the stories of Indigenous survival. We must join with tribal scholars and community-engaged historians in recovering the stories of Indigenous persistence and *adaptation* in the wake of the impacts of colonization, including these many wars. In Native planting grounds and fishing places, in executions and in enslavements, in postwar praying towns and children confined to service, colonial leaders sought to conquer and contain. But in small Native enclaves to the south, including at Pocasset and Hassanamesit, families regathered and survived. Their descendants still attest to the role of leaders like Weetamoo and James Printer, who enabled the protection of homelands and their kin. Across Wabanaki and Wôpanâak, the fabrics of kinship were and continue to be rewoven. In the reclamation of relations and in the expanse of northern refuges remain—the people who would not be contained.

NOTES

INTRODUCTION

1. Edward Winslow, *Good News From New England* (1924), ed. Kelly Wisecup (Amherst, MA: University of Massachusetts Press, 2014), 79–82. Kelly Wisecup, *Medical Encounters* (Amherst, MA: University of Massachusetts Press, 2013), 77–9. Matt Cohen, *The Networked Wilderness* (Minneapolis: University of Minnesota Press, 2010), 69–70, 75. Note that the Pocasset Mattapoisett (Swansea and Somerset, Massachusetts) is distinct from the contemporary Massachusetts town of Mattapoisett, east of Dartmouth. For maps and connections, http://ourbelovedkin.com/awikhigan/introduction

2. Winslow, *Good News*, 80. Even the order of words was transposed, with the suffix "skwa" always appearing at the end of an Algonquian word, to denote female. On *saunkskwa*, see ch. 1.

3. Winslow, *Good News*, 63, 80, 86. William Bradford, *Of Plymouth Plantation* (New York: Random House, 1981), 97–9. *Mourt's Relation: A Journal of the Pilgrims at Plymouth* (1622), ed. Dwight B. Heath (Bedford, MA: Applewood Books, 1986), 73–6.

4. Colin Calloway, *Dawnland Encounters* (Hanover, NH: University Press of New England, 1991), 27, 44. Jean O'Brien, *Firsting and Lasting: Writing Indians out of Existence in New England* (Minneapolis: University of Minnesota Press, 2010), 55–6. Patrick Wolfe, "Settler Colonialism and the Elimination of the Native," *Journal of Genocide Research* 8, no. 4 (2006): 387–409.

5. Nathaniel Saltonstall, *The Present State of New England With Respect to the Indian War* (London: Dorman Newman, 1675), 3. "Indian Deed," *Proceedings of the Massachusetts Historical Society* 48 (May 1915): 492–3. Francis Jennings, *The Invasion of America: Indians, Colonialism, and the Cant of Conquest* (Chapel Hill, NC: University of North Carolina Press, 2010), 128. Weetamoo is curiously absent from twentieth-century analyses of King Philip's War. Jennings mentioned Weetamoo only briefly in the body of his book and once in an erroneous footnote. Jill Lepore refers to Weetamoo twice in the landmark *The Name of War: King Philip's War and the Origins of American Identity* (New York: Knopf, 1998), and then only parenthetically. James

Drake's detailed *King Philip's War: Civil War in New England, 1675–1676* (Amherst, MA: University of Massachsetts Press, 1999) mentions Weetamoo fleetingly, at the initial outbreak of war. George Bodge, Douglas Leach, and Russell Bourne acknowledge Weetamoo's participation in the war, but they construct her in conformity with European gender conventions and downplay her leadership role, especially after the Pocasset swamp fight. However, Bourne does refer to Plymouth Court cases in which she participated. See George Madison Bodge, *Soldiers in King Philip's War* (Boston: Rockwell and Churchill, 1906); Douglas Edward Leach, *Flintlock and Tomahawk: New England in King Philip's War* (New York: Macmillan, 1958); Russell Bourne, *The Red King's Rebellion* (New York: Atheneum, 1990). Weetamoo does not appear at all in William Simmons's *Spirit of the New England Tribes: Indian History and Folklore, 1620–1984* (Hanover, NH: University Press of New England, 1986). *King Philip's War: The History and Legacy of America's Forgotten Conflict* (Woodstock, VT: Countryman Press, 2000) by Eric B. Schultz and Michael J. Tougias, although well written and especially valuable for its geographical focus, follows Leach's lead in regard to Weetamoo. Jenny Pulsipher's *Subjects unto the Same King: Indians, English, and the Contest for Authority in Colonial New England* (Philadelphia: University of Pennsylvania Press, 2005) refers to Weetamoo once in the body and once in a footnote. Even more surprisingly, Ann M. Little's *Abraham in Arms: War and Gender in Colonial New England* (Philadelphia: University of Pennsylvania Press, 2007) mentions Weetamoo only briefly, once acknowledging her participation in the war, and then in a limited reading of Rowlandson's representation.

6. Keith Basso, *Wisdom Sits in Places: Landscape and Language among the Western Apache* (Albuquerque: University of New Mexico Press, 1996), 6. Lisa Brooks, *The Common Pot: The Recovery of Native Space in the Northeast* (Minneapolis: University of Minneapolis Press, 2008), 245.

7. Anonymous, *A True Account of the Most Considerable Occurrences that have happened in the Warre between the English and the Indians in New-England* (London: Benjamin Billingsley, 1676), 5. Lepore, *Name*, 126, 136–48. Mary White Rowlandson, *The Sovereignty and Goodness of God: With Related Documents*, ed. Neal Salisbury (Boston: Bedford Books, 1997), 33–4, 49, 99, 122, 135.

8. Lepore, *Name*, 126. Pauline Turner Strong, *Captive Selves, Captivating Others* (Boulder, CO: Westview Press, 2000), 12. Margaret Ellen Newell, *Brethren by Nature: New England Indians, Colonists, and the Origins of American Slavery* (Ithaca, NY: Cornell University Press, 2015), 4.

9. Lepore, *Name*, 136–48. Daniel Gookin, "An Historical Account of the Doings and Sufferings of the Christian Indians in New England," in *Transactions and Collections of the American Antiquarian Society* 2 (Cambridge, MA: American Antiquarian Society, 1836), 455–9, 475–7, 486–91. Salisbury, ed., *Sovereignty*, 68–75.

10. Salisbury, ed., *Sovereignty*, 55.

11. O'Brien, *Firsting*, xxi–xxiii, 55–6. Lepore, *Name*, 119–223.

12. On Hawaiian history, see, for example, Noenoe K. Silva, *Aloha Betrayed: Native Hawaiian Resistance to American Colonialism* (Durham, NC: Duke University Press

2004); Noelani Arista, "Histories of Unequal Measure: Euro-American Encounters with Hawaiian Governance and Law, 1793–1827" (PhD diss., Brandeis University, 2010). On the Wôpanâak language, see the Wôpanâak Language Reclamation Project website: www.wlrp.org. See also Anna Ash, Jessie Little Doe Fermino, and Ken Hale, "Diversity in Local Language Maintenance and Restoration: A Reason for Optimism," in *The Green Book of Language Revitalization in Practice*, ed. Kenneth Hale (Boston: Brill Academic Publishing, 2001); Jennifer Weston and Barbara Sorenson, "Awakening a Sleeping Language on Cape Cod: The Wampanoag Language Reclamation Project," *Cultural Survival Quarterly* 35.4 (2011). On Wôpanâak texts, see Ives Goddard and Kathleen Bragdon, *Native Writings in Massachusett* (Philadelphia: The American Philosophical Society, 1988).

13. Pulsipher, *Subjects*, 128, 302, n. 44. Benjamin Church, *Entertaining History of King Philip's War* (Boston: B. Green, 1716). As Lepore notes of Church's "History," "This as-told-to, after-the-fact memoir is the single most unreliable account of one of the most well-documented wars of the Colonial period," although that has not prevented historians from relying on it as a primary source. Jill Lepore, "Plymouth Rocked," *New Yorker*, April 24, 2006. http://www.newyorker.com/archive/2006/04/24/060424crat_atlarge. Thanks to Christine DeLucia for recommending the review.

14. Lepore, *Name*, xv, xix, 48–9. Mary Beth Norton, *In the Devil's Snare: The Salem Witchcraft Crisis of 1692* (New York: Vintage Books, 2003), 11. Owaneco and Ben Uncas, "The Complaint and Prayer of Owaneco and Ben Uncas, 1700," in "Land Disputes between the Colony of Connecticut and the Mohegan Indians, 1736–1739," Ayer ms 459, Edward Ayer Manuscript Collection, Newberry Library, Chicago. Lepore does raise the question, "What would the Indians have called it?" However, her answer was mainly speculative, raised during a time when few historians turned to Indigenous language sources.

15. I use the Western Abenaki term for "human beings" here, although this is common to many Native languages. See Joseph Bruchac, *Roots of Survival* (Golden, CO: Fulcrum, 1996), 19–31, 179–94; Russell Handsman and Trudie Lamb Richmond, "Confronting Colonialism: The Mahican and Schaghticoke Peoples and Us," in *Making Alternative Histories: The Practice of Archaeology and History in Non-Western Settings*, ed. Peter R. Schmidt and Thomas C. Patterson (Santa Fe: School for Advanced Research Press, 1996), 87–117; Joseph Laurent, *New Familiar Abenaki and English Dialogues* (Quebec: L. Brousseau, 1884), 54, 58–9; Mohegan Tribe and Stephanie Fielding, "A Modern Mohegan Dictionary" (Uncasville, CT: Mohegan Tribe, 2006), 18, http://rmc.library.cornell.edu/collections/MoheganDictionary.pdf. "Language Keepers" (public event), featuring Wabanaki and Wôpanâak language teachers, including Carol Dana, Jessie Little Doe Baird, Roger Paul, Jesse Bruchac, and Gabe Paul, held at Harvard University in November 2010 and University of Maine, Farmington, in April 2012.

16. Joseph Aubery and Stephen Laurent, *Father Aubery's French Abenaki Dictionary* (Portland, ME: Chisholm Brothers, 1995), 288. Gordon M. Day, *Western Abenaki Dictionary* (Hull, PQ: Canadian Museum of Civilization, 1995), 1: 203–4, 2:437, 2:142.

"War," "*madôbakw*," "*migaka*," Western Abenaki Online Dictionary, www.western-abenaki.com. Winslow, *Good News*, 63, 106. Goddard and Bragdon, *Native Writings*, 3. Thanks to Jonathan Perry for discussion of the terms for "warrior."

17. Peter Hulme, quoted in Amy E. Den Ouden, *Beyond Conquest: Native Peoples and the Struggle for History in New England* (Lincoln, NE: University of Nebraska Press, 2005), 11.

18. Samuel Gardner Drake, *The Book of the Indians (BOI)* (Boston: Antiquarian Bookstore, 1841), 3:7–8.

19. Increase Mather, "A Brief History of the Warr with the Indians in New England," in *So Dreadfull a Judgment: Puritan Responses to King Philip's War 1676–1677*, ed. Richard Slotkin and James Folsom (Middletown, CT: Wesleyan Press 1978), 86.

20. Diana Taylor, *The Archive and the Repertoire: Performing Cultural Memory in the Americas* (Durham, NC: Duke University Press, 2003). Basso, *Wisdom*, 6. See also Yael Ben-Zvi, "Ethnography and the Production of Foreignness in Indian Captivity Narratives," *American Indian Quarterly* 32, no. 1 (Winter 2008): 5–32; James Cox, *Muting White Noise: Native American and European American Novel Traditions* (Norman, OK: University of Oklahoma Press, 2012); Daniel Heath Justice, *Our Fire Survives the Storm: A Cherokee Literary History* (Minneapolis: University of Minnesota Press, 2006); Robert Warrior, *The People and the Word* (Minneapolis: University of Minnesota Press, 2005), 3, 84; Craig Womack, *Red on Red: Native American Literary Separatism* (Minneapolis: University of Minnesota Press, 1999).

21. On colonization and objectivity, see Linda Tuhiwai Smith, *Decolonizing Methodologies: Research and Indigenous People* (London: Zed Books, 2012), 22, 39, 119.

PROLOGUE: CASKOAK

1. Christopher Levett, *A Voyage into New England* (1623), in *Maine in the Age of Discovery*, ed. Emerson Baker (Portland, ME: Maine Historical Society, 1988), 42, 46. Joseph Nicolar, *Life and Traditions of the Red Man* (1893), ed. Annette Kolodny (Durham, NC: Duke University Press, 2007), 199. Fannie Eckstorm,"Indian Place-Names of the Penobscot Valley and the Maine Coast," *Maine Bulletin* 44, no. 4 (1941): 168. Lisa T. Brooks and Cassandra M. Brooks, "The Reciprocity Principle and ITEK: Understanding the Significance of Indigenous Protest on the Presumpscot," *International Journal of Critical Indigenous Studies* 3, no. 2 (2010): 11–28. Levett's mission was "to locate a site for a 6,000-acre grant he had received from the Council of New England" and to investigate unregulated trade and related violence on the Maine coast. See Kenneth Morrison, *The Embattled Northeast: The Elusive Ideal of Alliance in Abenaki-Euramerican Relations* (Berkeley: University of California Press, 1984), 38–39. For maps, documents, images and connections, see http://ourbelovedkin.com/awikhigan/prologue.

2. Levett, *Voyage*, 42. Emerson Baker, "Finding the Almouchiquois: Native American Families, Territories, and Land Sales in Southern Maine," *Ethnohistory* 51, no. 1 (2004): 73–100. Brooks and Brooks, "Reciprocity Principle," 12–15. Emerson Baker and John Reid, "Amerindian Power in the Early Modern Northeast: A Reappraisal," *Wil-*

liam and Mary Quarterly 61, no. 1 (2004): 3, 11–12. Joseph Bruchac, *Roots of Survival* (Golden, CO: Fulcrum Publishing, 1996), 30. See also Lisa Brooks, *The Common Pot: The Recovery of Native Space in the Northeast* (Minneapolis: University of Minnesota Press, 2008), esp. 14–25. Colin Calloway, *The Western Abenakis of Vermont, 1600–1800: War, Migration, and the Survival of an Indian People* (Norman, OK: University of Oklahoma Press, 1990). William Cronon, *Changes in the Land: Indians, Colonists, and the Ecology of New England* (New York: Hill and Wang, 1983). David Ghere, "The 'Disappearance' of the Abenaki in Western Maine: Political Organization and Ethnocentric Assumptions," in *After King Philip's War: Presence and Persistence in Indian New England*, ed. Colin Calloway (Hanover, NH: University Press of New England, 1997), 72–89. Morrison, *Embattled*. Alice Nash, "The Abiding Frontier: Family, Gender and Religion in Wabanaki History, 1600–1763" (PhD diss., Columbia University, 1997), esp. 174–9. Nicolar, *Life*, 105–6, 134–9. Neal Salisbury, *Manitou and Providence: Indians, Europeans, and the Making of New England, 1500–1643* (New York: Oxford University Press, 1982), 30–49. John A. Strong, "Algonquian Women as Sunksquaws and Caretakers of the Soil: The Documentary Evidence in the Seventeenth Century Records," in *Native American Women in Literature and Culture*, ed. Susan Castillo and Victor DaRosa (Porto, Portugal: Fernando Pessoa University Press, 1997), 196–200. For the term *saunkskwa*, see ch. 1.

3. Baker, "Almouchiquois," 73–100. Brooks, *Common Pot*, 1–50. Brooks and Brooks, "Reciprocity," 15. Margaret M. Bruchac, "Earthshapers and Placemakers: Algonkian Indian Stories and the Landscape," in *Indigenous Archaeologies: Politics and Practice*, ed. Claire Smith and Martin Wobst (London: Routledge Press, 2003), 56–80. Calloway, *Western Abenakis*. William Cronon, *Changes*, 61–5. Morrison, *Embattled*, 29–31. Nash, "Abiding Frontier," 151, 196–7. Salisbury, *Manitou*, 19–49, 62, 77–8. David Stewart-Smith, "The Pennacook Indians and the New England Frontier, 1604–1733," (PhD diss., Union Institute, 1998), 52–61.

4. Emerson W. Baker, et al., eds. *American Beginnings: Exploration, Culture and Cartography in the Land of Norumbega* (Lincoln, NE: University of Nebraska Press, 1994), 132–46, 162, 173–7, 192–5, 203–8. Brooks, *Common Pot*, 3–7, 20–4, 57–8. Morrison, *Embattled*, 12–41, 72–5.

5. Levett, *Voyage*, 44. Morrison, *Embattled*, 29. For example, when the Jesuit Sebastien Rasle became a part of a Wabanaki extended family and sought to return to the college at Quebec, his "mother" demanded, "you were of our cabin . . . Why then did you leave us?" Morrison, *The Solidarity of Kin: Ethnohistory, Religious Studies, and the Algonkian-French Religious Encounter* (Albany, NY: State University of New York Press, 2002), 76.

6. Morrison, *Embattled*, 13–20. Nicolar, *Life*, 105–7. C. F. Waterman, *Fishing in America* (New York: Holt, Rinehart and Winston, 1975), 30–49.

7. Levett, *Voyage*, 45. Morrison, *Embattled*, 76, 102. Brooks and Brooks, "Reciprocity," 15. Baker, "Almouchiquois," 83. Nash, "Abiding Frontier," 174. Samuel Gardner Drake, *The Book of the Indians* (Boston: Antiquarian Bookstore, 1841), 2:48. William Willis, *History of Portland from 1632 to 1864* (Portland, ME: Bailey and Noyes, 1865), 35–6.

8. *York Deeds* (Portland, ME: John T. Hull, 1887), 1:83. *York Deeds* (Portland, ME: John T. Hull, 1892), 8:86. Francis Small's deposition (manuscript), May 10, 1683, Pejebscot Papers 6:67, Collections of Maine Historical Society. Deed from Warrabitta and Nanateonett to George Munjoy," June 4, 1666, and "Indenture . . . between Jhone an Indian Sister to Scaterey Gussett . . . and Anthony Brackett," January 15, 1670, Waldo Papers, box 1, coll. 34, folder 1/1, Collections of Maine Historical Society. F.S. Reiche,"Past activities at the mouth of Presumpscot River," Special Collections, Maine Historical Society. Leonard Chapman's Scrapbook: "Stroudwater," Coll 3343, Collections of Maine Historical Society. Baker, *Almouchiquois*, 83–6. Amy McDonald, ed., *Guide to the Presumpscot River: Its History, Ecology, and Recreational Uses* (Portland, ME: Presumpscot River Watch, 1994), 4–6. Sybil Noyes, Charles Libby, and Walter Davis, *Genealogical Dictionary of Maine and New Hampshire* (Baltimore, MD: Genealogical Publishing, 1979), 547. Brooks and Brooks, "Reciprocity," 15–16. Nash, "Abiding Frontier," 174, 181. Willis, *Portland*, 102–110. Eckstorm, "Place Names," 160. Joseph Aubery and Stephen Laurent, *Father Aubery's French Abenaki Dictionary* (Portland, ME: Chisholm Brothers, 1995), 400. On the complexity of deeds on the Wabanaki coast, see Emerson Baker, "'A Scratch with a Bear's Paw': Anglo-Indian Land Deeds in Early Maine," *Ethnohistory* 36, no. 3 (1989), and Nash, "Abiding Frontier," esp. introduction and ch. 3.

9. *York Deeds*, 2:114. Baker, "Almouchiquois," 82–6. Nash, "Abiding Frontier," 148–189. William Southgate, "History of Scarborough 1633–1783," in *Collections of the Maine Historical Society* (Portland, ME: Maine Historical Society, 1853), 1st ser., 3:99–177. Eckstorm, "Place Names," 171. Mary B. Pickard, "Scarborough: They Called it Owascoag," Maine Memory Network, http://scarborough.mainememory.net/page/1608/display.html.

10. *York Deeds*, 2:114. Morrison, *Embattled*, 29–31. Baker and Reid, "Amerindian Power," 77–106. Nash, "Abiding Frontier," 154. Brooks and Brooks, "Reciprocity," 16. Southgate, "Scarborough," 101.

11. Gordon M. Day, *Western Abenaki Dictionary* (Hull, PQ: Canadian Museum of Civilization, 1995), 2:173. Eckstorm, "Place Names," 170–1. Robin Wall Kimmerer, *Braiding Sweetgrass* (Minneapolis: Milkweed Editions, 2013), ix.

12. Nicolar, *Life*, 105, 134–9.

13. Nash, "Abiding Frontier," 153.

14. Nash, "Abiding Frontier," 186. Nicolar, *Life*, 105, 139.

1. NAMUMPUM, "OUR BELOVED KINSWOMAN"

1. "Indian Deed," *Proceedings of the Massachusetts Historical Society* 48: 492–3 (May 1915). On *awikhigan*, see Lisa Brooks, *The Common Pot: The Recovery of Native Space in the Northeast* (Minneapolis: University of Minnesota Press, 2008), 1–50. For maps, documents, images, and connections, see http://ourbelovedkin.com/awikhigan/chapter1.

2. Arthur Sherman Phillips, *The Phillips History of Fall River* (Fascicle 1) (Fall River, MA: Dover Press, 1941), 4–10, 95–6, 109. Arthur Phillips, "Pocasset and the Pocassets,"

Dec. 15, 1931, Rhode Island Historical Society (manuscript), 3–4. Henry M. Fenner, *History of Fall River* (New York: F. T. Smiley Publishing, 1906), 8–9. Kathleen Bragdon, *Native People of Southern New England, 1500–1650* (Norman, OK: University of Oklahoma Press, 1996), 56–7, 64, 121, 127. William Cronon, *Changes in the Land: Indians, Colonists, and the Ecology of New England* (New York: Hill and Wang, 1983), 27–8, 30–31. Eric Schultz and Michael Tougias, *King Philip's War: The History and Legacy of America's Forgotten Conflict* (Woodstock, VT: Countryman Press, 2000), 239. Ebenezer Peirce, *Brief Sketches of Freetown, Fall River and Fairhaven* (Boston: Dean Dudley, 1872), 17. Jeremy Dupertuis Bangs, *Indian Deeds: Land Transactions in Plymouth Colony, 1620–1691* (Boston: New England Historic Genealogical Society, 2008), 342. Laurie Lee Weinstein, "Indian vs. Colonist: Competition for Land in 17th Century Plymouth Colony" (PhD diss., Southern Methodist University, 1983), 20, 27, 76, 151–63, 200–2. *Mourt's Relation: A Journal of the Pilgrims at Plymouth*, ed. Dwight B. Heath (Bedford, MA: Appleton Books, 1963), 27. "Quacut," Francis Joseph O'Brien Jr., and Rhode Island USGenWeb Project, "American Indian Place Names in Rhode Island," http://rootsweb.ancestry.com/~rigenweb/IndianPlaceNames.html. For the document and associated map see http://ourbelovedkin.com/awikhigan/nonaquaket.

3. For wampum and writing, see Brooks, *Common Pot*.
4. Here, using Algonquian kinship terminology, "brother" means male cousin.
5. See, for example, Joseph Laurent, *New Familiar Abenaki and English Dialogues* (Quebec: L. Brousseau, 1884); Neal Salisbury, *Manitou and Providence: Indians, Europeans, and the Making of New England, 1500–1643* (New York: Oxford University Press, 1982), 41–3. On "Ndakinna" as an "exclusive" term, see Brooks, *Common Pot*, 202, 251; Laurent, *Dialogues*, 54, 58–9.
6. Cronon, *Changes*, 59–64. Bragdon, *Native People*, 46–7, 138–9. Laura Liebman, ed., *Experience Mayhew's Indian Converts* (Amherst, MA: University of Massachusetts Press, 2008), 51–2. Weinstein, "Indian vs. Colonist," 74. Salisbury, *Manitou*, 42–3. Brooks, *Common Pot*, 53, 68–9. David Stewart-Smith, "The Pennacook Indians and the New England Frontier, 1604–1733" (PhD diss., Union Institute, 1998), 24–9, 74–5.
7. Paul Campbell Research Notes, mss 369, folder 5, Rhode Island Historical Society.
8. *Mourt's Relation*, 56–7. *Plymouth Town Records* (Plymouth, MA: Avery and Doten, 1889), 1:36. Nathaniel Bradstreet Shurtleff, *Records of the Colony of New Plymouth, in New England (PCR)* (Boston: William White, 1855), 1:133. Mary Beth Norton, *Founding Mothers and Fathers: Gendered Power and the Forming of American Society* (New York: Alfred A. Knopf, 1996), 9, 12–13. Samuel Gardner Drake, *The Book of the Indians (BOI)* (Boston: Antiquarian Bookstore, 1841), 2:22. Phillips, *Fall River*, 1:23, 97. Virginia DeJohn Anderson, *Creatures of Empire: How Domestic Animals Transformed Early America* (Oxford: Oxford University Press, 2006), 53, 62–5, 166, 210. Cronon, *Changes*, 31, 58–68, 71. James Ronda, "Red and White at the Bench," *Essex Institute Historical Collections*, 110 (1974), 201–2. Norton, *Founding*, 12–13. H. Morse Payne, "New England Seventeenth Century Land Strategy," *NEARA Journal* 31, no. 2 (1997): 87–94. Salisbury, *Manitou*, 114–9. Weinstein, "Indian vs. Colonist," 120–6. *Native American Archaeology in Rhode Island* (Providence, RI: Rhode

Island Historical Preservation and Heritage Commission, 2002), 13, 14, 56. "Sapowett," "Espowet," American Indian Place Names in Rhode Island, http://rootsweb.ancestry .com/~rigenweb/IndianPlaceNames.html.

9. Anderson, *Creatures*, 215.

10. Rhode Island Historical Society, *Early Records of the Town of Portsmouth* (*Portsmouth Records*) (Providence, RI: E. L. Freeman and Sons, 1901), 16, 21, 47.

11. John Russell Barlett, *Records of the Colony of Rhode Island and Providence Plantations* (Providence, RI: A. Crawford Greene and Brother, 1856–65), 1:45–51. *Portsmouth Records*, 55–6, 64, 81. Samuel Greene Arnold, *History of the State of Rhode Island and Providence Plantations* (Providence, RI: Preston, 1894), 1:69–71, 125. Phillips, *Fall River*, 1:26–8. Glenn LaFantasie, *The Correspondence of Roger Williams* (Providence, RI: Brown/Rhode Island Historical Society, 1988), 1:163. *Archaeology in Rhode Island*, 27. Salisbury, *Manitou*, 228–9.

12. Norton, *Founding*, 358; see also ch. 1, 6, and 7. Arnold, *History*, 1:51–71. David D. Hall, ed., *The Antinomian Controversy* (Durham, NC: Duke University Press, 1990). Lyle Koehler, "The Case of the America Jezebels: Anne Hutchinson and Female Agitation during the Years of Antinomian Turmoil, 1636–1640," *William and Mary Quarterly*, Third Series, 31, no. 1 (Jan. 1974): 55–78. Samuel Atkins Eliot, *A History of Cambridge, Massachusetts, 1630–1913* (Cambridge, MA: The Cambridge Tribune, 1913), 42–3.

13. Norton, *Founding*, 374. Arnold, *History*, 1:69–71. Edward H. West, "Portsmouth, Rhode Island, before 1800," in *History of Portsmouth, 1638–1936* (Portsmouth, RI: J. Green, 1936), 9. *Portsmouth Records*, 1–2, 6, 23.

14. Norton, *Founding*, 10, 319, 392.

15. Cronon, *Changes*, 44, 75. Jane Mt. Pleasant, "A New Paradigm for Pre-Columbian Agriculture in North America," *Early American Studies* 13, no. 2 (Spring 2015). For maps, images, and connections, see http://ourbelovedkin.com/awikhigan/pocasset _pokanoket-placenames.

16. Arnold, *History*, 1:127–9, 135. *Records of the Colony of Rhode Island and Providence Plantations* (*RI Records*), 1: 53–64. *Portsmouth Records*, 35. Weinstein, "Indian vs. Colonist," 120–5, 130–1, 135–6. Cronon, *Changes*, 71–7, 128–9. Anderson, *Creatures*, 18, 144, 153–5, 158–9. Norton, *Founding*, 4–10. Darrett Rutman, *Husbandmen of Plymouth: Farms and Villages in the Old Colony, 1620–1692* (Boston: Beacon Press, 1967), 50.

17. Roger Williams, *A Key into the Language of America* (1643) (Bedford, MA: Applewood Books, 1997), 141. Edward Winslow, *Good Newes from New England* (Bedford, MA: Applewood Books, 1996), 33. Liebman, ed., *Indian Converts*, 56–8. Salisbury, *Manitou*, 36–40. John A. Strong, "Algonquian Women as Sunksquaws and Caretakers of the Soil: The Documentary Evidence in the Seventeenth Century Records," in *Native American Women in Literature and Culture*, ed. Susan Castillo and Victor DaRosa (Porto, Portugal: Fernando Pessoa University Press, 1997), 196–200. Norton, *Founding*, 4, 12, 360–1, 366, 398. For example, Mistress Anne Hutchinson's behavior was particularly threatening *because* she was a high-ranking woman, deriving her status as "Mistress" from her father, a minister in England, and her husband, a merchant and magistrate.

18. For interpretation of "saunkskwa," "sachem," and "sagamore" I am indebted to Roger Paul, who also helped me to see them as English variations of the same basic leadership term, drawn from Algonquian dialects; to Jessie Little Doe Baird; and to Melissa Tantaquidgeon Zobel and Lynn Malerba. (Roger Paul, personal communication, Orono, Maine, April 30, 2011; Jessie Little Doe Baird, "Wôpanâee Neekônuhshâeenun," presentation at the Harvard University Native American Program Commencement Dinner, May 26, 2011, Cambridge, MA; Melissa Tantaquidgeon Zobel, presentation for FM90j, Harvard University, Cambridge, MA, April 11, 2011; Lynn Malerba, "Native American Female Leadership" panel, University of Connecticut, Avery Point, March 17, 2011.) See also Melissa Tantaquidgeon Zobel (formerly Fawcett), *Medicine Trail: The Life and Lessons of Gladys Tantiquidgeon* (Tucson: University of Arizona Press, 2000), 21; and Strong, "Algonquian Women," 196–200.

19. Ebenezer Peirce, *Indian History, Biography and Genealogy* (North Abington, MA: Zerviah Gould Mitchell, 1878), 238–40. *Rhode Island Land Evidences* (Providence, RI: Rhode Island Historical Society, 1921), 1:145–6. "Massachusetts Land Records, 1620–1986," images, *FamilySearch* (https://familysearch.org/ark:/61903/3:1:3 QS7-99Z7-GL7?cc=2106411&wc=MCBR-PWY%3A361612701%2C362501701: 22 May 2014); Plymouth > image 268 of 677; county courthouses and offices, Massachusetts. "Massachusetts Land Records, 1620–1986," images, Family Search, (https:// familysearch.org/ark:/61903/3:1:3QS7-89Z7-G27?cc=2106411&wc=MCBR -PWY%3A361612701%2C362501701 : 22 May 2014), Plymouth > image 269 of 677; county courthouses and offices, Massachusetts. Richard Bowen, *Early Rehoboth: Documented Historical Studies of Families and Events in this Plymouth Colony Township* (Rehoboth, MA: Rumford Press, 1945), 1:82–4. Ebenezer Peirce, "The Original Owners and Early Settlers of Freetown and Assonet," *Collections of the Old Colony Historical Society* (Taunton, MA: C. A. Hack, 1882), 3:114–27. See also Bangs, *Deeds*, 291–3. For maps, images and connections, see http://ourbelovedkin.com/awikhigan/pocasset _pokanoket-placenames and http://ourbelovedkin.com/awikhigan/namumpum.

20. Peirce, *Indian History*, 238–9. "Tatapanum" may have even been a phrase akin to "this woman," as "phanem" (pronounced pa(h)anem) in the related Western Abenaki language, means "woman."

21. "Massachusetts Land Records, 1620–1986," image 268. "Massachusetts Land Records, 1620–1986," image 269.

22. *PCR*, 1:143. Anderson, *Creatures*, 154–5. Cronon, *Changes*, 128, 142–6. Weinstein, "Indian vs. Colonist," 151–60. Thomas Bicknell, *Sowams: With Ancient Records of Sowams and Parts Adjacent* (New Haven, CT: Associated Publishers of American Records, 1908), 173–4. Samuel Hopkins Emery, *History of Taunton, Massachusetts, From its Settlement to the Present Time* (Syracuse, NY: D. Mason and Co., 1893), 28, 55, 68–9, 95, 104. James Edward Seaver, "The Two Settlements of Taunton, Massachusetts," in *Collections of the Old Colony Historical Society* (Taunton, MA: C. A. Hack, 1899), 7:106–41. Henry Williams, "Was Elizabeth Poole the First Purchaser of the Territory, and Foundress, of Taunton?" in *Collections of the Old Colony Historical Society* (Taunton: C. A. Hack, 1880), 2:37–113. For maps, images, and connections, see http:// ourbelovedkin.com/awikhigan/plymouth-patuxet.

23. *Mourt's Relation*, 64. Fenner, *History of Fall River*, 8. Peirce, *Brief Sketches*, 17. Phillips, *Fall River*, 3:9. Weinstein, "Indian vs. Colonist," 151–62, 200–2.

24. PCR 3:167. Anderson, *Creatures*, 67–70, 145, 149–53, 159. Cronon, *Changes*, 77, 129, 134, 138–40. Weinstein, "Indian vs. Colonist," 56, 111, 120–141, 147, 237. Mt. Pleasant, "Paradigm," 381, 391–9. Rose T. Briggs, "The Court Houses of Plymouth," Pilgrim Society Note, Series One, No. 17, May 1966 at http://www.pilgrimhallmuseum.org/pdf/Court_Houses_Plymouth.pdf. Ann Marie Plane, *Colonial Intimacies: Indian Marriage in Early New England* (Ithaca, NY: Cornell University Press, 2000), 78–9.

25. *Mourt's Relation*, 64.

26. Weinstein, "Indian vs. Colonist," 111, 129. See also Norton, *Founding*, 5–15; Cronon, *Changes*; Anderson, *Creatures*.

27. Cronon, *Changes*, 37–53. Charles Robinson, *Asleep Beneath the Meadows* (Providence, RI: Universal Press, 1992), 45, 76. Duane Hamilton Hurd, *History of Bristol County, Massachusetts, with Biographical Sketches* (Philadelphia: J. W. Lewis, 1883), 214–5. *Archaeology in Rhode Island*, 14. Massachusetts Historical Commission, MHC Reconnaissance Survey Town Report: Dighton (1981), http://www.sec.state.ma.us/mhc/mhcpdf/townreports/SE-Mass/dig.pdf. Bragdon, *Native People*, 50, 108. Eva Butler, "Algonkian Culture and the Use of Maize," *Bulletin of the Archaeological Society of Connecticut* 22 (1948): 1–39. Cronon, *Changes*, 37–53. Edmund Burke Delabarre, "Early Interest in Dighton Rock," in *Publications of the Colonial Society of Massachusetts, Transactions, 1915–16* (Boston: The Society, 1917), 18:243–4. Weinstein, "Indian vs. Colonist," 53, 55–6. Samuel De Champlain, "Maine and Massachusetts" (1605), in *Sailors Narratives of Voyages Along the New England Coast*, ed. George Winship (Boston: Houghton, Mifflin and Company, 1905), 79–80, 83, 87. *Mourt's Relation*, 34, 41. William Wood, *New England's Prospect* (Amherst, MA: University of Massachusetts Press, 1993), 113. Martin Pring, "Plymouth Harbor" (1603), in *Sailors Narratives*, 58–9. Giovanni Da Verrazano, "Narragansett Bay" (1524), in *Sailors Narratives*, 139.

28. Cronon, *Changes*, 13, 28–9, 47–51, 57, 90–1, 118–9, 145–6. Anderson, *Creatures*, 47–8, 154–5. William A. Patterson III and Kenneth E. Sassaman, "Indian Fires in the Prehistory of New England," in *Holocene Human Ecology in Northeastern North America*, ed. George P. Nicholas (New York: Plenum Publishing Corporation, 1988), 107–22. *Archaeology in Rhode Island*, 14.

29. Francis Baylies, *A Historical Memoir of the Colony of New Plymouth* (Boston: Hilliard, Gray, Little, and Wilkins, 1830), 2:17, 20, 67–69. Bowen, *Early Rehoboth*, 79–80. Peirce, *Indian History*, 238–9.

30. PCR, 2:10–11, 3:84, 4:18–19. Bangs, *Deeds*, 63–5, 74–8, 238–9, 247. Bowen, *Early Rehoboth*, 79. Bicknell, *Barrington*, 42. Bicknell, *Sowams*, 125, 142–3, 152. Cronon, *Changes*, 71. Weinstein, "Indian vs. Colonist," 175, 208–9. Ralph V. Wood Jr., *Francis Cooke of the Mayflower: The First Five Generations* (Rockport, ME: Picton Press, 1996), 12:12–13. Payne, "Land Strategy," 87–94.

31. Weinstein, "Indian vs. Colonist," 74, 174–5, 182–4, 207, 244–5. Bragdon, *Native People*, 137–9. Cronon, *Changes*, 59–75. Salisbury, *Manitou*, 42–50, 116. Yasuhide Kawashima, *Igniting King Philip's War: The John Sassamon Murder Trial* (Lawrence, KS:

University Press of Kansas, 2001), 46–7, 63–4. Paul Robeson, "One Island, Two Places: Archaeology, Memory, and Meaning in a Rhode Island Town," in *Interpretations of Native North American Life: Material Contribution to Ethnohistory*, ed. Michael Nassaney and Eric Johnson (Gainesville, FL: University Press of Florida, 2000), 408. Bangs, *Deeds*, 75–7, 263–72. PCR, 2:49–50. Bicknell, *Sowams*, 26–7, 36–7. Leonard Bliss, *History of Rehoboth* (Boston: Otis Broaders and Co., 1836), 1, 22–3.

32. Bangs, *Deeds*, 76–77, 263–5, 293–6. PCR, 3:164–5. Plymouth men on the 1652 deed included John Winslow (Josiah's uncle), Thomas Southworth, John Cooke, and Myles Standish. Ekatebacke does not appear anywhere else in the records, suggesting this was not a man with a leadership role. Morris and Weetamoo appeared on different days, June 7 and 9, 1659. Morris did not formally accept Plymouth's offer and submit to their authority until the following spring.

33. PCR, 3:167, 192. Bangs, *Deeds*, 269–70. Anderson, *Creatures*, 160, 192, 223. Bicknell, *Barrington*, 38, 43. Bicknell, *Sowams*, 161, 174–5. Bliss, *History of Rehoboth*, 1–7. Cronon, *Changes*, 131–2, 134–5, 138. Guy Mannering Fessenden, *The History of Warren, Rhode Island, from the Earliest Times* (Providence, RI: H. H. Brown, 1845), 57. Liebman, *Indian Converts*, 46–55. Ronda, "Red and White," 208–9. Weinstein, "Indian vs. Colonist," 174–5, 182–4, 188, 208–11, 228, 244–5. Wright, *History of Swansea*, 23, 47, 51, 74.

34. Strong, "Algonquian Women," 196–200.

35. Norton, *Founding*, 72–3, 83–4, 139. Plane, *Colonial Intimacies*, 68.

34. Plane, *Colonial Intimacies*, 5.

36. Plane, *Colonial Intimacies*, 5.

37. Dennis Connole, *Indians of the Nipmuck Country in Southern New England, 1630–1750* (Jefferson, NC: McFarland and Company, 2001), 52–4. Nanamocomuck was released and shortly thereafter joined Wabanaki relations on the Androscoggin River.

38. PCR, 3:162. Peirce, *Indian History*, 238–40. Bangs, *Deeds*, 293–40. "Massachusetts Land Records, 1620–1986," image 269. Scott Richard Lyons, *X-Marks: Native Signatures of Assent* (Minneapolis: University of Minnesota Press, 2010), 1. Josiah Winslow and Constant Southworth were magistrates, as was Thomas Southworth, Constant's brother, who also was a grantee. Both their half-brother William Bradford and John Tisdale, a grantee, served as witnesses. John Barnes, the tavern keeper (and grantee), was on the docket of the court in June 1659, about to be disenfranchised "for his frequent and abominable drinking." PCR 3:167, 176. See also http://www.histarch.uiuc.edu/plymouth/BARNES2.htm.

39. Peirce, *Indian History*, 238–40. Bangs, *Deeds*, 297–9. Bowen, *Early Rehoboth*, 80. Hugo A. Dubuque, *Fall River Indian Reservation* (Fall River, RI: self-published, 1907), 10–11. Fenner, *History of Fall River*, 4–5, 8–10. Peirce, *Brief Sketches*, 1. Peirce, "Original Owners." Phillips, *Fall River*, 1: xv, 29, 62–96. Phillips, "Pocasset," 3–4. Weinstein, "Indian vs. Colonist," 171.

40. Phillips, *Fall River*, 3:9, 11. Bowen, *Early Rehoboth*, 80. Weinstein, "Indian vs. Colonist," 171. Friends of Historic Preservation, Report on Assonet Village Historic District, "First Settlement Period," http://www.assonetriver.com/preservation/dist_period.asp?P=COL.

41. Josiah Winslow later (falsely) claimed that their deeds had created just such a reserve at Pocasset. William Hubbard, *A History of the Indian Wars in New England*, ed. Samuel Gardner Drake (Roxbury, MA: W. E. Woodward, 1865), 66.

42. Phillips, "Pocasset," 3–4. Phillips, *Fall River*, 1: xv, 29, 62–96, 109. Fenner, *History of Fall River*, 4, 8. Weinstein, "Indian vs. Colonist," 171.

43. "Letter from Governor and Council of Massachusetts to Magnus, July 6, 1667" (manuscript), "Letter of Magnus to Governor, October 7, 1667" (manuscript), Facsimile Copies of Records of Massachusetts Archives (Photostats), #138, #139, #140, Massachusetts Historical Society. Drake, *BOI*, 3:64. Howard Chapin, *Sachems of the Narragansetts* (Providence, RI: Rhode Island Historical Society, 1931), 63, 68, 74. *Native American Archaeology in Rhode Island*, 53–4. Howard Chapin, "Queen's Fort," Rhode Island Historical Society Collections, 24:4 (1931). Sydney Rider, *The Lands of Rhode Island* (Providence, RI: printed by author, 1904), 58, 237–45.

44. *RI Records*, 1:464. Francis Jennings, *The Invasion of America: Indians, Colonialism, and the Cant of Conquest* (Chapel Hill, NC: University of North Carolina Press, 2010), 279. Chapin, *Sachems*, 68. Drake, *BOI*, 2:58. Usher Parsons and Rhode Island Historical Society, *Indian Place Names of Rhode Island* (Providence, RI: Knowles, Anthony and Co., 1861), 16. Lucinda Brockway, "Cultural Landscape Report for Cocumscussoc, Wickford, RI," (Kennebunk, ME: Past Designs, 2008). For members of the Atherton Company, see John Fredrick Martin, *Profits in the Wilderness: Entrepreneurship and the Founding of New England Towns in the Seventeenth Century* (Chapel Hill, NC: University of North Carolina Press, 1991), 62–73. For map and connections, see http://ourbelovedkin.com/awikhigan/quaiapin.

45. *RI Records*, 1:465. James N. Arnold, *The Records of the Proprietors of the Narragansett, or Fones Record* (Providence, RI: Narragansett Historical Publishing, 1894), 1:5–16. Chapin, *Sachems*, 70–4. Drake, *BOI*, 2:81. Richard Dunn, "John Winthrop, Jr. and the Narragansett Country," *William and Mary Quarterly*, Third Series, 13, no. 1 (Jan. 1956): 68–74, http://www.jstor.org/stable/1923390. Jennings, *Invasion*, 276, 279. Martin, *Profits*, 68–9. Paul Robinson, "The Struggle Within: The Indian Debate in Seventeenth-Century Narragansett Country" (PhD diss., State University of New York at Binghamton, 1990), 161–2, 179–80. The United Colonies was a quasi-legal political body led by representatives from the colonies of Massachusetts, Connecticut, New Haven, and Plymouth.

46. *RI Records*, 1:403, 418. Chapin, *Sachems*, 71. Society of Colonial Wars, *The Narragansett Mortgage: The Documents Concerning the Alien Purchases in Southern Rhode Island* (Providence, RI: E. R. Freeman Company, 1926), 35. Paul Campbell Research Notes, mss 369, folder 5, Rhode Island Historical Society. Jennings, *Invasion*, 278–86. Dunn, "Narragansett Country," 70–1, 74. David W. Conroy, "The Defense of Indian Land Rights: William Bolan and the Mohegan Case in 1743," *Proceedings of the American Antiquarian Society* 103 (1993): 403.

47. Massachusetts Archives, 30:102a.

48. Weinstein, "Indian vs. Colonist," 77. Wood, *New England's Prospect*, 38. See also Bragdon, *Native People*, 135–6; *Mourt's Relation*, 28–9; Verrazano, "Narragansett Bay," 139.

49. *RI Records*, 1:403, 418. Chapin, *Sachems*, 71.

50. Bangs, *Deeds*, 474, 476. *RI Land Evidences*, 1:189. PCR, 4:8. Durfee was then Tall-man's indentured servant.

51. Sidney Perley, *Historic Storms of New England* (Salem, MA: Salem Press Publishing and Printing, 1891), 14. William Tufts Brigham, "Historical notes on the earthquakes of New England" (Boston: Boston Society of Natural History, 1871), 3, http://www .worldcat.org/title/historical-notes-on-the-earthquakes-of-new-england/oclc/68775338. Paul Dudley, "An Account of the Several Earthquakes Which Have Happen'd in New-England," *Philosophical Transactions* (1735–6), 39:64. Anderson, *Creatures*, 54. "Earthquake," "nanamkiapoda," "nanam-," "poda-," Laurent, *Dialogues*, 17. Jelle Zeil-inga de Boer, *Stories in Stone: How Geology Influenced Connecticut History and Cul-ture* (Middletown, CT: Wesleyan Press, 2009), 132–3. Thanks to Rachel Sayet for her suggestions on sources related to the Moodus earthquakes.

52. Brigham, "Earthquakes of New England." RuthAlice Anderson, "Peter Tallman, A Footnote in History" (1984), http://www.skep.com/genealogy/PDFs/PeterTallman Footnote.pdf.

53. Anderson, "Peter Tallman." In 1652, Rhode Island passed a law prohibiting the per-manent enslavement of Africans in the colony, ordering that "no blacke mankind or white" could be held in bondage for "longer than ten years." *RI Records*, 1:243. Doug-las Harper, "Slavery in the North," http://www.slavenorth.com/rhodeisland.htm.

54. *RI Records*, 1:412–3. Harper, "Slavery." Margaret Ellen Newell, *Brethren by Nature: New England Indians, Colonists, and the Origins of American Slavery* (Ithaca, NY: Cornell University Press, 2015), 114–5.

55. *RI Records*, 2:85, 123, 187. *Portsmouth Records*, 361. William F. Reed, *Descendants of Thomas Durfee of Portsmouth, RI* (Washington, DC: Gibson Brothers, 1902), 6–8.

56. Bartholomew Gosnold, "Buzzard's Bay," in *Sailors Narratives*, 40–41. Cronon, *Changes*, 122–5, 147–8.

57. Cronon, *Changes*, 122–5, 147–8. Mt. Pleasant, "Paradigm," 390–9.

58. Plane, *Colonial Intimacies*, 5–6, 129–30. Norton, *Founding*, 89–90. Salisbury, *Mani-tou*, 40–1.

59. PCR, 4:16–17. See also Drake, *Aboriginal Races*, 187–8. Drake, *BOI*, 3:73. Phillips, *Fall River*, 31–3, 49, 100–3. Peirce, *Indian History*, 38. Jennings, *Invasion*, 280–1, 288–9.

60. PCR, 4:8. *Plymouth Town Records*, 1:46. In their recent town meeting, the Plymouth men had expressed concern over "the Incroachment of some Road Illand" settlers on "our lands att Puckateesett and places adjacent" and authorized John Cooke to intervene. Cooke had recently settled at Acushnet; he and his relations held shares in Pocasset Neck. Members of the court with interests included Josiah Winslow, whose uncle, John, and John's son-in-law, Edward Gray, had shares at Pocasset Neck; Thomas Hinckley, who held interest at Sakonnet; Thomas Southworth, who held a share in Pocasset Neck, along with his mother, Alice Bradford; and William Bradford Jr., Alice's son by William Sr. John Winslow and Thomas Southworth, with Cooke and Miles Standish, negotiated the deed with Ekatabacke in 1652. *Plymouth Town Records*, 1:36, 64–9. PCR, 3:164, 216, 4:8, 13–14. Bangs, *Deeds*, 76–7. Ralph Van Wood, *May-flower Families through Five Generations*, vol. 12 *(Francis Cooke)*, rev. ed. (Rockport,

ME: Picton Press, 1999), 75. Robert Wakefield, *Mayflower Families through Five Generations*, vol. 18 (Richard Warren) (Plymouth, MA: General Society of Mayflower Descendants, 1999). Wamsutta also confirmed Providence's rights "on the west side of Seecunk or Pawtuckqut river" in 1661, supporting Rhode Island's quest to secure a royal charter, which would include in its territories the contested lands at Pocasset and Seekonk. *Rhode Island Records*, 1:434–5, 574–5. Jennings, *Invasion*, 280–1, 288–9.

61. Drake, *BOI*, 3:7–8. Hubbard, *Indian Wars*, 60. Roland was brother to John Sassamon.

62. Drake, *BOI*, 3:7–8. Hubbard's account mainly agrees with Mather's on the points illustrated here.

63. Hubbard, *Indian Wars*, 60. Drake, *BOI*, 3:7–8. Although not certain, this wife was likely Weetamoo, and if so, Mather calls her "his squaw."

64. PCR, 4:8–24. Jennings, *Invasion*, 289–90. See also *RI Records*, 1:434–5, 574–575.

65. Hubbard, *Indian Wars*, 60. Drake, *BOI*, 3:7–8. John Easton, "A Relacion of the Indyan Warre" (1675), in *Narratives of the Indian Wars 1675–1699*, ed. Charles Lincoln (New York: Charles Scribner's Sons, 1913), 13. PCR, 3:216. *Mayflower Families*, 1:52. Matthew Fuller served as "physician" to the Plymouth troops during King Philip's War. Since the narrative names only "Fuller," Samuel Fuller Jr. (later Middleborough's first minister), whose house in Middleborough was burned during the war, is also possible. Samuel Sr. served as lay physician to the first settlers at Plymouth. Society for Colonial Wars, *Further Letters on KPs War* (Providence, RI: E. L. Freeman Co., 1923). Norman Gevitz, "Samuel Fuller of Plymouth Plantation: A 'Skillful Physician' or 'Quacksilver'?" *Journal of the History of Medicine and Allied Sciences* 47 (1992): 29–48. See also http://www.plimoth.org/sites/default/files/media/pdf/fuller_samuel.pdf.

66. Drake, *BOI*, 3:7.

67. Hubbard, *Indian Wars*, 60. Drake, *BOI*, 3:7–8.

68. *Collections of the Massachusetts Historical Society* (CMHS) (Boston: The Society, 1792–1888), 4th ser., 8 (1868): 233–4.

69. PCR, 4:25–26.

70. CMHS, 1st ser., 2 (1793): 40. Jennings, *Invasion*, 290–1. No date appears on this letter and Philip did sign agreements in the seven years following. Jennings argues that the letter refers to the 1662 council, but allows the letter could refer to the 1671 Taunton "Submission." Philip also signed deeds after that meeting. The interpreter, Tom, appears regularly on deeds beginning in 1667. Bangs, *Deeds*, 382, 388, 392, 447.

71. "The Trumbull Papers," CMHS, 5th ser., 9 (1885): 38–9. *Proceedings of the Massachusetts Historical Society*, 1867–9, 10 (Dec. 1868): 391. *Fones Record*, 19–22. Anderson, *Creatures*, 226–7. *Narragansett Mortgage*, 33–34. Dunn, "Narragansett Country," 78–81.

72. Anderson, *Creatures*, 157, 166, 210–227. Weinstein, "Indian vs. Colonist," 144, 155, 188, 208–12.

73. Anderson, *Creatures*, 150–1, 227. Clark Indian Manuscripts, box 1, folders 2, 3, 4, Rhode Island Historical Society. Martin, *Profits*, 62–74. *Portsmouth Records*, 398. Anderson, "Peter Tallman." Daniel A. Romani Jr., "The Pettaquamscut Purchase of 1657/58 and

the Establishment of a Commercial Livestock Industry in Rhode Island," in *Algonkians of New England: Past and Present*, ed. Peter Benes and Jane Montague Benes (The Dublin Seminar for New England Folklife Annual Proceedings), 18 (1993), 45–60. Note that "cattle" referred not only to cows, but to livestock in general.

74. Anderson, *Creatures*, 188–90, 210–11. Cronon, *Changes*, 131–2, 136. Russell Bourne, *The Red King's Rebellion: Racial Politics in New England 1675–1678* (Oxford University Press, 1991), 89. As Cronon notes, the Massachusetts Court reported in 1658 that "many children are exposed to great daingers of losse of life or limbe through the ravenousnese of swine." This referred to English children, but was likely true for Native children as well.

75. Anderson, *Creatures*, 190–2, 210–11, 223–4.

76. PCR, 3:192. Ronda, "Red and White," 208. Anderson, *Creatures*, 190–2, 210–11, 223–4. Cronon, *Changes*, 75–7, 129–31. *RI Records*, 1:412–3.

77. *RI Records*, 1:85, 454. *Portsmouth Records*, 113, 82, 83, 142, 153. PCR, 9:286. Clark Indian Manuscripts, box 1, folders 2, 3, 4, Rhode Island Historical Society. Anderson, *Creatures*, 227. Dunn, "Narragansett Country," 78–81. Martin, *Profits*, 69, 73–4. Elisha Potter, *The Early History of Narragansett* (Providence, RI: Marshall, Brown, 1886), 275–6. *Narragansett Mortgage*, 33–4. Romani, "Pettaquamscut Purchase," 45.

78. *Fones Record*, 5–6, 19–20, 23. "Petition of John Scott, John Winthrop, Simon Broadstreet, Daniel Denison, Josias Winslow, Thomas Willet & Richard Lord," *Proceedings of Massachusetts Historical Society*, 1867–9, 10 (Dec. 1868), 391. CMHS, 5th ser., 9:54–5. Edmund O'Callaghan, *Documents Relative to the Colonial History of the State of NY* (Albany, NY: Weed Parsons, 1853), 3:84. Martin, *Profits*, 69–70, 73–9. Potter, *History of Narragansett*, 275–6. Note that Prence's fellow Plymouth men, Thomas Willet, John Brown, and Josiah Winslow had purchased shares in the Atherton Company.

79. PCR, 9:283. *RI Records*, 1:36–8, 65, 451–3. CMHS, 5th ser., 9:38–9. *Narragansett Mortgage*, 33–34. Dunn, "Narragansett Country," 70–4, 78–81. Society of Colonial Wars, *Samuel Gorton's Letter to Lord Hyde in Behalf of the Narragansett Sachems* (Providence, RI: E. L. Freeman, 1931). Jennings, *Invasion*, 278–86.

80. PCR, 4:24. I am interpreting "Quiquequanchett" as a misspelling of Quequegunent. With no other reference to Quiquequanchett, a survey of the documents and secondary sources shows that Quequegunent is the closest match, a theory supported by contextual evidence. (Note that in a confirmatory Atherton deed, Quequegunent is referred to as "Ceshequansh," with a suffix similar to "-quanchett." All of these varied spellings give us a sense of how the Native name was *heard* by English ears.) Still, despite compelling evidence, it is possible that Quequequanchett was someone other than Quaiapin's son, a man who does not appear elsewhere in the records. *Fones Record*, 6–7.

81. PCR, 4:24. Drake, *BOI*, 2:81. On "the deed game," see Jennings, *Invasion*, 128.

82. Jennings, *Invasion*, 288. Newell, *Brethren*, 108.

83. Ronda, "Red and White," 206. Weinstein, "Indian vs. Colonist," 188. Jennings, *Invasion*, 282. Anderson, *Creatures*, 222–3. Herbert Osgood, *The American Colonies in the Seventeenth Century* (New York: Columbia University Press, 1907), 173, 143–92.

84. The Clarendon Papers, *Collections of the New York Historical Society, 1869* (New York: The Society, 1870), 90–1. *CMHS*, 5th ser., 9:70–1. John Hull, "Some Observable Passages of providence toward the Country [Diary of John Hull]," *Transactions and Collections of the American Antiquarian Society*, 3:216 (1857).

85. Clarendon Papers, 90–1. Hull, "Observable Passages," 3:216 (1857).

86. *RI Records*, 2:59. *Calendar of State Papers*, 5:274, 342, items 925 and 1103. *CMHS*, 2nd ser. (1815), 6:724–5. Clarendon Papers, 90–1. Samuel Maverick to Col. Richard Nicolls, March 5, 1664, Clark Family Papers, Rhode Island Historical Society, ms 351, box 4, Westerly Town Record Book, 8–12. O'Callaghan, *Documents*, 3:93. *RI Records*, 1:512–3. "Newport Historical Society Collections, Indian File," page 1937 in Paul Campbell Research Notes, Mss 369, folder 6, Rhode Island Historical Society. Jennings, *Invasion*, 281–5. Jenny Pulsipher, *Subjects unto the Same King: Indians, English, and the Contest for Authority in Colonial New England* (Philadelphia: University of Pennsylvania Press, 2005), 48–60. Osgood, *Colonies*, 179. *Archaeology in Rhode Island*, 54.

87. *RI Records*, 1:134–5, 2:59. *Calendar of State Papers*, 5:342, item 1103. Jennings, *Invasion*, 281–5. Pulsipher, *Subjects*, 55–6. Osgood, *Colonies*, 179. *CMHS*, 2nd ser., 6 (1815): 725.

88. Clark Family Papers, Rhode Island Historical Society, ms 351, box 4, Westerly Town Record Book, 13. *RI Records*, 2:4, 59. Jennings, *Invasion*, 285–6. Cronon, *Changes*, 57. King James Bible Online, http://www.kingjamesbibleonline.org/1611_Psalms-115-16.

89. Jennings, *Invasion*, 283, 288, 291. Weinstein, "Indian vs. Colonist," 208–12. O'Callaghan, *Documents*, 3:93. The Royal Commission did offer Plymouth a charter, in exchange for greater control over the composition of their governing body, but the Plymouth men "chose to be as they are." *Calendar of State Papers*, 5:344.

90. Bangs, *Deeds*, 326–7. *PCR*, 2:58. Henry Williams, "Elizabeth Poole," 47–48, 96–7, 105. Emery, *History of Taunton*, 122, 114, 117–9. As early as 1643, the Plymouth Court had "granted" the land at Assonet Neck to its men at Taunton, "provided leave can be procured from Ossamequin," which never occurred. For Assonet maps and connections, see http://ourbelovedkin.com/awikhigan/assonet.

91. Bangs, *Deeds*, 264, 339–43. "Massachusetts Land Records, 1620–1986," images, Family Search, (https://familysearch.org/ark:/61903/3:1:3QS7-99Z7-GYG?cc=2106411&wc=MCBR-PWY%3A61612701%2C362501701 : 22 May 2014), Plymouth > image 263 of 677; county courthouses and offices, Massachusetts. "Massachusetts Land Records, 1620–1986," images, Family Search, (https://familysearch.org/ark:/61903/3:1:3QS7-89Z7-GQ9?cc=2106411&wc=MCBR-PWY%3A61612701%2C362501701: 22 May 2014), Plymouth > image 417 of 677; county courthouses and offices, Massachusetts. Phillips, *Fall River*, 31. As Weinstein notes, the Mattapoisett near Acushnet/Dartmouth (contemporary Mattapoisett and Marion) should not be confused with Conbitant's seat of Mattapoisett in Pocasset (contemporary Gardner's Neck). Weinstein, "Indian vs. Colonist," 236.

92. *Plymouth Town Records*, 1:62, 73, 35. Bangs, *Deeds*, 339–43, 327–8. "Massachusetts Land Records, 1620–1986," image 263. Phillips, *Fall River*, 98–100. According to Phil-

lips, although the lots "had been 'laid out' to and 'entered upon' by the seventy-five freemen of Plymouth . . . no substantial structures had been built there" by the eve of King Philip's War. However, the Plymouth men apparently "leased" out those lands for pasturage in the interim. He adds, in another historical address, "Weetamoe's protest seems to have held up the partition of these lots." Phillips, "Pocasset," 52.

93. Jennings, *Invasion*, 275. For early writings see, for example, Ives Goddard and Kathleen Bragdon, *Native Writings in Massachusett*, Memoirs of the American Philosophical Society, vol. 185 (Philadelphia: American Philosophical Society, 1988).

94. Amie and Tuspaquin's grandson, Benjamin (II) Tuspaquin, married Sassamon's granddaughter, Mercy Felix. Peirce, *Indian History*, 212–4. Drake, *BOI*, 3:9–10.

95. Jill Lepore, *The Name of War: King Philip's War and the Origins of American Identity* (New York: Knopf, 1998), 30–2, 39. Drake, *BOI*, 3:9–10. PCR, 10:167, 4:25–26. Kawashima, *Igniting*, 76–87. Jennings, *Invasion*, 294–5. Phillips, "Pocasset," 28. John Easton, "Indyan Warre," 7. Bangs, *Deeds*, 287, 293, 326–7, 330–1, 339–43. Massachusetts Archives 30:102a.

96. *PCR*, 10:167. Drake, *BOI*, 3:9–10. Jennings, *Invasion*, 294–5. Lepore, *Name*, 30–2, 39. Kawashima, *Igniting*, 78–80.

97. Lepore, *Name*, 30–2, 39. Drake, *BOI*, 3:9–10. Bangs, *Deeds*, 287, 293, 326–7, 330–1, 339–43. "Massachusetts Land Records, 1620–1986," image 269. "Massachusetts Land Records, 1620–1986," image 417. Clark Indian Manuscripts, box 1, folders 2, 3, 4, Rhode Island Historical Society. *Fones Record*, 1:6–7. See also *RI Land Evidences*, 1:29, 68. The confirmatory documents included an additional statement by Namumpum, in October 1659, attesting that in the June court, she had "surrendered up all that right and title of such lands as Woosamequin and Wamsutta sould to the purchasers; as appears by deeds given under theire hands." This appeared as a blanket consent, not only to the Freeman's deed, but to all the deeds signed or confirmed by Ousamequin and Wamsutta. However, this statement was not recorded until 1674. See Chapter Three.

98. *RI Records*, 2:60. *Plymouth Town Records*, 1:73. Phillips, *Fall River*, 3:6. *Archaeology in Rhode Island*, 54.

99. *RI Records*, 2:96, 108, 122–3. *Portsmouth Records*, 127. Ruth Alice Anderson, "Peter Tallman, A Footnote in History," http://www.skep.com/genealogy/PDFs/PeterTallmanFootnote.pdf.

100. *RI Records*, 2:123–4. *PCR*, 4:168. Rick Durfee Balmer, "Revised Story of Ann Hill Tallman (c.1633–c.1683) & Thomas Durfee (1643–1712)," (June 26, 2008) http://www.genealogy.com/forum/surnames/topics/durfee/819/. If Ann Tallman had gone to Archer's home in Portsmouth, then Rhode Island, not Plymouth, would have asserted jurisdiction, under its law against harboring another man's wife. *Portsmouth Records*, 66. Plymouth did assert legal jurisdiction over Pocasset Neck, as evidenced by their demand of submission from Richard Morris. Archer was later called to Plymouth Court for "residing in the govment without order, and not attending the publicke worship of God, liveing lonely and in a heathenish way from good societie." PCR, 5:169.

101. *RI Records*, 2:187–8. Balmer, "Revised Story."

102. *RI Records,* 2:187–8. Balmer, "Revised Story," including Mary Beth Norton's email communication with Rick Durfee Balmer, posted by the author.

103. *PCR,* 4:168. "Dispose," www.oed.com.

104. *PCR,* 4:186. See also Drake, *Aboriginal Races,* 188.

105. Drake, *Aboriginal Races,* 188. Several years later, in 1671, the Sissons established the first settlement in Acoaxet, later "Westport," at the head of the Acoaxet River. http://wpthistory.org/timeline. For Sanford and Archer, see *Portsmouth Records,* 45–7, 58, 67–8, 75, 80, 85–9, 139, 358, 423, and *PCR,* 5:169. John Sanford was also involved in his half-brother Peleg's livestock trade.

106. *Portsmouth Records,* 80, 149–50. For a full account, see Anderson, *Creatures,* 199–211, 214–5, and Virginia Anderson, "King Philip's Herds: Indians, Colonialism, and the Problem of Livestock in Early New England," *William and Mary Quarterly* Third Series, 51, no. 4 (Oct. 1994), 601–24. See also David Silverman, "'We Chuse to Be Bounded': Native American Animal Husbandry in Colonial New England," *William and Mary Quarterly* Third Series, 60, no. 3 (Jul. 2003): 511–48. Chesawanocke, or Hog Island, had been granted to Richard Smith Jr. by Wamsutta in February 1653/4, a deed witnessed by John Sanford. Bangs, *Deeds,* 276–7.

107. *PCR,* 2:58. *RI Records,* 2:267, 272. Williams, "Elizabeth Poole," 47–8, 96–7, 105. Thomas Stanton to John Mason, July 8, 1669. Connecticut State Library, Connecticut Archives, Indian Series 1, 1:10. http://images.library.yale.edu:8080/neips/data/html/1669.07.08.00/1669.07.08.00.html. Emery, *History of Taunton,* 114, 117–9, 122. Weinstein, "Indian vs. Colonist," 171. Bowen, *Early Rehoboth,* 79–80, 84. Butler, "Algonkian Culture," 25. Hurd, *Bristol County,* 256. *A History of the Town of Freetown, Massachusetts* (Fall River, MA: J. H. Franklin, 1902), 207. Philips, *Fall River,* 29, 34–5, 48. Peirce, "Original Owners," 114. Delabarre, "Dighton Rock," 243–4.

108. *RI Records,* 2:267–71. West, "Portsmouth," 10. The Court included John Easton and John Sanford, as well as Governor Benedict Arnold. Ninigret relayed that "there was never a Mount Hope Indian there."

109. *RI Records,* 2:265, 270–3.

110. The group included John Sanford, Peleg Sanford, John Easton, Benedict Arnold, and John Clark, among others. *RI Records,* 2:292.

111. *RI Records,* 2:295–7. Philips, *Fall River,* 34–5.

112. *RI Records,* 2:420. Philips, *Fall River,* 34–5.

113. *PCR,* 12:242. Drake, *BOI,* 3:4. It is possible that Piowant is "Pianto," mentioned in the Freeman's survey. See Bangs, *Deeds,* 298.

114. *PCR,* 12:242. Delabarre, "Dighton Rock," 246–8. Phillips, *Fall River,* 34. Drake, *BOI,* 3:4, 55. For maps, documents and connections, see http://ourbelovedkin.com/awikhigan/assonet.

2. THE HARVARD INDIAN COLLEGE SCHOLARS

1. Note that Caleb and Joel were 10 and 11, respectively, when they entered the preparatory school, and 15 and 16 when they entered the college. My research on Harvard

Indian College, the preparatory schools, and the students has been extensive, and is richly informed by collaboration and conversation at Harvard University and with Native communities. I am especially grateful for research assistance from Tiffany Smalley. Sources consulted include: Hugh Amory, *First Impressions: Printing in Cambridge, 1639* (Cambridge, MA: Harvard University Press, 2005); Ethel Billie Branch, "From the Line to the Hoop: Harvard's History Through Native Eyes" (BA thesis, Harvard College, 2001); Michael Clark, ed., *Eliot Tracts with Letters from John Eliot to Thomas Thorowgood and Richard Baxter* (Westport, CT: Praeger, 2003), 67–8; Richard W. Cogley, "A Seventeenth-Century Native American Family: William of Sudbury and His Four Sons," *The New England Historical and Genealogical Register* 153 (April 1999): 171–9; Dennis Connole, *Indians of the Nipmuck Country in Southern New England 1630–1750* (Jefferson, NC: McFarlane, 2007); Samuel Gardner Drake, *The Book of the Indians (BOI)* (Boston: Antiquarian Bookstore, 1841), 2:118; John Ford, ed., *Some Correspondence between the Governors and Treasurers of the New England Company in London and the Commissioners of the United Colonies in America* (London: Spottiswood and Co., 1896); Daniel Gookin, "An Historical Account of the Doings and Sufferings of the Christian Indians in New England," in *Transactions and Collections of the American Antiquarian Society* (Cambridge, MA: American Antiquarian Society, 1836), 2:33–4; Daniel Gookin, *Historical Collections of the Indians of New England (1674)* (North Stratford, NH: Ayer, 2000); Lori M. Graham and Peter R. Golia, "In Caleb's Footsteps: The Harvard University Native American Program," in *Native American Studies in Higher Education*, ed. Duane Champagne and Jay Stauss (Walnut Creek, CA: Altamira Press, 2002), 123–43; Richard Walden Hale Jr., *Tercentenary History of the Roxbury Latin School* (Cambridge, MA: Riverside Press, 1946); Harvard University Bursar, Records of the Bursar, 1650–1957, Harvard University Archives (and the Harvard Archives generally); "Harvard College Records, 1636–1750," in *Publications of the Colonial Society of Massachusetts* (Boston: Colonial Society, 1925), vol. 15; William Kellaway, *The New England Company* (New York: Barnes and Noble, 1962); Laura Liebman, ed., *Experience Mayhew's Indian Converts* (Amherst, MA: University of Massachusetts Press, 2008), 36, 95–101, 111; George Emery Littlefield, *The Early Massachusetts Press, 1638–1711* (Boston: The Club of Odd Volumes, 1907); Walter Meserve, "English Works of Seventeenth-Century Indians," *American Quarterly* 8, no. 3 (Autumn 1956), 264–76; Samuel Eliot Morison, *Harvard College in the Seventeenth Century* (Cambridge, MA: Harvard University Press, 1936), 581 and entire volume; Samuel Morison, *Three Centuries of Harvard* (Cambridge, MA: Harvard University Press, 1936); Samuel Morison, *The Founding of Harvard College* (Cambridge, MA: Harvard University Press, 1935); Arthur R. Railton, "The Vineyard's First Harvard Men Were Indians" *Duke's County Intelligencer* 29, no. 3 (February 1988): 91–115; *Records of the Colony of New Plymouth in New England (PCR)* (Boston: William White, 1859), vol. 10; Neal Salisbury, "Red Puritans: The 'Praying Indians' of Massachusetts Bay and John Eliot," *William and Mary Quarterly* 31, no. 1 (January 1974): 27–54; Jerome D. Segel and R. Andrew Pierce, *The Wampanoag Genealogical History of Martha's Vineyard, Massachusetts* (Baltimore, MD: Genealogical

Pub, 2003), 133, 144, 288; John Langdon Sibley, *Biographical Sketches of Graduates of Harvard University* (Cambridge, MA: Charles William Sever, 1873), 2:201–4; David Silverman, *Faith and Boundaries: Colonists, Christianity, and Community among the Wampanoag Indians of Martha's Vineyard, 1600–1871* (New York: Cambridge University Press, 2007), 18–20, 54; Margaret O'Connell Szasz, *Indian Education in the American Colonies, 1607–1783* (Albuquerque: University of New Mexico Press, 1988); Isaiah Thomas, *The History of Printing in America* (Albany, NY: J. Munsell, 1874); George Parker Winship, *The Cambridge Press, 1638–1692* (Philadelphia: University of Pennsylvania Press, 1945); Hilary E. Wyss, *Writing Indians: Literacy, Christianity, and Native Community in Early America* (Amherst, MA: University of Massachusetts Press, 2000). For maps, documents, images, and connections, see http://ourbeloved kin.com/awikhigan/chapter2.

2. Lucius Robinson Paige, *History of Cambridge* (Boston: H. O. Houghton, 1877), 1–44. Charles M. Sullivan and Cambridge Historical Commission, "Harvard Square History and Development," http://www.cambridgema.gov/~Historic/hsqhistory1.html; John Smith, *A Description of New England, Or, Observations and Discoveries in the North of America, in the Year of Our Lord 1614* (London: Printed by Humfrey Lownes for Robert Clerke, 1616), 17. Richard Frothingham Jr., *The History of Charlestown, Massachusetts* (Boston: Little and Brown, 1845), 8–12. Morison, *Seventeenth Century*, 340. Meserve, "English Works," 272. Bernd Peyer, *The Tutor'd Mind: Indian Missionary-Writers in Antebellum America* (Amherst, MA: University of Massachusetts Press, 1997), 46. William Smith Tilden, *History of the Town of Medfield, Massachusetts, 1650–1886* (Boston: G. H. Ellis, 1887), 17. Anthony N. Penna and Conrad Edick Wright, eds., *Remaking Boston: An Environmental History of the City and its Surroundings* (Pittsburgh: University of Pittsburgh, 2009), 1, 84–6, 107–8, 133. Personal communication, Pam Ellis, December 7, 2009. Pam Ellis notes that her understanding is that the river has different names, based on distinct geographic features in different sections, as is the case with many Indigenous river names. Note that "Newtowne" spread to encompass the village of Nonantum, where Eliot first preached, now known as the city of Newton. For maps, documents, images, and connections, see http:// ourbelovedkin.com/awikhigan/harvard-indian-college.

3. Arthur Gilman, *The Cambridge of 1896: A Picture of the City and Its Industries Fifty Years after Incorporation* (Cambridge, MA: Riverside Press, 1896), 10. Paige, *Cambridge*, 383. Nathaniel Shurtleff, *Records of the Governor and Company of the Massachusetts Bay in New England* (Boston: W. White, 1853), 1:254, 394. Richard Frothingham Jr. *History of Charlestown* (Boston: C. C. Little and J. Brown, 1845), 35–6. William Bright, *Native American Place Names of the United States* (Norman, OK: University of Oklahoma Press, 2007), 306. Samuel Drake, *BOI*, 40–1. Dwight Health, ed., *Mourt's Relation: A Journal of the Pilgrims at Plymouth* (Bedford, MA: Applewood Books, 1986), 78–80. Neal Salisbury, *Manitou and Providence: Indians, Europeans, and the Making of New England, 1500–1643* (New York: Oxford University Press, 1982, 121, 199–201. David Stewart-Smith, "The Pennacook Indians and the New England Frontier, circa 1604–1733." (PhD diss., Union Institute, 1998), 29–30, 81–3, 91. See also

Ron Wiser's Research Home Page, "Descendants of Squa Sachem," http://freepages
.genealogy.rootsweb.ancestry.com/~raymondfamily/wiser/WiserResearch.html. The
New England Company encouraged the colony to acquire "purchase" of "title" from
Native leaders, which the colony then required of towns. The Massachusett Saunkskwa reserved planting grounds and hunting territory at Missitekw and fishing rights at
the weir above the ponds. For maps and connections, see http://ourbelovedkin.com/
awikhigan/missitekw

4. James Savage, Richard S. Dunn, and Laetitia Yeandle, eds., *The Journal of John Win-
throp, 1630–1649* (Cambridge, MA: Belknap Press of Harvard University Press, 1996),
35, 55, 86, 105. William Wood, *New England's Prospect* (Amherst, MA: University
Massachusetts Press, 1997) 64. Drake, *BOI*, 2:40–1, 47–9. Kathleen Bragdon, *Native
People of Southern New England, 1500–1650* (Norman, OK: University of Oklahoma
Press, 1996), 137–9. William Cronon, *Changes in the Land: Indians, Colonists, and
the Ecology of New England* (New York: Hill and Wang, 1983), 59–75. Frothingham,
Charlestown, 25, 28, 31–7. Yasuhide Kawashima, *Igniting King Philip's War: The John
Sassamon Murder Trial* (Lawrence, KS: University Press of Kansas, 2001), 46–7, 63–4.
Jean O'Brien, *Dispossession by Degrees: Indian Land and Identity in Natick, Mas-
sachusetts. 1650–1790* (Lincoln, NE: University of Nebraska Press, 1997), 43. Paul
Robeson, "One Island, Two Places: Archaeology, Memory, and Meaning in a Rhode
Island Town," in *Interpretations of Native North American Life: Material Contribution
to Ethnohistory* ed. Michael Nassaney and Eric Johnson (Gainesville, FL: University
Press of Florida, 2000), 408. Salisbury, *Manitou*, 42–50, 176, 183–4, 190–1, 199–201. Sil-
verman, *Faith*, 41. Stewart-Smith, "Pennacook," 29–30, 56–60, 81–8, 97–102, 134, 145.
Laurie Lee Weinstein, "Indian vs. Colonist: Competition for Land in 17th Century
Plymouth Colony" (PhD diss., Southern Methodist University, 1983), 74, 207.

5. Salisbury, *Manitou*, 190–2. Stewart-Smith, "Pennacook," 64–5, 90–2, 104–5. *Winthrop
Journal*, 35, 55, 105.

6. Stewart-Smith, "Pennacook," 52, 71.

7. Liebman, ed., *Indian Converts*, 96–100. Silverman, *Faith*, 20–24, 34–37. Lisa Brooks,
The Common Pot: The Recovery of Native Space in the Northeast (Minneapolis: University of Minnesota, 2008), 7–8. O'Brien, *Dispossession*, 31–2, 55.

8. Liebman, ed., *Indian Converts*, 28, 43, 96–104. Silverman, *Faith*, 7–13, 17–24, 34–7, 47,
59. David J. Silverman, "Indians, Missionaries, and Religious Translation: Creating
Wampanoag Christianity in Seventeenth-Century Martha's Vineyard, *William and
Mary Quarterly* 62, no. 2 (2005): 141–74. Neal Salisbury, "Religious Encounters in
a Colonial Context: New England and New France in the Seventeenth Century,"
American Indian Quarterly 16, no. 4 (Fall 1992). Brooks, *Common Pot*, 7–8. Jennifer
Monaghan, *Learning to Read and Write in Colonial America* (Amherst, MA: Univer-
sity of Massachusetts Press, 2007), 46–62.

9. Clark, ed., *Eliot Tracts*, 97. Liebman, *Indian Converts*, 28, 43, 96–104. Silverman,
Faith, 26–35, 50, 59, 72–3. Silverman, "Indians," 141–74. Salisbury, "Religious Encounters." Bragdon, *Native People, 1500–1650*, 187–207. Eva Butler, "Algonkian Culture and the Use of Maize," *Bulletin of the Archaeological Society of Connecticut*

22 (December 1948): 6. Monaghan, *Learning*, 46–7. Salisbury, *Manitou*, 35–7, 42–8. William Simmons, *Spirit of the New England Tribes* (Hanover, NH: University Press of New England, 1986), 38–44.

10. Liebman, ed., *Indian Converts*, 27–8, 36, 43, 62–4, 98–100, 104–5, 111. Silverman, *Faith*, 13, 26, 51, 54, 58, 60. Monaghan, *Learning*, 57. Graham and Golia, "Caleb's Footsteps," 123–43.

11. O'Brien, *Dispossession*, 54–8. Gookin, *Historical Collections*, 45. PCR, 10:167, 219, 238–43. Wawaus or James may have been among the first recruits brought to Dunster by Eliot, who reported in 1645 "he had sent two Indians—hopeful young plants . . . to Harvard," including a boy named "James." Massachusetts Archives, 30:9. As Pam Ellis explained to me, Speen was also known as Qualalanset, a title that recognized his leadership and knowledge. On the translation of *wabun* as wind, see Clark, ed., *Eliot Tracts*, 135, and James Hammond Trumbull, *Natick Dictionary* (Lincoln, NE: University of Nebraska, 2009), 178. On Wabun and early proselytizing, see Clark, ed., *Eliot Tracts*, 10, 16, 39–40, 83–7, 96–8, 122–6, 135, 271–2, 292–3, 374–6, 393–5. Drake, *BOI*, 53, 112, 115. O'Brien, *Dispossession*, 26–8. Peyer, *Tutor'd Mind*, 35–6, 43–4. For map, see http://ourbelovedkin.com/awikhigan/hassanamesit.

12. Drake, *BOI*, 2:53, 112. Clark, ed., *Eliot Tracts*, 83–7, 97. O'Brien, *Dispossession*, 27, 43. Silverman, "Indians," 141–74. Butler, "Algonkian Culture," 6. Bragdon, *Native People, 1500–1650*, 188–95, 207–8. Joseph Nicolar, *The Life and Traditions of the Red Man* (1893), ed. Annette Kolodny (Durham, NC: Duke University Press, 2007), 14. On multiple scholarly views of Eliot, see Drew Lopenzina, *Red Ink: Native Americans Picking Up the Pen in the Colonial Period* (Albany, NY: State University of New York Press, 2012), 93–7.

13. Clark, ed., *Eliot Tracts*, 83–4, 95, 99. Francis Samuel Drake, *The Town of Roxbury: Its Memorable Persons and Places, Its History and Antiquities* (Roxbury, MA: Municipal Print Office, 1908). Gookin, *Historical Collections*, 45, 48–9; Gookin, "Historical Account," 480. PCR, 10:167, 219, 238–43, 262, 323–31, 356. Kathleen Bragdon, *Native People of Southern New England, 1650–1775* (Norman, OK: University of Oklahoma Press, 2009), 29. Drake, BOI, 2:50. Ford, *Some Correspondence*, 28. Cogley, "Seventeenth-Century," 171–9. Although Cogley's research is essential for documenting James Printer's family, he mistakenly confused "Naoas," James's father, with another convert, "Nataos," or "William of Sudbury." Gookin's 1674 account, *Historical Collections*, clearly identifies them as two distinct individuals.

14. Pauline Turner Strong, *Captive Selves, Captivating Others* (Boulder, CO: Westview Press, 1999), 43–6. Clark, ed., *Eliot Tracts*, 59.

15. Williams quoted in O'Brien, *Dispossession*, 13. In Western Abenaki, *awani kia* means "who are you?" or *awanigik* = who, plural, perhaps, more accurately, "who are you," i.e., those we do not know. In the same language, *pilwaka* means "a stranger," so Roger Williams's phrase *may* have been closer to the former. www.westernabenaki.com.

16. *Winthrop Journal*, 105. Clark, ed., *Eliot Tracts*, 59, 222–3. Margaret Ellen Newell, *Brethren by Nature: New England Indians, Colonists, and the Origins of American Slavery* (Ithaca, NY: Cornell University Press, 2015), 65–9.

17. Drake, *BOI*, 3:9–10. *PCR*, 10:167. Steward's ledger, 1650–1659, Records of the Bursar, Harvard Archives. Jill Lepore, *The Name of War: King Philip's War and the Origins of American Identity* (New York: Knopf, 1998), 28–32, 39, and 19–45, generally. Kawashima, *Igniting*, 76–87. Morison, *Seventeenth Century*, 352–3. Newell, *Brethren*, 65.

18. See Kristina Bross, *Dry Bones and Indian Sermons: Praying Indians in Colonial America* (Ithaca, NY: Cornell University Press, 2004). Morison, *Three Centuries*. Winship, *Cambridge*. Clark, ed., *Eliot Tracts*. Roland Sanders, *Lost Tribes and Promised Lands: Origins of American Racism* (New York: HarperPerennial, 1992).

19. Clark, ed., *Eliot Tracts*, 58.

20. Bross, *Dry Bones*, 8, 148–52.

21. Clark, ed., *Eliot Tracts*, 97. Virginia Anderson, *Creatures of Empire* (Oxford: Oxford University Press, 2006), 159–63, 170, 188–92. Cronon, *Changes*, 131–2. O'Brien, *Dispossession*, 49–50. Anne Marie Plane, *Colonial Intimacies: Indian Marriage in Early New England* (Ithaca, NY: Cornell University Press, 2000), 5, 30, 42–64. Salisbury, *Manitou*, 187. Silverman, *Faith*, 14. Paige, *Cambridge*, 284. David Silverman, "'We Chuse to Be Bounded': Native American Animal Husbandry in Colonial New England," *William and Mary Quarterly*, Third Series, 60, no. 3 (July 2003): 511–48.

22. Railton, "Vineyard's First," 94. The Connecticut Commissioners were agents for the Society for the Propagation of the Gospel. "Yoke," *Oxford English Dictionary* http://dictionary.oed.com.

23. Bainbridge Bunting, *Harvard: An Architectural History* (Cambridge, MA: Belknap Press of Harvard University Press, 1985), 14. On Pequot War, see Laurence M. Hauptman and James D. Wherry, eds., *The Pequots in Southern New England* (Norman, OK: University of Oklahoma Press, 1990). Eric S. Johnson, "Uncas and the Politics of Contact," in Robert Steven Grumet, ed., *Northeastern Indian Lives, 1632–1816* (Amherst, MA: University of Massachusetts Press, 1996). Michael Leroy Oberg, *Uncas: First of the Mohegans* (Ithaca, NY: Cornell University Press, 2003), 34–72; Amy Den Ouden, *Beyond Conquest: Native Peoples and the Struggle for History in New England* (Lincoln, NE: University of Nebraska Press, 2005). Salisbury, *Manitou*, 203–35.

24. Bross, *Dry Bones*, 46. Morrison, *Three Centuries*, 11, 14–15. Winship, *Cambridge Press*, 67–9; Bunting, *Harvard*, 13. Graham and Golia, "Caleb's Footsteps," 125. Clark, ed., *Eliot Tracts*, 57, 65, 67, 99. Bobby Wright, "'For the Children of Infidels'?: American Indian Education in the Colonial Colleges," *American Indian Culture and Research Journal* 12, no. 3 (1988): 4–6.

25. *An Act for Promoting and Propagating the Gospel of Jesus Christ in New England* (London: Printed for Edward Husband, Printer to the Parliament of England, 1649). Clark, ed., *Eliot Tracts*, 223. Harvard University, Charter of 1650, Harvard University Archives. See http://library.harvard.edu/university-archives/using-the-collections/online-resources/charter-of-1650. For further analysis, see Bross, *Dry Bones*, 7; Morison, *Three Centuries*, 8; Wright, "Infidels," 6–7.

26. Railton, "Vineyard's First," 94. Winship, *Cambridge Press*, 138, 166. See also Bunting, *Harvard*, 13; Graham and Golia, "Caleb's Footsteps," 125; Gookin, *Historical Collections*, 32–3; Morison, *Seventeenth Century*, 340–8; Wright, "Infidels," 6–7. Re-

cent archaeological investigation has revealed that thick brick was used to create a lower wall for the Indian College, built to withstand the fluctuating water tables of Massachusett. See "The Indian College," "Digging Veritas" online exhibit, Peabody Museum, https://www.peabody.harvard.edu/node/2011.

27. Gookin, *Historical Collections*, 46. Duane Hamilton Hurd, *History of Bristol County, Massachusetts, with Biographical Sketches* (Philadelphia: J. W. Lewis, 1883), 3. Morison, *Seventeenth Century*, 352. Morison suggests that as many as twenty Indian students may have attended Weld's school in Roxbury between 1655 and 1672. At least four, perhaps more, of the students enrolled in the grammar school and in Corlett's Latin School died before the completion of their studies. Their names and nations, unfortunately, were not recorded in any extant documents. On the education of girls in the colonies, see Monaghan, *Learning*, 23, 41–3.

28. From 1659–1677, the vast majority of Harvard graduates went on to become ministers, doctors, and magistrates/political leaders. A handful became teachers and merchants. Morison, *Seventeenth Century*, 562.

29. PCR, 10:242. Hale Jr., *Tercentenary*, 17–20. Lepore, *Name*, 35. Liebman, ed,. *Indian Converts*, 21–2, 67, 71–2. Silverman, *Faith*, 51. Pilling, *Bibliography of the Algonquian Languages* (Washington, DC: Government Printing Office, 1891), 127–8. Monaghan, *Learning*, 84–90. Simmons, *Spirit*, 6.

30. Hale Jr., *Tercentenary*, 18. Silverman, *Faith*, 68. Liebman, ed., *Indian Converts*, 59–61.

31. Thomas Shepard, *A Short Catechism* (Cambridge, MA: Samuel Greene, 1654). Hale Jr., *Tercentenary*, 18. Morison, *Seventeenth Century*, 89–98. Joseph Bruchac, *Lasting Echoes: An Oral History of the Native American People* (New York: Harcourt, 1997). See also Joseph Laurent, *New Familiar Abenaki and English Dialogues* (Quebec: L. Brousseau, 1884) and Stephen Laurent, "The Abenakis: Aborigines of Vermont," in *Vermont Historical Journal* 23, no. 4 (Vermont Historical Soc. Proc., Oct 1955): 290.

32. Clark, ed., *Eliot Tracts*, 341–4. The phrase *Oohgôkje korâmen neh átta Mandouh?* was translated in print as "How prove you that there is a God?" This bilingual text was published in *A Further Account of the Progress of the Gospel* (London: M. Simmons, 1659), which also recounted the success of Joel and Caleb in the preparatory schools.

33. Hale, *Tercentenary*, 20, 98, citing W. A. L Vincent, *The Grammar Schools* (London: Murray, 1969). Liebman, ed., *Indian Converts*, 20, 59–62, 67–9. Morison, *Seventeenth Century*, 186–7.

34. PCR, 10:204–7. "Harvard College Records," 24–5. Clark, ed., *Eliot Tracts*, 67, 353. Szasz, *Indian Education*, 124. Railton, "Vineyard's First," 100–1. Ford, ed., *Some Correspondence*, 27–33. Gookin, *Historical Collections*, 32–34. Morison, *Seventeenth Century*, 354. Liebman, ed., *Indian Converts*, 58, 73. Monaghan, *Learning*, 41. The last record of Joane states, "Joane the Indian mayde now att Mr Welds is to bee with the Governor of the Massachusetts after her year is up until she be otherwise disposed he finding her clothes for her service." PCR, 10:204–7. On the history of women at Harvard, see Laurel Thatcher Ulrich, "Harvard's Womanless History," *Harvard Magazine* (November-December 1999), http://harvardmagazine.com/1999/11/womanless.html.

35. Clark, ed., *Eliot Tracts*, 67. Szasz, *Indian Education*, 124. Railton, "Vineyard's First," 100–1. *PCR*, 10:243, 251, 262, 296. Ford, ed., *Some Correspondence*, 27–33. Gookin, *Historical Collections*, 32–3, 45; Gookin, "Historical Account." Morison, *Seventeenth Century*, 349. Monaghan, *Learning*, 32–3. For a recent account of the struggling early years of the press within the context of the development of the missionary project and Harvard College, see Lopenzina, *Red Ink*, 106–10.

36. Winship, *Cambridge Press*, 151.

37. Peyer, *Tutor'd Mind*, 47. Lepore, *Name*, 29–39. Lopenzina, *Red Ink*, 106–23. Szasz, *Indian Education*, 113–4.

38. Winship, *Cambridge Press*, 157, 158, 161.

39. Szasz, *Indian Education*, 113–4. Peyer, *Tutor'd Mind*, 44–6. Lepore, *Name*, 29–39. Clark, ed., *Eliot Tracts*, 95–6. Pilling, *Bibliography*, 172. Jennifer Monaghan, *Learning*, 88.

40. Winship, *Cambridge Press*, 197, 200, 211. Lepore, *Name*, 34. Drake, *BOI*, 2:50–1. Peyer, *Tutor'd Mind*, 313. Morison, *Seventeenth Century*, 1:348.

41. For my understanding of the details and complexity of the colonial printing process I am indebted to Michael Kelly, who is quoted here. Email and personal communication, August 11, 2014, and February 18, 2015.

42. The language work and historical research of Wampanoag linguist Jessie Little Doe Baird and the Wôpanâak language project, as well as recent scholarship by Drew Lopenzina, strongly support this argument. See *Red Ink*, 106–23. Baird has identified Wôpanâak as the language of the Eliot bible and her research demonstrates that there were multiple speakers assisting in the translation. Although scholars often have used "Massachusett" to describe the language of the bible, this research demonstrates that the Wôpanâak language was spoken on the coast, from the islands and Cape Cod to the south side of the Merrimack River. Personal communication, Jessie Little Doe Baird and Judith Sanford-Harris. See also Helen Manning, "Language" (exc. from *Moshup's Footsteps*), in *Dawnland Voices*, ed. Siobhan Senier (Lincoln, NE: University of Nebraska Press, 2014).

43. Winship, *Cambridge Press*, 151–221. Lepore, *Name*, 29–38. Drake, *BOI*, 2:50–1. Morison, *Seventeenth Century*, 340–55. Hale, *Tercentenary*, 17–19. Silverman, *Faith*, 52. Monaghan, *Learning*, 78, 88–90. See also Clark, ed., *Eliot Tracts*. Great thanks to Michael Kelly for clarifying specific details and the great accomplishment of this endeavor. Note that special type had to be ordered in order to accommodate printing of the Indigenous language. See Lopenzina, *Red Ink*, 89.

44. Michael Wigglesworth, *Day of Doom: or A Poetical Description of the Great and Last Judgment* (1662) (Boston: Charles Ewer, 1828). Lepore, *Name*, 35. Liebman, ed., *Indian Converts*, 69; see also 62–72. Morison, *Seventeenth Century*, 349–50. Szasz, *Indian Education*, 117. Winship, *Cambridge Press*, 162. Monaghan, *Learning*, 34, 105–6.

45. Wigglesworth, *Day of Doom*, 13–19, 56 (Stanzas 8, 12–19, 21, 34, 183). Biblical references: John 5:28–29; Revelation 6:15–16; 2 Corinthians 5:10.

46. Craig Womack, *Red on Red: Native American Literary Separatism* (Minneapolis: University of Minnesota Press, 1999), 7.

47. A translation of Eleazar's elegy for minister Thomas Thatcher is published in Wolf-gang Hochbruck and Beatrix Dudensing-Reichel, "'Honoratissimi Benefactores': Na-tive American Students and Two Seventeenth-Century Texts in the University Tra-dition," in *Early Native American Writing: New Critical Essays*, ed. Helen Jaskoski (New York: Cambridge University Press, 1996). For another recent translation, see Robert Dale Parker, *Changing Is Not Vanishing: A Collection of Early American In-dian Poetry to 1930* (Philadelphia: University of Pennsylvania Press, 2011), 47–50. An excerpt appears in ch. 9 herein. On the recent finding of Larnell's poem, see Stuart M. McManus and Tom Keeline, "Benjamin Larnell, The Last Latin Poet at Harvard Indian College," *Harvard Studies in Classical Philology* 108 (2014). Caleb's address was included in a letter from John Winthrop Jr. to Robert Boyle in 1663, accompanied by a piece by Joel, which has not yet been recovered. Hochbruck and Dudensing-Reichel, "'Honoratissimi Benefactores,'" 2; Lopenzina, *Red Ink*, 129.

48. Boyle Correspondence (BL 2.12), Archive of the Royal Society, London, by permission of the Royal Society. This is a new, poetic translation of Caleb's address, produced with great insight and collaboration from Mark Schiefsky and Cassandra Hradil, to whom I owe great thanks for helping me to understand the Latin language and literary expression. Another translation can be found in Hochbruck and Dudensing-Reichel, "'Honoratissimi Benefactores,'" 3. Morison, *Seventeenth Century*, 355. Thanks to Pat-rick Johansson for gifting me with a copy of the original.

49. John Block Friedman, "Eurydice, Heurodis, and the Noon-Day Demon," *Speculum* 41, no. 1 (Jan. 1966): 22. John Friedman, "Syncretism and Allegory in the Jerusalem Or-pheus Mosaic," in *Traditio* 23 (1967): 3–6. Gary G. Gibbs and Florinda Ruiz, "Arthur Golding's *Metamorphoses*: Myth in an Elizabethan Political Context," *Renaissance Studies* 22, no. 4 (September 2008): 557–75. Hochbruck and Dudensing-Reichel, "'Honoratissimi Benefactores,'" 7. Mukhtar Ali Isani, "Edward Taylor and Ovid's 'Art of Love': The Text of a Newly-Discovered Manuscript" *Early American Literature* 10, no. 1 (Spring 1975): 68. Raphael Lyne, "Ovid in English Translation," in *Cambridge Companion to Ovid*, ed. Philip Hardie (Cambridge, MA: Cambridge University Press, 2003), 249–55. Morison, *Seventeenth Century*, 176–7. W. H. D Rouse, *Shakespeare's Ovid: Being Arthur Golding's Translation of the Metamorphoses* (London: De La More Press, 1904), i–vi. Thanks to Mark Schiefsky for pointing me to Ovid's *Metamorphoses* and Virgil's *Georgics* as the primary sources for the Orpheus myth.

50. Hochbruck and Dudensing-Reichel, "'Honoratissimi Benefactores,'" 6. For an alter-native reading of Caleb's address, see Drew Lopenzina, *Red Ink*, 129–33.

51. G. P. Goold, ed., Frank Justus Miller, trans., *Metamorphoses* (Harvard University Press, 1984), 71–2. Rouse, *Shakespeare's Ovid*, 203–4. "Barbarian," Oxford English Dictionary, http://dictionary.oed.com. "Barbărus," Lewis and Short, Latin Diction-ary, Pollux Archimedes Project Dictionary Access, http://archimedes.fas.harvard.edu/pollux/. Virgil (*Georgics*, Book IV) relates, in the translation by A. S. Klein, "They say he wept for seven whole months, / beneath an airy cliff, by the waters of desolate Strymon, / and told his tale, in the icy caves, softening the tigers' mood, / and gath-ering the oak-trees to his song." http://www.poetryintranslation.com/PITBR/Latin/VirgilGeorgicsIV.htm#_Toc534524384. It may be significant that in Caleb's native

language, trees and animals are categorized as animate, and the word *animantia* contains a similar connotation regarding the living beings' animacy. *Feras* denotes "wild animals" versus domesticated ones. Thanks again to Mark Schiefsky and Cassandra Hradil for interpretive insight.

52. Virgil, *Georgics*, Book IV. Gibbs and Ruiz, "Golding's *Metamorphoses*," 569. Friedman, "Syncretism," 2, 7–8. Graham and Golia, "Caleb's Footsteps," 123–43. Silverman, *Faith*, 20–6, 34–5. Liebman, *Indian Converts*, 102, 98–9.

53. Hochbruck and Dudensing-Reichel, "'Honoratissimi Benefactores,'" 6. Penna and Wright, eds., *Remaking Boston*, 108, 221. William B. Meyer, "Harvard and the Heating Revolution," *New England Quarterly* 77, no. 4 (December 2004): 588–606.

54. Goold, ed., *Metamorphoses*, 64–7. Virgil, *Georgics*, Book IV. Note that Virgil names both Pluto and Proserpina, while Ovid names "Persephone." Golding refers to "Persephone" as Pluto's "lady"; Sandys calls her "Hell's Queen." Rouse, *Shakespeare's Ovid*, 201–2. George Sandys, *Ovid's Metamorphosis* (Cambridge, MA: Chadwyck-Healey, 1992), 339.

55. Rouse, *Shakespeare's Ovid*, 201–2. Wigglesworth, *Day of Doom*, stanza 37. Hochbruck and Dudensing-Reichel, "'Honoratissimi Benefactores,'" 5. Friedman, "Eurydice," 22–4. Friedman, "Syncretism," 1–3, 7–10. Gibbs and Ruiz, "Golding's *Metamorphoses*," 557–75. Sandys follows Golding in describing Hades as "Hell." Sandys, *Ovid's Metamorphosis*, 338. In the Christian "philosophers'" readings, "Christ had finished" what Orpheus could not accomplish, bringing the human soul, symbolically associated with Eurydice, "home" to heaven.

56. Virgil, *Georgics*, Book IV. Gibbs and Ruiz, "Golding's *Metamorphoses*," 201. Goold, ed., *Metamorphoses*, 65. Sandys, *Ovid's Metamorphosis*, 338. Friedman, "Eurydice," 24. On the horned snake and three worlds, see, for example, Bragdon, *Native People, 1500–1650*, 187–190, 202; Daniel Heath Justice, "Notes Toward a Theory of Anomaly," *GLQ: A Journal of Lesbian and Gay Studies* 16, no. 1–2 (2010): 207–42; George E. Lankford, "World on a String: Some Cosmological Components of the Southeastern Ceremonial Complex," and F. Kent III Reilly, "People of Earth, People of Sky: Visualizing the Sacred in Native American Art of the Mississippian Period," in *Hero, Hawk, and Open Hand: American Indian Art of the Ancient Midwest and South*, ed. Richard F. Townsend and Robert V. Sharp (New Haven, CT: Yale University Press, 2004), 125–37, 207–18; Charles Godfrey Leland, *Algonquin Legends* (Boston: Houghton Mifflin, 1884); John R. Swanton, *Myths and Tales of the Southeastern Indians* (Washington, DC: US Government Printing Office, 1929), 21, 30–5; Womack, *Red on Red*, 32, 200–3, 239–51.

57. Simmons, *Spirit*, 173–203. Silverman, "Indians, Missionaries," 141–74. Silverman, *Faith*, 30–4. Bragdon, *Native People, 1500–1650*, 187–90, 202.

58. Goold, ed., *Metamorphoses*, 75. Gibbs and Ruiz, "Golding's *Metamorphoses*," 204. Friedman, "Syncretism," 5. Silverman, *Faith*, 32–4. Silverman, "Indians, Missionaries," 141–74. Bragdon, *Native People, 1500–1650*, 188–95, 206–8. Salisbury, "Religious Encounters."

59. Note that Caleb's use of "tigers" suggests, as other allusions do, that he was familiar with Virgil's version of the Orpheus myth, while the rhetoric of force follows Golding.

Virgil, *Georgics*, Book IV. The same philosophy was applied to children in the preparatory schools. See Liebman, *Indian Converts*, 20, 59–60.

60. Hochbruck and Dudensing-Reichel, "'Honoratissimi Benefactores,'" 38. I am indebted to Mark Schiefsky for these insights regarding parallelism and Caleb's creative use of "*matephorisin.*"

61. Goold, ed., *Metamorphoses*, 75.

62. Hochbruck and Dudensing-Reichel, "'Honoratissimi Benefactores,'" 3.

63. Hochbruck and Dudensing-Reichel, "'Honoratissimi Benefactores,'" 6. Goold, ed., *Metamorphoses*, 69.

64. Friedman, "Eurydice," 23. On the doctrine of "weaned affections," see Liebman, 48. Note that while in Ovid's telling, the gods of the underworld were "conquered by the song" of Orpheus, the Christian philosophers like William of Conches warned that Orpheus was ultimately "conquered" by the gods of hell, his own earthly desires turning his mind from the proper object of heaven above. Goold, ed., *Metamorphoses*, 67.

65. On "saints" and "goats," see Wigglesworth, *Day of Doom*, stanzas 22, 27, 34, and Liebman, *Indian Converts*, 35–9.

66. Morison, *Seventeenth Century*, 90–7. Personal communication, Christina Hodge, "Archeology of Harvard Yard" exhibit, Peabody Museum of Archaeology and Ethnology, Harvard University. "Table Troubles," in "Digging Veritas" online exhibit, https://www.peabody.harvard.edu/node/2007.

67. Silverman, *Faith*, 51, 68. Liebman, *Indian Converts*, 58, 64, 69–73, 128–9, 111–5. See also Bragdon, *Native People, 1500–1650*. James Axtell, *The Indian Peoples of Eastern America: A Documentary History of the Sexes* (New York: Oxford University Press, 1981). R. Todd Romero, "Colonizing Childhood: Religion, Gender, and Indian Children in Southern New England, 1620–1720," in *Children in Colonial America*, ed. James Alan Marten (New York: New York University Press, 2007).

68. Morison, *Three Centuries*, 28–9. Morison, *Seventeenth Century*, 94. Meyer, "Heating Revolution," 588–606.

69. Sibley, *Biographical Sketches*, 163–204. Gookin, *Historical Collections*, 34. Graham and Golia, "Caleb's Footsteps," 125. Caleb was apparently still living in Cambridge, although he "died of consumption in Charlestown," according to Gookin, "where he was placed by Thomas Danforth, who had inspection over him." Gookin notes that "Of this disease of the consumption sundry of those Indian youths died, that were bred up to school among the English." Yet it was not their encounter with civilization, but rather the social and environmental changes of colonization that most likely caused their deaths, including the radical change in diet, as well as "crowding and poor sanitation" in Boston and Cambridge. Penna and Wright, eds., *Remaking Boston*, 57–8, 221. Eric Jay Dolin, *Political Waters* (Amherst, MA: University of Massachusetts Press, 2008), 5–7, 10. Charles W. Schmidt, "Linking TB and the Environment: An Overlooked Mitigation Strategy," *Environmental Health Perspectives* 116, no. 11 (November 2008): A478–A485. See http://ourbelovedkin.com/awikhigan/harvard-indian-college.

70. Susan Power, "First Fruits," in *Roofwalker* (Minneapolis: Milkweed Editions, 2002), 132–3.

71. Silverman, *Faith*, 49–52, 56–60, 70. Liebman, *Indian Converts*, 21–2, 69–73. Segel and Pierce, *Wampanoag Genealogical*, 106, 122, 132–3, 142–4, 288, 330, 335–6.

72. Silverman, *Faith*, 57, 24–6. Len Travers and John Cotton Jr., "The Missionary Journal of John Cotton, Jr., 1666–1678," *Proceedings of the Massachusetts Historical Society*, 3rd ser., 109 (1997): 74, 80. Note that Caleb's father Cheeshateaumuck was tied politically to Towanquatick, the "first Christian sachem" on the island. Segel and Pierce, *Wampanoag Genealogical*, 132, 177, 335. Liebman, *Indian Converts*, 95, 113–5, 129, 173–6.

73. Silverman, *Faith*, 57. Travers and Cotton, *Journal*, 68, 71, 74, 88. Liebman, ed., *Indian Converts*, 128–9.

74. Liebman, ed., *Indian Converts*, 129, 177, 185–9. Segel and Pierce, *Wampanoag Genealogical*, 142, 330.

75. Caleb Seaton was the grandson of Abigail, and likely the son of Thomas Sissetom. He lived at Sanchakantacket. Liebman, ed., *Indian Converts*, 111–4, 239–42, 254–6. Segel and Pierce, *Wampanoag Genealogical*, 106, 144, 279, 335–6.

76. Gookin, *Historical Collections*, 44–5, 48–9. Gookin, "Historical Account," 481. Ford, *Some Correspondence*, 28–9. Clark, ed., *Eliot Tracts*, 403–4. "A Memorandum of Indian Children Put Forth into Service to the English, August 10, 1676," *Proceedings of the Colonial Society of Massachusetts* 19 (1916–17): 25–8. Morison, *Seventeenth Century*, 356–7. On Wampus, see Connole, *Nipmuck*, ch. 8.

INTERLUDE: NASHAWAY

1. Mary White Rowlandson, *The Sovereignty and Goodness of God: With Related Documents*, ed. Neal Salisbury (Boston: Bedford Books, 1997), 14, 209. David Jaffee, *People of the Wachusett* (Ithaca, NY: Cornell University Press, 1999), 34–5, 38–40, 48–9. Henry Nourse, ed., *Early Records of Lancaster 1643–1725* (Lancaster, MA: self-published, 1884), 9–10, 33. Henry Nourse, *Lancastriana I. A Supplement to the Early Records and Military Annals of Lancaster Mass* (Lancaster, MA: self-published, 1900) 6. Samuel Morison, "The Plantation of Nashaway—An Industrial Experiment," in *Publications of the Colonial Society of Massachusetts: Transactions 1927–1930* (Boston, Published by the Society, 1932), 23:205–15. Dennis Connole, *Indians of the Nipmuck Country in Southern New England 1630–1750* (Jefferson, NC: McFarlane, 2007), 52, 141–3. For maps, documents, images and connections, see http://ourbelovedkin.com/awikhigan/interlude-nashaway.

2. Nathaniel Shurtleff, ed., *Records of the Governor and Company of the Massachusetts Bay in New England* (Boston: W. White, 1853), 2:11. Nourse, *Records*, 10–13. Connole, *Nipmuck*, 52, 143. Jaffee, *Wachusett*, 32–4. Morison, "Nashaway," 23:205–15. Salisbury, ed., *Sovereignty*, 12–13, 17. Neal Salisbury, "Contextualizing Mary Rowlandson: Native Americans, Lancaster and the Politics of Captivity," in *Early America Re-explored: New Readings in Colonial, Early National and Antebellum Culture*, ed. Klaus H. Schmidt and Fritz Fleishmann (New York: Peter Lang International Academic Publishers, 2002), 107–50. The 1641 Act for Encouraging Mines supported resource extraction, but also required "purchase of the interest" from Native people.

3. Connole, *Nipmuck*, 52, 61–5. Jaffee, *Wachusett*, 41. Nourse, *Records*, 10–13. Salisbury, "Contextualizing," 112–4. Salisbury, ed., *Sovereignty*, 12. David Stewart-Smith, "The Pennacook Indians and the New England Frontier, 1604–1733," (PhD diss. Union Institute, 1998), 130–3.

4. Shurtleff, *Massachusetts Records*, 3:365–6. Jaffee, *Wachusett*, 44, 47, 51–3. Nourse, *Records*, 10, 25–7. Salisbury, "Contextualizing," 112–4. Salisbury, ed., *Sovereignty*, 7–10, 15–6.

5. Jaffee, *Wachusett*, 44, 49, 55–8. Nourse, *Records*, 10, 17, 41–4, 60–1, 66, 68–9, 91, 261–4. Salisbury, "Contextualizing," 119–20. Salisbury, ed., *Sovereignty*, 18. John Pendergast, *The Bend in the River* (Tyngsborough, MA: Merrimac River Press, 1992), 46, 67.

6. Daniel Gookin, *Historical Collections of the Indians of New England (1674)* (North Stratford, NH: Ayer, 2000), 24–7, 53. Salisbury, ed., *Sovereignty*, 17–20.

7. Gookin, *Historical Collections*, 24–7, 53. Salisbury, "Contextualizing," 119–20. Salisbury, ed., *Sovereignty*, 17–20. For a different account of the raid, highlighting Mohawk perspectives, see Ruben G. Thwaites, ed., *The Jesuit Relations and Allied Documents* (Cleveland: Burrows Brothers Co., 1896–1901), 53:137. See also Jon Parmenter, *The Edge the Woods: Iroquoia, 1534–1701* (East Lansing, MI: Michigan State University Press, 2014), 137.

3. THE QUEEN'S RIGHT AND THE QUAKER'S RELATION

1. Letter by John Easton to Josiah Winslow, Mss C 357, R. Stanton Avery Special Collections, New England Historic and Genealogical Society (NEHGS). For maps, documents, images, and connections, see http://ourbelovedkin.com/awikhigan/chapter3.

2. Arthur Phillips, "Pocasset and the Pocassets," Dec. 15, 1931, Rhode Island Historical Society (manuscript), 2–14. Arthur Phillips, *The Phillips History of Fall River* (Fall River, MA: Dover Press, 1941–1946), fascicle 1 (1941): xv, 7–8, 29; fascicle 3 (1946): 1, 9. Benjamin Church, *The History of King Philip's War*, ed. Henry Dexter (Boston: John Wiggin, 1865), 14.

3. Easton to Winslow, NEHGS.

4. Nathaniel Bradstreet Shurtleff, *Records of the Colony of New Plymouth, in New England (PCR)* (Boston: William White, 1855), 5:159, 167. *Collections of the Massachusetts Historical Society (CMHS)* (Boston: The Society, 1792–1888), 1st ser., 6 (1800): 94. John Easton, "A Relacion of the Indyan Warre" (1675), in *Narratives of the Indian Wars 1675–1699*, ed. Charles Lincoln (New York: Charles Scribner's Sons, 1913), 7–8. John Brown to Josiah Winslow, June 11, 1675, Winslow Family Papers II, item 89, Massachusetts Historical Society (MHS). Samuel Gardner Drake, *The Book of the Indians (BOI)* (Boston: Antiquarian Bookstore, 1841), 3:10–12. Jill Lepore, *The Name of War: King Philip's War and the Origins of American Identity* (New York: Knopf, 1998), 21–5. Francis Jennings, *The Invasion of America: Indians, Colonialism, and the Cant of Conquest* (Chapel Hill, NC: University of North Carolina Press, 2010), 294–6. Yasuhide Kawashima, *Igniting King Philip's War: The John Sassamon Murder Trial* (Lawrence, KS: University Press of Kansas, 2001), 88–101.

5. Jeremy Dupertuis Bangs, *Indian Deeds: Land Transactions in Plymouth Colony, 1620–1691* (Boston: New England Historic Genealogical Society, 2008), 452, 465–7, 474–8. PCR, 7:191, 5:162, 170–1. Francis Baylies, *A Historical Memoir of the Colony of New Plymouth* (Boston: Hilliard, Gray, Little, and Wilkins, 1830), 2:62–5.

6. Phillips, "Pocasset," 14. Drake, *BOI*, 3:64–6. Bangs, *Deeds*, 159–60, 282, 434, 458, 460, 465, 477–9. PCR, 7:191. Richard Bowen, *Early Rehoboth* (Rehoboth, MA: Rumford Press, 1945), 58. B. Church, *History*, ed. Dexter, xviii–xxiv, 2–5, 11. Society of Colonial Wars in Rhode Island and Providence Plantations, *Purchase of Lands in Little Compton RI 1672/3 from the Saconet Indians*, tr. Philip Baldwin Simonds (Providence, RI: Society of Colonial Wars, 1977). Benjamin Church, "Entertaining Passages Relating to Philip's War," in *So Dreadfull a Judgment: Puritan Responses to King Philip's War 1676–1677*, ed. Richard Slotkin and James Folsom (Middletown, CT: Wesleyan Press 1978), 395.

7. Slotkin and Folsom, eds., *Dreadfull*, 397. Almy held "rights" at Sakonnet and Pocasset Neck. He was living in the area by 1669, his settlement protested by Wampanoag people, in part due to damage his cattle caused. Bangs, *Deeds*, 402–3. He claimed further land from Awashonks through debt, and by the spring of 1675 was planting on Pocasset Neck, the site of the "pease field fight," narrated by Church.

8. Bangs, *Deeds*, 414–5, 417–420, 426–7, 453, 460–3, 465–6, 471, 477–83. PCR, 5:126. B Church, *History*, ed. Dexter, xvii–xxiv, 2–5, 11. Phillips, *Fall River*, 100. See also David J. Silverman, *Faith and Boundaries: Colonists, Christianity, and Community among the Wampanoag Indians of Martha's Vineyard, 1600–1871* (New York: Cambridge University Press, 2007), 100.

9. Jill Lepore, "Plymouth Rocked: Of Pilgrims, Puritans and Professors," *New Yorker* (April 24, 2006), http://www.newyorker.com/archive/2006/04/24/060424crat_atlarge.

10. PCR, 3:216, 5:73–5, 64. B Church, *History*, ed. Dexter, 2–5, 26. CMHS, 1st ser., 5 (1798): 193–4. Ebenezer Peirce, *Indian History, Biography and Genealogy* (North Abington, MA: Zerviah Gould Mitchell, 1878), 247–54. Thomas Hinckley and Nathan Bacon to Governor Prence, July 7, 1671, Winslow Family Papers II, MHS. Douglas Edward Leach, *Flintlock and Tomahawk: New England in King Philip's War* (Hyannis, MA: Parnassus Imprints, 1996), 27.

11. PCR, 5: 75. CMHS, 1st ser., 5 (1798): 193–7. Peirce, *Indian History*, 247–54.

12. CMHS, 1st ser., 5:195–7. Peirce, *Indian History*, 247–54. Awashonks's brother Tatacomuncah "appeared" in Plymouth Court in November, "with Phillip," to sign a similar agreement. PCR, 5:80.

13. PCR, 7:191. Bangs, *Deeds*, 452, 465–7. Drake, *BOI*, 3:72. Peirce, *Indian History*, 247. B. Church, *History*, ed. Dexter, xviii, 2–5. For a deed to Sakonnet with Awashonks's mark, excepting her town at the point, see Society of Colonial Wars, "Purchase of Lands." By 1675, Mammanuah signed a deed relinquishing the same territory, from Pocasset Neck "south to Sakonnet Point" and the "Main Sea," extending "east to Dartmouth bounds." Bangs, *Deeds*, 477–9.

14. PCR, 7:191. Drake, *BOI*, 3:67. Bangs, *Deeds*, 460–1, 452.

15. PCR, 7:190–1.

16. Bangs, *Deeds*, 342, 463, 472–3. "Massachusetts Land Records, 1620–1986," images, FamilySearch, (https://familysearch.org/ark:/61903/3:1:3QS7-89Z7-GQ9?cc=2106411& wc=MCBR-PWY%3A61612701%2C362501701: 22 May 2014), Plymouth > image 417 of 677; county courthouses and offices, Massachusetts. According to this document, John Cooke gave Namumpum "one third of the pay" (the remainder allotted to Wamsutta and Ousamequin) and engaged her "promise" to "remove the Indians of[f] from those lands," a stipulation in the original Dartmouth deed.

17. Bangs, *Deeds*, 460–3, 471. Peirce, *Indian History*, 189.

18. Increase Mather, "A Brief History of the War with the Indians in New England," in *So Dreadfull a Judgment*, ed. Slotkin and Folsom, 87. Lepore, *Name*, 23. Kawashima, *Igniting*, 99–100.

19. *PCR*, 5:138. Bangs, *Deeds*, 463–4, 469–71.

20. Peirce, *Indian History*, 189. The deed records that "the Indians of Assowamsett" had "agreed amongst themselves" to "leave out homelots," from a larger grant to the colony, however, the only "Indians" allotted lots in these deeds were Sassamon and his daughter and son-in-law. Bangs, *Deeds*, 469.

21. Bangs, *Deeds*, 467–8. Easton, "Relacion," 7. Note that Winslow's claim that Sassamon reported Philip's "endeavouring to engage all the Sachems round about in a war against some of the English" appears only in the narratives written after the war began, not in any of the documents surrounding the trial. *PCR*, 10:362.

22. Bangs, *Deeds*, 476–7, 481–4.

23. Lepore, *Name*, 24. Southworth and Thompson simultaneously acquired consent to settle Nemasket from Thomas Hunter and Popanahoe, or Peter, allegedly for the Massachusett people under Josiah Wampatuck, who died in the 1669 raid against the Mohawks. Bangs, *Deeds*, 480.

24. Easton to Winslow, NEHGS. Easton does not specify which river(s) Weetamoo referred to.

25. Frederick Smith, et al., *A Look at Westport Through Four Centuries* (Westport, RI: Westport Bicentennial Commission, 1976).

26. B. Church, *History*, ed. Dexter, 11. Phillips, "Pocasset," 2–14, 49–52.

27. Bangs, *Deeds*, 467.

28. Easton to Winslow, NEHGS.

29. Easton to Winslow, NEHGS.

30. *PCR*, 5:167. Slotkin and Folsom, eds., *Dreadfull*, 87. Easton, "Relacion," 8. Lepore, *Name*, 22

31. *PCR*, 5:169.

32. Easton, "Relacion," 8. Leach, *Flintlock*, 34. Brown to Winslow, June 11, 1675, MHS. *PCR*, 10:363. For insightful analysis regarding the impact of this "trial" on Wampanoag jurisdiction (and the opening of war), see Silverman, *Faith*, 103.

33. *CMHS*, 1st ser., 6:94. *PCR*, 10:363–4. Leach, *Flintlock*, 34. Glenn LaFantasie, *The Correspondence of Roger Williams* (Providence, RI: Brown/Rhode Island Historical Society, 1988), 691. Hubbard later claimed that "no answer could be obtained" from Philip "otherwise than threatening of war." Hubbard, *Narrative*, 72.

34. Josiah Winslow to "Weetamoo, and Ben her husband, Sachems of Pocasset," June 15, 1675, Winslow Family Papers II, item 89, MHS. Leach, *Flintlock*, 37–40. Bowen, *Early Rehoboth*, 53. Although he cited it, Leach essentially disregarded Winslow's letter to Weetamoo, its content and implications, instead privileging Church's account. To his credit, Drake foregrounds the letter in his analysis of Pocasset's "waver[ing]" position on the eve of war, although it appears he was not aware of the letter from Easton. James Drake, *King Philip's War: A Civil War in New England 1675–76* (Amherst, MA: University of Massachusetts Press, 2000), 97–8. See document at http://ourbeloved kin.com/awikhigan/right-relation.

35. *PCR*, 10:363. Slotkin and Folsom, eds., *Dreadfull*, 397–8, 400. B. Church, *History*, ed. Dexter, xix.

36. Brown to Winslow, June 11, 1675, MHS. Slotkin and Folsom, eds., *Dreadfull*, 400.

37. Nathaniel Saltonstall, *The Present State of New England With Respect to the Indian War* (London: Dorman Newman, 1675), 3. Slotkin and Folsom, eds., *Dreadfull*, 400. Winslow to Weetamoo, June 15, 1675, MHS. If Weetamoo did report to Church that they had all gone "to the dances," she may have strategically hid the number of her "men" from him, preventing him from attempting to make a count.

38. Slotkin and Folsom eds., *Dreadfull*, 400. Winslow to Weetamoo, June 15, 1675, MHS.

39. PCR 12: 242. Slotkin and Folsom, eds., *Dreadfull*, 400. Bangs, *Deeds*, 489. Roger Williams, *A Key into the Language of America* (Bedford, MA: Applewood Books, 1997), 142. Samuel G. Drake, *The Aboriginal Races of North America* (New York: Hurst, 1880), 189.

40. Slotkin and Folsom, eds., *Dreadfull*, 400. Peirce, *Indian History*, 44. Josiah Winslow to John Freeman, June 28, 1675, Winslow family papers II, item 91, MHS.

41. John Easton, "A Relacion of the Indyan Warre" (1675), in *Narratives of the Indian Wars 1675–1699*, ed. Charles Lincoln (New York: Charles Scribner's Sons, 1913), 7. Note that Easton's orthography has been modernized for ease of reading. Easton wrote his narrative, recalling this meeting and other events of the war, in February 1676, still advocating for mediation. Lepore, *Name*, 49. For significant readings, see Virginia DeJohn Anderson, *Creatures of Empire: How Domestic Animals Transformed Early America* (Oxford: Oxford University Press, 2006), 233–4. Silverman, *Faith*, 89, 99–100. Jennings, *Invasion*, 295–7. For Easton's "Relacion," see http://ourbelovedkin.com/awikhigan/right-relation.

42. Easton, "Relacion," 9.

43. Easton, "Relacion," 6–9. Neal Salisbury, *Manitou and Providence: Indians, Europeans, and the Making of New England, 1500–1643* (New York: Oxford University Press, 1982), 115.

44. Easton, "Relacion," 9. PCR, 5:63–80. CMHS, 1st ser., 6 (1800): 211. William Hubbard, *A Narrative of the Troubles with the Indians in New England* (1677) (Brattleboro, VT: William Fessenden, 1814), 61–4. Drake, *BOI*, 18–19. Silverman, *Faith*, 89, 100–2. Jennings, *Invasion*, 293. Peirce, *Indian History*, 56–7. Patrick M. Malone, *The Skulking Way of War: Technology and Tactics Among the New England Indians* (Lanham, MD:

Madison Books, 1991), 49, 54, 60–4. Anderson, *Creatures*, 232. Personal communication, Elizabeth Perry, October 19, 2015.

45. *CMHS*, 1st ser., 5 (1798): 196, 198, 200–1. Silverman, *Faith*, 84–5, 102. Jenny Pulsipher, *Subjects unto the Same King: Indians, English, and the Contest for Authority in Colonial New England* (Philadelphia: University of Pennsylvania Press, 2005), 95. Anderson, *Creatures*, 232.

46. *PCR*, 5:63–80. Drake, *BOI*, 3:18–21. Hubbard, *Narrative*, 61–4. Silverman, *Faith*, 89, 100–102. Peirce, *Indian History*, 56–7. Easton, "Relacion," 8–9.

47. *CMHS*, 1st ser., 5:195–8, 201–3. *PCR*, 5:64–5, 76–9. Drake, *BOI*, 3:21. Peirce, *Indian History*, 58. Cogley, *John Eliot's Mission to the Indians Before King Philip's War* (Cambridge, MA: Harvard University Press, 1999), 201–3. Jennings, *Invasion*, 293–4. Pulsipher, *Subjects*, 96–8. Silverman, *Faith*, 85, 102.

48. *PCR*, 5:77. Silverman, *Faith*, 85. *CMHS*, 1st ser., 5:199–200. Jennings, *Invasion*, 293–4. Cogley, *Eliot*, 202–3. Pulsipher, *Subjects*, 97–8.

49. *CMHS*, 1st ser., 5:199. *PCR*, 5:76–9. Drake, *BOI*, 19–23. Leach, *Flintlock*, 28. Anderson, *Creatures*, 232–3. Cogley, *Eliot*, 200–3. Jennings, *Invasion*, 292–4. Pulsipher, *Subjects*, 99–100. Silverman, *Faith*, 102. Kawashima, *Igniting*, 59–65.

50. Easton, "*Relacion*," 10–11. See, for example, Leach, *Flintlock*, 26–9; Pulsipher, *Subjects*, 94–100. Ebenezer Peirce maintained that Metacom "never had intended to carry out the agreement." Peirce, *Indian History*, 59.

51. *PCR*, 5:63–80. Easton, "Relacion," 9. Hubbard, *Narrative*, 61–4. Leach, *Flintlock*, 15, 25–9. Jennings, *Invasion*, 294. Silverman, *Faith*, 85, 84–101. Bangs, *Deeds*, 421–31. Pulsipher, *Subjects*, 95. Also, according to the agreement, Metacom could not sell land or engage in war without their approval. Note that Plymouth used the agreement in precisely this way postwar, asserting that Montaup was theirs not by right of conquest but because Philip broke the articles. See *PCR*, 2:369 and Salisbury, *Manitou*, 120.

52. Easton, "Relacion," 10.

53. Easton, "Relacion," 10–11.

54. Easton, "Relacion," 7–8, 10–11. Silverman, *Faith*, 89, 100, 102. Cogley, *Eliot*, 200–3.

55. Easton, "Relacion," 11. Silverman, *Faith*, 100–1.

56. Easton, "Relacion," 11. Anderson, *Creatures*, 233.

57. Anderson, *Creatures*, 233. See, for example, the case of Samuel, who drowned after drinking in Portsmouth, which Wootensauke witnessed. Inquest and verdict, July 17, 1670, manuscript 9001-Sa, Rhode Island Historical Society.

58. Charles Lincoln, editor of the "Relacion," remarks, "In no contemporary account of the war do we find more evidence of a desire to be impartial." Lincoln, ed., *Narratives*, 5.

59. *CMHS*, 4th ser., 7 (1865): 630.

60. Easton, "Relacion," 7.

61. Saltonstall, *Present*, 9.

62. Salstonstall, *Present*, 9. Eric Schultz and Michael Tougias, *King Philip's War: The History and Legacy of America's Forgotten Conflict* (Woodstock, VT: The Countryman Press, 2000), 21.

63. Hubbard, *Narrative*, 72. See also Mather, "Brief History," 88; Lepore, *Name*, 50–1, 106–10.

64. Thomas Church, *The History of King Philip's War*, ed. Samuel Drake (Exeter, NH: J & B Williams, 1843), 30–1. Lepore, *Name*, 17.
65. Easton, "Relacion," 12.

4. HERE COMES THE STORM

1. Note that fictionalized historical reconstruction/storytelling is indicated here and throughout the text by italics. For maps, documents, images, and connections, see http://ourbelovedkin.com/awikhigan/chapter4.
2. Ann Marie Plane, *Colonial Intimacies: Indian Marriage in Early New England* (Ithaca, NY: Cornell University Press, 2000), 1–4. Silverman, *Faith and Boundaries: Colonists, Christianity, and Community among the Wampanoag Indians of Martha's Vineyard, 1600–1871* (New York: Cambridge University Press, 2007), 90–1. My understanding of the conditions on the eve of war is informed by conversations at Montaup and in Wampanoag territory with Elizabeth and Jonathan Perry, to whom I am grateful.
3. George Madison Bodge, *Soldiers in King Philip's War* (Boston: Rockwell and Churchill, 1906), 88. Douglas Edward Leach, *Flintlock and Tomahawk: New England in King Philip's War* (Hyannis, MA: Parnassus Imprints, 1996), 37. John Easton, "A Relacion of the Indyan Warre" (1675), in *Narratives of the Indian Wars 1675–1699*, ed. Charles Lincoln (New York: Charles Scribner's Sons, 1913), 10, 12. Glenn LaFantasie, ed., *The Correspondence of Roger Williams* (Providence, RI: Brown/Rhode Island Historical Society, 1988), 694.
4. William Bradford, *A Letter from Major William Bradford to the Rev. John Cotton* (Providence, RI: S.P.C. for the Society of Colonial Wars, 1914), 15. Richard Bowen, *Early Rehoboth* (Rehoboth, MA: Rumford Press, 1945), 73, 71. Roger Williams, *A Key in the Language of America* (1643) (Bedford, MA: Applewood Books 1997), 182.
5. Bowen, *Early Rehoboth*, 53–4. Howard Chapin, *Sachems of the Narragansetts* (Providence, RI: Rhode Island Historical Society, 1931), 75–6. *Collections of the Massachusetts Historical Society* (CMHS) (Boston: The Society, 1792–1888), 5th ser., 9 (1885): 74–6. Elisha Potter, *Early History of Narragansett* (Providence, RI: Marshall, Brown, 1886), 71.
6. Bowen, *Early Rehoboth*, 53–4. Eric Schultz and Michael Tougias, *King Philip's War: The History and Legacy of America's Forgotten Conflict* (Woodstock, VT: The Countryman Press, 2000), 41. Leach, *Flintlock*, 41.
7. Bowen, *Early Rehoboth*, 53–4.
8. Bowen, *Early Rehoboth*, 53–4. See also Samuel Gardner Drake, *The Book of the Indians (BOI)* (Boston: Antiquarian Bookstore, 1841), 75–6.
9. Bowen, *Early Rehoboth*, 53–4. LaFantasie, *Correspondence*, 690–2.
10. Bowen, *Early Rehoboth*, 53–4.
11. Bowen, *Early Rehoboth*, 53–4.
12. Bowen, *Early Rehoboth*, 55. John Brown to Josiah Winslow, June 11, 1675, Winslow Family Papers II, item 89, Massachusetts Historical Society (MHS). J. Hammond Trumbull and Charles J. Hoadly, eds., *The Public Records of the Colony of Connecticut, 1636–1776* (Hartford, CT: Lockwood and Brainard, 1850–90), 2:336.
13. Bowen, *Early Rehoboth*, 54–5, 68, 76.

14. *A Court Martial Held at Newport* (Albany, NY: Munsell, 1858), 12–3. Nathaniel Bradstreet Shurtleff, *Records of the Colony of New Plymouth, in New England* (Boston:
William White, 1855), 5:169, 10:364. William Hubbard, *A History of the Indian Wars
in New England*, ed. Samuel Gardner Drake (Roxbury, MA: W. E. Woodward, 1865),
39. Patrick Malone, *The Skulking Way of War: Technology and Tactics Among the New
England Indians* (Lanham, MD: Madison Books, 1991), 18, 29. The historical narratives by Hubbard and Winslow conflate and confuse John Archer and John Lawton,
both of whom were living at Pocasset on the eve of war.

15. *Court Martial*, 12–13.

16. *Court Martial*, 12–13.

17. Daniel Gookin, "An Historical Account of the Doings and Sufferings of the Christian
Indians in New England," in *Transactions and Collections of the American Antiquarian
Society* 2 (Cambridge, MA: American Antiquarian Society, 1836), 441. Bodge, *Soldiers*,
27, 48, 80–1. Bowen, *Early Rehoboth*, 62. Mary White Rowlandson, *The Sovereignty and
Goodness of God: With Related Documents*, ed. Neal Salisbury (Boston: Bedford Books,
1997), 120. Alonzo Lewis, *The History of Lynn* (Lynn, MA: George Herbert, 1890), 39,
40. David Stewart-Smith, "The Pennacook Indians and the New England Frontier,
1604–1733" (PhD diss., Union Institute, 1998), 86. Sidney Perley, *The Indian Land Titles
of Essex County Massachusetts* (Salem, MA: Essex Book and Print Club, 1912), 8–9. For
location of Winisimet, see http://ourbelovedkin.com/awikhigan/revolt-map.

18. Bowen, *Early Rehoboth*, 53, 55–62. Leach, *Flintlock*, 37–40, 45–7. Bodge, *Soldiers*, 27,
59–63, 88–90, 460. Malone, *Skulking*, 54–64.

19. Salisbury, ed., *Sovereignty*, 122. Daniel Gookin, *Historical Collections of the Indians
of New England (1674)* (North Stratford, NH: Ayer, 2000), 24–7. Malone, *Skulking*,
20–4, 52, 59, 61, 66, 80, 82, 100. Barbara Mann, *Iroquois Women: The Gantowisas*
(New York: Peter Lang, 2004), 117, 179–82. Arthur Parker, "The Constitution of the
Five Nations," in *Parker on the Iroquois*, ed. William Fenton (Syracuse, NY: Syracuse
University Press, 1968). Jon Parmenter, *The Edge of the Woods: Iroquoia, 1534–1701*
(East Lansing, MI: Michigan State University Press, 2010), 137.

20. Bowen, *Early Rehoboth*, 62. George Ellis and John Morris, *Easton's Relation of the
Causes of King Philip's War* (New York: Grafton Press, 1906), 20n21. For eclipse, see
http://ourbelovedkin.com/awikhigan/mapping-war.

21. Bowen, *Early Rehoboth*, 62. Leach, *Flintlock*, 43, 47–8, 53. Gookin, "Historical Account," 438.

22. Bradford, *Letter to Cotton*, 4. Bowen, *Early Rehoboth*, 62–3. Schultz and Tougias,
King Philip's War, 98–101. Leach, *Flintlock*, 42–3. Thomas Church, *The History of
King Philip's War*, ed. Samuel Drake (Boston: Thomas Wait and Son, 1827), 30–3.

23. Bradford, *Letter to Cotton*, 5. Josiah Winslow to John Freeman, June 28, 1675, Winslow Family Papers II, item 91, Massachusetts Historical Society. Bowen, *Early Rehoboth*, 55, 57–8. Church, *History*, ed. Drake, 31–3. Leach, *Flintlock*, 43, 50. Schultz and
Tougias, *King Philip's War*, 62–3, 101–2. Ebenezer Peirce, *Indian History, Biography
and Genealogy* (North Abington, MA: Zerviah Gould Mitchell, 1878), 84. Benjamin
Church, *The History of King Philip's War*, ed. Henry Dexter (Boston: John Wiggin,

1865), 20. Thomas Williams Bicknell, *A History of Barrington, Rhode Island* (Providence, RI: Snow and Farnham, 1898), 159. Note that two more men were "ambushed and killed when they rode" toward Rehoboth "in search of a surgeon" following the ambush.

24. Bodge, *Soldiers*, 80–1. Bowen, *Early Rehoboth*, 62–3. Gookin, "Historical Account," 441. Church, *History*, ed. Drake, 32–3.

25. Salisbury, ed., *Sovereignty*, 122. Malone, *Skulking*, 21–2, 52, 59, 61, 66, 80, 82, 100.

26. Those colonial soldiers still using matchlocks were especially hindered by rainfall, as rain often "extinguished burning match tips" and "could also ruin one's spare match" and soak priming powder. As Malone notes, Native men discerned long before settlers that the flintlock, which did not require a lighted match and was "faster" and less cumbersome "to fire," was more adaptable to woodland warfare, putting them at a military advantage. Malone, *Skulking*, 33.

27. Richard Slotkin and James Folsom, eds., *So Dreadfull a Judgment: Puritan Responses to King Philip's War 1676–1677* (Middletown, CT: Wesleyan Press, 1978), 88–9. Bowen, *Early Rehoboth*, 62. Gookin, "Historical Account," 441–2. Jill Lepore, *The Name of War: King Philip's War and the Origins of American Identity* (New York: Knopf, 1998), 99–104.

28. Bowen, *Early Rehoboth*, 63. Malone, *Skulking*, 21. See also Slotkin and Folsom, eds., *Dreadfull*, 401, 403.

29. Slotkin and Folsom, eds., *Dreadfull*, 403. Bodge, *Soldiers*, 87. Bowen, *Early Rehoboth*, 59, 63. Leach, *Flintlock*, 53. Note that Church's account, in this instance, appears more likely than Hubbard's, as Drake concluded in his 1827 edition of Church. Church, *History*, ed. Drake, 34.

30. Massachusetts Archives 67:207. Bowen, *Early Rehoboth*, 63–4. Leach, *Flintlock*, 53.

31. Bowen, *Early Rehoboth*, 64. Church, *History*, ed. Drake, 34–5. Leach, *Flintlock*, 43, 54. Lepore, *Name*, 99–104, 118–9. Personal communication, Linda Coombs, April 21, 2017.

32. Bowen, *Early Rehoboth*, 64, 55. Church, *History*, ed. Drake, 35. Josiah Winslow to James Cudworth, July 6, 1675, Winslow Family Papers, item 92, Massachusetts Historical Society. Anderson, *Creatures*, 234. Leach, *Flintlock*, 40, 55–6.

33. Bowen, *Early Rehoboth*, 64–5. Bradford, *Letter to Cotton*, 5. Leach, *Flintlock*, 40, 54.

34. Bowen, *Early Rehoboth*, 65. Leach, *Flintlock*, 54. Bodge, *Soldiers*, 90.

35. Salisbury, ed., *Sovereignty*, 120. Peirce, *Indian History*, 85. Bowen, *Early Rehoboth*, 65. Gookin, "Historical Account," 441–2.

36. Bowen, *Early Rehoboth*, 64. Church, *History*, ed. Drake, 26.

37. Bradford, *Letter to Cotton*, 5. Church, *History*, ed. Drake, 26–33, 39. B. Church, *History*, ed. Dexter, 26. Bowen, *Early Rehoboth*, 58, 69. Gookin, "Historical Account," 442. For maps, documents, images, and connections, see http://ourbelovedkin.com/awikhigan/mapping-war.

38. James Cudworth to Josiah Winslow, July 9, 1675, Winslow Family Papers II, item 93, Massachusetts Historical Society. Church, *History*, ed. Drake, 39–47. B. Church, *History*, ed. Dexter, 30–4. Schultz and Tougias, *King Philip's War*, 238–41. Malone,

Skulking, 21, 90. Arthur Phillips, *The Phillips History of Fall River* (Fall River, MA: Dover Press, 1941–1946), fascicle 1 (1941), 34, 100, 103

39. Cudworth to Winslow, July 9, 1675, MHS. Winslow to Cudworth, July 6, 1675, MHS. Church, *History*, ed. Drake, 47.

40. Malone, *Skulking*, 22, 80. Schultz and Tougias, *King Philip's War*, 114–7. Lepore, *Name*, 78. Leach, *Flintlock*, 66. The garrison house of John Cooke was among those few excepted.

41. Bowen, *Early Rehoboth*, 65, 73. Nathaniel Saltonstall, *The Present State of New England With Respect to the Indian War* (London: Dorman Newman, 1675), 13. Lepore, *Name*, xxv. Schultz and Tougias, *King Philip's War*, 115.

42. Bowen, *Early Rehoboth*, 66. LaFantasie, *Correspondence* (Providence, RI: Brown/Rhode Island Historical Society, 1988), 701. Francis Jennings, *The Invasion of America: Indians, Colonialism, and the Cant of Conquest* (Chapel Hill, NC: University of North Carolina Press, 2010), 305. Gookin, "Historical Account," 444. Wait Winthrop, *A Letter Written by Capt. Wait Winthrop from Mr. Smiths in Narragansett to Govr. John Winthrop of the Colony of Connecticut* (Providence, RI: Standard Printing for the Society of Colonial Wars, 1919), 13.

43. LaFantasie, *Correspondence*, 701–2. Charles Lincoln, ed., *Narratives of the Indian Wars 1675–1699* (New York: Charles Scribner's Sons, 1913), 13. Howard Chapin, *Sachems of the Narragansetts* (Providence, RI: Rhode Island Historical Society, 1931), 77. Bowen, *Early Rehoboth*, 56, 66, 77. Jennings, *Invasion*, 302–7. Bodge, *Soldiers*, 59–62. Drake, *BOI*, 79. "Acts of the Massachusetts Council about Narragansett Sachems, Sept. 5, 1668," Rhode Island Historical Society manuscript 9004, 2:43. Wait Winthrop and Richard Smith represented Connecticut.

44. Chapin, *Sachems*, 77. Bowen, *Early Rehoboth*, 58–9, 66. Jennings, *Invasion*, 306.

45. Bowen, *Early Rehoboth*, 67–8. Josiah Winslow to John Leverett, July 18, 1675, Winslow Family Papers II, item 97, Massachusetts Historical Society.

46. Bowen, *Early Rehoboth*, 56. Jennings, *Invasion*, 306. Wait Winthrop had traveled on a parallel mission to secure a pledge of "neutrality" from Ninigret, whose counselor Cornman was present at the Pettaquamscut meeting. Chapin, *Sachems*, 77.

47. Winslow to Leverett, July 18, 1675.

48. Easton, "Relacion," ed. Lincoln, 12. Ellis and Morris, *Easton's Relation*, 18n20. Bradford, *Letter to Cotton*, 15. Jeremy Dupertuis Bangs, *Indian Deeds: Land Transactions in Plymouth Colony, 1620–1691* (Boston: New England Historic Genealogical Society, 2008), 486.

49. Easton, "Relacion," ed. Lincoln, 12–14. Bradford, *Letter to Cotton*, 15. Bowen, *Early Rehoboth*, 96. Bangs, *Deeds*, 486. Church, *History*, ed. Drake, 26, 36. Easton and Peter Awashonks's accounts provide an important counterpoint to Church's narrative, wherein he insists he went over to Sakonnet in part to fulfill a promise of protection he made to Awashonks.

50. Cudworth to Winslow, July 9, 1675, MHS. Bangs, *Deeds*, 486, 490. Church, *History*, ed. Drake, 47, 50. Mammanuah later testified that "himself and his men, in number fifteen, had, during our late troubles, continewed faithfull to the English, and some of

his men had all the time bin in our service." See also Mammanuah's grant of 100 acres to Alderman, "now liveing neer Punckatest pond," "for service done . . . in the late warr." Dorothy Worthington, *Rhode Island Land Evidences*, 1648–1696 (Providence, RI: Rhode Island Historical Society, 1921), 1:263.

51. Bowen, *Early Rehoboth*, 71, 73. Church, *History*, ed. Drake (1827 ed.), 50. Malone, *Skulking*, 10–11, 87.

52. Bowen, *Early Rehoboth*, 73, 77. Church, *History*, ed. Drake, 48–9. Bodge, *Soldiers*, 81, 395. Peirce, *Indian History*, 94. Bangs, *Deeds*, 479–81. Gookin, "Historical Account," 441–4. Malone, *Skulking*, 53–4, 58–66. Schultz and Tougias, *King Philip's War*, 238–9.

53. Gookin, "Historical Account," 441. Bowen, *Early Rehoboth*, 71. Malone, *Skulking*, 20–1, 52. Schultz and Tougias, *King Philip's War*, 238–9.

54. Cudworth to Winslow, July 9, 1675. Bradford, *Letter to Cotton*, 15. Bowen, *Early Rehoboth*, 71, 73. Church, *History*, ed. Drake (1827 ed.), 49. Malone, *Skulking*, 21, 30–2, 34–5, 65–6, 89.

55. Bradford, *Letter to Cotton*, 15. Bowen, *Early Rehoboth*, 71, 73. Malone, *Skulking*, 11.

56. Bradford, *Letter to Cotton*, 15. Bowen, *Early Rehoboth*, 71, 73. Church, *History*, ed. Drake, 49. Church later claimed they had "come within hearing of the Crys of their Women, and Children" but "were commanded back by their Captain." No evidence in Cudworth or Bradford's letter supports this romanticized claim. Slotkin and Folsom, eds., *Dreadfull*, 411.

57. Malone, *Skulking*, 7, 22, 58, 60. Bradford, *Letter to Cotton*, 15. Kevin Sweeney, "Military Uses of Firearms in Seventeenth-Century New England," 17th Century Warfare, Diplomacy, & Society in the American Northeast Conference, Pequot Museum, Connecticut, October 2013. Kevin Sweeney, personal communication, April 14, 2017. Elizabeth Perry, personal communication, October 19, 2015.

58. John Freeman to Josiah Winslow, July 18, 1675, Winslow Family Papers II, item 95, Massachusetts Historical Society. Josiah Winslow to James Cudworth, July 18, 1675, Winslow Family Papers II, item 96, Massachusetts Historical Society. Josiah Winslow to John Leverett, July 18, 1675, Winslow Family Papers II, item 97, Massachusetts Historical Society. Bowen, *Early Rehoboth*, 71.

59. Freeman, "Freeman to Winslow, July 18, 1675". Gookin, "Historical Account," 81.

60. Freeman, "Freeman to Winslow, July 18, 1675". Bowen, *Early Rehoboth*, 71, 73.

61. Bowen, *Early Rehoboth*, 73. Bradford, *Letter to Cotton*, 5–6, 16. Gookin, "Historical Account," 444. Bodge, *Soldiers*, 81. On location of Pocasset swamp, see Schultz and Tougias, *King Philip's War*, 121–4.

62. Bowen, *Early Rehoboth*, 71.

63. Bradford, *Letter to Cotton*, 8, 16. Bowen, *Early Rehoboth*, 56–7, 71, 73, 77. Church, *History*, ed. Drake (1827 ed.), 50. Leach, *Flintlock*, 68.

64. Saltonstall, *Present State*, 13. Malone, *Skulking*, 66. Gookin, "Historical Account," 444. Salisbury, ed., *Sovereignty*, 126.

65. Bradford, *Letter to Cotton*, 16. Gookin, "Historical Account," 444. Lepore, *Name*, 97–100, 104, 118–9.

66. Bradford, *Letter to Cotton*, 16. Bowen, *Early Rehoboth*, 71, 73. Church, *History*, ed. Drake (1827 ed.), 50.

67. Bradford, *Letter to Cotton*, 8, 16. Church, *History*, ed. Drake, (1827 ed.), 50. Bowen, *Early Rehoboth*, 71, 73. Leach, *Flintlock*, 69.

68. Bowen, *Early Rehoboth*, 72, 82, 89–91, 94, 96. Phillips, *Fall River*, 3:95–6. Church, *History*, ed. Drake (1827 ed.), 50. Leach, *Flintlock*, 71–2. Schultz and Tougias, *King Philip's War*, 124.

69. Bowen, *Early Rehoboth*, 91–2, 94. Gookin, "Historical Account," 445. Leach, *Flintlock*, 71–2, 75–7. Michael Leroy Oberg, *Uncas: First of the Mohegans* (Ithaca, NY: Cornell University Press, 2006), 174–5. Nathaniel was the son of Captain Thomas.

70. For more on Nipsachuck, see Christine DeLucia, "The Memory Frontier: Uncommon Pursuits of Past and Place in the Northeast after King Philip's War (1675–1678)," *Journal of American History* 98:4 (March 2012): 975–97; and National Park Service, American Battlefield Protection Program, Technical Report: "The 1676 Battle of Nipsachuck: Identification and Evaluation" (GA-2255-11-016), April 12, 2013, 27–9, 40–1, 83–5, 91, 94, 108, http://kpwar.org/wp-content/uploads/2015/04/FINAL-REPORT -Nipsachuck.pdf.

71. Bowen, *Early Rehoboth*, 78, 91, 94–5. Gookin, "Historical Account," 445–6. Leach, *Flintlock*, 76. Lepore, *Name*, 86.

72. Bowen, *Early Rehoboth*, 95. Oberg, *Uncas*, 176. Leach, *Flintlock*, 76–7. Malone, *Skulking*, 21.

73. Bowen, *Early Rehoboth*, 83, 98–99. A captured Pocasset man, apparently Metacom's "uncle," reportedly returning "to Pocasset" when Mosely's company "met him," reported that the troops had killed 23 men, including the 4 captains.

74. Lincoln, ed., *Narratives*, 26.

5. THE PRINTER'S REVOLT

1. Samuel Morison, *Harvard College in the Seventeenth Century* (Cambridge, MA: Harvard University Press, 1936), 69. Daniel Gookin, "An Historical Account of the Doings and Sufferings of the Christian Indians in New England," in *Transactions and Collections of the American Antiquarian Society* (Cambridge, MA: American Antiquarian Society, 1836), 2:455–9. Henry Nourse, ed., *Early Records of Lancaster 1643–1725* (Lancaster, MA: W. J. Coulter, 1884), 99. Jill Lepore, *The Name of War: King Philip's War and the Origins of American Identity* (New York: Knopf, 1998), 137. For maps, documents, images, and connections, see http://ourbelovedkin.com/awikhigan/chapter5.

2. Daniel Gookin, *Historical Collections of the Indians of New England (1674)* (North Stratford, NH: Ayer, 2000), 45.

3. Gookin, *Historical Collections*, 45, 48–9, 54. Gookin, "Historical Account," 480. Nathaniel Bradstreet Shurtleff, *Records of the Colony of New Plymouth, in New England* (PCR) (Boston: William White, 1855), 10:323–31, 356. John Ford, ed., *Some Correspondence between the Governors and Treasurers of the New England Company in London and the Commissioners of the United Colonies in America* (London: Spottiswood and

Co., 1896), 28. Michael Clark, ed., *The Eliot Tracts* (Westport, CT: Praeger, 2003), 403–4. Richard W. Cogley, "A Seventeenth-Century Native American Family: William of Sudbury and His Four Sons," *The New England Historical and Genealogical Register*, 153 (April 1999), 174–5. "A Memorandum of Indian Children Put Forth into Service to the English," in Mary White Rowlandson, *The Sovereignty and Goodness of God: With Related Documents*, ed. Neal Salisbury (Boston: Bedford Books, 1997), 144.

4. Massachusetts Archives, 30:146. For map, document, and connections, see http://our belovedkin.com/awikhigan/1668-covenant.

5. Massachusetts Archives, 30:146. See, for example, Jenny Pulsipher, *Subjects unto the Same King: Indians, English, and the Contest for Authority in Colonial New England* (Philadelphia: University of Pennsylvania Press, 2005), 108.

6. Dennis Connole, *Indians of the Nipmuck Country in Southern New England, 1630– 1750* (Jefferson, NC: McFarland and Company, 2001), 20–3. Louis Roy, *Quaboag Plantation alias Brookefield: A Seventeenth-Century Massachusetts Town* (Brookfield, MA: L. E. Roy, 1965), 9–11. Levi Chase, *The Bay Path and Along the Way* (Norwood, MA: Plimton Press, 1919) 175–211. Gookin, *Historical Collections*, 45–52. Josiah Howard Temple, *History of North Brookfield, Massachusetts* (Brookfield, MA: North Brookfield, 1887), 24–6.

7. "Wotowsaukwas to Massachusetts Governor and Council, October 1667," facsimile copies of the Records of the Massachusetts Archives, #140, Massachusetts Historical Society. Gookin, *Historical Collections*, 50–2. Connole, *Nipmuck*, 79–82. Michael Leroy Oberg, *Uncas: First of the Mohegans* (Ithaca, NY: Cornell University Press, 2003), 169. Joseph Laurent, *New Familiar Abenaki and English Dialogues* (Quebec: L. Brousseau, 1884), 23.

8. Massachusetts Archives, 30:146. Gookin, "Historical Account," 436. Clark, ed., *Eliot Tracts*, 403. David Stewart-Smith, "The Pennacook Indians and the New England Frontier, 1604–1733," (PhD diss., Union Institute, 1998), 136, 155, 161–9. David Jaffee, *People of the Wachusett* (Ithaca, NY: Cornell University Press, 1999), 59–66. Personal communication, Kahntineta Horn, Norridgewock and Kahnawake, August 2013 and November 2014. See also Jon Parmenter, *The Edge of the Woods: Iroquoia, 1534–1701* (East Lansing, MI: Michigan State University Press, 2010).

9. Connole, *Nipmuck*, 55. Oberg, *Uncas*, 169. John Pendergast, *The Bend in the River* (Tyngsborough, MA: Merrimac River Press, 1992), 50, 67, 69. William Willis, *History of Portland from 1632 to 1864* (Portland, ME: Bailey and Noyes, 1865), 134. Gookin, *Historical Collections*, 37. Nathaniel Shurtleff, *Records of the Governor and Company of the Massachusetts Bay in New England* (Boston: W. White, 1853), vol. 4, pt. 2, 385–6. Elias Nason, *A History of the Town of Dunstable, Massachusetts* (Boston: Alfred Mudge and Son, 1877), 9–11. Willard's son married Tyng's daughter.

10. Kristina Bross, *Dry Bones and Indian Sermons: Praying Indians in Colonial America* (Ithaca, NY: Cornell University Press, 2004), 152. Clark, ed., *Eliot Tracts*, 15–16, 368, 387–9. Jean O'Brien, *Dispossession by Degrees: Indian Land and Identity in Natick, Massachusetts, 1650–1790* (New York: Cambridge University Press, 1997), 26–43. Pam

Ellis, Tribal Historian for Natick Nipmuc Tribal Council, personal communication, May, 2009.

11. O'Brien, *Dispossession*, 12, 44–8. Laurent, *Dialogues*, 54. James Hammond Trumbull, *Natick Dictionary* (Lincoln, NE: University of Nebraska Press, 2009), 6, 104. As O'Brien notes, Christian Nipmucs continued to rely on hunting and fishing, which made the maintenance of their land at the falls and along the river even more critical to their survival.

12. "Letter of John Eliot, July 3, 1667," facsimile copies of the Records of the Massachusetts Archives, #138, Massachusetts Historical Society. Ann Marie Plane, *Colonial Intimacies: Indian Marriage in Early New England* (Ithaca, NY: Cornell University Press, 2000), 1–3.

13. O'Brien, *Dispossession*, 27.

14. Gookin, *Historical Collections*, 45–9. Samuel Gardner Drake, *The Book of the Indians* (*BOI*) (Boston: Antiquarian Bookstore, 1841), 2:51.

15. Massachusetts Archives: 30:169. George Madison Bodge, *Soldiers in King Philip's War* (Boston: Rockwell and Churchill, 1906), 104. Pulsipher, *Subjects*, 108. Douglas Edward Leach, *Flintlock and Tomahawk: New England in King Philip's War* (New York: Macmillan, 1958), 73–4. Temple, *Brookfield*, 74. Curtis's expedition went out at the same time as Hutchinson's first commission to Narragansett, with the same purpose.

16. For a reading that emphasizes "ethnicity" and racial "identity," see Pulsipher, *Subjects*, 108.

17. Massachusetts Archives 30:169. Bodge, *Soldiers*, 104–5.

18. Temple, *Brookfield*, 75–80. Lucius R. Paige, *History of Hardwick, Massachusetts* (Boston: Houghton, Mifflin and Co., 1883), 6–7. Bodge, *Soldiers*, 104–5. Gookin, "Historical Account," 436, 442–3, 445. For map, see http://ourbelovedkin.com/awikhigan/revolt-map.

19. Temple, *Brookfield*, 75–80. Paige, *Hardwick*, 6–7. Oberg, *Uncas*, 174. J. Hammond Trumbull and Charles J. Hoadly, eds., *The Public Records of the Colony of Connecticut, 1636–1776* (*CT Records*) (Hartford, CT: Lockwood and Brainard, 1850–90), 2:336. Bodge, *Soldiers*, 104–5. Gookin, "Historical Account," 442, 445.

20. Temple, *Brookfield*, 76. Bodge, *Soldiers*, 104–5. Gookin, "Historical Account," 450.

21. Temple, *Brookfield*, 76. Bodge, *Soldiers*, 104–5. Eric B. Schultz and Michael J. Tougias, *King Philip's War: The History and Legacy of America's Forgotten Conflict* (Woodstock, VT: Countryman Press, 2000), 143–5. For maps, images, and connections, see http://ourbelovedkin.com/awikhigan/menimesit_quaboag.

22. Temple, *Brookfield*, 100.

23. Temple, *Brookfield*, 76–7. Connole, *Nipmuck*, 22.

24. Temple, *Brookfield*, 77–8.

25. Temple, *Brookfield*, 77.

26. Temple, *Brookfield*, 77.

27. Temple, *Brookfield*, 77–8.

28. Temple, *Brookfield*, 77–8. Bodge, *Soldiers*, 104–5.

29. Bodge, *Soldiers*, 105. Gookin described Matoonas as a "grave and sober Indian," chosen to serve as "constable" at Pakachoag. Gookin, *Historical Collections*, 52–3. The

title "constable" may have been given to men who were already war chiefs, since several led raids during the war, including Black James and Matoonas.

30. Temple, *Brookfield*, 79.

31. Temple, *Brookfield*, 78–80. Bodge, *Soldiers*, 106. Massachusetts Archives, 67:227. This report later "proved false." Connole, *Nipmuck*, 166.

32. Richard Bowen, *Early Rehoboth: Documented Historical Studies of Families and Events in this Plymouth Colony Township* (Rehoboth, MA: Rumford Press, 1945), 97–9. Gookin, "Historical Account," 446. Temple, *Brookfield*, 99. Leach, *Flintlock*, 76–7. Oberg, *Uncas*, 176.

33. Temple, *Brookfield*, 79. Gookin *Historical Collections*, 49–50. Gookin, "Historical Account," 447. The sons of Hassanamesit ruler Robin Petavit, Sampson had first taught with Job at Okkanamesit, and by 1674 he taught at Webquasset while Joseph taught at Chabanakongkomun. For maps, documents, images, and connections, see http://ourbelovedkin.com/awikhigan/menimesit_quaboag.

34. Temple, *Brookfield*, 79–81. Connole, *Nipmuck*, 135, 166, 281. Gookin, "Historical Account," 447–9. Schultz and Tougias, *King Philip's War*, 142, 147–8. These settlers included John Ayres, William Pritchard, and Richard Coy.

35. Temple, *Brookfield*, 32, 91, 100. Connole, *Nipmuck*, 164, 167. Paige, *Hardwick*, 79.

36. "Great David," *The New England Indian Papers Series* (NEIPS), Paul Grant-Costa and Tobias Glaza, eds., Yale University Library Digital Collections, http://images .library.yale.edu/walpoleweb/footnote.asp?db=a&id=202. Gookin, "Historical Account," 456–8. Drake, *BOI*, 3:81–2.

37. Virginia DeJohn Anderson, "King Philip's Herds: Indians, Colonialism, and the Problem of Livestock in Early New England," *William and Mary Quarterly* 51:4 (Oct. 1994): 614.

38. Temple, *Brookfield*, 81, 89. Schultz and Tougias, *King Philip's War*, 147–55. Gookin "Historical Account," 447–8. Roy, *Quaboag*, 9–11. Special thanks to Ed Lonergan for guiding me through the crucial sites of Quaboag and Menimesit.

39. Temple, *Brookfield*, 79, 81, 91. Schultz and Tougias, *King Philip's War*, 150–5.

40. Temple, *Brookfield*, 81–2, 89–90. Gookin, "Historical Account," 447–8, 456–7. William Hubbard, *A History of the Indian Wars in New England*, ed. Samuel Gardner Drake (Roxbury, MA: W. E. Woodward, 1865), 98.

41. Temple, *Brookfield*, 82, 89–90. Gookin, "Historical Account," 447–8. Halsey Thomas, *Notes from The Diary of Samuel Sewall: 1674–1729* (New York: Farrar, Straus, and Giroux, 1973), 1:23.

42. Temple, *Brookfield*, 89. Increase Mather, "A Brief History of the Warr with the Indians in New England," in *So Dreadfull a Judgment: Puritan Responses to King Philip's War 1676–1677*, ed. Richard Slotkin and James Folsom (Middletown, CT: Wesleyan Press 1978), 91.

43. Drake *BOI*, 2:29. Temple, *Brookfield*, 89. Gookin, "Historical Account," 447–8. Thanks to Pam Ellis for observing that "Memecho" was likely Camecho, a common Nipmuc surname, appearing in the records after the war. See O'Brien, *Dispossession*, 95.

44. Bowen, *Early Rehoboth*, 94–8, 107.

45. Bodge, *Soldiers*, 50. Bowen, *Early Rehoboth*, 94–8. Hubbard, *Indian Wars*, 94–5.

46. Temple, *Brookfield*, 83, 91. Drake *BOI*, 3:29. Hubbard, *Indian Wars*, 99. Roy, *Quaboag*, 73, 158–9. Schultz and Tougias, *King Philip's War*, 155, 157–8. Personal communication, Ed Lonergan, West Brookfield.

47. Temple, *Brookfield*, 83–7, 90. Drake *BOI*, 3:29–30. Hubbard, *Indian Wars*, 99. Roy, *Quaboag*, 73, 158–9. Schultz and Tougias, *King Philip's War*, 155, 157.

48. Temple, *Brookfield*, 83–5, 90. Drake *BOI*, 3:29. Hubbard, *Indian Wars*, 99. Roy, *Quaboag*, 73, 158–9, 161. Schultz and Tougias, *King Philip's War*, 157.

49. Temple, *Brookfield*, 85. Bowen, *Early Rehoboth*, 94–8.

50. Hubbard, *Indian Wars*, 98–101. Temple, *Brookfield*, 83–8. Leach, *Flintlock*, 83–4. Personal communication, Ed Lonergan, West Brookfield, June 25, 2013. My reading is a reversal of Wheeler's original attempt to turn a defeat into a victory. Asserting that the warriors' goal was to "destroy them by fire," he created a narrative of divine intervention, marked by the rain and Willard's arrival, despite the fact that Willard was driven inside and the rain did not stop the warriors from burning the church. He wrote, "When they saw their divers designs" to "destroy" them "unsuccessful, and their hopes therein disappointed, they then fired" the remaining buildings and left "towards the breaking of the day," as if in defeat. Wheeler either obfuscated or missed the point of the "siege," although he sorely felt its impacts. Wheeler seemed especially concerned with portraying himself in good light, having failed in both of his missions. Although attributing their salvation to God, he did give himself credit for sending Curtis to seek help. Temple, *Brookfield*, 87–8.

51. Slotkin and Folsom, eds., *Dreadfull*, 91–2. Drake, *BOI*, 3:30. Temple, *Brookfield*, 100–1.

52. Drake, *BOI*, 3:30, 32. Nathaniel Saltonstall, *The Present State of New England With Respect to the Indian War* (London: Dorman Newman, 1675), reprinted in *Old Indian Chronicle: Chronicles of the Indians from the Discovery of America to the Present Time*, ed. Samuel Drake (Boston: Antiquarian Institute, 1836), 13. Henry Nourse, ed., *The Narrative of the Captivity and Restoration of Mrs. Mary Rowlandson* (Cambridge, MA: J. Wilson, 1903), 89. See also Bowen, *Early Rehoboth*, 101, and Russell Bourne, *The Red King's Rebellion: Racial Politics in New England 1675–1678* (Oxford University Press, 1991), 126–9.

53. Joseph Nicolar, *The Life and Traditions of the Red Man* (Bangor, ME: C. H. Glass, 1893), 64. Neal Salisbury, *Manitou and Providence: Indians, Europeans, and the Making of New England, 1500–1643* (New York: Oxford University Press, 1982), 13. For the Great Beaver see "Amiskwôlowôkoiak—the People of the Beaver-tail Hill," http://1704.deerfield.history.museum/voices/stories.do; Margaret Bruchac, "Earthshapers and Placemakers: Algonkian Indian Stories and the Landscape," *Indigenous Archaeologies: Politics and Practice*, ed. H. Martin Wobst and Claire Smith (London: Routledge Press, 2003); and Lisa Brooks, *The Common Pot: The Recovery of Native Space in the Northeast* (Minneapolis: University of Minnesota Press, 2008), 17–24.

54. *Collections of the Massachusetts Historical Society* (Boston: The Society, 1792–1888), 3rd ser., 3 (1833): 154. Salisbury, *Manitou*, 13, 49, 231, 236. See also Virginia DeJohn

Anderson, *Creatures of Empire: How Domestic Animals Transformed Early America* (Oxford: Oxford University Press, 2006), 206–8. Brooks, *Common Pot*, 59–64.

55. Great thanks to J. Kēhaulani Kauanui for helping me to clarify and develop these ideas.

56. Bowen, *Early Rehoboth*, 99. Hubbard, *Indian Wars*, 95. Drake, *BOI*, 3:30.

57. Bodge, *Soldiers*, 66–7. Hubbard, *Indian Wars*, 95, 104–5. *CT Records*, 2:353.

58. Bodge, *Soldiers*, 66, Gookin, "Historical Account," 443, 464. Hubbard, *Indian Wars*, 95–6, 103–4. James Phinney Baxter, ed., *Documentary History of the State of Maine* (*Baxter Manuscripts*) (Portland, ME: Maine Historical Society, 1900), 6:88–9.

59. Gookin, "Historical Account," 443, 455, 460. Drake *BOI*, 3:81–2. Note Gookin describes Aaron as Andrew's "son-in-law."

60. Saltonstall, *Present State*, 25. Gookin, "Historical Account," 448, 456–7. Drake *BOI*, 81–2. Schultz and Tougias, *King Philip's War*, 150.

61. Gookin, "Historical Account," 458–9. Slotkin and Folsom, eds., *Dreadfull*, 92. Salisbury, ed., *Sovereignty*, 21.

62. Gookin, "Historical Account," 457. Drake *BOI*, 3:81. Hubbard, *Indian Wars*, 86. Leach, *Flintlock*, 148. "Great David," NEIPS.

63. CT Records, 2:353. Slotkin and Folsom, eds., *Dreadfull*, 94. Gookin, "Historical Account," 450. Hubbard, *Indian Wars*, 103–5. Drake *BOI*, 3:31. Bodge, *Soldiers*, 128–9. Temple, *Brookfield*, 91–2. Schultz and Tougias, *King Philip's War*, 161–3. Leach, *Flintlock*, 85–7. Oberg, *Uncas*, 154, 171, 177–8. Alice Nash, "Quanquan's Mortgage of 1663," in *Cultivating a Past: Essays on the History of Hadley Massachusetts*, ed. Marla R. Miller (Amherst, MA: University of Massachusetts Press, 2009), 31. For maps, images, and connections, see http://ourbelovedkin.com/awikhigan/connecticut-river-valley-1675.

64. Gookin, "Historical Account," 455–61. Drake, *BOI*, 3:81. Hubbard, *Indian Wars*, 86. Oberg, *Uncas*, 179. Lepore, *Name*, 137. Leach, *Flintlock*, 148–9.

65. CT Records, 2:355. Oberg, *Uncas*, 178. Drake, *BOI*, 3:81. Gookin, *Historical Collections*, 53. Gookin notes "some conjecture" that this arrest was motivated by Marlborough settlers' desire for adjoining Okkanamesit, a "fair tract of land" "belonging to" the Native inhabitants "not only by natural right but by a grant from the General Court." Gookin, "Historical Account," 456.

66. Lepore, *Name*, 138, 299. Gookin, "Historical Account," 450–1, 455. Anderson, *Creatures*, 235.

67. Temple, *Brookfield*, 101. Gookin, "Historical Account," 450, 455.

68. Husband to the poet Anne Bradstreet, Simon was also on the court that banished Anne Hutchinson.

69. *Records of the Court of Assistants of the Colony of Massachusetts Bay* (Boston: Rockwell and Churchill, 1901) 1:52–4. Gookin, "Historical Account," 459–60. Saltonstall, *Present State*, 26–7. Lepore, *Name*, 138. Leach, *Flintlock*, 148–9.

70. Gookin, "Historical Account," 465.

71. Slotkin and Folsom, eds., *Dreadfull*, 96–7. Leach, *Flintlock*, 87. Hubbard, *Indian Wars*, 106–7. Drake *BOI*, 3:31. For more on the Connecticut River Valley, see Evan

Haefeli and Kevin Sweeney, *Captors and Captives: The 1704 French and Indian Raid on Deerfield* (Amherst, MA: University of Massachusetts Press, 2005); Calloway, *Western Abenaki*; Brooks, *Common Pot*; Margaret M. Bruchac, "Historical erasure and cultural recovery: Indigenous people in the Connecticut River Valley" (PhD diss., University of Massachusetts, 2007).

72. Oberg, *Uncas*, 178–9. Hubbard, *Indian Wars*, 108. Slotkin and Folsom, eds., *Dreadfull*, 98. Leach, *Flintlock*, 87. *Court of Assistants*, 1:52.

73. *Court of Assistants*, 1:53–4. Gookin, "Historical Account," 458–9. Saltonstall, *Present State*, 27. Margaret Ellen Newell, *Brethren by Nature: New England Indians, Colonists, and the Origins of American Slavery* (Ithaca, NY: Cornell University Press, 2015), 145. See also Margaret Ellen Newell, "The Changing Nature of Indian Slavery in New England, 1670–1720," in *Reinterpreting New England Indians and the Colonial Experience*, ed. Colin Calloway and Neal Salisbury (Boston: Colonial Society of Massachusetts, 2003), 106–29.

6. THE ROADS LEADING NORTH

1. Richard LeBaron Bowen, *Early Rehoboth: Documented Historical Studies of Families and Events in This Plymouth Colony Township* (Concord, NH: Rumford Press, 1945), 101. See also Daniel Berkeley Updike, *Richard Smith: First English Settler of the Narragansett Country, Rhode Island* (Boston: The Merrymount Press, 1937), 110. For maps, images, and connections, see http://ourbelovedkin.com/awikhigan/chapter6.

2. Updike, *English Settler*, 111. Eric Schultz and Michael Tougias, *King Philip's War: The History and Legacy of America's Forgotten Conflict* (Woodstock, VT: The Countryman Press, 2000), 246. Julie Fisher and David Silverman, *Ninigret, Sachem of the Niantics and Narragansetts* (Ithaca, NY: Cornell University Press, 2004), 118.

3. The Council of Connecticut to Richard Smith, August 8, 1675. Charles Hoadly, comp., *Hoadly Memorial Early Letters and Documents Relating to Connecticut 1643–1709* (Hartford, CT: Connecticut Historical Society, 1932), 18. Douglas Edward Leach, *Flintlock and Tomahawk: New England in King Philip's War* (Hyannis, MA: Parnassus Imprints, 1996), 113. Bowen, *Early Rehoboth*, 53.

4. Updike, *English Settler*, 110–11. Fisher and Silverman, *Ninigret*, 119, 121. *Collections of the Massachusetts Historical Society* (CMHS) (Boston: The Society, 1792–1888) 4th ser., 7 (1865): 578–9, my emphasis. OED, "kind," www.oed.com.

5. Robert Stanton to Richard Smith, September 19, 1675 and Stanton to John Winthrop Jr., September 22, 1675, Winthrop Family Papers, reel 11, box 20, Massachusetts Historical Society (MHS). Leach, *Flintlock*, 115. Updike, *English Settler*, 50, 110–11. David Stewart-Smith, "The Pennacook Indians and the New England Frontier, 1604–1733," (PhD diss., Union Institute, 1998), 184.

6. Bowen, *Early Rehoboth*, 67. Updike, *English Settler*, 50, 110–11. CMHS, 4th ser., 7:578–9. Stanton to Smith and Stanton to Winthrop, September 1675, MHS. Leach, *Flintlock*, 115. Jenny Pulsipher, *Subjects unto the Same King: Indians, English, and the Contest for Authority in Colonial New England* (Philadelphia: University of Pennsylvania Press, 2005), 120, 133.

7. Stanton to Winthrop, September 22, 1675, MHS. CMHS, 4th ser., 7:578–9. Leach, *Flintlock*, 115. Pulsipher, *Subjects*, 133. Fisher and Silverman, *Ninigret*, 115, 121.

8. Stanton to Smith and Stanton to Winthrop, September, 1675, MHS. CMHS, 4th ser., 7:578–9. Massachusetts Archives, 30:177. Edward Rawson, "Massachusetts General Court Decision against William Smith, September 29, 1675" (1675.09.29.03). Grant-Costa, Paul, et al., eds., *The New England Indian Papers Series* (NEIPS), Yale University Library Digital Collections, http://jake.library.yale.edu:8080/neips/data/html/167 5.09.29.03/1675.09.29.03.html. Nathaniel Saltonstall, "The Present State of New England with Respect to the Indian War" (1675), in *Narratives of the Indian Wars 1675–1699*, ed. Charles Lincoln (New York: Charles Scribner's Sons, 1913), 44–5. Leach, *Flintlock*, 115. Pulsipher, *Subjects*, 120, 133. Fisher and Silverman, *Ninigret*, 122–3.

9. Daniel Gookin, "An Historical Account of the Doings and Sufferings of the Christian Indians in New England," in *Transactions and Collections of the American Antiquarian Society* (Cambridge, MA: American Antiquarian Society, 1836), 2:467. Gookin notes that their orders were to "destroy the enemies' cornfields that they had deserted" and that "they were cautioned by their instructions not to spoil anything belonging to the poor Christian Indians, that lived among us." As he notes, they did just the opposite, destroying the harvest at the praying towns, and leaving those at Pakachoag and Quaboag "untouched, which after, in the winter, afforded relief to the enemy."

10. James Phinney Baxter, ed., *Documentary History of the State of Maine* (*Baxter Manuscripts*) (Portland, ME: Maine Historical Society, 1900), 6:91–2. William Hubbard, *A History of the Indian Wars in New England*, ed. Samuel Gardner Drake (Roxbury, MA: W. E. Woodward, 1865), 96–8, 154–5. Emerson Baker and John Reid, "Amerindian Power in the Early Modern Northeast: A Reappraisal," *William and Mary Quarterly* 61, no. 1 (January 2004): 85. Kenneth Morrison, *The Embattled Northeast* (Berkeley: University of California Press, 1984), 89, 109. Emerson Baker, "Trouble to the Eastward: The Failure of Anglo-Indian Relations in Early Maine" (PhD diss., College of William and Mary, 1986), 173, 188–9. Alvin Morrison, "Tricentennial, Too: King Philip's War Northern Front (Maine, 1675–1678)" in *Actes Du Huitième Congrès Des Algonquinistes (1976)*, ed. William Cowan (Ottawa: Carleton University Press, 1977), 208–12. William Williamson, *History of the State of Maine* (Hallowell, ME: Glazier, Masters and Co., 1832) 518–9. John Noble Jr., "King Philip's War in Maine" (master's thesis, University of Maine, 1970), 13–5, 21–2. Gardner had operated the Pemaquid trading post for about a decade. He was from a merchant family in Salem and had previously traded on the Penobscot and in Acadia. Baker, "Trouble," 117–9.

11. *Baxter Manuscripts*, 6:92, 118, 178. Mary Beth Norton, *In the Devil's Snare: The Salem Witchcraft Crisis of 1692* (New York: Vintage Books, 2003), 86–7. Baker, "Trouble," 173, 188–9. Hubbard, *History*, 92–3. Samuel Gardner Drake, *The Book of the Indians* (*BOI*) (Boston: Antiquarian Bookstore, 1841), 3:104. Morrison, *Embattled*, 89, 108–9.

12. *Baxter Manuscripts*, 6:92–3. Baker, "Trouble," 188. Morrison, *Embattled*, 89, 108–9.

13. Massachusetts Archives, 30:182. Stewart-Smith, "Pennacook," 86, 87, 175, 179. Daniel Gookin, *Historical Collections of the Indians of New England (1674)* (North Stratford, NH: Ayer, 2000), 46. Michael Clark, ed., *Eliot Tracts* (Westport, CT: Praeger, 2003), 404–5. Colin Calloway, "Wanalancet and Kancagamus: Indian Strategy and Leader-

ship on the New Hampshire Frontier," *Historical New Hampshire* 43, no. 4. (1988): 274. For maps, images, and connections, see http://ourbelovedkin.com/awikhigan/winnipesaukee.

14. Massachusetts Archives, 30:182. Henry Nourse, ed., *Early Records of Lancaster 1643–1725* (Lancaster, MA: W. J. Coulter, 1884), 16. Joseph Laurent, *New Familiar Abenaki and English Dialogues* (Quebec: L. Brousseau, 1884), 51–4. John Daly, "No Middle Ground: Pennacook-New England Relations in the Seventeenth Century" (masters thesis, Memorial University of Newfoundland, 1997), 56–7.

15. Calloway, "Wanalancet," 268–9, 273–4. Stewart-Smith, "Pennacook," 34. Emerson Baker, "Finding the Almouchiquois: Native American Families, Territories, and Land Sales in Southern Maine," *Ethnohistory* 51, no. 1 (2004): 91.

16. Gookin, "Historical Account," 462. P.-André Sévigny, *Les Abénaquis: habitat et migrations, 17e et 18e siècles* (Montréal: Bellarmin, 1976), 201. See also Evan Haefeli and Kevin Sweeney, "Watanummon's World: Personal and Tribal Identity in the Algonquian Diaspora c. 1660–1712," in *Papers of the Twenty-fifth Algonquian Conference*, ed. William Cowan (Ottawa: Carlton University, 1994), 212–24. For maps, images, and connections, see http://ourbelovedkin.com/awikhigan/wannalancet.

17. Massachusetts Archives, 30:182. George Madison Bodge, *Soldiers in King Philip's War* (Boston: Rockwell and Churchill, 1906), 296. Hubbard, *History*, 275–7. Noble, "Phillips War" 23–8.

18. Hugh McLellan, *History of Gorham*, ed. Katharine Lewis (Portland, ME: Smith and Sale Printers, 1903). Lisa T. Brooks and Cassandra M. Brooks, "The Reciprocity Principle and ITEK: Understanding the Significance of Indigenous Protest on the Presumpscot," *International Journal of Critical Indigenous Studies* 3, no. 2 (2010). Gideon Ridlon, *Saco Valley Settlements and Families: Historical, Biographical, Genealogical, Traditional, and Legendary* (1895) (Somersworth, NH: New England History Press, 1984), 15, 19. Baker notes that Francis Small ran a trading post at the confluence "as late as the 1660s" but it was not in operation in 1675. Baker, "Trouble," 96–7. For maps, images, and connections, see http://ourbelovedkin.com/awikhigan/1676-raid.

19. *Baxter Manuscripts*, 6:89. Jill Lepore, *The Name of War: King Philip's War and the Origins of American Identity* (New York: Knopf, 1998), 74–6, 83. Emerson Baker and Mary Beth Norton, "The Names of the Rivers: A New Look at an Old Document," *New England Quarterly* 80, no. 3 (September 2007), 178, 186. Norton, *Devil's Snare*, 86–7. Williamson, *History of Maine*, 520–2. William Willis, *History of Portland from 1632 to 1864* (Portland, ME: Bailey and Noyes, 1865), 196. Charles P. Isley Manuscript, coll. 79, ch. 5, box 1/5, Collections of Maine Historical Society. Note that Thomas Wakely was John's elderly father.

20. Drake, *BOI*, 3:102. Increase Mather, "A Brief History of the Warr with the Indians in New England," in *So Dreadfull a Judgment: Puritan Responses to King Philip's War 1676–1677*, ed. Richard Slotkin and James Folsom (Middletown, CT: Wesleyan Press 1978), 100. Hubbard, *History*, 263, 269, 291–2. Morrison, *Embattled*, 108. Sévigny, *Les Abénaquis*, 152–4, 173. Baker, *Almouchiquois*, 87.

21. Hubbard, *History*, 269. Baker, "Trouble," 5. Hubbard's dramatic story of "Squando's" revenge is repeated more often than his confusing account of the nameless Indian

killed near Casco Bay. No surviving documents confirm the drowning of Squando's son, which may have been merely a circulating story. One 1677 document does suggest that some "injury" was committed against "his child at Saco," to which Massachusetts would not answer, but it likely occurred during the war. See *Baxter Manuscripts*, 6:187–8.

22. F. S. Reiche, "Past activities at the mouth of Presumpscot River" (1978), Special Collections, Maine Historical Society. Willis, *History of Portland*, 98, 102–3, 106–8, 113, 138, 157. William Barry and Patricia Anderson, *Deering: A Social and Architectural History* (Portland: Greater Portland Landmarks, 2010), 32. Baker, "Almouchiquois," 83–4. Brooks and Brooks, "The Reciprocity Principle," 12. Willis records Jenkin Williams and Humphrey Durham as the other two, but only includes a deed for Williams, authorizing the sale of a large tract of land between the south boundary of Munjoy's deed and Wakely's house. There is no reference to a deed for Wakely.

23. *Baxter Manuscripts*, 6:90–5. *York Deeds* (Portland, ME: John T. Hull, 1887–1910), 2:114. Baker, *Almouchiquois*, 84–6. Emerson Baker, *The Clarke and Lake Company* (Augusta, ME: Maine Historic Preservation Commission, 1985), 12. Willis, *History of Portland*, 197. Williamson, *History of Maine*, 523. William Southgate, "History of Scarborough," in *Collections of the Maine Historical Society* (Portland, ME: Maine Historical Society, 1853), 1st ser., 3:101–6.

24. Drake, *BOI*, 3:102–3. *Baxter Manuscripts*, 6:94. Hubbard, *History*, 271. Mather, *Brief History*, 100. Williamson, *History of Maine*, 522–3. Bodge, *Soldiers*, 297. Some of these raids may have been carried out by Wabanaki men who appeared on Saco River deeds, including Mogg Hegone, a leader in the war. *York Deeds*, 8:220–1, 2:45–6. Baker, "Almouchiquois," 86–7. Baker, "Trouble," 96–7, 196–8. Drake, *BOI*, 3:126.

25. Norton, *Devil's Snare*, 85. Ridlon, *Saco Valley*, 191. Hubbard, *History*, 250. Baker, "Trouble," 81. See also James Sullivan, *History of District of Maine* (Boston: Thomas and Andrews, 1795), 246.

26. *Baxter Manuscripts*, 6:99. Hubbard, *History*, 278–9, 280–1. Noble, "Phillips War" 28. Williamson, *History of Maine*, 525. Bodge, *Soldiers*, 297. Sullivan, *History*, 246, 249.

27. Drake, *BOI*, 3:115. Baker "Trouble," 142–6, 144–5. Morrison, "Tricentennial," 208–12. Morrison, *Embattled*, 89.

28. Hubbard, *History*, 275, 280–1. Calloway, "Wanalancet," 276. Bodge, *Soldiers*, 300. Chester Price, *Historic Indian Trails of New Hampshire* (1974), in *The Indian Heritage of New Hampshire and Northern New England*, ed. Tadeusz Piotrowski (Jefferson, NC: McFarland, 2002), 160.

29. Hubbard, *History*, 275, 280–1, 283. Drake, *BOI*, 3:110. Williamson, *History of Maine*, 524–7. Baker, "Trouble," 189. Jeremy Belknap, *History of New Hampshire* (Dover, NH: Crosby and Varney, 1812), 1:111–14. Sullivan, *History*, 249.

30. Baker, "Almouchiquois," 74, 82, 91. Baker and Reid, "Amerindian Power," 79–80. Norton, *Devil's Snare*, 10.

31. Williamson, *History of Maine*, 516. Charles Starbird, *The Indians of Androscoggin Valley: Tribal History, and Their Relations with the Early English Settlers of Maine* (Lewiston Journal Printshop, 1928), 35. For maps, images, and connections, see http://ourbelovedkin.com/awikhigan/wannalancet.

32. Nathaniel Shurtleff, *Records of the Governor and Company of the Massachusetts Bay in New England (MA Records)* (Boston: W. White, 1853), 4:45, 57. Gookin, "Historical Account," 471–2. The court included Leverett, Gookin, Willard, Edward Tyng, Dennison, and Hathorn.

33. Massachusetts Archives, 30:182. Gookin, "Historical Account," 471, 482. "Nathaniel," the leader of this first raid on Chelmsford, would continue to lead raids on the colonial town.

34. Gookin, "Historical Account," 472–5. *MA Records*, 4:58, 5:68. Stewart-Smith, "Pennacook," 179–82. Massachusetts Archives, 30:184a. "Memorandum from the Committee of the Massachusetts Court Regarding the Wives and Children of Indian Captives," November 5, 1675, (*NEIPS*). http://images.library.yale.edu:8080/neips/data/html/1675 .11.05.00/1675.11.05.00.html.

35. Gookin, "Historical Account," 462–4, 475. *MA Records*, 4:58. Gookin, *Historical Collections*, 46–7. Stewart-Smith, "Pennacook," 180. Gookin suggests more men may have been deemed "suspicious" strangers, estimating that only "about twenty" men returned to Wamesit. Knight was subsequently tried and acquitted.

36. *MA Records*, 4:46–7, 54–7. Nathaniel Bradstreet Shurtleff, *Records of the Colony of New Plymouth, in New England (PCR)* (Boston: William White, 1855), 2:360–1. Bodge, *Soldiers*, 301, 303. On Deer Island, see Gookin, "Historical Account"; Christine DeLucia, "The Memory Frontier: Uncommon Pursuits of Past and Place in the Northeast after King Philip's War (1675–1678)," *Journal of American History* (Spring 2012); Lepore, *Name*, 138–45.

37. Glenn LaFantasie, ed., *The Correspondence of Roger Williams* (Providence, RI: Brown/ Rhode Island Historical Society, 1988), 2:704–6. On "Idolatrous Quakers" and the October Court, see Mather in Slotkin and Folsom, eds., *So Dreadfull*, 105. By November, the court passed numerous restrictive orders, including an order to imprison anyone found at a Quaker meeting. During the October court, they also made strict rules for soldiers, not only regarding military conduct, but offenses such as "blasphemy" and "fornication." *MA Records*, 4:49–50, 60.

38. LaFantasie, *Correspondence*, 704–6. "Commotion," www.oed.com. Lepore, *Name*, 91, 113.

39. Lepore, *Name*, 74

40. Lepore, *Name*, 60. LaFantasie, *Correspondence*, 705. *CMHS*, 5th ser., 1 (1871): 105–6.

41. *Baxter Manuscripts*, 6:91, 96. Updike, *English Settler*, 113. Lepore, *Name*, 83, 91. Bodge, *Soldiers*, 298.

42. *Baxter Manuscripts*, 4:348–9. Isley Manuscript, 83–4. *MA Records*, 4:51.

43. LaFantasie, *Correspondence*, 705, 707. Leach, *Flintlock*, 115. Pulsipher, *Subjects*, 120.

44. LaFantasie, *Correspondence*, 705, 707. Roger Williams, *A Key in the Language of America* (1643) (Bedford, MA: Applewood Books 1997), 108–9.

45. *Further Letters on King Phillips War* (Providence: E. L. Freeman for the Society of Colonial Wars, 1923), 12, 14–16.

46. Massachusetts Archives, 30:184a. "Memorandum," *NEIPS*.

47. *CMHS*, 4th ser., 7:578–9. *PCR*, 10:361. Schultz and Tougias, *King Philip's War*, 247.

48. *CMHS*' 5th ser., 1:106–9.

49. Gookin, "Historical Account," 475–7. Mary White Rowlandson, *The Sovereignty and Goodness of God: With Related Documents*, ed. Neal Salisbury (Boston: Bedford Books, 1997), 121.

50. Gookin, "Historical Account," 475.

51. Gookin, "Historical Account," 473–4, 485. Lepore, *Name*, 136, 138–9. Pam Ellis, quoted in Julia Spitz, "Nipmucs Add History to Memorial to Deer Island Internment," *MetroWest Daily News*, October 24, 2010, http://www.metrowestdailynews.com/article/20101024/NEWS/310249951. Jean O'Brien, *Dispossession by Degrees: Indian Land and Identity in Natick, Massachusetts, 1650–1790* (New York: Cambridge University Press, 1997), 61–2. Salisbury, ed., *Sovereignty*, 121. In the November 3 session, the court prohibited Indians from leaving the island, "upon pain of death," and also passed an order to provide provisions to prevent "their perishing" by "extremity" for "want of absolute necessities." The first order was enforced, the second only sporadically. *MA Records*, 4:64.

52. Gookin, "Historical Account," 476. Daniel Gookin to Richard Smith, November, 1675, Facsimile Copies of Records of Massachusetts Archives (Photostats), #188, Massachusetts Historical Society. Special thanks to Andrea Cronin for assistance in locating this document. Salisbury, ed., *Sovereignty*, 121. Leach, *Flintlock*, 118. Pulsipher, *Subjects*, 147.

53. Gookin, "Historical Account," 476.

54. Salisbury, ed., *Sovereignty*, 121. Gookin, "Historical Account," 476–7. Lepore, *Name*, 138.

55. Gookin, "Historical Account," 476–7. Lepore, *Name*, 136–45. James Drake, *King Philip's War: A Civil War in New England 1675–76* (Amherst, MA: University of Massachusetts Press, 2000), 104.

56. Leach, *Flintlock*, 118. Pulsipher, *Subjects*, 146–7. Updike, *English Settler*, 112.

57. Gookin to Smith, November, 1675, MHS. Leach, *Flintlock*, 118. Pulsipher, *Subjects*, 146–7.

58. Updike, *English Settler*, 112–3. Leach, *Flintlock*, 118. Pulsipher, *Subjects*, 146–7.

59. Gookin to Smith, November, 1675, MHS.

60. *PCR*, 10:357. *CMHS*, 5th ser., 9:99. Leach, *Flintlock*. Douglas Leach, "A New View on the Declaration of War Against the Narragansetts," *Rhode Island History* 15 (April 1956): 33–41.

61. *CMHS*, 3rd ser., 1 (1825): 67. *CMHS*, 4th ser., 7:579. *CMHS*, 5th ser., 9:100. *PCR*, 10:357, 361.

62. Saltonstall, "Present State," 25. This image contrasts with more recent historical portrayals, which described Weetamoo as a "noncombatant" and emphasized her need for "protection," constructing a more conventional gender role for the saunkskwa. See Leach, *Flintlock*, 85, 113–4; Douglas Leach, ed., *A Rhode Islander Reports on King Philip's War: The Second William Harris Letter of August, 1676* (Providence, RI: Rhode Island Historical Society, 1963), 24n14; and Russell Bourne, *The Red King's Rebellion: Racial Politics in New England 1675–1678* (Oxford University Press, 1991), 125.

63. Saltonstall, "Present State," 34.

64. Saltonstall, "Present State," 34, 44–5, 48. Church's narrative elides this motivation, attributing the military expedition to justified suspicion that the Narragansetts "designed mischief" and needed to be "suppressed." Slotkin and Folsom, eds., *Dreadfull*, 412. Note that Saltonstall confused Cornman and Quinnapin in this report.

65. Saltonstall, "Present State," 48.

66. Saltonstall, "Present State," 48. PCR, 10:357. CMHS, 5th ser., 9:98. Bodge, *Soldiers*, 177, 180–4. Many of the soldiers who fought at Great Swamp became original proprietors of the "Narragansett townships" in Massachusetts, New Hampshire, and Maine, listed in early records and histories as "Narragansett No. 1," "Narragansett No. 2," etc. For a list of soldiers who claimed these lands, see Bodge, *Soldiers*, appendix 1, 406–41.

67. Nathaniel Saltonstall, "A Continuation of the State of New England" (1676), in Lincoln, ed., *Narratives*, 55. Note that Saltonstall incorrectly identified Weetamoo's new husband as "Ninicroft's Eldest Son."

68. Bodge, *Soldiers*, 53–4, 267. Gookin, "Historical Account," 477.

69. Bodge, *Soldiers*, 267. CMHS, 5th ser., 1:105–10. Kristina Bross, *Dry Bones and Indian Sermons: Praying Indians in Colonial America* (Ithaca, NY: Cornell University Press, 2004), 163–8.

70. John Metcalf, comp., *Annals of the Town of Mendon from 1659–1880* (Providence, RI: E. L. Freeman, 1880), 172–3. Gookin, "Historical Account," 478–9. Bodge, *Soldiers*, 54–5. Gookin to Smith, November 1675, MHS. Leach, *Flintlock*, 118. Pulsipher, *Subjects*, 146–7.

71. Gookin, "Historical Account," 477–8. Bodge, *Soldiers*, 268. Gookin letter, Nov. 1675.

72. Gookin, "Historical Account," 478.

73. Gookin, "Historical Account," 478–80. Bodge, *Soldiers*, 268. Salisbury, ed., *Sovereignty*, 120.

74. Metcalf, *Annals of Mendon*, 73–4. Gookin, "Historical Account," 480. Salisbury, ed., *Sovereignty*, 123.

75. Gookin, "Historical Account," 480–1.

76. Gookin, "Historical Account," 480.

77. Gookin, "Historical Account," 481. Bodge, *Soldiers*, 55, 398.

78. Gookin, "Historical Account," 483.

79. Gookin, "Historical Account," 482–5. Daly, "No Middle Ground," 53. Stewart-Smith, "Pennacook," 86, 134, 175. Proceedings of the Littleton Historical Society, no. 1, 97. Sarah was the daughter of a Wamesit sachem, John, "who was a great friend to the English," and she had been married consecutively to two "pious" rulers. Two of the Chelmsford men were "afterward" tried for murder, but "the jury pretended want of clear evidence" and they were acquitted. Note that some of Numphow's people did return to Wamesit the next month, reportedly going no further than Penacook. See http://ourbelovedkin.com/awikhigan/sarah-of-wamesit.

80. David Stewart-Smith, "Pennacook-Pawtucket Relations: The Cycles of Family of Alliance on the Merrimack River in the 17th century," in *Actes Du Vingt-cinquième Congrès Des Algonquinistes*, ed. William Cowan (Ottawa, Ontario: Carleton University Press, 1995), 457.

81. Bross, *Dry Bones*, 146–8, 156, 167–9. Elizabeth was John Wakely's daughter, carried north in the raid.

82. Neal Salisbury, *Manitou and Providence: Indians, Europeans, and the Making of New England, 1500–1643* (New York: Oxford University Press, 1982), 31.

83. Slotkin and Folsom, eds., *Dreadfull*, 106. Salisbury, *Manitou*, 48–9, 232–3. James Axtell, *The Indian Peoples of Eastern America: A Documentary History of the Sexes* (New York: Oxford University Press, 1981), 71. Morrison, *Embattled*, 31. Robert Grumet, "Sunksquaws, Shamans, and Tradeswomen: Middle Atlantic Coastal Algonkian Women During the Seventeenth and Eighteenth Centuries," in *Women and Colonization*, ed. Mona Etienne and Eleanor Leacock (New York: Praeger, 1980), 53. Gordon Sayre, "Native American Sexuality in the Eyes of the Beholders, 1535–1710," in *Sex and Sexuality in Early America*, ed. Merril D. Smith (New York: New York University Press, 1998), 39–40. Richard Godbeer, "Eroticizing the Middle Ground: Anglo-Indian Sexual Relations," in *Sex, Love, Race*, ed. Martha Hodes (New York: New York University Press, 1999). Plane, *Colonial Intimacies*, 5, 30. Miantonomi had pursued a similar strategy, with less success. See Salisbury, *Manitou*, 41.

84. Bodge, *Soldiers*, 203. Franklin B. Hough, ed., "Record of a Court Martial held in Newport, R.I. in August 1676," in *A Narrative of the Causes that Led to Philip's Indian War, 1675 and 1676, by John Easton with Other Documents* (Albany, NY: J. Munsell, 1858), 178. Paul Robinson, "A Narragansett History from 1000 B.P. to the Present," in *Enduring Traditions: The Native Peoples of New England*, ed. Laurie Lee Weinstein (Westport, CT: Bergin and Garvey, 1994), 83.

85. Saltonstall, "Continuation," 57–8. LaFantasie, *Correspondence*, 713. Bourne, *Red King*, 155. Schultz and Tougias, *King Philip's War*, 247.

86. *Baxter Manuscripts*, 23:1. Sybil Noyes, Charles Libby, and Walter Davis, *Genealogical Dictionary of Maine and New Hampshire* (Baltimore, MD: Genealogical Publishing, 1979), 711–2. Norton, *Devil's Snare*, 89. Baker, "Trouble," 194. Frank T. Siebert Jr., "The First Maine Indian War: Incident at Machias," in *Actes du 14e Congrès des Algonquinistes*, ed. William Cowan (Ottawa: Carleton University Press, 1983), 139–40. As Baker notes, it is not clear if Waldron received Gardner's warning. For maps, documents, images, and connections, see http://ourbelovedkin.com/awikhigan/machias.

87. *Baxter Manuscripts*, 6:118. Noyes, *Genealogical Dictionary*, 1. Norton, *Devil's Snare*, 89. Baker, "Trouble," 194.

88. Williamson, *History of Maine*, 1:530. Hubbard, *History*, 287. Saltonstall, "Continuation," 56. Bodge, *Soldiers*, 303.

89. Saltonstall, "Continuation," 57. Bodge, *Soldiers*, 192. Hubbard, *History*, 128.

90. Bodge, *Soldiers*, 192. Leach, *Flintlock*, 125. Hubbard, *History*, 127–8.

91. Bodge, *Soldiers*, 174, 180–1, 192. Leach, *Flintlock*, 125–6. Hubbard, *History*, 128.

92. Schultz and Tougias observe that Smith seemed entirely unaware of any preparations or "fort construction" at Great Swamp, which might seem "unlikely, until we recognize that neither Smith nor any of his countrymen ever discovered the Queen's Fort, a Narragansett installation located less than four miles from Smith's trading post." Schultz and Tougias, *King Philip's War*, 247–8.

93. Sidney Rider, *The Lands of Rhode Island*, Providence, 1904. *Native American Archaeology in Rhode Island* (Providence, RI: Rhode Island Historical Preservation and Heritage Commission, 2002), 53–4. Howard Chapin, "Queen's Fort," *Rhode Island Historical Society Collections*, 24, no. 4 (Oct. 1931), 144. "The Queen's Fort" (pamphlet), presented by "The Old Stone Bank," Providence, RI, Rhode Island Historical Society (RIHS). Susan F. Berman, "Towards a History of Exeter" (manuscript), RIHS. Saltonstall, "Continuation," 57. Bodge, *Soldiers*, 180–1, 192. Schultz and Tougias, *King Philip's War*, 252–4. Leach, *Flintlock*, 126. Hubbard, *History*, 128.

94. LaFantasie, *Correspondence*, 711. "Pessicus his messenger's examination, April 29, 1676," *Collections of the Connecticut Historical Society* (Hartford, CT: 1924) 21:241–242. Paul Robinson, "The Struggle Within: The Indian Debate in Seventeenth-Century Narragansett Country" (PhD. diss., State University of New York at Binghamton, 1990), 251. Colin A Porter, "The Jireh Bull House at Pettaquamscutt: Archaeology of a Fortified House in Narragansett Country," public talk given at the Rhode Island Historical Society, Providence, RI, October 26, 2011. Thanks to the author for sharing his manuscript. Bodge, *Soldiers*, 174. Schultz and Tougias, *King Philip's War*, 255. Peirce, *Indian History*, 128. Hubbard, *History*, 129.

95. Peirce, *Indian History*, 128. Bodge, *Soldiers*, 174, 181. *A Court Martial Held at Newport, Rhode Island* (Albany, NY: J. Munsell, 1858). LaFantasie, *Correspondence*, 711–2. Hubbard, *History*, 129. Leach, *Flintlock*, 127. Schultz and Tougias, *King Philip's War*, 255. Porter, "Jireh Bull."

96. Bodge, *Soldiers*, 174.

97. Leach, *Flintlock*, 126. Bodge, *Soldiers*, 174, 192. Saltonstall, "Continuation," 57. Schultz and Tougias, *King Philip's War*, 252–4.

98. Bodge, *Soldiers*, 192. Schultz and Tougias, *King Philip's War*, 255.

99. Bodge, *Soldiers*, 174, 192–3. Leach, *Flintlock*, 125–6. Davenport was commander of 5th Massachusetts company, including Cambridge and Watertown men. "Great Swamp Fight Regiments," http://minerdescent.com/2011/12/04/great-swamp-fight-regiments/.

100. Bodge, *Soldiers*, 174, 193.

101. Mather, *Brief History*, 108. Bodge, *Soldiers*, 58, 193–4. Leach, *Flintlock*, 126.

102. Saltonstall, "Continuation," 58.

103. Bodge, *Soldiers*, 193–4.

104. Bodge, *Soldiers*, 187.

105. Bodge, *Soldiers*, 193–4.

106. Bodge, *Soldiers*, 174, 187, 191. See also Francis Jennings, *The Invasion of America: Indians, Colonialism, and the Cant of Conquest* (Chapel Hill, NC: University of North Carolina Press, 2010), 312.

107. DeLucia, "Memory Frontier," 980.

108. Saltonstall, "Continuation," 66. Bodge, *Soldiers*, 175. Leach, *Flintlock*, 133.

109. LaFantasie, *Correspondence*, 712–3. Gookin, "Historical Account," 488. J. Hammond Trumbull and Charles J. Hoadly, eds., *The Public Records of the Colony of Connecticut, 1636–1776* (Hartford, CT: Lockwood and Brainard, 1850–90), 2:403. Lepore, *Name*, 131–3.

INTERLUDE: "MY CHILDREN ARE HERE AND I WILL STAY"

1. Daniel Gookin, "An Historical Account of the Doings and Sufferings of the Christian Indians in New England," in *Transactions and Collections of the American Antiquarian Society* (Cambridge, MA: American Antiquarian Society, 1836), 2:486. George Madison Bodge, *Soldiers in King Philip's War* (Boston: Rockwell and Churchill, 1906), 399–400. Neal Salisbury, "The Examination and Relation of James Quannapaquait," in Mary White Rowlandson, *The Sovereignty and Goodness of God: With Related Documents*, ed. Neal Salisbury (Boston: Bedford Books, 1997), 119–20. For maps, documents, images, and connections, see http://ourbelovedkin.com/awikhigan/interlude-my-children.
2. Salisbury, ed., *Sovereignty*, 121–2.
3. Salisbury, ed., *Sovereignty*, 122. Gookin, "Historical Account," 487.
4. Salisbury, ed., *Sovereignty*, 122. Gookin, "Historical Account," 487–9. *Collections of the Massachusetts Historical Society* (Boston: The Society, 1861), 4th ser., 5:1. Massachusetts Archives 30:211, 215–7.
5. Salisbury, ed., *Sovereignty*, 121. Gookin, "Historical Account," 489.
6. Salisbury, ed., *Sovereignty*, 122, 126. Gookin, "Historical Account," 488–9.
7. Salisbury, ed., *Sovereignty*, 24, 123–4. Colin G. Calloway, *The Western Abenakis of Vermont, 1600–1800: War, Migration, and the Survival of an Indian People* (Norman, OK: University of Oklahoma Press, 1990), 77. Gordon Day, *In Search of Native New England's Native Past: Selected Essays* (Amherst, MA: University of Massachusetts Press, 1998), 142. Nathaniel Saltonstall, "A New and Further Narrative of the State of New England" (1676), in *Narratives of the Indian Wars*, ed. Charles Lincoln (New York: Barnes and Noble, 1966), 87–8. Francis Jennings, *The Invasion of America: Indians, Colonialism, and the Cant of Conquest* (Chapel Hill, NC: University of North Carolina Press, 1975), 314.
8. Salisbury, ed., *Sovereignty*, 123–4. Gookin, "Historical Account," 488. Gordon Day, *The Identity of the St. Francis Indians* (Ottawa: National Museums of Canada, 1981), 13, 15. Nathaniel Saltonstall, "A Continuation of the State of New England" (1676), in Lincoln, ed., *Narratives*, 64, 68. Jennings, *The Invasion*, 313. Ruben G. Thwaites, ed., *The Jesuit Relations and Allied Documents* (73 vols.) (Cleveland: Burrows Brothers Co., 1896–1901), 60:133–5.
9. Salisbury, ed., *Sovereignty*, 124.
10. Salisbury, ed., *Sovereignty*, 125–6. Gookin, "Historical Account," 488.
11. Salisbury, ed., *Sovereignty*, 126–7. Gookin, "Historical Account," 488–9.
12. Salisbury, ed., *Sovereignty*, 127. Gookin, "Historical Account," 489.
13. Salisbury, ed., *Sovereignty*, 127. Gookin, "Historical Account," 487–9.
14. Salisbury, ed., *Sovereignty*, 123. Gookin, "Historical Account," 488.
15. Gookin, "Historical Account," 489–90. Salisbury, ed., *Sovereignty*, 24, 64, 68. Douglass Edward Leach, *Flintlock and Tomahawk: New England in King Philip's War* (New York: Macmillan, 1958), 157–8. Abijah Perkins Marvin, *History of Worcester County, Massachusetts* (Boston: CF Jewitt and Company, 1879), 2:103–7.

16. Salisbury, ed., *Sovereignty*, 24–5. Gookin, "Historical Account," 489–90. Leach, *Flint-lock*, 157–8.

17. David Jaffee, *People of the Wachusett* (Ithaca, NY: Cornell University Press, 1999), 48–9.

7. THE CAPTIVE'S LAMENT

1. Mary White Rowlandson, *The Sovereignty and Goodness of God: With Related Documents*, ed. Neal Salisbury (Boston: Bedford Books, 1997), 70–1. Samuel Eliot Morison, "The Plantation of Nashaway," *Publications of the Colonial Society of Massachusetts* (Boston: Colonial Society of Massachusetts, 1932), 28:205, 209. David Jaffee, *People of the Wachusett* (Ithaca, NY: Cornell University Press, 1999), 34. For maps, documents, images, and connections, see http://ourbelovedkin.com/awikhigan/chapter7.

2. Salisbury, ed., *Sovereignty*, 71. Roderick Nash, *Wilderness and the American Mind* (New Haven: Yale University Press, 1982), 2–3, 8, 34, 37. Mark David Spence, *Dispossessing the Wilderness: Indian Removal and the Making of the National Parks* (New York: Oxford University Press, 1999). Pauline Turner Strong, *Captive Selves, Captivating Others* (Boulder CO: Westview Press, 2000), 35. Kristina Bross, *Dry Bones and Indian Sermons: Praying Indians in Colonial America* (Ithaca, NY: Cornell University Press, 2004), 65. Jaffee, *Wachusett*, 17–19.

3. Salisbury, ed., *Sovereignty*, 70. O'Brien, *Dispossession by Degrees: Indian Land and Identity in Natick, Massachusetts. 1650–1790* (Lincoln, NE: University of Nebraska Press, 1997), 22. Yael Ben-Zvi, "Ethnography and the Production of Foreignness in Indian Captivity Narratives," *American Indian Quarterly* 32, no. 1 (Winter 2008): 5–32. Kathryn Zabelle Derounian, "A Note on Mary (White) Rowlandson's English Origins," *Early American Literature* 24 (1989): 70–2. Kathryn Zabelle Derounian and David L. Greene, "Additions and Corrections to 'A Note on Mary (White) Rowlandson's English Origins,'" *Early American Literature* 25 (1990): 306.

4. Salisbury, ed., *Sovereignty*, 74.

5. Salisbury, ed., *Sovereignty*, 74.

6. Salisbury, ed., *Sovereignty*, 75. Strong, *Captive Selves*. See also Margaret Davis, "Mary White Rowlandson's Self-fashioning as Puritan Goodwife," *Early American Literature* 27 (1992): 56. Teresa Toulouse, "'My Own Credit': Strategies of (E)Valuation in Mary Rowlandson's Captivity Narrative," *American Literature* 64, no. 4 (1992): 656–8. Michelle Burnham, "The Journey Between: Liminality and Dialogism in Mary White Rowlandson's Captivity Narrative," *Early American Literature* 28 (1993): 60–75.

7. Gordon M. Day, *Western Abenaki Dictionary* (Hull, PQ: Canadian Museum of Civilization, 1995), 1:47. Joseph Aubery and Stephen Laurent, *Father Aubery's French Abenaki Dictionary* (Portland, ME: Chisholm Brothers, 1995), 513, 232. Salisbury, ed., *Sovereignty*, 15–17, 97.

8. Salisbury, ed., *Sovereignty*, 76.

9. Daniel Gookin, "An Historical Account of the Doings and Sufferings of the Christian Indians in New England," in *Transactions and Collections of the American Antiquar-*

ian Society (Cambridge, MA: American Antiquarian Society, 1836), 2:490, 506. Jaffee, *Wachusett*, 67.

10. William Smith Tilden, *History of the Town of Medfield, Massachusetts, 1650–1886* (Boston: G. H. Ellis, 1887), 83–6, 42–3. Dennis Connole, *Indians of the Nipmuck Country in Southern New England 1630–1750* (Jefferson, NC: McFarlane, 2007), 185. Massachusetts Archives, 30:205–6.

11. Noah Newman to John Cotton, March 14, 1676, Curwen Family Papers, American Antiquarian Society. Gookin, "Historical Account," 494. Samuel Gardner Drake, *The Book of the Indians* (*BOI*) (Boston: Antiquarian Bookstore, 1841), 3:37. Massachusetts Archives, 30:205–6. Jill Lepore, *The Name of War: King Philip's War and the Origins of American Identity* (New York: Knopf, 1998), 89–94, 283.

12. Tilden, *Medfield*, 23, 34–5. Virginia DeJohn Anderson, *Creatures of Empire: How Domestic Animals Transformed Early America* (New York: Oxford University Press, 2004), 235–6. Drew Lopenzina, *Red Ink: Native Americans Picking Up the Pen in the Colonial Period* (Albany, NY: State University of New York Press, 2012), 179. See also Lisa Brooks, *The Common Pot: The Recovery of Native Space in the Northeast* (Minneapolis: University of Minnesota, 2008), ch. 1

13. Bross, *Dry Bones*, 168. Anonymous, *A True Account of the Most Considerable Occurrences that have happened in the Warre between the English and the Indians in New-England* (London: Benjamin Billingsley, 1676), 5.

14. Tilden, *Medfield*, 82. George Madison Bodge, *Soldiers in King Philip's War* (Boston: Rockwell and Churchill, 1906), 80–1, 84–5. Samuel Eliot Morison, *Harvard College in the Seventeenth Century* (Cambridge, MA: Harvard University Press, 1936), 418. Nathaniel Shurtleff, *Records of the Governor and Company of the Massachusetts Bay in New England* (Boston: W. White, 1853), 5:31. Matt Cohen, *The Networked Wilderness: Communicating in Early New England* (Minneapolis: University of Minnesota Press, 2010), 7. Oakes had served under Prentiss in the Montaup and Pocasset campaigns.

15. Gookin, "Historical Account," 504.

16. Increase Mather, "A Brief History of the Warr with the Indians in New England," in *So Dreadfull a Judgment: Puritan Responses to King Philip's War 1676–1677*, ed. Richard Slotkin and James Folsom (Middletown, CT: Wesleyan Press 1978), 86. Cathy Rex, "Indians and Images: The Massachusetts Bay Colony Seal, James Printer, and the Anxiety of Colonial Identity," *American Quarterly* 63 (2011): 83–4. Hilary Wyss, *Writing Indians: Literacy, Christianity and Native Community in Early America* (Amherst, MA: University of Massachusetts, 2003), 31. Philip Round, *Removable Type: Histories of the Book in Indian Country, 1663–1880* (Chapel Hill, NC: University of North Carolina Press, 2010), 41, 42.

17. Gookin, "Historical Account," 494. See also Lepore *Name*, 89–94. Ben-Zvi, "Production of Foreignness," 5–32.

18. Salisbury, ed., *Sovereignty*, 76.

19. Salisbury, ed., *Sovereignty*, 98.

20. Salisbury, ed., *Sovereignty*, 77. Connole, *Indians*, 186. Josiah Howard Temple, *History of North Brookfield, Massachusetts* (Brookfield, MA: North Brookfield, 1887), 118–9.

Daniel Gookin, *Historical Collections of the Indians of New England (1674)* (North Stratford, NH: Ayer, 2000), 500–5.

21. Salisbury, ed., *Sovereignty*, 78. Mabel Cook Coolidge, *The History of Petersham, Massachusetts* (Hudson, MA: Powell Press, 1948), 18. Henry Nourse, ed., *The Narrative of the Captivity and Restoration of Mrs. Mary Rowlandson* (Cambridge, MA: J. Wilson, 1903), 92. Douglass Leach, "The 'Whens' of Mary Rowlandson's Captivity," *New England Quarterly* 34, no. 3 (1961): 356. William Bright, *Native American Placenames of the United States* (Norman, OK: University of Oklahoma Press, 2004), 326.

22. Salisbury, ed., *Sovereignty*, 78.

23. Salisbury, ed., *Sovereignty*, 78–9.

24. Henry Nourse, ed., *The Narrative of the Captivity and Restoration of Mrs. Mary Rowlandson* (Cambridge, MA: J. Wilson, 1903), 92.

25. Salisbury, ed., *Sovereignty*, 96–7.

26. Salisbury, ed., *Sovereignty*, 29–30, 96–7.

27. Salisbury, ed., *Sovereignty*, 32. Ben-Zvi, "Production of Foreignness," 5–32.

28. Salisbury, ed., *Sovereignty*, 85.

29. John Pynchon, *The Pynchon Papers*, ed. Carl Bridenbaugh (Boston: Colonial Society of Massachusetts, 1982), 1:167.

30. Salisbury, ed., *Sovereignty*, 80. Nourse, *Narrative*, 92. J. H. Temple and George Sheldon, *A History of the Town of Northfield, Massachusetts* (Albany, NY: Joel Munsell, 1875), 50.

31. Salisbury, ed., *Sovereignty*, 72, 80. Temple and Sheldon, *Northfield*, 50. Nourse, *Narrative*, 92. Coolidge, *Petersham*, 18.

32. Salisbury, ed., *Sovereignty*, 80.

33. Temple and Sheldon, *Northfield*, 73, 79; see also ch. 1 and 2. William Haviland and Marjory Power, *The Original Vermonters: Native Inhabitants, Past and Present* (Hanover, NH: University Press of New England, 1994), 149, 152, 227–8. Nourse, *Narrative*, 92. Colin Calloway, *The Western Abenakis of Vermont* (Norman, OK: University of Oklahoma Press, 1990), 76–7. Gordon Day, *The Identity of the Saint Francis Indians* (Ottawa: National Museums of Canada, 1981), 12–15. Salisbury, ed., *Sovereignty*, 80–1.

34. On Sokwakik see Brooks, *Common Pot*, ch. 1; Calloway, *Western Abenakis*; Day, *Identity*; Margaret M. Bruchac, "Historical Erasure and Cultural Recovery: Indigenous People in the Connecticut River Valley" (PhD diss., University of Massachusetts, 2007), ch. 2 and 3; Temple and Sheldon, *Northfield*, 2.

35. Salisbury, ed., *Sovereignty*, 81, 83.

36. Salisbury, ed., *Sovereignty*, 32, 81–2. Nourse, *Narrative*, 92. Charles Lincoln, ed., *Narratives of the Indian Wars 1675–1699* (New York: Barnes and Noble, 1966), 133n2. Coolidge, *Petersham*, 18. Temple, *Brookfield*, 110. Temple and Sheldon, *Northfield*, 41.

37. Salisbury, ed., *Sovereignty*, 32. Calloway, *Western Abenakis*, 78. Nourse, *Narrative*, 92. Coolidge, *Petersham*, 18. Temple, *Brookfield*, 110.

38. Salisbury, ed., *Sovereignty*, 83. Temple and Sheldon, *Northfield*, 41. Calloway, *Western Abenakis*, 78. Michelle Burnham, "The Journey Between: Liminality and Dialogism

in Mary White Rowlandson's Captivity Narrative," *Early American Literature* 28, no. 1 (1993): 65–6.

39. Salisbury, ed., *Sovereignty*, 83, 96. Laurel Thatcher Ulrich, *Good Wives: Images and Reality in the Lives of Women in Northern New England, 1650–1750* (New York: Alfred Knopf, 1982), 8.

40. Carroll Smith-Rosenberg, "Captured Subjects, Savage Others: Violently Engendering the New American," *Gender and History* 5, no. 2 (June 1993): 183. Davis, "Mary White," 50. Ben-Zvi, "Production of Foreignness," 5–32.

41. Salisbury, ed., *Sovereignty*, 40. See also Joseph Nicolar, *The Life and Traditions of the Red Man* (1893), ed. Annette Kolodny. (Durham, NC: Duke University Press, 2007), and Melissa Tantaquidgeon Zobel (formerly Melissa Jayne Fawcett), *Medicine Trail: The Life and Lessons of Gladys Tantaquidgeon* (Tucson, AZ: University of Arizona Press, 2000).

42. Salisbury, ed., *Sovereignty*, 82–4. Elizabeth Chilton, "'Towns They Have None': Diverse Subsistence and Settlement Strategies in Native New England," in *Northeast Subsistence-Settlement Change: A.D. 700–A.D. 1300*, ed. J. P. Hart and C. B. Reith (Albany, NY: New York State Museum Bulletin, 2002), 293, 295. Elizabeth Chilton, "Mobile Farmers of Pre-Contact Southern New England: The Archaeological and Ethnohistoric Evidence," in *Current Northeast Paleoethnobotany*, ed. John P. Hart (New York: New York State Museum Bulletin, 1999), 163. Temple and Sheldon, *Northfield*, 32–54. See also Brooks, *Common Pot*; Bruchac, "Historical Erasure"; Calloway, *Western Abenakis*.

43. J. Hammond Trumbull, *The Public Records of the Colony of Connecticut (1636–1776)* (*CT Records*) (Hartford, CT: F. A. Brown, 1852), 2:48–9, 397–8, 406. "Statement of Thomas Warner Concerning His Captivity with the Indians," in *The Andros Papers: 1674–1676*, ed. Peter Christoph and Florence Christoph (Syracuse, NY: Syracuse University Press, 1989), 1:330–1. Salisbury, ed., *Sovereignty*, 143–5. Rueben Gold Thwaites, ed., *The Jesuit Relations and Allied Documents* (73 vols.) (Cleveland: Burrows Brothers, 1896–1901), 60:133. Edmund O'Callaghan, *The Documentary History of the State of New York* (*NYCD*) (Albany, NY: Weed, Parsons, 1850), 3:255, 13:528. Calloway, *Western Abenakis*, 67–77. Brooks, *Common Pot*, 14–24. Robert S. Grumet, *Historic Contact: Indian People and Colonists in Today's Northeastern United States in the Sixteenth through Eighteenth Centuries* (Norman, OK: University of Oklahoma Press, 1995), 97. Francis Jennings, *The Invasion of America: Indians, Colonialism, and the Cant of Conquest* (Chapel Hill, NC: University of North Carolina, 1975), 313–14. Nathaniel Saltonstall, "A New and Further Narrative of the State of New England" (1676), in *Narratives of the Indian Wars 1675–1699*, ed. Charles Lincoln (New York: Charles Scribner's Sons, 1913), 87–8. George Sheldon, *History of Deerfield: The Times When and the People by Whom it was Settled, Unsettled and Resettled* (Deerfield MA: 1895), 128–9, 142.

44. Robert Stanton to Richard Smith, September 19, 1675, Winthrop Family Papers, reel 11, box 20, Massachusetts Historical Society. Saltonstall, *Narrative*. *CT Records*, 2:406. *NYCD*, 13:528, 3:254–65. Jennings, *Invasion*, 313–4. Calloway, *Western Abenakis*, 78.

Franklin B. Hough, ed., *A Narrative of the Causes that Led to Philip's Indian War, 1675 and 1676, by John Easton with Other Documents* (Albany, NY: J. Munsell, 1858), 146. Jon Parmenter, *The Edge of the Woods: Iroquoia, 1534–1701* (East Lansing, MI: Michigan State University Press, 2010), 149–51. Michael Leroy Oberg, *Uncas: First of the Mohegans* (Ithaca, NY: Cornell University Press, 2003), 188. Michael Oberg, *Dominion and Civility: English Imperialism, Native America, and the First American Frontiers, 1585–1685* (Ithaca, NY: Cornell University Press, 1999), 163.

45. NYCD, 13:491. *CT Records*, 2:398. Gookin, *Historical Collections*, 26–7. Jennings, *Invasion*, 313–4. Ted Brasser, *Riding on the Frontier's Crest: Mahican Indian Culture and Cultural Change* (Ottawa: National Museums of Canada, 1974), 22–4. Parmenter, *Edge*, 137, 143–4. Thwaites, *Jesuit Relations*, 52:123, 135–57. Darren Bonaparte, "Turtles, Bears, and Wolves: Mohawk Resettlement of the Northern Frontier," Wampum Chronicles, http://www.wampumchronicles.com/sevennations.html.

46. *CT Records*, 2:397–406, 436. NYCD, 3:255, 257, 265, 13:494, 528–9. Robert Livingston, *The Livingston Indian Records, 1666–1723* (Gettysburg, PA: Pennsylvania Historical Association), 165–6. Salisbury, ed., *Sovereignty*, 89. Jennings, *Invasion*, 314–15. Parmenter, *Edge*, 149–51. No documents support Increase Mather's claim that Mohawk action was prompted by a failed ruse by Philip to kill some Mohawks and blame it on the English. See George Ellis and John Morris, *King Philip's War* (New York: Grafton Press, 1906), 167. By April 15, Andros reported that the Mohawks "had returned from following the North Indians," NYCD, 13:496.

47. Christoph, *Andros Papers*, 330–1. Saltonstall, *Narratives*, 87–8. Calloway, *Western Abenakis*, 77. Gordon M. Day, *In Search of New England's Native Past*, ed. Michael K. Foster and William Cowan (Amherst, MA: University of Massachusetts Press, 1998), 141–7. Judy Dow, personal communication. See also Margaret Bruchac and Peter Thomas, "Locating 'Wissatinnewag' in John Pynchon's Letter of 1663," *Historical Journal of Massachusetts* 34, no. 1 (Winter 2006): 56–82; Margaret Bruchac, "Historical Erasure."

48. Christoph, *Andros Papers*, 330–1. Saltonstall, *Narratives*, 87–8. Day, *Search*, 142.

49. Christoph, *Andros Papers*, 330–1. Saltonstall, *Narratives*, 87–8. Warner reported that Philip's men were "not above one Hundred" and that Philip was "very sickly" at that time.

50. Bodge, *Soldiers*, 236.

51. Salisbury, ed., *Sovereignty*, 84. Nourse, *Narrative*, 91, 93. Saltonstall, *Narratives*, 90–1. *CT Records*, 2:420–32. Richard LeBaron Bowen, *Early Rehoboth: Documented Historical Studies of Families and Events in This Plymouth Colony Township* (Concord, NH: Rumford Press, 1945), 12–14, 19. William Hubbard, *A Narrative of the Indian Wars in New England* (Brattleboro, VT: William Fessenden, 1814), 156–62. Douglas Edward Leach, *Flintlock and Tomahawk: New England in King Philip's War* (New York: Norton, 1966), 171–2. Ebenezer Peirce, *Indian History, Biography and Genealogy* (North Abington, MA: Zerviah Gould Mitchell, 1878), 48. Eric Schultz and Michael Tougias, *King Philip's War: The History and Legacy of America's Forgotten Conflict* (Woodstock, VT: The Countryman Press, 2000), 286–7.

52. Salisbury, ed., *Sovereignty*, 85. These included raids on Groton, in Nipmuc territory, Clark's garrison, in Wampanoag territory, and Warwick, in Narragansett territory.

Leach, *Flintlock*, 153, 165. Schultz and Tougias, *King Philip's War*, 124–5. *CT Records*, 2:421. See also Craig S. Chartier, Plymouth Archaeological Rediscovery Project, "Clarke Garrison House Massacre." http://plymoutharch.tripod.com/id16.html.

53. Brooks, *Common Pot*, ch. 1. Temple, *Brookfield*, 110. Lisa Brooks, Donna Moody, and John Moody, "Native Space," in *Where the Great River Rises: An Atlas of the Upper Connecticut River Watershed in Vermont and New Hampshire*, ed. Rebecca Brown (Hanover, NH: University Press of New England, 2009), 136. Personal communication, Judy Dow, Brattleboro, VT, March 18, 2016.

54. This disease killed several colonial leaders and speculators, including Simon Willard and John Winthrop Jr. Leach, *Flintlock*, 170. Mather, "Brief History," 118, 121.

55. John Easton, *A Relacion of the Indyan Warre* (Albany, NY: J. Munsell, 1858), 10.

56. John A. Strong, "Algonquian Women as Sunksquaws and Caretakers of the Soil: the Documentary Evidence in the Seventeenth Century Records," in *Native American Women in Literature and Culture*, ed. Susan Castillo and Victor DaRosa (Porto, Portugal: Fernando Pessoa University Press, 1997), 191–2. Gordon Sayre, "Native American Sexuality in the Eyes of the Beholders, 1535–1710," in *Sex and Sexuality in Early America*, ed. Merril D. Smith (New York: New York University Press, 1998), 39.

57. Salisbury, ed., *Sovereignty*, 82, 86, 88.

58. Salisbury, ed., *Sovereignty*, 86.

59. Salisbury, ed., *Sovereignty*, 87.

60. Salisbury, ed., *Sovereignty*, 87–9, 91.

61. Noel Sainsbury, ed., *Calendar of State Papers, Colonial Series, America and West Indies, 1669–1674, preserved in the Public Record Office* (New York: Kraus Reprint Ltd., 1964), 406. See also Calloway, *Western Abenakis*; Evan Haefeli and Kevin Sweeney, *Captors and Captives: The 1704 French and Indian Raid on Deerfield* (Amherst, MA: University of Massachusetts Press, 2005), 129. Both Ktsi Mskodak and Koasek fit within the framework of Quinnapin's promised return in "three days."

62. Salisbury, ed., *Sovereignty*, 89.

63. Salisbury, ed., *Sovereignty*, 91.

64. See Christine DeLucia, "The Sound of Violence: Music of King Philip's War and Memories of Settler Colonialism in the American Northeast," *Common Place* 13, no. 2 (Winter 2013).

65. Mary Beth Norton, *Founding Mothers & Fathers: Gendered Power and Forming of American Society* (New York: Alfred Knopf, 1996), 143. Marilyn C. Wesley, "Moving Targets: The Travel Text in *A Narrative of the Captivity and Restauration of Mrs. Mary Rowlandson*," *Essays in Literature* 23, no. 1 (1996): 42–61.

66. Salisbury, ed., *Sovereignty*, 92–4, 132–3.

67. Henry Nourse, *The Military Annals of Lancaster, Massachusetts* (Clinton, MA: W. J. Coulter, 1889), 135–6.

68. Salisbury, ed., *Sovereignty*, 97–98, 130–5.

69. Daniel Gookin, "Historical Account," 498, 500, 508. *CT Records*, 2:438–9. John Allyn, "Examination of Pessicus's Messenger, Wuttawawaigkessuek Sucqunch," April 29, 1676, Paul Grant-Costa, et al., eds., *The New England Indian Papers Series* (NEIPS), Yale University Library Digital Collections, http://jake.library.yale.edu:8080/neips/

data/html/1676.04.29.01/1676.04.29.01.html. *Collections of the Connecticut Historical Society* (Hartford, CT, 1924), 21:241–2. Leach, *Flintlock*, 178–9. Salisbury, ed., *Sovereignty*, 33–4, 98, 134. Connole, *Nipmuck*, 200–1.

70. Salisbury, ed., *Sovereignty*, 136. On use of "I," see, for example, Hilary Wyss, *Writing Indians: Literacy, Christianity and Native Community in Early America* (Amherst, MA: University of Massachusetts, 2003), 42; Connole, *Nipmuck*, 201; Lopenzina, *Red Ink*, 179; Brooks, *Common Pot*, 114, 129, 155, 158. James was responding on behalf of the sachems to the council's second letter, now lost, a reply to the letter the sachems sent with Tom Neponet on his return. See Salisbury, ed., *Sovereignty*, 132–3.

71. Lepore, *Name*, 146. On Peter Jethro, see chapter 9. See also Gookin, *Historical Collections*, 53. Jaffee, *Wachusett*, 63.

72. Gookin, "Historical Account," 506. Salisbury, ed., *Sovereignty*, 105. Leach, *Flintlock*, 170. LaFantasie, *Correspondence*, 723. *Calendar of State Papers*, 9:350, 371 (items 816, 876).

73. LaFantasie, *Correspondence*, 720–4. Drake, *BOI*, 3:90. Gookin, "Historical Account," 508. Schultz and Tougias, *King Philip's War*, 202. Hubbard, *Narrative*, 176–7. Connole, *Nipmuck*, 188. Leach, *Flintlock*, 165. Williams, *Letter*. Neal Salisbury, "Embracing Ambiguity: Native Peoples and Christianity in Seventeenth-Century North America," *Ethnohistory* 50, no. 2 (2003): 248.

74. Massachusetts Archives, 30:190a. Gookin, "Historical Account," 501–2. Salisbury, ed., *Sovereignty*, 130–1. The widow may have been a daughter or kinswoman of Pumham, in whose house Job's children were living in January.

75. Massachusetts Archives, 30:190a. Salisbury, ed., *Sovereignty*, 130–1. Lepore, *Name*, 141–2.

76. Gookin, "Historical Account," 500–1, 505–6. Salisbury, "Embracing Ambiguity," 249. Drake, *BOI*, 124–5. Nathaniel Bradstreet Shurtleff, *Records of the Colony of New Plymouth, in New England* (Boston: William White, 1855), 10:294. Bodge, *Soldiers*, 97. Leach, *Flintlock*, 153. Lisa Brooks, "Peace medal," in *Infinity of Nations: Art and History in the Collections of the National Museum of the American Indian*, ed. Cecile Ganteaume (New York: HarperCollins Publishers, 2010), 189.

77. Gookin, "Historical Account," 501.

78. Massachusetts Archives, 30:190a. Gookin, "Historical Account," 501.

79. Others suspected Job of informing the "enemy" of the army's impending arrival, to explain their failure at Menimesit, however Gookin reported the opposite from both Savage and the army's minister, arguing that these were false rumors. Gookin, "Historical Account," 501, 502, 505, 506. Lepore, *Name*, 142.

80. Lepore, *Name*, 142. Margaret Ellen Newell, *Brethren by Nature: New England Indians, Colonists, and the Origins of American Slavery* (Ithaca, NY: Cornell University Press, 2015), 152. Massachusetts Archives, 30:200.

81. Gookin's report is inconsistent as to the number of Joseph's children.

82. Lepore, *Name*, 142–3. Bross, *Dry Bones*, 156. Anderson, *Creatures*, 235. Salisbury, "Embracing Ambiguity," 251.

83. Lepore, *Name*, 142.

84. Salisbury, "Embracing Ambiguity," 257.

85. Salisbury, ed., *Sovereignty*, 100. Lepore, *Name*, 97–8.

86. Gookin, "Historical Account," 506, 509. Brooks, "Peace Medal," in *Infinity of Nations: Art and History in the Collections of the National Museum of the American Indian*, ed. Cecile Ganteaume (New York: HarperCollins, 2010), 189. My understanding of the men who served in this company is informed by attendance at the Deer Island memorial, and informal conversations with descendants of the people who were interned, including Natick Nipmuc tribal historian Pam Ellis.

87. Gookin, "Historical Account," 510.

88. Salisbury, ed., *Sovereignty*, 100. Gookin, "Historical Account," 511. Nathaniel Saltonstall, *The Present State of New England With Respect to the Indian War* (London: Dorman Newman, 1675), 91–2. Schultz and Tougias, *King Philip's War*, 206–19. Bodge, *Soldiers*, 213–6, 218–31. Leach, *Flintlock*, 174. Connole, *Nipmuck*, 189–90.

89. Gookin, "Historical Account," 511–2. Leach, *Flintlock*, 174–5.

90. Salisbury, ed., *Sovereignty*, 100–1. Gookin, "Historical Account," 506. Bodge, *Soldiers*, 223. Jaffee, *Wachusett*, 67.

91. Jaffee, *Wachusett*, 66.

92. Leach, *Flintlock*, 165, 168, 170. James Drake, *King Philip's War: A Civil War in New England 1675–76* (Amherst, MA: University of Massachusetts Press, 2000), 124. Bodge, *Soldiers*, 98, 99, 101. Brooks, *Common Pot*, 13–14, 25, 34–5. Both of these proposals were "shouted down" or ignored by settlers from towns in the Connecticut River Valley or outside the perimeter. Plymouth, too, considered and rejected an invitation to remove to Cape Cod. Bowen, *Early Rehoboth*, 3:16.

93. Leach, *Flintlock*, 170. Bodge, *Soldiers*, 99. Gookin, "Historical Account," 507–8. Connole, *Nipmuck*, 200.

94. Salisbury, ed., *Sovereignty*, 101.

95. Gookin, "Historical Account," 495–6. Salisbury, ed., *Sovereignty*, 102–4, 136.

96. Salisbury, ed., *Sovereignty*, 104. Connole, *Nipmuck*, 202. Nourse, *Military Annals*, 112.

97. Gookin, "Historical Account," 509.

98. Salisbury, ed., *Sovereignty*, 107. Gookin, "Historical Account," 501–3.

99. Salisbury, ed., *Sovereignty*, 103. Massachusetts Archives, 30:202. "Peter Ephraim's Report to the Massachusetts Council on the Allegience of the Narragansett, June 1, 1676," *NEIPS*, http://findit.library.yale.edu/yipp/catalog/digcoll:3617.

8. UNBINDING THE ENDS OF WAR

1. An allusion to Ovid's *Amore*, Book III Elegy IX: "Elegy for the Dead Tibullus," http://poetryintranslation.com/PITBR/Latin/AmoresBkIII.htm#_Toc520536665. Thanks to Cassandra Hradil for this insight and for poetic vision and precision. For maps, documents, images, and connections, see http://ourbelovedkin.com/awikhigan/chapter8.

2. The elegy for minister Thomas Thatcher was originally published by Eleazar's classmate, Cotton Mather, in *Magnalia Christi Americana* (1702). This excerpt is from an

original translation of Eleazar's poem, with major contributions by Cassandra Hradil, Sally Livingston, and Vanessa Dube. Our work was informed by the translation in Wolfgang Hochbruck and Beatrix Dudensing-Reichel, "'Honoratissimi Benefactores': Native American Students and Two Seventeenth-century Texts in the University Tradition," in *Early Native American Writing: New Critical Essays*, ed. Helen Jaskoski (Cambridge: Cambridge University Press, 1996). For another recent translation, see Robert Dale Parker, *Changing Is Not Vanishing: A Collection of Early American Indian Poetry to 1930* (Philadelphia: University of Pennsylvania Press, 2011), 47–50.

3. See William Hubbard, *A Narrative of the Indian Wars in New England* (Brattleboro, VT: William Fessenden, 1814), 203–4, 206–7. David Jaffee, *People of theWachusett* (Ithaca, NY: Cornell University Press, 1999), 67. Eric Schultz and Michael Tougias, *King Philip's War: History and Legacy of America's Forgotten Conflict* (Woodstock, VT: The Countryman Press, 2000), 59. Jenny Pulsipher, *Subjects unto the Same* King (Philadelphia: University of Pennsylvania, 2007), 201, 205. Although providing substantive analysis, James Drake concludes that "the will to fight fizzled among most of the rebels before it had a chance to among the English," while more recently Katherine Grandjean proclaims, "What happened, it seems, was that Native people lost heart." James Drake, *King Philip's War: A Civil War in New England 1675–76* (Amherst, MA: University of Massachusetts Press, 2000), 141. Grandjean, *American Passage: The Communications Frontier in Early New England* (Cambridge, MA: Harvard University Press, 2015), 164.

4. Douglas Leach, ed., *A Rhode Islander Reports on King Philip's War: The Second William Harris Letter of August, 1676* (Providence, RI: Rhode Island Historical Society, 1963), 60.

5. Joseph Laurent, *New Familiar Abenaki and English Dialogues* (Quebec: L. Brousseau, 1884), 66. Jean O'Brien, *Firsting and Lasting: Writing Indians Out of Existence in New England* (Minneapolis: University of Minnesota Press, 2010), 55–6.

6. J. Hammond Trumbull, *Public Records of the Colony of Connecticut* (Hartford, CT: F. A. Brown, 1852) (*CT Records*), 2:425, 435, 438–40, 466. Henry Nourse, ed., *Early Records of Lancaster 1643–1725* (Lancaster, MA: W. J. Coulter, 1884) 16, 112–3. Massachusetts Archives, 30:202. "Peter Ephraim's Report to the Massachusetts Council on the Allegience of the Narragansett," June 1, 1676, (1676.06.01.00), Paul Grant-Costa, et al., eds., *The New England Indian Papers Series* (*NEIPS*), Yale University Library Digital Collections, http://jake.library.yale.edu:8080/neips/data/html/1676.06.01.00/1676.06.01.00.html. Nathaniel Shurtleff, ed., *Records of the Governor and Company of the Massachusetts Bay* (MA Records) (Boston: William White, 1854), 5:82–3, 93–4. Franklin B. Hough, ed., "Papers Relating to King Philip's War," in *A Narrative of the Causes that Led to Philip's Indian War, 1675 and 1676, by John Easton* (Albany, NY: J. Munsell, 1858), 165. Dennis Connole, *Indians of the Nipmuck Country in Southern New England 1630–1750* (Jefferson, NC: McFarlane, 2007), 199–204.

7. "Letter from the Residents of Hadley Giving Notice of the Release of Mrs. Rowlandson," May 15, 1676, (1676.05.15.00), *NEIPS*, http://jake.library.yale.edu:8080/neips/data/html/1676.05.15.00/1676.05.15.00.html. Colonial War Series 1, vol. 1:71, Con-

necticut State Archives. George Madison Bodge, *Soldiers in King Philip's War* (Boston: Rockwell and Churchill, 1906), 244. Nathaniel Saltonstall, A *New and Further Narrative of the State of New England*, in *Narratives of the Indian Wars, 1675–1699*, ed. Charles Lincoln (New York: Charles Scribner's Sons, 1913), 94. Mary White Rowlandson, *The Sovereignty and Goodness of God: With Related Documents*, ed. Neal Salisbury (Boston: Bedford Books, 1997), 34, 108. Great thanks to Paul Grant-Costa and NEIPS for generously sharing a draft transcription of the Hadley letter. The sachems' collective letter apparently has not survived.

8. "Residents of Hadley," May 15, 1676, *NEIPS*. Bodge, *Soldiers*, 236–8, 241–4; Salisbury, ed., *Sovereignty*, 89–90. Evan Haefeli and Kevin Sweeney, *Captors and Captives: The 1704 French and Indian Raid on Deerfield* (Amherst, MA: University of Massachusetts Press, 2005), 12, 15–19. George Sheldon, *History of Deerfield: The Times When and the People by Whom it was Settled, Unsettled and Resettled* (Deerfield, MA: 1895), 12–4. Elizabeth Chilton, Tonya B. Largy, and Kathryn Curran, "Evidence for Prehistoric Maize Horticulture at the Pine Hill Site, Deerfield, Massachusetts," *Northeast Anthropology* 59 (2000). Elizabeth Chilton, personal communication, April 29, 2014. O'Brien, *Firsting*. On Mather's editorial influence, see also Billy J. Stratton, *Buried in Shades of Night: Contested Voices, Indian Captivity, and the Legacy of King Philip's War* (Tucson, AZ: University of Arizona Press, 2013). On just war doctrine, see Jill Lepore, *The Name of War: King Philip's War and the Origins of American Identity* (New York: Knopf, 1998), 105–13; and Margaret Ellen Newell, *Brethren by Nature: New England Indians, Colonists, and the Origins of American Slavery* (Ithaca, NY: Cornell University Press, 2015), 10.

9. Great thanks to Melissa Tantaquidgeon Zobel for discussion and insights on these concepts. See, for example, The Mohegan Tribe and Stephanie Fielding, *aquyá* and *áwipun* in the Mohegan-English Dictionary and the English-Mohegan Word Finder on http://www.moheganlanguage.com; *wlakamigen, wlakamigezo*, and *wlakamigenok* in the Western Abenaki online dictionary, www.westernabenaki.com; *olakamigenoka, olakamigenokawôgan, olakamigezo*, and *olakamigezowôgan* in Gordon Day, *Western Abenaki Dictionary* (Hull, QC: Canadian Museum of Civilization, 1994), 1:399, 2:283; *Aquene* in John C. Huden, *Indian Place Names of New England* (New York: Museum of the American Indian/Heye Foundation, 1962), 377; Roger Williams, A *Key in the Language of America* (1643) (Bedford, MA: Applewood Books 1997), 182.

10. *MA Records*, 5:82–3. Nourse, *Lancaster*, 112–3. *CT Records* 2:439.

11. *MA Records*, 5:93–4. Nourse, *Lancaster*, 112–3. Connole, *Nipmuck*, 202–3.

12. *MA Records*, 5:93–4. Nourse, *Lancaster*, 112–3. Connole, *Nipmuck*, 199–200, 203. "Residents of Hadley," May 15, 1676, *NEIPS*.

13. Massachusetts Archives, 30:279. Nourse, *Lancaster*, 113–4. Salisbury, ed., *Sovereignty*, 140–1. Ephraim's Report, June 1, 1676, *NEIPS*. A *True Account of the Most Considerable Occurrences that have happened in the Warre between the English and the Indians in New-England* (London: Benjamin Billingsley, 1676), 3. Connole, *Nipmuck*, 203–4. Lemuel Shattuck, A *History of the Town of Concord, Middlesex County, Massachusetts* (Acton, MA: Russell, Odiorne, and Company, 1835), 60. Captives had been

steadily released from Wachusett since Rowlandson's return, and the remaining captives held there were returned with this council.

14. *True Account*, 3. *CT Records*, 2:471. Bodge, *Soldiers*, 236, 244–6. Connole, *Nipmuck*, 204. "Residents of Hadley," May 15, 1676, NEIPS. Howard Mansfield, *Turn and Jump: How Time and Place Fell Apart* (Rockport, ME: Downeast, 2010), 153–7. "Assault on Peskeompskut," Raid on Deerfield: The Many Stories of 1704, http://1704.deerfield. history.museum/scenes/scene.do?title=Peskeompskut. Marge Bruchac, personal communication, Turner's Falls, August 3, 2014. Hope Atherton, Caleb's classmate, served as the chaplain. John Langdon Sibley, *Biographical Sketches of Graduates of Harvard University* (Cambridge, MA: Charles William Sever, 1873), 2:194.

15. *True Account*, 3–4. *CT Records*, 2:471. Bodge, *Soldiers*, 241–7. "Residents of Hadley," May 15, 1676, NEIPS. Leach, *Flintlock*, 200. Schultz and Tougias, *King Philip's War*, 63. Mansfield, "Turn and Jump," 153–7. "Peskeompscut." Marge Bruchac, personal communication, Turner's Falls, August, 2014. Captured Native women later reported four hundred died at the falls. Turner died while crossing the Green River, northwest of the falls.

16. Connecticut had also urged against an "attack on the enemy whilst so many captives remain in their hands." *CT Records*, 2:440; Bodge, *Soldiers*, 244–5. "Residents of Hadley," May 15, 1676, NEIPS.

17. *MA Records*, 5:94–5. Bodge, *Soldiers*, 77. *CT Records*, 2:444, 455. "Residents of Hadley," May 15, 1676, NEIPS. Francis Jennings, *The Invasion of America: Indians, Colonialism, and the Cant of Conquest* (Chapel Hill, NC: University of North Carolina, 1975), 319.

18. *CT Records*, 2:466. *MA Records*, 5:97. *True Account*, 3–4. Bodge, *Soldiers*, 270–1. Connole, *Nipmuck*, 204. Schultz and Tougias, *King Philip's War*, 62, 66.

19. *True Account*, 5–6. Salisbury, ed., *Sovereignty*, 140–1. Connole, *Nipmuck*, 204–5. Leach, *Flintlock*, 205–6, 214. Jaffee, *Wachusett*, 68. George Ellis and John Morris, *King Philip's War* (New York: Grafton Press, 1906), 242. Abenaki and Mohegan concepts of "stillness" are related to the words for peace and peacemaking; see note 9 above. Special thanks to Timothy Gaura for vital conversations that informed this reading.

20. Massachusetts Archives, 30:204. Bodge, *Soldiers*, 303–4. *MA Records*, 5:92, 96–7.

21. When Massachusetts had first sent its messengers to Wachusett, Shoshanim said, "Philip and Quinnapin sent [said?] to kill them," but Shoshanim had said that "if any kill them," it would be him, asserting jurisdiction in his territory. In a third letter, Magunkaquog leader Pomham conveyed that the Numphows and Wamesit men blamed Philip for drawing "so many people to him" and had even been willing to "kill Philip." Salisbury, ed., *Sovereignty*, 141. *True Account*, 6–7. Connole, *Nipmuck*, 204–5.

22. *True Account*, 6–7. *MA Records*, 5:97. *CT Records*, 2:447. Massachusetts Archives, 30:202a, 203. *Collections of the Massachusetts Historical Society* (CMHS) 4th ser., 5 (1861): 9.

23. *CT Records*, 2:465. *True Account*, 4. Bodge, *Soldiers*, 57, 270–1. Connole, *Nipmuck*, 204. Leach, *Flintlock*, 206. *True Account* says they took 27 and killed 6, but the official

Massachusetts report notes the "surprisal of thirty sixe Indians." The numbers above are taken from Bodge. Shoshanim was betrayed not only by Massachusetts but also by their messenger, Tom Dublet, who is credited with revealing to Henchman the location of the people who were fishing at Weshawkim. For maps, documents, images, and connections for this chapter section, see http://ourbelovedkin.com/awikhigan/cambridge-boston-nipmuc.

24. Daniel Gookin, "An Historical Account of the Doings and Sufferings of the Christian Indians in New England," in *Transactions and Collections of the American Antiquarian Society* (Cambridge, MA: American Antiquarian Society, 1836), 2:513. *CMHS*, 4th ser., 5:9. *CT Records*, 2:450, 465, 469. Bodge, *Soldiers*, 226, 348. Michael Leroy Oberg, *Uncas: First of the Mohegans* (Ithaca, NY: Cornell University Press, 2003), 187–9. The Mohegans were reluctant to rejoin the Connecticut forces; they had not been properly compensated and were grieving the recent loss of Uncas's son Attanwood.

25. *True Account*, 3–5, 7. *CT Records*, 2:469. *MA Records*, 5:84–7. Gookin, "Historical Account," 513, 524–5. Shattuck, *History of Concord*, 61–2. Bodge, *Soldiers*, 226. Pulsipher, *Subjects*, 195. Massachusetts Archives, 30:201b.

26. Massachusetts Archives, 30:172. Daniel Gookin, *Historical Collections of the Indians of New England (1674)* (North Stratford, NH: Ayer, 2000), 53. J. H. Temple, *History of Framingham, Massachusetts* (Town of Framingham, 1887), 60. J. H. Temple, *History of North Brookfield, Massachusetts* (Brookfield, MA: North Brookfield, 1887), 24. Shattuck, *History of Concord*, 62.

27. Massachusetts Archives, 30:172. Temple, *Framingham*, 6–7, 45, 58–61, 83. Connole, *Nipmuck*, 22, 206–7. Salisbury, ed., *Sovereignty*, 139.

28. The "election" was on the same day that Rowlandson arrived in Boston, with the sachems' message. All other magistrates held their seats. "Residents of Hadley," May 15, 1676, *NEIPS*. Massachusetts Archives, 30:172, 203, 204, 205. Temple, *Framingham*, 60. Connole, *Nipmuck*, 206–7. Salisbury, ed., *Sovereignty*, 139. Lepore, *Name*, 143–4.

29. Gookin, "Historical Account," 528–9. Salisbury, ed., *Sovereignty*, 137–8.

30. Gookin, "Historical Account," 528–9. Salisbury, ed., *Sovereignty*, 137–8.

31. Salisbury, ed., *Sovereignty*, 140. Connole, *Nipmuck*, 206, 208. See Lepore, *Name*, 144. for gender analysis of Tom's judgment and the release of both Rowlandson and Nehemiah's wife.

32. Lisa Brooks, "Peace Medal," in *Infinity of Nations: Art and History in the Collections of the National Museum of the American Indian*, ed. Cecile Ganteaume (New York: HarperCollins, 2010), 189. Newell, *Brethren*, 167.

33. *True Account*, 4–5. *The Diary of Samuel Sewall: 1674–1729*, ed. M. Halsey Thomas (New York: Farrar, Straus, and Giroux, 1973), 1:18. Massachusetts Archives, 30:203. Temple, *Framingham*, 61. Connole, *Nipmuck*, 207. Lepore, *Name*, 145.

34. *True Account*, 5.

35. Massachusetts Archives, 30:207, 215. *True Account*, 5.

36. Increase Mather, "A Brief History of the War with the Indians in New England," in *So Dreadfull a Judgment: Puritan Responses to King Philip's War 1676–1677*, ed. Richard Slotkin and James Folsom (Middletown, CT: Wesleyan Press 1978), 130. On Mather

and Hubbard's narratives and colonial narration of just war, see Lepore, *Name*, 48–60, 105–13.

37. Hubbard, *Narrative*, 211–2.

38. Hubbard, *Narrative*, 211–3. Samuel Gardner Drake, *The Book of the Indians (BOI)* (Boston: Antiquarian Bookstore, 1841), 2:50–1. Lepore, *Name*, 47. Note that Hubbard further displaced this context in his narrative, as he moved rhetorically from Massachusetts's declaration to the military expeditions against Philip and Quaiapin, claiming that those who did not come in understood they were guilty. Thus, the offer of amnesty was portrayed as a stage in just war, with "mercy" offered before assaults were carried out.

39. Sewall, *Diary*, 18. *True Account*, 5. Church portrayed Awashonks's surrender with great romanticism, emphasizing his chivalry in offering her amnesty, but Peter Awashonks testified that their primary purpose in surrendering was their "desire" to "settle" at Sakonnet "again," insisting that they had not fought with Philip but were rather driven from their places. Jeremy Dupertuis Bangs, *Indian Deeds: Land Transactions in Plymouth Colony, 1620–1691* (Boston: New England Historic Genealogical Society, 2008), 485–7.

40. *True Account*, 5. Hubbard, *Narrative*, 202–3. In early May, Henchman's troop had killed eleven or twelve people about Hassanamesit, the scouts credited with having "well acquitted themselves as men and friends to the English." *True Account*, 3. "Residents of Hadley," May 15, 1676, *NEIPS*. On June 5, Talcott's Connecticut and Mohegan forces attacked people who had newly planted fields at Chabonkongamog, where "they killed and captured 52." Peter Ephraim reported that he had been in the midst of meeting with the sachems in "the Nipmug woods" on June 4, as part of the peace negotiations, when the "Connecticut Army fell upon us seized our party my horse and cart." Massachusetts Archives, 30:203. On June 7, they took "27 women and children, prisoners" from Quaboag, all on their way to Hadley to reconnoiter with the Massachusetts troops. *CT Records*, 2:453

41. Massachusetts Archives, 30:211, 215–7. William T. Forbes, "Manteo and Jackstraw," *Proceedings of the American Antiquarian Society* (December 1901), 14:240–7. Temple, *Framingham*, 41–3, 57, 61–2, 65, 70–79.

42. Massachusetts Archives, 30:211, 216–7. Forbes, "Manteo and Jackstraw," 245–6. Temple, *Framingham*, 38, 45, 49–50, 61–5, 72–83, 91–7, 109–10. Drake, *BOI*, 3:80. "Historic USGS Maps of New England & New York," Framingham, MA Quadrangle, UNH Dimond Library, Documents Department and Data Center, http://docs.unh.edu/nhtopos/Framingham.htm.

43. Massachusetts Archives, 30:211, 211a, 215–7. "Residents of Hadley," May 15, 1676, *NEIPS*. Temple, *Framingham*, 73–8, 90–3. Forbes, "Manteo and Jackstraw," 245–7. William Barry, *A History of Framingham, Massachusetts, Including the Plantation, from 1640 to the Present Time* (Boston: James Munroe, 1847), 24–5.

44. *True Account*, 8. Salisbury, ed., *Sovereignty*, 141–4. Hubbard, *Narrative*, 221. Gookin, "Historical Account," 532. Drake, *BOI*, 3:79–80. Connole, *Nipmuck*, 208–10, 228.

45. Temple, *Framingham*, 76–7. Salisbury, ed., *Sovereignty*, 141–4. Newell, *Brethren*, 5–7, 12–13, 53, 109. Daniel Mandell, *Behind the Frontier: Indians in Eighteenth-*

Century Eastern Massachusetts (Lincoln, NE: University of Nebraska Press, 1996), 25–37, 47.

46. Salisbury, ed., *Sovereignty*, 141–4. Hubbard, *Narrative*, 240. Gookin, "Historical Account," 513, 532. Connole, *Nipmuck*, 209. Newell, *Brethren*, 12–13.

47. Massachusetts Archives, 30:216–7. Temple, *Framingham*, 77–8.

48. Massachusetts Archives, 30:211, 215–7. Temple, *Framingham*, 77–8. Lepore, *Name*, 116–7. In their testimony, the Wannukhows had a court-appointed interpreter, James Speen, suggesting they were not highly fluent.

49. Forbes, "Manteo and Jackstraw," 245. Temple, *Framingham*, 90, 93, 96–7. Increase Mather, *Diary*, ed. Samuel A. Greene (Cambridge, MA: J. Wilson, 1900), 46. Sewall, *Diary*, 22. Shattuck, *History of Concord*, 63. On the murder of the wives and children of scouts, including Andrew Pittimee and Thomas Speen, see Gookin, "Historical Account," 513–4, and Jenny Pulsipher, "Massacre at Hurtlebury Hill, *William and Mary Quarterly*, Third Series, 53, no. 3 (July 1996): 450–86.

50. Massachusetts Archives, 30:224a. Salisbury, ed., *Sovereignty*, 144. Sewall, *Diary*, 25. Increase Mather's *Brief History* had recently been published and formal reports, such as William Harris's letter, were circulating. For Stoughton and Buckley's mission, see also Nathaniel Bouton, ed., *New Hampshire Provincial Papers* (Concord, MA: George E. Jenks, 1867), 1:333–8, 345, and Pulsipher, *Subjects*, 197–9. On the continuation of "involuntary servitude," including of children, see Margaret Ellen Newell, "The Changing Nature of Indian Slavery in New England, 1670–1720," in *Reinterpreting New England Indians and the Colonial Experience*, ed. Colin Calloway and Neal Salisbury (Boston: Colonial Society of Massachusetts, 2003), 117, and in the same volume, Ruth Wallis Herndon and Ella Wilcox Sekatau, "Colonizing the Children: Indian Youngsters in Servitude in Early Rhode Island," 137–73.

51. *Calendar of State Papers, Colonial Series, America and West Indies 1675–1676* (1893), ed. W. Noel Sainsbury (Vaduz: Kraus Reprint, 1964), 9:467. Lepore, *Name*, 126, 136, 147–8. Salisbury, ed., *Sovereignty*, 48–9, 135. Kathryn Zabelle Derounian, "The Publication, Promotion, and Distribution of Mary Rowlandson's Indian Captivity Narrative in the Seventeenth Century," *Early American Literature* 23 (1988): 239–61. Richard W. Cogley, "A Seventeenth-Century Native American Family: William of Sudbury and His Four Sons," *The New England Historical and Genealogical Register* 153 (April 1999): 177–8. Cheryll Toney Holley, personal communication, Hassanamisco, June 21, 2014. Thanks also to Bruce Curliss for many conversations about James Printer and Nipmuc continuance. "Hassanamesit" changed to "Hassanamisco" over time. As Nipmuc leaders explained it to me, Hassanamesit was the original place name, but Hassanamisco has emerged as the name of the community. It also now refers to the small reservation which that community still holds.

52. Massachusetts Archives, 30:265, 300. Grafton (Mass.) Records, 1743–1948, folders 1 & 2, John Milton Earle Papers, box 1, American Antiquarian Society. *CMHS*, 1st ser., 10:134. Cogley, "Seventeenth-Century," 178. Jean O'Brien, *Dispossession by Degrees: Indian Land and Identity in Natick, Massachusetts. 1650–1790* (Lincoln, NE: University of Nebraska Press, 1997), 74–8. Mandell, *Behind the Frontier*, 25–36, 43–7. Drew Lopenzina, *Red Ink: Native Americans Picking up the Pen in the Colonial Period*

(Albany, NY: State University of New York Press, 2012), 191–3. Connole, *Nipmuck*, 124–37, 232–50. Cheryll Toney Holley, personal communication, Hassanamisco, June 21, 2014 and July 27, 2015.

53. *CT Records*, 2:447–9, 458–9. National Park Service, American Battlefield Protection Program, Technical Report: "The 1676 Battle of Nipsachuck: Identification and Evaluation" (GA-2255–11–016), April 12, 2013, 27–9, 40–1, 83–5, 91, 94, 108, http://kpwar .org/wp-content/uploads/2015/04/FINAL-REPORT-Nipsachuck.pdf. "Dress," *Oxford English Dictionary*, www.oed.com.

54. *CT Records*, 2:447–50, 458–9, 466. Jennings, *Invasion*, 320. Mather, "Brief History," 136–7. Hubbard, *Narrative*, ed. Fessenden, 242. Leach, *Flintlock*, 210, 215, 221. Oberg, *Uncas*, 190. "Battle of Nipsachuck," 85, 87, 91–2. *Collections of the Connecticut Historical Society* (Hartford, CT: 1924), 21:241–2. John Allyn, "Examination of Pessicus's Messenger, Wuttawawaigkessuek Sucqunch," April 29, 1676, NEIPS, http://jake .library.yale.edu:8080/neips/data/html/1676.04.29.01/1676.04.29.01.html.

55. *CT Records*, 2:459, 466, 473–4. "Residents of Hadley," May 15, 1676, NEIPS. Hough, "Papers," 165–7. *Calendar of State Papers*, 9:444. Jennings, *Invasion*, 320–1. Leach, *Flintlock*, 211–2. Independent of this research, the Nipsachuck Battlefield Project report suggests that "it is quite possible the Connecticut War Council (or Talcott at his discretion) targeted Quaiapan and Potucke to derail any peace overtures," pointing to the "respect and fear" Quaiapan commanded and the threat her "return to Narragansett Country" to "possibly seek a peace agreement with Massachusetts Bay" posed to "Connecticut's plans to claim Narragansett territory by the doctrine of Right of Conquest and Vacuum Domicilium." "Battle of Nipsachuck," 37, 21–2. See also Paul Robinson, "The Struggle Within: The Indian Debate in Seventeenth-Century Narragansett Country" (PhD. diss., State University of New York at Binghamton, 1990), 257.

56. Sheila McIntyre and Len Travers, ed., *The Correspondence of John Cotton Junior* (Boston: The Colonial Society of Massachusetts, 2009), 154, 164–5. Leach, *Rhode Islander*, 68. Thomas Walley to John Cotton Jr., July 18, 1676, John Davis Papers, Massachusetts Historical Society (MHS).

57. McIntyre and Travers, *Correspondence*, 159. Leach, *Flintlock*, 215–6. Leach, *Rhode Islander*, 83–4. Bodge, *Soldiers*, 263. See also Church's account of his expeditions in Drake, ed., *History*, 92–140. Wootonakanuske and Philip's son was sold into slavery, after months of imprisonment and colonial debate over his fate. No surviving sources record what happened to Wootenanuske. Lepore, *Name*, 150–3.

58. Franklin B. Hough, ed., "Record of a Court Martial held in Newport, R.I. in August 1676," in *A Narrative of the Causes that Led to Philip's Indian War, 1675 and 1676, by John Easton* (Albany, NY: J. Munsell, 1858), 173–8, 183. Richard Hutchinson, *The Warr in New-England Visibly Ended* (1677), in Lincoln, ed., *Narratives*, 105. See also Hubbard, *Narrative*, 223; Mather, "Brief History," 136. John Easton was present on the court that tried Quinnapin and several others. A "sister" of Weetamoo's, not mentioned elsewhere, was also present, likely as a prisoner, testifying regarding another accused man.

59. Leach, *Rhode Islander*, 85. Edward Rawson to Josiah Winslow, August 28, 1676, Winslow Family Papers II, 103, Massachusetts Historical Society. *CT Records*, 2:471. See also Mather, "Brief History," 138–9; Drake, *History*, 126.

60. Hubbard, *Narrative*, ed. Fessenden, 224. Leach, *Flintlock*, 210, 215, 218, 231. McIntyre and Travers, *Correspondence*, 159.

61. McIntyre and Travers, *Correspondence*, 154, 159. Hough, "Court Martial," 187–8. Rawson to Winslow, August 28, 1676, MHS. Newell, *Brethren*, 152.

62. George Faber Clark, *History of the Town of Norton* (Boston: Crosby, Nichols and Company, 1859), 52–3. Samuel Hopkins Emery, *History of Taunton, Massachusetts, From its Settlement to the Present Time* (Syracuse, NY: D. Mason and Co., 1893), 388, 404–5, and "Map of Taunton, ALS Cohannet" (drawn by James Edward Seaver for Emery's *History*), also Massachusetts Archives #4680. Great thanks to Andy Anderson, Maggie King, and Cassandra Hradil for locating the map and for thinking through its implications with me. Leach, *Flintlock*, 229, 231; Bodge, *Soldiers*, 263, 464. Schultz and Tougias, *King Philip's War*, 94. Ruth Goold, George Yelle, and Christopher Cox, "History of the Community," Town of Norton Open Space and Recreation Plan, 2005–2010, http://www.nortonma.org/sites/nortonma/files/uploads/section_3 _community_setting_.pdf. Michael Gelbwasser, "Historical War Site Marked in Norton," *Sun Chronicle*, May 25, 2010, http://www.thesunchronicle.com/news/historical -war-site-marked-in-norton/article_e9e5808e-08fb-5bee-807b-55255f838074.html. For map and connections, see http://ourbelovedkin.com/awikhigan/lockety-fight.

63. Mather, "Brief History," 137–8, 71.

64. Mather, "Brief History," 137–8. Hubbard, *Narrative*, 224.

65. Leach, *Rhode Islander*, 2, 83. For settlers' "deference" to the "official" accounts of wartime violence, see Lepore, *Name*, 53.

66. Hubbard, *Narrative*, 224. Clark, *Norton*, 52–3. Emery, *History of Taunton*, 388, 404–5, "Map of Taunton." Schultz and Tougias, *King Philip's War*, 94. McIntyre and Travers, *Correspondence*, 226.

67. Bangs, *Deeds*, 485, 488–9, 495–502, 507, 517–20. "Boundaries of lots in Pocasset, April 1681," Tiverton Town Records Collection, mss 219, folder 6, Rhode Island Historical Society. Arthur Sherman Phillips, *The Phillips History of Fall River* (fascicle 1) (Fall River, MA: Dover Press, 1941), 109–112. Duane Hamilton Hurd, *History of Bristol County, Massachusetts with Biographical Sketches* (Philadelphia: J. W. Lewis, 1883), 746. Arthur Sherman Phillips Papers, "Pocasset Purchase" folder, Fall River Historical Society.

68. See "Residents of Hadley," May 15, 1676, NEIPS; *Calendar of State Papers*, 9: 250–5, 274–5, 317–23, 350–3, 366–88, 402–19.

69. Edmund O'Callaghan, *The Documentary History of the State of New York* (NYCD) (Albany, NY: Weed, Parsons, 1850), 4:744, 902; 13:497, 501–4, 514–30, 538. Colin Calloway, *The Western Abenakis of Vermont* (Norman, OK: University of Oklahoma Press, 1990), 80–4. Gordon Day, *Identity of the Saint Francis Indians* (Ottawa: National Museums of Canada, 1981), 19–20. Schultz and Tougias, *King Philip's War*, 184. The Mohawks would continue to pursue raids under the Great Law for years to come, including on the praying towns, contrary to New England's desires.

9. THE NORTHERN FRONT

1. Quoted in Jean O'Brien, *Firsting and Lasting: Writing Indians Out of Existence in New England* (Minneapolis: University of Minnesota Press, 2010), 108. For maps, documents, images, and connections, see http://ourbelovedkin.com/awikhigan/chapter9.

2. O'Brien, *Firsting*, xxi–xxiv, 27, 32–5, 42, 94, 108–9. Thomas Church, *The History of King Philips War*, ed. Samuel Gardner Drake (Boston: Howe and Norton, 1825), 25–6.

3. "Owaneco and Ben Uncas, "The Complaint and Prayer of Owaneco and Ben Uncas, 1700" in "Land Disputes between the Colony of Connecticut and the Mohegan Indians, 1736–1739," Ayer ms 459, Edward Ayer Manuscript Collection, Newberry Library, Chicago. Evan Haefeli and Kevin Sweeney, *Captors and Captives: The 1704 French and Indian Raid on Deerfield* (Amherst, MA: University of Massachusetts Press, 2005), 2, 28, 215. Emerson Baker and John Reid, "Amerindian Power in the Early Modern Northeast: A Reappraisal," *William and Mary Quarterly* 61, no. 1 (January 2004): 102. See also Margaret M. Bruchac, "Historical Erasure and Cultural Recovery: Indigenous People in the Connecticut River Valley" (PhD diss., University of Massachusetts, 2007); Colin Calloway, *The Western Abenakis of Vermont* (Norman, OK: University of Oklahoma Press, 1990); David L. Ghere, "The 'Disappearance' of the Abenaki in Western Maine: Political Organization and Ethnocentric Assumptions," in *After King Philip's War: Presence and Persistence in Indian New England*, ed. Colin Calloway (Hanover, NH: University Press of New England, 1997), 72–89; Alvin Morrison, "Tricentennial, Too: King Philip's War Northern Front (Maine, 1675–1678)," in *Actes Du Huitième Congrès Des Algonquinistes (1976)*, ed. William Cowan (Ottawa: Carleton University Press, 1977), 208–12; Kenneth Morrison, *The Embattled Northeast* (Berkeley: University of California Press, 1984); Alice Nash, "The Abiding Frontier: Family, Gender and Religion in Wabanaki History, 1600–1763" (PhD diss., Columbia University, 1997); Mary Beth Norton, *In the Devil's Snare: The Salem Witchcraft Crisis of 1692* (New York: Vintage Books, 2003); Frank Siebert, "The First Maine Indian War: Incident at Machias (1676)," in *Actes Du Quatorzième Congrès Des Algonquinistes (1982)*, ed. William Cowan (Ottawa: Carleton University Press, 1983), 137–9, 143; David Stewart-Smith, "The Pennacook Indians and the New England Frontier, 1604–1733," (PhD diss., Union Institute, 1998), 52–61.

4. Massachusetts Archives, 30:204. George Madison Bodge, *Soldiers in King Philip's War* (Boston: Rockwell and Churchill, 1906), 304. Joshua Scottow to John Leverett, September 15, 1676, S-888, misc. box 33/21, Collections of Maine Historical Society. Charles P. Isley Manuscript, coll. 79, box 1/5, Collections of Maine Historical Society. Edward Rawson to Josiah Winslow, August 28, 1676, Winslow Family Papers II, item 103, Massachusetts Historical Society. William Williamson, *History of the State of Maine* (Hallowell, ME: Glazier, Masters and Co., 1832), 533–5. William Willis, *History of Portland from 1632 to 1864* (Portland, ME: Bailey and Noyes, 1865), 200–3. William Hubbard, *A History of the Indian Wars in New England*, ed. Samuel Gardner Drake (Roxbury, MA: W. E. Woodward, 1865), 134–46. Samuel Gardner Drake, *The*

Book of the Indians (BOI) (Boston: Antiquarian Bookstore, 1841), 3:110–2. Richard R. Westcott, *A History of Harpswell, Maine* (Harpswell, ME: Harpswell Historical Society, Curtis Memorial Library and Blackberry Books, 2010), 14. Norton, *Devil's Snare*, 88. P.-André Sévigny, *Les Abénaquis: habitat et migrations, 17e et 18e siècles* (Montréal: Bellarmin, 1976), 17, 121. Church's expedition from Portsmouth, Rhode Island, to Montaup began on the evening of August 11, and Philip was killed in the early morning of August 12, according to Leach. Douglas Edward Leach, *Flintlock and Tomahawk: New England in King Philip's War* (Hyannis, MA: Parnassus Imprints, 1996), 232–5.

5. James Phinney Baxter, ed., *Documentary History of the State of Maine (Baxter Manuscripts)* (Portland, ME: Maine Historical Society, 1900), 6:118. "Indenture" between Warrabitta and Anthony Brackett, January 15, 1670, Waldo Papers, box 1, coll. 34, folder 1/1, Collections of Maine Historical Society. Hubbard, *History*, 134–46. Williamson, *History of Maine*, 533–5. Willis, *Portland*, 200–3. Bodge, *Soldiers*, 304. Emerson Baker, "A Scratch with a Bear's Paw: Anglo-Indian Land Deeds in Early Maine," *Ethnohistory* 36 (1989): 242. Hubbard is the main source for this account of Symon's involvement in the raid, leaving it suspect. Drake notes that Brackett or other settlers had reported the cattle killing to Waldron, and that this "secret" application for "a force" may have prompted the raid. Drake, *BOI*, 3:112.

6. Nathaniel Bouton, ed., *New Hampshire Provincial Papers (NHPP)* (Concord, NH: George E. Jenks, 1867), 1:318. *Baxter Manuscripts*, 6:118. Nathaniel Shurtleff, ed., *Records of the Governor and Company of the Massachusetts Bay* (Boston: William White, 1854), 5:106–7. Ruben G. Thwaites, ed., *The Jesuit Relations and Allied Documents* (Cleveland: Burrows Brothers Co., 1896–1901), 60:133. Hubbard, *History*, 134–46. Williamson, *History of Maine*, 533. Sévigny, *Abénaquis*, 153, 126, my translation. Bodge, *Soldiers*, 301–4. Solon B. Colby, *Colby's Indian History: Antiquities of the New Hampshire Indians and Their Neighbors* (Conway, NH: Walkers Pond Press, 1975), 73, 104–7, 275. Gordon Day, *Identity of the Saint Francis Indians* (Ottawa: National Museums of Canada, 1981), 16–17. Franklin B. Hough, ed., "Papers Relating to King Philip's War," in *A Narrative of the Causes that Led to Philip's Indian War, 1675 and 1676, by John Easton* (Albany, NY: J. Munsell, 1858), 168. Nash, "Abiding Frontier," 6–7. Norton, *Devil's Snare*, 86. Willis, *Portland*, 202.

7. Williamson, *History of Maine*, 535–7, 540. *Baxter Manuscripts*, 6:116–20, 149–50. Isley Manuscript, coll. 79, box 1/5, Collections of Maine Historical Society. W. Southgate, "History of Scarborough," in *Collections of the Maine Historical Society* (Portland, ME: Maine Historical Society, 1853), 1st ser., 3:109. Baker, "Scratch," 240, 245. Emerson Baker, *The Clarke and Lake Company* (Augusta, ME: Maine Historic Preservation Commission, 1985), 6–15. Morrison, "Tricentennial," 208–12. Siebert, "Indian War," 137–9, 143. Thomas Lake participated in confiscating Kennebec guns at the beginning of war. Hubbard, *History*, 98.

8. *Baxter Manuscripts*, 6: 178–9. Norton, *Devil's Snare*, 89–91. Siebert, "Indian War," 147. Elizabeth was the wife of Kennebec River trader Richard Hammond. Spelling and punctuation in the document, likely written by Elizabeth Hammond, have been altered for the sake of clarity.

9. *Baxter Manuscripts*, 6:118–9. Hubbard, *History*, 211–23. Norton, *Devil's Snare*, 82–93. Emerson Baker, "Trouble to the Eastward: The Failure of Anglo-Indian Relations in Early Maine" (PhD diss., College of William and Mary: 1986), 207–10. Bodge, *Soldiers*, 305–14. Colin Calloway, "Wanalancet, and Kancagamus: Indian Strategy and Leadership on the New Hampshire Frontier," *Historical New Hampshire* 43, no. 4. (1988): 275, 282–3. Sybil Noyes, Charles Libby, and Walter Davis, *Genealogical Dictionary of Maine and New Hampshire* (Baltimore, ME: Genealogical Publishing, 1979), 711–2. Evan Haefeli and Kevin Sweeney, "Revisiting *The Redeemed Captive*: New Perspectives on the 1704 Attack on Deerfield," in *After King Philip's War: Presence and Persistence in Indian New England*, ed. Colin G. Calloway (Hanover, NH: University Press of New England, 1997), 41–5. As Baker notes, the events of February 1677 are difficult to discern, since the primary source is a perplexing account by Waldron, recounted by Hubbard, although Madoasquarbet's statement sheds light on how Wabanaki people understood Waldron's actions.

10. Anonymous, *A True Account of the Most Considerable Occurrences that have hapned in the Warre Between the English and the Indians in New-England* (London: Benjamin Billingsley, 1676), 5. Hubbard, *History*, 103–6. Bodge, *Soldiers*, 303, 307. Calloway, *Western Abenaki*, 81. Calloway, "Wanalancet," 275. Day, *Identity*, 17. Evan Haefeli and Kevin Sweeney, "Wattanummon's World: Personal and Tribal Identity in the Algonquian Diaspora c. 1660–1712," in *Actes Du Vint-cinquième Congrès Des Algonquinistes*, ed., William Cowan (Ottawa: Carlton University Press, 1994), 215. Nourse, *Annals*, 114–5. Mary White Rowlandson, *The Sovereignty and Goodness of God: With Related Documents*, ed. Neal Salisbury (Boston: Bedford Books, 1997), 109–10, 170. Willis, *Portland*, 196. Rowlandson's daughter was "brought to Seakonk" by a Native woman and "got home" shortly thereafter.

11. Richard Waldron to Massachusetts Council, September 6, 1676, coll. 77, "Autographs of Special Note," box 2/42, Collections of Maine Historical Society, courtesy Kevin Sweeney. Norton, *Devil's Snare*, 90. Jeremy Belknap, *The History of New Hampshire* (Dover, NH: S. C. Stevens and Ela & Wadleigh, 1831), 116–8. *Baxter Manuscripts*, 6:116–7, 119. Hubbard, *History*, 131–2. Bodge, *Soldiers*, 305, 271. Williamson, *History of Maine*, 1:538.

12. Waldron to Council, September 6, 1676, Collections of Maine Historical Society. *Baxter Manuscripts*, 6:116–7, 119, 121. Norton, *Devil's Snare*, 89–90. The same ruse (i.e. "under pretension of Imploying ym in ye Country Service" which "gave us ye fit opportunity of Surprisal") is noted in Shapleigh and Daniel's letter, written the same day on the opposite side of Waldron's letter. Syll and Hathorne had recently arrived, joining with Waldron and Frost, of Kittery, to "protect the settlements" and "repel and destroy" the enemy. Belknap suggests their order was to "seize" all Indian enemies. Although many historians have taken Belknap's narrative at face value, others, including Bodge and Norton, have questioned its validity, based on review of the primary sources. Stewart-Smith suggests Belknap may have recorded a settler "oral tradition." "Pennacook," 190.

13. Waldron to Council, September 6, 1676, Collections of Maine Historical Society. Bodge, *Soldiers*, 307, my emphasis. Norton, *Devils' Snare*, 351. Both Norton and

Bodge discerned from Waldron's correspondence that the judgment took place in Boston, contradicting Belknap and Hubbard's narratives regarding the "separation." Norton further discerned that Waldron and the Massachusetts officers acted under orders from Boston, and did not devise the stratagem at Cocheco, as Hubbard suggested. As Norton observes, Hubbard's narrative thus displaces blame for the deceit from the Massachusetts magistrates and ministers. See Hubbard, *Narrative*, 289, 324.

14. Waldron to Council, September 6, 1676, Collections of Maine Historical Society. *Baxter Manuscripts*, 6:123–4. Gookin, "An Historical Account of the Doings and Sufferings of the Christian Indians in New England," in *Transactions and Collections of the American Antiquarian Society* (Cambridge, MA: American Antiquarian Society, 1836), 2:515–6. Bodge, *Soldiers*, 307. Williamson, *History*, 1:538–9. Dennis Connole, *Indians of the Nipmuck Country in Southern New England 1630–1750* (Jefferson, NC: McFarlane, 2007), 223.

15. *Baxter Manuscripts*, 6:116–7, 122–9, 138. *NHPP*, 1:360. Gookin, "Historical Account," 515–6. Bodge, *Soldiers*, 271, 320–1. Stewart-Smith, "Pennacook," 192. Siebert, "Indian War," 144. Williamson, *History*, 1:539–40. Hubbard, *History*, 178–82.

16. *Baxter Manuscripts*, 6:116–131, 138, 150–1. Hubbard, *History*, 182–8. Bodge, *Soldiers*, 310–1. Calloway, *Western Abenakis*, 81. Southgate," Scarborough," 108–9. Willis, *Portland*, 210. Williamson, *History of Maine*, 1:540–1. Siebert, "Indian War," 145, 151.

17. *The Diary of Samuel Sewall: 1674–1729*, ed. M. Halsey Thomas (New York: Farrar, Straus, and Giroux, 1973), 23. Drake, *BOI*, 3:83. This news arrived in a letter from John Reyner Jr. of Dover, sent from Salisbury, MA. *NHPP*, 1:365.

18. Gookin, "Historical Account," 515–6. Massachusetts Archives, 30:214. "Massachusetts Council Order to Major Gookin regarding Spies," August 28, 1676, (1676.08.28.00), Paul Grant-Costa, et al., eds., *The New England Indian Papers Series* (NEIPS) Yale University Library Digital Collections, http://jake.library.yale.edu:8080/neips/data/html/1676.08.28.00/1676.08.28.00.html.

19. Bodge, *Soldiers*, 309. Temple, *Framingham*, 53. Salisbury, ed., *Sovereignty*, 134. Gookin, *Historical Collections*, 53. Drake, *BOI*, 2:81. Connole, *Nipmuck*, 225. Peter Jethro had previously been recruited by Gookin and Eliot to extend their mission to Nashaway.

20. Increase Mather, *A Relation of the Troubles Which Have Happened in New England*, ed. Samuel G. Drake (Boston, 1864), 257–8. *Diary of Increase Mather, March, 1675-December, 1676*, ed. Samuel A. Green (Cambridge, MA: J. Wilson, 1900), 47. Hubbard, *History*, 133.

21. Bodge, *Soldiers*, 309. Drake, *BOI*, 3:82–3. Temple, *Framingham*, 52–3. J. H. Temple, *History of North Brookfield, Massachusetts* (Brookfield, MA: North Brookfield, 1887), 133. Connole, *Nipmuck*, 225.

22. Hubbard, *History*, 162, 165n190. Rufus King Sewall, *Ancient Dominions of Maine* (Bath, ME: Elisha Clark and Company, 1859), 162n1. Thomas Lake was a merchant in Boston but maintained a major trading post on the Kennebec with his partner, Thomas Clarke. Lake had helped disarm Wabanaki people at the outset of war. For more on Lake and his trading post, see Baker, *Clarke and Lake*. Alvin Morrison, "Tricentennial," 8. Although at the time John believed his brother had been taken

captive, Thomas was slain while attempting escape during the raid, as Hubbard later recorded.

23. Sewall, *Diary*, 23. *Baxter Manuscripts*, 6:118, 120. Temple, *Framingham*, 52. Drake, *BOI*, 3:83. Connole, *Nipmuck*, 225. With Gookin's advocacy, Peter Jethro ultimately earned his "life and liberty," later appearing on numerous deeds when Massachusetts needed to confirm its titles to land in Nipmuc country. Bodge, *Soldiers*, 309. See also Mary de Witt Freeland, *The Records of Oxford, Massachusetts* (Albany, NY: Joel Mun-sell's Sons, 1894), 126.

24. Shurtleff, *Massachusetts Records*, 5:104–17. Hubbard, *History*, 132. Mather, *Diary*, 46. Sewall, *Diary*, 21. Margaret Ellen Newell, *Brethren by Nature: New England Indians, Colonists, and the Origins of American Slavery* (Ithaca, NY: Cornell University Press, 2015), 10–3, 53, 109, 168–70. Of Mather's report, the editor Green notes, "These were taken at Cocheco by a stratagem of Major Waldron." Although none of the people he helped capture at Cocheco appeared in the court records, Hathorne's rights to Native land were recognized by the court during the September session.

25. Gookin, "Historical Account," 492. Massachusetts Archives, 30:219, 219a. Bodge, *Soldiers*, 304, 307–9. Drake, *BOI*, 2:117. Norton, *Devil's Snare*, 90, 351. Salisbury, ed., *Sovereignty*, 141. Stewart-Smith, "Pennacook," 190. For more on captives taken at Cocheco, see http://ourbelovedkin.com/awikhigan/wabanaki-coast.

26. Massachusetts Archives, 30:228. "Order re: Mary Namesit and Jacob Indian," November 23, 1676, photostats, Massachusetts Historical Society. Bodge, *Soldiers*, 309. Stewart-Smith, "Pennacook," 190. Sidney Perley, *The Indian Land Titles of Essex County Massachusetts* (Salem, MA: Essex Book and Print Club, 1912), 9, 10. "Biography of Kancamagus," *Farmer's Monthly Visitor* 13, no. 5 (Manchester, NH: Rowell, Prescott & Co., 1853). George may have been among those gathered at Cocheco because he had been married to Wanalancet's sister. A group of documents from the 1680s, related to the title of Salem/Naumkeag, offer a glimpse of the kinship network to which the two men belonged. See Perley, *Land Titles*, 8–12.

27. *Baxter Manuscripts*, 4:378. Gookin, "Historical Account," 520–1. Franklin Benjamin Hough, *Papers Concerning the Attack on Hatfield and Deerfield by a Party of Indians from Canada September Nineteenth 1677* (New York: privately printed, 1859), 51–7. Martin Moore, ed., *Memoirs of the Life and Character of Rev. John Eliot* (Boston: Flagg and Gould, 1822), 126–9. Edward Ballard, "Character of the Penacooks," *Collections of the New Hampshire Historical Society* 8 (1866): 433. George Sheldon, *A History of Deerfield, Massachusetts: The Times When and the People by Whom it was Settled, Unsettled and Resettled* (Deerfield, MA: 1895), 183. Calloway, *Western Abenakis*, 81–2, 84–5. Calloway, "Wanalancet," 276. Colby, *Indian History*, 104–6. Day, *Identity*, 17–8, 22–3, 29–30. Drake, *BOI*, 3:113–8. Evan Haefeli and Kevin Sweeney, *Captive Histories: English, French and Native Narratives of the 1704 Deerfield Raid* (Amherst, MA: University of Massachusetts Press, 2006), 34–48. Haefeli and Sweeney, "Wattanummon's World," 215–6. John Pendergast, *The Bend in the River* (Tyngsborough, MA: Merrimac River Press, 1992), 67. Stewart-Smith, "Pennacook," 36, 199–214. For maps, documents, images, and connections, see http://ourbelovedkin.com/awikhigan/connecticut-river-valley.

28. *Baxter Manuscripts*, 6:164, 177–9, 268. Siebert, "Indian War," 147.

29. *Baxter Manuscripts*, 6:177–9. Baker, "Trouble," 211.

30. *Baxter Manuscripts*, 6:178–9.

31. *Baxter Manuscripts*, 6:148–56, 169–76. *NHPP*, 1:361–4. Hubbard, *History*, 211–23, 226–37. Plymouth Council to John Leverett, June 6, 1677, Davis Papers, Massachusetts Historical Society. *CT Records*, 492–8, 502–4. *MA Records*, 5:138. Gookin, "Historical Account," 516. Thwaites, ed., *Jesuit Relations*, 60:133. Baker, "Trouble," 207–10. Bodge, *Soldiers*, 311–5. A. Morrison, "Tricentennial,"10. K. Morrison, *Embattled*, 110. Pulsipher, *Subjects*, 229. Siebert, "Indian War," 145–8. Williamson, *History of Maine*, 545–52. Jon Parmenter, *The Edge of the Woods: Iroquoia, 1534–1701* (East Lansing, MI: Michigan State University Press, 2010), 151. Horation Hight, "Mogg Heigon—His Life, His Death, and its Sequel," in *Collections of the Maine Historical Society* (Portland, ME: Maine Historical Society, 1895, 2nd ser., 6:256–80. Some of the "praying Indians under Captain Hunting" participated in Waldron's February 1677 expedition ("their council not attended to") and the June 1677 expedition. Kennebec leaders may have received word of Massachusetts's petition to the Mohawks from their kin who traded on the St. Lawrence, where the French also expressed concern for the impact of Mohawk raids on Abenaki towns, and the threat to it posed to their own.

32. Baker and Reid, "Amerindian Power," 84–5, 88–9. Gordon Day, *Western Abenaki Dictionary* (Hull, QC: Canadian Museum of Civilization, 1994), 1:31. Joseph Aubery and Stephen Laurent, *Father Aubery's French Abenaki Dictionary* (Portland, ME: Chisolm Brothers, 1995), 299. Joseph Laurent, *New Familiar Abenaki and English Dialogues* (Quebec: L. Brousseau, 1884), 54. Note that the word conveying "ownership" in the Abenaki language, *debaldamwôgan*, conveys "independence" and "mastery," which Wabanaki people asserted and achieved. Day, *Dictionary*, 1:160.

33. *Baxter Manuscripts*, 6:179–80, 185–6, 189–93; 4:376–8. Edmund O'Callaghan, *The Documentary History of the State of New York* (NYCD) (Albany, NY: Weed, Parsons, 1850), 3:248–9; 13: 497, 501–4, 538. Joshua Scottow, "Narrative of a Voyage to Pemaquid," coll. 420, vol. 8, f.57, Collections of Maine Historical Society. Charles P. Isley Manuscript, coll. 79, ch. 5, box 1/5, Collections of Maine Historical Society, 91–2. Baker, "Trouble," 219. Calloway, *Western Abenakis*, 82–3. Day, *Identity*, 16–21. Fannie Eckstorm, *Indian Place-Names of the Penobscot Valley and the Maine Coast* (Orono, ME: University of Maine, 1941), 102–3, 129. Hough, "Papers," 166–7. Jennings, *Invasion*, 317. A. Morrison, "Tricentennial," 10. K. Morrison, *Embattled*, 110–1. Parmenter, *Edge*, 149. Siebert, "Indian War," 150. Williamson, *History of Maine*, 552. Helen Ainslie Smith, *The Colonies: Historical Series, Book 2* (New York: Morse Company, 1899), 203.Hubbard undermines the importance of this treaty in his *History*, 238–9. For the New York commissioners' experience in diplomacy, see, for example, NYCD, vols. 3 and 13. In pursuing diplomacy, Andros, who had a close relationship to James, the Duke of York, also sought to bolster his power and English defense against Quebec. Historians have revealed the ways in which the colonies highlighted and exaggerated the possibility of French involvement, in order to draw England's attention. See Emerson Baker, "New Evidence on the French Involvement in King Philip's War," *Maine Historical Society Quarterly* 28, no. 2 (Fall 1988): 85–91.

34. *Baxter Manuscripts*, 6:171–6, 6:185–90.
35. *Baxter Manuscripts*, 6:189, 23:2. Siebert, "Indian War," 140.
36. Scottow, "Narrative." *Baxter Manuscripts*, 6:191. For maps, documents, images, and connections, see http://ourbelovedkin.com/awikhigan/wabanaki-coast.
37. *Baxter Manuscripts*, 6:186–92. Scottow, "Narrative." Baker, "Trouble," 219.
38. *Baxter Manuscripts*, 6:191–3. Scottow, "Narrative." NYCD, 3:249.
39. *Baxter Manuscripts*, 6:191–3, 23:2. Scottow, "Narrative."
40. *Baxter Manuscripts*, 6:191–3, 4:378. Scottow, "Narrative." Siebert, "Indian War," 145.
41. *NHPP*, 1:365. Massachusetts Archives, 69:185. Isley Manuscript, 91–2. Baker and Reid, "Amerindian Power," 85–6. Charles Starbird, *The Indians of Androscoggin Valley: Tribal History, and Their Relations with the Early English Settlers of Maine* (Lewiston Journal Printshop, 1928), 56. Williamson, *History of Maine*, 552–3. Willis, *Portland*, 214. George Ellis and John Morris, *King Philip's War* (New York: Grafton Press, 1906), 314. *Collections of the Maine Historical Society* (Portland, ME: Maine Historical Society, 1868), 4th ser., vol. 8: 631–2. Mather, *Diary*, 52. In 1683, Joshua Scottow wrote to Increase Mather with news he had received of the deaths of Squando and Symon, concluding, "so let all thine enemies perish, O Lord!"
42. On "resisting" versus "replacement," see O'Brien, *Firsting*, ch. 4.
43. Baker and Reid, "Amerindian," 84, 102–3. See also Calloway, *Western Abenakis* and *Dawnland Encounters: Indians and Europeans in Northern New England* (Hanover, NH: University Press of New England, 1991).

INDEX